No Business without Communication

Freiberger Beiträge zur interkulturellen und Wirtschaftskommunikation

A Forum for General and Intercultural Business Communication

Edited by Michael B. Hinner

Band 9

Michael B. Hinner (ed.)

No Business without Communication

How Communication Can Shed Additional Light on Specific Business Contexts

PETER LANG
Lausanne - Berlin - Bruxelles - Chennai - New York - Oxford

Bibliographic Information published by the Deutsche Nationalbibliothek
The Deutsche Nationalbibliothek lists this publication in the Deutsche Nationalbibliografie; detailed bibliographic data is available in the internet at http://dnb.d-nb.de.

Library of Congress Cataloging-in-Publication Data
A CIP catalog record for this book has been applied for at the Library of Congress.

Herausgegeben von: TU Bergakademie Freiberg

ISBN 978-3-631-89766-9 (Print)
E-ISBN 978-3-631-90227-1 (E-Book)
E-ISBN 978-3-631-90229-5 (E-Pub)
DOI 10.3726/20836

Published by Peter Lang GmbH, Berlin, Deutschland

info@peterlang.com http://www.peterlang.com/

This publication has been peer reviewed.

Michael B. Hinner (ed.)

No Business without Communication

How Communication Can Shed Additional Light on Specific Business Contexts

PETER LANG

Lausanne - Berlin - Bruxelles - Chennai - New York - Oxford

Bibliographic Information published by the Deutsche Nationalbibliothek
The Deutsche Nationalbibliothek lists this publication in the Deutsche Nationalbibliografie; detailed bibliographic data is available in the internet at http://dnb.d-nb.de.

Library of Congress Cataloging-in-Publication Data
A CIP catalog record for this book has been applied for at the Library of Congress.

Herausgegeben von: TU Bergakademie Freiberg

ISBN 978-3-631-89766-9 (Print)
E-ISBN 978-3-631-90227-1 (E-Book)
E-ISBN 978-3-631-90229-5 (E-Pub)
DOI 10.3726/20836

Published by Peter Lang GmbH, Berlin, Deutschland

info@peterlang.com http://www.peterlang.com/

This publication has been peer reviewed.

Table of Contents

Part IV Communication at the Workplace

Part V Politeness and Emotion at the Workplace

Part VI Intercultural Communication Competence and Cultural Adaptation

Communication about Intercultural Communication – A Preface in Honor of Michael B. Hinner

"Intercultural communication is a subject that was introduced in Germany relatively recently by researchers who had visited North American universities" (Hinner, 2017, p. 1). As it turned out, Freiberg, Saxony, was the place where this introduction happened. Moreover, above-cited *Michael B. Hinner* was the researcher getting the job done. Naturally, someone who had been at a North American university not as a temporary guest researcher but as a full member of a faculty turned out the perfect solution to overcome the missing link. Twenty-five years later, we now celebrate the silver jubilee of *Michael Hinner's* career as a full professor of a German university as well as the introduction of intercultural communication in Germany. This collection of papers authored by various distinguished researchers belonging to his network of leading intercultural and communication scholars from around the world is an impressing acknowledgment of his contributions to teaching and researching intercultural communication. It is not only my pleasure but an honor to contribute this brief preface.

Born in Germany but having grown-up on the East Coast of the United States, *Michael Hinner* studied Anthropology, Comparative Studies, English, German, History, and Linguistics at the State University of New York (SUNY) and Law at St. John's University, School of Law. After receiving his master's degree and a Ph.D. from SUNY Stony Brook, he moved back to Germany, where he relocated in the Hannover region to work for corporate employers and, more importantly, for various academic institutions. He then joined the Faculty of Business Administration at the Technische Universität Bergakademie Freiberg in 1997, taking the position as head of the Chair of Intercultural Communication. Having detected the shortcomings of Economics/Business Management programs concerning communication (for details, please see Hinner, 1998, 2002. The gap detected already back then has not been closed yet – please see the recent analysis of Hinner, 2020c, esp. pp. 228–229), he undertook to fill the gap in the ways a university professor can pursue: by teaching, researching/publishing, and as a member of various institutions of his university's self-administration.

Having excelled in teaching at Stony Brook already, *Michael Hinner* quickly became a highly appreciated lecturer and has been awarded by considerable numbers of students taking his courses – and requesting thesis supervision – ever since. His lectures, especially those on Professional Communication, Business Communication, and Intercultural Communication, attracted students from Freiberg's German bachelor/master classes and international MBA programs. Whereas the lectures mentioned above represent traditional parts of his chair's curriculum, it also contained a most unusual element in the best possible sense: the film seminar, during which the student participants produce a short film, including a movie poster. The public presentation of the movies "started as a byproduct of a course [and] evolved into an exciting spectacle that draws large audiences and evokes public notice. A jury [...] awards Ottos in such categories as "Best Actress", "Best Actor", "Best Supporting Role", "Best Production", "Best Humor", etc. The Ottos are then awarded during the public showing of the films in the university's Alte Mensa."[1] Supported by the enthusiastic team of his chair, *Michael Hinner* thus established a true Freibergian institution, making the award ceremony of the "Otto Night" a highlight of any academic calendar until 2019, when the final curtain fell (Freie Presse, 2019).

Regarding topics, his earlier research concentrated on the intercultural aspect of communication problems, putting "Intercultural Competence in a Business Context"(see the eponymous book chapter by Hinner, 2014). Surrounded by chairs of business administration ("Betriebswirtschaftslehre") and economics ("Volkswirtschaftslehre") – and communicating with their team members –, he quite naturally applied his expertise to several areas linking him with these disciplines, such as (cultural aspects of) customers' price/value perceptions (Hinner, 2016; Stępień et al., 2016), their (communication/consumer) behavior on social networks (Bartosik-Purgat et al., 2017), or the (cultural challenges of) mergers & acquisitions (Hinner, 2019). In doing so, he displayed his openness to current interdisciplinary research topics. The up-to-dateness of his research becomes extremely obvious in his recent papers on intolerance (Hinner, 2020b)[2]

1 See the former Otto website of *Michael Hinner's* chair, i.e., https://tu-freiberg.de/fakult6/intercultural-communication/otto-awards (accessed Nov 17, 2021).

2 Even though he starts with the pessimistic insight that "[r]esearch has shown consistently over the past sixty years that once intolerance is lodged in a person, many well intended efforts designed to counterbalance and overcome such intolerance are not very effective and often fail" (p. 181), which does not create much hope with regard to intolerant people, especially those acting as presidents, his attempt to elaborate on a "curriculum which is designed to help overcome intolerance" (p. 181, also p. 193) could help fight intolerance in the future, albeit the complexity and the necessary individualization of the approach (see pp. 193–197) are considerable.

and prejudice (Hinner, 2020a), which he published in times characterized by new levels of these phenomena observable not only but most prominently in politics.

Regarding publication styles, *Michael Hinner* proceeded according to the culture of his discipline, meaning that he remained steadfast in his appreciation for books, be it monographs or edited volumes. He did so, and he does so, even when surrounded by the journal-paper-euphoria of our times. One prominent example is the series of books designed to provide "A Forum for General and Intercultural Business Communication" ("*Freiberger Beiträge zur interkulturellen und Wirtschaftskommunikation*")[3]. Further prominent examples are the numerous book chapters authored by *Michael Hinner*, such as, most recently, his contributions to two volumes on cultural conceptualization (Hinner, 2020a, 2020c) or his four contributions to "*The International Encyclopedia of Intercultural Communication*" (Hinner, 2017)[4].

Michael B. Hinner supervised an above-average number of Ph.D. projects dealing with intercultural communication problems. Following the traditional approach, all of them were book-based rather than paper-based, and several of these books achieved the highest degrees or even a university award (most recently, see Boehnisch, 2021; Meschke, 2021). Based on the hitherto achievements of his candidates, the probability of further outstanding dissertations written under *Michael Hinner's* guidance appears significant.

Throughout the Freiberg chapter of his academic career, *Michael B. Hinner* also practiced communication in his daily university life. One prominent example is his membership in several institutions of Freiberg University's self-administration. Besides the usual suspects, such as the faculty council ("Fakultätsrat") or the university parliament ("Konzil", today known as the extended senate), he also joined the Fulbright Selection Committee, the Study Abroad Selection Committee, and became Freibergs's representative of the ERASMUS Sokrates program. Furthermore, he acted as a liaison between his

3 The series consists of eight books, seven of which have been edited by Michael B. Hinner, reaching from Hinner (ed., 2005) to Hinner (ed., 2014). For further information, see the respective website of the publisher, i.e., https://www.peterlang.com/series/6136 (accessed Nov 17, 2021).

4 The other three chapters addressed "Communication Modes, German", "Organizational Communication in Germany and the United States", and took a "Social Ecological Perspective on Intercultural Communication", see the publisher's website https://onlinelibrary.wiley.com/browse/book/10.1002/9781118783665/title?startPage=&ContribRaw=Hinner%2C%20Michael%20B (accessed Nov 17, 2021).

students and the German-American-Chamber-of-Commerce, thus supporting students to achieve internships in the United States of America.

Altogether, *Michael Hinner* is an academic who has taught, researched, and lived communication in general, and intercultural communication in particular. He has done so for 25 years, and he already was an established member of Freiberg's faculty of business administration when the author of this preface was allowed to join it. To be asked to deliver a preface to a volume he edited would have been nothing but an honor, and to deliver a note on the occasion of a silver jubilee nothing but pure pleasure. In the particular case of *Michael B. Hinner*, however, both come with a bittersweet taste, as they also mean a farewell. Consequently, this preface closes with a combination of congratulation and regret: Well done, but you will leave a gap – maybe in your field of research, definitely in our faculty.

Andreas Horsch
Dean of the Faculty of Business Administration
Technische Universität Bergakademie Freiberg

References

Bartosik-Purgat, M., Filipchuk, O., & Hinner, M. B. (2017). Communication and Consumer Activities of Social Networking Sites Users: Cases from Germany, Poland, and Russia. *Managing Global Transitions, 15*(4), 341–363.

Boehnisch, A. (2021). *Health Communication Management: The Interface between Culture and Scientific Communication in the Management of Ebola in Liberia*. Freiberger Forschungshefte D253, Freiberg: TU Bergakademie Freiberg, https://nbn-resolving.org/urn:nbn:de:bsz:105-qucosa2-758738 (accessed Nov. 17, 2021).

Freie Presse. (2019). Vorhang fällt für letzte Otto-Nacht. *Freie Presse*, July 06, 2019, https://www.freiepresse.de/vorhang-f-llt-f-r-letzte-otto-nacht-artikel10557455 (accessed Nov. 17, 2021).

Hinner, M. B. (1998). *The Importance of Intercultural Communication in a Globalized World*, Freiberg Working Papers No. 1998/06. Freiberg: Faculty of Economics and Business Administration.

Hinner, M. B. (2002). *Communication Science: An Integral Part of Business and Business Studies?*, Freiberg Working Papers No. 2002/13. Freiberg: Faculty of Economics and Business Administration.

Hinner, M. B. (Ed.). (2005). *Introduction to Business Communication*. Frankfurt/M. et al.: Peter Lang.

Hinner, M. B. (2014a). Perceiving Intercultural Competence in a Business Context. In X. Dai & G.-M. Chen (Eds.), *Intercultural Communication Competence: Conceptualization and Its Development in Cultural Contexts and Interactions* (pp. 293–314). Newcastle upon Tyne: Cambridge Scholars Publishing.

Hinner, M. B. (Ed.). (2014b). *Chinese Culture in a Cross-Cultural Comparison*. Frankfurt/M. et al.: Peter Lang.

Hinner, M. B. (2016). Relationships and Trust in Perceiving Price Fairness: An Exploratory Study. *Economics and Business Review, 2*(2), 54–73.

Hinner, M. B. (2017). Intercultural Communication Study in Germany. In Y. Y. Kim (Ed.), *The International Encyclopedia of Intercultural Communication* (3 Vols.). Hoboken, NJ: Wiley. https://doi.org/10.1002/9781118783665.ieicc0083

Hinner, M. B. (2019). The Cultural Perspective of Mergers & Acquisitions: An Exploratory Study. In J. Stumpf-Wollersheim & A. Horsch (Eds.), *Forum Mergers & Acquisitions 2019*, (pp. 119–143). Wiesbaden: Springer Gabler.

Hinner, M. B. (2020a). Can the Social Ecological Model Help Overcome Prejudices? In B. Lewandowska-Tomaszczyk (Ed.), *Cultural Conceptualizations in Language and Communication* (pp. 239–258). Cham: Springer.

Hinner, M. B. (2020b). Developing a Curriculum Designed to Overcome Intolerance: A Conceptual Approach. *Lodz Papers in Pragmatics* (Special issue on (In)tolerance and (in)civility in public discourse from multidisciplinary perspectives), *16* (2), 181–201.

Hinner, M. B. (2020c). Integrating Cultural Conceptualization and Communication Courses into Business Administration Curricula. In B. Lewandowska-Tomaszczyk (Ed.), *Cultural Conceptualizations in Translation and Language Applications* (pp. 227–248). Cham: Springer.

Meschke, S. (2021). *Employee Loyalty – Intercultural Comparison of European and East Asian Approaches*. Cham: Springer.

Stępień, B., Pinto Lima, A., Sagbansua, L., & Hinner, M. B. (2016). Comparing Consumers' Value Perception of Luxury Goods: Is National Culture a Sufficiently Explanatory Factor? *Economics and Business Review, 2*(2), 74–93.

Introduction

According to Robert Kent, the former Dean of the Harvard Business School, "in business, communication is everything" (Stuart et al., 2007, p. 381). In other words, business is not possible without communication. Communication, thus, assumes a central, if not *the* central role in business. That is why an understanding of communication is crucial. But surprisingly, communication did not and still does not play a central role in most business curricula at German universities (Hinner, 2020). One can only speculate as to why that is when such complementary subjects as computer science, law, mathematics, etc. are integral components of business curricula at German universities, but not communication science which is also relevant as Robert Kent notes. And it is not as if business students had received extensive background knowledge in communication science while attending secondary schools which could have been a reason why communication science is not included in business curricula. So if in the words of Robert Kent communication is everything in business, then it would be foolish to neglect communication. That is why it is necessary to integrate communication into business curricula.

For a number of years now, the TU Bergakademie Freiberg has included communication as a part of its business curriculum. Not surprisingly, many students acknowledged the need to better understand communication so as to better understand the interaction of the various stakeholders in the world of business. In today's global world, it is also necessary to understand how culture influences human behavior and communication. After all, intercultural encounters occur not only abroad, but also within local companies. That was why the *Freiberger Beiträge zur interkulturellen und Wirtschaftskommunikation* were launched in 2005. The *Beiträge* invited prominent researchers from the field of communication and intercultural communication to contribute texts on a variety of topics revolving around culture and communication to show how culture and communication influence human interaction and, thus, also business. This tradition is continued with this volume. However, this time the scope was expanded to include not only researchers from communication and intercultural communication, but also from linguistics. Such an interdisciplinary extension provides a broader base for understanding human interaction because one perspective seldom provides a comprehensive view of a phenomenon.

Wherever and whenever people come together, communication is needed. Communication occurs at all levels inside and outside companies between all stakeholders. Within companies, colleagues communicate with one another, subordinates with their supervisors and vice versa, diversity increasingly assumes a greater role within companies, and the advent of social media has had considerable impact on how people communicate with one another in companies. Communication also assumes a central role in building and maintaining customer relations or in supply chain management – whether it be locally or globally. Nor can one ignore the significance of communication in the interaction between companies and public authorities and/or the scientific community. These are just some examples of where communication comes into play in the world of business. And that is why no business is possible without communication.

The following chapters can be helpful in understanding how communication and culture influence human interaction in the world of business. The eclectic collection of texts is grouped into several categories. The first four chapters introduce the most fundamental aspects of intercultural communication. In the first chapter, Malgorzata Bartosik-Purgat provides a general introduction to personal communication and how culture influences business interactions. Svetlana Kurtes reviews Hofstede's cultural dimensions, Hall's cultural dichotomies as well as Brown and Levinson's linguistic politeness theory. In doing so, she provides a foundation for topics which will be discussed in more detail in later chapters. Edwin R. McDaniel broadens the base further to include various tools that have been developed over time to permit cross-cultural comparisons and communication. One of Hall's cultural dimensions, namely high versus low context communication, is examined closer by Adam Komisarof who uses Japanese and American business communication to illustrate the difference. Xiaodong Dai and Xiaohong Lyu take closer look at face and facework. They explain in detail what is meant by face and facework and why both are so important for an understanding East Asian cultures.

After having provided a general foundation for some basic aspects of (intercultural) communication, the focus of the next group of chapters shifts towards worldview and perception to help explain how they influence the communication directly and indirectly. Jim Neuliep briefly describes ethnocentrism, i.e. seeing and evaluating the world from one's own cultural perspective. He points out that ethnocentrism can lead to problems because people do not take the perspective of another person. Elena Steiner develops the concept further by examining the impact of worldviews on the beliefs and values. She points out that these differences influence cognition which is why it is necessary to understand why people behave and communicate the way they do. David Katan notes that people tend to attribute and apply their own ways of seeing the world and thinking to the behavior and communication of others even though such attribution is faulty because members of different cultures hold different worldviews. Guo-Ming Chen uses the example of the Belt and Road Initiative of the Chinese government to illustrate how different worldviews can influence the perception of a large scale government project. From these chapters it should become apparent that perception influences not only how we "see" the world around us, but also how we react to what we think we see.

The next group of texts examines the meaning of messages – whether it be via translation or in discourse. Barbara Lewandowska-Tomaszczyk points out that it is not possible to transfer an identical meaning directly from one text to another due to linguistic and cultural differences. She presents many examples to illustrate the difficulties associated with translations. Craig Frayne examines natural resource projects from the perspective of intercultural communication. While much traditional research has focused on the power relationship of the stakeholders, little attention has been given to the various cultures of the stakeholders. By presenting a few examples, Frayne is able to demonstrate that the respective discourse consists of multiple culturally embedded language games which need to be considered when trying to navigate through the shifting contexts, distinguishing between the different levels, and integrating these variants into understanding the meaning communicated between diverse stakeholders. Douglas Ponton examines legal discourse to show how meaning is constructed in situational factors associated within a text. He notes that not everyone takes, for example, metaphors into consideration – even though they should since metaphors are quite common in human communication, but vary from culture to culture. Noémie Hermeking uses French fables to illustrate how they are used in French discourse and so help explain the habits, customs, beliefs, and normative behavior of native speakers. Ling Chen takes a closer look at formulations. Formulations refer to the rewording of previous messages to ensure that the proper meaning of messages has been conveyed from one speaker to another. They, thus, help facilitate framing which would otherwise create problems in the transfer of meaning from one language to another. Juana Du and Zhenyi Li point out that the use of language in an international work environment is often associated with a number of challenges. While knowledge of the host countries language can be helpful in building positive relationships, one should also not neglect learning a company's own jargon and acronyms because it is often used in the day-to-day business of that company. And knowledge of that jargon and those acronyms can be helpful in becoming better integrated into the company's internal networks due to code sharing.

This brings us to the next category of texts that take a closer look at various aspects associated with communication at the workplace. Xiaowei Shi and Yang Soo Kim examine upward communication, in particular upward influence and impression management communication, within companies. Their research indicates that employees have a need to feel comfortable when talking to their supervisors. An atmosphere of trust is essential in creating a positive work environment. They note that this communication, though, is influenced to a large extend by the culture of the interlocutors – which needs to be considered when trying to avoid misunderstandings. Haoyang Chen, Vivian C. Sheer, and Tien Ee Dominic Yeo applied Sheer's leader-member exchange communication model in a corporate context. Not surprisingly, they found that communication is critically important in developing, maintaining, and strengthening supervisor-subordinate relationships because it builds trust which facilitates corporate learning due to that trust. In the next chapter, Vivian Sheer looks at sex stereotyping and its role in perceived managerial effectiveness. Her study revealed that while men use a more assertive style of communication than women, women use more immediate and supportive cues in their communication than men. While assertiveness can be important for some situations, supportive communication is not inconsequential either. In fact, Sheer found that communication immediacy is actually more important than assertiveness when it comes to the perceived effectiveness of leaders. While Ee Lin Lee examines discrimination within educational organizations, the findings can also be applied, more or less, to business organizations where discrimination can also hamper positive relationships. Lee makes a case to legitimize everyone's personhood because such a policy fosters solidarity and, thus, reduces the creation of out-groups. How complex and at what various levels discrimination can occur within a company is revealed by Hanna and Razzante. They take a closer look intersectionality and its role in inclusion and diversity at the workplace. Intersectionality refers to the meeting of diversity at various corporate levels ranging from corporate strategies to corporate practices and discursive actions. This makes discrimination complex because it involves these different levels. That is why discrimination has to be addressed at all of these levels if it is to be overcome.

The next chapters examine politeness and emotions at the workplace. Carmen Santamaria-García reviews the current state of research in the field of (im)politeness with a particular focus on social media. Social media have assumed an ever increasing role in workplace communication which is why their characteristic features need to be taken into consideration when examining the transfer of meanings. Santamaria-García also points out that that one cannot always translate the meaning of a message directly from one language to another – this needs to be considered when attempting to translate politeness from one language to another. Hairong Feng notes that politeness is a complex, multi-dimensional social phenomenon that involves language and culture. She discusses in detail how pragmatics, interpersonal communication, and intercultural communication can reveal the complexity of politeness and how the findings from these three scientific disciplines can make one more aware of what needs to considered when trying to be polite across cultures. Meina Liu, Mengyuan Chen, and Yi Ren examine the role of emotions in negotiations. They point out that while emotions are often universally recognizable, the actual display of emotions in specific contexts varies from culture to culture. That is why knowledge of other cultures can be helpful because such knowledge allows one to be more precise in properly reading the emotions and intentions of one's counterpart.

And finally, the last category of chapters examines intercultural communication competence and cultural adaptation to show how cultural differences may be recognized and overcome. Darla K. Deardorff provides an overview of the topic which actually consists of several characteristics ranging from respect to knowledge and the ability to properly apply that knowledge in one's interaction with others. Kris Acheson, Sundae Schneider-Bean, and Jennifer Wiley present a means of improving one's intercultural communication competence. This includes also a discussion of various tools that are currently available which allow one to assess one's abilities. Thus, it is possible to determine how competent one is and what needs to be done to overcome specific deficits. Young Yun Kim notes that almost everyone undergoes some form of cross-cultural adaptation when coming into contact with another culture. While most individuals encounter stress in such situations, it is also possible to reduce this stress by becoming knowledgeable of the host language and culture. This knowledge coupled with a positive attitude and the ability to effectively and appropriately implement the proper behavior and communication to specific situations makes the adjustment to another culture easier and encourages personal growth. L. Ripley Smith focuses on social networks and their role in adjusting to a foreign culture. Smith notes that while many new arrivals seek to establish contact to members of their home culture, which can be helpful in learning the new culture, it is also a good idea to establish contact to members of the host culture because these contacts support and foster the integration into the host culture. Noriko Hasegawa and Teruyuki Kume present a case study from Japan that shows how cooperation among members of a multicultural community helped reduce prejudices and created a mutually beneficial work environment. The creation of diverse work groups and active communication amongst all participants were instrumental in developing and maintaining a friendly, open, and empathetic work environment.

It is hoped that these chapters provide some new and important insights into communication and how cultural differences can influence human behavior and communication. Insights that are important in understanding why others behave and communicate the way they do because these insights could be helpful in avoiding misunderstandings. Misunderstandings that can result in mistakes that might have been avoided had there been a better knowledge and understanding of how culture influences communication – also in the world of business. After all, as Robert Kent points out: "In business, communication is everything."

As noted above, the chapters are grouped into categories of related topics. Each chapter is preceded by a brief introduction to and summary of the chapter's contents as well as a brief biography of the author(s). While there is a general thread uniting all the chapters and while some of the chapters build on the contents of previous chapters, it is also possible to read individual chapters because the chapter topic interests the reader.

At this point, I would like to thank my colleagues for having participated in this project. All are experts in their fields which is why I am glad that they had agreed to participate in this project and were willing to share their expert knowledge so that we will have a better understanding of culture and its impact on communication. After all, in order to better understand human interaction, it is necessary to have different perspectives. These different perspectives provide a fuller view and a better understanding of what is happening during any such interaction. I am, therefore, thankful that these experts provide these perspectives.

I had mentioned above that the first volume of the *Freiberger Beiträge* was published in 2005. Many colleagues have contributed to the volumes over the years. Unfortunately, a number of dear colleagues who had contributed to past volumes are no longer with us. These include Charles R. Berger, Martin Fishbein, William B. Gudykunst, Edward T. Hall, Geert Hofstede, Tadasu Todd Imahori, and Arthur B. VanGundy. In addition to being acknowledged experts in their respective fields, all were fantastic human beings. It is a distinct honor to have known them.

At this point, I would like to thank everyone who contributed to the *Beiträge* in the past and to this volume:

> "I can no other answer make but thanks,
> And thanks; and ever thanks"
>
> (Shakespeare, *Twelfth Night*, III, 3)

References

Hinner, M. B. (2020). Integrating Cultural Conceptualization and Communication Courses into Business Administration Curricula. In B. Lewandowska-Tomaszczyk (Ed.), *Cultural Conceptualizations in Translation and Language Applications* (pp. 227–248). Cham: Springer.

Stuart, B. E., Sarow, M. S., & Stuart, L. (2007). *Integrated Business Communication in a Global Marketplace.* Chichester, UK: Wiley.

Part I General Introduction to Culture and Communication

Introduction to Cross-Cultural Personal Communication: Diversity and Business Implications

By Małgorzata Bartosik-Purgat

The first chapter provides a general overview and summary of the most important elements of interpersonal communication and how culture influences that communication. Bartosik-Purgat points out that communication is essential to business which is why it is important to have an understanding of the communication principles and how they are influenced by culture. The chapter covers all the important aspects of communication, including verbal and nonverbal communication, and the role of culture in such communication. The reader is, thus, given a general introduction to human interpersonal communication.

In addition, this chapter also provides a foundation for the subsequent chapters that examine specific aspects of communication and culture closer, ranging from specific intercultural communication topics to linguistic principles applicable to a variety of business contexts and situations all the way to communication competence.

Michael B. Hinner

Małgorzata Bartosik-Purgat, Professor in the Department of International Management at Poznan University of Economics and Business, Poland. Her research addresses: cultural aspects in international business, cross-cultural communication, cross-cultural consumer behavior, consumer ethnocentrism, acceptance of innovations in the consumers` decisions, the significance of new media in marketing, and personal communication. Member of EIBA – European International Business Association, IAIR - International Academy for Intercultural Research, ABC - Association for Business Communication, SIETAR Poland - Society for Intercultural Education Training and Research, IT&FA - International Trade and Finance Association, AIB - Academy of International Business. Author and co-author of publications in (e.g.) *International Journal of Emerging Markets, European Journal of International Management, Technology Analysis & Strategic Management, Entrepreneurial Business and Economics Review, Economics and Business Review.*

Małgorzata Bartosik-Purgat

Cross-Cultural Personal Communication: Diversity and Business Implications

Introduction

Communication is one of the most important elements of our lives, for both individuals and organizations (Macnamara, 2004; Guang Tian, 2011; Weaver, 2013; Vemou & Karyda, 2020). It helps people to gather and share information about anything and everything that concerns or interests them. In particular, personal communication allows for establishing and maintaining contact between people and friendships, as well as the general functioning of organizations and societies (Xue, 2019; Vemou & Karyda, 2020; Qian et al., 2021).

The development of new technologies and new media (especially social media) have made it possible to stay in touch with friends all over the world (Park & El Mimouni, 2020; Vemou & Karyda, 2020; Bartosik-Purgat; 2020; Camilleri, 2021). McLuhan (1964) emphasized has the importance of the media used during communication – as the saying goes, the medium is the message – which indicates the need to use the type of media that the receiver prefers. Although we usually communicate using telephones or Internet videophones now, we still value direct contact the most (Xue, 2019; Bartosik-Purgat, 2019). The coronavirus pandemic has also led to, indeed necessitated, many new possibilities for people to communicate with others in different countries and cultures (Camilleri, 2021), and the use of communication platforms and programs such as Zoom, MS Teams, Google Meets have increased considerably. This is not to say that people were unaware of these platforms before, rather that they were not used with so much frequency. These platforms allow for audio-video contact, through which other people can be both seen and heard. In the case of communication between people from diverse cultures some difficulties associated with different cultural backgrounds may appear.

The globalization and internationalization processes have, unsurprisingly, led to global and international cooperation between people. They not only live and work together in one organization, or community, but also learn and teach one another in institutions such as schools and universities. In other words, cultural diversity is common and can be met in many situations today. As such, understanding people from different cultures and trying to develop one's skills for more efficient communication is an important element of today"s societies (Macnamara, 2004; Guang Tian, 2011; Weaver, 2013; Meyer, 2016; Park & El Mimouni, 2020).

The main purpose of this chapter is to explain the personal cross-cultural communication process, including its instruments and diversification. The chapter is structured as follows: firstly, some general aspects of the communication process are described, after which, cultural differences are presented; and then language and the problem of context in multicultural communication are introduced, and finally, the tools of verbal and non-verbal communication in cross-cultural contexts are described. Business implications are highlighted throughout all parts of the chapter.

Personal Communication

Personal communication (from the Latin *comunicatio* i.e. conversation, exchange) is a process where people share meanings through symbols (as sounds, letters, words, gestures). The general process of personal communication consists of the transmission of a message (verbal or non-verbal) by the sender and the reception of it by the recipient (Bartosik-Purgat; 2020; Qian et al., 2021). Shannon and Weaver (1949) postulated that the message sent by the sender is more effective when it suits the recipient's needs and preferences.

Thus, we can say that sender, receiver, and the message are the three main elements of the personal communication process, without the existence of which communication cannot occur. In more detail, the components of the communication process are sender, coding, message, channel, receiver, decoding, and feedback (Bartosik-Purgat; 2020; Qian et al., 2021). The sender is a person who has particular information, formulates the message, and transfers it to the receiver using the most adequate channel. Formulating the message means encoding it in symbols. The main purpose of encoding is to choose the right communication tools i.e. gestures and words that work coherently together. Verbal language, written language, and non-verbal behavior – such as gestures, facial expressions, personal distance, touch, or inarticulate sounds – can be distinguished among various communication tools (Weaver, 2013; Ronen & Shenkar, 2017; Steers et al., 2018). These are used to deliver a message through different channels. They are the means of transmitting information from one person to another and depend on the preferences, habits, and possibilities of both sender and receiver. Among the most popular message channels today are in-person conversations, phone calls, text messages, emails, audio and video internet platforms, social media, and digital communities. Encoded in such a way, the message reaches the receiver (a person), whose task is to read (decode) the meaning of the symbols used (Bartosik-Purgat, 2019; Park & El Mimouni, 2020). Decoding relies on interpreting the message, then processing it so that it is understood. This is a two-phase activity: firstly, receiving the message, and secondly, processing it. Decoding depends on many determinants, including, e.g.: the ability to interpret diverse symbols and gestures, attitudes, the relationship with the sender, and cultural differences. When the decoding is successful the receiver will usual formulate feedback to the sender (but their roles in the communication process change).

Depending on the accuracy of the message, the means used, and the possible occurrence of any disturbances, the feedback may be immediate, delayed, or may not occur at all. Difficulties in understanding the message and giving the right answer may be caused by a filter of cultural differences (Figure 1).

Cultural background (e.g. perceptions, attitudes, values, beliefs) may be a barrier in the personal communication between people coming from different cultures (Qian et al., 2021). This aspect can cause misunderstandings, the wrong answer, or simply not replying at all. People who cooperate with others from diverse cultures should be aware of such obstacles (Meyer, 2016; Steers et al., 2018; Park & El Mimouni, 2020). There is no, one best solution and advice for such situations, but one thing is true – we should try to find out as much as

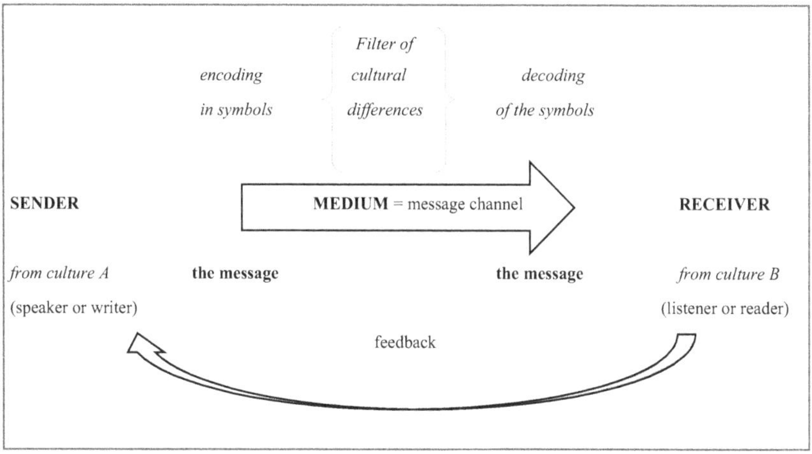

Figure 1: Cross-Cultural Communication Process
Source: Own

possible about the characteristic cultural traits of our interlocutor in cross-cultural communication.

National Culture and Language as an Element of It

Cultural elements are an important filter between encoding and decoding the message among parties belonging to different cultures (Gudykunst et al., 1996; Ronen & Shenkar, 2017), primarily because culture shapes people's thinking, feeling and communicating (Gudykunst et al., 1996; Park & El Mimouni, 2020; Ronen & Shenkar, 2017). Culture has been the subject of scientific research for a considerable period of time now, including in anthropology, economics, management, sociology, and psychology (Steers et al., 2018). The English anthropologist E.B Tylor (1873), was one of the first to propose a definition of national culture and over time it became the cannonical definition, widely used in academia. According to Tylor (1873) the culture is "that complex of whole which includes knowledge, belief, art, law, morals, custom, and any other capabilities and habits acquired by man as a member of society." However, there are still discrepancies when defining this term, which results in a large number of interpretations. Kluckhohn and Kroeber (1952) gathered and categorized 164 different interpretations of culture, dividing them into several types, and only then formulating their own definition of national culture. According to the authors national culture is related to schematic ways of thinking, acquired and transmitted mainly through symbols, which are creations of groups of people and containing their concretization in the form of artifacts, which can be understood artificial cultural creations (Kluckhohn & Kroeber, 2020). In other definition, Leung et al. (2005) define culture as values, beliefs, and norms, as well as patterns of behavior specific to a nation.

Taking into account the main purpose of this chapter, communication, the definition offered by Hall (1976) – a specialist in cross-cultural communication – is particularly salient. In the presentation of national culture, he focuses mainly on those areas related to communication, claiming that culture is a human medium and shapes (influences) all aspects of human life. Culture manifests itself in a person's personality, and affects how a person expresses themself (i.e. the overall communication framework – words, actions, poses, gestures, tone and timbre, facial expression), as well as the way they treat time, space and the ways of working, playing, loving and defending themself (Hall, 1976). In other words, culture is "somehow the other side of communication", it is often shaped in the process of social communication. Similarly, Hollensen (2004) mainly advises looking for cultural differences concerning communication aspects, as they are the most visible. He includes among them both the verbal language used by a given society, and non-verbal language, which can include the use of spatial distance, touch, eye contact and various gestures (Hollensen, 2004).

Language is one of the most important elements of national culture (Ronen & Shenkar, 2017; Steers et al., 2018; Konara & Wei, 2021). It is defined as a socially generated collection of meaningful symbols, both verbal and non-verbal (Bartosik-Purgat, 2010). Hall (1976) emphasizes that language is not a system for transmitting thoughts and meanings from one brain to another, but a system that organizes information and triggers thoughts and reactions in other organisms. This feature of language makes communication between people possible, and thus understanding the whole culture depends on it. Language – the main element of the culture of any nation is its "mirror" in which all its smallest details are reflected (Samovar, 1999, p. 225). Language helps in communication between people, and thus allows active participation in public life, and so constitutes the main cultural difference between societies. As a result it is also of great importance for the activities of enterprises in international markets. The language of any culture is related to the way a nation perceives the world. Konara and Wei (2021, p. 276) proved that language difference has "a negative impact on subsidiary performance. The positive effects of cultural distance on performance become stronger when the language difference is smaller".

Language"s ignorance of the recipients of "messages" (e.g. during business meetings or when preparing advertisements addressed to foreign consumers) may lead to misunderstanding the intentions of the sender (Macnamara, 2004; Guang Tian, 2011; Ronen & Shenkar, 2017; Steers et al., 2018). This is caused, among others things, by the large number of languages in the world, as well as their diversity and complexity. The meanings of individual words may differ between languages and an incorrect translation may change them. Indeed, bad translation and misuse of language are common traps in the activities of enterprises in foreign markets (Ronen & Shenkar, 2017; Steers et al., 2018).

When preparing for a meeting or other form of cooperation with people from other countries, it is worth answering the following questions: what language(s) are the official ones there? what language do my interlocutors use (e.g. during negotiations)?; what language is used by the purchasers of our products to whom, for example, a promotional campaign will be directed?; and are there any regional dialects (varieties of the official language) in the given market? etc. (Konara & Wei, 2021)

Many societies have two (or more) official languages (Chaika, 1994). The labelling on products targeted at these markets usually have to be prepared in these languages. The examples of such countries are Switzerland (German,

Italian and French), Belgium (Dutch, French and German), Finland (Finish and Swedish), Canada (French and English), India (Hindi and English), Malta (Maltese and English) and many others. Moreover, many countries belong to the so-called linguistically heterogeneous, in which the society uses different languages (apart from official ones) or dialects. It is therefore necessary to check which part of the country your business partner comes from and where your product will be delivered. This is also important in order not to make a cultural faux pas.

Context in the Cross-Cultural Communication

Context is also a significant barrier in communication between people from different cultural groups. This consists of the directness of communication, and the degree of use of symbols, signs, and metaphors which are specific for a particular culture (society). Based on the degree of context"s use, Hall (1976, 1992) distinguished low-context cultures (communicating at the low-context level) and high-context cultures (communicating at the high-context level). Figure 2 (below) indicates where different countries can be placed on this high-low context scale.

High-context cultures are known for indirect communication, "coding" their conversation by using many metaphors, euphemisms and sayings that are sometimes misinterpreted, particularly by people from other context cultures (Hall, 1992; Tian, 2012; Steers et al., 2018). They usually say less rather more and expect the other party is able to "read between lines". Some words, especially those with negative connotations, are not used at all. Instead of "no", words, such as statements like "I don"t know", "we don"t want to sell it", "we don"t want to cooperate", one can instead hear "it is a problem", "we will think about it", "we will answer shortly", etc. Showing negative emotions in public may have very important on face, which pertains to honor and good image in society (Kavanagh, 2016; Tian, 2012). The concept of face is called *Mianzi* in China and may cause many difficulties and misunderstandings in communication between persons from Western and Eastern cultures (Tian, 2012; Steers et al., 2018). *Mianzi* is usually interpreted as compliance with the rules adopted by the group, and the "loss of face" by an individual is also a disgrace to the group (Hofstede et al., 2010; Tian, 2012). Westerners are not accustomed to such behavior and way of communication.

The most contextual culture are the Japanese (Kavanagh, 2016). Because they carefully "hide" what they think, are courteous and appear extremely grateful, do not rush decisions, and rarely use the word "no" (Zimmerman, 1985; Kavanagh,

2016.). Saying no is a loss of face for a Japanese person. Saying "yes" means that a person respects their interlocutor and is kind to them, therefore the Japanese "hai" ("yes") is heard very often during conversations. However, saying "hai" for a Japanese means that they understand what is being said or that they hear what is being said, but does not necessarily imply they agree with it (similar behavior is found in many Asian countries, especially East Asia).

High-context cultures also use more non-verbal expressions during conversations (Tian, 2012; Verluyten, 2014). Sometimes, these signs are not recognized or interpreted easily and correctly by people from other cultures. Moreover, elements of non-verbal communication replace spoken words but may

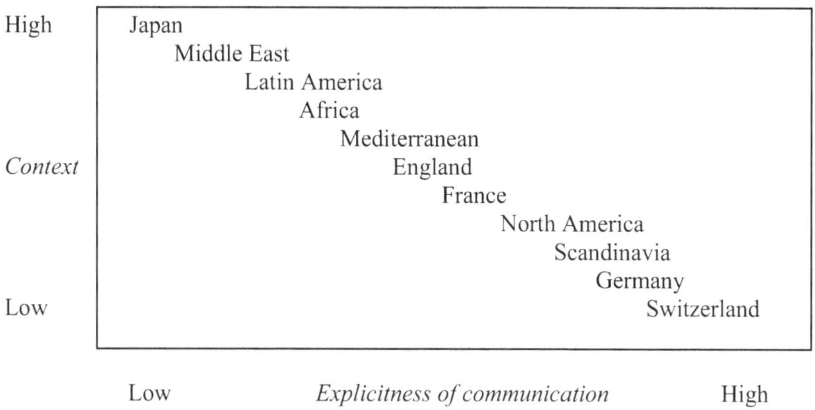

Figure 2: Context and Explicitness of Communication – Examples of Cultures
Source: (Hall & Hall, 1990).

differ among cultures in interpretation (meanings). Examples of high-context societies are Japan and other Asian societies, Middle East, Latin American and African countries, and others

Low-context cultures tend to communicate directly without the use of a wide variety of symbols, signs, and sayings that can be interpreted differently by people from diverse cultures (Hall, 1992). Context is not needed for the correct understanding of the message, which should, however, contain a lot of information, arguments, and data. From the "practical point of view", for members of low-context cultures, "yes" means "yes", "no" means "no", "tomorrow" means "tomorrow", etc. They tend to use negations and the word "no" if necessary. Low context societies are characterized by the individuality of expressing features (representatives of these cultures are individualists, on their own and responsible) and "face" is a much less salient concept (Hofstede et al., 2010). Examples of low-context cultures are Scandinavian countries, Switzerland, Germany, and the United States, (Figure 2). On top of this, representatives of low-context cultures do not use non-verbal expressions to such a great extent as high-context societies. Instead, they say directly and verbally what they want to say to their interlocutors (Verluyten, 2014).

Low and high-context communication is usually compared to the level of explicitness. High-context messages are usually related to low a level of explicitness and, vice versa, low-context messages are associated with a high level of directness (Figure 2).

Knowledge of high- and low- context cultures allows for a better understanding and decoding of the messages between parties belonging to different cultural groups and we should be aware that not everyone (even in business) have the same perceptions, attitudes, preferences, and ways of presenting their thoughts. Such knowledge can help to prepare people for different situations and the reactions of other parties. It can also make those involved more attuned to a particular form of behavior of other parties, which without such knowledge might be unnoticed or misinterpreted (Ferraro, 2002).

Styles of Verbal Communication in Culturally Diverse Backgrounds

Effective verbal communication between people from different cultures requires learning and mutual respect for the communication style that is characteristic of

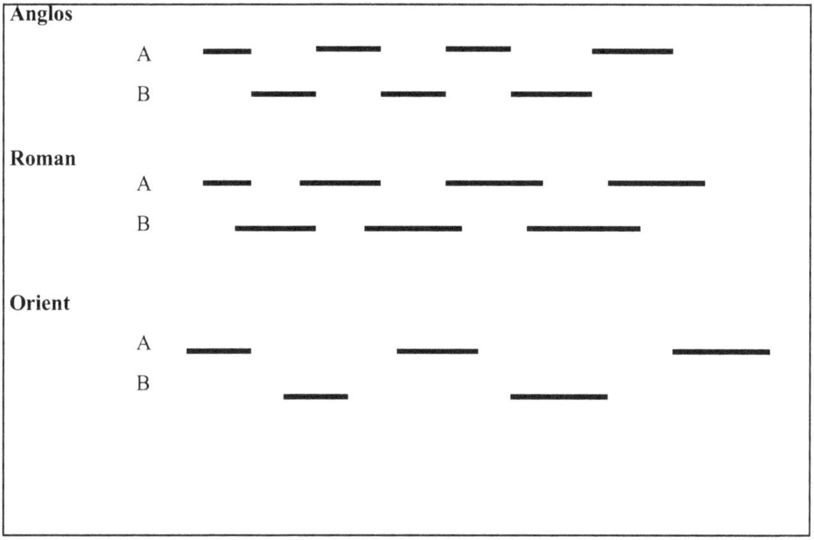

Figure 3: Styles of Verbal Communication
Source: (Trompenaars & Hampden-Turner, 2001).

the other party (Samovar & Porter, 1991). Trompenaars and Hampden-Turner (2001) distinguished three styles of formal verbal communication: Anglos, Roman and Orient (Figure 3).

The Anglos style of communication means not interrupting while another person is speaking. As soon as the first person (A) finishes speaking, the second person (B) begins their talk. For people from these cultures, interruption of speech and the so-called "breaking someone's word" is seen as particularly uncultured and rude. Waiting for your turn is a form of showing respect to your partner in conversation (Trompenaars & Hampden-Turner, 2001). This style is used, among others, in the United Kingdom, but also in the northern and central European countries. A majority of these cultures can also be considered to moderately expressive or restrained nations with regard to the level of expressiveness (Gesteland, 2012) .

The Roman style differs significantly from the Anglos way of communication. Here, participants of the conversation often interrupt each other. This behavior is connected with showing a great interest and engagement in what the other person is saying (Trompenaars & Hampden-Turner, 2001). Such way of communicating is found in emotional cultures, and is prevalent, among others, in Mediterranean and Latin American countries (Gesteland, 2012).

The Orient style of communication styles includes moments of silence between active turns in the conversation. After person A finishes their turn the second interlocutor (B) thinks about what the first interlocutor (A) just said. These cultures understand this moment of silence as a way of showing respect for the conversation partner (Trompenaars & Hampden-Turner, 2001; Tian, 2012). Members of Orient societies often fail to understand how representatives of Western cultures can understand each other well. In their opinion, it is very difficult and sometimes rude that they do not have time to think about what the interlocutor has just said. This style is used, among others, in many the many Asian countries which belong to reserved (no emotional) cultures (Gesteland, 2012).

Cross-Cultural Non-Verbal Communication

Verbal communication is the basis for good understanding between people from different countries. However, non-verbal communication, otherwise known as wordless communication, is equally important, as it complements the verbal form, and in some countries, it even it (Gabbott & Hogg, 2000; Steers et al., 2018; Park & El Mimouni, 2020).

Mehrabian (1981) introduced a sequence of numbers 7-38-55 to the theory of communication, which means that in the communication of attitudes, feelings and emotions, the percentage contribution of these elements to the final message is as follows: spoken words 7 %, voice sounds 38 % and non-verbal communication 55 %. He emphasized the significance of non-verbal communication in the process of personal conversation (Mehrabian, 1981). Taking into account that the voice sound belongs to non-verbal communication, it should be underlined that non-verbal communication can be up to 93 % of the entire communication.

A non-verbal message is an indirect message, with every movement of the body of the message sender being a certain symbol, which has a given social meaning, and a correct reading of which sometimes replaces direct communication with the use of words (Gabbott & Hogg, 2000).

Non-verbal communication includes many elements which are distinguished in scientific classifications (e.g. Gabbott & Hogg, 2000; Ferraro, 2002; Verluyten, 2014; Lin et al., 2020). They usually include:

- Kinesics – This pertains to movement and covers a wide range of movement-based behavior. Kinesics examines the “messages” sent by the human body and includes:
  - gestures – hand gestures, head gestures, posture, etc.;

- oculesics – facial expressions and eye contact during conversation;
- proxemics – the human use of space, i.e. the personal distance in conversation;
- haptics – the behavior of an individual related to touch

- Paralanguage – tone, speed and volume of speech, silence (the meaning of being silent when communicating), and other, non-linguistic behavior, e.g. yawns, grunts, etc.

Gestures

Each conversation involves many hand gestures. It is an integral part of communication. A lot of information is conveyed by hand gestures, each of which have specific meanings (often characteristic for a particular cultural group). The use of such non-verbal signs can shorten a conversation, because one gesture (one hand movement or the entire hand) sometimes replaces a few or even a dozen words (Axtel, 2007; Tian, 2012 Verluyten, 2014; Lin et al., 2020). Correct interpretation can therefore contribute to quick understanding of the statement by the other party, as long as the other party reads the sender's intentions correctly. Hand gestures are also very often complementary to verbal communication. As illustrators they present what is being talked about or what has just been said in a non-verbal (demonstrative) way (Steers et al., 2018; Verluyten, 2014). However, the meaning of gestures does not always have the same interpretation in another culture. For example, the "thumbs up"gesture can mean "OK" or "good" in many societies, but in some cultures (like Iran, Bangladesh and Thailand) it is the equivalent of showing the "middle finger".

Head movements are another element of non-verbal speech that may be confusing or misunderstood. For example, during a conversation with a Bulgarian, one should be aware that the accepted gestures of acceptance and negation are opposite in this culture. Nodding up and down means "No" for them (for most cultures it is a gesture of approval "Yes"), whilst turning the head from side to side is a symbol of consent, acceptance, approval – "Yes" (for most cultures it is a gesture of negation, the denial of "No").

Oculesics

Facial expressions apply to all types of expressions created with the use of facial muscles (Gabbott & Hogg, 2000). They "accompany" every conversation and often appear automatically in connection with experiencing and expressing various feelings and emotions. They play a special role when communicating with people from different cultural groups, among which the greatest diversity is found in smiling and eye contact.

In a cross-cultural communication a smile on our face is not a universal sign of friendship or joy. Although in many Western cultures a smile is the "initiator" of communication, in the Far East it can be used to hide embarrassment, sadness, anxiety or anger (Novinger, 2001; Axtel, 2007; Tian, 2012). For example, when negotiating with Japanese, Chinese or Indonesians, a smile on their faces may not mean acceptance and satisfaction with the goal achieved. On the contrary, it can be polite behavior covering dissatisfaction and anger. Showing anger or dissatisfaction would be a sign of "losing face" and thus a disgrace to the group to which they belong. Differences in the interpretation of these behaviors may lead to conflict situations. Along with long silences, the smile on a Japanese person's face can be a sign of nervousness. Such a state often causes anxiety for the other party. Instead, we should t respect the moment of silence and respond with a gentle smile, if everything on our part has been properly fulfilled.

Maintaining intense eye contact during intercultural communication can also contribute to discomfort, especially when our partner is a person from restrained culture (Verluyten, 2014). Looking at someone directly in the eye for extended periods of time can be a sign of hostility, intimidation and provocation in most Asian cultures (Axtel, 2007; Tian, 2012) and such behavior can be a sign of disrespect for the person. Therefore, Western businesspeople are advised to only glance briefly at the other person's face, and focus their eyesight on other elements. On the other hand, in more expressive countries, especially in Latin American and Arab cultures, intense eye contact is commonly found (Ferraro, 2002; Gesteland, 2012; Verluyten, 2014), and it may be a symbol of showing respect and a sign of understanding your communication partner. In these cultures, maintaining eye contact is very important both when speaking and when an interlocutor responds. By contrast, Japanese and Koreans avoid looking directly at interlocutors during a conversation (Axtel, 2007; Gesteland, 2012), believing it is a sign of weakness. Americans, on the other hand, say that looking a person directly in the eye shows the honesty and truthfulness of the other person, and in Latin American cultures, intense eye contact between men may be perceived as a challenge or a sign of aggression (Gesteland, 2012).

Proxemics

Proxemics concerns the use of space and physical distance by the parties in the communication process, i.e., the distance that a person keeps in relation to other interlocutors (Jones, 1984; Lin et al., 2020). Each individual has a zone of spatial distance created around them. Depending on cultural differences, such a distance is larger (available to a larger number of people – family, friends, etc.) or smaller (usually only the closest ones have access to it). Personal distance is perceived and used differently among different societies.

When the area of intimacy is disturbed by another person to whom they have no access (permission), defensive reactions may occur, e.g. stepping back. When dealing with cultures that prefer "close" contact during conversations, care should be taken before making such a sudden "backward" motion. This can be interpreted as a sign of enmity and hostility. In turn, if we ourselves are "close distance" people, and we talk to representatives who prefer a large distance, we should also be careful not to be taken as an insistent communication partner. A small distance is characteristic of, among others, Latin American, Mediterranean and Arab cultures, whereas a moderate or large spatial distance is found, e.g., among North American societies, and countries of northern, central and eastern Europe, and the greatest personal distance is characteristic of most Asian countries (Gesteland, 2012; Tian, 2012).

Haptics

Haptics is a branch of science that studies the behavior of people in relation to touch. As with othe forms of non-verbal communication, the behavior of people from different countries is very often varied in this area (Gabbott & Hogg, 2000). There are societies for which touching (e.g. while greeting, standing or sitting next to each other) during conversation is common, and others who limit it to a minimum in contact with others. The latter group is more sensitive about being touched, especially by strangers, i.e. from outside the immediate family. Touching during a conversation can cause discomfort and lead to offense. Most Asian and Scandinavian cultures are good examples of cultures who prefer not to be touching, whilst touching is often observed in Mediterranean, Latin American, and Arab cultures (Tian, 2012; Gesteland, 2012).

Knowing the various rules regarding the manner of greeting, frequency of touch, etc. in our business partner's culture is an expression of respect for them, as well as an opportunity to show our knowledge of the intercultural business protocol. On the other hand, ignorance of the meaning of various gestures can lead to disagreement and drawing the wrong results of business conversation.

Paralanguage

Paralanguage consists of the auditory components of a conversation that have meaning independent of the content of the words, such as: intonation, articulation, tempo, volume, sighs, grunts, laughter, and silence. These elements are culturally grounded. For example, Asian cultures may use silence for face-saving, hiding emotions or a moment for thinking about what was said before (Tian, 2012; Verluyten, 2014; Kavanagh, 2016). Roman cultures (e.g. Latin American countries, some Mediterranean countries), on the other hand, are characterized by the use of different voice intonations; often their utterances move swiftly from a quiet to a very loud tone. In turn, representatives of the Orient cultural group (e.g. most East and South-East Asian countries) speak using an even voice modulation and a rather quiet manner of speaking. Representatives of the Roman group believe that their manner of speaking indicates a high degree of commitment to the matter, while restrained societies (including the Orient group) consider people from the Roman group and such behavior as not serious. According to them, respect for the interlocutor is instead shown when the conversation takes place in a calm and subdued mood.

The differentiation in the verbal and non-verbal behavior of cultural groups contributes to the degree of their expressiveness. Cultures can be distinguished as either expressive (emotional) or restrained based on criteria associated with touching, personal distance, eye contact, and paralanguage, (Trompenaars & Hampden-Turner, 2001; Gesteland, 2012). Highly expressive (emotional) cultures are societies that show their emotions and feelings using a whole range of elements of non-verbal communication (Gesteland, 2012; Verluyten, 2014; Kavanagh, 2016). They are characterized, inter alia, by small personal distance between people, high acceptance of tactile contact, intense eye contact and a loud tone of speaking. These include: Mediterranean, Latin American, and some Arab countries. By contrast, representatives of restrained cultures do not reveal their emotions (especially feelings), but rather try to scrupulously hide them (Trompenaars & Hampden-Turner, 2001; Gesteland, 2012; Tian, 2012; Kavanagh, 2016). These are societies characterized by a large personal distance between people, a lack of acceptance of tactile contact, indirect eye contact, and a rather quiet and calm tone of speech. These include Southeast Asians, as well as Nordic and Germanic Europeans. The following cultures can be categorized as displaying moderate expressiveness: the United States, Canada, Australia, Eastern European countries and African countries (Trompenaars & Hampden-Turner, 2001; Gesteland, 2012).

Conclusions

Culture influences the way people speak, gesticulate, use space, touch one another, etc. It is an important barrier in communication among people coming from different cultural backgrounds (Tian, 2012; Bartosik-Purgat; 2020). Cultural obstacles may cause problems in understanding the message and giving a proper reply, and sometimes, the usage of improper gestures or other signs can offend one's interlocutor(s).

Knowing the meaning of international cultural aspects of verbal and non-verbal communication can help both in the professional and private lives of people who cooperate with members of different cultures (e.g. during negotiating with a foreign partner or just communicating with a colleague from another culture).

The range of a culture"s influence on the intercultural communication process is so great that it is impossible to describe all its features in one chapter. However, the author would have been at least somewhat successful if readers, and especially those who communicate with members of different cultures, are sensitized to the existence of cultural differences in this area. In economic and business life, these factors are still very often ignored and before starting cooperation with people coming from diverse foreign markets, it is worth thoroughly analyzing all the cultural aspects and communication features of a particular society.

References

Axtel, R. E. (2007). *Essential Do's and Taboos: The Complete Guide to International Business and Leisure Travel.* New York: Wiley Publ.

Bartosik-Purgat, M. (2019). *New Media in the Marketing Communication of Enterprises in the International Market.* Warsaw: PWN Publ.

Bartosik-Purgat, M. (2020). External Factors of New Media Tools' Usage in Personal Communication across Countries. *International Journal of Emerging Markets* (Vol. ahead-of-print No. ahead-of-print). https://doi.org/10.1108/IJOEM-10-2019-0865.

Camilleri, M. A. (2021). Strategic Dialogic Communication Through Digital Media During COVID-19 Crisis. In M. A. Camilleri (Ed.), *Strategic Corporate Communication in the Digital Age* (pp. 1–18). Bingley: Emerald Publishing Limited. https://doi.org/10.1108/978-1-80071-264-520211001.

Chaika, E. (1994). *Language, the Social Mirror.* London: Heinle&Heinle Publ.

Ferraro, G. P. (2002). *The Cultural Dimension of International Business* (4th ed.). New Jersey: Prentice Hall.

Gabbott, M., & Hogg, G. (2000). An Empirical Investigation of the Impact of Non-Verbal Communication on Service Evaluation. *European Journal of Marketing, 34*(3/4), 384–398. Retrieved from: https://doi.org/10.1108/03090560010311911.

Gesteland, R. R. (2012). *Cross-Cultural Business Behavior: A Guide for Global Management*, 5th ed. Copenhagen: Business School Press.

Guang Tian, R. (2011). International Communications Strategy: Development in Cross-Cultural Communications, PR and Social Media. *Journal of Consumer Marketing, 28*(3), 242–244. Retrieved from: https://doi.org/10.1108/07363761111127699.

Gudykunst, W. B., Matsumoto, Y., Ting, Toomey, S., Nishida, T., Kim, K., & Heyman, S. (1996). The Influence of Cultural Individualism & Collectivism, Self Construals, and Individual Values on Communication Styles across Cultures. *Human Communication Research, 22*(4), 510–543.

Hall, E. T. (1976). *Beyond Culture*. New York: Anchor Books.

Hall, E. T. (1992). *An Anthropology of Everyday Life*. New York: Doubleday: Anchor Books.

Hall, E. T., & Hall, M. R. (1990). *Understanding Cultural Differences*. Yarmouth: Intercultural Press.

Hofstede G., Hofstede G. J., & Minkov M. (2010). *Cultures and Organizations; Software of the Mind* (3rd ed.). New York: McGraw-Hill.

Hollensen, S. (2004). *Global Marketing. A Decision Oriented Approach* (3rd ed.). Harlow: Prentice Hall.

Jones, L. (1984). Proxemics: The Language of Space. *Education + Training 26*(1), 6–10. https://doi.org/10.1108/eb002119.

Kavanagh, B. (2016). Emoticons as a Medium for Channeling Politeness within American and Japanese Online Blogging Communities. *Language and Communication, 48*, 53–65.

Kluckhohn, C., & Kroeber, A. (1952). Culture: A Critical Review of Concepts and Definitions. *Peabody Museum Papers*. Cambridge, MA: The Peabody Musuem Press, *47*(1).

Kluckhohn, C., & Kroeber, A. (2020). *Culture: A Critical Review of Concepts and Definitions – The History of Human Culture, Its Role in Social Sciences*. Pantianos Classics Publ.

Konara, P., & Wei, Y. (2021). Does Language Matter to Foreign Subsidiary Performance? *International Marketing Review, 38*(2), 276–299. Retrieved from: https://doi.org/10.1108/IMR-05-2019-0129.

Leung, K. Bhagat, R. S., Buchan, N. R., Erez, M., & Gibson, C. B. (2005). Culture and International Business: Recent Advances and Their Implications for Future Research. *Journal of International Business Studies*, *36*(4), 357–378.

Lin, H., Zhang, M., & Gursoy, D. (2020). Impact of Nonverbal Customer-to-Customer Interactions on Customer Satisfaction and Loyalty Intentions. *International Journal of Contemporary Hospitality Management, 32*(5), 1967–1985. Retrieved from: https://doi.org/10.1108/IJCHM-08-2019-0694.

Macnamara, J. R. (2004). The Crucial Role of Research in Multicultural and Cross-Cultural Communication. *Journal of Communication Management, 8*(3), 322–334. Retrieved from: https://doi.org/10.1108/13632540410807727.

McLuhan, M. (1964). *Understanding Media: The Extensions of Man.* New York: McGraw-Hill.

Mehrabian, A. (1981). *Silent Messages: Implicit Communication of Emotions and Attitudes* (2nd ed.). Belmont: Wadsworth.

Meyer, E. (2016). *The Culture Map.* New York: Public Affairs.

Novinger, T. (2001). *Intercultural Communication.* Austin: University of Texas Press.

Park, J. R., & El Mimouni, H. (2020). Emoticons and Non-Verbal Communications across Arabic, English, and Korean Tweets. *Global Knowledge, Memory and Communication 69*(8/9), 579–595. Retrieved from: https://doi.org/10.1108/GKMC-02-2020-0021.

Qian, C., Seuring, S., Wagner, R., & Dion, P. A. (2021). Personal and Organizational Level Relationships in Relational Exchanges in Supply Chains – A Bottom-Up Model. *Supply Chain Management, 26*(1), 32–47. Retrieved from: https://doi.org/10.1108/SCM-12-2019-0441.

Ronen, S., & Shenkar, O. (2017). *Navigating Global Business. A Cultural Compass.* Cambridge: University Press.

Samovar, L. A. (1999). *Intercultural Communication: A Reade*r (9th ed.). Belmont: Wadsworth Publ.

Samovar, L., & Porter, R. (1991). *Communicating Between Cultures.* Belmont: Wadsworth.

Shannon, C. E., & Weaver, W. (1949). *The Mathematical Theory of Communication.* Urbana, IL: University of Illinois Press.

Steers, R. M., Nardon, L., & Sanchez-Runde, C. J. (2018). *Management across Cultures Developing Global Competencies* (3rd ed.). Cambridge: University Press.

Tian, X. (2012). *Managing International Business in China.* Cambridge: University Press.

Trompenaars, F., & Hampden-Turner, C. (2001). *Riding the Waves of Culture* (3rd ed.). Nicholas Brealey Publishing.

Tylor, E. B. (1873). *Primitive Culture: Researches into the Development of Mythology, Philosophy, Religion, Language, Art, and Custom* (2nd ed.). London: John Murray.

Vemou, K., & Karyda, M. (2020). Requirements for Private Communications over Public Spheres. *Information and Computer Security, 28*(1), 68–96. Retrieved from: https://doi.org/10.1108/ICS-01-2019-0002.

Verluyten, S. P. (2014). *Intercultural Skills for International Business and International Relations. A Practical Introduction with Exercises*. Haag: Acco Publ.

Weaver, G. R. (2013). *Intercultural Relations: Communication, Identity, and Conflict*. New York: Pearson Learning Solutions.

Xue, F. (2019). Facebook News Feed Ads: A Social Impact Theory Perspective. *Journal of Research in Interactive Marketing, 13*(4), 529–546.

Zimmerman, M. (1985). *How to Do Business with the Japanese*. New York: Random Mouse.

Introduction to Cultural Universals and Human Interaction: Supporting Global Professionals on Their Intercultural Journey

By Svetlana Kurteš

The following chapter introduces Hofstede's Cultural Dimensions, Hall's Cultural Dichotomies, and Brown and Levinson's Linguistic Politeness Theory so that some fundamental aspects of communicating successfully across cultures is assured. It is pointed out that Hofstede had been given the task of identifying why IBM employees misunderstood one another despite proficiency in the English language. He revealed that the cultural values and norms of the employees as well as their communicative styles and interactional behavior could be explained by the employees' national culture. Hofstede concluded that all other things being the same, i.e. corporate culture, professional background and experience, led to his conclusion that the differences in behavior and communication he had identified in his survey could be explained by differences in the employees' culture. Hall was interested in nonverbal communication and discussed the perception of time, space, and context from a cultural perspective which, in turn, influences the communicative behavior across different cultures. The specific dimensions of Hofstede and Hall are explained in detail so that it is possible to identify the various forms of behavior and communication exhibited in different cultures around the globe. With the help of these dimensions it is possible to not only understand the differences, but to also predict how someone from a particular culture might behave and communicate. The chapter also introduces Brown and Levinson's Theory of Linguistic Politeness which is a theoretical framework designed to explain some universal features of human interaction. The theory postulates that politeness is a universal feature observed by interlocutors whenever they communicate with one another. But what is considered polite communication is very culture specific which explains why what might be considered polite in one culture may not be perceived as such another culture. The chapter ends with suggestions for some hands-on activities designed to illustrate how the presented information might be applied. This chapter, thus, provides an additional introduction to and foundation for some fu ndamental aspects of intercultural communication and politeness that will be discussed in detail in a number of the subsequent chapters of this book.

Michael B. Hinner

Svetlana Kurteš is a UK-based scholar with an extensive international experience in the area of linguistic and intercultural education, spanning over almost three decades. She has held academic positions at universities in Europe, Asia and the Middle East. She is currently affiliated with the University of Madeira, where she is engaged on an invited basis, teaching on a number of units in the area of English and Comparative Linguistics, English for Specific Purposes, Business and Intercultural Communication, etc. The focus of her research interests clusters around interdisciplinary approaches to communication, culture and society and issues surrounding their pedagogical applications. She regularly presents and publishes internationally.

Svetlana Kurteš

Cultural Universals and Human Interaction: Supporting Global Professionals on Their Intercultural Journey

Introduction

The chapter intends to put a spotlight on some cornerstones of human interaction in intercultural and cross-cultural contexts, primarily having in mind young global professionals and future business leaders as its intended readership. It specifically focuses on some theoretical approaches dealing with the concept of cultural universals and communication, enabling the reader to get a better understanding of their interdependence and internal structure. More concretely, the chapter looks into key characteristics of Hofstede's Cultural Dimensions, Hall's Cultural Dichotomies and Brown and Levinson's Linguistic Politeness Theory, assuming no previous knowledge in the area. Using her own pedagogical experience and practice, the author argues that the chosen theoretical approaches bring about the threshold level of knowledge and competences, necessary to function effectively in global intercultural and cross-cultural contexts. Once the reader has acquired basic concepts of cultural universals, they will be able to understand more profoundly what motivates our communicative behaviour and interpret correctly the interlocutor's communicative intentions.

The chapter is structured in the following way: each theoretical approach is briefly presented and illustrated with examples that young global professionals can find intriguing and eye-opening. The chapter ends with a suggested activity that is suitable both for a classroom-based setting or independent work, discussion and reflection.

Cultural Universals 1: Geert Hofstede's Cultural Dimensions

Originally put forward by Dutch anthropologist Geert Hofstede (1928–2020), Cultural Dimensions revolutionised our understanding of culture and communication, bringing about the notion of universality of their fundamental features. That is to say, Hofstede's framework provided necessary tools for interpreting human interaction in cross- and intercultural contexts, allowing us not only to see patterns in our communicative behaviour across the globe, but also to be able to understand, explain and, possibly more importantly, predict typical ways of communicative behaviour characteristic of a speech community. Hofstede's research was originally commissioned by the IBM, one of the largest American multinational technology corporations, prompted by senior management's observation that a number of communicative failures their staff were experiencing on a daily basis could not be explained by the lack of their language proficiency skills. Hofstede was asked to investigate the reasons behind this growing issue. He embarked on the investigation in the late 1960's, collecting a large amount of data consisting of IBM employees' surveys that looked into their cultural values and norms, communicative styles and interactional behaviour. The data collected was one of the biggest to date, consisting of over 100,000 questionnaires taken from more than 70 international IBM branches worldwide. The results of the investigation were published in 1980 in the volume entitled *Culture's consequences: international differences in work-related values* (Hofstede, 1980), postulating 4 major cultural dimensions indicating behavioural patterns characteristic of multinational professional contexts. Specifically, they were: Individualism vs Collectivism, Power Distance (Low vs High), Masculinity vs Femininity and Uncertainty Avoidance. The framework was subsequently expanded, with two more dimensions added. Here we will briefly present the original 4 dimension and refer the reader to relevant literature elaborating on the additional ones.

Individualism vs Collectivism refers to the continuum whose one end represents cultural values having a focus on the individual, while the other end of the spectrum, the collectivist one, represents "we-cultures", that is to say, cultures in which collective interests take priority (Larina et al., 2017). In other words, "Individualism is the extent to which people feel independent, as opposed to being interdependent as members of larger wholes" (www.geerthofst ede.com). Collectivism, on the other hand, "means that one 'knows one's place' in life, which is determined socially" (ibid.). Having analysed a large amount of collected data, Hofstede and his associates were able to identify culture-specific scores on the scale from 1 to 100, defining a place for each observed country of the Individualism-Collectivism continuum. The results, presented on a world map, do not necessarily take into account regional differences within a country, so should perhaps be taken as "rough 'climate maps' of culture" (www.geerth ofstede.com). Countries scoring high on the Individualist end of the spectrum are the United States of America, Canada, Australia, the United Kingdom, etc. Typical representatives on the opposite end of the spectrum are China, Russia, some Latin American, African and South Asian countries (see Figure 1 for further details).

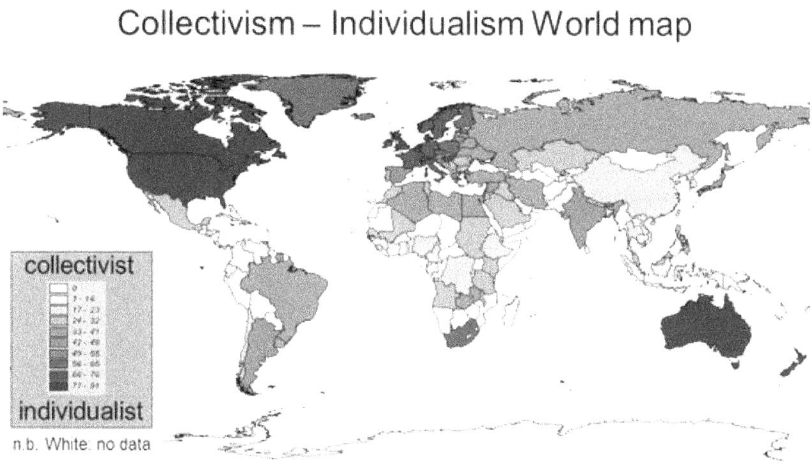

Figure 1: Individualism-Collectivism in the World
Retrieved from: https://geerthofstede.com/culture-geert-hofstede-gert-jan-hofstede/6d-model-of-national-culture/.

Power distance, the second major cultural dimension originally proposed by Hofstede, refers to the hierarchical stratification of a society, that is to say, how perceived power and status of individuals are distributed. If a country has a low level of power distance, one can say it is a "flat" society, in which our perceived social status does not play a crucial role. Similarly, countries with a high level of power distance are rather hierarchical, which means that our perceived power, coming from our attributed social status, is very important, determining our role in society and, consequently, our communicative behaviour. In Hofstede's own words "Power Distance is the extent to which the less powerful members of organizations and institutions (…) accept and expect that power is distributed unequally" (ibid.). Typical representatives of the High Power Distance end of the spectrum are countries of the Far East and Middle East, South East Asia, etc, while a number of Low Power Distance countries are in Western and North Western Europe, North America, etc (see Figure 2).

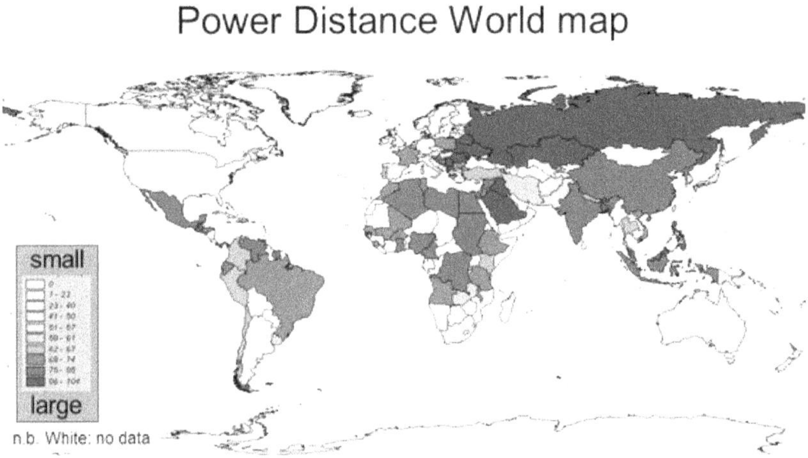

Figure 2: Power Distance in the World

Retrieved from: https://geerthofstede.com/culture-geert-hofstede-gert-jan-hofstede/6d-model-of-national-culture/.

The third cultural dimension is the *Masculinity-Femininity* continuum, referring to what extent a country values the use of force, competitiveness and well divided gender and socially imposed roles, on the one hand, or empathy, general well-being, social care and no visible division, even fluidity of gender roles. In other words, "(i)n a masculine society, men are supposed to be tough. (…) In a feminine society, the genders are emotionally closer. Competing is not so openly endorsed, and there is sympathy for the underdog" (ibid.). Hofstede sees masculine societies as rather "gendered", that is to say, gender roles are very firmly defined and strictly observed. In feminine societies the opposite is valid: the social imposition and determination of gender roles are hardly there, allowing individuals to express their gender identity and define their social roles freely. Geographically speaking, countries on the Masculine end of the spectrum are in the Far East, Middle East, some Central American, Latin American and African countries, while a prototypical example of a feminine society would be countries of Northwest Europe and Scandinavia (see Figure 3).

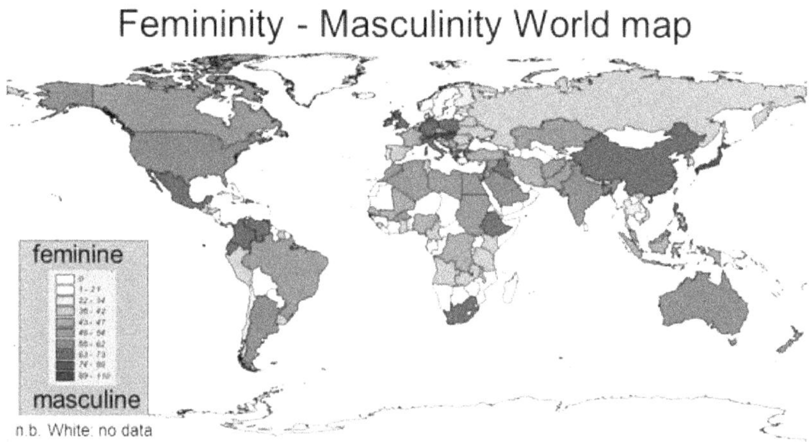

Figure 3: Masculinity-Femininity in the World
Retrieved from: https://geerthofstede.com/culture-geert-hofstede-gert-jan-hofstede/6d-model-of-national-culture/.

The fourth cultural dimension originally proposed by Hofstede is *Uncertainly Avoidance*, referring to how a society deals with a prospect of uncertainty. Hofstede stresses out that this dimension is not about "risk avoidance, nor with following rules. It has to do with anxiety and distrust in the face of the unknown, and conversely, with a wish to have fixed habits and rituals, and to know the truth" (ibid.). Countries with a very high level of Uncertainty Avoidance are Russia and Portugal. The opposite end of the spectrum are countries with a very low Uncertainty Avoidance, China and Sweden being typical representatives (see Figure 4).

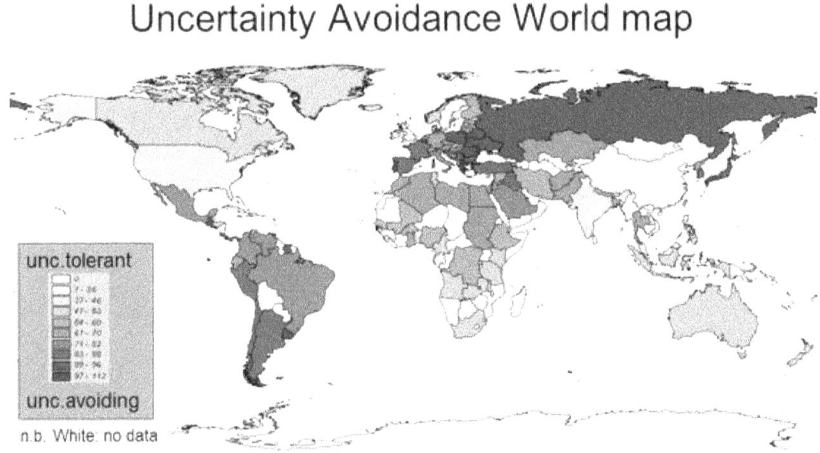

Figure 4: Uncertainty Avoidance in the World

Retrieved from: https://geerthofstede.com/culture-geert-hofstede-gert-jan-hofstede/6d-model-of-national-culture/.

Suggestions for Further Activities

If you are interested in exploring Hofstede's cultural dimensions further, a good starting point could be his website https://geerthofstede.com/culture-geert-hofstede-gert-jan-hofstede/6d-model-of-national-culture/. where you can find short video clips in which he talks about each dimension in his own words. This is a rather unique opportunity to hear about a theoretical framework directly from the author, so take a listen and then check individual countries' scores for each of the dimensions. This is the website: https://www.hofstede-insights.com/product/compare-countries/. You can also compare scores of two or more different countries, reflect on them and, finally, engage in a discussion with your classmates about the possible implications. Specifically, think about if knowing the cultural dimensions can help us understand better and predict communicative behaviour of interlocutors in inter- and cross-cultural contexts.

Cultural Universals 2: Edward Hall's Dichotomies

Edward T. Hall (1914–2009) was an American anthropologist. Having received his doctoral degree from Columbia University in 1942, he embarked on a very prolific career as a scholar and university professor. He taught at a number of universities, including Harvard Business School, Northwestern University, the

University of Denver, etc. Hall spent many years doing anthropological field work around the world, which enabled him to be in close contact with cultural diversity of communities worldwide, subsequently prompting him to focus his research on culture-specific differences in our perception of time and space and, in turn, how these differences influence our interactional behaviour, both verbal and, perhaps even more so, non-verbal. His contribution to the study of non-verbal communication is particularly noteworthy, to a great extent considered to be pioneering and seminal.

Hall's framework, also known as Hall's *cultural dichotomies*, puts forward a profound, rather revolutionary, insight into our perception of time, space and context, bringing a new dimension – the cultural one – into our understanding and interpretation of these concepts. In other words, Hall's framework looks into aspects of objective physical reality and identifies their culture-specific interpretation, postulating two opposing divisions – dichotomies – in our perception of these segments of reality and, consequently, our communicative behaviour influenced by it. We present the dichotomies in more detail below.

Perhaps one of the most widely known dichotomies is the so-called *monochronic and polychronic cultural concept of time*. Starting from the premise that time is a segment of universal physical reality we all share, Halls postulates two separate divisions in our perception of time, both very culture-specific. He elaborated on these concepts in his book entitled *The Silent Language*, originally published in 1959, and further expanded on in his book *The Dance of Life* (1983). All subsequent references to Hall in this section refer to information from both of these books which is why there is no further reference to Hall in this section. The monochronic vs polychronic perception of time is essentially our "cultural lens" through which we observe the concept of time and, consequently, how we behave, interact with each other and engage with our environment. More specifically, the monochronic perception of time is essentially a linear timeline dedicated to a specific singular activity, carefully planned and scheduled. Prototypical representatives of a monochronic culture are Germany, Switzerland and the United States of America, countries in which punctuality, time-keeping and commitment to previously agreed deadlines are highly valued. This is particularly well observed in business and professional contexts, where adhering to an agreed and pre-planned schedule, milestones and deliverables is sacrosanct. On the other hand, in polychronic cultures, specifically in professional contexts, the focus is not on a specific task done within a specific time slot, but rather diffused, allowing several projects and tasks to be happening parallelly and simultaneously. It is important to notice that polychronicity should not be interpreted as synonymous with sloppiness, laziness, unprofessionalism, but simply as a different cultural universal, valuing not so much the process, its stages and steps set out within a meticulously defined timeframe, as is the case with monochronicity, but rather the end result, which can be reached and achieved in a number of different ways. Polychronic cultures around the world are numerous, the most prototypical representatives being countries in Central and Latin America, Mediterranean countries, countries of the Middle East, Southeast Asia, Africa and others (see Figure 5).

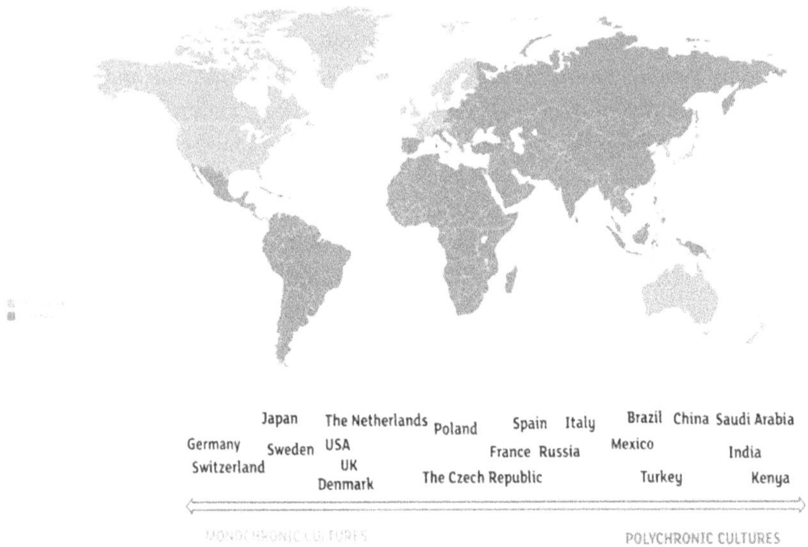

Figure 5: Monochronic and Polychronic Cultures in the World

Retrieved from: https://www.ericsson.com/en/blog/2019/10/the-power-of-agile. (Based on Morden, 1999; Kotabe & Helsen, 2001).

Hall is widely acclaimed as the founder of *proxemics*, a study field exploring our engagement with the space around us. He makes an important distinction between a *high territoriality* and *low territoriality* cultures, highlighting the difference in which our sense of belonging and personal space is considered of utmost importance, as is the case in high territoriality cultures, and the opposite, in which this is not considered of great importance. In business and professional contexts this could come to the fore, specifically in case of culturally diverse teams. Hall proposes concepts of *intimate and personal space* and, more widely, *social and public space*, indicating their proximal values (see Figure 6). It should be noted, though, that borderlines between individual zones are also quite culture specific, particularly the concepts of personal and social space, which may significantly vary across cultures. Typically, Central and Latin American countries would have smaller personal and social space zones, with interlocutors coming rather close to each other while interacting verbally. On the other hand, Great Britain can be taken as a typical representative of a culture in which the concept of personal space is very important and interlocutors are expected to observe it and keep the distance (approximately 1m/3ft 2').

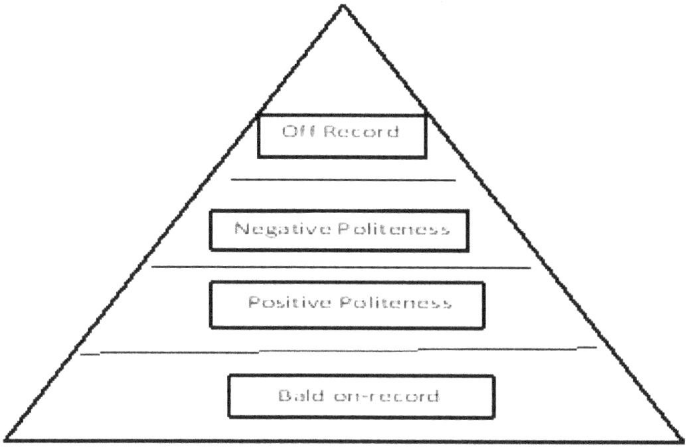

Figure 6: Hall's Proxemics Zones
Source: (Marquardt & Greenberg, 2012).

There is another cultural dichotomy that Edward Hall has been widely known for. It focuses on *context* and how important it is to take it into account when interpreting a message. Cultures in which it is important to take the wider context of the communicative event into account when interpreting the message are known as *high context* or implicit communication cultures, and cultures in which context does not play an important part, because communication is rather explicit and direct, are known as *low context* cultures. Looking at the global professional arena, one can easily see that this cultural dichotomy is another very important and relevant one, particularly in culturally diverse teams. It is necessary to possess a high level of awareness of these issues and agree on the appropriate communicative style that will be acceptable for and accessible to all member of the team, thus assuring successful and efficient exchange of ideas during the communicative process. Typical representatives of high context

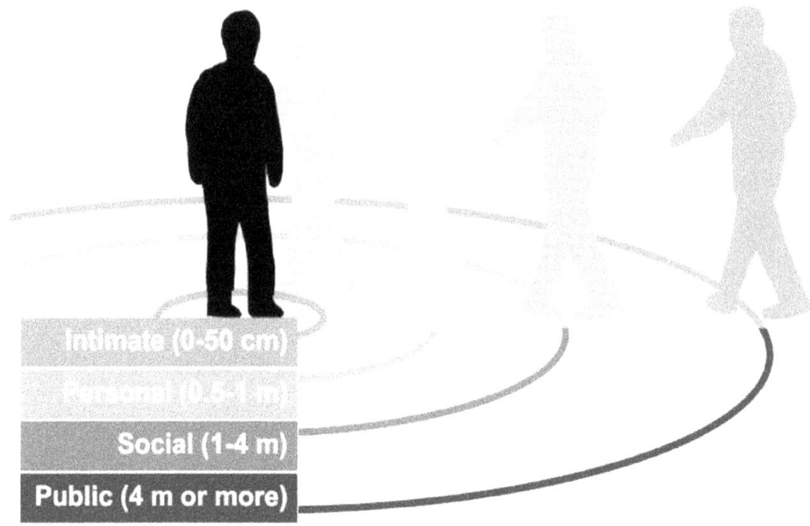

Figure 7: Hall's High Context vs Low Context Culture World Map
Source: (Duncan Chapple, 2006. Retrieved from: https://www.influencerrelations.com/209/mid-atlantic-reading-on-the-english).

cultures are countries in the region of Asia, Japan being the most prominent one, while countries typically representing low context cultures, favouring explicit and direct communicative styles, are Germany, Switzerland and the United States of America (see Figure 7 for further details).

Suggestions for Further Activities

Now that you know more about Hofstede's Cultural Dimensions and Hall's Cultural Dichotomies, you can begin to see patterns in cultural geographical diversity and understand the reasons behind our communicative behaviour cross- and interculturally. You can now take a look at each cultural dimension and each dichotomy and examine the likelihood of their compatibility. For example, if a society is on the High Power Distance end of the spectrum, their Masculinity index also tends to be higher. At the same time, they also tend to be high context cultures as well. Japan is a good example. Think about your country/region or the country/region you lived in or are familiar with. What are their scores in Hofstede's cultural dimensions and where do they stand in terms of Hall's dichotomies?

Cultural Universals 3: Brown & Levinson's Theory of Linguistics Politeness

Penelope Brown (b. 1944) and Stephen Levinson (b. 1947) are two internationally renowned scholars whose long-term collaboration has brought forward what is known as the *Theory of Linguistic Politeness*, a framework explaining some universal features of human interaction. More specifically, Penelope Brown is an American anthropological linguist, who has devoted her whole academic career to exploring issues in language, culture and cognition. She was awarded her doctoral degree in Anthropology from the University of California at Berkeley in 1979, having subsequently spent most of her professional academic career at the Max Planck Institute for Psycholinguistics in Nijmegen, The Netherlands, where she is now an Emeritus Professor. Stephen Levinson is a British-born social scientist, anthropologist and linguist. He was educated at the University of Cambridge, UK, where he received his BA, and then at the University of California at Berkeley, where he was awarded his doctorate in Anthropological Linguistics. He has held academic positions at a number of universities, including the University of Cambridge, the University of Stanford and the Max Planck Institute for Psycholinguistics in Nijmegen, where he was Academic Director until his retirement in 2017. Penelope Brown and Stephen Levinson are both prolific authors, but they are internationally known for their seminal and influential book *Politeness: some universals in language usage*, published in 1987. They presented their theoretical framework postulating that politeness in communication is a universal feature observed by interlocutors whenever they engage in communicative exchange. In other words, politeness is a universal concept, cherished and valued by speech communities world-wide, but what type of communicative behaviour is considered polite in an individual community is very culture-specific. This distinction is very important to understand. It might be fair to say that the universality and ubiquity of politeness at the conceptual level makes it one of the building blocks of successful and effective communicative behaviour; however, what happens on the "surface" level, the level of day-to-day communicative exchange, specifically in inter- and cross-cultural contexts, may turn politeness into a rather difficult stumbling block, preventing communicative events from being successfully executed and delivered. That is why understanding basic principles of the Theory of Politeness and, more specifically, politeness strategies put forward by Brown and Levinson, is very beneficial and eye-opening. We present these strategies below.

The Theory of Politeness takes into account the concept of "face", derived originally from Erving Goffman's framework of "facework" (Goffman, 1967), one of the very influential sociological theories. Here face should not be taken in its literal meaning, but rather as our public persona, the way we project ourselves, how we would like to be seen and perceived by the others. Face plays a very important part in East Asian cultures, China, Japan, Korea and Vietnam being some of the most prominent representatives. The English language has expressions such as "to lose face", denoting a situation causing one to feel embarrassed or humiliated publicly or, in case of the expression "to save face", a situation in which one was able to avoid public humiliation and/or embarrassment. Brown and Levinson make a distinction between the so-called *positive* and *negative face*. Again, the labels should not be taken literally. In other words, a positive face should not be interpreted as a "good, pretty face", and a negative face as a "bad, ugly face". Rather, in order to understand the meaning of these labels in the Theory of Politeness we should move away from these literal interpretations of their meaning and look at the explanations given by the authors. Positive face is a type of communicative behaviour in which the overarching value is to show solidarity, appreciation and approval. Interlocutors intend to establish common ground and make each other feel welcome, part of the team. On the other hand, negative face is a type of communicative behaviour in which the overarching value the interlocutors tend to observe is respecting each other's autonomy, privacy and space, avoiding any imposition of personal views on the participant in the communicative event. This is also very important to notice: any communicative event is potentially *face threatening*, that is to say, it can cause the interlocutors to feel embarrassed, damaging their public persona and breaking the expected rules of behaviour. Successful communication is, therefore, characterised by the interlocutors' intention to minimise the threat to either their positive or negative face. They do so by employing specific communicative strategies in order to redress the so-called *face threatening acts*, making choices in language use that give the interlocutors space and/or showing a friendly attitude to them. Face threatening acts can be verbal (i.e. expressed by spoken or written language), but also non-verbal (expressed by facial expressions, body language, etc) or extra-linguistic (expressed by features such as intonation, tone, voice pitch, etc).

When we communicate, we employ specific strategies ensuring our communicative intentions are relayed and interpreted correctly. These strategies are the pillars of the Theory of Politeness, characterising any communicative event that happens at any given moment anywhere in the world. Similar to the concept of face, politeness can also be positive and negative. *Positive politeness* essentially refers to communicative strategies aiming to minimise the effects of threats to the interlocutor's positive face. *Negative politeness*, on the other hand, implies communicative strategies we employ in an attempt to minimise the effects of threats to our interlocutor's negative face. There are four politeness strategies, universal in nature, but culture specific in their geographical distribution (see Figure 8). We present their key characteristics below.

Bald on record is a positive politeness strategy characterised by the highest level of *directness* in communication. The speaker practically makes no attempt to minimise the face threatening act on their interlocutor. This could be required by the communicative situation. For example, in emergencies, when a maximum level of efficiency is of paramount importance, we may hear a command such as:

1. Fire! Get out!
   Giving instructions also requires clarity and simplicity, as is the case in (2):
2. Add two cups of flour to the mix and stir gently.
   Both utterances are very direct, which is contextually not only justifiable, but also appropriate. We may wish to argue that this level of directness is universally acceptable in the mentioned contexts. In other words, it would be hard to imagine utterances such as (1a) and (2a), both of which could be marked as contextually and situationally inappropriate and utterly ineffective in communicative terms:
   (1a) *I'm terribly sorry to bother you, but there's fire on the second floor, so would you awfully mind leaving the building, please?
   (2a) *It would be a good idea to add two cups of flour to the mix and then we would strongly suggest you stir it gently.

However, directness in everyday communication is highly culture-specific and is particularly favoured by cultures that consider *honesty* and *truthfulness* as major cultural values. In other words, in order to show respect and be polite in daily interaction, one has to express their thoughts and feelings openly and honestly. Some Eastern European culture belong to this category, Russian being the most prominent representative (Larina, 2008, 2015; Wierzbicka, 2003). Take, for example, the utterance in (3), said by a university administrator at a UK university to an international graduate student coming from Russia:

3. Hello, good to see you! How are you?

The student, fluent in English and familiar with communicative conventions characteristic of British English, correctly understood the communicative intention of the university administrator, which was to greet the student and simply sound pleasant and welcoming. However, the student, coming from a typical "bald on record" culture, perceived the utterance as insincere and, therefore, impolite and, potentially, even disrespectful and offensive. Why would the administrator be happy to see the student? Did the administrator truly want to know how the student really was? This was unlikely the case, so from the point of view of a representative of the culture that favours honesty as the key value, being openly and obviously insincere is perceived as rude and disrespectful. This is yet another very relevant point to be borne in mind in professional contexts when communicating with culturally diverse teams.

On record with positive politeness is another politeness strategy, which is, as the name suggests, still on the positive, and also rather direct, end of the communicative spectrum. Put simply, it is a strategy characterised by the speaker's intention to show respect to the interlocutor's public image by making them feel welcome, appreciated and part of the team. The speaker tries to establish common ground, identifying mutual interests, viewpoints and making the interlocutor feel accepted as a member of the team. A very common communicative strategy achieving this goal is giving compliments or agreeing with what the interlocutor has said. The United States of America could be taken as a typical representative of this politeness strategy. Take, for example, the following utterances:

4. Oh my gosh, I love your shoes!
5. Great job! Awesome!

What is valued in a culture like this one is not the truthfulness, as was the case in "bald on record" cultures, but the intention to *make the interlocutor feel good about themselves, welcome and appreciated*. The speaker may not truly mean what they say, but that is not culturally expected at all. Again, this is another very important point to be borne in mind in professional contexts. If one receives a lot of positive comments and compliments, it should not be immediately interpreted "on the face value", literally. It could simply mean that the speaker would like to make the interlocutor feel welcome and create a positive atmosphere. Why? Because that is what is considered polite in that particular culture.

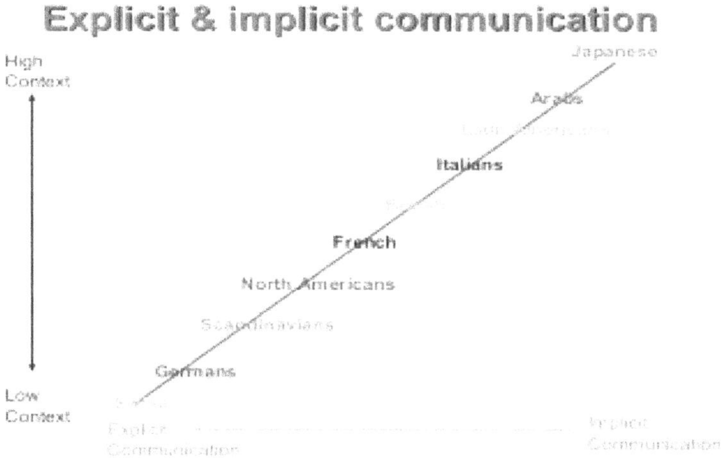

Figure 8: Brown and Levinson's Politeness Strategies

Source: (Aisyadatina et al, 2018. Retrieved from: https://www.researchgate.net/figure/Level-of-Politeness-Strategy-adapted-on-Brown-and-Levinsons-Theory_fig1_327898918).

On record with negative politeness is, again as the name suggests, a negative politeness strategy belonging to the indirect end of the communicative spectrum. The speaker's intention is to minimise any kind of imposition on the interlocutor, respecting their *autonomy*, *freedom of choice* and *personal space*, as key cultural values. This can be achieved in a variety of ways, but typically it would be either by giving options (6), apologising (7) or showing pessimism (8):

6. Would it be possible for me to book a room for next Tuesday?
7. Sorry to bother you, could I just ask if Mary is coming over too?
8. I don't suppose you would know if there's a meeting this afternoon.

A prototypical representative of a negative politeness culture and this specific communicative strategy is Great Britain, and ever more so, England. What is important to notice, specifically in professional context, is that requests will normally take a form of a question, or a vague suggestion, giving the interlocutor the impression that they have an option of accepting or refusing. Thus, utterances such as:

9. Would you like to show John around?
10. You may wish to revise section two.
11. Why don't you take a day off?

should not be taken literally, but rather interpreted as a request (9) or instructions (10–11), given by a representative of a negative politeness culture, in which autonomy, personal space and freedom of choice are highly valued.

Off record is another negative politeness communicative strategy, which is characterised by the highest level of *indirectness*. The speaker's intention is not only to minimise the face threatening act on their interlocutor, but to make it practically invisible. The speaker's communicative intention is given only as a vague hint, leaving it to the interlocutor to interpret it. Take, for example, the following utterances:

12. It's a bit chilly in here, isn't it?
13. It's getting dark. I wonder if the cat is still out in the garden.

In both cases, the speaker is actually making an indirect request. In (12), the request is to do something about the room temperature (e.g. close the window, turn the heating on, etc.), while in (13) the speaker is effectively asking the interlocutor to check if the cat is still out in the garden. A prototypical representative of the "off record" culture is England, but also some countries of East Asia, such as Japan, Korea, Vietnam and China. In professional contexts, misinterpreting this communicative strategy could be rather problematic. It is, therefore, always advisable, particularly if working with culturally diverse teams, to familiarise oneself with key cultural values and communicative styles of members of the team and, if appropriate, agree on the communicative strategy that will be culturally acceptable for all team members, thus avoiding any misinterpretations or communicative breakdowns.

Suggestions for Further Activities

Now that you are familiar with key principles of Politeness Theory, it is important to note that politeness strategies can vary not only cross-culturally and cross-linguistically, but also intra-linguistically, that is to say, within the same language, specifically if it is very diffused geographically. English is a very good example. Thus, for instance, speakers of British English and American English typically use different politeness strategies in everyday communication. To find out more about this, take a look at a TEDx presentation by Professor Lynne Murphy (2012) about British and American politeness: https://www.youtube.com/watch?v=Jbu-eMcEF3s. Now think about politeness strategies typically used by speakers of languages you know or are familiar with. Would you say there is one dominant strategy characteristic of that language, or can you identify some regional differences? If so, how are they manifested?

Instead of a Conclusion… Hands-On Activities

The chapter has given you an opportunity to familiarise yourself with some key concepts in intercultural communication, showing you that culture is not just a random, shapeless and confusing conglomerate of do's and don'ts, but rather a well organised system of values, beliefs and norms, the underpinnings of which can easily be explained within theoretical frameworks dealing with cultural universals. We have looked at three of them: Hofstede's Cultural Dimensions, Hall's Cultural Dichotomies and Brown and Levinson's Theory of Politeness, in an attempt to help you gain deeper insights into interconnectedness between culture and communication. These insights can further contribute to your professional development, paving your way to your international career in an ever increasingly globalised world. By understanding this profound connection between culture and communication and the universal laws lying it its foundations, your intercultural communicative skills will become more sophisticated, facilitating your development as a confident and successful communicator in intercultural contexts, professional or otherwise. The road can sometimes seem to be long and winding, but your ultimate goal is to become an open minded, tolerant and non-judgemental citizen of the world.

Here is a hands-on activity that can help you implement your skills, competences and knowledge you have just developed. It can be performed as a classroom-based group activity, or used for autonomous, independent work and reflection. The activity is a case study, inviting you to analyse and suggest a solution to a real-life situation that happened in 2017. Namely, a French-born waiter living and working in Canada lost his job in a restaurant, having been accused of being rude and disrespectful to his co-workers. The case ended up in court, where the waiter claimed that he had been dismissed simply for being French and communicating in the way that is "normal" for the culture he came from. You can find more about the case here: https://www.bbc.com/news/world-us-canada-43507949.

Suggestions for a Classroom-Based Group Activity

Divide into two groups and organise a simulation mediation meeting, representing the waiter and his team (including roles plays such as a lawyer, a union representative, friends, family members, etc) and the employer and their team (with role plays such as the manager, an HR representative, a lawyer, co-workers, etc). There should also be someone acting as a mediator (e.g. the teacher). Try making the mediation meeting as realistic as possible. For example, the mediator can start by inviting both parties to present their case, explaining also some ground rules (e.g. confidentiality, no offensive language, no shouting or interrupting, etc). Once the parties have presented the case from their respective points of view, the mediator can invite both parties to propose a solution, saying how the case ideally should be resolved (e.g. "if you had a magic wand…"). Each party should then be given a chance to say what they think about the proposal of the opposite team and the role of the mediator would then be to try to establish some common ground and bring the two standpoints closer, if possible. If the discussion might seem to have reached a deadlock, the mediator could suggest that the parties take a short break and discuss the situation in private (make sure there is a breakout room for this to happen). For example, if the employer's team made an offer, the employee's team should consider it and, if appropriate, come up with a counter-offer. Similarly, if the employee's team made a specific request (e.g. severance package, damages claim, etc), the employer's team should consider it and, if appropriate, come up with their counter-offer. The second round of the discussion should be progressing in the direction of a compromise, encouraging both parties to be open minded and flexible. Hopefully, the mediation session will reach a favourable agreement, making both parties satisfied. If such an agreement seems impossible, the mediator should suggest further steps (e.g. additional sessions after the current offers and counter-offers have been discussed with each party's legal teams). The session could finish by the mediator's invitation to both parties to reflect on the experience and think of possible steps to prevent a similar situation in the future. For example, would some intercultural training sessions for staff and management be a step in the right direction?

Suggestions for Individual Work and Reflection

Imagine you are an expert in intercultural communication advising businesses on issue in diversity management and interculturality. You have been contacted by the Head of HR of the restaurant, asking you to suggest how they should proceed in this case. Try to suggest (1) a short-term solution (e.g. should they offer the job back to the employee, or perhaps offer a new job in a different section of the company? Or perhaps offer a severance package and promise that the employee's reputation will not be tarnished?), (2) a mid-term solution (e.g. should a mediation meeting trying to defuse the tension and pacify both parties be a good idea?) and, finally, (3) a long-term solution, making sure that a similar situation does not happen again (e.g. by suggesting intercultural communication training for staff and management, induction sessions for new members of staff that will include diversity awareness and intercultural communicative competence, etc). Suggest how both parties can learn from the experience and reflect on it in a positive, formative way.

Enjoy your intercultural journey!

References

Aisyadatina, A., Susilo, S., & Asih, Y. (2018). The English Pre-service Teachers Politeness Strategies of Offering Context Across Genders. *Proceedings of the 2017 International Conference on Education and Technology (2017 ICEduTech).* https://doi.org/10.2991/icedutech-17.2018.41.

Brown, P., & Levinson, S. C. (1987). *Politeness: Some Universals in Language Usage.* Cambridge: Cambridge University Press.

Chapple, D. (2006). Mid-Atlantic Reading on the English. *Influencer Relations.* Retrieved on September 15, 2021, from: https://www.influencerrelations.com/209/mid-atlantic-reading-on-the-english.

Fired Vancouver waiter: I'm not rude, just French. (2018, March 26). *BBC News.* Retrieved on September 15, 2021, from: https://www.bbc.com/news/world-us-canada-43507949.

Goffman, E. (1967). *Interaction Ritual: Essays on Face-to-Face Behavior.* New York: Doubleday.

Hall, E. T. (1959). *The Silent Language.* New York: Doubleday.

Hall, E. T. (1983). *The Dance of Life: The Other Dimension of Time.* New York: Anchor Press.

Hofstede, G. (1980). *Culture's Consequences: International Differences in Work-Related Values.* London: Sage Publications Ltd.

Hofstede, G. (n.d.). *The 6-D Model of National Culture.* Retrieved September 15, 2021, from: https://geerthofstede.com/culture-geert-hofstede-gert-jan-hofstede/6d-model-of-national-culture/.

Hofstede Insights. (n.d.). *Compare Countries.* Retrieved September 15, 2021, from: https://www.hofstede-insights.com/product/compare-countries/.

Kotabe, M., & Helsen, K. (2001). *Global Marketing Management.* New York: Wiley.

Larina, T. (2008). Directness, Imposition and Politeness in English and Russian. *Cambridge ESOL Research Notes, 33*, 33–38.

Larina, T. (2015). Culture-Specific Communicative Styles as a Framework for Interpreting Linguistic and Cultural Idiosyncrasies. *International Review of Pragmatics, 7*(2), 195–215. https://doi.org/10.1163/18773109-00702003.

Larina, T. V., Ozyumenko, V. I., & Kurteš, S. (2017). I-Identity vs We-Identity in Language and Discourse: Anglo-Slavonic Perspectives. *Lodz Papers in Pragmatics, 13*(1), 109–128. https://doi.org/10.1515/lpp-2017-0006.

Marquardt, N., & Greenberg, S. (2012). Informing the Design of Proxemic Interactions. *IEEE Pervasive Computing, 11*(2), 14–23. https://doi.org/10.1109/MPRV.2012.15.

Morden, T. (1999). Models of National Culture – A Management Review. *Cross Cultural Management: An International Journal*, 6 (1), 19–44; https://doi.org/10.1108/13527609910796915.

Murphy, L. (2012). British and American Politeness. *TEDx Sussex University* [Youtube video]. Retrieved September 15, 2021, from: https://www.youtube.com/watch?v=Jbu-eMcEF3s.

Wierzbicka, A. (2003). *Cross-Cultural Pragmatics: The Semantics of Human Interaction*. Berlin: Mouton de Gruyter.

Introduction to Cultural Values: The Foundation of Cross-Cultural Communication

By Edwin R. McDaniel

The next chapter introduces and summaries the theories of intercultural communication and cross-cultural management. It is pointed out that knowledge of another language is often not enough to facilitate communication across cultures. More is needed; namely, understanding cultural values which attach different meaning to a message. That is why it is important to have an understanding of how such values influence human communication. Shared values and beliefs, it is pointed out, create a system of cultural patterns which help identify and explain a culture's worldview and guide societal activities. These patterns allow one to compare the norms and behaviors of different cultures with one another. It is, though, also pointed out that individuality has to be considered because not everyone behaves and communicates in an identical fashion.

McDaniel introduces seven cultural pattern typologies that are most often cited in research; namely, Hall's cultural context and time orientation, six cultural dimensions of Hofstede and Minkov, Trompenaars' and Hampden-Turner's cultural value orientation, Lewis' model of cultural values and communication styles, Ting-Toomey's facework and face negotiation theory, the Global Leadership and Organizational Behavior Effectiveness (GLOBE) study initiated by House, Gelfand's tight and loose cultures, and Nisbett's cognitive differences. McDaniel, thus, provides an excellent overview of the most common methods used today to facilitate cross-cultural comparisons. These methods allow one to anticipate potential differences in communication and behavior and also provide the means of overcoming these differences. However, as McDaniel also points out, these methods refer to the most probable behavior and communication derived from a cultural average. These methods do not predict the behavior and communication of each and every individual because different people from the same culture can and do behave and communicate differently. Anyone conducting business in today's global economy ought to have some background in intercultural communication since intercultural encounters are inevitable. This chapter provides such a background.

Michael B. Hinner

Edwin R. McDaniel received his Ph.D. in communication from Arizona State University and is a Visiting Senior Lecture at Peking University HSBC Business School, Shenzhen, China. He also teaches in a summer program at Harbin Institute of Technology, Harbin, China. He is the co-author/co-editor of eight intercultural communication textbooks and a public speaking textbook; his articles and book chapters have been published in China, Germany, Korea, and Japan, as well as the United States. His works have been translated into Chinese and Korean. Dr. McDaniel is frequently invited to speak at international forums on the role of culture and intercultural communication across a variety of contexts, including cross-culture management. He has been a Professor of Intercultural Communication at Aichi Shukutoku University, in Nagoya, Japan, and a Japan ICU Foundation Visiting Scholar at the International Christian University in Tokyo, as well as teaching for several years at San Diego State University. Dr. McDaniel also holds an MA in history, concentrating on Russia and Northeast Asia and has lectured and written on contemporary China. Before beginning an academic career, he was in government service, working, travelling, and living in more than 40 countries.

Cultural Values: The Foundation of Cross-Cultural Communication

By Edwin R. McDaniel

Given today's awareness of global society interconnectedness, there seems little need to point out the benefits, indeed necessity, of understanding cultural differences. The demands of global cooperation in response to the Covid-19 pandemic remain salient. It has illustrated the requirement for effective communication, cooperation, and mutual effort across cultural and state borders, both domestically and internationally. In the ever-nearing future, international challenges, such as climate change, natural disasters, large scale migration, and national security issues, will continue to mandate cross-cultural collaboration. Additionally, the growth of domestic diversity resulting from south to north migration requires increased intercultural awareness and sensitivity. But it is not enough to just recognize the existence of cultural differences. There is a need to understand the motivations behind those differences. From that perspective, this chapter is designed to introduce and provide an overview of the theories most commonly used in the contemporary study and application of intercultural communication and cross-cultural management.

The terms culture, intercultural, and cross-culture are used throughout the chapter and call for some definition. "Culture," simply refers to those values that underpin the attitudes, norms, and behaviors of a group of people. "National culture" is used to generalize to the population of an entire nation but actually characterizes the dominant culture of that country. In a purely academic sense, "intercultural" and "cross-cultural" have slightly different meanings. "Intercultural communication" refers to what occurs when individuals from two different cultures engage in a communicative act, i.e., someone from culture A sends a message to someone from culture B. "Cross-culture" connotes a comparison of two or more cultures, i.e., a contrast of values, communication styles, non-verbal behaviors, conflict management, decision making, etc. However, the two terms are often used interchangeably, with the context left to specify the specific meaning.

Cultural differences have beset interactions since humans began roaming the earth, as attested to by archeological records and early historical accounts of warfare, trade, and migration. The historical chronicles of early explorers, merchants, travelers, missionaries, and conquers offer ample evidence of the world's widely variant peoples and their beliefs and behaviors. Words attributed to the Chinese philosopher Confucius (c. 551–479) point this out: *Human beings draw close to one another by their common nature, but habits and customs keep them apart.* However, it was not until the 1800s that systematic, scientific based studies of cultural differences were undertaken, primarily by western anthropologist. Much of their work was theoretical, with any empirical evidence gained from participant-observant studies, albeit often through the lens of colonialism.

World War II and its aftermath saw the early application of cultural studies across a variety of contexts. Individuals involved in post war international reconstruction, national security, and economic activities soon realized that simply knowing a language was not enough to guarantee successful engagement and outcomes. To help overcome the problem, study and training in intercultural communication was initiated. Contemporary internationalization of the global economy, increasing workforce diversity, and emerging issues of social justice have promoted and expanded the study of cross-cultural topics. Today, culture's influence on communication and behavior is being researched across many academic disciplines, and practical application is taught using a wide array of training programs.

Understanding Cultural Values and Cultural Pattern

Comprehending the complexities of culture can be a challenging task. However, research has disclosed that within each culture the dominant group's shared values and beliefs create a system of similar social characteristics, often referred to as cultural patterns. These patterns help identify and explain the values that inform a culture's worldview (*Weltanschauung*) and guide societal activities. As such, the patterns provide a means of predicting and understanding dissimilar cultural structure, norms, and behaviors.

While these cultural patterns aid in recognizing the differences of others, some caveats should be kept in mind. *First* in importance is that individuals are generally more than their culture. In other words, an individual may not fully adhere to the dominant values for a variety of reasons, such as age, gender, education, past experiences, or other factors. Therefore, in any intercultural exchange, one should be aware that the individuals may or may not subscribe to the dominant culture norms. *Secondly*, the patterns are dynamic; they can evolve and produce social change. In the increasingly integrated world, people are being exposed to other values and social structures, which can generate a desire for change. *Third*, in order to simplify understanding, the cultural patterns treat values individually, but in life they are integrated and act in concert. *Finally*, in some instances, they can appear contradictory. That is, a culture may rhetorically espouse a particular value but practice behaviors in opposition to that value, e.g., the touted value of "equal opportunity" and "equality" in the USA versus actual conditions for minorities.

Cultural Pattern Typologies

While a number of different cultural pattern typologies have been created by work across several disciplines, the seven discussed here are considered the most popular among cross-cultural practitioners and the most often cited by researchers. It will quickly become obvious that a degree of overlap exists between the various classification systems. Some of the cultural dimensions, or variations thereof, are found in several of the typologies, and this should be expected as they are addressing the dominant values found in a culture. In using the typologies to better understand cultural values, however, two considerations should remain salient. First, the dimensions are generalizations, often derived from a standard-distribution model. Accordingly, as previously mentioned, not every individual in a culture will practice a particular dimension. Secondly, in actuality the value dimensions are continuums, not polar opposites, and individuals within a culture may adopt one, or all, to varying degrees.

Discussions of the different value taxologies below are structured to provide a brief summary of the author'(s) background, a short explanation of each value dimension, and a few practical examples. Where available, critiques of the typologies are included.

E. T. Hall – Cultural Context and Time Orientation

E.T. Hall, an American anthropologist, is generally considered to be one of the founders of the study of culturally influenced communicative interactions, especially nonverbal, between members of different cultures. His work on how communication meaning can be embedded in the context and the role of space and time (Hall, 1976, 1983) remains seminal to the field. His early research involved field work among Native American tribes in the US Southwest. Subsequent work was conducted in Europe and Asia. In formulating his different concepts, Hall combined anthropological methods, linguistics, and personal observations (Cardon, 2008; Hall & Trager, 1953; Rogers et al., 2002).

Hall posited that "context," defined as "the information that surrounds an event" played an essential role in how meaning was constructed during a communication exchange (Hall & Hall, 1990, p. 6). Additionally, he considered the degree of reliance on context to vary across national cultures, existing along a *high- to low-context* continuum. Northeast Asian cultures were placed at the high end, with USA and Northern European cultures at the low end (Hall, 1976).

In high-context cultures, communication is often characterized by vague or ambiguous verbal exchanges and the intended meaning is largely imbedded in the context or the individuals themselves. People from high-context cultures commonly emphasize in-group relations, have a significant degree of similarity, and follow well defined social protocols, resulting in widely shared perceptions, experiences, behaviors and societal expectations. Their commonalities enable interactants to communicate without the need for explanatory or complete background information. In other words, the intended meaning is derived more from the context than the actual words. How something is said is often more important than what is actually said. The implicit meaning is imbedded in inferences, gestures, or even what is ***not*** said. An ability to discern the unspoken meaning is a much-admired trait among Northeast Asians.

Conversely, low-context communication relies on detailed, explicit exchanges to make the meaning clear, and the context is of much lesser importance. Countries that practice low-context interactions tend to be more individualistic and have diverse populations, resulting in a significant level of dissimilar experiences. Therefore, the normative practice is to use more direct, forceful communication and rhetorical are skills seen as a positive attribute.

Another area of Hall's (1983) research focused on how cultures use time as a form of communication and defined two categories – *monochronic* and *polychronic* time – referred to as M-time and P-time. A culture with a monochronic orientation will approach time in a linear, sequential manner. Time is viewed as a commodity, to be measured and used proportionally by close adherence to schedules and appointments. Tasks are generally approached individually and managed sequentially. Cultures commonly considered as monochronic include Germany, Switzerland, Scandinavian countries, and the USA (Hall & Hall, 1990).

As the term implies, P-time cultures are quite in contrast to M-time adherents. There is a more relaxed attitude toward time and greater importance is placed on human relations than tasks. Because time is considered to be flexible, people in polychronic cultures often engage in multiple tasks, with fluid deadlines and schedules. As a result, plans are subject to frequent change and can be impacted by the people involved in a particular event. One study found that cultural time orientation can influence an individual's attitude toward e-commerce webpage download times, with P-time consumers being more patient than those with an M-time perspective (Rose et al., 2003). Arabic, Asian, and Latin American cultures are more prone to a polychronic time orientation (Browaeys & Price, 2015; Hall & Hall, 1990)

Selected characteristics of Hall's two cultural classifications are provided in Table 1.

Table 1: Hall's Cultural Characteristics

Influence of Hall's Cultural Classifications	
Low vs. High Context Communication	
Low Context (Direct) (e.g., Germany, UK, USA) • Meaning inherent in verbal message • Nonverbal communication of low importance • Silence is avoided • Communication is normally direct	*High Context* (Indirect) (e.g., China, ROK, Japan) • Meaning dependent on context • Nonverbal communication highly important • Silence is normal • Communication is often indirect
Monochronic vs. Polychronic (Use of Time)	
Monochronic (e.g., Germany, Norway. UK, USA) • Time is linear and segmented • Time is a commodity • Focus on a single task • Committed to the task • Adherence to schedules	*Polychronic* (e.g., Arabs, Africans, China, France) • Time is flexible • Time is relative • Focus on multiple tasks • Committed to people and relationships • Weak ties to schedules

Source: (Adapted from Hall, 1976, 1983).

The implications of contrasts in high- and low-context communications can be illustrated by Japanese-USA business negotiations. In addition to the project under consideration, the Japanese are likely concerned about establishing and maintaining long term positive relations for potential future business opportunities. But their USA counterparts will be focused only on the current proposal. Should the USA side make an offer that the Japanese consider untenable, they might reply with "We will need to study that…" or "That might be difficult…", either of which is intend to convey a negative inclination toward the proposal. However, the USA negotiators, being more accustomed to direct yes or no replies, may interpret the Japanese as simply needing more time to consider the proposition. Thus, a stalemate is likely to develop, with the USA side awaiting a more conclusive response and the Japanese waiting for a change in the proposal.

The trials of a monochronic German business representative embarking on a series of meetings in France can be used to demonstrate the consequences of varied time orientations. The German will likely prepare a structured itinerary of meetings, allotting a specific amount of time to each, and a list of subjects to be addressed. As much official activity as possible will be packed into each day. Unfortunately, interactions with the polychronic French are likely to bring disarray to the envisioned schedule. The German will expect appointments to begin and end on time, with discussions quickly turning to business topics. For the French, however, it is not important for the meeting to adhere to the specified time schedule, nor is it necessary to quickly begin discussing the business aspects. The meeting may begin, experience some interruptions as the French attend to other tasks, and run overtime. The French could even propose going to lunch, which the German had not anticipated. As a result, the German's finely tuned schedule will likely need to be repeatedly amended.

Hall's cultural classifications continue to enjoy broad acceptance and application across intercultural communication and other cross-cultural fields of study. However, his concepts are not without their critics. A frequent criticism is Hall's reliance on anecdotal evidence and the continuing lack of empirical data to support the categorizations (e.g., Cardon, 2008; Kittler et al., 2011). Another cited shortfall is that assigning the concepts to national cultures tends to stereotype by overlooking the domestic diversity found in many of those nations. Despite these calls for greater analytical research, Hall's work continues to be widely cited.

Hofstede and Minkov – Cultural Dimensions

One of the early research studies using statistical analysis on large data bases to identify cultural values was conducted by Geert Hofstede (1928–2020), a Dutch social psychologist. Drawing on attitude surveys of over 100,000 IBM international employees, in the late 1960s and early 1970s, he initially identified four cultural value dimensions. A fifth dimension was discovered by a subsequent survey of 23 countries. Results from each study rank-ordered the nations based on the importance given to the bi-polar dimensions. This work identified the cultural dimensions importance in the respective countries and enabled a country-to-country comparison (Hofstede, 2001; Hofstede et al., 2010)

Drawing on statistical analysis of data from the World Values Survey (WVS), Michael Minkov, a Bulgarian social anthropologist, identified additional bi-polar dimensions, which complemented Hofstede's earlier research. Here, only the *industry (restraint) vs. indulgence* value will be discussed (Minkov, 2011).

The following paragraphs offer a brief theoretical discussion of the six cultural dimensions from the research of Hofstede and Minkov. Table 2 provides additional insight into the cultural traits.

The *individualism vs. collectivism* dimension has been the subject of extensive research projects and, for some people, represents a basic concept to help explain and understand cultural differences. Succinctly, individualism gives primacy to the individual as fundamental to any social setting, and values independence over interdependence. Each individual is considered unique and personal rights often take precedence over group considerations. In contrast, collectivistic societies (group orientation) characterize most of the world's populations. The defining traits of collectivism are close in-group ties and reliance on social relations for support, which creates a strong sense of mutual-obligation and group harmony. These traits tend to moderate the expression of personal opinions and feelings. But individualist, unburdened by the need to sustain positive relations, are generally unrestrained in voicing personal opinions.

High vs. low power distance is easily explained by the degree of acceptance of differences in social inequality. In high power cultures, such as Asian and Middle East countries, variations in power, authority, and privilege are considered normal. Both superiors and subordinates view each other differently and generally act according to their respective positions. Social hierarchies can be the result of family name, age, profession, level of education, organizational position, etc. Relationships between individuals of different social strata are usually kept on a formal level and the use of professional titles is common. Members of low power societies, like Western Europe and the USA, believe that inequalities should be minimized, which is reflected in numerous laws, regulations, rules, and social customs designed to minimize power differentials. Professional titles are used only in certain situations (e.g., medical) and normally relationships move to an informal level soon after initial meetings.

Low vs high uncertainty avoidance is used to characterize the degree to which ambiguity and unpredictability is managed in a culture. Countries with a high degree of population diversity, such as the USA, the UK, and Singapore, generally exhibit low uncertainty avoidance tendencies. The people do not feel threatened by different idea and values, are generally more tolerant of changes, and are less constrained by social protocols. High uncertainty avoidance cultures usually have a relatively homogeneous population. These cultures are characterized by numerous social rules, rituals, and ceremonies, as well as established social behavioral and communication norms. Adherence to the many protocols is expected and deviation can create difficulties. Contrasting USA and Japan employment patterns offers insight to this dimension. The low uncertainty avoidance USA employees are focused on their own careers and will often change jobs in order to advance. There is no hesitancy about, or stigma attached to, moving from one organization to another. However, in Japan, a high-uncertainty culture, life-time employment has been the post-WW II norm, with advancement largely based on age. Someone with a resume suggesting job-hopping will likely be viewed with caution. [*caveat*: The situation of Japanese lifetime employment is changing due to multiple domestic and international factors (Schaede, 2020)].

Masculinity vs. femininity is Hofstede's label for the degree to which a society values masculine or feminine traits. However, some consider that designation limiting and suggest "career success" and "quality of life" more accurately represent the dimension's broader meaning (Adler & Gunderson, 2008). Cultures where the dominant social values stress a male-orientation are classified as masculine. Common characteristics include well defined assertiveness, a focus on achievement and material success, and clearly defined male-female gender roles. Ideally, females should be modest, nurturing, and more concerned with care-giving. In feminine cultures, quality of life is emphasized, gender roles tend to overlap, workers try to find an equitable balance between professional achievement and family life. According to Hofstede's research, an attractive work environment in a masculine culture would include the opportunity for a high income, appropriate recognition, the chance for promotion, and offer challenging tasks. Conversely, a feminine work environment would have an emphasis on positive working relations between managers and co-workers, the ability to live in a desirable area, and offer job security. The former set of work characteristics can be found in Germany, the UK and the USA, all considered masculine; the latter ideals are exemplified in the Scandinavian nations, which score the highest on the feminine scale (Hofstede et al., 2010) and have the lowest gender-gaps ("World", 2021).

The *long vs. short-term* dimension was not discovered in Hofstede's original IBM study. It was initially revealed by a study of twenty-three nations (Chinese Cultural Connection, 1987) and further refined by Minkov and Hofstede (2010) using World Values Survey data from thirty-eight countries. Succinctly, this dimension looks at how cultures either prioritize the future or focus more on the present and past. A long-term oriented nation will prepare for future rewards through thrift, self-discipline, and lasting personal relations. However, a country with a short-term national culture will be more concerned with immediate achievements, self-determination, meritocracy, and short-term beneficial relations. In Northeast Asia (China, Korea, and Japan), the long-term orientation is evident in the high personal saving rate, stress on education, and importance of interpersonal relations. In short-term national cultures, such as Ireland and the USA, people tend to be more individualistic and concerned with their immediate environment. A frequent example used to the contrast long and short-term dimension is how corporations in China and the West often view their objectives differently. The Chinese are likely be more motivated to grow their organization to gain market share and willing to forego immediate profits. In contrast, corporations in the USA are intently focused on increasing profits and raising stock prices for each quarterly report, which is often the criteria for determining executive pay.

Industry vs. indulgence is concerned with how work and leisure are valued differently across national cultures. In an industrious national culture, hard work and savings will take precedence over leisure and personal enjoyment. People in an indulgent country will place greater value on personal freedom and the opportunity to relax and engage in and social activities. Industrious countries are characterized by more governmental control and adherence to societal norms. Indulgent societies tend to chafe at government interference (Minkov, 2011). A good example of an industrious culture is China. In many of the mom and pop businesses, the owners both work and live in their establishment, which is commonly open seven days a week. The Chinese are willing to forfeit many personal freedoms in return for the promise of personal and national economic growth. This drive can be explained by Minkov's (2011) findings that lesser developed nations typically reflect a higher industry score, but as national wealth increases and people gain greater financial security, there is an increase in indulgence scores, as can be seen in most highly developed countries.

Table 2: Hofstede's Cultural Dimensions

Influence of Selected Hofstede Cultural Dimensions	
Individualism vs. Collectivism	
Individualism (e.g., USA, UK, Germany, Italy) • Focuses on the individual and self- promotion • Independency • Task dominates relationship • Weak organizational ties • Social obedience through sense of guilt	*Collectivism* (e.g., ROK, China, Mexico, Russia) • Focuses on the group/affiliations and self-criticism • Interdependency • Relationship dominates task • Strong organizational ties • Social obedience through sense of shame

(*Continued*)

Table 2: Continued

Influence of Selected Hofstede Cultural Dimensions	
High vs. Low Power Distance (Egalitarian vs. Hierarchal)	
Egalitarian (e.g., Australia, Canada, USA) • Horizontal relationships • Equality expected • Informal work relations • Relaxed student-teacher relationship	*Hierarchal* (e.g., China, India, Russia, ROK) • Vertical relationships • Inequality accepted • Formal work relations • Structured student-teacher relationship
Low vs. High Uncertainty Avoidance	
Low Uncertainty Avoidance (e.g., China, India, USA) • Differences can interesting • Change is normal and good • Few behavioral protocols • Greater cultural diversity	*High Uncertainty Avoidance* (e.g., France, Greece, Japan) • Differences can be threatening • Change is disruptive and disliked • Many behavioral protocols • Less cultural diversity
Masculinity (Achievement) vs. Femininity (Quality of life)	
Masculine (e.g., Japan, Germany, Italy, USA) • Competition • Material progress • Specific gender roles • Success equals material rewards • Assertiveness • Live to work	*Femininity* (e.g., Scandinavian nations, Chile, Thailand) • Cooperation • Social progress • Gender equality/interchangeable roles • Quality of life • Consensus oriented • Work to live
Long vs. Short Term Orientation	
Long Term (e.g., China, Japan, ROK, Germany) • Focus on future • Willingness to delay gratification • Increase market share • Savings and investing • Success and failure a function of effort	*Short Term* (e.g., US, South Africa, Egypt, Australia) • Focus on immediate past or present • Seek immediate gratification • Increase profits and stock price • Social spending and consumption • Success and failure influenced by luck
Industry vs. Indulgence	
Industry (e.g., India, China, Indonesia) • Hard work over leisure (personal gratification) • Strict social norms • Thrift is important • Firm governmental controls	*Indulgence* (Mexico, Sweden, UK, Germany) • Leisure (personal gratification) over hard work • Relaxed social norms • Thrift less important • Loose governmental controls

Source: (Adapted from Hofstede 2001; Hofstede et al., 2010; Minkov, 2011).

Hofstede's work remains a prominent feature of academic and commercial literature on cross-cultural issues. It has inspired countless studies and is commonly cited in both academic textbooks and business literature (Kirkman et al., 2006). Despite this widespread acceptance, it is not without criticism, which has been both varied and extensive. The more common complaints include the original study being conducted in a single company (IBM) but the results being applied nationally, conflating national and organizational cultures, insufficient consideration of a nation's co-cultures, and, of course, methodological issues, and there is also concern that the original data is now some 50 years old and may not be representative of contemporary values. More comprehensive explanations of perceived shortfalls of Hofstede's cultural model are provided by Fang (2003), Kirkman et al. (2006), McSweeney (2002), McSweeney et al. (2016), Nakata (2009), and Orr and Hauser (2008).

Trompenaars and Hampden-Turner – Cultural Value Orientations

Frons Trompenaars is a Dutch born cross-cultural management consultant and academic. To help explain and understand national and corporate cultural differences, he worked with Charles Hampden-Turner, an English academic and management theorist, to develop a typology of fundamental bi-polar cultural dimensions. In constructing their model, the two authors have drawn on 25 years of research, which includes survey data from corporate executives and managers, analysis of nearly 10,000 actual case studies, and anecdotal material collected during more than 1,500 cross-cultural training sessions in over 25 countries. Collectively, their data base contains information from over 60 different countries, with input from 140,000 participants (Trompenaars & Hampden-Turner, 2020).

Drawing on their very formidable database and experience, the authors identified seven cultural value dimensions which provide a foundation for understanding cross-cultural issues in business and management contexts. Five of the dimensions focus on relations between people, one concerns the way a cultural group uses time, and another is how people consider and react to their contextual environment. Following a brief discussion of each, Table 3 provides a synopsis of the dimensions.

At its core, the *universalism vs. particularism* dimension asks the basic question of which is more important, rules or relationships? People from universalist cultures believe social rules, regulations, and laws should apply equally to everyone, regardless of the situation or consequences. Comprehensive legal contracts are used to conduct business and any changes require renegotiation. In contrast, particularists give priority to relationships and circumstances, which may necessitate exceptions to the rules. Realizing that relations and situations evolve, contracts are more easily modified. A rather simplistic example, often used to illustrate the distinction between the two cultural values, is how pedestrians will likely react to a red light in the absence of traffic. In Germany or Switzerland, it is common to see people quietly waiting for the light to turn green. However, in India or Vietnam people will be crossing well before the light changes.

In *individualism vs. communitiarism* the emphasis is on which should take precedence, the individual or the group? Is personal choice more or less important that the collective good? Since this dimension is very similar to Hofstede's individualism vs. collectivism, there is no need to expand the discussion here.

The *neutral vs. emotional (affective)* dimension considers whether cultural groups value restrained or expressive emotional displays. Varied communicative styles provide numerous examples of this value. In neutral cultures, facial expressions, voice tone, and other nonverbal behaviors are generally much less demonstrative than in an emotional culture. Unfortunately, interactions between members from the two cultural groups can be unnecessarily influenced by the differences. In negotiations between individuals from China or Korea and the USA, the former may misinterpret the latter's expressive facial displays and rising voice level as anger. And the USA negotiator may see his "inscrutable" Chinese counterpart's lack of facial displays as insincerity or even deceitfulness.

An easy way of understanding the *specific vs. diffuse* dimension is to look at the degree to which professional and private lives are separated or overlapping. Specific cultures see a distinct difference between their work and private life, but among diffuse cultures there is more integration. Although there are signs of change, work life in China and Japan has traditionally been very diffuse, and managers would frequently function as a matchmaker between company employees. However, among the specific cultures of the USA, Western Europe, and Scandinavia this practice is frowned upon and today could well result in an HR complaint.

The way a culture assigns status is the focus of the *achievement vs. ascription* dimension. In an achievement-oriented culture, status and reputation are earned through personal accomplishments which is often an ongoing process. Status in ascription-based cultures is frequently a product of who the person is, which can be a function of family background, university attended, social connections, or even their profession. In some situations, a national culture will exhibit a degree of both achievement and ascription. In Northeast Asia, for example, scores on the exams for admission to university are individual achievements, but the reputation of the college attended will be a source of lifelong status. In the USA, admission to higher education is a result of personal effort and the university graduated from will initially open doors. But ultimately, the individual will have to prove themselves through workplace activities. In Latin America and South Korea, a person's family name may offer enduring social privilege, but among the Scandinavian nations, it will matter little.

Moving away from cross-cultural personal relationships with others, *the sequential vs. synchronic* dimension examines how cultures relate to time. Sequential cultures consider and relate to the past, present, and future. Time is a product to be managed and activities are undertaken in a lineal progression. Synchronic cultures tend to multitask and view time more abstractly with relationships taking precedence over schedules. This dimension reflects Hall's work on mono- and polychronic time cultures and is similar to what Hofstede identified as long- and short-term time orientations.

Internal vs. external, the final dimension proposed by Trompenaars and Hampden-Turner, deals with the cultural attitude toward management of one's natural and social environment. An inner-directed culture believes the environment can be controlled and shaped to their personal advantage, but outer-directed cultures think that one should try to adapt and live in harmony with the environment. The USA has historically felt that nature could and should be controlled. This belief is evident in the early immigrants "taming" the wilderness, and that attitude persists today as the USA seeks to "conquer" space. The UK's similar perception is articulated in William Ernest Henley's poem *Invictus*, which declares, *I am the master of my fate, I am the captain of my soul.* This is carried over to the business context, where organizations are managed by top-down directives, exercise an aggressive management strategy which seeks to control situations, and where managers endeavor to convince subordinates of the best way of fulfilling a task. The implementation of sales strategies designed to convince consumer to purchase a particular product is common. Consider the algorithms used by online advertisers to identify and appeal to potential customers.

In an outer-directed culture, such as Japan, positive relations and cooperation are important. Decisions are often arrived at through both horizontal and vertical workplace discussion and consensus among the involved individuals. Japanese sales are driven by the axiom that "the customer is god", which indicates that organizations must adapt to outside influences.

Additional characteristics of the seven cultural orientations are offered in Table 3, along with a few national cultures that practice the values.

Table 3: Trompenaars' and Hampden-Turner's Cultural Orientations

Influence of Trompenaars' & Hampden-Turner's Cultural Orientations	
Universalism Versus Particularism	
Universalism (e.g., Northern EU, USA, Australia) • Rules/regulations apply equally to all in every situation • Relationship is subordinate to principle • There is only one truth; reality is objective • Definitive legal contracts	*Particularism* (e.g., China, Morocco, Poland) • Adherence to rules/regulations is situational • Relationship obligations may take precedence over principle • Truth is perception based; reality is subjective • Generalized, easily modifiable contracts
Individualism vs. Communitiarism	
Individualism (Australia, Germany, USA) • Frequent use of "I" in communication • Broadly delegated authority; quick decisions • Personal decisions, responsibility and achievement • Leisure time commonly spent in couples, nuclear family, or alone	*Communitiarism* (Japan, Brazil, Spain) • "We" common in communication • Decisions by group consensus or top management • Group decisions, responsibility, and achievement • Leisure time commonly spent in groups or extended family
Affective vs. Neutral	
Neutral (e.g., Northeast and Southeast Asia, Scandinavia) • Thoughts and feelings are not openly disclosed • Restrained self-control is considered positive trait • Any stress revealed nonverbally is accidental • Suppressed emotions sometimes explode	*Emotional (Affective)* (USA, Western Europe, Latin America, Middle East, Russia) • Thoughts/feeling readily revealed • Open emotional expression is normal • Public, intense arguments common and can be beneficial
Specific vs. Diffuse	
Specific (e.g., USA, Western Europe, Scandinavia) • Professional and private self are separate • Individuals are open, precise, logical, and definitive • Principles and morality are consistent and apart from the person and context	*Diffuse* (e.g., NEA, SEA, Russia, Middle East) • Professional and private self are clearly integrated • Individuals are tactful, ambiguous, and even opaque • Principles and morality are situational, dependent on the person and context

Table 3: Continued

Influence of Trompenaars' & Hampden-Turner's Cultural Orientations	
Achievement vs Ascription	
Achievement (e.g., USA, Western EU, Scandinavia) • Status based on personal performance • Age, gender, family, and social connections matter little • Rewards/privileges based on proven results • What you did in university is important • Promotion based on merit	*Ascription* (e.g., NEA, SEA, France, Italy, Middle East) • Status based on who a person is • Age, gender, family, and social connections are important consideration • Rewards/privileges based on position • Which university attended is important • Promotion based on background
Sequential vs Synchronic Time Orientations	
Sequential time (e.g., U.S., Germany, Russia) • Engage in one activity at a time – lineal • Time is a product to be managed • Appointments and schedules adhered to • Schedules take precedence over relationships	*Synchronic time* (e.g., NEA, Southern EU, Middle East) • Engage in multiple activities – holistic • Time is continuous and diffuse • Appointments and schedules are approximate • Relationships take precedence over schedules
Internal vs. External Orientation	
Internal (e.g., USA, UK, Switzerland, Israel) • People can control nature and the environment • Conflict and resistance are normal and can be good • Focus is on self, own group, own organization • Winning is important – tend to be dominant	*External* (e.g., China, Russia, Middle East) • People should live in harmony with nature and the environment • Harmony and cooperation are paramount over conflict • Focus is on the "other" – i.e., relationships • Relationships are important – flexibility is important

Source: (Adapted from Trompenaars & Hampden-Turner, 2020).

Quite naturally, there are critiques of Trompenaars' and Hampden-Turner's research, such as their data base is derived from only corporate participants, and therefore the dimensions cannot apply to the general population. Hofstede (1996) voiced several methodological concerns and has pointed out that Trompenaars' and Hampden-Turner's survey questions were constructed in a manner that directed participants toward preconceived concepts, rather than letting those concepts emerge naturally from the data.

Richard D. Lewis – Categorizing Cultures

The Lewis model uses cultural values and communication styles to explain organizational behaviors from a macro perspective. The objective of the model is to offer a general structure to facilitate communication and enhance understanding between people of varied cultural backgrounds.

Originally from England, Richard Lewis was educated in the UK and France. He speaks 11 languages and has worked and lived in numerous countries, including Finland, Japan, Norway, and Portugal. A prolific author, Lewis's *When Cultures Collide* has been published in 15 different languages and has sold over one million copies. He is the founder a worldwide consultancy specializing in cross-cultural communication and language. In constructing his model, Lewis integrated previous cultural communication research, extensive international experience abroad, language training, and personal observations (Lewis, 2018).

The Lewis model offers a general framework for classifying and understanding culturally diverse behaviors. Perhaps its greatest utility lies in the recognition of cultural variances and recommendations on how to bridge those differences. The model consists of three distinct categories (*Linear-active, Multi-active, and Reactive*). *Linear-active* cultures approach tasks sequentially and focus on schedules and organizing. They are data driven. *Multi-active* cultures are not bound by time schedules, consider relationships to carry more importance, and excel at multitasking. They are motivated by interaction. *Reactive-cultures* endeavor to understand the intentions of others and, accordingly, consider listening to be important. Reactive-cultures are cautious, methodical, and consider courtesy and respect in relationships to be important (Lewis, 2018).

To visually illustrate how national cultures may adhere to the characteristics of his categories to varying degrees, Lewis constructs a triangle diagram with a category in each corner. National cultures are then spaced along the connecting lines to the degree that they reflect values of a particular category. This illustration is reportedly the produce of "decades-long observation and thousands of assessments of cultural profiles with respondents of 68 nationalities" (Lewis, 2018, pp. 32–33). He presents numerous examples to help define the three different cultural categories and provides lengthy discussions on what can occur during interactions by participants from different categories. Specifically, the model is used to explain the cultural impact on national business cultures across team building, motivating and promoting trust among employees, and how status is accorded, as well as leadership and negation styles.

Table 4 delineates some of the characteristics of each of Lewis' three cultural categories.

Table 4: Lewis' Cultural Categories

Lewis' Cultural Categories Model	
Linear-active Cultures	
• Task oriented	• Highly organized
• Adhere to plans and schedules	• Focus on one project at a time
• Prefer direct discussion	• Confrontation is OK
• Logic over emotion	• Rely on official channels over relations
• Results are paramount	• Compromise when necessary
(e.g., Swiss, Dutch, German, UK, USA)	
Multi-active Cultures	
• Impulsive	• Emotional/feelings are important
• Relationships/people are important	• Compassionate
• Loose adherence to agendas	• Good at multitasking
• Discussions are indirect	• Talkative and animated
• Dislike silence	• Frequent interruptions
(e.g., Arab, African, & Hispanic cultures, Italy, Russia)	
Reactive Cultures	
• Listen carefully	• Establish understanding of other's intent
• Use a period of silence to evaluate	• Ask for additional information
• React in a constructive manner	• Maintain a degree of inscrutability
• Imitate other's strengths/products	• Improve/refine them
• Perfect if possible	• Face is highly important
(e.g., China, Korea, Japan, Singapore, Vietnam)	

Source: (Lewis, 2018).

Lewis' model is clearly intended and designed more for the practitioner than as an academic work. It has been criticized for lacking a scientific research background and generalizing to entire national populations. However, Lewis does acknowledge the existence of individual differences within a culture and warns that the broad generalizations of national characteristics carry the risk of stereotyping (Lewis, 2018)

Ting-Toomey – Facework and Face Negotiation Theory

The concept of "face" has a particularly long history, reaching back as far as the 4th century BCE in China, according to Hu (1944). In the context of cultural values, the term refers to the self-image an individual presents to others. "Face" is used as a metaphor for a person's social image, which means it is commonly acquired, maintained, and lost as a function of social interactions, particularly through communication, referred to as "facework." According to Domenici and Littlejohn, face work is "a set of coordinated practices in which communicators build, maintain, protect or threaten personal dignity, honor, and respect" (2006, p. 10). In other words, when you take actions to acquire or sustain your own face or to influence the face of someone else, you are engaging in facework.

U.S. communication scholar Stella Ting-Toomey posits that face considerations influence communicative interactions in every culture. Working with colleagues, her empirical research has produced the Face Negotiation Theory, which explicates culturally varied face concerns during conflict situations. According to the theory, three possible face concerns can arise during a dispute – (1) *self-face*, (2) *other-face*, and (3) *mutual-face* – and are influenced by the interactants cultural orientation. Self-face, or concern for one's own face, is most common in individualistic cultures. Other-face gives priority to the other person in the disagreement and mutual-face, which takes into consideration the face of everyone in the conflict, are more common among collectivistic cultures. These three different cultural concerns for face can exert a noticeable influence on how the conflict is managed (Ting-Toomey, 1994, 2005).

Face Negotiation Theory research indicates that people from individualistic cultures emphasize self-face and when dealing with conflicts will lean more toward a dominating, or confrontational position. Conversely, in collective societies the tendency is to adopt a more accommodating, conflict avoidance strategy, with a stress on other and mutual facework. This can be explained by the importance that collectivistic cultures place on relationships. As a result, one's identity, social status, and social support is often derived from group membership. Maintaining harmony within the group becomes a paramount consideration, mitigating against aggressive, discordant behaviors. In contrast, self-image in individualistic cultures is normally derived from personal efforts and results in communicative styles designed to protect one's own face (Ting-Toomey, 2005). Table 5 briefly describes the differences of low vs. high face concerns.

Table 5: Ting-Toomey's Face Concerns

Influence of Ting-Toomey Face Concerns	
Low vs. High Face	
Low Face Concerns (e.g., Australia, Germany, USA) • Conflict/disagreement is constructive • Concern for self-face	*High Face Concerns* (e.g., China, Japan, Korea) • Conflict/disagreement is threatening • Concern for mutual and other-face

Source: (Adapted from Ting-Toomey, 2005).

The value that an individual places on face is often evident in behaviors exhibited in various social contexts. From a communication perspective, a Japanese negotiator, can be expected to use strategies to avoid or mitigate potential conflict while focusing on mutual and other face issues. This could include the use of indirect language, avoiding a direct no response, or even indicating that time was needed to further study the proposal. This is quite in contrast to a Western representative, who is more likely to use a direct, solution-oriented communication style, which favors self-face. Research by Oetzel empirically demonstrated these different face concerns (Oetzel et al., 2001, 2008).

The cultural importance of face can also play out on a macro level, influencing the way a society approaches problem solving. A nation culture's prevalence for litigation serves as an example. Table 6 provides the citizen-lawyer ratio for Japan and four Western nations, which suggests that the greater the value on self-face (e.g., the USA) the greater the number of lawyers. This is borne out by the US propensity to use legal venues to resolve even minor disputes. In Japan, where face and social harmony are valued, there is a greater inclination to avoid conflicts or to employ non-legal mitigation measures. In China, another national culture where face issues are important, a government report projects that by 2022 there be only 4.2 attorneys per every 10,000 citizens, across a population of approximately 1.4 billion ("Japan", 2019; Ju, 2020).

Originally, the major premise of Face Negotiation Theory posited that culture was the primary factor influencing face in conflict situations. However, subsequent research has found that other issues, such as self-construal and emotions, also play a role, although culture remains a major impetus (Oetzel et. al., 2001, 2008; Zhang et al., 2014). Therefore, research continues to further identify, and better define, the role of culture and other variables that bear on face concerns in cross-cultural conflict scenarios (e.g., Neuliep & Johnson, 2016; Nguyen-Phuong et al., 2014; Zhang et al., 2019)

Table 6: Number of Citizens per Attorney by Country

Country	Citizens per attorneys
Japan	3075
France	999
Germany	498
United Kingdom	382
United States	260

Source: ("Japan", 2019).

Contemporary Theories

The GLOBE Project

An extremely large, complex, and innovative international research program is the ongoing Global Leadership and Organizational Behavior Effectiveness (GLOBE) study, which was envisioned in the early 1990s by Robert J. House, an academic at the Wharton School of Business at the University of Pennsylvania. Conducted by a large international team of researchers using a variety of quantitative and qualitive methods, the project is described as, "A unique large-scale study of cultural practices, leadership ideals, and generalized and interpersonal trust in more than 170 countries in collaboration with more than 500 researchers" (GLOBE, 2020).

To date, there have been three phases of data collection completed, resulting in three major books and numerous articles. The initial publication, *Culture, Leadership, and Organizations: The GLOBE Study of 62 Societies* (House et al., 2004), provided the results of the first study, which drew data from 17,000 mid-level managers in 62 countries. The second book, *Culture and Leadership, Across the World: The GLOBE BOOK of In-depth Studies of 25 Societies* (Chhokar et al., 2007), surveyed 18,000 middle managers from 62 nations across 1,000 organizations. The most recent publication, *Strategic Leadership Across Cultures: The GLOBE Study of CEO Leadership Behavior and Effectiveness in 24* Countries (House et al., 2014), involved over 1,000 CEOs and more than 6,000 corporate managers from 24 countries. An ongoing data collection effort is intended to extend the earlier findings. This investigation involves 120 countries and has a focus on lesser studied nations in Africa and the Middle East. (GLOBE, 2020).

Each of the studies examined a particular aspect of cross-cultural management from several perspectives. The results published to date have proven insightful, beneficial, and extensive. The findings being well beyond the scope and space of this chapter, the preceding was intended to offer only a concise overview of the project. Those seeking additional information are encouraged to visit the GLOBE Project website (GLOBE, 2020).

Gelfand – Tight and Loose Cultures

Anthropologist introduced the concept of classifying cultures as *tight* and *loose* in the mid-1900s. More recently, Michele Gelfand, a psychologist at Stanford university, and her associates analyzed survey data from thirty-three nations. The quantitative survey sample included over 6800 respondents from a variety of social classes, religions, occupations, and organizations. The results substantiated two cultural classifications.

National cultures classified as *tight* are characterized by a very defined set of established societal norms. People are expected to adhere to these norms, and there is little tolerance for any form of deviance. Japan, which has specific protocols for nearly every social situation, provides an excellent example of a *tight culture*. For instance, at initial formal meetings cultural rules dictate who bows first, lowest, and longest based on each participants' status level.

In contrast, *loose cultures*, have less defined social norms and afford greater tolerance for aberrations. For example, at business meetings in the USA a handshake is the normal procedure, but who initiates it is of little consequence. The use of titles offers another example of the contrast between tight and loose cultures. In Mexico, a *tight* culture, official titles are expected to be used, and initial meetings proceed along formal lines until the participants establish a relationship. However, in the USA and Australia titles are often eschewed in favor of first names at the first encounter, which often moves quickly to informal participant interaction. (Gelfand et al., 2011; Gelfand, 2018)

Although it has been positively received, Gross (2018) points out that the theory attempts to be too all inclusive and does not consider additional factors, such as materialism, that sometimes drives human behavior. As another example, Gelfand frequently cites Singapore as a tight culture but never points out that the country's current form of authoritarian governance was instituted in 1965 by the Prime Minister in an effort to institute Confucianism political values (Hai, 2). It was not a natural evolution of values.

Nisbett – Cognitive Differences

The above discussions of varied values demonstrate how people from different cultures can have contrasting worldviews, perceive issues differently, and employ dissimilar problem-solving practices. While not considered a "value", how people think about issues can also impact their perceptions and behaviors. And there is a body of evidence that suggests culture does influence some cognitive organizing processes.

Although empirical data supporting this concept is relatively recent, it has long been recognized that differences between East and West in values, beliefs, and behaviors produce dissimilar worldviews. There is also some early literature, albeit anecdotally, contending that people in Northeast Asia, specifically China, Korea, and Japan, actually think differently than their Euro-American counterparts. In a cogent treatise, the Swiss journalist and longtime Asia resident

Lily Abegg, posited that Chinese and Japanese were psychologically different from Westerners (Abegg, 1952). The Japanese scholar Hajime Nakamura, drew on language, logic and cultural products to argue that thought patterns could vary among cultures (Nakamura, 1964).

More recently, the USA social psychologist Richard Nisbett and his colleagues brought empirical evidence to bear on this topic. His research suggests that culture does guide how people think and reason, referred to as cognitive patterns. The data indicated that a holistic pattern of reasoning was common among Chinese, Koreans, and Japanese. This style considered events and relations to be complex and interconnected. The whole was emphasized more than the individual parts. For the Northeast Asians, the relationship between the parts mattered more than the individual components. By contrast, Euro-Westerns (primarily US Americans) tended to use a more lineal logical approach, which prioritized comprehension of the discrete parts, rather than the greater context (Nisbett, 2003, 2010; Nisbett & Masuda, 2003).

To illustrate, when deciding on the composition of a workgroup, the individual talents of each person will often be the major consideration for USA managers. However, among Japanese managers, the skills of the people *and* their ability to effectively work together will likely receive equal weight. The difference in cognitive patterns can also influence how cross-cultural interactions play out. Research by McDaniel (2001) revealed that during Japanese-US negotiations, the Japanese side would often ask for additional information and frequently request to revisit previously discussed issues. From their holistic perspective, the introduction of each new topic carried the potential to influence and change the perception of the previous decisions. The USA negotiators considered these incidents disruptive, frustrating, and in some instances duplicitous. They approached negotiations from a lineal perspective and once discussion of an issue had concluded considered it settled.

These varied ways of thinking can lead to an event or a situation being viewed dissimilarly and carry clear implications for intercultural interactions. The challenges this brings to cross-culture management are discussed by Kase et al. (2011). Ji and Yap (2016) offer an overview of the origins of the contemporary study of cognition and culture and suggest areas of future research.

Conclusion – Understanding Cultural Value Motivations

Literature, both professional and popular, on interculture and cross-culture topics has become common over the past several decades. Driven largely by economic globalization, the Internet and libraries are replete with information reporting how to effectively interact with peoples of other cultures. Too often, however, these works only delineate the proper protocol for a particular cross-cultural interaction, such as a business meeting, dining etiquette, or pointing out that a particular culture prefers to work in groups rather than independently. Unfortunately, someone with only a topical knowledge of culture may well consider these protocols as just different, strange, improper, or even misguided. To overcome this pitfall, it is important to have a better understanding of *why* cultural differences exist.

The material discussed in this chapter was intended and designed to bring readers additional insight into the values that motivate varied behaviors, but even the discussed typologies do not provide unambiguous, definitive reasons for *why* a particular cultural value is held, or how it came to be and evolved. That knowledge is acquired through a more comprehensive examination of a culture's history, geography, environment, political-economy, social development, cross-cultural contact, etc. Understanding the *why* behind a particular set of cultural values demands time and effort, but offers significant benefits, leading to long term, mutually fulfilling intercultural relationships.

References

Abegg, L. (1952). *The mind of East Asia* (A. J. Crick & E. E. Thomas, Trans.). London; New York: Thames and Hudson. (Originally published as *Ostasien denkt anders*, 1949).

Adler, N. J., & Gunderson, A. (2008). *International Dimensions of Organizational Behavior* (5th ed.). Mason, OH: Thomson South-Western.

Browaeys, M.-J., & Price, R. (2015). *Understanding Cross-Cultural Management* (3rd ed.). New York: Pearson.

Cardon, P.W. (2008). A Critique of Hall's Contexting Model: A Meta-Analysis of Literature on Intercultural Business and Technical Communication. *Journal of Business and Technical Communication*, *22*(4), 399–428.

Chhokar, J. S., Brodbeck, F. C., & House, R. J. (Eds.). (2007). *Culture and Leadership, Across the World: The Globe Book of In-depth Studies of 25 Societies.* Mah-wah, NJ: Lawrence Erlbaum Associates.

Chinese Cultural Connection. (1987). Chinese Values and the Search for Culture-Free Dimensions of Culture. *Journal of Cross-Cultural Psychology*, *18*(2), 143–164. https://doi.org/10.1177/0022002187018002002

Domenici, K., & Littlejohn, S. W. (2006). *Facework: Bridging Theory and Practice.* Thousand Oaks, CA: Sage.

Fang, T. (2003). A Critique of Hofstede's Fifth National Culture Dimension. *International Journal of Cross Cultural Management*, *3*(3), 347–368. https://doi.org/10.1177/1470595803003003006.

Gelfand, M. (2018). *Rule Makers, Rule Breakers: How Tight and Loose Cultures Wire Our World*. New York: Scribner.

Gelfand, M., Raver, J., Nishii, L. Leslie, L., Lun, J., Lim, B., Duan, L., Almaliach, A., Ang, S., Arnadottir, J., Aycan, Z., Boehnke, K., Boski, P., Cabecinhas, R., Chan, D., Chhokar, J., D'Amato, A., Ferrer, M., Fischlmayr, I., & Yamaguchi, S. (2011). Differences between Tight and Loose Cultures: A 33-Nation Study. *Science*, *332*, 1100–4.

GLOBE. (2020). *Global Leadership and Organizational Behavior Effectiveness*. Retrieved September 01, 2021, from: https://globeproject.com/publications.

Gross, N. (2018, September 14). Is Your Culture 'Tight' or 'Loose'? The Answer Could Explain Everything. *New York Times*. Retrieved September 27, 2021, from: https://www.nytimes.com/2018/09/14/books/review/michele-gelfand-rule-makers-rule-breakers.html.

Hai, H. (2019). *The Rule of Culture: Corporate and State Governance in China and East Asia*. London: Routledge.

Hall, E. T. (1976). *Beyond Culture*. New York: Anchor (Originally published 1976).

Hall, E. T. (1983). *The Dance of Life: The Other Dimension of Time*. New York: Anchor.

Hall, E. T., & Hall, M. R. (1990). *Understanding Cultural Differences: Germans, French, and Americans*. Yarmouth, ME: Intercultural Press.

Hall, E. T., & Trager, G. L. (1953). *The Analysis of Culture*. New York, NY: American Council of Learned Science (Prepublication Edition).

Hofstede, G. (1996). Riding the Waves of Commerce: A Test of Trompenaars' "model" of National Cultural Differences. *International Journal of Intercultural Relations*, *20*(2), 189–198.

Hofstede, G. (2001). *Culture's Consequences* (2nd ed). Thousand Oaks, CA: Sage.

Hofstede, G., Hofstede, G. J., & Minkov, M. (2010). *Cultures and Organizations: Software of the Mind*. New York: McGraw-Hill.

House, R. J., Hanges, P. J., Javiad, M., Dorfman, P. W, & Gupta, V. (Eds.). (2004). *Culture, Leadership, and Organizations: The GLOBE Study of 62 Societies*. Thousand Oaks, CA: Sage.

House, R. J., Dorfman, P. W., Javidan, M., Hanges, P. J., & Sully de Luque, M. F. (Eds.). (2014). *Strategic Leadership across Cultures: The GLOBE Study of CEO Leadership Behavior and Effectiveness in 24 Countries*. Thousand Oaks, CA: Sage.

Hu, H. C. (1944). The Chinese Concepts of Face. *American Anthropologist*, *46*(1), 45–64.

Japan Federation of Bar Association. (2019). *White Paper on Attorneys 2019*. Retrieved from: https://www.nichibenren.or.jp/en/about/publications/whitepaper_2019.html.

Ji, L.-J., & Yap, S. (2016). *Culture and Cognition. Current Opinion in Psychology*, *8*, 105–111. https://doi.org/10.1016/j.copsyc.2015.10.004.

Ju, G.-D. (2020, September 27). Rocketing Up: Chinese Lawyers Increasing 148% in Ten Years. China Justice Observer. *China Justice Observer*. Retrieved September 05, 2021, from: https://www.chinajusticeobserver.com/a/rocketing-up-chinese-lawyers-increasing-148-percent-in-ten-years.

Kase, K., Slocum, A., & Zhang, Y. Y. (2011). *Asian versus Western Management Thinking: Its Culture Bound Nature*. London: Palgrave Macmillan.

Kirkman, B. L., Lowe, K. B., & Gibson, B. L. (2006). A Quarter Century of Culture's Consequences: A Review of Empirical Research Incorporating Hofstede's Cultural Values Framework. *Journal of International Business Studies*, *37*, 285–320.

Kittler, M. G., Rygl, D., & Mackinnon. (2011). Beyond Culture or Beyond Control? Reviewing the Use of Hall's High-/Low-Contest Concept. *International Journal of Cross Cultural Management*, *11*(1), 63–82.

Lewis, R. D. (2018). *When Cultures Collide: Leading across Cultures* (4th ed.). Boston; London: Nicholas Brealey.

McDaniel, E. R. (2001). *Japanese Negotiating Practices: Low Context Communication in a High Context Culture*. San Diego State University Center for International Business Education and Research (CIBER). Working Paper Series 1–112.

McSweeney, B. (2002). Hofstede's Model of National Cultural Differences and Their Consequences: A Triumph of Faith – A Failure of Analysis. *Human Relations*, *55*(1), 89–118. https://doi.org/10.1177/0018726702551004.

McSweeney, B., Brown, D., & Lliopoulou, S. (2016). Claiming Too Much, Delivering Too Little: Testing Some of Hofstede's Generalizations. *Irish Journal of Management*, *35*(1), 34–57. https://doi.org/10.1515/ijm-2016-0003.

Minkov, M. (2011). *Cultural Differences in a Globalizing World*. Bingley, UK: Emerald.

Minkov, M., & Hofstede, G. (2010). Hofstede's Fifth Dimension: New Evidence from the World Values Survey. *Journal of Cross-Cultural Psychology*, *43*, 3–14. https://doi.org/10.1177/0022022110388567.

Nakamura, H. (1964). *Ways of Thinking of Eastern Peoples: India, China, Tibet, Japan*. Delhi, India: East-West Center.

Nakata C. (2009). Going beyond Hofstede: Why We Need to and How. In C. Nakata (Ed.), *Beyond Hofstede*. London, UK: Palgrave Macmillan. https://doi.org/10.1057/9780230240834_1.

Neuliep, J. W., & Johnson, M. (2016). A Cross-Cultural Comparison of Ecuadorian and United States Face, Facework, and Conflict Styles During Interpersonal Conflict: An Application of Face-Negotiation Theory. *Journal of International & Intercultural Communication*, *9*(1), 1–19.

Nguyen, P. M., Terlouw, C., & Pilot, A. (2014). Revisiting Facework with a New Analysis Instrument: Face Strategies and Face Negotiation in Intercultural Communication. *Journal of Intercultural Communication*, *36*. Retrieved September 06, 2021, from: https://immi.se/oldwebsite/nr36/nguyen.html.

Nisbett, R. E. (2003). *The Geography of Thought*. New York: Free Press.

Nisbett, R. E. (2010). *Intelligence and How to Get It*. New York: W.W. Norton.

Nisbett, R. E., & Masuda, T. (2003). Culture and Point of View. *Proceedings of the National Academy of Sciences, 100*(19), 11163–11170. https://doi.org/10.1073/pnas.1934527100.

Oetzel, J, Garcia, A. J., & Ting-Toomey, S. (2008). An Analysis of the Relationships among Face Concerns and Facework Behaviors in Perceived Conflict Situations. *International Journal of Conflict Management, 19*(4), 382–403.

Oetzel, J., Ting-Toomey, S., Masumoto, T., Yokochi, Y, Pan, X.-H, Takai, J., & Wilcox, R. (2001). Face and Facework in Conflict: A Cross-Cultural Comparison of China, Germany, Japan, and the United States. *Communication Monographs*, *68*, 235–258. https://doi.org/10.1080/03637750128061.

Orr, L. M., & Hauser, W. J. (2008). A Re-Inquiry of Hofstede's Cultural Dimensions: A Call for 21st Century Cross-Cultural Research. *The Marketing Management Journal*, *18*(2), 1–19.

Rogers, E. M., Hart, W. B., & Miike, Y. (2002). Edward T. Hall and the History of Intercultural Communication: The United States and Japan. *Keio Communication Review*, *24*, 3–26.

Rose, G. M., Evaristo, R., & Straub, D. (2003). Culture and Consumer Responses to Web Download Time: A Four-Continent Study of Mono and Polychronism. *Engineering Management, IEEE Transactions, 50*(1), 31–44. https://doi.org/10.1109/tem.2002.808262.

Shaede, U. (2020). *The Business Reinvention of Japan: How to Make Sense of the New Japan and Why It Matters*. Stanford: Stanford University Press.

Ting-Toomey, S. (1994). Face and Facework: An Introduction. In S. Ting-Toomey (Ed.), *The Challenge of Facework: Cross-Cultural and Interpersonal Issues* (pp. 1–14). Albany: State University of New York Press.

Ting-Toomey, S. (2005). The Matrix of Face: An Updated Face-Negotiation Theory. In W. B. Gudykunst (Ed.), *Theorizing about Intercultural Communication* (pp. 71–92). Thousand Oaks, CA: Sage.

Trompenaars, F., & Hampden-Turner, C. (2020). *Riding the Waves of Culture: Understanding Diversity in Global Business* (4th ed.). London: McGraw-Hill.

World Economic Forum. (2021, March). *Global Gender Gap Report*. Retrieved September 14, 2021, from: http://www3.weforum.org/docs/WEF_GGGR_2021.pdf.

Zhang, Q., Ting-Toomey, S., & Oetzel, J. G. (2014). Linking Emotion to the Conflict Face-Negotiation Theory: A U.S.-China Investigation of the Mediating Effects of Anger, Compassion, and Guilt in Interpersonal Conflict. *Human Communication Research*, *40*, 373–395.

Zhang, Q., Oetzel, J. G., Ting-Toomey, S., & Zhang, J. (2019). Making Up or Getting Even? The Effects of Face Concerns, Self-Construal, and Apology on Forgiveness, Reconciliation, and Revenge in the United States and China. *Communication Research*, *46*(4), 503–524.

Introduction to Context Matters: High- Low Context Orientation as Expressed in Japanese and American Business Communication

By Adam Komisarof

The following chapter takes a closer look at high versus low context communication. Low context communication means that the entire message is typically encoded as words which means that little or nothing of the message is contained in nonverbal cues or the setting. High context communication, in contrast, means that much of the message can actually be contained in the nonverbal cues or the setting and less so in the words. This means that low context communication is very explicit and detailed whereas high context communication is implicit and vague. As Komisarof points out, context plays a central role in intercultural communication. He uses Japanese and American communication to illustrate how context influences the communication. But it is also pointed out that high versus low context communication can and does occur in different situations with different people; for example, an American (low context communication culture) might use low context communication when negotiating a business deal at work, but high context communication when talking to the partner at home. After having explained the fundamentals of high versus low communication, Kamisarof goes to great lengths to explain the various aspects of context and uses many examples from the real world to illustrate the differences. These communication aspects include nonverbal communication cues which assume a greater and more relevant role in high context communication than in low context communication. This also includes silence which is often associated with ambiguity in low context communication, but often sends very clear signals in high context communication. The chapter ends with some recommendations for high and low context communicators so as to avoid possible misunderstandings.

Michael B. Hinner

Adam Komisarof, PhD, is Professor in Keio University's Faculty of Letters in Tokyo. His research interests are in intercultural communication, acculturation psychology, and intercultural education. He spent a sabbatical at the University of Oxford (2012–13), where he conducted research as a Visiting Academic at the Nissan Institute of Japanese Studies, St. Antony's College. Professor Komisarof has published 3 books, the newest being *Crossing Boundaries and Weaving Intercultural Work, Life, and Scholarship in Globalizing Universities* (Routledge, with Prof. Zhu Hua), as well as numerous journal articles and book chapters with publishers such as Cambridge University Press, Wiley, and Taylor-Francis. He recently served as the co-editor of a special issue in Elsevier's *International Journal of Intercultural Relations* entitled "Viewing Intercultural Adaptation and Social Inclusion Through Constructs of National Identity." Dr. Komisarof is a Fellow and President of the International Academy for Intercultural Research, an academic organization whose members are dedicated to advancing research in intercultural studies and intergroup understanding in the world. However, taken together a member of a low context culture is in sum total more likely to use low context communication than high context communication because the larger socio-cultural environment prefers low context communication over high context communication.

Adam Komisarof

Context Matters: High-Low Context Orientation as Expressed in Japanese and American Business Communication

Contextual communication orientation, more commonly referred to as high-low context, is a central concept in the field of intercultural communication and can be used to understand tendencies in communication styles and communication-related values among various cultural groups. This had decided implications for the study and practice of international business, for example, grasping cultural differences in the fields of management and marketing (Kim et al., 1998). The goal of this chapter is to explicate this concept, illustrating its meaning primarily using examples from Japan and the United States. I will draw from my 25-year career as a corporate trainer and university educator, employing examples from the literature in intercultural communication, international business, and Japan studies, as well as my own experiences as a US American living in Japan for nearly 25 years. By the end of this chapter, readers should have a clear grasp of what constitutes context, differences between high and low context communication styles, and a richer understanding of how such communication style differences impact business communication among Japanese and Americans as well as between them. I will conclude with brief recommendations as to how such differences can be bridged to realize more effective, positive communication outcomes between people experiencing challenges in communicating across the high-low context divide.

Before Context: Language, Symbols, Messages, and the Construction of Meaning

First, it is critical to lay the groundwork for explaining high-low context by providing some definitions from the field of intercultural communication: language, symbols, messages, and culture – as well as explaining their relationships. According to Gudykunst and Nishida (1994), language constitutes a system of rules for

> how the sounds of the language are made, how sentences are formed, the meaning of words or combinations, and how the language is used. When the rules of language are translated into a channel of communication (e.g., the spoken word) using symbols, messages are created. (p. 4)

Symbols of particular interest in this chapter include words and nonverbal signals such as gestures, eye contact, or facial expressions. All symbols refer to something, whether it is an idea or an object, yet the relationship between a symbol and that to which it refers is arbitrarily constructed by human beings, and often the meaning assigned to symbols differs from culture to culture. For instance, the same symbol, a thumbs up gesture, can be a show of approval in some cultures but a grave insult in others. Another symbol, the word "difficult," typically means "impossible" in Japan but "challenging yet possible" in North America.

Symbols are combined into messages, which are in turn transmitted to others who then interpret them. Depending upon the cognitive framework of the receiver, one may perceive the meaning of that message differently from how the sender intended it. Because each individual has their own unique cognitive makeup, which is a combination of their life experiences (nurture) and hereditary characteristics (nature), no two individuals transmit or interpret messages in exactly the same way. Those cognitive frameworks used for both deciding how to transmit messages and how to interpret them are shaped in part by culture – one aspect of nurture.

Hall and Hall (1987) described culture as "a system for creating, sending, storing, and processing information" (p. 3), whereas Barnlund (1989) argued that culture gives its members "a commitment to similar ways of managing meanings" (p. xiii). Thus, culture adds another layer of complexity to the already complex processes of message transmission and interpretation. While countries can be useful proxies for cultural groups existing roughly on the level of nation, a culture can be formed by any group of regularly interacting people who, in the process of such interactions, establish their own communicative norms, beliefs, and associated practices; therefore, cultures may exist on many levels of abstraction such as geographic region, ethnic group, work organization, and family (Bennett, 2013). How we transmit and interpret messages can vary from one cultural group to another – whether on the level of nation, region, organization, family, or whichever types of groups are being compared.

Defined by Gudykunst and Nishida (1994), communication refers to the "exchange of messages and the creation of meaning (e.g., assigning significance or interpreting the messages)," and it is only effective to the extent that the person who interprets the message attaches "a meaning to the message that is similar to what the transmitter intended" (p. 5). Given the complexity of the processes of encoding and interpretation, as well as the potentially infinite variation in human cognitive frameworks for deriving meaning from communication, co-constructing similar or identical meanings to the same message is no small task, and differences between what is termed high and low context communication play a significant role in making the overall process of communication more challenging. High-low context orientation forms a dimension of cultural variability that can be used to explain how people communicate differently across cultures (Gudykunst & Nishida, 1994), and if these two forms of encoding and interpreting messages are better understood and capably bridged, intercultural communication can become more effective in the process, engendering more positive relational outcomes.

Context Defined

What exactly is context? According to Hall and Hall (1987), it constitutes "the information that surrounds an event and is inextricably bound up with the meaning of that event" (p. 7). Hall (1976) explained that a high context message is one in which "most of the information is either in the physical context or internalized in the person, while very little is in the coded, explicit, transmitted part of the message" (p. 79); therefore, in high-context communication, meaning is communicated, as per Condon (1984), "in the *context* within which words are spoken – such as who says the words, where and how they are spoken and so on" (p. 45). Alternately, Condon clarified, a low context message is one in which "the mass of information is vested in the explicit code" (p. 70). Because low context communicators tend not to presume that the listener shares unsaid context, to facilitate accurate, effective communication, they explicitly verbalize their message so the meaning of messages can be gleaned from the words themselves.

Cultures on the level of nation can influence the use of context to communicate intended meanings. For instance, Hall (1976), Condon (1986), and Ramsey (1998) asserted that Americans tend to place a strong trust in words to communicate and rely little on context to do so (i.e., they tend to be low context communicators), whereas Japanese often follow the opposite pattern (i.e., they are apt to be high context communicators). However, reliance upon context to communicate is not just a function of cultural patterns; context can be utilized in relational dyads or groups simply due to their greater familiarity with other(s) in that dyad or group. For example, even among low context communicators, spouses may communicate through context to a much higher extent than they would in other relationships, simply because they have built such an extensive foundation of shared experiences and meanings that they can readily tap into, thus relying on a few words or just a facial expression to encode messages to each other.

Therefore, high context communication presumes a large degree of collective knowledge and assumptions that do not need to be made explicit because communicative partners assume, at least unconsciously, that both are aware of or can readily tap into such shared bodies of information and the meanings commonly derived from them. The conditioning that makes such communication possible may occur through socialization in a specific society or even a work organization. In Japan, for example, corporate newcomers are indoctrinated in organizational culture through an extensive orientation period, or *shinyuu shain kenshuu*. Once ensconced in the company, continuous efforts are made to build upon the foundation of shared information, leading to similar cognitive frameworks for encoding and decoding such information. For instance, a Japanese client once told me that upon joining his company he was trained that it was his job – and that of everyone in the same section – to listen to other colleagues' conversations on the office phones to be current on all work-related business.

High-Low Context: Not a Dualism But a Continuum

US American communication patterns are utilized in this chapter as a primary counterpoint to Japanese ones; however, high-low context is not conceived as dualistic concept, but as a continuum. As Hall and Hall (1987) wrote, "The elements that combine to produce a given meaning – events and context – are in different proportions depending on the culture. It is thus possible to order the cultures of the world on a scale from high to low context" (p. 7). Therefore, low-context communicators, for example, are not all created the same – those closer to the low-context extreme of the scale incorporate greater proportions of explicit messages in their communication, while those high-context communicators nearer to the high-context extreme rely more on context in theirs. If one imagines a continuum from low to high context (illustrated in Figure 1), one could plot national group tendencies as Hall and Hall proposed, or individual communication styles. When plotting countries, if one were to assess high-low context using a quantitative instrument, for example, Japan's group average would presumably be near (but not at) the extreme end of the high context continuum as indicative of a strong high context communication style compared with most other national averages, and America situated clearly on the low context end of the continuum but comparatively higher in context than the points representing Swiss, German, and Scandinavian averages (Gudykunst & Nishida, 1994).

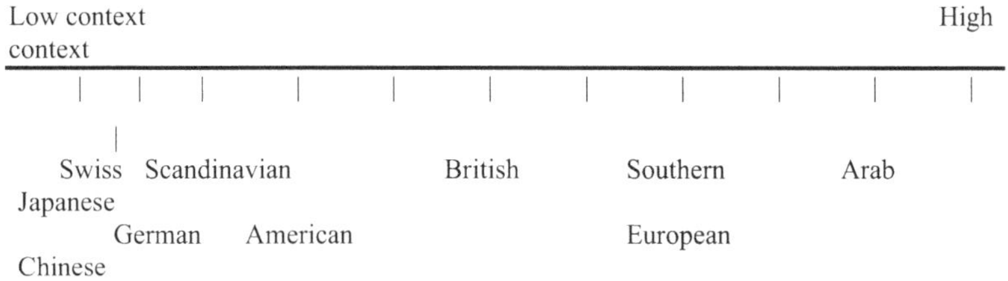

Figure 1: The High-Low Context Continuum with National Groups Plotted
Source: (Adapted from Hall & Hall, 1990).

Thus, there are degrees of low and high context, and the relative positions of individuals and the groups to which they belong on this continuum help to shape their reactions to others in everyday communication. For instance, many Japanese businesspeople perceive Americans and Britons as low context, yet in Figure 1, the British tend to be placed in a higher context position than Americans, yet still on the low context half of the continuum. I was confronted by such differences regularly when I lived in Oxford, England for one year while on sabbatical. The first two months, I was quite confused, as people frequently seemed to omit information that I needed to grasp what they were saying – typically intimating something that appeared obvious to them but unknown to me. One day, an American friend who had lived a decade in the UK and two decades in Japan advised me, "When the British talk to you, just imagine they are speaking Japanese." Eureka! When my colleagues spoke, I imagined their words in Japanese (instead of American English), and using this high context framework for interpretation, their implied meanings grew much clearer.

The high-low context continuum raises several important issues and implications. First, when plotting countries, a group's point on the continuum only represents an average score for all members tested within a group – not necessarily individual communication styles. This also means that all gradations of high and low context on the continuum may be found among individuals in that national group. For example, if we examined the predominant communication style of a large group of Americans (or Japanese), we would expect to identify people whose primary communication tendencies could be plotted all over the continuum, demonstrating a diversity of individual styles. One would also likely find a cluster of individual American (or Japanese) scores at or near their group average – signifying a common communication style within the group, though not one that is indicative of every person in it. In other words, it is important to remember that low and high context communication patterns exist in all cultural groups, but one style that has been conditioned during members' primary socialization tends to be shared broadly among those members. Thus, high-low context is a dimension of cultural variation that can be used to describe the predominant communication style in a specific national culture while at the same time recognizing that the individual with whom we are communicating may or may not align with such patterns, or that tendencies at the group cultural level are not necessarily held at the individual level (Komisarof & Zhu, 2016; Richardson & Smith, 2007).

The continuum can also be used similarly to visualize the communication style of any given individual. For instance, if we examined someone's communication style, we would likely find that person employs both high and low context styles: in specific situations (e.g., expressing one's opinion at a meeting, negotiation, or handling difficult requests from customers) or with particular conversational partners (e.g., one's boss vs. a subordinate), they are likely to assume a communication style represented by different gradations along the high-low context continuum. However, if we plotted a large number of communication scenarios, then a dominant individual high or low context style would likely emerge, which could be expressed as a plot on the continuum indicating that person's primary communication tendency.

Tests of Hall's Original Positions for American and Japanese Culture

Empirical tests of Hall's original assertion of Japan as an extremely high context culture and America as a moderately strong low context culture have generally showed mixed results. For instance, Richardson and Smith (2007) measured individual tendencies in high-low context among Japanese and Americans, finding significantly different mean group scores between them, with Japanese scoring higher on the scale; however, this difference was modest, and the Japanese sample's mean score was only at the scale midpoint. They concluded that Japan may be considered higher in context than America, but not necessarily high context in any absolute sense.

Kim, Pan, and Park (1998) attempted to empirically assess whether Americas are low context (and Chinese and South Koreans high context). With the caveat that their samples were not representative (comprising business managers enrolled in 3 separate MBA programs) and modest in size, differences were statistically significant between Americans (comparatively low context) and Chinese as well as Koreans, respectively (comparatively high context). Thomas

(1998), however, could not confirm high-low context differences between Americans and South Koreans, though this study comprised an analysis of written texts produced by participants in only a small sample.

Thus, empirical support of Americans as low context and Japanese as high context is inconclusive, though these positions are often assumed in research (Cardon, 2008). Though a significant portion of the literature supporting Hall's original assertions about these two national cultures is theoretical and/or anecdotal as opposed to empirical, this does not render it invalid. First, empirical studies of Japan's and America's position on the high-low context continuum, particularly in comparison with one another, are scant. Moreover, theoretical and anecdotal descriptions of Japanese high context and American low context communication styles have helped countless numbers of people to adapt to communication patterns in the other – whether it was Americans trying desperately to understand Japanese people or Japanese struggling to adjust to Americans. Further empirical research is recommended to better understand high-low context tendencies in both countries, particularly in cross-cultural comparison, as well as studies testing the efficacy of various strategies for bridging their differences.

Differentiating High and Low Context

High and low context were originally distinguished by Hall (1976) as summarized in Figure 2. In the subsequent sections, these differences will be discussed in turn, illustrated with examples, and elaborated upon.

	High Context	**Low Context**
Organization	Indirect, circular	Direct, linear
Use of language	Implicit (how you say it is more important than what you say)	Explicit (what you say is more important than how you say it)
Emphasis	Nonverbal communication, shared knowledge, and role expectations	Words
Purpose of communication	Establish and maintain good relations	Exchange ideas and information
Attitude toward conflict	Should be avoided or resolved through consensus. Judgments of person and their ideas are not separate.	Conflict can be acknowledged openly. Person and their ideas often separate.
Communicative focus	Receiver-oriented: receiver must interpret the message accurately.	Sender-oriented: sender must clearly convey the message.

Figure 2: High and Low Context Communication Styles

Direct vs. Indirect Communication

The first difference between high and low context relates to how verbal communication is organized: high context tends to be circular and indirect with low context being linear and direct. Over 50 years ago, Nakane (1970) observed the central importance of shared context in Japanese relationships and how it enables indirect communication to be understood: "Members of a group know each other exceedingly well… . Among fellow members a single word would suffice for the whole sentence." (p. 121).

Once such knowledge of the other is gained, then one can often infer what the other means to communicate without them needing to do so explicitly. For instance, a Japanese manager once told me that when he wanted a subordinate to handle a problem, he would just say, "Take care of it" (in Japanese, *Nantoka shite oite*). He reasoned that a trusted, competent subordinate would know what to do without the details needing to be enumerated. Low context communication, in stark contrast, tends to be direct, detailed, and unambiguous, with managers generally expected to explain precisely what they want done and how.

One Japanese high context expression that typically causes confusion to those unaccustomed to doing business there is "It's a little difficult" (*Sore wa chotto muzukashii desu*), which means that something is impossible or undesirable. Quite simply, it means no. By stating this indirectly, the face is saved of both the speaker and listener and interpersonal harmony maintained.

Naturally, there are exceptions to Japanese communicating in a high context manner: as previously discussed, there are Japanese who utilize primarily low context communication styles, and we can also observe diverse styles employed by the same individual. For example, even if Japan's most high context communicator sees a fire rapidly approaching, s/he would not say, "Do you feel it is getting a bit hot?" to imply that a fire is about to engulf them. Screaming "Fire!" and running away is culturally universal.

Another important difference in the organization of high and low context styles is that the former tends to be circular and the latter linear. Japanese people often describe details of a situation or event without explicitly stating the main point, expecting that listeners who understand the context, or the body of knowledge related to the issue, will be able to infer what the speaker is alluding to. In this sense, the speaker is "moving around" the main point without verbalizing it – thus utilizing a "circular" style. North American communicators tend to state the main point first and provide pertinent reasons and examples afterward, thus becoming frustrated with their Japanese counterparts who do not "get to the point," while Japanese may feel that the predominant North American style is invasive and/or pushy for its overly linear, direct approach (Ramsey, 1998).

Verbal Communication and Words vs. Nonverbal Communication, Shared Knowledge and Role Expectations

While low context communication is heavily dependent upon words to communicate meaning, high context communication tends to reference bodies of unstated context that the speaker elicits in the mind of the listener. There are 3 ways this is usually achieved: through 1. nonverbal communication, 2. allusions to collective knowledge, and 3. shared role expectations. From here, each is considered in turn.

Sugiyama Lebra (1976) asserted that Japanese place a premium upon implicit, nonverbal, intuitive communication, rather than that which is explicit and verbal: "The Japanese … feel that speech is a poor substitute for an intuitive understanding of what is going on in other people's minds" (p. 46), and "only an insensitive uncouth person needs a direct, verbal, complete message" (p. 47). Hall and Hall (1987) emphasized Japanese predilections toward having prodigious needs for "information about human relationships and how people are feeling … [and possessing] quite sensitive antennae for perceiving emotional reactions" (p. 75).

Nonverbal communication is achieved through various channels including body language (e.g., facial expressions, gestures, and body posture), eye language (e.g., eye movements or frequency of eye contact), space language (e.g., standing distance between conversational partners), touch language (e.g., the places on the body considered appropriate to be touched and the frequency of such touching), and paralanguage – or the non-lexical aspects of speech communication (e.g., tone and volume of voice) (Yashiro et al., 2001).

High context communicators are commonly socialized to be extremely sensitive to nonverbal signals. For instance, when my wife and I were engaged and still had different last names, we gave an intercultural communication workshop as co-trainers. To maintain an air of professionalism, we decided that we would not acknowledge our relationship to the participants and behave neutrally toward each other. After the workshop, a group of Americans and a Japanese participant approached us. One American asked if we knew each other well, to which I responded, "Actually, we are engaged." Everyone's mouth dropped open in surprise except for the Japanese man, who said with a small smile, "I thought that you were not just training partners." When I asked him how he knew, he told us it was in how we gestured toward each other. Despite our best efforts to camouflage our relationship, we could not deceive his high context nonverbal observational skills.

Another form of nonverbal communication which plays a large role in high context communication, particularly in Japan, is silence. In low context cultures such as the US, silence tends to be seen as uncomfortable and something to be avoided because of its ambiguity. In Japan, silence is often employed as an important tool in communication. In business, silence can be used to indicate agreement (as when no one objects to a proposal) or as disagreement (as when a speaker at a meeting implores agreement with their position but others remain silent). As Barnlund (1989) explained, "There are silences [in Japan] as damning, eloquent, reassuring or confirming as any remark one might make" (p. 129).

In addition to nonverbal channels, references to shared knowledge play an important role in high context communication. In Sakamoto and Naotsuka (1982), an American recounted when she asked a Japanese teacher whether he had any discipline problems in his high school, to which he replied, "Our school is an old school." Baffled, she repeated the question, thinking he had misunderstood. He gave the same answer. To the American, an old school had no relationship to discipline problems – it was merely old. From his perspective, he was communicating quite clearly that his school was an old school, or one with a long history, which meant it was a college preparatory school with high admissions standards and students aspiring to go to Japan's best universities; therefore, he expected the listener to share this commonplace knowledge and grasp that he did not have major discipline problems with the utterance that his school was old.

Shared role expectations constitute another critical aspect of high context communication. To demonstrate this point in my corporate workshops, I often give the following scenario: Imagine that you live in an apartment building with your partner and your 8-year-old daughter, who loves to practice the piano every afternoon. One day, you exit your apartment and by chance run into the woman who lives next door. After exchanging greetings, she says, "Your daughter plays piano so well." When I ask American participants how they interpret this statement, typically 80–90 % respond that the neighbor is complimenting their daughter's piano playing. Yet with Japanese audiences, 80–90 % say that the neighbor is complaining that their daughter plays too noisily. Why? In Japanese society, a key role expectation is that neighbors will not cause any inconvenience or trouble (in Japanese, *meiwaku*) for each other. Excessive noise is one form of *meiwaku*, so when neighbors in Japan communicate, their antennas are raised, so to speak, to detect subtle messages that hint of any sources of trouble needing to be ameliorated.

Likewise, providers are expected to offer their customers service that minimizes any form of inconvenience – a smooth user experience – and if some form of inconvenience is pointed out, the vendor will usually try to remedy the problem, which is a key to getting repeat business as well as referrals to new clients. For instance, I have hired several Japanese moving companies (6 times in total) with extremely consistent experiences. When moving, some of the most common sources of potential trouble are a scratch to the property that one is moving out of, the property being moved into, or to one's possessions. Therefore, as soon as moving companies arrive on a property, most will set up easily removable covers all over the walls to make sure that they are not inadvertently scratched when carrying furniture in or out. The furniture itself is wrapped in elastic covers made of padded protective material. Finally, even the slightest movers are stunningly strong and agile, moving large furniture seamlessly through narrow spaces, blending grace and power as they navigate twisting halls and cramped stairwells – all the while avoiding scratches or bumps anywhere – in a country that is famous for small living spaces.

A final example of shared role expectations that impacts Japanese business communication is the role of a manager, who is presumed to know the projects being currently addressed by each of their subordinates, thus implicitly understanding everyone's current workload. In low context cultures such as the US, if a manager asks an employee to take on extra work and the employee feels overloaded, they are generally expected to say so, reminding the manager about other projects in which they are involved. In Japan, however, since the manager is supposed to be conscious of everyone's workload, subordinates often assume that requests are being made with that workload already in their manager's mind. Given this role expectation and the sensitivity to keeping harmonious collegial relations, subordinates frequently will accept such burdensome assignments. This leaves potential for misunderstandings (and a burned-out workforce) when low context American managers assume that Japanese subordinates will let them know if their request is not feasible, yet the high context employee assumes that their boss understands exactly what is being asked and is requesting them to complete this task despite the overwork they are sure to encounter.

Conflict Avoidance vs. Conflict Acknowledgement

The next major differences between high and low context communication styles described in Figure 1 relate to the purpose of communication and attitude toward conflict. As for high context communication, especially in Japan, one of *the* primary purposes is establishing and maintaining harmonious human relationships (Dalsky & Su, 2020), so differences of opinion, especially arguments, are usually seen as disruptive to positive interactions and conflict is generally avoided (Gercik, 1992; Goldman, 1994; Morisaki & Gudykunst, 1994). Barnlund (1989) observed that Japanese tend to search for what is mutually agreeable, at least in initial stages of conversation, with differences of opinion being expressed indirectly and gingerly. This is not to say that diverse ideas and contrary information are never shared, but when they are, great attention is paid to keeping positive relations through protecting the face of one's communicative partner. In groups, consensus-based decision making is preferred, and in discussions, a person and their idea are often considered one and the same; in other words, if you express disfavor towards another's idea, you could easily be construed as attacking their personhood.

In contrast, the primary purpose of low context communication is generally thought to be exchanging information and ideas, where differences of opinion can be frankly considered (Condon, 1984), particularly because low context communicators are more likely than high context communicators to see another's personhood and their ideas as distinct. In the workplace, as long as norms for polite language and professional behavior are adhered to, people are more likely to receive disagreements without feeling attacked or that their face needs are in jeopardy. Barnlund (1989) characterized American communication as an instrument of analysis, utilized for "clarifying positions, … comparing and contrasting views, and a way, ultimately, of testing the relative merits of different opinions" (p. 42). Ramsey (1998) described how these tendencies manifest in business:

> The persuasive function is highly emphasized in North American corporate communication style. Selling a product or promoting an action relies heavily on the assumption that if one can be shown the facts, the numbers, the details, or the direct correlation between cause and effect logically or objectively, he or she will accept the point… . All parties to a conversation are responsible for their own opinions; active give-and-take is expected. (p. 123)

Such observations may be connected to what is termed the *independent* and *interdependent self*. Markus and Kitayama (1991) distinguished the former (common in Western countries such as the United States) as a conception of the self as "an independent, self-contained, autonomous entity," while the latter, common in Japan, as one that insists upon the "fundamental relatedness of individuals to each other" (p. 224) and constitutes a self that "changes structure with the nature of the particular social context" (p. 227). As the self is characterized as embedded in context and shifting, "relationships between individuals and interactively defined meaning are prioritized over the individual self and 'private' meaning" (Bachnik, 1994, p. 18).

Moreover, Japan is broadly thought to be a collectivistic society in which maintaining harmony within groups is at a premium (Dalsky & Su, 2020; Gudykunst & Nishida, 1994). When ingroup differences of opinion arise, people tend to tread carefully, often utilizing indirect statements and questions to hint at an alternative view. Another frequent rhetorical strategy is making utterances that stimulate empathy in one's communicative partner to convince them of the speaker's perspective. In contrast, low context communication tends to predominate in individualistic cultures such as the United States, as it is important for one to state opinions clearly so others can know how that person stands as an individual (Gudykunst & Nishida, 1994). In such cultures, instead of the empathy-eliciting approach often employed by Japanese, persuasive logic is used to argue to the efficacy or correctness of the speaker's position.

I have seen these tendencies clash innumerable times when Americans propose controversial changes in Japanese companies. Typically, Americans support their viewpoint with reasons, data, and examples. If Japanese remain unconvinced, rather than risk overt conflict, they often drop the matter – appearing to assent to the American view but in fact quietly continuing the status quo. Invariably, this eventually comes to light, followed by Americans charging they have been deceived and Japanese feeling further besieged with unreasonable demands. Moreover, the Japanese often become less transparent about other matters that could lead to discord, which inflames American feelings of exclusion from the organization's daily workings (Komisarof, 2011).

Another example comes from a former client – a newly arrived American executive manager of an American company's Tokyo office that was populated almost entirely with Japanese employees. Relationships with "Ronald's" Japanese subordinates were quite strained after several months, so he read extensively about Japanese culture to decipher how to repair them. He discovered what he thought was clearly a panacea for doing so: taking a corporate trip together at the organization's expense. Such events are a traditional mainstay in Japanese companies for building positive relations as people stay overnight at a hotel eating, drinking, and singing karaoke together.

When Ronald proudly proposed this idea at his sectional meeting the next week, he was greeted with silence. He repeated his idea. Once again, silence. Ronald had spent so much time coming up with this solution, and people were not even willing to tell him what they thought! He exploded in frustration. Unfortunately, his outburst further soured intercultural relations. I was brought in several months later to help. After interviews with Ronald's managers, I learned that the Japanese were silent at the meeting because they had not had time first to gauge their coworkers' opinions. Offering individual opinions about a proposal that affects an entire group of people would be seen as inconsiderate of those with a divergent point of view: in this case, those against the trip could be required to go if someone spoke out in favor of the idea, or those wanting to attend might be disappointed if the first speakers rejected the proposal. Furthermore, if anyone publicly opposed the executive's proposal, from a high context perspective, they could be seen as repudiating his leadership and personhood – which could destroy their relationship. On multiple levels, Japanese employees tried to avoid conflict with Ronald and with each other.

So how do Japanese people express contrarian opinions yet circumvent conflict at meetings? Dalsky and Su (2020) detail one common method:

> In a Western setting, a meeting is typically a forum to exchange ideas and opinions, or to develop plans for moving forward. In a Japanese setting, a meeting … is usually a formality in which all parties involved meet to agree on a predetermined course of action. This action has been planned and discussed beforehand in a practice called *nemawashi*. Typically, an individual will have discussed a proposal with relevant members and superiors, considered their opinions, and gained their acceptance before raising the proposal for formalization in the meeting. (p. 592)

Thus, *nemawashi* promotes social cohesion through the interaction between coworkers and superiors that it requires. It also maintains harmony within meetings by avoiding potentially awkward disagreements that have already been aired and negotiated beforehand.

Challenges to Notions of Conflict Avoidance and Acknowledgment

While Japanese tendencies towards conflict avoidance and American ones towards conflict acknowledgement have been described by the scholars cited so far, other studies have challenged or refined these ideas. For example, Ward et al. (2016) tested the premise that the higher context the communication style, the less likely one is to express contrarian opinions. They found among a robust sample of faculty members at US universities (including both American and foreign citizens) that there are two important boundary conditions of this relationship: the type of voice being considered (i.e., promotive voice that offers novel, additive ideas and solutions vs. prohibitive voice that criticizes existing plans and strategies), as well as relational context (i.e., whether the speaker sees oneself as part of the same ingroup as the message's receiver). While high context communicators reported using prohibitive voice less frequently than those who are low context, they did not necessarily voice suggestions (i.e., use the promotive voice) less frequently. Moreover, high context communicators voiced suggestions less frequently than low context communicators when they did not share ingroup status with others, but they "may practice non-face damaging upward communication when in an in-group context" (p. 1505) with comparable frequency. Thus, while there is evidence that high context communicators attempt to preserve harmony through conflict avoidance with greater urgency than low context communicators, these tendencies relent when they feel close to others and are using the promotive voice, as such suggestions are less likely to conflict with their deference, face maintenance, and harmony goals.

Thomas (1998) analyzed stylistic differences in written communication among Americans and South Koreans using central criteria from Hall's original definition of high-low context, such as use of politeness strategies to avoid offending others, direct vs. indirect organizational patterns in explaining one's main point, and linear vs. recursive lines of reasoning. Though the study itself has numerous limitations including a small sample, she found that Americans employed politeness strategies with similar frequency to South Koreans. This begs the question whether and in which situations Americans are indeed direct and openly acknowledge conflict.

Such caveats and contradictory findings about conflict avoidance vs. acknowledgment merit a final comment on the body of research validating the high-low context concept. Though a comprehensive review of the literature is beyond the scope of this chapter, Cardon's (2008) meta-analysis concluded that while high-low context is the most important concept in intercultural business and technical communication (given its numerous citations and central role in so many studies), it has not yet been empirically validated. Specifically, "Most of the contexting categories simply have not been researched enough to make firm conclusions" (p. 422). However, he also asserted that the propositions of the high-low context model deserve serious attention given the large body of diverse intercultural communication researchers across the globe who have developed them. I would add that the experiential validation from innumerable practitioners who have found the concepts useful to make sense of and improve their daily intercultural communication dynamics also speaks to the need for further research of this promising concept. Future studies will presumably probe the differences between high and low context, clarifying if and when they are significant and how they transform based upon various boundary conditions. This is best achieved by developing more rigorous measures of the high-low context concept and using them to examine more countries (most literature focuses upon the US, Japan, Australia, and South Korea), studying more dimensions of contexting than that of directness-indirectness, and clarifying within specific cultures when high and low context messages tend to be utilized (Cardon, 2008).

Sender and Receiver Orientations

In Japan, there is a famous saying, "Hear 1 understand 10" (*ichi ieba juu wakaru*). In other words, if you hear 1 piece of information, you should be able to understand 10 implications from it. A good communicator listens carefully and can grasp their partner's intended meaning without them needing to verbalize it explicitly. In Japanese, inferring such messages is called "reading the air" (*kuuki wo yomu koto*), and those unable to do so are derisively called "K.Y." meaning *kuuki wo yomenai*, or someone who cannot read the air. Thus, the burden for successful communication lies firmly with the message receiver, who must fill information gaps to understand the sender's meaning. For low context communicators, this burden rests squarely on the message's sender, who is expected to clearly articulate their message so their intended meaning is accurately received. To "say what you mean" is the hallmark of an effective communicator in societies where low context communication is valued.

An American client demonstrated the importance of hearing 1 and understanding 10 in Japanese business communication. As the representative of the Japanese office of an American company, he was leading the talks between his organization and the Japanese government about a potential joint project. Going into the initial meeting with an important Japanese government official, his biggest concern was whether his current proposal allowed enough time to execute the project – particularly since his firm was tied up with other commitments at the moment and would have trouble starting right away. Accompanied by his trusted number two manager, a Japanese national, the American was relieved by the Japanese official's great enthusiasm for the project. As he was praising the project, the official paused for one moment, saying almost incidentally, "My motto is speed," then continuing along his previous line of thought. The meeting ended amicably. Afterwards, once they were alone, the American confided to his Japanese manager, "I was worried for nothing. The official was positive from the start, and he never mentioned any problem with our proposed schedule." Immediately, the Japanese manager's face turned ashen as he interjected, "No! He was very clear that we must move more quickly when he said, 'My motto is speed.'" From that one brief comment during a 30-minute meeting, the Japanese manager had grasped the essence of what the official had intended to communicate: the project was highly desirable, but only if it could be executed rapidly.

Differences between receiver and sender orientations can be further illustrated through the role of questions in high and low context communication. In low context communication, a question is usually precisely that – a question. If a low context communicator proposes modifications in their company's customer service model and they are asked, "What will our customers think?", then they will likely explain how they anticipate the customers will react to the changes – in other words, they will answer the question as it has been stated. However, in high context communication, a question can potentially be a question, but it frequently has a different function: expressing disagreement. By asking "What will the customer think?", my high context communicative partner might be saying that they believe customers will find the proposed changes undesirable. Such questions are a form of face-saving communication, as they allow the questioner to state their disagreement without doing so directly and the listener to process this objection without being overtly challenged.

Another function of questions in Japanese high context communication is making requests (Sakamoto & Naotsuka, 1982). A Japanese corporate trainer arrived for the first time at the office of his American client. He needed materials for that day's workshop to be copied – a situation which he assumed was understood. When he asked the American coordinator of the workshop, "Can you tell me where the copy machine is?", he expected his client to infer that he was actually requesting for someone from the company to make copies for him; in Japanese companies, to walk through an organization's office space and use their copier unaccompanied would typically be considered inappropriate if one is not an employee. The trainer was quite surprised when his request went completely unrecognized and the client simply responded, "It's on the second floor on the left after you exit the elevator."

Naturally, low context communicators use questions as requests or indirect statements of disagreement, too. However, the frequency differs. Consequently, low context communicators may not be ready to regularly interpret questions as requests or disagreements – mistakenly assuming that they are straightforward inquiries with no further interpretation necessary. In other words, their sender orientation dictates that it is the speaker's responsibility to clearly state requests or disagreements as such, so they might fail to detect these other uses of questions when they are employed. High context communicators, especially in Japan, encounter these uses of questions regularly and are hence quite accustomed to activating their receiver orientation to recognize and decode them.

Shifting Along the High-Low Context Continuum: Power Dynamics and Insider Status

As stated earlier in the chapter, individuals may shift their communication style along the high-low context continuum based upon the situation, including their conversational partner. This next section attunes readers to how such shifts can occur in Japan: specifically, depending upon the status differences between them and the extent that they share membership in the same ingroup. In other words, one's choice of style on the high-low context continuum among Japanese is dynamic and hence cannot be understood or estimated without clarifying the nature of the relationship between the communicating parties.

Hierarchical ranking in Japan is dependent upon various factors such as age, gender, and job status (Bachnik, 1994), and such ranking decidedly influences conversational dynamics – for example, those higher in rank than their conversational counterparts will commonly speak for much longer amounts of time, expecting their partner to take the role of listener (Nakane, 1970). As a faithful listener of lesser status, relational subordinates commonly adopt a high context style specifically by avoiding the expression of opposing views and listening attentively to discern the wishes and opinions of the higher status speaker. Conversely, those higher in status are much less likely to hesitate in scolding their subordinates (Yashiro et al., 2001) and tend to express differences of opinion with little hesitation. Thus, tendencies to speak indirectly, avoid conflict, and be a faithful listener are all high context features that are far more likely to be adopted by those lower in status as a display of deference.

Another key factor in Japanese relationships in determining the degree of high context communication utilized can be traced to *uchi-soto* (literally "inside-outside"), or the insider-outsider continuum of human relationships. As Bachnik (1994) explained, "One is constantly constraining or expressing 'self,' in relation to the degree of social constraint, or relaxation of constraint, that is perceived appropriate" (p. 25) in a particular social setting with one's communicative partner(s). Such dynamic tension between the relaxation and tightening of constraint depends in part upon one's insider or outsider status in relation to the other, and this dynamic accentuates different facets of communication on the high-low context continuum. For instance, if people share an ingroup, they can enjoy relations characterized by spontaneity (Bachnik, 1994), thus enabling a certain degree of freedom to express differences of opinion (Ward et al., 2016) – a characteristic associated with a low context style. On the other hand, mutual ingroup status provides numerous opportunities through common experiences to develop shared knowledge and assumptions that they can reference through indirect verbal or nonverbal communication – i.e., high context communication. Thus, insider relationships reveal aspects of both high and low context communication. Outsider relationships similarly combine both high and low context facets: lacking the same degree of familiarity as insiders, those with an outsider relationship may need to verbalize more, so as to make themselves understood; however, as they rely more on standardized social rituals, they draw upon high-context elements in that norms for avoiding differences of opinion tend to be quite stringent (Bachnik, 1994).

Ultimately, *uchi-soto* relations are fluid: one is constantly calculating based on circumstantial conditions who is on the inside and outside relative to the self (Wetzel, 1994), and the same conversational partner might be inside one moment and outside the next depending upon who is sharing a social space. For instance, two members of the same company in different departments might consider each other outsiders, or *soto,* if they are discussing an interdepartmental matter in which they are each representing the distinct and somewhat conflicting interests of their respective ingroups. However, if they meet several hours later with someone from another company, and they must work collaboratively to represent their own company's unified interests to the outsider, then they will reposition in this new situation to an *uchi*, or insider relationship. As such insider-outsider dynamics shift between people, so may their use of various facets of high or low context communication, dynamically and fluidly moving them along the high-low context continuum.

Commonly Encountered Context Impacting Japanese Business Communication

When encountering Japanese high context communicators, even the most detailed understanding of high-low context is incomplete without grasping the assumptions and information to which high context messages so frequently refer. The purpose of the following sections is to explain three common themes that impact Japanese high context communication in business so that those trying to decipher such messages are better prepared to do so.

Context in Business Theme 1: Empathy, Hospitality, and Customer Service

Every businessperson must understand how to treat their customers in order to keep them. Indeed, the mutual expectations embedded in the customer-provider relationship in Japan are quite specific, and they frequently impact business communication. The first key is grasping the importance of empathy in Japanese high context communication, as well as its relationship to hospitality generally and more specifically to customer service. Though dated, Sugiyama Lebra's (1976) description of empathy and hospitality's role in everyday communication still holds true today:

> Empathy is manifested in Ego's readiness to anticipate and accommodate Alter's need. Ego tries to optimize Alter's comfort by providing what Alter needs or likes and by avoiding whatever might cause discomfort for him… . The Japanese concept of hospitality is to have everything arranged ahead of time … [and] should be done on the basis of an understanding of Alter's feelings without verbal communication. (p. 40)

This notion of empathy infusing hospitality can be used whether hosting a business partner or building relationships with colleagues in the same organization. For example, when I first arrived in Japan, a teacher at my high school of employment kindly offered to give me Japanese lessons, during which he would often ask me about my hobbies, habits, and the types of Japanese food I liked (and disliked), which made perfect practice for my rudimentary speaking skills. One day, he invited me to his home for a meal his wife had meticulously prepared. I was shocked and profoundly moved when I sat down at the dinner table to find every type of food that I had told him over the past 6 months I liked, and none of the foods for which I had expressed antipathy. I immediately realized that our conversations had never been just about language practice; rather, they were vital sources of information for him to understand me through my food preferences, and once he built up that reservoir of context, he could work with his wife to execute the perfect menu for this thankful guest.

Thus, in Japan, the ideal experience as a guest in someone's home, and by extension, a customer of any business, is having one's needs understood, remembered, and fulfilled without needing to ask or repeat them. This is the spirit of *omotenashi*, or a traditional code of conduct for the guest-host relationship. Such hospitality includes the anticipation of the needs of others fused with modesty by not displaying one's extensive efforts to create such an environment. *Omotenashi* forms a core element of the context in the Japanese business world. For instance, impeccable customer service stems from an impeccable grasp of one's customers' needs.

In America, the belief prevails that each individual knows best what they want, so service usually gives the customer a broad array of options that they are empowered to select at any moment, allowing them to choose anew each time there is a service encounter. While the American model provides for choices to be made anytime at an individual's whim, the Japanese model places a premium on predictable behavior based on preferences that have been defined at the onset of the customer-provider relationship (without the need to be reiterated because the vendor remembers them). Thus, empathy allows one to anticipate and satisfy customer needs with minimal explanation. This starkly contrasts with the widespread American assumption that one should not presume another person's needs, intentions, or preferences without confirming them first (Ramsey, 1998).

Context in Business Theme 2: Sincerity

Another critical aspect of context in the Japanese business world is that of treating customers with absolute sincerity or "trueheartedness" *(magokoro)*. Providers are expected to dedicate themselves to customer care, which in turn inspires customer trust and loyalty. Illustrating as much, a close friend shared a story about when he bought a home in Tokyo. The deal would be sealed at a meeting between the realtors of my friend and the seller, the seller himself, and the bank providing my friend's loan. Bringing together so many parties at a mutually convenient time was extremely challenging but required by law, so any change in the meeting date was out of the question.

As the day approached, the health of my friend's realtor's father declined rapidly in a hospital that was a 2-hour plane ride from Tokyo. Though he knew he might not be able to see his father in the hospital before his impending death, the realtor stayed for the meeting, though my friend would have certainly understood if the realtor had asked one of his colleagues from the same office to represent their company. As soon as the meeting ended, the realtor went straight to the airport to book the next available flight, but it was too late – his father passed away while he was waiting for a plane with an open seat. Weeks afterward and the realtor met my friend again, he explained his reason for staying in Tokyo: his father had always taught him to be sincere toward his customers, so the realtor felt that he was honoring his father by staying for the meeting and giving the best possible customer service. While this may be an extreme example, it is safe to say that Japanese vendors are often prepared (and expected) to go to great lengths for their customers – a keystone in such relationships which shapes context when providers make pledges to their customers, or customers make requests to those serving them.

Context in Business Theme 3: Humility

A third value that frequently influences Japanese high context communication both in business and beyond is humility. When asked to take on an important job, many Japanese downplay their credentials or even profess that they lack the ability to handle such an assignment or post. If they go on to say they will humbly accept, then the listener can rest assured that the person is just being self-effacing and is indeed well-qualified. As the Japanese proverb says, "The larger the fruit on an ear of grain, the deeper its head bows," meaning "The greater the person, the humbler" (Yashiro et al., 2001).

This brings to mind an experience I had shortly after arriving in Japan in 1990 at the high school where I worked. One day, I was greeted by a physical education teacher, whom I will fictitiously call "Mr. Sato." During our conversation, I asked him his favorite sport. He replied "soccer." I probed further: "Are you good at soccer?" to which he said, "I am not so good." He must have noticed my twisted facial expression, as I thought how utterly pathetic it was that a PE teacher was *bad* at his own favorite sport. The next day, another PE teacher approached me, saying he had overheard my conversation with Mr. Sato. He gently informed me that Mr. Sato had been the captain of his university soccer team, which had won the Japanese national championship, after which he had gone on to play for Japan's national team.

My jaw must have dropped to the floor as I received my first lesson in the depth of Japanese humility. In fact, I later learned that Mr. Sato was a bit of a celebrity at our school for his decorated soccer career and still possessed mesmerizing skill. Since it would have been untoward for Mr. Sato to explain all of this himself when I asked him, he had humbly deflected my question, assuming that I would know from his demeanor that he was indeed talented. When it was obvious from my facial expression that I had misunderstood, it was only through a third party a factual message could be directly communicated in a way attuned to my low context style. Mr. Sato was a deeply bowing ear of grain, and in business communication, when someone replies with humility about questions related to their competence in a skill that can help the company, this is often a good sign that you have found the right person.

Minding the Gap: Bridging High-Low Context

After detailing differences between high and low context communication styles, particularly in terms of how they tend to manifest themselves in Japan and the US, it is only fair to conclude by sharing some ways that these differences can be bridged. First, many low context communicators have found that focusing on the nonverbal signals of their high context counterparts helps them to understand their partner's intended message more frequently and accurately (Komisarof, 2011). Strategies include paying extra attention to vocal inflections, facial expressions, silence, and even verbal hints to discern subtle signs of discomfort or disagreement.

Low context communicators can also ask questions to solicit opinions from high context colleagues. Open-ended questions are recommended, or those that begin with "how," "what," or "why," as they tend to elicit more detailed responses and do not indicate the preferred answer of the questioner (thus avoiding answers in which the responder guesses the opinion of the questioner and provides a complementary answer). Asking open-ended questions to elicit high context coworkers' opinions before asserting one's own is an essential means of gathering critical information from one's colleagues to make the best decision.

For high context communicators attempting to adjust to low context communication, putting into words more than they do usually can help them to construct explicit messages that are more easily interpreted by sender-oriented low context communicators. Also, asking whether one's communicative partner has received the information that they need, while taking the time to clarify any requested information, can go a long way in bridging the communication gap. Since conflict aversion is not as common among low context communicators, it is essential to realize that differences of opinion do not necessarily indicate a rejection of you as a person – just a concern about your idea; moreover, expressions of contrary views by coworkers are not necessarily final rejections that idea but may actually serve as openings to further discuss your diverging views and come to a mutually agreeable solution.

By employing some of these simple, yet powerful strategies, both low and high context communicators can enjoy smoother communication with each other and ultimately build more positive, productive relationships. Indeed, the gap between those who prefer nonverbal, non-confrontational, and receiver-oriented communication and those who tend to employ verbal, conflict acknowledging, and sender-oriented communication can be great, but armed with an understanding of both the self and the other, as well as the determination and curiosity to bridge this divide, great rewards in business and interpersonal relations await.

References

Bachnik, J. (1994). Self, Social Order, and Language. In J. Bachnik & C. Quinn, Jr. (Eds.), *Situated Meaning: Inside and outside in Japanese Self, Society, and Language* (pp. 3–37). Princeton, NJ: Princeton University Press.

Barnlund, D. (1989). *Communicative Styles of Japanese and Americans*. Belmont, CA: Wadsworth Publishing Company.

Bennett, M. J. (2013). A Constructivist Frame for Intercultural Communication. In M. J. Bennett (Ed.), *Basic Concepts of Intercultural Communication: Paradigms, Principles, and Practices* (2nd ed., pp. 3–22). Yarmouth, ME: Intercultural Press.

Cardon, P. (2008). A Critique of Hall's Contexting Model: A Meta-Analysis of Literature on Intercultural Business and Technical Communication. *Journal of Business and Technical Communication, 22*(4), 399–428. https://doi.org/10.1177/1050651908320361

Condon, J. (1984). *With Respect to the Japanese*. Yarmouth, ME: Intercultural Press.

Dalsky, D., & Su, J. (2020). Japanese Psychology and Intercultural Training: Presenting *wa* in a Nomological Network. In D. Landis & D. P. S. Bhawuk (Eds.), *The Cambridge Handbook of Intercultural Training* (4th ed., pp. 584–597). Cambridge, UK: Cambridge University Press.

Gercik, P. (1992). *On Track with the Japanese: A Case-by-Case Approach to Building Successful Relationships*. New York: Kodansha International.

Goldman, A. (1994). The Centrality of "ningensei" to Japanese Negotiating and Interpersonal Relationships: Implications for U.S.-Japanese Communication. *International Journal of Intercultural Relations, 18,* 29–54. https://doi.org/10.1016/0147-1767(94)90003-5

Gudykunst, W., & Nishida, T. (1994). *Bridging Japanese/North American Differences*. Thousand Oaks, CA: Sage.

Hall, E. T. (1976). *Beyond Culture*. New York: Doubleday.

Hall, E. T., & Hall, M. R. (1987). *Hidden Differences: Doing Business with the Japanese*. New York: Anchor-Doubleday.

Hall, E. T., & Hall, M. R. (1990). *Understanding Cultural Differences: Germans, French and Americans*. Yarmouth, ME: Intercultural Press.

Kim, D., Pan, Y., & Park, H. S. (1998). High- versus Low-Context Culture: A Comparison of Chinese, Korean, and American Cultures. *Psychology & Marketing, 15*(6), 507–521. https://doi.org/10.1002/(SICI)1520-6793(199809)15:6<507::AID-MAR2>3.0.CO;2-A.

Komisarof, A. (2011). *On the Front Lines of Forging a Global Society: Japanese and American Coworkers in Japan.* Kashiwa, Japan: Reitaku University Press.

Komisarof, A., & Zhu, H. (2016). Introduction. In A. Komisarof & H. Zhu (Eds.), *Crossing Boundaries: Weaving Intercultural Work, Life, and Scholarship in Globalizing Universities* (pp. 1–20). London: Routledge.

Markus, H. R., & Kitayama, S. (1991). Culture and the Self: Implications for Cognition, Emotion and Motivation. *Psychological Review, 98*(2), 224–253. https://doi.org/10.1037/0033-295X.98.2.224.

Morisaki, S., & Gudykunst, W. (1994). Face in Japan and the United States. In S. Ting-Toomey (Ed.), *The Challenge of Facework: Cross-Cultural and Interpersonal Issues* (pp. 47–93). Albany, NY: State University of New York Press.

Nakane, C. (1970). *Japanese Society.* Oakland, CA: University of California Press.

Ramsey, S. J. (1998). Interactions between North Americans and Japanese: Considerations of Communication Style. In M. J. Bennett (Ed.), *Basic Concepts of Intercultural Communication: Selected Readings* (pp. 111–130). Yarmouth, ME: Intercultural Press.

Richardson, R. M., & Smith, S. W. (2007). The Influence of High/Low Context Culture and Power Distance on Choice of Communication Media: Students' Media Choice to Communicate with Professors in Japan and America. *International Journal of Intercultural Relations, 31*(2007), 479–501. https://doi.org/10.1016/j.ijintrel.2007.01.002.

Sakamoto, N., & Naotsuka, R. (1982). *Polite Fictions*. Tokyo: Kinseido.

Sugiyama Lebra, T. (1976). *Japanese Patterns of Behavior*. Honolulu, HI: University Press of Hawaii.

Thomas, J. (1998). Contexting Koreans: Does the High/Low Model Work? *Business Communication Quarterly, 61*(4), 9–22. https://doi.org/10.1177/1080569998061004 03.

Ward, A.-K., Ravlin, E. C., Klass, B. S., Ployhart, R. E., & Buchan, N. R. (2016). When Do High-Context Communicators Speak Up? Exploring Contextual Communication Orientation and Employee Voice. *Journal of Applied Psychology, 101*(10), 1498–1511. https://doi.org/10.1037/apl0000144.

Wetzel, P. J. (1994). A Movable Self: The Linguistic Indexing of *Uchi* and *Soto*. In J. Bachnik & C. Quinn, Jr. (Eds.), *Situated Meaning: Inside and Outside in Japanese Self, Society, and Language* (pp. 73–87). Princeton, NJ: Princeton University Press.

Yashiro, K., Araki, S., Higuchi, Y., Yamamoto, C., & Komisarof, K. (2001). *Ibunka komyunikeishyon waakubuuku* [Intercultural Communication Workbook]. Tokyo: Sanshuusha.

Introduction to Face, Facework and Intercultural Facework Competence

By Xiaodong Dai and Xiaohong Lyu

The next chapter examines facework in an intercultural context. While most people in the world wish to present a positive image of themselves, how this is done and perceived by others varies from one culture to another. This chapter describes in detail what face is, what is meant by facework, and what constitutes facework competence in order to introduce this important topic to the interested reader. While in many Western cultures, face is associated with one's self-worth and loss of face is associated with oneself, in many Eastern cultures face assumes a broader, more collectivistic meaning so that loss of face also affects one's family and group. Facework, in turn, refers to the verbal and nonverbal communication that is undertaken to maintain and/or restore face. And intercultural facework competence is the ability to apply the right facework in the right context and situation. Dai and Lyu explain in detail as to what needs to be considered and applied in order to achieve intercultural facework competence. Knowledge of these factors is a first step in the right direction.

Clearly, understanding face and facework assumes an important role in building and maintaining good international business relationships. That is why anyone unfamiliar with the concept of face and facework ought to read this chapter carefully so as to avoid possible mistakes and misunderstandings that could otherwise escalate into conflicts. After all, conflicts are often detrimental to mutually beneficial business relationships.

Michael B. Hinner

Xiaodong Dai, a Fulbrighter, is Associate Professor of Foreign Languages College of Shanghai Normal University. Presently he serves as the Vice President of China Association for Intercultural Communication (CAFIC). His major research interests are intercultural competence, identity negotiation, and intercultural communication theories. He has published numerous journal articles. His recent books include *Intercultural Communication Competence: Conceptualization and Its Development in Cultural Contexts and Interactions* (2014, co-edited with Guo-Ming Chen, Cambridge Scholars), *Conflict Management and Intercultural Communication: The Art of Intercultural Harmony* (2017, co-edited with Guo-Ming Chen, Routledge), and *A Study on Intercultural Competence* (2018, Foreign Language Teaching and Research Press).

Xiaohong Lyu is Lecturer of Foreign Languages College of Shanghai Normal University. She has been engaged in English Language Education for 30 years, teaching *Teacher Talk, English Teaching Methodology and Intercultural Communication*. She has presented papers in international conferences. Her research interests are English language education and intercultural competence.

Xiaodong Dai and Xiaohong Lyu

Face, Facework and Intercultural Facework Competence

Introduction

Face is a universal value that is intuitively meaningful to people (Haslett, 2020; Spencer-Oatey, 2000). People in all cultures want to display positive images in social communication. The need to recognize other's face and enhance one's own constitutes an integral part of human dignity (Ting-Toomey, 2017). However when culturally different individuals encounter each other, they often run into face conflict due to incompatible value orientations and disparate social preferences. Face is culturally defined and socially constructed. Different cultures tend to have different definitions of face and differing facework styles. For example, while Americans who embrace individualism tend to regard face as an individual image, Chinese who follow collectivism tend to regard face as both an image of self and the group they belong to. In social communication, Americans prefer the direct style of communication. By contrast, Chinese prefer the indirect style of communication. Face conflict frequently arises in intercultural encounters, and it is one of the most problematic issues of intercultural communication (Dai, 2017; Ting-Toomey, 2005; Ting-Toomey & Kurogi, 1998). This chapter first defines the concepts of face and facework respectively with their connections to culture, then discusses how culture shapes the definitions of face and facework styles, and finally identifies the key components of intercultural facework competence.

Face and Culture

The concept of face is Chinese in origin, and another name for Chinese personhood (Ho, 1976; Jia, 2001). Scholars from East and West have studied this complex construct for decades (e.g., Brown & Levinson, 1987; Chen, 2010; Goffman, 1955; Haslett, 2020; He & Zhang, 2011; Hwang, 1987; Jia, 2001; Spencer-Oatey, 2007; Ting-Toomey & Kurogi, 1998). They have interpreted the meaning of face and explored its connections to culture. For example, Goffman (1955) defined face as "the favorable social impression that a person wants others to have of him or her during a particular contact" (p. 213). Similarly, Brown and Levinson (1987) regarded face as the public self-image that every individual wants to claim for himself. Ting-Toomey and Kurogi (1998) referred to it as "a claimed sense of favorable social self-worth that a person wants others to have of her or him" (p. 187). Haslett (2012) considered face to be the positive value one assumes during a social encounter which is confirmed or denied by others.

These definitions embody typical Western cultural values. Rooted in Greek and Roman tradition, Western cultures predominantly embrace individualism. Individualism is a set of cultural values that gives priority to personal goals over group goals, and emphasizes the importance of "I" identity over "We" identity (Ting-Toomey & Kurogi, 1998; Triandis, 1995). Within the individualistic cultural framework, self is construed as an independent, coherent, stable and free entity (Markus & Kitayama, 1991). People tend to view face as an individual, equal and rationally based construct. They judge a person's face by his or her ability, competitiveness, social performance and achievements. While gaining face improves one's social functioning, it helps little to enhance the social image of one's family or the group he/she belongs to. The loss of face, in turn, only means a decrease in one's social worth, seldom leads to personal, family or group disgrace (Jia, 2001). By contrast, Eastern cultures, particularly those influenced by Confucianism, primarily follow collectivism. Collectivism is a set of cultural values that gives priority to collective goals over personal goals, and emphasizes the importance of "We" identity over "I" identity (Ting-Toomey & Kurogi, 1998; Triandis, 1995). Within the collectivistic cultural framework, self is construed as an interdependent, flexible, variable, and committed being who is bound to others (Miyahara, 2000).

Eastern cultures that have interdependent self-construal tend to view face as a person's social respectability (Cheng, 1986; Dai, 2017; He & Zhang, 2011). It is hierarchical, relational, emotionally sensitive and highly moralistic. People need to meet the basic moral standard and fulfill social obligations in order to have face in collectivistic societies such as China, Japan and South Korea. A person's face is determined by their social status, family prestige, virtuous behavior, and personal ability (Jia, 2001; Liu, 2008). When a person gains face, both himself and his family or group benefit, and accordingly their social functioning is enhanced. The loss of face has negative consequences that range from the loss of symbolic resources to the loss of whole personhood and to family or group disgrace. Face plays such a crucial role in the Eastern social communication that people would use all possible means to maintain or save it (Chen, 2002; Hwang, 2011).

The above discussion demonstrates that culture affects people's conception of face and different cultures tend to have different face definitions. In general, Western cultures emphasize the individual claim, exhibiting a face that is relatively equal and rational; in contrast Eastern cultures emphasize the social recognition, displaying a face that is relational and hierarchical, full of emotional and moral implications. Culture not only shapes how people define face, but also how they behave in keeping and enhancing face. The following part addresses the concept of facework and the major differences of facework styles between the East and the West.

Facework and Culture

Scholars generally regard facework as a communication behavior, albeit with some varied wordings. For example, Goffman (1967), Bargiela-Chiappini (2003), and Merkin (2006) all defined facework as actions taken to gain or maintain face. Tracy (1990) referred to it as "communicative strategies that are the enactment, support, or challenge of those situated identities" (p. 210). Similarly, Ting-Toomey (2005) defined it as "specific verbal and non-verbal behaviors that we engage in to maintain or restore face loss and to uphold and honor face gain" (p. 73).

In social communication people often perform three types of facework: self-oriented, other-oriented and mutually oriented facework. Self-oriented facework is the face behavior to gain or keep positive self-image; other-oriented facework is the face behavior to protect or enhance other's image; and mutually oriented refers to the face behavior to maintain or honor both parties' images, focusing on relationship development (Ting-Toomey, 2005). Face in the first place is a self-presentation, thus self-oriented facework constitutes the basic form of face behavior. Given that face is socially accorded, people need to take others into account and show due respect to others' faces when display self-image. Moreover as social communication is characterized by reciprocal behavioral expectations (Charon, 1998), mutually oriented facework becomes necessary in developing interpersonal relationships. It is of particular importance in building social harmony (Dai, 2017; Dai & Chen, 2015; Haslett, 2020).

Although people in all cultures endeavor to display positive images in communication, how people enact facework differs from one culture to the other. Many empirical evidences show that cultural value orientations are positively associated with facework styles in communication (e.g., Kaushal & Kwantes, 2006; Merkin, 2006; Oetzel et al., 2008; Oetzel & Ting-Toomey, 2003; Zhang & Wu, 2021). People from Western individualistic cultures that construe self as an independent being tend to prioritize self-interest and pay more attention to self-face than to other-face, hence their facework is more self-oriented. By contrast, people from Eastern collectivistic cultures that construe self as an interdependent entity tend to prioritize collective interest and show more concern to other-face and mutual face in order to maintain interpersonal harmony.

Besides self-construal, differences in facework styles are also produced by power distance. According to Hofstede (2001), power distance refers to the extent to which members of a culture expect and accept status inequalities and social hierarchies. While most of Western cultures are small power distance cultures, most of Eastern cultures are large power distance cultures. Western people tend to minimize status differences, treat all social members as equals, and enact horizontal facework. By contrast Eastern people tend to accept unequal power distributions and asymmetrical relations, and enact vertical facework (Ting-Toomey, 2005).

In social communication, people use various facework strategies to maintain and enhance face which can be either verbal or non-verbal in form, either direct or indirect in style (Ting-Toomey, 2017). According to Hall (1976), communication styles are broadly categorized into high-context and low-context. In a low-context communication, much of the information is encoded in the language and the importance of explicit verbal message is emphasized; in a high-context communication, much of the information is encoded in the context or internalized in the person, and the importance of non-verbal cues and the multilayered contexts are emphasized. People from the Western individualistic cultures tend to use the low-context style and perform direct verbal facework. By contrast, people from the Eastern collectivistic cultures tend to use the high-context style and perform indirect facework, particularly when expressing disapproval or dissatisfaction. Hence, the enactment of facework in collectivistic cultures entails more interpersonal sensitivities and skills of interpreting those non-verbal cues such as gift, seating, timing and distance. (Ho, 1994; Jia, 1997/1998).

When people run into face conflict, they often use three kinds of strategies to defend face: dominating, avoiding and integrating. Dominating facework focuses on self-interest and personal control. It is an aggressive strategy of saving face by directly defending one's positive image or displaying one's strength and competitiveness. Avoiding facework focuses on interpersonal harmony. It is a passive way of saving face by keeping away from face-loss situations or resorting to a third party help. Integrating facework is the compromising way of saving face which focuses on mutual image and conflict resolution. The integrative strategies include "mindful listening, intentional reframing, collaborative dialogue, and mutual interest problem solving" (Ting-Toomey, 2005, p. 78). As face conceptions, the strategies people use to defend face are also culturally shaped. Western people who embrace individualism tend to perform the aggressive facework, by contrast Eastern people who follow collectivism tend to use the passive or compromising facework. Because in resolving face conflicts, while the individualistic Western people place emphasis on achieving justice, the collectivistic Eastern people place emphasis on maintaining harmonious relationships (Ohbuchi et al., 1999).

The above discussion demonstrates that there are salient differences between the Eastern and Western facework. In general, the individualistic Western people focus more on individual image and self-identity. By contrast, the collectivistic Eastern people focus more on social relationships and interpersonal harmony. Furthermore, the former tend to perform direct and aggressive facework, and the latter tend to enact indirect and passive facework in communication. It should be noted that the Eastern facework is less consistent than the Western one, showing more variations across communication contexts. For example, Chinese are highly direct when interacting with intimates; they tend to be very aggressive when face is broken and personal disgrace ensues in social interactions (Chen, 2010).

Intercultural Facework Competence

In intercultural encounters, misunderstandings and conflicts often arise as a result of different face conceptions and behaviors. Only through cultivating facework competence can culturally differing individuals achieve successful communication. In this chapter, intercultural facework competence is defined as the ability to use appropriate facework to effectively protect and enhance face with the purpose of developing harmonious relationships in intercultural contexts. Four key components are included in intercultural facework competence: the ethical, affective, cognitive and behavioral abilities.

The ethical ability constitutes the foundational dimension of intercultural facework competence, regulating the affective, cognitive and behavioral dimensions. It refers to the moral norms and principles that govern intercultural facework interactions. All human communication possesses the ethical dimension as the foundation for reaching a more satisfactory outcome of interpersonal interactions, the ethical ability is critical when differences are large and power differentials are important (Casmir, 1997; Dai & Chen, 2015; Deetz, 1983). It plays a key role in cultivating the appropriate communication behavior and paving the way for genuine intercultural encounters (Haslett, 2014, 2020).

The ethical ability includes four elements: respect, equality, trust, and reciprocity. The importance of respecting others has been emphasized by both Western and Eastern cultures (Haslett, 2020; Spencer-Oatey, 2007). It is the basis of just and rightful intercultural communication (Dai & Chen, 2015). A respectability face always presents in interaction and the mutual respect facilitates interpersonal harmony (Spencer-Oatey, 2020). The respect principle dictates that individuals recognize others' dignity, treat them as decent partners, and be ready to explore their insights and wisdoms. This ethical ability enables culturally different individuals to engage in friendly and rewarding interactions, and co-manage the process with a spirit of solidarity (Black, 2008; Pasquali, 1997).

Given that there still exist discriminations and power differentials in intercultural communication, equality principle that grants communicators the right of free expression and equal participation needs to be stressed (Haslett, 2017; Nakayama & Martin, 2014). The equality principle requires that individuals take self and other as equal participants, and give them equal chance to join the interactions. Communication equality allows culturally different individuals to engage in subject to subject dialogue, and both parties make due contribution to the interactive process, interculturality thus can be truly fulfilled and intercultural interactions become more productive (Pasquali, 1997; Dai & Chen, 2015).

Competent intercultural facework communication also entails trust. Trust refers to a moral tendency of viewing others as kind, honest, competent and dependable persons (Hofstede, 2009; Haslett, 2014). This principle dictates that we make our own words and behaviors trustworthy to others and believe that others would do the same to us in return. Mutual trust fosters a vital bond between culturally different individuals which enables them to speak out the truth. Hence communication reveals more than it conceals (Pines, 1996; Richards, 2014). Since intercultural communication must begin with a fundamental trust in mutual dignity and an accompanying mutual vulnerability among interactants, the well-founded trust smoothens the communicative process, and is conducive to any effective and appropriate facework interaction (Ting-Toomey & Kurogi, 1998).

Ethical intercultural communicators attend to others in addition to self. Reciprocity is not only a moral principle that characterizes Eastern social communication but also a socially endorsed moral norm in the Western cultures (Chen, 2010; Goffman, 1967; Ho, 1976; Morin, 2017). Since communication is a dialogic encounter that involves both self and other, it implies a reciprocity of coding and decoding, giving and taking, teaching and learning, which cannot be separated (Christians, 1997, 2014). The reciprocity principle dictates that individuals pay due attention to maintaining both self-face and other-face, and honor them in a reciprocal way. Interpersonal reciprocity serves to remove the conflict between the needs of self-face and other-face, enhance communication mutuality, and facilitate the development of harmonious relationships (Dai & Chen, 2015).

The second dimension of intercultural facework competence is the affective ability. The affective ability refers to individuals' emotional tendency in communication. It is the motivational force that pushes individuals to ceaselessly acquire knowledge and skills in order to be appropriate and effective in intercultural interactions. Four elements are included in the affective dimension: open-mindedness, positive self-concept, cultural sensitivity, and cultural empathy.

Open-mindedness is the starting point for individuals to develop intercultural facework competence (Deardorff, 2006; Van de Zee & van Oudenhoven, 2000). It refers to the willingness to experience new things, accept different views and behaviors and make changes (Dai & Chen, 2020). Open-minded individuals recognized the complexity of culture and communication. They are open to differences, willing to suspend judgment, ready to expand the range of acceptable face orientations and behaviors, and constantly adapt themselves to culturally different others in intercultural communication (Dai & Chen, 2015; Haslett, 2014; Spitzberg & Cupach, 1984).

When individuals cross cultural borders to communicate with others, they redefine their self-concepts. Self-concept refers to how we view ourselves. Positive self-concept plays a key part in intercultural facework enactment. It helps individuals to enhance self-esteem, remove anxiety and contribute to confident interactions. Empirical evidences show that individuals with a positive self-concept tend to think well of others, are more likely to be accepted by others, and more effective in getting themselves understood by others (Adler & Towne, 1987; Chen, 1989).

Given that face is particularly vulnerable and problematic in intercultural encounters (Ting-Toomey, 2005; Ting-Toomey & Kurogi, 1998), cultural sensitivity becomes crucial to facework competence. Cultural sensitivity refers to the ability to accurately perceive similarities and differences between culturally differing individuals in terms of face conception and behavior. Culturally sensitive communicators reject stereotypes and ethnocentric views. They are capable of perceiving what face orientation and facework style are appropriate to a specific communication scenario, and how they subtly vary across communication contexts and among different individuals, being ready to attend to their face needs.

Empathy has long been regarded as a core element of the affective ability (Chen & Starosta, 1996, 1997). It refers to the ability of putting ourselves in others' shoes. Human sociality is basically grounded on our ability to empathize and emote with others (Haslett, 2020; Langholtz & Lochner, 2013). The ability to empathize allows us to experience and participate in others' life, and cultivate shared emotions and feelings. In facework interactions, this ability helps individuals cultivate appropriate attitude, facilitate mutual understanding, and motivate them to honor others' face so as to develop harmonious relationships (Dai & Chen, 2015, 2020).

The third dimension of intercultural facework competence is the cognitive ability. It refers to individuals' awareness or understanding of communication information and behavior (Wiseman, 2003). This cognitive ability, functioning as a cultural map, enables individuals to understand both their own and others' ways of thinking and patterns of behavior. It consists of four elements: sociocultural knowledge, multiple perspectives, self-other awareness, and reflective thinking.

To be competent in facework interactions, individuals need to acquire the requisite sociocultural knowledge (Ting-Toomey, 2005; Ting-Toomey & Kurogi, 1998), which includes the knowledge about our own face culture and social norms as well as about other's face culture and social expectations. Such knowledge helps culturally different individuals to understand their respective value orientations and social preferences, and facilitate competent facework in intercultural communication (Dai & Chen, 2015; Wiseman, 2003).

As people tend to approach face from different perspectives in intercultural encounters, individuals need to be aware of the possibility of different interpretations on the same face behavior or communication event. Multiple perspectives refer to the ability to construe face and facework from both our own and other's perspectives as well as from a third party's perspective. The development of multiple perspectives serves to broaden individuals' horizon, enhance mutual understanding, and facilitate meaningful facework interactions (Dai & Chen, 2015, 2020).

Self-other awareness refers to the ability to be aware of how we view ourselves and others, how others view themselves and us, and the possible gaps between the two views. In intercultural communication, individuals tend to view things from their own perspectives, more often than not producing cultural prejudices and misunderstandings (Bennett, 1993; Samovar et al., 2000). The cultivation of self-other awareness, along with the development of multiple perspectives, helps culturally different individuals to identify the similarities and differences between self and other, reduce ethnocentric bias, and develop reciprocal relationships via respectful, inclusive and mindful facework.

Reflective thinking refers to the critical evaluation of both one's own and other's view of face on the basis of explicit criteria and perspectives (Byram, 1997; Haslett, 2014). Such practice prevents individuals from blindly accepting cultural differences without rejecting the negative elements from other cultures. As mentioned before, while people from Western individualistic cultures prefer an equal and rationally based face, people from Eastern collectivistic cultures prefer a hierarchical, emotional and moralistic face. The former well expresses individual agency and social justice, but lacks human warmth and shows inadequate appreciation of the social basis of communication. The latter well expresses human warmth and connection but has insufficient regard to individual agency and social equity. Reflective thinking facilitates the integration of positive cultural elements and the development of intercultural personhood, which allows individuals to rise above the mono-cultural lens and become competent communicators in facework interactions (Dai & Chen, 2015; Evanoff, 2006; Haslett, 2020).

The fourth dimension of intercultural facework competence is behavioral ability. Individuals need to acquire behavioral ability in order to honor each other's face and foster harmonious relationships in intercultural encounters. Behavioral ability refers to the skill to put positive emotion and requisite knowledge into practice so as to meet communication goals. As other three abilities, this ability also includes four elements: skill to listen and observe, skill to adapt and adjust, skill to negotiate, and skill to build rapport.

Skill to listen and observe refers to the audio and visual ability to collect information. Individuals need to listen and observe in order to collect verbal and non-verbal information and keep track with the development of communication event. Competent individuals are good listeners and observers. They engage in active listening and careful observation (Arasaratnam & Doerfel, 2005; Deardorff, 2006), accurately capturing communication cues in intercultural facework interactions.

The skill to adapt and adjust refers to the ability to display adaptive behavior and make necessary adjustment. Culturally different individuals tend to apply different facework styles and strategies in intercultural communication. Flexible adjustment helps them develop mutually expected patterns of behavior and facilitates interpersonal synchrony (Dai & Chen, 2020; Kim, 2001, 2015). Empirical evidences show that when communicators have similar patterns of behaviors and their behaviors are highly predictable to partners, the interactive process usually becomes efficient, productive and enjoyable (Burgoon, 1993; Burgoon & Hubbard, 2005).

Individuals negotiate to maintain and honor face in intercultural communication. Skill to negotiate refers to the ability to use facework strategies to protect, save, and enhance face (Ting-Toomey & Kurogi, 1998). The key to successful face negotiation lies in the balance of self-image maintenance and mutual gain enhancement (Ho, 1994; Spencer-Oatey, 2007; Ting-Toomey, 2005). Competent individuals make use of verbal and non-verbal faceworks that are in line with their respective value orientations to validate and support each other's face. They are capable of defending face when encountering face threatening acts and repairing face damage or loss. Moreover, they are capable of integrating other's strategies into their own to create more inclusive face-saving strategies in dealing with face conflicts (Dai, 2017; Haslett, 2020).

Skill to build rapport is the ability to create a harmonious and smooth relation between people (Spencer-Oatey, 2000). As individuals often encounter tension and conflict in intercultural face communication, they need to be highly sensitive to how their behaviors are perceived by others (Ho, 1994), and act in accordance with their expectations (Burgoon & Hubbard, 2005). Skill to build rapport functions to avoid face threatening acts, display mutual support, and help communicators to develop friendly intercultural relationships (Dai & Chen, 2015). The above four dimensions of intercultural facework competence are equally important and work together to reach successful intercultural communication.

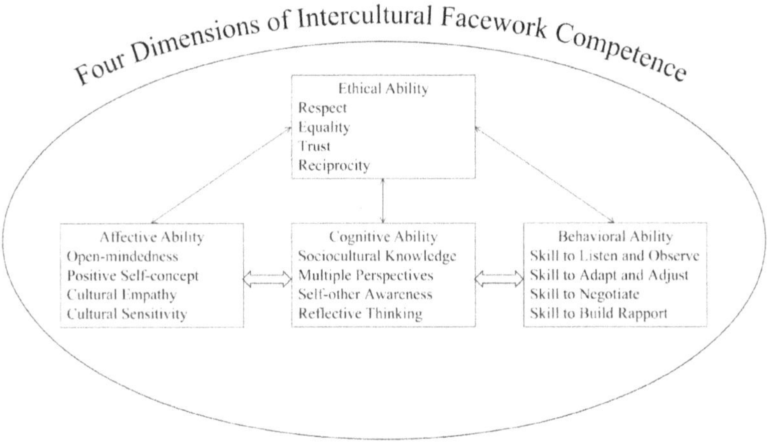

Figure 1: Four Dimensions of Intercultural Facework Competence

Conclusion

This chapter addresses the concepts of face, facework and intercultural facework competence. In defining face and facework, we highlight that face is people's social respectability, and facework is the communication behavior to maintain and enhance people's dignity, both of which are culturally shaped. Major differences between the East and the West in terms of face conceptions and facework styles are examined, and the possible explanations are explored.

Generally speaking, Western people tend to regard face as an individual image and enact more self-oriented facework. By contrast, Eastern people tend to view face as both the image of self and the group they belong to, and they tend to enact more other-oriented and mutually-oriented facework. Different value orientations, self-construals and power distances between the East and the West significantly account for these cross-cultural differences.

In identifying the key components of intercultural facework competence, we emphasize that the ethical ability constitutes the foundational dimension, and the affective, cognitive and behavioral abilities are the essential parts of intercultural facework competence. Competent individuals are capable of using appropriate facework to effectively negotiate their desired face and develop harmonious relationships with others in intercultural contexts. With the blurring of cultural boundaries in globalization, intercultural communication has become a mundane part of people's daily life. Although people around the world share increasing similarities in face conception and face behavior (Dai, 2017; Zhang & Wu, 2021), the East-West differences tenaciously remain, which often produce communication barriers and intercultural conflicts. This chapter clarifies some of the face issues, leaving many questions unanswered. Research on face merits continuous scholarly attention.

References

Adler, R. B., & Towne, N. (1987). *Looking Out/Looking In*. New York, NY: Holt, Richard &Winson.

Arasaratnam, L. A., & Doerfel, M. L. (2005). Intercultural Communication Competence: Identifying Key Components from Multicultural Perspectives. *International Journal of Intercultural Relations, 29*(2), 137–163.

Bargiela-Chiappini, F. (2003). Face and Politeness: New (Insights) for Old (Concepts). *Journal of Pragmatics, 35*, 1453–1469.

Bennett, M. J. (1993). Towards Ethnorelativism: A Developmental Model of Intercultural Sensitivity. In M. Paige (Ed.), *Education for the Intercultural Experience* (pp. 21–71). Yarmouth, ME: Intercultural Press.

Black, L. W. (2008). Deliberation, Storytelling, and Dialogic Moments. *Communication Theory 18*, 93–116.

Brown, P., & Levinson, S. C. (1987). *Politeness: Some Universals in Language Usage*. Cambridge, UK: Cambridge University Press.

Burgoon, J. K. (1993). Interpersonal Expectations, Expectancy Violations, and Emotional Communication. *Journal of Language and Social Psychology, 13*, 30–48.

Burgoon, J. K., & Hubbard, A. S. E. (2005). Cross-Cultural and Intercultural Application of Expectancy Violation Theory and Interaction Adaptation Theory. In W. B. Gudykunst (Ed.), *Theorizing about Intercultural Communication* (pp. 149–171). Thousand Oaks, CA: Sage.

Byram, M. (1997). *Teaching and Assessing Intercultural Communicative Competence.* Clevedon, UK: Multilingual Matters.

Casmir, F. L. (1997). Ethics, Culture, and Communication: An Application of the Third-Culture Building Model to International and Intercultural Communication. In F. L. Casmir (Ed.), *Ethics in Intercultural and International Communication* (pp. 89–117). Mahwah, NJ: Lawrence Erlbaum Associates, Publishers.

Charon, J. M. (1998). *Symbolic Interactionism: An Introduction, an Interpretation, an Integration.* Upper Saddle River, NJ: Prentice Hall.

Chen, G. M. (1989). Relationships of the Dimensions of Intercultural Communication Competence. *Communication Quarterly, 37*(2), 118–133.

Chen, G. M. (2002). The Impact of Harmony on Chinese Conflict Management. In G. M. Chen, & R. Ma (Eds.), *Chinese Conflict Management and Resolution* (pp. 3–19). Westport, CT: Ablex.

Chen, G. M. (2010). *Study on Chinese Communication Behaviors.* Hong Kong: China Review Academic Publishers.

Chen, G. M., & Starosta, W. J. (1996). Intercultural communication competence: A synthesis. *Communication Yearbook, 19*, 353–383.

Chen, G. M., & Starosta, W. J. (1997). A review of the Concept of Intercultural Sensitivity. *Human Communication, 1*(1), 1–16.

Cheng, C.-y. (1986). The Concept of Face and Its Confucian Roots. *Journal of Chinese Philosophy, 13*, 329–348.

Christians, C. G. (1997). The Ethics of Being in a Communication Context. In C. Christians, & M. Traber (Eds.), *Communication Ethics and Universal Values* (pp. 3–23). Thousand Oaks, CA: Sage.

Christians, C. G. (2014). Primordial Issues in Communication Ethics. In R. S. Fortner, & P. M. Fackler (Eds.), *The Handbook of Global Communication and Media Ethics* (pp. 1–19). Malden, MA: Blackwell Publishing.

Dai, X. D. (2017). The Development of Interculturality and the Management of Intercultural Conflict. In X. D. Dai, & G. M. Chen (Eds.), *Conflict Management and Intercultural Communication: The Art of Intercultural Harmony* (pp. 85–97). Abingdon, UK: Routledge.

Dai, X. D., & Chen, G. M. (2015). On Interculturality and Intercultural Communication Competence. *China Media Research, 11*(3), 100–113.

Dai, X. D., & Chen, G. M. (2020). Conceptualizing Cultural Integration Competence. *China Media Research, 16*(2), 13–24.

Deardorff, D. K. (2006). Identification and Assessment of Intercultural Competence as a Student Outcome of Internationalization. *Journal of Studies in International Education, 10*, 241–266.

Deetz, S. (1983). Keeping the Conversation Going: The Principle of Dialectic Ethics. *Communication, 7*, 263–288.

Evanoff, R. (2006). Integration in Intercultural Ethics. *International Journal of Intercultural Relations, 30*(4), 421–437.

Goffman, E. (1955). On Face-Work: An Analysis of Ritual Elements in Social Interaction. *Psychology Journal for the Study of Interpersonal Processes, 18*(3), 213–231.

Goffman, E. (1967). *Interaction Ritual: Essays on Face-to Face Behavior*. New York, NY: Pantheon Books.

Hall, E. T. (1976). *Beyond Culture*. Garden City, NY: Anchor.

Haslett, B. (2012). A Structurational Interaction Approach to Investigating Culture, Identity and Mediated Communication. In P. Cheong, J. N. Martin, & L. Macfadyen (Eds.), *New Media and Intercultural Communication: Identity, Community and Politics* (pp. 39–60). New York, NY: Peter Lang.

Haslett, B. (2014). A Face Model of Intercultural Communication Competence. In X. D. Dai, & G. M. Chen (Eds.), *Intercultural Communication Competence: Conceptualization and Its Development in Cultural Contexts and Interactions* (pp. 118–143). Newcastle upon Tyne, UK: Cambridge Scholars Publishing.

Haslett, B. (2017). Transforming Conflict Through Communication and Common Ground. In X. D. Dai, & G. M. Chen (Eds.), *Conflict Management and Intercultural Communication: The Art of Intercultural Harmony* (pp. 85–97). Abingdon, UK: Routledge.

Haslett, B. (2020). A Face Model of Intercultural Communicative Competence: Integrating Non-Western and Western Communication. *China Media Research, 16*(2), 24–39.

He, M., & Zhang, S. J. (2011). Re-Conceptualizing the Chinese Concept of Face from a Face-Sensitive Perspective: A Case Study of a Modern Chinese TV Drama. *Journal of Pragmatics, 43*, 2360–2372.

Ho, D. (1976). On the Concept of Face. *American Journal of Sociology, 81*, 867–884.

Ho, D. (1994). Face Dynamics: From Conceptualization to Measurement. In S. Ting-Toomey (Ed.), *The Challenge of Facework: Cross-Cultural and*

Interpersonal Issues (pp. 269–286). Albany, NY: State University of New University Press.

Hofstede, G. (2001). *Culture's Consequences: Comparing Values, Behaviors, Institutions, and Organizations across Nations* (2nd ed.). Thousand Oaks, CA: Sage.

Hofstede, G. (2009). The Moral Circle of Intercultural Competence: Trust across Cultures. In D. K. Deardorff (Ed.), *The SAGE Handbook of Intercultural Competence* (pp. 85–99). Thousand Oaks, CA: Sage.

Hwang, K.-K. (1987). Face and Favor: The Chinese Power Game. *American Journal of Sociology, 92*, 944–974.

Hwang, K.-K. (2011). Face Dynamism in Confucian Society. *China Media Research, 7*(4), 13–24.

Jia, W. (1997/1998). Facework as a Chinese Conflict-Preventive Mechanism: A Cultural/Discourse Analysis. *Intercultural Communication Studies, 7*(1), 43–61.

Jia, W. S. (2001). *The Remaking of the Chinese Character and Identity in the* 21st *Century*. Westport, CT: Ablex Publishing.

Kaushal, R., & Kwantes, C. (2006). The Role of Culture and Personality in Choice of Conflict Management Strategy. *International Journal of Intercultural Relations, 30*, 579–603.

Kim, Y. Y. (2001). *Becoming Intercultural: An Integrative Theory of Communication and Cross-Cultural Adaptation*. Thousand Oaks, CA: Sage.

Kim, Y. Y. (2015). Achieving Synchrony: A Foundational Dimension of Intercultural Communication Competence. *International Journal of Intercultural Relations, 48*, 27–37.

Langholtz, A., & Lochner, M. (2013). The Role of Emotions in Relational Work. *Journal of Pragmatics, 58*, 87–107.

Liu, J. F. (2008). Re-Defining the Concept of Face. *Social Psychology Sciences, 23*(5), 30–35.

Markus, H. R., & Kitayama, S. (1991). Culture and the Self: Implications for Cognition, Emotion, and Motivation. *Psychological Review, 98*, 224–253.

Merkin, R. S. (2006). Power Distance and Facework Strategies. *Journal of Intercultural Communication Research, 35*, 139–160.

Miyahara, A. (2000). Toward Theorizing Japanese Interpersonal Communication Competence from a Non-Western Perspective. *American Communication Journal, 3*(3), 1–18.

Morin, E. (2017). *Ethics* (S. Yu, Trans.). Shanghai, China: Xuelin Press.

Nakayama, T., & Martin, J. N. (2014). Ethical Issues in Intercultural Communication Competence: A Dialectical Approach. In X. D. Dai, & G.

M. Chen (Eds.), *Intercultural Communication Competence: Conceptualization and Its Development in Cultural Contexts and Interactions* (pp. 97–117). Newcastle upon Tyne, UK: Cambridge Scholars Publishing.

Ohbuchi, K., Fukushima, O., & Tedeschi, J. T., (1999). Cultural Values in Conflict Management: Goal Orientation, Goal Attainment, and Tactical Decision. *Journal of Cross-Cultural Psychology, 30*(1), 51–71.

Oetzel, J. G., & Ting-Toomey, S. (2003). Face Concerns in Interpersonal Conflict: A Cross-Cultural Empirical Test of Face-Negotiation Theory. *Communication Research, 30*(6), 599–624.

Oetzel, J. G., Garcia, A., & Ting-Toomey, S. (2008). An Analysis of the Relationships among Face Concerns and Facework Behaviors in Perceived Conflict Situations: A Four-Culture Investigation. *International Journal of Conflict Management, 19*, 382–403.

Ohbuchi, K., Fukushima, O., & Tedeschi, J. T., (1999). Cultural Values in Conflict Management: Goal Orientation, Goal Attainment, and Tactical Decision. *Journal of Cross-Cultural Psychology, 30*(1), 51–71.

Pasquali, A. (1997). The Moral Dimension of Communicating. In C. Christians, & M. Traber (Eds.), *Communication ethics and Universal Values* (pp. 24–45). Thousand Oaks, CA: Sage.

Pines, M. (1996). Dialogue and Selfhood: Discovering Connections. *Group Analysis 29*, 327–341.

Richards, I. (2014). The Dilemmas of Trust. In R. S. Fortner, & P. M. Fackler (Eds.), *The Handbook of Global Communication and Media Ethics* (pp. 247–262). Malden, MA: Blackwell.

Samovar, L. A., Porter, R. E., & Stefani, L. A. (2000). *Communicating between Cultures*. Beijing, China: Foreign Language Teaching and Research Press.

Spencer-Oatey, H. (2000). Rapport Management: A Framework for Analysis. In H. Spencer-Oatey (Ed.), *Culturally Speaking: Managing Rapport Through Talk across Cultures* (pp. 11–46). London, UK: Continuum.

Spencer-Oatey, H. (2007). Theories of Identity and the Analysis of Face. *Journal of Pragmatics, 39*, 639–656.

Spencer-Oatey, H. (2020). Intercultural Competence and Harmonious Intercultural Relations: Interdisciplinary Perspectives and Insights. *China Media Research, 16*(2), 1–12.

Spitzberg, B. H., & Cupach, W. R. (1984). *Interpersonal Communication Competence*. Beverly Hills, CA: Sage.

Ting-Toomey, S. (2005). Identity Negotiation Theory: Crossing Cultural Boundaries. In W. B. Gudykunst (Ed.), *Theorizing about Intercultural Communication* (pp. 211–233). Thousand Oaks, CA: Sage.

Ting-Toomey, S. (2017). Conflict Face-Negotiation Theory: Tracking Its Evolutionary Journey. In X. D. Dai, & G. M. Chen (Eds.), *Conflict Management and Intercultural Communication: The Art of Intercultural Harmony* (pp. 123–143). Abingdon, UK: Routledge.

Ting-Toomey, S., & Kurogi, A. (1998). Facework Competence in Intercultural Conflict: An Updated Face-Negotiation Theory. *International Journal of Intercultural Relations, 22*, 187–225.

Tracy, K. (1990). The Many Faces of Facework. In H. Giles, & P. Robinson (Eds.), *Handbook of Language and Social Psychology* (pp. 209–220). Chichester, UK: John Wiley.

Triandis, H. C. (1995). *Individualism and Collectivism.* Boulder, CO: Westview.

Van der Zee, K. I., & van Oudenhoven, J. P. (2000). The Multicultural Personality Questionnaire: A Multidimensional Instrument of Multicultural Effectiveness. *European Journal of Personality, 14*(4), 291–309.

Wiseman, R. L. (2003). Intercultural Communication Competence. In W. B. Gudykunst (Ed.), *Cross-Cultural and Intercultural Communication* (pp. 191–208). Thousand Oaks, CA: Sage.

Zhang, M., & Wu, D. (2021). Self-Oriented and Other-Oriented Facework on Social Media. *Modern Foreign Languages, 44*(2), 196–207.

Part II Worldview and Perception

Introduction to Ethnocentrism

By James W. Neuliep

The following chapter briefly introduces ethnocentrism and briefly sketches its academic history back to the beginning of the 20th century. Ethnocentrism plays an important role in many realms of the business world. This includes all aspects ranging from a diverse workforce within a small local company all the way to marketing strategies designed to span the globe. In fact, ethnocentrism can occur even when a person or a company does not deliberately seek to discriminate against others and considers, for example, their traditional ways as being appropriate and correct – maybe because things have always been done that way successfully in the past. While this may not be considered condescending by the company or its representative, it could be perceived as such because it rules out other options or means. Ethnocentrism essentially applies an arbitrary reference point, but it has to be understood that other reference points are also possible. Who is to say which viewpoint is the right one? And most people are unaware that they are ethnocentric because they consider their way to be natural and correct because it feels right and natural to them. This assumption can often lead to misunderstandings or even conflicts in an intercultural context. That is why ethnocentric behavior ought to be avoided – especially in the world of business where one of the key slogans is: "The customer is always right." Awareness is a first and important step towards overcoming one's ethnocentrism.

Michael B. Hinner

James W. Neuliep is Professor Emeritus of Communication and Media Studies at St. Norbert College. During his tenure at St. Norbert College, Dr. Neuliep has been awarded the Leonard Ledvina Award for Excellence in Teaching, the Donald B. King Distinguished Scholar Award, the Outstanding Advisor to a Student Organization Award, and the Wisconsin Academic Advising Association's Faculty Advising Excellence Award.

Jim has presented dozens of papers at national and international conferences, published dozens of articles in academic journals, and published eight books. His most current book, *Intercultural Communication: A Contextual Approach* (Sage Publications, 2021) is now in its 8th edition and is used in university and college classrooms across the United States and abroad and is regarded as a best seller among intercultural communication textbooks.

Jim is the past editor of the *Journal of Intercultural Communication Research*. He is also past chair of the Intercultural Communication Division of the International Communication Association. Jim currently sits on several editorial boards and is an Associate Editor of *International Journal of Intercultural Relations*.

James W. Neuliep

Ethnocentrism[1]

Introduction

Nearly 70 years ago, the painter and author Wyndham Lewis described a global village in his book titled *America and Cosmic Man* (Lewis, 1948). Several years later, his friend Marshall McLuhan also used the term to describe how technological advances of mass media would eventually disintegrate the natural time and space barriers inherent in human communication. To be sure, technological changes have made the world a smaller planet to inhabit. The technological feasibility of mass media and the Internet to bring events from across the globe into the homes, businesses, and schools across the planet dramatically reduces the distance between people of different cultures and societies. Telecommunication systems, e-mail, texting, Skype, and social networking sites connect people in milliseconds throughout the world via satellites and fiber optics.

One of the essential effects of this technology is its decentralizing role in disseminating information across local, regional, national, and international borders. This means that billions of people across the planet now have access to information that was not available to them only a few years ago. Information empowers people. The ease and speed with which people of differing cultures can now communicate is stunning. Technology has linked the world (Neuliep, 2010, 2015).

Although technological advances facilitate the initiation and maintenance of cross-cultural relationships, decades ago the late noted historian and Pulitzer Prize winner Arthur Schlesinger (1993) warned us that history tells an ugly story of what happens when people of diverse cultural, ethnic, religious, or linguistic backgrounds converge in one place. Schlesinger argued that the hostility of one group of people against another, *different* group of people is among the most instinctive of human drives. Xenophobia, the fear or contempt of that which is foreign or unknown, especially of strangers or those perceived as foreigners, is believed by many to be an innate biological response to intergroup competition.

1 Permission to reprint this text has been granted by De Gruyter Mouton. It was previously published as: Neuliep, James W. Ethnocentrism and intercultural communication. *Intercultural Communication*, edited by Ling Chen, Berlin, Boston: De Gruyter Mouton, 2017, pp. 331–348. https://doi.org/10.1515/9781501500060-015

Indeed, Schlesinger (1993) argued that unless a common goal binds diverse people together, tribal hostilities will drive them apart.

Ethnocentrism

One of the central concepts in understanding outgroup attitudes, intergroup relations, and intercultural communication is ethnocentrism (Neuliep & McCroskey, 1997). The term stems from the Greek words *ethnos,* which refers to nation, and *kentron,* which refers to center. Over a hundred years ago Sumner (1906) defined ethnocentrism as "the technical name for this view of things in which one's own group is the center of everything, and all others are scaled and rated with reference to it" (p. 13). Sumner (1906) argued that ethnocentrism nourished a group's pride and vanity while looking on outsiders, or outgroups, with contempt. Franz Boas, who is considered the founder of modern anthropology, believed that humans are necessarily ethnocentric and that observations of other cultures are necessarily biased in favor of one's own native cultural background (Boas, 1932). For example, people raised in Culture A are taught that their cultural traditions, values, and customs are the preferred and accepted standards by which they should conduct their lives. Consequently, individuals from Culture A cannot draw conclusions about some other Culture B's traditions, values, and customs without some inherent bias. To some degree everyone is ethnocentric.

The Study of Ethnocentrism in the Social Sciences

The first systemic social scientific research on ethnocentrism began some 70 years ago with the publication of *The Authoritarian Personality* (Adorno et al., 1950). In the wake of World War II, Adorno and his colleagues focused on the psychology of fascism, anti-Semitism, and what they labeled the *antidemocratic* personality. They collected data from thousands of questionnaires and clinical interviews and concluded that (a) nationalism is a species of ethnocentrism, (b) ethnocentrism is an expression of authoritarianism, and (c) authoritarianism is a personality defect. Refining and extending Sumner's original definition of ethnocentrism, Levinson (1950) argued that ethnocentrism is:

> ...based on a pervasive and rigid ingroup-outgroup distinction; it involves stereotyped, negative imagery and hostile attitudes regarding outgroups, stereotyped positive imagery and submissive attitudes regarding ingroups, and a hierarchical, authoritarian view of group interaction in which ingroups are rightly dominant, outgroups subordinate (Adorno et al, 1950, p. 150).

Adorno and his colleagues forwarded the argument that that prejudices against outgroups was a generalized personality profile and that such prejudices should be not be studied in isolation. They maintained that an individual's prejudice toward any specific outgroup is representative of an overall cognitive orientation of negative attitudes about all outgroups. They labeled this generalized attitude profile ethnocentrism. In the decades following their ground breaking work,

Adorno and his colleagues were criticized for their methodology and conclusions but many researchers today agree that prejudices against outgroups constitute a general attitudinal profile (c.f., Bierly, 1985; Murphy & Likert, 1938; Ray & Lovejoy, 1986; Rubinstein, 1996).

In much more current research, yet consistent with past findings for example, Wrench and his colleagues (2006) have found a consistent and significant and positive correlations between ethnocentrism, religious fundamentalism and homonegativity. That is, ethnocentrism and religious fundamentalism are linked together, and ethnocentrism and homonegativity are linked together. They also report a negative relationship between ethnocentrism and tolerance for religious disagreement; that is, as ethnocentrism increases, one's tolerance for religious disagreements decreases.

Measurement of Ethnocentrism

In both the natural and social sciences, whenever some new phenomena or concept has been discovered great amounts of time and energy are spent trying to measure and operationalize it. Historically, there have been two significant attempts to develop a scale that measures and operationalizes ethnocentrism. In their influential work, Adorno and his colleagues designed and constructed a scale labeled the E scale. The scale is a series of 34 Likert like items that were subdivided into three subscales, including the Negro subscale, the minority subscale, and the patriotism subscale. Upon extensive reliability and item analyses, a 20-item final version of the E scale was constructed that included a 6-item Jew subscale, a 6-item Negro subscale, and an 8-item other minority and patriotism subscale. Adorno et al., treated the combined scores from the three subscales as a global measure of ethnocentrism. Representative items from the Jew subscale included "To end prejudice against Jews, the first step is for Jews to try sincerely to get rid of their harmful and irritating faults," "There may be exceptions, but in general, Jews are pretty much alike," and "I can hardly imagine myself marrying a Jew." Representative items from the Negro subscale include "Negroes have their rights, but it is best to keep them in their own districts and schools and to prevent too much contact with whites," "Negro musicians may sometimes be a good as white musicians, but it is a mistake to have mixed Negro-white bands," and "It would be a mistake to have Negroes for foreman and leaders over whites." Finally, representative items from the other minority and patriotism scale include "Filipinos are all right in their place, but they carry it too far when they dress lavishly and go around with white girls," "Zootsuiters prove that when people of their type have too much money and freedom, they just take advantage and cause trouble," and "Certain religious sects who refuse to salute the flag should be forced to conform to such a patriotic action or else be abolished." As Neuliep and McCroskey (1997) point out, because the E scale was designed for white populations in the United States nearly 70 years, it is outdated and ironically ethnocentric.

References

Adorno, T. W., Frenkel-Brunswik, E., Levinson, D. J., & Sanford, R. N. (1950). *The Authoritarian Personality.* New York: Harper & Brothers.

Bierly, M. M. (1985). Prejudice toward contemporary outgroups as a generalized attitude. *Journal of Applied Social Psychology, 15*(2), 189–199. https://doi.org/10.1111/j.1559-1816.1985.tb02344.x

Boas, F. (1932). *Anthropology and Modern Life.* New York: Norton.

Lewis, W. (1948). *America and Cosmic Man.* London: Nicholson & Watson

Murphy, G., & Likert, R. (1938). *Public opinion and the individual: A psychological study of student attitudes on public questions with a re-test five years later.* New York, NY: Harper Books

Neuliep, J. W. (2010). Ethical and Cultural Relativism. In R. L. Jackson (Ed.), *Encyclopedia of Identity* (pp. 252–253). Thousand Oaks, CA: Sage Publications.

Neuliep, J. W. (2015). *Intercultural Communication: A Contextual Approach* (6th ed). Los Angeles, CA: Sage Publications.

Neuliep, J. W., & McCroskey, J. C. (1997). The Development of a US and Generalized Ethnocentrism Scale. *Communication Research Reports, 14*, 385–398.

Ray, J. J., & Lovejoy, F. H. (1986). The generality of racial prejudice. *The Journal of Social Psychology, 126*(4), 563–564. https://doi.org/10.1080/00224545.1986.9713627

Rubenstein, L. S. (1996). Discrimination by any other name. *Psychiatric services (Washington, D.C.), 47*(6). https://doi.org/10.1176/ps.47.6.557

Schlesinger, A. M. (1993). *The Disuniting of America: Reflections of a Multicultural Society*. New York: Norton.

Sumner, W. G. (1906). *Folkways*. Boston: Ginn.

Wrench,J.S., Corrigan, M.W., McCroskey.J.C. & Punyanunt-Carter, N.M. (2006) Religious Fundamentalism and Intercultural Communication: The Relationships Among Ethnocentrism, Intercultural Communication Apprehension, Religious Fundamentalism, Homonegativity, and Tolerance for Religious Disagreements, *Journal of Intercultural Communication Research, 35:1*, 23–44, DOI: 10.1080/17475740600739198

Introduction to Deep Culture: Linguistic Markers of Worldview for Business in the Real World

By Elena Steiner

The next chapter focuses on worldview and how it influences our thinking, language, and behavior often without us being consciously aware that it is doing so. In doing so, Steiner shows how relationships and trust may be built across dynamic, nuanced, multi-layered settings. It is pointed out that people have multiple identities and essentially cannot be put into a single box with predetermined categories. At the same time, it needs to be considered that what we see only reflects a complex interior which includes values and belief systems, i.e. worldviews. In other words, a person's belief system influences the values that person accepts which in turn affects how that person lives and interacts with others. Steiner uses the earth as an example and likens the crust to visible attributes of culture. The earth's mantle are the sociocultural institutions that refer to the organizations and infrastructure of a society which permit it to function. The outer core represents the values that influence the visible on the crust and are supported by the institutional mantle. And the molten center are the worldviews which explain why life is like it is in this world. Specific examples are used to illustrate this concept. From these examples it becomes clear that worldview is a cognitive framework that contains tacit assumptions about morality or reasons for particular behavior, agency within the environment, and positionality in relation to other people, groups, institutions, nature, etc. And it is the various narratives that people are exposed to throughout their lives which essentially conveys and reinforces the worldview. Steiner proposes and describes a method of overcoming possible misunderstandings due to different worldviews which she calls the MAP matrix – that is, Morality: Why? For what purpose? Agency: How? By what means? and Positionality: Who? What? Where? When? This might be a useful tool to analyze cultural misunderstandings. Steiner's final advice in applying the MAP matrix is to follow the ODIS principle; namely, observe, describe, interpret, and suspend judgment. Very helpful advice.

Michael B. Hinner

Elena Steiner is a Social Science Research Specialist at Arizona State University's Global Security Initiative focused in the Center for Narrative, Disinformation, and Strategic Influence and holds a PhD in communication. She facilitates team research across humanities, social science, and computer science to learn how information is used in the digital space to guide attitudes, beliefs, and behavior. At ASU's Center for Strategic Communication, previous research included hate speech detection, precursors to social unrest, and the connection between communication and productivity in organizations.

A self-identified pracademic, Elena has a concurrent affiliation with Steinbeis Center of Management and Technology in Stuttgart, Germany. Her focus is worldview analysis of narratives in organizations to better understand socio-cultural difficulties in global management teams and develop strategies and instructional modules to prevent, alleviate, or recover from them. She has worked, lived in, or studied in 27 countries, and has presented across academic, non-profit, public, and private sector audiences on the influence of culture on communication, leadership, management, negotiation, and risk and security.

Elena has substantial humanitarian and crisis experience across five organizations and 28 years. These include National Ski Patrol as a trainer and first responder in mountain rescue, Court Appointed Special Advocates for children of abuse and neglect, and Jesuit Worldwide Learning serving communities at society's margins due to poverty or forced displacement.

Elena Steiner

Deep Culture: Linguistic Markers of Worldview for Business in the Real World

Introduction

Consider this riddle: What is possessed by everyone, surrounds us like the air we breathe, influences everything we think, say, and do, but lies outside our awareness? Every day, we make dozens of snap judgments and take action without much or any forethought. Such taken-for-granted ways of thinking and acting are necessary to avoid constantly questioning why things are as they are and relearning everything in our environment. At the same time, this spontaneity is at the core of intercultural difficulties. Being on auto-pilot can sometimes be a hindrance rather than an aid.

The answer is the deepest part of culture – all-powerful worldview. Is it too complex to consider? Yes. But it is also too important to ignore and doing so is to our detriment. Think about the following headlines and excerpts from news articles in which worldview is invoked:

Bosch manufactures a data-driven culture with Salesforce Tableau analytics (Lauchlan, 2021)

> For us, the basic argument is that while physical products will continue to exist, they will be superseded by software which extends or enhances the value they're delivering. That's a worldview that has some serious implications for the work of Florian Bankoley, Executive Vice President for Corporate IT at manufacturer Bosch.

How do wealthy investors feel about their good fortune during the pandemic? The answer may surprise you (Albrecht, 2021)

> Affluent investors say they're reassessing their worldview – and financial goals…There was a gender and generational divide among those who reported that the pandemic had significantly altered their worldview.

Taking the knee and holding heads high (Sheridan, 2021)

> Growing up in the West of Ireland, I was pretty much unaware of class and race…There was no fear of gang violence or kidnap…Undoubtedly there were social issues, just like everywhere else, but to my innocent eyes, they were hidden from view…There were two black people in my life… It never occurred to me that their worldview might be different to mine.

In, *What Biden's first foreign trip tells us about his worldview* (Semanski, 2021), readers are left with a cliffhanger. Although featured in the headline, nowhere in the article is worldview ever mentioned! What *does* the trip tell us about Biden's worldview? Tools and terms are needed to unpack the article and draw conclusions to answer that question. By contrast, in *What business leaders can learn from an indigenous worldview* regarding unmarked graves of indigenous children at a Canadian residential school (Bansal, 2021), the term is invoked 18 times, suggesting its extreme importance. Knowing what worldview means or what elements are included would enhance our interpretations of these and the other references.

The purpose of this chapter is to accomplish just that – succinctly define worldview, describe three universal composite elements, and experiment with identifying them in story examples from everyday life and business experiences. Doing so paves the way for thinking about how to adapt thoughts, language, and actions in intercultural settings. The potential is the ability to avoid or mitigate difficulties resulting from auto-pilot perceptions and action. Here is a brief story about how this chapter came into being.

During many years living in Europe coaching executives and global teams in "U.S. culture" and business English, subsequent graduate work on the impact of culture on business, and training and teaching in the field, I began to sense something was missing. Intercultural practitioners tended to focus on impossible-to-remember lists of do's and don'ts in various regions of the world which could easily lead to oversimplifications and stereotypes. Leaning on the idea of national culture was a way to make it all more manageable, but this approach has its limitations as well. There has to be something more. What macro level understanding and tools of culture are flexible across all culture groups and can be applied in myriad settings? How can professionals working in complex global environments make sense of deep culture implications without becoming a cultural anthropologist? These experiences and questions inspired my doctoral studies, which in turn inform practical application in the real world.

This chapter represents a condensed version of my resulting dissertation – a worldview approach to building relationship and trust across dynamic, nuanced, multi-layered settings in which actors are from multiple nations and do not speak the same language. Rather, they have multiple identities, transition between cultural settings, adhere to various political and religious beliefs, and cannot be placed into any single box with neat categorical labels. The description of a novel worldview foundation paves the way to narrative analysis and serves as a heuristic tool for gaining clarity in global settings. The impetus for doing so is to prevent conflict, understand and minimize it when it does occur, and then to recover and learn from it.

A Variation on the Origin Story of Earth

In university classrooms and organizations, I have had the challenge of introducing the seemingly all-encompassing concepts of culture and worldview in 50 minutes to audiences who often have never considered what either means much less their impact on communication and business. Participants have tight schedules, are under stress, and need solutions for immediate problems that can be put into practice fairly quickly and easily so they can focus on the business at hand. Perhaps this scenario resounds with readers of this volume.

Earth Layers of Culture

Many professionals working in global settings are familiar with the iceberg metaphor for culture. What is seen on the surface is quite miniscule when compared to the unseen mass of ice beneath and supporting it. The deeper the dive under the surface, the more complex and important the forces of culture and worldview become. Instead of an iceberg, imagine four basic layers of the earth: A relatively thin outer crust, followed by the mantle, the outer core, and a molten hot inner core. The earth's crust is only a small fraction of the total earth's depth. So, too, what one sees of culture is also quite small, and most is deep inside the molten core (Strauss & Strauss, 2019).

The crust layer of culture consists of external and therefore observable behaviors – what people do, say, what they wear and eat, even nonverbal cues like eye contact or proximity. Anyone who has traveled or worked abroad has readily noticed such different patterns, some more obvious or striking than others. One step further, in culture's mantle layer are sociocultural institutions. These comprise the organizations, government, businesses, religious institutions, legal systems, education, and so on that provide the platforms for society to function. Sociocultural institutions are the places, the stages, on which life is acted out.

The outer core consists of values that influence what is observed in the crust and supported by the institutional mantle. Values are not only hidden from outsiders entering into a new cultural context, but they are also taken-for-granted by a culture's own members. Values such as individualism and collectivism or high/low power distance may be quite familiar. Less frequently mentioned are fate and control of the environment, conceal or reveal, patron and client relations, or power/fear dynamics. These will resurface later in the chapter.

Finally, at culture's molten center are worldviews – tacitly assumed and strongly-held understandings of what is and is not real. It is how reality undeniably is or should be for the person holding them. Worldview is a lens to make sense of all of life. Because of their unstated nature, identifying worldviews – both our own and those of others – is a formidable challenge at best. Yet worldview differences are at the root of every misunderstanding or conflict across cultures. Anthropologist, Hall (1959, p. 39) stated, "Culture hides more than it reveals, and strangely enough, it hides most effectively from its own participants."

Every culture consists of these four layers (Barney, 1973; Strauss & Strauss, 2019), but the focus of this paper is the worldview core, the universal elements that constitute it, and how to identify them when encountered in daily life and business settings. When considering the invisible values beneath what is experienced on the outside together with deep culture worldview assumptions, it becomes clear that focusing on lists of behavioral rules – dos and don'ts – although necessary, are far from sufficient. They merely scratch the surface. Here is a story example.

While attending a lecture at a university in Japan, I experienced the elusive nature of worldview firsthand. The audience consisted of graduate students from several European and Asian countries. The speaker wanted to convey the importance of apology in Japan and the idea that apology is not always concerned with fault or wrongdoing. Some confusion ensued. A European student questioned the professor, an act that is itself embedded with worldview assumptions, but I leave that for later consideration. "Would you apologize even if you did nothing wrong? Why would I do that?" she asked. The idea of doing so was confusing if not downright disagreeable, and behavioral adaptation, that is, apologize and comport with local expectation seemed unlikely.

The presenter appeared somewhat perplexed. "Because it's just what you do," he said. "An apology is needed in this culture to mend relationships." The Asian students sat in silence while the European student pressed on, indicating more worldviews on both sides. Shifting uneasily in my seat, I wanted to stand up, press the imaginary pause button, and suggest that we take the balcony view of the discussion itself. Worldview was not only the topic of the presentation, purpose of apology, but it was also driving the interaction *about* it. Could we peel back the layers and see how worldview is embedded right here and directing this Q&A? What was transpiring in this professor to student debate? The answers are found in three universal and composite elements of worldview.

Positionality: "The Pale Blue Dot" Positionality

"The Earth is a very small stage in a vast cosmic arena," offered Carl Sagan in *The Pale Blue Dot*. "Think of the endless cruelties visited by the inhabitants of one corner of this pixel on the scarcely distinguishable inhabitants of some other corner…think of the rivers of blood spilled by all those generals and emperors so that, in glory and triumph, they could become the momentary masters of a fraction of a dot." This famous excerpt is rife with examples of positionality – various sociocultural groups in conflict with each other, the actors' location in various "corners of this pixel," their place in a certain time frame (momentary), the idea that one group is master over another, and the position of the entire Earth within a vast cosmic expanse – a fraction of a dot.

Consider global conflicts, that is, between nation states. Arguably, most conflicts center around positionality: Borders, the nation state, land, or sociocultural groups to which people belong, the alliances to which nation states belong such as NATO or the United Nations. What are the relationships? Who are the opposition forces?

While researching disinformation and adversarial framing in mass media, I encountered the following news statement, "…the Donetsk People's Republic command also accused servicemen of Ukraine's Azov regiment of shelling the Ukrainian army's positions…in order to accuse the DPR of breaching the truce…" Several readings were required to untangle the relationships. Who are the actors? What are the claims? DPR accused Ukraine of firing on itself to stage and claim a ceasefire breach on DPR. That's a lot of finger-pointing – all of which point to positionality.

In business, positionality can look like market share, branding with respect to all other competing brands, pricing, manufacturing sites, and who is aligned with whom. Is status in the organization achieved or ascribed? That is, does one gain rank and title by working hard and demonstrating capabilities, or is it determined by relationships or one's name? Is one an employer or employee, a patron or client? Perhaps an organization's members value egalitarian and low power distance rather than hierarchical relationships.

Use of space points to relationship between people and things – open floor concept, sectioned-off work cubbies, open door policies, glass doors and walls or solid. Likewise, is some level of physical contact or non-contact the expectation in the organization? And finally, attention to meeting start times and deadlines or lack thereof indicates the human relationship with time.

Positionality then, is the relationship between entities, individuals, countries, and companies. It describes who, where, and when. In every story, actors are in relationship with each other, for better or worse. Their actions, or the story's events, take place in particular settings and at a certain time. The relationships between actors, place, time, and all elements of the environment such as plants or animals are a part of positionality. Humans may be in relationship (or lack thereof) with unseen spirit beings or forces.

Agency: Be Confident! Be More Like Me!

Actors are nothing if they are not acting. Returning to the above examples. In the news, DPR made accusations. Shelling took place. Someone breached a truce. Cruelties were carried out. Rivers of blood were spilled. In business, actors are growing market share, protecting a brand, engaging in price wars, building manufacturing sites, resolving conflict, leading teams and launching or dissolving ventures.

Working with global teams across Europe and Asia, I collected hundreds of narratives from team members about both their challenges and successes. Reflection questions, designed to elicit stories reflecting all elements of worldview included the following: Reflect on a time when the team was working together very well. Describe it. What signs suggested the work was going well? Describe a time when you thought a teammate was doing or saying the wrong thing or a negative thing? What would you do differently or how would you change it to make it right? Describe your ability to communicate and work together across differences in language and culture. Describe a teammate's ability to do the same. What did he or she do well?

Analysis of these narratives revealed implicit expectations about agency. Specifically, participants storied about what constitutes effective, productive communication and what does not. For example, when asked "what would you change" to improve a negative event or difficulty, many Europeans expressed the wish for their counterparts to be more direct and open, to participate in discussions more actively, freely admit when they do not understand, and offer their opinions unabashedly in the open group forum. In short, be more confident. Also, be more like *me*! Direct, open, and transparent communication shows leadership and is beneficial for the team project, and reserved behavior is ineffective. Interestingly, a pattern across Asian participants' answers indicated the same; careful thought before contributing aloud and silence were somehow weak or ineffective. I should be more like you.

Single sentences revealed worldviews about what kind of communication is appropriate in this business context, and how concealed they can be. Naturally, everyone knows that in business, one must speak up, speak often, be straightforward, and confidence wins the day. Agency is the means by which actors act and events take place. It consists of acts or forces that produce a particular effect, one's ability to cause or prevent a particular effect (self-efficacy), and the means by which change occurs or status quo is maintained. The locus of control can be internal or external. Agency works together with positionality as would be expected in any film or novel plot. Actors in relationship with others and elements in the environment and in particular settings act or refraining from acting.

The next and likely most critical question is why do actors act as they do? To achieve a preferred outcome or resolution to a conflict. What makes a certain outcome more desirable than all others? Why more or less confident, direct, and open? Why reticent, thoughtful, hesitant, silent? Knowing what behaviors are customary and what the actors performing them are trying to achieve are necessary for skillful navigation in different cultural settings. Understanding why is critical.

Morality, a Necessary Evil

The third worldview element, morality, attends to the purpose for which one acts. It is the rationale governing what one should say and how one should behave – a code of ethics. Morality is the actor's motivation, the driving force behind standards of behavior. Exploring morality requires venturing into deeper worldview waters. Doing so might be concern or even trepidation of appearing judgmental. For example, cultural relativism adherents argue that one cannot evaluate the practices and values of another culture using the lens of one's own.

Considering morality, however, is necessary to unravel the profound assumptions at the root of cultural miscommunication and conflict. The aim here is to observe and describe differences not pass judgment on them. Recall the story about the student and lecturer debating the purpose of an apology – to repair relationship or to admit guilt due to a wrongdoing. Following is a personal cultural story that takes this idea a step further.

Southwest, United States. A campsite in the middle of the desert. I had finished my work for the week and wanted to escape town a little early to extend my weekend. Of course, my cell phone beeped – a text from a colleague. It was my direct supervisor. He asked if I was coming to the regular weekly meeting. I was instantly mortified as I imagined the large group of participants sitting around a conference table. I take pride in being reliable and felt terrible. Driving back was not even a remote possibility.

On auto pilot, my immediate response was something like: "I'm not sure how I made this mistake. I must have confused it with the holiday schedule, and

I was off a week. I thought I had it in my calendar..." Well, there were no good explanations. He reassured me it was perfectly ok; it was just a mistake and could happen to anyone. But to my surprise he added that it would have been much better to just apologize instead of coming up with excuses. I felt taken aback and worse, having committed two wrongs, rather than reassured.

Being a practitioner and academic of intercultural communication my entire adult life, I mentally stepped back, took the balcony view and asked, what had really happened. What did I miss and why does this feel so disagreeable? There were no good excuses. In my mind, they were necessary explanations. I automatically and unconsciously assumed the remedy for the situation was to respond to the (unasked) question, "Why did you do that?" My motivation was to discover and share the real reason I missed the meeting. He was not interested in a reason and focused instead on an apology as a remedy. Both of us had acted from tacit worldviews about two things: What one does and says in cross-cultural interactions and also why one does so – the morality element of worldview.

Applying MAP to unravel this interaction, it became clear I had been operating from an innocence and guilt, or justice morality orientation – very common in my native United States. My colleague's orientation was honor and shame – likewise common in his native Korea. Both are powerful forces that govern behavior. I grew up with the expectation that when one broke a commitment, there must be a good reason, and one must be forthcoming with it. Right versus wrong. Letter of the law. My colleague, on the other hand, was raised with the understanding that a broken commitment dishonors and shows a lack of respect others in the group. Loss of face occurs not because of legalistic thinking about dates, times, and meetings. Rather, it occurs in the context of relationships among the people affected by the mistake – even if that mistake is completely outside of one's control.

Consider a related story about how differences in morality orientations also governs how one makes reparations to missteps. Back at the Japanese university with an audience of graduate students from several European and Asian countries, the teams experienced a real-world cultural difficulty that provided far more insight to culture, worldview, and global team communication than any planned cultural competence lecture or activity could ever accomplish. For orientation, I was working on behalf of the European side.

After a long day of meetings and case study discussions, the students enjoyed some free time and relaxation – perhaps a bit too much. In the middle of the night, some unfortunate events took place. Early the next morning, the German staff received the bad news that one or more people caused some damage to property in the building. Imagine my first reaction Again, acting on jet lag, time pressure, and cultural auto pilot, I immediately asked how much money it would cost to fix it. My second question was, who did it? In other words, who is guilty, and who needs to pay?

The monetary cost and the physical damage were of far less concern to the Japanese leadership. Their obvious urgent need was to identify the person and arrange a face-to-face apology. No one stepped forward. Who from an innocence/guilt-based culture would want to admit to a wrongdoing, especially if there might be legal consequences? Time went by, and we moved on to another city. Still, no one took responsibility for the damage. The critical face-to-face apology would now require a 2-hour train ride to begin the process of restoring face and making reparations. It was of little consequence to the Japanese; an apology was required.

All the while, I was thinking about the physical property damage, fixing and paying for it, and that somehow, doing so would restore a kind of order. It would – from an innocence/guilt morality lens where truth is paramount, offense takes the form of lawbreaking, and offenses are remedied by confessing, correcting the issue, or enduring a legal judgment. From a predominantly honor/shame morality lens, reputation in society and family is paramount, offense takes the form of harming those relationships and breaking the community's expectations and conventions. Offenses are remedied through public shame and apology or excluding oneself from the group. Ultimately, someone did step forward, embarked on the train ride, and apologized as was culturally necessary, but the ripple effects were still felt years later.

Both stories display indicators of worldview and specifically, two types of morality that govern the behavior of actors (agency) and their relationships (positionality). In addition to innocence/guilt and honor/shame, a third morality lens is power and fear. Actors are concerned with access to and control over resources – those who have power or aspire to have it. They are engaged in reciprocal relationships and are driven by the need for security, fear avoidance, or maintaining or increasing dominance. Offense takes the form of challenging those in power and is remedied by appeasing, placating, or manipulating (see Appendix).

In the first story, interacting with my direct supervisor power/fear could have governed our behavior via my performance rating anxiety. Likewise, he could have exerted power and withheld overtures for future cooperation. However, the focus on apology (as opposed to excuses) was an indicator of the overarching morality innocence/guilt and honor/shame lenses.

Scholars suggest all three morality lenses, or subdimensions are found in every culture, but one is more predominant than the others. Further, the predominant subdimension varies according to the context (James & McLeod, 2014; Muller, 2000). Although the power/fear subdimension was not predominant in the above stories, the concepts are established in the literature (James & McLeod, 2014; Muller, 2000; Shweder et al., 1997; Wilson, 2013). Recognizing the fundamental morality orientation that governs behavior within a given culture and context is key to first understanding intercultural difficulties and then to improving intercultural competence (see Appendix).

To this point, worldview can be defined as a cognitive framework of the natural and supernatural environment containing tacit assumptions about morality, or rationale for behavior, agency within the environment, and positionality in relation to elements in the environment, which includes other people, groups, institutions, objects, nature, other living beings, and supernatural beings. Two additional elements are yet to be addressed. First, I describe how the three worldview elements were derived and the source of worldviews.

Why Every Worldview Consists of Morality, Agency, and Positionality

Early in my cultural studies and career, a colleague offered a book I would normally not pick up on my own, *Understanding Folk Religion* (Hiebert et al., 1999). I had been well versed in cultural value dimensions like individualism and collectivism, low and high context communication, and fate and control of the environment, but is soon became clear there is far more to culture. Values are not just preferences; they come from a deeper place, and that place is worldview, the deep culture element that lies outside our awareness and yet controls everything we think, say, and do.

Convinced that deep worldview perceptions of reality were at the core of culture and of every intercultural difficulty, I reviewed literature on its origins and conceptualizations across multiple disciplines. Scholars in philosophy, cultural anthropology, missiology (the study of religious missions), cross-cultural psychology, and communication all contributed. When taken as a whole, the literature essentially focused on three main approaches: Philosophical questions which every worldview must answer, values – often expressed as binary opposites on a continuum, and universal categories such as self, other, relationship, and causality.

Looking across these traditional approaches, three themes emerged. Each philosophical question, value, and category was concerned with either actors and their settings/environment, actions of the actors, or the actor's purpose or motivation for acting. As a result of the comprehensive review across the literature, I posit that every worldview can be both identified and described via these three universal composites, morality, agency, and positionality. Table 1 details how three main approaches to worldview fit under each.

Table 1: Origin of MAP Universal Composites Based on Three Existing Worldview Approaches

	Morality (why?)	**Agency (how?)**	**Positionality (who? what? where? when?)**
Philosophical questions	How are we to act and to create in this world? What is right and wrong? What are life-orienting core commitments? What are the general principles by which we should organize our actions? By what criteria are we to select possible futures? How do we assess global reality and the role of our species in it? Is human nature good, evil, or both?	Why is our world the way it is, and not different? How does the world function? We are we the way we are, and not different? What kind of global explanatory principles can we put forward? How can we influence and transform the world? What future is open to us and our species in this world? What happens to a person at death? What is the preferred personality: Doing, growing, or being? Why do we feel the way we feel in this world?	What is the nature of external reality? How is it structured? What is a human being? What is the meaning of human history? What is the relationship between humans and nature? What is the relationship between humans? What is the orientation toward time? What is the orientation toward space?
Cultural value dimensions	Honor/shame Innocence/guilt Power/fear	Fate/control of the environment Uncertainty avoidance Masculinity/femininity (gender role differentiation) High/low context communication styles Doing/being Task/relationship	Patron/client Hierarchy/egalitarianism Achieved/ascribed status Proxemics Contact/noncontact Individualism/collectivism Time orientation Power distance
Worldview universal categories	Values	Causality	Self, nonself/other, relationship, allegiance, space, time, and classification

Narrative: It Goes Without Saying

Approximately eleven stories are woven throughout this paper. The intent was to be engaging and insightful and show, rather than simply tell the power of story. Each illustrates examples of what one knows to be true. Not surprisingly, story is also the means by which we acquire that knowledge. From the beginning of language formation as infants, books, school teachers, church leaders, mass media consumption, and more provide an endless stream of narratives and source of worldview.

Narrative, or a coherent system of stories, is a way of knowing, "a meaning structure that organizes events and human actions into a whole" (Polkinghorne, 1988, p. 18). Because the creation, telling, and hearing of stories is a basic human mechanism for making sense of reality, narrative is integral to communication in general and intercultural communication in particular (Entman, 1993; Van Gorp, 2007). Narrative has been linked to the earliest forms of human learning and language acquisition (Abbott, 2008) and shapes cognition, societies, and culture (Dautenhahn, 2001). Likewise, language and worldview are circularly informing; language shapes worldview, and worldview influences language (Fantini, 1995). Adding on to the proposed definition above, worldview is a *narrative-based* cognitive framework. One last feature of the definition remains.

In my earliest academic attempts at developing a construct to identify worldviews, I conducted interviews with Catholics regarding their Lenten practices. The research question was: What is the connection between the outward observable practice and the outcome of those actions – perceived or otherwise – and why is that outcome desirable? The focus was to uncover assumptions about causality, but revealing them given that they lie outside our awareness was a formidable challenge. "Culture hides much more than it reveals, and strangely enough, it hides most effectively from its own participants" (Hall, 1959, p. 39).

Using the Earth layers of culture metaphor (Barney, 1973; Strauss & Strauss, 2019), I started by eliciting stories related to the outer crust and working toward the molten core, peeling back layer after layer. Unveiling the first layer was simple. What do you do? What can you see others doing? These questions resulted in various descriptions of church services, fasting on Fridays, special prayers, and creating family activities around the Lenten season.

Then, what were you taught to do as a child at home, at school, and in church? Participants storied about the sociocultural institution level – home, school, church, and family. Values embedded in the practices and institutions began to emerge. These centered around love of family, God, and community, a desire for peace, the importance of sacrifice to gain appreciation for all of one's blessings.

Moving into the molten core of culture, worldview, is where it became more perplexing. Why do you do this practice? What does it get you? Posing such pointed questions aimed at diving into less conscious levels, confusion or irritation sometimes ensued. The answers were intuitively obvious – to them. Although, bringing these ideas to the conscious, surface level took some time and effort, it ultimately resulted in moments of true interest and revelation. It created insights into their own worldviews. Regarding prayer, one participant emphatically said it brings God's grace down from heaven to become manifest in the world and change things for the good.

This was a strong statement at the intersection of positionality, agency, and morality. The actors are the human Catholics and God. Acts of agency, showing cause and effect, were praying and attending a service known as Stations of the Cross. The result was grace from God entered the natural, physical world bringing goodness. Morality themes revolved around justice insofar as prayer and ritual invoked God's hand in the natural world to rectify wrongs. Power and fear were evident in the human request for an omnipotent spirit being to ease suffering in the world. When probing to the same depths with another participant and asking why he attends certain services or follows certain practices, he responded, "Why do I buy a Christmas tree every year? Because I buy a Christmas tree every year." Circular and profound. Both stories revealed the final part of the definition of worldview. It is learned and transmitted within communities of others; that is, it is socially-learned. One anthropologist said it well, "It goes without saying because it comes without saying" (Bourdieu, 1977). One is simply born into it.

Adding on, a comprehensive and succinct worldview definition is: A socially-learned and narrative-based cognitive framework of the natural and supernatural environment containing tacit assumptions about morality, or rationale for behavior, agency within the environment, and positionality in relation to elements in the environment, which includes other people, groups, institutions, objects, nature, other living beings, and supernatural beings. Recall the news headlines in the introduction in which worldview was invoked and left for readers to assume only a face value meaning – view of the world – or to derive some other meaning perhaps from the article's context. Given the proposed theoretical foundation demonstrated through story, how could the headlines and articles differently be interpreted differently? How might MAP lead to a clearer, more conscious awareness of deep culture difficulties experienced in cross-cultural interactions? To answer these, an opportunity to experiment with application follows.

Doing Things with Worldview: Mapping MAP to Narratives

Since narrative is a way of knowing and source of worldview, analyzing narrative aids in detecting worldviews hidden beneath observable behavior. With a definition and construct of worldview and its subdimensions, I turn to application. Presented in this section is a story example using Table 1 as a type of codebook to guide investigation. In the following and final section, is an opportunity for readers to replicate the process drawing on personal and/or professional experiences.

In, *Earth Layers of Culture,* recall the lecture hall story at the Japanese university. The professor was explaining the importance of apology, while the student questioned why apology is necessary if one has done nothing wrong. Here is an excerpt:

> "...The speaker wanted to convey the importance of apology in Japan, including the idea that apology is not always concerned with fault or wrongdoing. Some confusion ensued. A European student questioned the professor, an act that itself is embedded with worldview assumptions, but I leave that for later consideration. "Would you apologize even if you did nothing wrong? Why would I do that?" she asked. The idea of doing so was confusing at best and downright disagreeable at worst. Not only did apology in the absence of wrongdoing not make sense in her mind, but the expectation that she would ever adapt her outward behavior, that is, apologize, to comport with the local practice was unlikely.
>
> The presenter seemed a little bit stumped – because it's just what you do. An apology is needed in this culture to preserve or mend relationships. The Asian students sat in silence while the European student pressed on (more worldview indicators on both sides.) I shifted uneasily in my seat, wanting to stand up, press the pause button, suggest that we "step outside of this exchange" and take the balcony view of the discussion itself. I wanted to show how worldviews are beneath not only the topic of the presentation, apology, but that worldview was also driving the interaction *about* it."

Going through my mind while shifting uneasily in my seat were the three universal composites and how they could have clarified not only the topic of apology in honor/shame and innocence/guilt (as well as power/fear) cultures, but also how the exchange itself exhibited worldview. What are the positionality indicators – actors, their relationships, and the setting in time and place? A student (from a European country), a professor (Japanese by birth but living in Austria and married to a European), the setting is a large, open lecture hall, a raised stage with a screen, podium, and microphone, and a total of approximately 100 participants from multiple countries, all facing forward, including several prominent professors, business leaders, and staff, and me.

What are agency indicators – means by which actors behave? A European student questioned the professor. The professor offered explanation. The Asian students sat in silence – a subtle and easy to miss non-action. Likewise, I refrained from inserting myself into the debate as did all other faculty and staff. The professor to student debate had effectively leveled the position of both to peers, rather than that of expert and learner. Positionality and agency are connected; it is difficult to describe one without the other. Both are included in any investigation into morality, the code of conduct that governs behavior.

What are morality indicators? Innocence/guilt and honor/shame were apparent in two ways. The first is quite explicit. The topic of the seminar was apology and the underlying reasons for it. The professor's stance: Apology is not necessarily concerned with wrongdoing; rather, it is intended to preserve relationship and reputation of self and other within the group to which one belongs. The participant's stance: Apology is used to admit wrongdoing and restore innocence. Guilt is to be avoided, as is admitting to guilt via apology, especially when one is innocent. Doing so could itself be viewed as a lie.

The second way innocence/guilt and honor/shame are apparent is within the style of the interaction. Since morality governs behavior, then conversely, interaction reveals morality. More concretely, the European student directly challenged the professor in an open forum, pointing to the high importance of truth, justice, and what is right or wrong. The professor, having been raised in an honor/shame culture, seemed unable recognize how critically important it was to her to maintain innocence. To her, the cost of an apology is high when the aspiration is to maintain innocence. In his view, the cost of an apology is quite low when the aspiration is to preserve or restore reputation. Honor also likely explains why the Asian students remained silent. It ensures the professor's reputation cannot be diminished; speaking up and directly questioning may imply a weakness in the professor's skills.

This experience shed light on a previous interaction years before at my university in the U.S. Hosting a graduate student from Japan, she was struck by the differences in classroom patterns. Debate and energetic participation contrasted with her expectation of students to quietly listen while the professor delivers a lecture. Leaving class that night, she was quite stunned by the student behavior and asked about their lack of respect. I had not anticipated such a cultural divide and therefore had failed to prepare her and avoid an uncomfortable evening. Missing were the concepts of agency and underlying morality as well as the differences in both between the two cultures.

Taking the Balcony View: More MAP Application

After working on consulting projects in a global team, participants engage in a final reflection activity about intercultural aspects. Experience without reflection does not translate to learning; it is simply an experience. Revisiting the post-seminar questions mentioned previously, conduct an analysis from a professional intercultural experience.

- Reflect on a time when you thought the team was not working together very well or when a teammate was doing or saying a wrong or negative thing.
- Describe it in a few sentences or paragraphs.
- What made it wrong or negative?
- How would you change it to make it right?
- That is, what would you have done differently?

Write down a story in response to the above prompts. Referring to Table 2 as a guide, highlight keywords or phrases indicating positionality. This is easiest and quickest to identify because and is found in single words or short phrases. Who are the actors and what is their positionality to each other? What was the setting? Were the hierarchies? Did some members know each other a long time, or were some brand-new introductions? Was there a time element involved, like a deadline, time zone difference, or jetlag? What about physical space – too close? Too distant? Consider all elements of the environment that seem relevant.

With a different highlighter color, mark keywords indicating agency. Agency is typically found in slightly longer text segments, such as phrases or complete sentences. What was done? What was not done? What do you wish you or others had done differently? Lastly, and perhaps most importantly, highlight story sections indicating the morality influence exhibited in the actions. Morality is often revealed in longer passages of many sentences. What deep values motivated the actors? What linguistic markers underpin innocence/guilt, honor/shame, or power/fear?

Table 2: MAP Detailed Description

	Morality: Why? For what purpose? (see Appendix)	**Agency: How? By what means?**	**Positionality: Who What? Where? When**
What is it?	System of values and principles that guide behavior. Rationale for behavior. Code of conduct. Why an outcome is desirable or not.	What actors do or refrain from doing. Perceptions about causality. Means by which change occurs or status quo is maintained.	Relationship between self, others, and elements in the environment: Other people, sociocultural groups, organizations, city, state, nation, world, universe, nature, animals, supernatural beings, time, and place/setting.
Linguistic Markers in Narratives	Evaluative markers: Ashamed, bad, benefit, better, decency, embarrass, ethical evaluate, fair, fear, good, guilt, honor, important, innocence, loyalty, must, necessary, negative, opinion, ought, policy, polite, power, qualities, righteousness, relaxed, reputation, required, respect, right, rules, shame, should, standards, succeed, successful, worse, wrong	Event markers: Ability, affect, agency, agree, capability, cause, change, choose, decide, dismantle, divide, effect, how, ignore, impetus, improve, must (in terms of causality), responsibility, result,	Identity markers: Class, race, gender, and identity markers. ancestors, animals, another perspective, characteristic, city names, colleague, community, comparison/compared to, country, culture, different, environment, everyone, family, global, god, hierarchy, kinship, location, nature, no one organization, Other, partner, place, quality, social group, space, spirit, supernatural beings, teammate, time,

Identifying three worldview composites illuminates much about cultural differences and how various tacit assumptions about how reality is or should be are at the root of misunderstanding and conflict. As a final step, refer to the Morality Matrix (see Appendix). Consider how the highlighted story segments are illuminated by or are connected to the concepts in the Morality Matrix. Given your current understanding of culture and worldview, what was the source of or reason for the difficulty? If you were faced with the same situation, what might you do or say differently?

A Final Word

Any attempt to operationalize worldview is bound by one's own worldview. How readers will understand and apply the concepts within are likewise so.

A second limitation is that no single chapter can comprehensively address the vast literature on culture, worldview, and intercultural communication, nor provide sufficient guidance on applying that knowledge in real world settings. However, the purpose was to shine a light on the critical importance of deeply-held worldviews at the core of every cultural interaction and secondly, to provide a memorable tool to discover ways to enter into any cultural setting flexibly and successfully. More specifically, the objectives were:

1. Be able to describe the features of deep culture worldview using MAP.
2. Connect elements of stories to worldview concepts.
3. Interpret narratives/stories through the lens of a 3-part worldview framework.
4. Apply worldview concepts to global business situations to make sense of difficulties and create avenues for solving them.

Optimistically, brief stories of real-world experiences in organizations intertwined with theoretical, academic work will inspire readers to share knowledge, discover the worldviews of others, consider their own, and further investigate deep culture. The next time unmet expectations, surprises, or difficulties in cross-cultural settings arise, stop, turn off auto pilot, and observe. Describe what is happening as objectively as possible starting with actors and setting (positionality) and actions (agency). Apply the Morality Matrix to interpret motivations beneath the actions and determine the predominant morality subdimension. Lastly, suspend judgment and ask what could be happening here? Every behavior makes sense if there is enough information. The process is ODIS: Observe, describe, interpret, and suspend judgment.

We storied about intercultural difficulties and identified morality, agency, and positionality to shed a light on underlying worldview assumptions. Higher order abilities include using that information to improve intercultural competence.

References

Abbott, H. P. (2008). *The Cambridge Introduction to Narrative* (2nd ed.). New York, NY:Cambridge University Press.

Albrecht, L. (2021, June 5). How Do Wealthy Investors Feel about Their Good Fortune during the Pandemic? *Morningtar*. Retrieved from: https://www.marketwatch.com/story/the-pandemic-has-prompted-wealthy-investors-to-contribute-more-to-society-but-some-more-than-others-11622721772.

Bansal, T. (2021, June 15). What Business Leaders Can Learn From An Indigenous Worldview. *Forbes*. Retrieved from: https://www.forbes.com/sites/timabansal/2021/06/15/what-business-leaders-can-learn-from-an-indigenous-worldview/?sh=47b28fc5c2fc.

Barney, G. L. (1973). The Supracultural and the Cultural. In *The Gospel and Frontier Peoples*, ed. B. R. Pierce. Pasadena, CA: William Carey Library; pp. 48–57.

Bourdieu, P. (1977). *Outline of a Theory of Practice* (R. Nice, Trans.). New York, NY: Cambridge University Press.

Dautenhahn, K. (2001). The Narrative Intelligence Hypothesis: In Search of the Transactional format of Narratives in Humans and Other Social Animals. In M. Beynon, C. L. Nehaniv, & K. Dautenhahn (Eds.), *Cognitive Technology: Instruments of Mind* (pp. 248–266). Berlin, Germany: Springer.

Entman, R. M. (1993). Framing: Toward Clarification of a Fractured Paradigm. *Journal of Communication, 43*(4), 51–58. Retrieved from: https://doi.org/10.1111/j.1460-2466.1993.tb01304.x.

Fantini, A. E. (1995). Introduction-Language, Culture and World View: Exploring the Nexus. *International Journal of Intercultural Relations, 19,* 143–153. Retrieved from: https://doi.org/10.1016/0147-1767(95)00025-7

Hall, E. T. (1959). *The Silent Language.* Garden City, NY: Doubleday.

Hiebert, P. G., Shaw, R. D., & Tiénou, T. (1999). *Understanding Folk Religion: A Christian Response to Popular Beliefs and Practices.* Grand Rapids, MI: Baker Books.

James, A., & McLeod, C. (2014). An Analysis of the Three Colors Worldview Mapping Tool: Contrasting Emirati and Non-Emirati Worldviews. *Intercultural Communication Studies 23(1)*: 165–186.

Lauchlan, S. (2021, June 1). Bosch Manufactures a Data-Driven Culture with Salesforce Tableau Analytics. *Diginomica*. Retrieved from: https://diginomica.com/bosch-manufactures-data-driven-culture-salesforce-tableau-analytics.

Muller, R. (2000). *Honor and shame: Unlocking the door.* Bloomington, IN: XLibris

Muller, R. (2015). *The Messenger, the Message, & the Community: Three Critical Issues for the Cross-Cultural Church Planter* (4th ed.). Independent Scholars Press.

Polkinghorne, D. E. (1988). *Narrative Knowing and the Human Sciences.* Albany: State University of New York Press.

Semanski, P. (2021, June 17). What Biden's First Foreign Trip Tells Us about His Worldview. *CNN*. Retrieved from: https://kesq.com/news/national-politics/cnn-us-politics/2021/06/17/what-bidens-first-foreign-trip-tells-us-about-his-worldview/.

Sheridan, C. (2021, June 13). Taking the Knee and Holding Heads High. *Irish Examiner*. Retrieved from: https://www.irishexaminer.com/opinion/columnists/arid-40312892.html.

Shweder, R. A., Much, N. C., Mahapatra, M., & Park, L. (1997). The "big three" of morality (autonomy, community, divinity) and the "big three" explanations of suffering. In A. M. Brandt & P. Rozin (Eds.), *Morality and health* (pp. 119–169). Abingdom on Thames, UK: Taylor & Frances/Routledge.

Steffen, T. (2015). Minimizing Crosscultural Evangelism Noise. *Missiology*, *43*(4), 413–428.

Strauss, R. (2017). *Introducing Story-Strategic Methods.* Eugene, OR: Wipf & Stock.

Strauss, R., & Strauss, C. (2019). *Four Overarching Patterns of Culture: A Look at Common Behavior*. Wipf & Stock Publishers.

Van Gorp, B. (2007). The Constructionist Approach to Framing: Bringing Culture Back In. *Journal of Communication, 57,* 60–78. Retrieved from: https://doi.org/10.1111/j.0021-9916.2007.00329.x.

Wilson, J. K.(2013). Exploring the Past, Present, and Future of Cultural Competency Research: The Revision and Expansion of the Sociocultural Adaptation Construct. Open Access Te Herenga Waka-Victoria University of Wellington. Thesis. https://doi.org/10.26686/wgtn.17004835.v1

Appendix

Morality Matrix, A Deeper View

	Honor/shame	Innocence/guilt	Power/Fear
Metaphor	Society	Courtroom	Combat
Conscience: The Inner Voice is…	Grandmother "For shame! I'm so embarrassed! I let everyone down!"	Lawyer "That's wrong! You'll get caught! You'll get in trouble!"	Demon: "Fear me! I will punish you!"
Focus	Reputation in community & family	Legality & individual rights	Resources & exchange
Actions driven by… (Muller, 2015, p. 88)	…preserving face, honor code, and community expectation.	…legality and the individual conscience informed by rules, regulations, and policies.	…need for security or to increase or maintain dominance.
Decisions are based on…	…needs of the in-group.	…internal code of conduct.	…perceived threat.
Objective	Avoid disloyalty and insubordination to prevent disgrace and humiliation	Avoid lawbreaking to prevent punishment	Avoid subjugation and minimize uncertainty
Goals of relationships	Build group solidarity and build or maintain reputation	Achieve the task	Obtain resources, favors, pardons, promotions

	Honor/shame	Innocence/guilt	Power/Fear
Key observable behavior, key indicators	Indirect communication Group accountability Relationship-centric negotiation Historical events drive today's relationships Performance assessment is linked to the group Relationship often placed over rules Verbal commitment builds relationships	Direct communication Individual accountability Goal/issue-centric negotiation Laws are used to establish innocence and argue for individual rights Performance is linked to individuals Rules often placed over relationship Telling the truth Written agreements, codes, contracts, and standards	Aggressive, direct, strong communication Benefactor/beneficiary accountability Resources and benefits-centric negotiation Position of power used to instill fear to achieve compliance of to empower others Performance is linked to dominance or control of resources. Relationship is focused on exchange and benefits.
Key Sociocultural Institutions (2nd layer in the Earth model)	family extended family kinship	codified law justice system law enforcement	family religion political groups, military, police

Muller, 2015; Shweder et al, 1997; Steffen, 2015; Strauss, 2017; Strauss & Strauss, 2019; Wilson, 2013.

Introduction to The English Are All Cold Fish: The Reattribution Generator and the Creation of Alternative Models of Meaning

By David Katan

The next chapter introduces a 6-stage language-based Reattribution Generator. This generator permits individuals to become more consciously aware of cultural differences in perceiving the world around themselves. In line with Heider's Attribution Theory, individuals tend to attribute the behaviour of others due to internal or personal factors while they tend to attribute their own behaviour as being influenced by external factors. Katan notes that while executives may consider their inability to complete a task on time to such external factors as having too much work to do, these same executives will probably assume that subordinates who do not complete their assigned duties one time are disorganized or lazy. This is a fundamental attribution error, and it is often found in prejudices. Quite often, prejudices directed at others are based on attributing one's own meaning to the behaviour of the other. Without knowing much about the other, this can, of course, often result in misunderstandings. What we consider to be appropriate will also be applied as a standard for evaluating the behaviour of others - even though we know little or nothing of the other. That is why the Rettribution Generator can help one overcome these misperceptions. Katan uses a specific example to demonstrate how the Generator works, but he points out that it can also be applied to many other situations and intercultural encounters. The Generator allows people to isolate their perception from (faulty) attribution, interpretation, and evaluation by having them suspend their own beliefs and values. It, thus, permits individuals to put themselves into the position of others to see the world from the perspective of the others. In other words, the Generator permits one to avoid automatic attribution and to think recursively outside one's model of the world. It, thus, permits one to respect other worldviews as logical within those worlds and, thus, accepting alternative worldviews without having to give up one's own beliefs and values. This makes the Generator an ideal tool for intercultural encounters in the world of business.

Michael B. Hinner

David Katan taught at the Interpreters' School, University of Trieste for 20 years before taking up the chair in English Language and Translation at the University of Salento (Lecce), where he teaches translation, intercultural communication and tourism. His publications include contributions for the Routledge Encyclopaedias of *Translation* (2nd and 3rd eds.), *Translation and Conflict* and *Translation and Globalisation*, the Benjamins *Handbook of Translation Studies* (1st and 2nd eds.) and for the Wiley-Blackwell *Encyclopedia of Applied Linguistics* (1st and 2nd eds.). His volume *Translating Cultures: An Introduction for Translators, Interpreters and Mediators* has just been updated to its 3rd edition (Routledge, 2021). He has also worked for over 25 years in intercultural business training with TCO International and Worldwork, which also involved long engagements with *Benetton* and *Generali*. He is now a licensee of the TCO Intercultural Competence diagnostic tool, "The International Profiler". He has been keynote speaker for a variety of international conferences in Australia, Columbia, Italy and South Africa, and is currently Visiting Researcher at the University of South Africa. He has been editor-in-chief of *Cultus: the Journal for Intercultural Mediation and Communication* since its inception in 2008. Professionally he works as a translator, specializing in museum and tourism guides, which has now led him to research on heritage translation, and translation as narrativity.

David Katan

The English are All Cold Fish: The Reattribution Generator and the Creation of Alternative Models of Meaning

Introduction

The aim of this paper is to show how limiting instinctive reactions to culture-bound behaviour can become progressively more reflective when guided through a 6-stage language-based Reattribution Generator. The Generator constitutes a framework for individuals to create more positive and conscious evaluations of perceived behaviour through guided disassociation and the generation of hypotheses to reattribute meaning. At a later stage of intercultural development, individuals can become more autonomous in using the reattribution language exercises themselves to disassociate not only from their own culture-bound model of the world, but also from immediate interpretation and evaluation of perceived behaviour.

The theory behind the model and the techniques themselves are adapted mainly from Neurolinguistic Programming (NLP), and are explained below.

The Theory

Attribution Theory

Our natural ethnocentric approach to other cultures (Bennett 1993, Paige & Martin 1996, p. 46) means that we tend to blame individuals and their culture for our own internal response. This process, known in psychology as the Attribution Theory, was discussed first by Fritz Heider in 1958, and has since been a mainstream concept in intercultural studies (e.g. Gudykunst, 2004). Heider had already documented the human need to bring order out of chaos (Heider & Simmel, 1944, p. 256). In an experiment almost all the participants, when asked to 'describe', interpreted the random movements of geometrical figures as "actions of animated beings, chiefly of persons" (Heider & Simmel, 1944, p. 259). The participants had attributed volition, or "causal origins" to the inanimate shapes (e.g. he tries to catch, hiding, congratulating,...). The Attribution Theory itself focusses on the similar need "to make sense out of the manifold of proximal stimuli by ordering them in terms of distal invariants and their relevant dispositional properties" (Heider & Simmel, 1944, p. 296).

Importantly, to give order, "constancy" is required. So the mind tends to make sense of an individual behaviour by fitting it in to a trait. Consequently, the mind tends to treat the transient social world (an individual behaviour) as a constant in the same way as the physical world may be seen as a constant no matter how you look at it (e.g. a table). Heider also suggested that perception of behaviour changes according to whether we are the actor or the observer.[1] Crucially, in observing others, we will tend to attribute others' behaviour as dispositional, meaning the cause of the behaviour will be internal and due to volition or other personal factors regarding the other's personality. On the other hand, as actor, we will tend to attribute our own behaviour as situational, the cause being external. A good example is the manager or university professor who is unable to complete a job on time due to overwork, pressing engagements, etc. The subordinate, or participant, who likewise is unable to complete his or her task will, on the other hand, be thought of as lazy, badly organised or untrustworthy. In some cases this may match the reality, but what we are focussing on is the automatism of the judgement, which without objective evidence, is a "fundamental attribution error" (FAE) (Ross, 1977).

The importance of FAE cannot be underestimated when it comes to fostering prejudice in cross-cultural communication (see also Selby 1975; Lalljee 1987), and will be further exacerbated when at least one of the participants is not a native speaker. If the other speaks at a low level of the native language, then the native speakers can usually contextualise and accommodate communication inaccuracies, reducing the probability of FAE. However, the participants are unlikely to have the same conscious contextual awareness of native levels when it comes to command of linguistic or behavioural *appropriacy* (rather than accuracy), especially when the stranger involved has a reasonable, if not fluent, command of the language in question. As a result, the native speaker is likely to attribute the inappropriacy to some personal factor rather than to the stranger's communication or cultural competence.

Appropriacy

Every time we have a negative reaction to another person's behaviour we are attributing our own meaning to the other's behaviour, and hence we are applying

1 As explained this observation was not Heider's main argument. In Intercultural Communication, however, it is often taken as such.

an aspect of our own congruent logical level system[2] to another. The Logical Levels theory (see below) is an extension of the Iceberg Theory, often attributed to E. T. Hall (1959/1990, p. 63). What Hall did was to discuss the visible (external/conscious) features of culture, comparing them with those features that are completely hidden (internal/unconscious) adding an intermediate layer. This middle layer is what Hall calls "the taken for granted" level – the tacit, generally accepted (appropriate) norms – and has been likened to the area just under the floating iceberg that at times can become visible. Heider also discusses appropriacy. He lists one's understanding of "ought or ought not", or standards of behaviour, is one of the basic concepts affecting our perception of others, having a very direct bearing on our evaluation (1958, p. 17). Below this "ought"/tacit level are the hidden beliefs and values that "logically" motivate the norms. So, if we value time, when we notice a stranger's visible behaviour (arriving at 09:25 for a 09:00 meeting) without no mention of "the time", this behaviour is logically linked to flouting of the norms (timekeeping or apologising, etc.). A default response is to presume that our logical level system is universal, and therefore that the stranger has consciously flouted the norms.

Within long-term relationships and with people from the same cultural background this may well be the case. However, this response is "mindless" (Langer & Minhea, 2000, p. 2; Gudykunst, 1995, p. 16) in the sense that "rules and routines are more likely to govern our behavior, irrespective of the current circumstances". It is this default recourse to (culture-bound) norms that triggers FAE. The less interlocutors share of each other's world the more they will need to be "mindful", which means, following Langer again "drawing novel distinctions" through:

1. a greater sensitivity to one's environment,
2. more openness to new information,
3. the creation of new categories for structuring perception, and
4. enhanced awareness of multiple perspectives in problem solving (Langer & Minhea, 2000, p. 2)

The question that we will attempt to answer here is how can we stimulate awareness of multiple perspectives, especially when we have already triggered

2 The Logical levels model or theory is central to NeuroLinguistic Programming (NLP) See, e.g., Dilts 1990, Chapter 1: "The Nature of Belief" and Katan & Taibi (2021, pp. 61–99) for a fuller discussion.

the automatic mindless response towards strangers and their inappropriate behaviour.

NLP

One branch of cognitive psychology, Neuro-Linguistic Programming (NLP), has developed an extremely useful tool for identifying lack of explicitness and potential attribution problems due to the misunderstanding of context. According to Dilts et al. (1980, p. 2), the co-founders of the discipline:

> "'Neuro' stands for the fundamental tenet that all behaviour is the result of neurological processes. 'Linguistic' indicates that neural processes are represented, ordered, and sequenced into models and strategies through language and communications systems. 'Programming' refers to the process of organising the components of a system to achieve a specific outcome."

NLP is based on a number of basic tenets, the most basic of which is: "the map is not the territory". The theory, according to its developers originated with the Kantian scholar Hans Vaihanger (1924, pp. 159–60):[3] "It must be remembered that the object of the world of ideas as a whole is not the portrayal of reality – this would be an utterly impossible task – but rather to provide us with an instrument for finding our way about more easily in the world". The second source of the map/territory metaphor was Korzybski (1958, pp. 58–60): "A map is not the territory it represents, but, if correct, it has a similar structure to the territory, which accounts for its usefulness…" Those who suffer from a mindless reaction, or more specifically from culture shock (Paige, 1993, p. 2), are, though, convinced that they are being affected by external reality. Instead, they are responding to their own internal – and very poor, distorted and generalised – model of reality. So, we begin by accepting that there is (probably) an objective reality, and that there is an internalised idea or subjective model of that reality, known as "model of the mind", "a mental model" or "a map of reality" (see Katan & Taibi, 2021).

A second tenet of NLP is that these learnt maps can be modified and enlarged through language. O'Connor (2001, p. 3), for example, recounts a story to illustrate NLP, finishing with these words "You changed how he felt with a few words. That's NLP". The linguistic part of NLP is based loosely on Chomsky's generative grammar, and in particular on the assumption that all sentences are composed of a deep and surface structure. The surface structure contains the language necessary

3 The concept of map or mental model itself, now enshrined in the cognitive sciences, originates with Kant himself (Brook, 2004).

for communication with others. It is, however, transformed (through deletion and rearrangement) from a deep structure, which is the potential full linguistic realisation, "spelling out in words", of the conscious thoughts and coherent links attached to the words uttered. We may locate the deep structure, at the tacit "taken for granted" layer in the Iceberg model. As mentioned above, below this layer are the presuppositions, core values or truths about the world that make what we say and do logical (at least to us).

Korzybski suggested a series of "who, what, when, where, and how" questions to recover information deleted in the verbal description of a person's mental map, to correct or clarify distortions, and to limit unwarranted generalizations. He thought that we would understand each other better (and behave more sanely) if we used language to create more complete, more accurate mental and verbal maps of our reality.

Bandler and Grinder (1975) developed this framework of questions and coined the term "Meta Model" to refer to the fact that these questions probe an individual's model of the world at a "meta" level. O'Connor (2001, p. 140; see also Katan & Taibi 2021, p. 151) defines the Meta Model as a "set of language patterns and questions that reconnect the deletions, distortions and generalisations with the experience that generated them". The Model was also influenced by Chomsky's transformational grammar. The deep structure is a full linguistic representation, and will contain a complete, "well-formed"[4] rendition of "what or who did what exactly". Any utterance that is not well-formed represents a Meta Model violation, which will automatically in the trainer's mind trigger a Meta Model challenge to produce a full description of the subject, a specification of the action and of the object of the action unambiguously contextualised as if part of a police report.

According to Furduescu (2017, p. 171), the Meta Model is considered the most important tool in the NLP repertoire. Originally designed for therapists as a set of tools that question, or in NLP terms "challenge", the client's limited world it is now used to offer more clarity and choice in thinking about solutions to problems in a wide variety of areas, such as business (Campbell, 2021), education (Menon & Nagalakshmi, 2020), interview design (Knight, 2012), intercultural communication (Katan & Trickey, 1996; Katan, 1999) and translation (Katan &

4 'well-formed' is taken from Chomsky but while Chomsky was concerned with the underlying syntactic regularities of sentences, NLP focusses on 'well-formed' as representing the fullest disambiguation of the language so that one person's model of the world is as clearly represented to others as possible.

Taibi, 2021; Katan forthcomimg). Here, the aim will be to separate those rules and beliefs about behaviour that are culture-bound from those which are more objectively true about the world.

As already hinted, there are three main modelling processes that sever links with the external world: generalisation, deletion and distortion. "Generalisation" (Bandler & Grinder, 1975, p. 14) is "the process by which elements or pieces of a person's model become detached from their original experience and come to represent the entire category of which the experience is an example". Hence, the apparent "rudeness" of one person can easily become a frozen stereotype applied to all people from that culture.

Secondly, "Deletion" (*ibid*: 15) is a "process by which we selectively pay attention to certain dimensions of our experience and exclude others". In cross-cultural communication our perception of "the other" language and behaviour is necessarily limited to our own competence. So, if we are not native or "insiders" we will necessarily not perceive, or rather delete, part of the observable world.

Thirdly, "distortion" is a "process which allows us to make shifts in our experience of sensory data" (Bandler & Grinder, 1975, p. 16). Hence, distortion allows us to focus our full attention on what we can make sense of, without the clutter of other and less meaningful aspects of reality. This filter is, in fact, at the heart of attribution: culture-2 behaviour is "shifted" inside the viewer's/listener's model, distorted into a culture-1 type behaviour and then, logically, treated to an internal response.

Positive Intent

A third tenet of NLP is that all animate behaviour is trying to achieve something, and will therefore be congruent within its own logical system: "at some level all behavior is (or at one time was) 'positively intended' " (Dilts, n.d.). The idea of a logical system, originally termed 'Logical Levels' and later neurological levels, was introduced by Robert Dilts (1990; see also Katan & Taibi, 2021, pp. 61–99). The idea came originally from theories of logical typing by Bertrand Russell and Gregory Bateson (see Katan & Taibi, 2021, pp. 61–62). The theory parallels the Iceberg theory (ibid: 67) in that behaviour is visible while the motives are hidden. In all cases though, the hidden motives will be based on values that are, in themselves, positive.

Usually, in the cognitive sciences, intention is classified not only as positive but also as neutral or negative. NLP, however, takes its cue from two family therapists. First, Carl Rogers (1959), who introduced the concept of "unconditional positive regard" (UPR), which entails the need to distinguish the person from their behaviour. The person is to be unconditionally respected or valued as someone who is attempting to construct something, however ineffective or destructive the actual behaviour is. Luthman (1974) continues in the same vein, stating that however dysfunctional the behaviour may appear, the intent is positive. So, while a behavioural outcome may well be that of destruction such as any war or terrorist attack, behind the destruction there will always be a "fighter for the cause".

More useful, however, as a principle for intercultural communication is the 80–20 principle – which tempers the "unconditional" in the UPR, and makes the activity that follows more acceptable for those whose views are (for the moment) unshakable. The principle was discovered in 1896 by economist Vilfredo Pareto. He calculated that 80 % of the land in 13th-century England was in the hands of 20 % of the people. He then went on to hypothesise that this 80-20 division was, in fact, a general principle. He discovered, among other things, that 80 % of his garden-pea production was generated by only 20 % of his plants. Business books now abound with this "rule" in terms of time management and problem solving. Simons et al. (1993) also sustain that in cross-cultural encounters, in 80 % of the cases the culture-2 behaviour that seems incongruent or even rude is not – when framed in the appropriate context. This tempering of the UPR avoids the controversy surrounding cultural relativity, where interculturalists are often accused of accepting all behaviour, however inappropriate or even destructive. The reason for this tempering is simply to reassure the participants that they will be allowed to react negatively – and that the exercise is not one of whitewashing or of total acceptance of cultural difference.

We should also add that we are not concerned here with armed conflict or with individual idiosyncratic, or clearly dysfunctional behaviour, but with those behaviours that give rise to culture shock. The important point here is that generally individuals behave to achieve something that they value, and that much of the behaviour that is noticed by cultural others rests on a different set of culturally shared values. Also, the Reattribution Generator, in itself, is a diagnostic tool, and does not entail condonation of behaviour.

Disassociation

To make an informed decision regarding the other, individuals must be able to disassociate from the anchoring context of one culture, and be able to construct another context of culture from which to evaluate and respond. Disassociation, through change in perceptual position, will always lower the emotional involvement and anxiety – and automatically reduces the "fight or flight" response to perceived threat. In this position, an individual is able to adopt another frame of reference, or rather a meta-position, from which s/he is able to perceive, interpret and evaluate both the model of the world of "self" and that of the "other". In Cognitive Science, this is called "recursive thinking", and has been defined as the uniquely human ability to conceive of our own minds and the minds of others (Corballis, 2011).

This ability to disassociate, to move above one particular mindset, is what Michael Hall (1995, pp. 12–13) calls a meta-state, adding that it "creates the ability to transcend one's immediate time, space, being, values, experiences, etc. and to bring other awareness to bear upon things". According to NLP World (2021), "the ability to be dissociated is useful for … preventing emotional reactions to triggers, controlling nerves, gaining a more objective view of a situation and many more situations". NLP then distinguishes 3 perceptual positions. That of associating with one's own mind (1st postion), associating with an other's (2nd position) and then disassociating from both (3rd position) (O'Connor, 2001, pp. 33–34; see also Katan, 1999, 2001, 2002; Katan & Taibi, 2021, pp. 361–362)

With disassociation comes the final NLP concept used here: "reframing", which can be divided into 3 aspects: "as if", "content reframing" and "context reframing". The *as if* frame is explained in more detail in most NLP books (e.g. O'Connor, 2001, p. 224). The concept is taken from Vainger's volume *The Philosophy of "As If"* (1924, pp. 159–160), which purports that we cannot actually know the world, but we do act is if we do, so we behave "as if" the world matches our models. NLP uses the *as if* to encourage a person to explore possibilities and ideas internally. The specific effect sought is to allow "a person's limiting beliefs to be temporarily set aside for the purpose of exploring alternate possibilities, without having to threaten or challenge their existing conceptual world-view in the process". (Wikia, n.d.).

Specifically we can distinguish between 2 forms of *as if* by reframing the content or the context (e.g. O'Connor, 2001, p. 232). With content (or meaning) reframing, the behaviour is interpreted *as if* the outcome were positive. This helps in separating the experience perceived from instant interpretation and the automatic evaluation, laying the path for an analysis of how the FAE works in practice. The context reframe retains the behaviour but encourages participants to observe from a wider perspective. So, the focus here is on in what ambits could this (revolting / unpolite) behaviour actually be useful.

These techniques are used in the popular NLP "Six-step reframe", first described in detail by Bandler and Grinder (1979, pp. 138–151). Since then, it has become a standard NLP technique to find positive intentions behind what appears to be undesirable behaviour – which clearly matches most culture shock situations. Below, I describe the "Reattribution Generator", an adaptation of the "Six-step reframe" specifically designed for culture shock trainings.

The Practice

The 6 Stage Reattribution Generator

The Reattribution Generator helps individuals reassess their instinctive attribution through separating the process of perception and evaluation, thus disassociating from their default emotive (and negative) response. Once the individual is in this position, s/he is more likely to be able to create alternative behaviour-value connections with the help of specific guided questions.

There are 6 basic guided stages to go through, and the Generator like any other system also has a regulatory feedback loop, which tests the effectiveness of the process. Though the Generator can be used for any culture-shock situation, in the first instance, individuals will need to be guided by a trainer as part of a cross-cultural training programme or specifically on re-entry after a period abroad. With time and further cognitive experience the process can be internalised, and will help individuals in facilitating their own cross-cultural encounters.

Pre Stage 1: The Culture Shock

For the exercise, trainers will need one or more culture-shock examples to work with. The trainer may use, for example, participant experience of a sojourn abroad, stereotypical "truths" about others or culture shock simulations in the training room. During the description of this activity here, I will use refer to training room comments following culture-shock reactions to an extract from a BBC (1989) film and verbatim replies to the Reattribution Generator questions. In the film is a "typical" English birthday party scene. In brief, the scene shows a number of 30-something professional couples in a private room of a Chinese restaurant. Birthday presents are given over dinner and at the end there is a birthday cake and "Happy Birthday" is sung. The camera focuses on the bill and the guests are seen discussing the bill and the amount to pay. The participants are asked to imagine that they too are sitting round the table at the event. I have shown this extract to Italian schools, universities, and to business trainees for over 30 years, and surprisingly, the fly-on-the-wall emotional reactions have not changed. While comments about the outmoded hairstyles of the characters on film have become more apparent, the "Birthday Boy" has remained "mean" and the English are still (in 2021) "cold fish", meaning calculating machines lacking human warmth and personal feelings. For Italians, and for many other cultures, the only person who should be paying is the person celebrating the birthday. We now turn to the activity itself.

Bad (Negative) Behaviour of Other(s) Noted Verbatim

Participants are asked to discuss their culture shocks or to take part in a cross-cultural incidant as above, and report what they saw and felt. The trainer asks: "what did you see exactly?" or "what happened exactly". A flip chart or screen is then covered with verbatim reports of their comments. It is important that the *exact words* are recorded. To give an example, some of the most useful statements written on the flip chart (regarding the film extract) related to the fact that some things didn't happen ("The birthday boy didn't pay"), perceived obligations ("The guests had to pay for the dinner"), or value judgements ("It wasn't a real birthday party" or, as reported above, "the English are all cold fish and stingy"). Along with this, a set of "How did you feel" and (in the film extract case) "What do you think about the English?" questions should be asked. Here, participants should feel free to vent their own shocks, levels of feeling and emotional response. It is extremely useful to keep the original teacher-led questions and (where possible) responses visibly displayed without necessarily referring to them during this feedback stage.

Non Judgemental Description of Behaviour

This stage entails a good understanding of the Meta Model. The objective will be to challenge the subjective (ill-formed) responses, on the flip chart into more objective (well-formed responses) and to allow the participants to see how changing the use of language can actually begin to change perception, interpretation and evaluation. The idea of well-formedness can be initiated using the Meta Model challenges for syntactic well formedness, beginning with a demonstration how ill-formed "Tell me what you see" is. The task here is for participants to become adept at recognising these possible communication dragons (Katan & Trickey, 1996). Challenges to the "ill-formed" question may be as follows:

Surface language	Missing details:
Tell me	How exactly? *informally? in English?*
	Where exactly? *here?*
	When exactly? *immediately, on reflection, next week?*

(what)	
you	Who exactly? *me singular, us plural?*
see	Where exactly? *anywhere on the screen, in this room, in my mind's eye?*
	How exactly? *A summary? A blow by blow of every frame? What I noticed that was significant? Focussing on…. the people? the conversation? the quality of the acting? the director's gaze? the camera work?*

Returning to the Birthday Boy responses, the first thing that is often to be commented on is that the responses tend to related only to what was significant or made an impact, rather than an actual description of what was seen. For example, no participant has ever mentioned that the new boyfriend at the birthday dinner, a total outsider, is seen to order a beer while all the rest were drinking wine from the visible bottles on the table, nor did the participants mention that there was a disapproving look from another of the guests. Logically, though, if the film director is guiding our gaze to this series of events it does have significance within the story. If nothing else, it tells us something about the character's wilful individualism and outsider status.

The principal areas of Meta Model violation found with regard to the Birthday Party sequence were in terms of, modal operators of necessity, presuppositions with non-specified nouns and verbs, (value) judgements s and simple deletions.

Modal operators of necessity are very useful to indicate the limits of a model of the world. for example, participants generally noted "The guests have to pay". The use of "have to" suggests that the guests were forced to pay. In reality, the modal used tells us about the speaker's rules regarding the world than the other's world. A more descriptive observation would be "The guests paid". Clearly, this is equally ill-formed. We have not made the context explicit (what they pay for, how they pay, who to, when, and so on). The resulting well-formed sentence will consequently be on the lines of: "The guests divide the bill equally in the restaurant after the dinner (for the birthday boy)".

We still have a Meta Model violation, a presupposition that the people seen are indeed "guests". There is no overt cue in the extract to suggest that the birthday boy has invited these people (and indeed he probably hadn't). This particular presupposition limits the participants' responses to the norms concerning "a guest" and their socially sanctioned rights and duties at a "birthday party". In Italy, and in many other countries of the world, "guests" do not pay. So, the extract watched can only lead to culture shock and negative attribution. So, the participants will be encouraged to reformulate "guest" into an objective description of reality, avoiding as far as possible any term that represents a potentially culture-bound interpretation. A more objective representation of the reality here would be to talk of "people" or "participants".

It will also be necessary at this stage 1 to challenge the value judgements. This exercise will help move attention linguistically from attribution of traits ("S/he is rude/untrustworthy …", "The English are cold fish") to attribution of behaviour ("She didn't look at me" or "he never offered to help"). Often, as in these examples, when not attributing traits, participants will focus on what they expected to see but was missing. Reference, instead must be made to what they actually did see (e.g. "she looked at the others" or "she continued reading her book").

The participants then look at the list again and note to what extent their "Tell me what you see" responses could be counted as either positive or negative. Following the Attribution theory, almost all the responses to a culture-shock incident will be negative evaluations, even a number of the "descriptions". For example, participants describing the birthday cake noted that it had light-blue decorations. On questioning, it became clear that the decoration would have been appropriate for a children's party, but not for adults. The mind's ability to focus on the inappropriate rather than on objective description is a point which any group involved in intercultural encounters could usefully consider.

Having, at the end of stage one purged the language of value judgements, modals of possibility and necessity, and unspecified language in general, we should have a relatively objective account of the behaviour seen, and we can move on to Stage 2.

Stage 2: Own Culture Appropriate Behaviour

Stage 2 should be a relatively quick and automatic stage. Participants are asked to clearly state what the appropriate behaviour should have been. In this case: "The Birthday Boy should pay". We instantly notice the modal of necessity signalling the socio-cultural rules, which are (so far) regarded as normal.

Stage 3: Effect/Meaning (in Your Culture) When Not Respected

It is here that the emotional responses are framed, which will help the participants focus on their model of the world, which highlights the (culture-bound) response to the behaviour rather than the behaviour itself. For example: "You will be seen/thought of as *cold fish, stingy, hypocritical*".

Stage 4: Values behind Preferred Behaviour

It will be more difficult to ask participants to analyse why they prefer their behaviour. The question may not make sense, as it automatically obliges them to step out of their state and move into a meta-state to comment on their logical model of the world. Replies will tend to be in terms of "*because that's normal /right/a tradition/...*" If this is the case, it may also be useful to ask: "What positive intentions can makes this behaviour normal/right/..?", or, "What does this preferred behaviour show?" The answers now should be in terms of positive values such as "*generosity*", "*warmth*", "*friendship*" and so on.

Stage 5: As If ... Possible Positive Reasons for Culture-2 Behaviour

This stage mirrors Bennett's (1993, p. 45) "major conceptual shift" from ethnocentric to ethnorelative thinking. This is the stage of partial disassociation from culture-1 response and the beginnings of a first enquiry into possible culture-2 realities. Participants are asked to wonder, and to imagine *as if* there were a world where culture-1 behaviour would be perceived as positive. Here it is useful to repeat the 80/20 principle, and suggest that that there might just be in a weird but certainly not wonderful world in which this negatively attributed behaviour just might make sense. The participants will need to be assured that they are not being asked to approve or like this imagined world, but to consider "What positive intention could make that behaviour normal/good/right/a useful tradition for them?" Positive values for the Birthday sketch were in terms of "equality" and "charity, in the sense that the participants might club together to help out the Birthday Boy if he himself cannot pay." If the *as if* produces very little then more specific content/context reframing may be tried, as below.

Optional 5a. Content Reframing

Using the guided question below, participants can be encouraged to literally see the Culture shock in a different light. The language patterns simply need to be filled out with appropriately positive alternatives:

> It is good to know that/Isn't it interesting/useful for *Culture-2* that they can [*behaviour*]. For them it could mean [*outcome*]

An example from the Birthday extract is as follows:

> "It's interesting to know that the *English pay for the birthday boy*. For them it could mean that *no one is burdened with a huge payment*".

Optional 5b. Context Reframing

This reframing requires a search for imagined alternative contexts where, for example, dividing the bill equally among participants is not inherently "bad". The intent is to limit the negatively attribution of "dividing the bill" to one particular context. The question for the trainer to ask in all cases is "In what context could this behaviour be positively valued?" The Italian participants readily agreed, for example, that if the scene were that of a group of equally penniless participants rather than a group of moneyed professionals, it would be normal for the "guests" to share the bill. This behaviour can also be seen as positive in many other contexts such as more financially onerous group holidays (where maybe one member of the group is the guide and would not be expected to pay); entertaining foreign visitors in a business context, or alternatively surprise events in honour of a particular person.

Stage 6: Unsatisfied Values?

This stage focuses on the missing values themselves. Though the values mentioned in Stage 4 may not be visible in the behaviour witnessed, they may very possibly be found elsewhere in culture-2. The object at this stage is twofold. The guided questions, in the first place, help the participants to disassociate from their automatic behaviour-value evaluation; and secondly, they implicitly encourage the idea that all cultures not only have access to all values, but that all values will also be present somewhere in the culture (Kluckhohn & Strodtbeck, 1961). What makes a culture different is the way values are hierarchically clustered, or, as Kluckhohn puts it, which values are dominant and which are recessive. Some less-preferred or recessive values may only be visible in culture-2 in other contexts. In the Birthday Party extract, participants only need to switch their attention away from the birthday boy's "ungenerous" behaviour to note that the other participants (guests) are clearly satisfying the missing value through their "generosity" in paying for the birthday boy. They may also note that "tradition" is also valued in this particular sequence, through the cake, candles and so on.

Ecological Check

Having gone through the 6 stages, the participants' present level of disassociation can be ascertained through checking the emotional pulse. The same basic questions as asked in Stage 1 can be repeated: "What did you see" and "How do you feel now?" Alternatively, their original verbatim comments about culture-1 behaviour can be repeated back to the participants for their reaction. The extent to which the participants are able to disown these comments will indicate the success of this exercise. If there is no discernable change of opinion then the participants should be asked to repeat from Stage 1 in the hope of rectifying overlooked Meta Model violations, of creating more useful alternative models of meaning or of classifying the behaviour as part of that 20 % of bad behaviour present across all cultures.

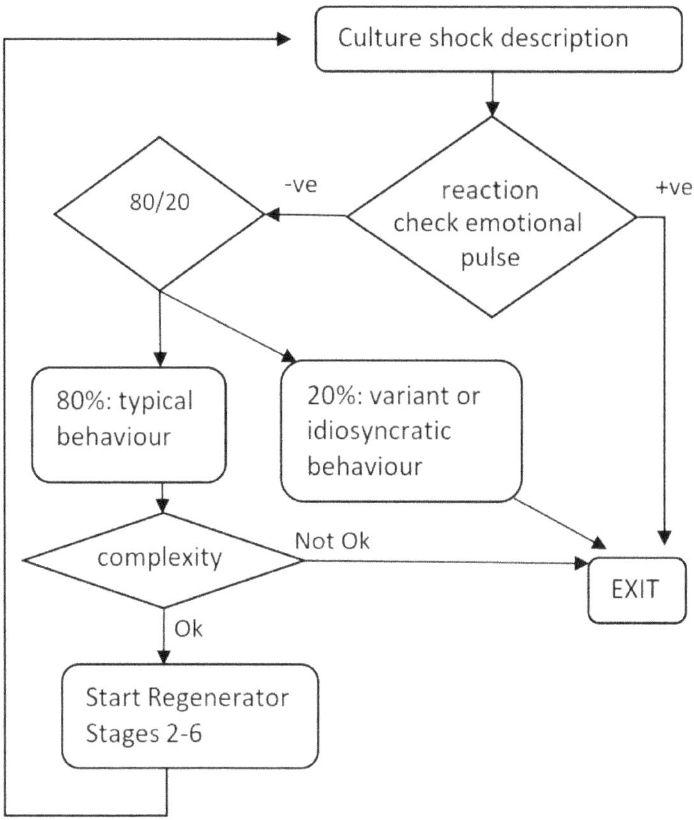

If no changes in participant response can be made, and the above checks have been made, then the particular behaviour picked may be considered too challenging or complex for this level of intercultural sensitivity (Bennett, 1993). The group will need the assurance of more similarities across cultures before they are ready to manage these particular differences.

Conclusion

In conclusion, the fact that a group of participants can change their beliefs about perceived behaviour, and can isolate their perception from interpretation and evaluation, does not automatically entail a change of belief about the people in general. The shift that is looked for here is the reduction or total avoidance of the automatic attribution, or "fundamental attribution error" regarding culture-bound behaviour. In doing so, participants became able to think recursively outside of their normal model of the world and not only imagine other models but begin to respect them as logical within those worlds. So, the object of the exercise is not to suggest that the typically English birthday party is, in fact, a sign that the English are "warm, generous and passionate" but rather that there are alternative models of meaning, and are worth enquiring into before culture-bound evaluation becomes the automatic response.

References

Bandler, R., & Grindler, J. (1975). *The Structure of Magic I.* Palo Alto, CA: Science and Behavior Books.

Bandler, R., & Grinder, J. (1979). *Frogs Into Princes.* Moab, UT: Real People Press.

Bennett, M. J. (1993). Towards Ethnorelativism: A Developmental Model of Intercultural Sensitivity. In R. M. Paige (Ed.), *Education for the Intercultural Experience* (pp. 21–72). Maine: Intercultural Press Yarmouth.

Brook, A. (2004). Kant, Cognitive Science and Contemporary Neo-Kantianism. *Journal of Consciousness Studies, 11*(10–11) (pp. 1–25).

Campbell, F. (2021). Advanced Communication Skills for Business Leaders and Coaches. *The Professional Growth Company.* Retrieved 08/10/2021, from: https://www.nlpbusinesscircle.com/how-to-use-the-nlp-meta-model-in-business.

Corballis, M. C. (2011). *The Recursive Mind: The Origins of Human Language, Thought, and Civilization.* Princeton, NJ: Princeton University Press.

Dilts, R. (n.d.). Positive Intention – Bringing Light into the Darkness: The Principle of Positive Intention. In R. Dilts (Ed.), *NLP University International.* Retrieved 06/10/2021, from: http://www.nlpu.com/Articles/article2.htm.

Dilts, R. (1990). *Changing Belief Systems with NLP.* Cupertino CA: Meta Publications.

Dilts, R., Grinder, J., Bandler, R., Cemeron-Banler, L., & DeLozier, J. (1980). *Neuro-linguistic Programming, Vol. I.* Cupertino, CA: Meta Publications.

Furduescu, B.-A. (2017). Using the 3M Method for the Optimization of the Managerial Act. In M. Sampaio de Alencar (Ed.), *Communication Management and Information Technology* (pp. 171–178). London: CRC/Balkema

Gudykunst, W. (1995). Anxiety/Uncertainty Management (AUM) Theory: Current Status. In R. L. Wiseman (Ed.), *Intercultural Communication Theory* (pp. 8–58). Thousand Oaks, CA: Sage.

Gudykunst, W. B. (2004). *Bridging Differences: Effective Intergroup Communication* (4th ed.). Thousand Oaks, CA: Sage.

Hall, E. T. (1959/1990). *The Silent Language*. New York, NY: Anchor Books, Doubleday.

Hall, M. (1995). *Meta-States: A Domain of Logical Levels*. Grand junction, CO: Empowerment Technologies.

Heider, F. (1958). *The Psychology of Interpersonal Relations*. New York, NY: John Wiley & Sons.

Heider, F., & Simmel, M. (1944). An Experimental Study of Apparent Behavior. *The American Journal of Psychology*, *57*, 243–259.

Kane, G. (2017). *Accelerating Sustainability Using the 80/20 Rule*. Oxford: Routledge.

Katan, D., & M. Taibi. (2021). *Translating Cultures: An Introduction for Translators, Interpreters and Mediators* (3rd ed). Oxford: Routledge.

Katan, D., & Trickey, D. (1996). Negotiating Meaning across Cultures: Using the Meta Model in NLP as an International Business Communication Tool. In D. Evans (Ed.), *Communicative Ability and Cultural Awareness: A Key to International Corporate Success*. VIII International ENCoDe Conference (pp. 114–119). Nice: Groupe EDHEC.

Katan, D. (2002). Mediating the Point of Refraction and Playing with the Perlocutionary Effect: A Translator's Choice?. Critical Studies, Vol. 20. In S. Herbrechter, (Ed.), *Cultural Studies, Interdisciplinarity and Translation* (pp. 177–195). Amsterdam: Ridolphi.

Katan, D. (2001). When Difference Is Not Dangerous: Modelling Intercultural Competence for Business. *Textus XIV*, 2 (Cortese, G. & D. Hymes, Ed.), 287–306.

Katan, D. (1999). What Is It That's Going on Here?: Mediating Cultural Frames in Translation. In S. Bassnett, R. M Bolletteri Bosinelli, & M. Ulrych (Eds.), *Textus* XII*: Translation Studies Revisited, Towards Ethnorelativism: A Developmental Model of Intercultural Sensitivity* (No. 2, pp. 409–426). Genova: Tilgher.

Kluckhohn, F. R., & Strodtbeck, F. L. (1961). *Variations in Value Orientations*. Evanston, IL: Peterson.

Knight, J. (2012). Deletion, distortion and data collection: The application of the neuro-linguistic programming (NLP) meta-model in qualitative interviews. *Australasian Journal of Market & Social Research*, 20(1), 15–21.

Langer, E. J., & Minhea, M. (2000). The Construct of Mindfulness. *Journal of Social Issues*. Vol. *56*(1), 1–9.

Korzybski, A. (1958). *Science and Sanity* (4th ed.). Englewood, NJ: The International Non-Aristotelian Library Publishing Company.

Lalljee, M. (1987). Attribution Theory and Intercultural Communication. In K. Knapp, W. Enninger, & A. Knapp- Potthoff (Eds.), *Analyzing Intercultural Communication* (pp. 37–49). Berlin: Mouton de Gruyter.

Luthman, S. (1974). *The Dynamic Family*. Palo Alto, CA: Science & Behavior Books.

Menon, S., & Nagalakshmi, M. (2020). Using NLP to Eliminate Negative Self-Belief of Students during English Language Acquisition. *Journal of Critical Reviews, 7*(18), 3297–3305.

NLP World. (2021). *Glossary*. Retrieved 19/10/2021, from: https://www.nlpworld.co.uk/nlp-glossary/d/dissociated/.

O'Connor, J. (2001). *The NLP Workbook: The Practical Guide to Achieving the Results You Want*. London: Thorsons.

Paige, R. M., & Martin, J. N. (1996). Ethics in Intercultural Training. In D. Landis, & R. S. Bhagat (Eds.), *Handbook of Intercultural Training* (2nd ed., pp. 35–60). Thousand Oaks, CA: Sage.

Paige, M. R. (1993). On the Nature of Intercultural Experiences and Intercultural Education. In M. R. Paige (Ed.), *Education for the Intercultural Experience* (pp. 1–21). Yarmouth, ME: Intercultural Press.

Rogers, C. (1959). A Theory of Therapy, Personality, and Interpersonal Relationships, as Developed in the Client-Centred Framework. In S. Koch (Ed.), *Psychology: A Study of a Science. Formulations of the Person and the Social* Context (Vol. 3, pp. 184–256). New York, NY: McGraw-Hill.

Ross, L. (1977). The Intuitive Psychologist and His Shortcomings: Distortions in the Attribution Process. In L. Berkowitz (Ed.), *Advances in Experimental Social Psychology* (pp. 173–220). New York, NY: Academic Press.

Selby, H. (1975). Semantics and Causality in the Study of Deviance. In M. Sanches & B. G. Blount (Eds.). *Sociocultural Dimensions of Language Use* (pp. 11–24). London: Academic Press Inc.

Simons, G. F., Vazques, C., & Harris, P. (1993). *Empowering the Diverse Workforce*. Houston, Texas: Gulf Publishing.

Vaihanger, H. (1924). *The Philosophy of 'as if'*. London: Routledge, Kegan and Paul.

Wikia. (n.d.). As-If. *Psychology Wiki*. Retrieved 14/10/2021, from: https://psychology.wikia.org/wiki/As-if_(NLP).

Film

BBC. (1989). *One Way Out*, director Robert Young, Screen One 10 September.

A Six Step Re-Attribution Strategy

This is a useful strategy to help to reduce negative attribution and reduce potential culture shock.

Two presuppositions will need to be accepted before this strategy can be effective. First there will need to be a belief in the possibility that it is the context which defines appropriate behaviour rather than personal beliefs. Second, we need to take note of the 80/20 rule.

According to the economist Alfredo Pareto, 80 % of the wealth of Italy was in the hands of 20 % of the people. This become known as the 80/20 principle and has been since used in many different contexts. Business consultants, Simons et al. (1993), point out that in cross-cultural encounters, in 80 % of the cases the behaviour that seems incongruent or even rude probably is not – when framed in the appropriate environment. There will, therefore, be a positive reason for the strange, unusual, or even unbelievable behaviour. Logically, too, like in one's own culture there will be a minority of people (the 20 %) whose behaviour will be deemed offensive by the rest of their culture.

The most important strategy to learn in the Re-Attribution strategy is that of disassociation. "to develop a third perspective", which is neither culture one nor culture two. Only by stepping outside the usual interpretative frame can behaviour be objectively evaluated.

The Six Step Reattribution Strategy

1. (Bad, negative) behaviour of other(s) noted verbatim

For this activity, any strange behaviour should be noted exactly as reported along with all avaluative comments and resulting feelings

2. **Non-judgmental description of behaviour.**
   The strange behaviour is now purged of any judgmental language, and should be simply a technical statement of what was seen or heard. All metamodel violations are (informally) checked
3. **Own culture appropriate behaviour, and effect/meaning when not respected**
   What should be the appropriate behaviour, and what is the effect or the meaning when someone does not respect that behaviour.
4. **Values behind culture-1 behaviour**
   We now need to consider own beliefs and values underlying own culturally acceptable behaviour in this context: Why do we behave in this way, in what way is it appropriate? Note particularly those values which are felt to be missing in the other culture. A list of values should be written down, ready for step five.
5. **Possible positive reasons (values) for the strange behaviour**.
   It is very important here that these reasons are couched in the positive, both grammatically and semantically. This will give you the positive internal response to their external behaviour. Also, check how this behaviour could fit in to a wider context, and therefore be "logical" within that culture.
6. **Culture-1 values satisfied by culture-2 behaviour**
   At this point we need to investigate creative alternatives. Look for any other behaviour (either during the same event or not) in the other culture which could satisfy the values listed under step three.

Check: Culture-2 Behaviour Re-Viewed

The "strange" behaviour is looked at once more, and differences in perception are noted. If the perception is still negative, the process is repeated from step 2, and a check is made that the behaviour is not totally idiosyncratic, or the 20 % of the 80/20 rule.

This exercise makes use of the natural ability to frame a behaviour to give it meaning. Another useful reframing exercise is to extend Step 4, and concentrate on the possible outcome, using the following:

> Isn't it interesting/useful/nice for the [*pick culture of choice*] that they can [*behaviour*]. For them it can mean [*positive outcome*]

Alternatively we can reframe the context. In this case we accept that all behaviour can be positive or useful in some context, and so the task is to reframe the context so that the behaviour now elicits a positive response.

This behaviour [*behaviour*] is actually useful/necessary in [*pick alternative contexts*]

In all cases we are opening up options, and enlarging the boundaries of our map of the world. Conscious reattribution is an essential task for anyone working cross-culturally. In fact, one of the most important steps in cross-cultural awareness, as Kramsch (1993, *passim*) amongst others suggests, is to be aware of one's own map of the world, and to what extent it can serve to orient appropriately abroad.

Example: The Guests at the Birthday Party Had to Pay

1. The bill was divided equally among the participants.
2. In Italy… the birthday boy should pay. If not, the effect is embarrassment, and the meaning is: stingy…
3. The reason is: generosity, "that's part of the birthday party", tradition
4. In Britain, the event could be interpreted as meaning equality or another present for the birthday boy. In a wider context, by the end of the year everyone will have paid for one entire birthday: just like the Italian system
5. generosity (the guests); tradition: the cake, "Happy Birthday" song.

Introduction to The Belt and Road Initiative (BRI): An Intercultural Communication Perspective

By Guo-Ming Chen

The following text examines the Belt and Road Initiative (BRI) of the People's Republic of China from an intercultural perspective. The study focuses on cultural values. It is argued that different cultures have evolved different cultural values and evaluating another culture with the values of another culture is bound to create problems. These problems arise when the cultural values reflect essentially polar opposites as is often the case when Western and Eastern cultural values are compared and contrasted with one another. That is why Chen argues real cultural adaptation occurs in a space located between both polar opposites, a space he calls interculturality. Interculturality refers to the establishment of a flexible cultural identity without rigidly holding one's own cultural values; in other words, it is space that transcends a specific culture. Chen calls this space intercultural communication competence, i.e. effective and appropriate communication. However, misunderstandings and even conflicts are essentially inevitable especially if the cultural differences are considerable. With regard to the BRI, Chen argues that the Chinese government has a negative image which it needs to overcome if the benefits of the BRI are to be communicated effectively. The problem, though, is that the Chinese government employs essentially propaganda methods which essentially seek to promote its ideology. The analysis of the BRI from an intercultural perspective does offer some interesting insights as to what interculturality is and what characteristics are typically associated with intercultural communication competence. Herein lies the strength of this text because it summarizes some important insights of cross-cultural dialogue. That is what makes this analysis so perceptive.

Michael B. Hinner

Guo-Ming Chen is Professor of Communication Studies at the University of Rhode Island. He was the recipient of the 1987 outstanding dissertation award presented by the NCA International and Intercultural Communication Division. Chen is the founding president of the Association for Chinese Communication Studies. He served as Chair of the ECA Intercultural Communication Interest Group and at-large member of the SCA Legislative Council, and the President of International Association for Intercultural Communication Studies (IAICS). He also served as the co-editor of the journal of *China Media Research*.

Chen's primary research interests are in intercultural/organizational/global communication and Chinese communication behaviors. In addition to receiving various awards and honors, Chen has published numerous papers, book chapters, and essays in *Communication Quarterly, Communication Yearbook, Journal of Asian Communication, International Journal of Intercultural Relations, Journal of Cross-Cultural Psychology, Journal of Psychology, China Media Research, Death Studies, Communication Research Reports, Intercultural Communication Studies* and others.

Chen (co)authored and (co)edited more than 40 books and journal special issues, including *Foundations of Intercultural Communication, Communication and Global Society, Dialogue among Diversities, A Study of Intercultural Communication Competence, Chinese Conflict Management and Resolution, Introduction to Intercultural Communication, Theories and Principles of Chinese Communication, Chinese Perspective of Conflict Management and Resolution, Asian Perspective of Culture and communication, Communication Research Methods, and Communication Theories.*

Chen continues to be active in teaching, scholarship and in professional, university, and community services.

Guo-Ming Chen

The Belt and Road Initiative (BRI): An Intercultural Communication Perspective[1]

Introduction

The ideas of "Silk Road Economic Belt" and "21st Century Maritime Silk Road", known as the Belt and Road Initiative (BRI), the One Belt One Road (OBOR), or Yi Dai Yi Lu (一带一路) in Chinese, were first announced by President Xi Jinping (习近平, 2013a, 2013b) in September and October during his visits to Kazakhstan and Indonesia

respectively in 2013. Followed by the move of Premier Li Keqiang to include this global economic cooperation initiative in the Chinese government annual report in March 2015, the BRI officially became a major part of Chinese economic development. Since then, more and more economic explorations and cooperation between the People's Republic of China (PRC) and other countries have been launched and implemented. According to Xi's (习近平, 2017a) report, until 2017 more than 100 countries and regions have joined the BRI. Today, the number has reached 138 (Green Belt and Road Initiative Center, 2020).

The "Belt" refers to the overland trade route, proceeding along the Chinese traditional Silk Road. It goes through the region of central Asia from China to Europe, which is called "the Silk Road Economic Belt". There are two routes for the "Belt". The north route starts from cities such as Xian and Lanzhou in the northwestern area of China, extends to central Asia and Russia, and then reaches Europe. The south route starts from provinces in southwestern China, extends to central and west Asia, and then reaches countries in the areas of Persian Gulf and Mediterranean Sea. The "Road" follows the Chinese traditional Maritime Silk Road, which starts from major seaports, e.g., Guangzhou and Fuzhou, in the southeast China through South China sea, Indian ocean, then reaches Africa and extends to Europe (See Figures 1 and 1a).

1 Permission has been granted to reprint this text which had originally been published in: Chen, G. M. (2021). The Belt and Road initiative (BRI): An intercultural communication perspective. *China Media Research, 17*(1), 1–27.

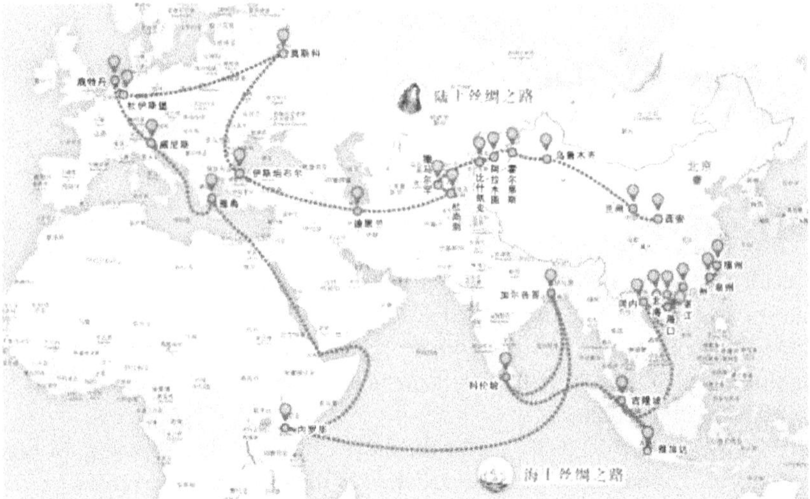

Figure 1: The Belt and Road Initiative Map
Source: (Xiuhanet, 2021).

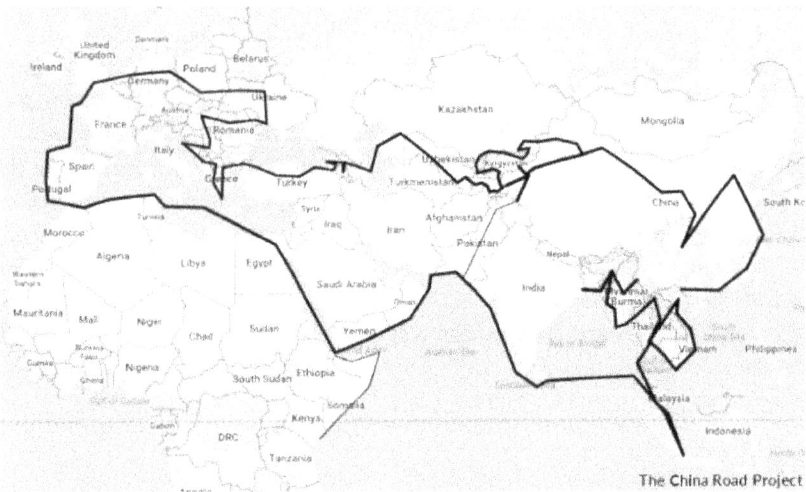

Figure 1a: The Belt and Road Initiative Map
Source: (CSIS, 2021)

As Kwang (邝志良，2018) estimated, in the early 2018 the BRI has covered 65 countries with the area of 5,539 square kilometers (about 41.3 % of the area of the earth). It includes 4.67 billion people (about 66.9 % of the global population), and the overall volume of regional economy has reached 27.4 trillion dollars (about 38.2 % of the global aggregate economic volume). The statistics indicate the widespread influence of the BRI, and it will continue to greatly impact the development of human societies in a global scale. According to the report of the PRC National Development and Reform Commission (NDRC) (中华人民共和国国家发展和改革委员会, 2015), the BRI aims at "embracing the trend towards a multipolar world, economic globalization, cultural diversity and greater IT application, is designed to uphold the global free trade regime and the open world economy in the spirit of open regional cooperation", and it "upholds the Five Principles of Peaceful Coexistence: mutual respect for each other's sovereignty and territorial integrity, mutual nonaggression, mutual noninterference in each other's internal affairs, equality and mutual benefit, and peaceful coexistence". In addition, the BRI is "a way for win-win cooperation that promotes common development and prosperity and a road towards peace and friendship by enhancing mutual understanding and trust, and strengthening all-round exchanges", through which the PRC government "advocates peace and cooperation, openness and inclusiveness, mutual learning and mutual benefit. It promotes practical cooperation in all fields, and works to build a community of shared interests, destiny and responsibility featuring mutual political trust, economic integration and cultural inclusiveness". In a nutshell, the goal of the BRI is to "promote policy coordination, facilities connectivity, unimpeded trade, financial integration and people-to-people bond" through the strengthening of cooperation among the joining countries and regions. It will provide a way for all human societies in the 21st century to reach a state of "mutual respect, win-win cooperation, and mutual learning of different civilizations".

Because the BRI is such a huge global plan, involves so many countries and regions, promotes a great scale of benefits, and impacts various aspects of international communities, it is not surprising to see the increasing reports in media and research in academic community. The BRI by nature is an initiative for economic exchanges, thus, most media reports and academic research as well focus on the economic aspect of the BRI. However, more and more reports and research are found to extend the investigation of the BRI from economic to political, foreign affair, social, and military perspectives (e.g., 何茂春、张冀兵、张雅芃、田斌， 2015；纽约时报中文网，2017；袁新涛，2014； Overholt, 2015; Perdinand, 2016; Swine, 2015). Unfortunately, very few of them examine the BRI from the perspective of civilization (e.g., 每日头条，2017；Winter, 2016), even President Xi (习近平, 2017b) mentioned 15 times of "civilization" in his speech at the 2017 Belt and Road Forum for International Cooperation. In the speech Xi indicated that Fifth, we should build the Belt and Road into a road connecting different civilizations. In pursuing the Belt and Road Initiative, we should ensure that when it comes to different civilizations, exchange will replace estrangement, mutual learning will replace clashes, and coexistence will replace a sense of superiority. This will boost mutual understanding, mutual respect and mutual trust among different countries. Worse, after scrutinizing the existing literature we found that there is even fewer articles dealing with the BRI from the concepts of "culture" and "communication" (e.g., 希文，2017; 张恒军、吴秀峰, 2019)。

It is obvious that from the goal of the BRI mentioned previously, which is to "promote policy coordination, facilities connectivity, unimpeded trade, financial integration and people-to-people bond", we can easily detect all the five sub-goals in the quote concern the basic issues that are directly related to the concepts of "culture" and "communication". For example, "promote policy coordination" refers to the gaining of support for infrastructure plans from counterparts; "facilities connectivity" refers to smoothly going through different construction projects; "unimpeded trade" refers to the removal of barriers for the cross-national investment and economic cooperation; 'financial integration' refers to the negotiation of currency policy and the enhancement of financial cooperation; and "people-to-people bond" refers to the promotion of intercultural exchanges and mutual understanding of people in different countries (HKTDC, 2020). A common word included in all the five sub-goals of the BRI is "tong" (通) in Chinese, which means "going through via interactional or communication process". In other words, all the activities in promoting the goal of the BRI are about interaction or communication in an intercultural context.

The concept of interaction or communication denotes the process of reaching mutual understanding between two objects through the exchange of symbols (Chen & Starosta, 2005). The "two objects" represent two persons or groups from human communication perspective, and their communication can be face-to-face or mediated. Moreover, the process of human communication is dictated by culture, especially the cultural values interactants carry during intercultural interaction. Together, it shows that the success of the BRI is founded on effective and appropriate intercultural communication. However, although a round table panel was held to discuss the important role intercultural communication plays in the BRI in 2018 (时晓莉、张赛， 2018), up to this time we still do not see any published scholarly articles that examine the BRI from the perspective of intercultural communication. In order to improve this problem this paper attempts to study the BRI from five different aspects of intercultural communication.

The Belt and Road Initiative: An Intercultural Communication Perspective

As a relatively young field in the discipline of Communication Studies, the origin of the study of intercultural communication can be traced back to scholars' research in the field of Cultural Anthropology in the late 1950s. The research legacy from Cultural Anthropology was inherited and extended by scholars in Communication Studies in the West (especially in the United States), though the study of intercultural communication may be situated in different academic disciplines (e.g., it is mainly situated in the discipline of Foreign Language in the PRC). Nevertheless, the impact of globalization trend since the early 1990s has demanded students in all academic disciplines to acquire knowledge and skills of intercultural communication in order to become a competitive and productive citizen in global society (陈国明, 2007).

Intercultural communication refers to the exchange of verbal and nonverbal symbols between people from differing cultures (Chen & Starosta, 2005). As previously mentioned, the process of communication can be either face-to-face or mediated. They may include interpersonal communication between two persons and group communication between organizations or between countries. Hence, the content of intercultural communication can cover international communication, interracial communication, interethnic or minority communication, cross-cultural communication, and comparative mass communication (Gudykunst, 1987; Rich, 1974).

As the term "intercultural communication" illustrates, "culture" and "communication" form the key concepts for the study of the subject, and "cultural value" is the foundation of the two key concepts, which is applied to examine other concepts relating to the study of intercultural communication through the representation of linguistic symbols in order to achieve the ultimate goal, i.e., intercultural communication competence, of interaction (Chen & Starosta, 2005). Because the BRI involves different cultures and is a process of intercultural communication, this paper employs the five main concepts of intercultural communication to analyze the BRI: cultural values, intercultural adaptation, intercultural relationship, cultural flow and media, and intercultural communication competence.

Cultural Values

Culture is the foundation of human communication, and its essence is embodied in the values it attributes. Cultural values serve as the guidance of thoughts and behaviors of members of a cultural group. They give the direction for human action and the choice of decision making in the process of communication. From the perspective of international communication, as Jiang and Huang (姜飞、黄廓, 2018) stated, cultural values serve as the foundation for a nation to claim its own identity; they form theory or principle of the nation's international discourse and further construct image of the nation.

Like the concept of culture, cultural value is a highly abstract concept, thus in order to empirically study cultural value scholars have to narrow down the scope of the concept to "cultural value orientation", which allows scholars to mirror it on the basis of direct or indirect observation of human behaviors. Over the years, scholars in different disciplines have tried to establish a variety of models that can be used to study cultural values (e.g., Condon & Yousef, 1975; Hall, 1976; Hofstede, 1984; Kluckhohn & Strodbeck, 1961). Chen and An (2009) further listed the differences of cultural values based on paradigmatic assumptions between East and West (see Figure 2).

Ontology	
East	**West**
Holistic	Atomistic
submerged collectivistic	discrete individualistic

Axiology		**Epistemology**		**Methodology**	
East	**West**	**East**	**West**	**East**	**West**
Harmonious	Confrontational	Inter- connected	Reductionistic	Intuitive	Logical
indirect subtle adaptative consensual agreeable	direct expressive dialectical divisive sermonic	reciprocity we hierarchical associative ascribed	independent I equal free will achieved	subjective nonlinear ambiguous ritual accommo- dative	objective linear analytical justificatory manipulative

Figure 2. A List of Cultural Values between East and West

Source: (Chen & An, 2009, p. 204).

The figure clearly shows the contrast of cultural values between Eastern and Western cultures, and the differences often cause barriers of mutual understanding in the process of intercultural communication, which in turn lead to unnecessary confrontation or conflict.

The study of cultural values has important implication to the BRI. The BRI is a cross- national project on a global scale, in which participants are from different countries and regions with a different set of cultural values. Although the BRI mainly involves in economic activities, there is no question that the awareness of differences of each other's cultural values is the basis of successful interaction and cooperation for achieving the goal of the BRI. It will also directly affect the outcome of intercultural adaptation, the development and maintenance of intercultural relationship, and other aspects of intercultural communication in the process of implementing the BRI. As Chen (2010) argued, knowing the differences of cultural values and effectively applying them to one's behaviors in interaction is the decisive factor for being competent in intercultural communication to achieve communication goals.

A caution is that from the perspective of human communication it is crucial to know that the differences of cultural values between two cultures do not infer an insurmountable gap for reaching mutual understanding. It will be impossible for people or countries to reach mutual respect and trust if the chasm caused by cultural differences cannot be bridged. As Chen (2009a) pointed out, people should avoid dichotomizing the differences of cultural values by treating them as an "either-or" situation. In other words, differences and similarities simultaneously exist among cultures. The key to successful intercultural communication is to "seek common grounds while accepting differences" or "seek harmony but not conformity" (和而不同) that is based on the universal aspect of human cultures (Chen, 2015a).

Chen continued to argue that to tackle the problem of "either-or" or dichotomy thinking on the differences of cultural values, it is necessary to use "as if" or "tend to" when addressing cultural differences. For instance, we should say that Asian people "tend to" be more indirect or act "as if" they are more subtle than Westerners in interaction. The expression leaves a space of commonality for people from differing cultures to reach rapport, rather than demonstrates the stereotype that all Asians "are" indirect, agreeable, or reciprocal, and all Westerners "are" direct, expressive, or independent in the process of communication. Chen (2009a) further criticized that for the convenience of research intercultural communication scholars tend to dichotomize cultural values into two opposite extremes. The dichotomy problem often results in the pessimistic view that misunderstanding is inevitable, or mutual respect and understanding are unreachable in the process of intercultural communication. To understand this first and foremost misperception about cultural values is essential for the success of the BRI.

The bottleneck the BRI faces recently also can be explained from the perspective cultural values, in addition to other factors. A report by Shi (施予, 2018) shows the RWR Advisory Group found that from 2013 to 2018 there are about 234 out of 1,673 infrastructure projects of the BRI encounter resistances or obstacles in participating countries and regions along the Belt and Road. It was found that most of the problems were triggered by the mismanagement embedded in differences of cultural values between the PRC and other BRI participants.

In addition, the negative impact on the BRI due to different cultural values was also reflected in the criticism of James N. Mattis, the former U.S. secretary of defense, who claimed that the PRC is using the BRI to expand its geographical territory as exercised in the Ming Dynasty and demand its participating countries to become the PRC tributary states (皇金, 2018). Nevertheless, from the perspective of the PRC government the BRI is founded on the traditional Chinese cultural value of "world harmony" (shi jie da tong, 世界大同), which aims to promote cultural diversity and destiny on the basis of acceptance, tolerance, and empathy. How to improve the problem of lacking attention on the potential impact of cultural values on the BRI that leads to the unexpected predicament should be a good lesson to learn for the future development of the BRI.

Intercultural Adaptation

Intercultural adaptation or adjustment is the primary concept in the early study of intercultural communication. In the early stage of preaching God's words to the aboriginal groups in remote areas, Catholic priests must face different languages and cultures, thus how to adapt to aboriginal societies in order to accomplish the mission of God becomes the first problem they need to overcome. From that moment, some of the priests with the background of cultural anthropology have started to observe and study the process of intercultural adaptation. Since Oberg (1954) coined the term "culture shock" in 1951 in an academic convention to describe the nature of intercultural adaptation, research on the concept has created a large amount of literature, including theories, principles, and practical information.

Nevertheless, most research of the concept treats the process of intercultural adaptation as a one-way adjustment. By focusing only on how sojourners adapt to the host culture when they enter a new culture, it neglects that intercultural adaptation also involves the way how the host nationals adapt to the newcomers. In other words, intercultural adaptation should be a mutual process in which both sojourners and host nationals make efforts to adapt to each other. Hence, Chen (2013a) proposed a heuristic argument that intercultural adaptation is a process of boundary game. It is a "process in which two cultural beings carrying different cultural values endeavor to reach a state of harmonious equilibrium through equal interaction" (陈国明, 2014, pp. 591–592). Intercultural adaptation is therefore built on the basis of mutual understanding, respect, and acceptance of cultural differences, and moves to develop a holistic, equal space of co-existence. Through this continuing, interdependent, and transforming process of interaction, the boundary line between the two cultures is gradually developing into a new interdependent space, which was labelled the "third culture" (Casmir, 1993) or "interculturality" (Dai, 2012).

Chen (2015b) theorized this new co-existing space as the ideal "global community" of future human society, which is characterized by the landscape of cultural integration. Chen employed the Chinese Taji Yin-Yang Model to further explicate the space (see Figure 3). A and B in the figure symbolize yin and yang and represent two different cultures; and the curve line between A and B indicates the boundary line between the two sides. It is assumed that the boundary line will be gradually expanded from a line into a culturally overlapping area or border, and further to a frontier through constant interpenetrative and transformative interaction between the two cultural beings.

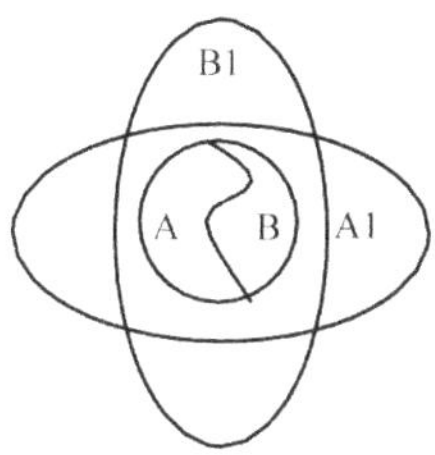

Figure 3: The Taiji Yin-Yang Model of Intercultural Adaptation
Source: (Chen, 2013a, p. 4).

Figures 4 and 5 illustrate the development from the two isolated cultures of non-contact before interaction to an integrated culture after interaction. The diamond area refers to the integrated space, the third space, or the space of interculturality, and to maximize the area becomes the ultimate goal of future global community in the new century (Chen, 2017). Chen (2015b) argued that the larger the area is, the more successful intercultural adaptation is, and it is the guarantee of a peaceful co-existence of human beings in the space. It is worth mentioning that this new interdependent area does not infer the diminishing of one's cultural identity. Instead, it refers to the establishment of a flexible cultural identity without rigidly holding one's own cultural values. As Starosta and Chen (2003) pointed out, only in this space can people temporarily release the clench of one's own culture values through peaceful and productive interaction to reach the goal of intercultural communication.

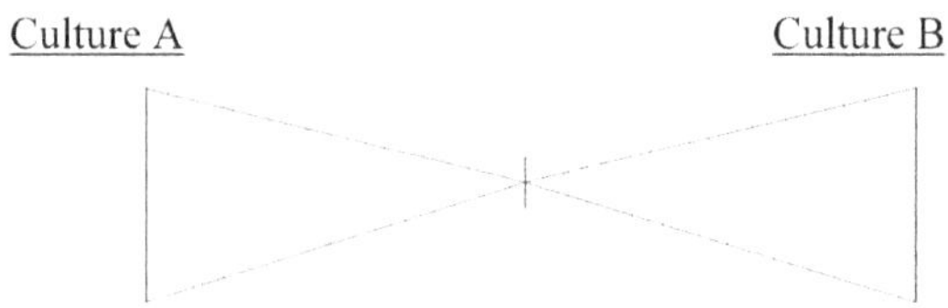

Figure 4: Two Isolated Cultures before Interaction
Source: (Chen, 2017, p. 150）.

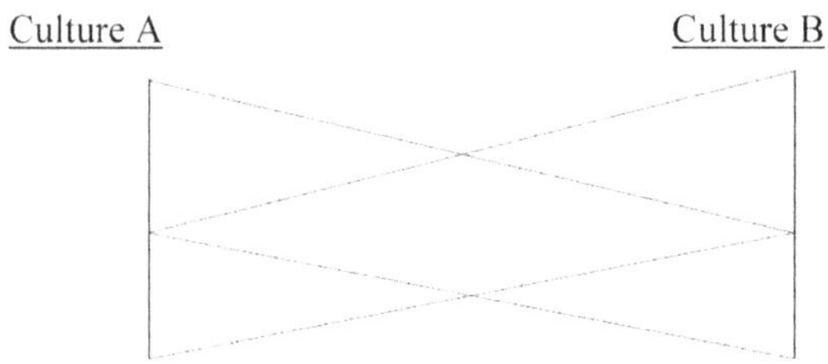

Figure 5: Integration of Two Cultures after Interaction
Source: (Chen, 2017, p. 151）.

A productive boundary game between two cultures based on intercultural communication is dependent on the acquirement of "boundary wisdom" (bian ji zhi hui, 边际 智 慧). Because of cultural differences, the contact or border line area between two cultures often shows a higher degree of ambiguity and uncertainty, which in turns will increase stress and difficulty in the process of interaction. "Boundary wisdom" provides the mechanism for uncertainty reduction and converts the unfamiliar "abnormal" situation into a controllable normal circumstance (陈 国 明， 2009). Chen (2015b) asserted that "boundary wisdom" is equivalent with the concept of "intercultural communication competence." Looking the concept of "boundary wisdom" from the perspective of Chinese history of territory expansion in different dynasties, we can find that the genuine combination of "boundary wisdom" and "expansion consciousness" (tuo bian yi shi, 拓边意 识) witnesses a way of using open-mindedness to face and accept "odd things from foreign lands" (su fang yi wu, 殊方异物).

The launch of the BRI is identical with the boundary game of intercultural adaptation.

When people of two cultures with different cultural values engage in economic activities, as indicated in Figures 3–5, they are playing the intercultural boundary game. If Culture A in the figures represents the PRC, it includes those people such as infrastructure workers, management, negotiation team, media representatives, and other employees in the workforce of the BRI. How to equip this group of frontline employees with an appropriate degree of boundary wisdom will be a measure of the success of their intercultural adaptation and the overall implementation of the BRI. Although there is no scholarly research on intercultural adaptation directly about the BRI, a few studies have been done in the context of the Confucius Institutes (CI). For example, scholars and practitioners have been investigating and developing the effective way of training CI's Chinese management, language teachers, and volunteers to foster the ability of intercultural adaptation in the host culture. In other words, it is to train and educate CI's employees to acquire the abilities of knowing cultural values, respecting cultural differences, and appropriate behavioral skills in the process of intercultural interaction, so that the cultural boundary line can be expanded to a larger area of mutual understanding (陈国明， 2011), and the goal of CI in promoting Chinese culture and language can be obtained (安然、刘程、王丽虹, 2015； 黄湄, 2016; An et al., 2018).

It is hoped that this expanded boundary space embedded in the implementation of the BRI can be maximized and ultimately becomes the co-center of global community. People living in this culturally integrated community will not be marginal persons or strangers anymore (Park, 1928; Rogers, 1999). Instead, they are like members in the same family, co-sharing the responsibility for constructing sustainable intercultural relationships, participating in the process of continuous production, and enjoying shared cultural meanings (Chen, 2015b). It is only in this ideal state of intercultural adaptation, can the BRI be empowered with cultural relativity characterized by cultural interpenetration, integration and transformation, and move beyond the traditional confinement of center vs. periphery, power vs. powerless, authentic vs. inauthentic between different countries (Cohen, 2000; Shils, 1975). In the arenas of politics and foreign affairs Fernandez (2000) developed the theory of "peripheral wisdom" to stipulate the boundary wisdom, which may also serve as a good reference for promoting the BRI.

Intercultural Relationship

People cannot be an isolated island; we need to live in an interrelated network in order to survive as human beings. Similar to this, any groups, including organizations, cultures and countries, as well need to rely on a sound relationship with other groups to sustain and develop their own life and history. The purpose of relationship development is to satisfy the three universal needs of inclusion, control, and affection for human beings (Schutz, 1966). In the process of intercultural communication, it is more difficult to develop relational ties than in an intracultural context due to the impact of different cultural values. It demonstrates that intercultural relationship development is a highly complicated and dynamic process, in which more misunderstanding and conflicts will appear.

As discussed previously, the development of equally co-existing third space is based on the concept of "cultural synergy" (Casmir, 1993). According to Adler (1980), cultural synergy demands mutual understanding of the two interactants, and through the process of mutual adaptation and negotiation to integrate both cultural values for the development of mutual cooperation and achievement of the task goal. Casmir (1993) indicated that the development of intercultural relationship in the third space usually follows the stages from contact, need, dependence, to interdependence; and cultural dialogue is the foundation for smooth movement of the four stages (Dai, 2010). It is undeniable that intercultural relationship in the third space embedded in cultural synergy is an intricated connector, and only the establishment of this connector can activate "the holistic nature of interaction and lead to the emergence of mutual identification, so that a sustainable mutual adaptation can be unlocked to alleviate cultural tension and conflict and transform cultural differences into a dynamic and creative factor" (陈国明, 2014, p. 593).

The description above shows the degree of difficulty for the development of intercultural relationship in the third space. However, it is even more difficult to examine the process from Orbe's (1998) co-cultural theory, which involves the concept of power in the process of intercultural communication. Because the power structure usually is unequal before the interaction of two parties, how to keep the balance and equality of power to release oppress or being oppressed for both sides or the predetermined strong or weak power between two countries through assimilation and acculturation processes is a critical question the BRI needs to answer.

It is inevitable that misunderstanding and conflict often are apparent in the process of intercultural relationship development, because cultural values are embedded in thinking patterns, language expression, and communication behaviors of interactants (单波、肖珺, 2015; Dai & Chen, 2017). For example, during the 2008 Beijing Olympic games the PRC government attempted to utilize success of the event to transform its national image of authoritarianism, backward, air pollution, and political corruption into a positive one. Unfortunately, although the PRC government used "New Beijing, New Olympics" as the propaganda slogan, dubbed the game as "Green Olympics", "Humanistic Olympics", and "Technology Olympics", and has begun to polish the city, build green Olympic stadium, and give international news agencies more open access years before the game, it was still unable to achieve the expectations of changing the national image (Syed, 2010). The reason for this misperception is that a different set of cultural values dictate the way of broadcasting that results in the reporter's focus on issues such as the violation of human right, environmental pollution, and political corruption in China and ignores the agenda set by the PRC government (Dai & Chen, 2014a). A suggestible view is that the misunderstanding was not caused by the intentional discrimination or attack on the PRC, but instead caused by the reporters' Western cultural values of free expression and human right that are reflected in their news reports (Murray, 2011).

It can be seen from the example of the 2008 Beijing Olympics that the development of intercultural relationship in the process of the BRI is closely related to inherent national image of the PRC. As Fan (2002) mentioned, the success of a brand is associated with the national image of the country it belongs to. Therefore, it will be beneficial to the BRI if a highly visible and positive national image of the PRC can be created through the making of an effective agenda setting on the issues of domestic and international policies and the promotion of public relations of the PRC and the BRI (Manheim & Albritton, 1984).

National image is also inseparable with the concept of soft power. Soft power mirrors a national image that is based on the deeds of virtue. The difference between soft power and hard power is that soft power relies on four elements while dealing with one's counterparts: (1) use communication and negotiation to persuade, (2) use the foresight of policy to attract, (3) use a high degree of emotional quotients to understand, and (4) has the ability to develop and promote a productive mutual relationship; while hard power employs organizational or national power to overcome its counterparts (Nye, 2006). Nye (2008) also emphasized that in this highly complicated global society, a more effective way to build a positive national image is to use both soft and hard power interchangeably based on the need of the situation. Nye (2008) used "smart power" to name the integration of soft and hard power, and the concept is closely linked to public diplomacy. He specified that the practice of traditional public policy mainly aims to develop soft power, but in order to succeed in contemporary world it needs to rely on "smart power" through the understanding and practice of trust, self-reflection, and civility rooted in the heart of soft power.

For the implementation of the BRI, it is urgent for the PRC to evaluate its own public diplomacy policy, so that a positive national image and a sound intercultural relationship with participating countries and regions can be established. The concept of "public diplomacy" was first mentioned by Edmund Gullion in 1965. It deals with how a government influences the public attitudes via implementation of a foreign policy by focusing on the cross-national movement of information and ideas. Gullion asserted that public diplomacy has a broad scope, which mainly incudes non-traditional international relations, public opinions formed by a government in other countries, interaction with private interest groups of another country, concern and report of the impact of foreign affairs and policy, interaction with foreign diplomats and news agencies, and handling cross-cultural communication process. Later in the United States more emphasis was laid on the concept of communication for the content of public diplomacy. For instance, Tuch (1990) stipulated that public diplomacy is the process of a government's attempt to create a favorable communication environment in a foreign country, and its major goal is to improve outsiders' misperception or misunderstanding towards the United States. Moreover, the meaning of public diplomacy used in the earlier time is more similar to the concept of "propaganda" (Stephens, 1955). Although the two concepts were separated later, their relationship is still close in recent years, denoting that it needs to go through the process of propaganda in order to achieve the goal of public diplomacy.

Research on the Chinese practice of public diplomacy over the years found that the expected outcome was not reached, even if the PRC invested a huge amount of personnel, materialistic, and financial resources to promote its national image through different channels such as the Xinhua News Agency, the China Daily, and CCTV/CGTN to promote public diplomacy. As Creemers (2015) found, two reasons can be accounted for the less successful outcome of the PRC public diplomacy. First, the PRC public diplomacy is operated by its propaganda agency; and second, the PRC treats soft power as a commercial concept, which is a quantifiable, absolute, and can be used as a defensive and offensive tool.

It is well known that the communication system of the PRC Propaganda Department is a top-down process dictated by the central government. The disadvantage of this kind of operational system is reflected in the lack of taking care of needs of the market and issues concerned by people. The credibility of propaganda is therefore reduced, and public opinions are often neglected. This in turn leads to the failure of soft power because of passive, authoritarian, and inconsistent problems of the propaganda system. As a result, the PRC continues to struggle in peacefully participating in the international communication process for global governance which is founded on the political and social ideas of global citizenship (Zhao, 2013).

In addition, Shambaugh (2007) pointed out that the PRC propaganda operation continues to show improvement, but it still incapable of facing the impact of globalization. The PRC Propaganda Department is a bureaucratic unit controlled by the Communist Party, the information is always scrutinized, and the process of message dissemination is not opaque enough. It becomes highly difficult for this system to face challenges from the rapid development of commerce and technology and the complexity of global public affairs. Obviously, it is hard for the system to establish a positive intercultural relationship in the global society; and sadly, a positive intercultural relationship is an indispensable element for the success of the BRI.

Although the PRC has gained some success in promoting its national image by means of soft cultural diplomacy, it is still a long way to go for a satisfactory result. According to Tian and Deng's (2018) analyses, it is Peng Li Xuan, the PRC first lady, who is constantly promoting the PRC national image though cultural diplomacy. Mitchell (1986) indicated that culture as a significant part of public diplomacy often creates a beneficial eternal environment and boosters the effect of public diplomacy that increases the power of a nation's influence and a positive national image. Tian and Deng (2018) found that through her graceful behaviors rooted in elegant Chinese culture and playing the role of a humanitarianism advocate during President Xi's foreign trips in recent years, Peng Li Xuan effectively assisted her husband to promote public diplomacy and convert the negative national image of the PRC. Nevertheless, although this does not indicate the victory of the PRC foreign policy, the integration of soft cultural diplomacy and traditional public diplomacy may serve as a good example to follow for the strategy of promoting the PRC public diplomacy in the future. This also includes the newly use of social media, such as the digital "panda engagement" through Twitter, for the promotion of the PRC public diplomacy (Huang & Wang, 2020).

It is no doubt that the constant criticisms and predicaments of the BRI urge the PRC government to contemplate a more effective way to improve its national image through public diplomacy by means of building a mutually benefitted relationship with countries and regions along the sides of the BRI. Examples of criticisms include, for example, Page and Shah's (2018) report in the Wall Street Journal. The report describes the setback of the BRI in Pakistan, and the accusation of Western countries that blames the BRI as the resurrection of colonialism in Africa. It also reports that when James N. Mattis visited Africa in March of 2018, he openly criticized that the BRI in Africa is a kind of neo-colonialism that brings about dependency to the PRC, and African countries need to be alert on the future development of the BRI in African Continent. The report from Thu (2018) also referred to the aggressiveness of the PRC military in the South China Sea and other regions has caused counterattack from other countries.

No matter what these incidents arisen from the BRI are true or not, the problem gives the PRC government a great opportunity to reevaluate the project and produce a more sustainable strategy for the implementation of the BRI. In other words, as Zhou (周公瑾, 2018) suggested, it is necessary for the PRC government to have a holistic and objective

analysis on the new challenge the BRI is facing with a calm and clear mind.

Cultural Flow and Media

The rapid development of communication technologies, especially the new media, has pushed the trend of globalization to its highest level. Chen (2012) stated that the emergence of new media not only greatly intensifies relationships among human societies to a highly interrelated and intricate level, but also simultaneously challenges the meaning and practice of intercultural communication in traditional sense. New media is changing the nature and application of cultural values, intercultural adaptation, and intercultural relationship discussed in this paper. Thus, it is vitally important to consider the relationship between media and culture when dealing with human affairs at the present time, including the project like the BRI.

Culture is dynamic; it flows within a country and between nations carried by different media through various channels. Similar to the ancient Chinese Silk Road, through which commodities and merchandises were delivered to foreign lands by means of humans, animals, and ships, culture is moving around with the breakthrough of time and space. Although the pace of movement was slow, after the accumulation over a thousand years a through silk road was formed. The constant and prolonged cultural and economic exchanges on the silk road in turn increase and promote cross-continental cultural activities and the development of human civilization.

After the Industrial Revolution in Europe and the United States in the early 19th century, the expeditious development of communication and transportation technologies completely has transformed cultural, economic, and other activities in human society. The recent development of new media, with its distinctive characteristics of digitalization, convergence, interactivity, hypertextuality and virtuality, has maximized the impact of globalization (Chen & Zhang, 2010; Flew, 2005). The integration of new media and globalization trend has shrunk the world, compressed time and space, linked every corner of the world, and enhanced competitive and cooperative relations among people everywhere (Chen & Starosta, 2000). It has greatly expedited the speed and complexity of cultural flow. According to Zhang (张玉佩, 2017), there are three types of cultural flow, namely, media imperialism, cross-national flow, and diachronic movement, and they are built respectively on the theories of internationalism, Marxist paradigm, theories of representation, theories of reception, and theories of identity (Alleyne, 2009).

The media imperialism model of cultural flow is originated from Marx's economic theory on the exploitation of labor. It dictates that the exploitation of workers by capitalists led to the flood of cultural and commercial products from the West to the third world in the last century. The dominance of Western power over the Third World made the flow of commodities, culture, and media a one-way direction, and tragically further resulted in the colonization and marginalization in politics and economy of the Third World (Straubhaar, 1991). The cross-national flow of culture is based on the theories of cultural relationship and proximity. It claims that geographical proximity provides an opportunity for the easy access of cultural products, but the convenience of cultural contact and commodity exchanges also produces the problem of asymmetrical dependency. Moreover, the proximity or relationship woven by the flow of culture also illustrates the fact that it becomes easy for culture to break through geographical boundary and closely connects two distant countries to initiate mutual influence between them (Straubhaar, 1991). Finally, in addition to the synchronic or horizontal movement among geographical areas, the flow of culture also shows its diachronic or vertical movement within a nation. The diachronic movement of culture not only reflects, but also promotes the transformation of a society and the life change of ethnic groups within the culture (张玉佩, 2017).

The media imperialism model of cultural flow apparently has become obsolete in contemporary interdependent global society. It is inappropriate for any country trying to resurrect the soul of this model, and the chance of success for any attempt of this in modern time is also extremely slim. Unfortunately, the BRI suffers from criticisms embedded in this model from its inception.

The neo-colonialism criticism mentioned by Page and Shah (2018) above is a good example of employing the model of media imperialism of cultural flow by Western countries to criticize the BRI as a kind of cultural and economic colonialism. In addition, unequally historical phrases such as "chaogong" (朝贡) and "kowtou" (叩头) were used to describe the BRI (Schuman, 2018). Targeting this problem, President Xi affirmed in a 2009 overseas Chinese social gathering in Mexico that the PRC never had the intention to export revolution, hunger and poverty, or to torture Chinese people. Unfortunately, Xi's claim seems still unable to relieve the worry and suspicion from the West.

The issue becomes even more entangled when the criticism is related to President Xi's idea on Chinese "Tianxia Guan" (World View, 天下观). It is the intention of the PRC that through the BRI the PRC can propose its traditional worldview of openness, inclusiveness, responsibility, shared destiny, and righteousness to promote the construction of a harmonious world (董明利，2016) and serve as the guideline of the PRC geopolitical relations with other countries (储殷，2018). The problem is that the Tianxia Guan is colored with the character of traditional China-centrism. Even the PRC government argued that the Tianxia Guan is a historical thought based on the concept of harmony, which is completely different from the ideas of cultural imperialism or colonialism, in the eyes of Western countries the Tianxia Guan is equal to concepts like monarchy, colonization, chaogong, or kowtou. Western countries' concern that the execution of the Tianxia Guan will challenge the existing world order by replacing their leading role in constructing the coming global society. Therefore, it is an urgent task for the PRC government to first let Western countries understand, via the channels of propaganda and public diplomacy, that the Tianxia Guan is the pursuit of a mutually beneficial and co-existing human society; and then moves one step further, through the process of negotiation and dialogue, to attract and persuade Western countries and those participating members of the BRI to co-build a cooperative relationship. This is also a way to warrant the success of the PRC "Zou Chu Qu" (go global, 走出去) strategy in the process of reconstructing the new world order.

Intercultural Communication Competence

Intercultural communication competence (ICC) is the ruler for the measurement of successful intercultural interaction. The ultimate goal of intercultural communication education or training is to equip participants with ICC in order to become successful and productive global citizens. The success of the BRI, as a process of intercultural communication, is as well greatly dependent on the degree of ICC participants possess. The significance of the concept has resulted in a large amount of literature from the research of ICC (Dai & Chen, 2014b; Deardorff, 2009). Among the studies of ICC, the triangular model of ICC (Chen, 2010) shown in Figure 6 is the most suitable one applied to the analysis of the BRI.

Figure 6: Triangular Model of Intercultural Communication Competence
Source: (Chen, 2010, p. 180).

The model is comprised of three dimensions: intercultural awareness, intercultural sensitivity, and intercultural adroitness or effectiveness (Chen & Young, 2012). Intercultural awareness refers to the cognitive aspect of ICC. It is the process of understanding one's own and counterpart's cultural values through learning in the process of intercultural communication. The awareness of one's own cultural values and based on the understanding of people as cultural beings to learn about one's counterparts' culture is the key to opening the door of successful intercultural communication. Intercultural sensitivity represents the affective aspect of ICC, which shows the ability to, in addition to intercultural awareness, acknowledge, respect, and even accept different thoughts and behaviors caused by cultural differences in the process of intercultural communication. Intercultural adroitness demonstrates the behavioral aspect of ICC. It requires the ability to apply both intercultural awareness and intercultural sensitivity to the context of intercultural communication by knowing how to act appropriately and effectively during the interaction.

Thus, for the BRI to succeed how to train its employees to equip with the ability of ICC becomes a significant factor. As mentioned previously, the BRI covers more than one hundred countries and regions in the continents of Africa, Asia, and Europe, which shows a great diversity of cultures. Only through intercultural awareness of customs and beliefs in different countries involving in the BRI, fostering the ability of intercultural sensitivity towards cultural differences, and further displaying intercultural adroitness in the process of intercultural interaction, can harmonious relationships be established to reduce mutual misunderstanding and conflict to a minimum level.

From a different angle we can see that the acquisition of ICC provides the BRI an opportunity to reinforce the importance and necessity of cultural diversity and the connectivity of local and global cultures (Sorrells, 2013). This also allows the BRI to challenge the predicaments caused by the Eurocentrism, which is characterized by aggressive individualism, chauvinistic rationalism, and ruthless culturalism and leads to the marginalization of non-Western countries (Asante, 2006). This by no means refers to the attempt of using the BRI as a tool to create an Asian or African cultural center through the acquisition of ICC (Asante, 2007; Miike, 2006). Instead, it alludes to the opportunity for establishing a multicultural co-existing human society in the process of dialogue or even confrontation with the Eurocentrism. In other words, it demands that in the process of co-governing and reforming the world system, the PRC needs to embody the ideal of global community based on the distinguishing feature of Chinese culture. This ideal global community also displays the principle, strategy, and mission of the PRC public diplomacy (杨晖， 2018).

Discussion and Conclusion

From Deng Xiaoping's "hiding its light" (tao guang yang hui, 韬光养晦) and "wading across the stream by feeling the way" (mo shi guo he, 摸石过河) policies to Xi Jingping's "China Dream" (zhong guo meng, 中国梦) and "go global" (zuo chu qu, 走出去), and to the slogan of "made in China 2025" (中国制造 2025)（国务院发布"中国制造 2025", 2015), it clearly shows the PRC ambition to join the global society to co-govern world affairs. It also displays that the rapid development of the PRC in the last five decades has moved the country to a well-off level and is gradually leading the country to a great power, and the BRI is the mark of the development in this process. The BRI not only represents the PRC key economic and political plan, but also shows that it will give the PRC a great potential of future development in economy, politics, and culture. However, it also will be accompanied with uncertainty mainly due to the worries and criticisms from especially countries in the West, who tend to consider the BRI as a means the PRC uses to influence global politics.

It is important to understand that facing international doubts and negative views on the BRI call for both a peaceful solution from the PRC government and attention from news report and academic research. Unfortunately, the existing literature from news report and research of the BRI mostly focuses on the aspects of economy, foreign affairs, politics, and military, very few of them deal with the issue from the perspective of intercultural communication. This is the reason why this paper aims to explore the BRI from the five perspectives of intercultural communication, namely, cultural values, intercultural adaptation, intercultural relationship, cultural flow and media, and intercultural communication competence. By doing so, it is not the intention of the author to over highlight or exaggerate the crucial role of intercultural communication in the implementation of the BRI. The author only wishes to argue that intercultural communications should be the foundation of the BRI. It is hoped that the analyses of the BRI from the perspective of intercultural communication can produce some positive contribution to understanding and implementation of the project, which may also help to develop a future world of mutual trust, mutual benefit, and peaceful co-existence.

Three related issues regarding the BRI deserve discussion here. First of all, the uncertainty of the BRI continues to increase due to the criticisms of Western countries, and is getting worse owning to the trade war between the PRC and the United States. More and more discussions have emerged on how the PRC should proceed the BRI while facing these barriers. For example, recently the *Global Times* proposed some rational solutions on the problems caused by the trade war between the PRC and the United States (张 迪, 2018). The report triggers hot discussions on the claim of the "neo-hiding its light" (新韬光养晦) (凌云, 2018). The idea of the "neo-hiding its light" seems to be a thoughtful and acceptable suggestion, which may function to correct the myth or fallacy of slogans like "comprehensive transcendence" (全面超越论) and "amazing China" (厉害了, 我的国) based on the overzealous claim from the populism. It is a fact that the PRC is a large country, but it is still questionable whether the PRC is already a superpower. Hence, knowing the real situation of the country with a clear and calm mind through self-reflection, improvement, and breakthrough should be a good way for the PRC to sustain its steady development.

The hexagram of Qian (乾卦) of the Book of Changes or I Ching can be used to explain this situation. The original practice of the "hiding its light" is mirrored by the first line (爻) of the hexagram, which is the moment of "潜龙勿用" (qian long wu yong), meaning that the dragon is hiding in deep water, or it is not time for action yet. The present condition can be represented by the second line. The line states that "见龙在田" (xian long zai tian), referring to the dragon is appearing in the field. It reflects the strength of the PRC produced by the rapid development of economy over the last decades. However, the emergence as a strong game player will be inevitable to encounter the resistance or criticism from surrounding countries. To a certain point the PRC needs to decide how far it can go to face the challenge. In other words, the PRC needs to see if the situation demands the change of strategy or make a detour by entering the third line of the hexagram. The third line conveys the message of "continuing to make earnest efforts days and nights with vigilance" (zhong ri qian qian, xi ti ruo, 终日乾乾, 夕惕若) to avoid unnecessary conflicts with others, and then "jumping back to the deep water" (huo yue zai yuan, 或跃在渊) dictated by the fourth line of the hexagram to temporarily be a hiding dragon or "hiding its light" again while being observant and diligent. When the time comes, as the fifth line of the hexagram says, "it is the right moment now for the dragon to fly in the sky" (fei long zai tian,飞龙在天) to peacefully and productively work with other countries in the global society.

Zhou (周 山, 2014) argued that although the Qian hexagram is characterized by its emphasis on exerting oneself constantly or striving unceasingly, the progress of this earnest effort to improve oneself is actually conditioned by the three concepts of endurance (ren, 忍), worry (you, 忧), and repentance (hui, 悔). It illustrates the flexibility of adapting to the situation embedded in the interplay between Yin and Yang forces, and this flexibility can serve as a workable reference for the BRI.

Second, the BRI brings about the debate on the so-called "China model" (zhong guo mo shi, 中国模式). From the perspective of intercultural communication, we can see that there exist universal values, such as the pursuit of power, achievement, and hedonism, in different cultures (Schwartz, 1992), but it is difficult to find a universal model of problem solving in human societies. Although the domination of Western models in the world has been over two centuries, it by no means infers that the Western models are fit or can be transplanted to other societies due to the differences of cultural values. Similarly, it is also not valid to argue that non-Western models, e.g., the Asian economic or cultural model, can be applied or transplanted to Western societies. Thus, any model tinted with a specific culture's feature will be subject to the challenge of competition and adaptation in the application to a different society. Because the Western models are considered as invalid for the BRI to follow, scholars have begun to ponder and discuss what then will be a suitable China model the BRI can rely on for its sustainable development.

More and more scholars from different disciplines have endeavored to construct various models based on Chinese culture (e.g., 邵培仁, 姚锦云, 2018; 谢清果, 陈昱成, 2018). On the micro- or middle-range level, in addition to the above example of using the hexagram of Qian to explain the discourse of "hiding its light" applied to the BRI, more attempts for developing a China model were found in the fields of interpersonal communication and management. They include, e.g., Cheng's (成中英, 1995) C theory of Chinese management, Zeng's

(曾仕强, 2005) theory of I Ching management, Chen's (陈 国 明, 2004a, 2004b) theories of human relationship development based on the eight hexagrams of I Ching and Chinese harmony, Chen's (2009b) I Ching theory of human communication, Chen and An's (2009) Chinese model of global leadership, and G. Chen's (2013b) and M. Chen's (2002) Chinese models of the middle-way (中道) management. In the areas of economy and politics the Chinese "World View" (天 下 观) or "Tian-Xia Doctrine" (天 下 主 义) and "China Model" are the two theories most explored that are directly related to the BRI. The efforts to develop models or theories from the Chinese cultural perspective that are used to explain the rapid development of the PRC reflects China's ambition to co-govern the global society with other countries.

Based on the interpretation of the statement of "Looking at the world, we are facing a major change that has not been seen in a century" of President Xi's talk (习近平, 2017c), the theory of Chinese "World View" is considered as a strong sense of mission delineated in Confucian teachings, though Western countries criticized it as the reemergence of "chougong" or "kowtou". Nevertheless, from the perspective of Chinese history, the Chinese "World View" is rooted in the spirit of "li" (rite, propriety, 礼), which denotes an unequal relationship but specifies a system of peaceful co-existence with the emphasis of righteousness rather than greed. Yang (杨晖, 2018) contended that the system can provide protection of economy, culture, and politics for participating countries and regions in the process of implementing the BRI.

It is a good effort for using the Confucian concept of "li" to interpret the Chinese "World View" of the BRI, which can connect the process of China's new modernization with Chinese traditions. The question is that how can this Chinese "World View" successfully dialogue and integrate with presently dominating Western civilization remains a great challenge. As mentioned previously, facing the impact of negative national image presently, it is crucial for the PRC government to seek an effective way to tackle this predicament through the process of intercultural propaganda and constructive public diplomacy, which is based on ethical human relationship and world order originated from the Chinese "World View".

The "China Model" aims to answer the question raised by President Xi (习 近 平, 2017b): "What is the socialism with Chinese characteristics for a new era". It should be a model of major country diplomacy with Chinese characteristics, but opinions are still varied for how to apply this Chinese model to the world stage. Undoubtedly, the successful transformation of Chinese society due to the rapid development of economy in the last five decades must refer to that there is an objective model existing in it that guides the great achievement in China.

The dilemma is that a more accurate face or map of the model still remains to be drawn, which also indicates that this hidden model is still on the stage of change. In other words, it shows that the model of economic development in China is still an unstable one and subjects to constant revisions when the PRC continues to interact with other countries globally.

As Yao (姚 洋, 2011) pointed out, it seems to be more appropriate to use "China experience" (zhong guo jing yan, 中国经验) or "Chinese way" (zhong guo dao lu, 中国道路) to replace "China Model", but no matter which term is used, they ought to include four common elements: elitism, meritocracy, effective system, and neutral government. Zheng (郑 永 年, 2015) further indicated that the soul of all the various perceptions of "China Model" shares the same idea that it is a unique type of mixed Chinese economic and political model, and it is not a fixed universal model so far. As the PRC is rising in this global society, it can be expected that competition, cooperation, and confrontation between the "China Model" and other existing models will increase. It is worth keeping an eye to observe how the "China Model" is embodied through the BRI in the future.

Finally, the unexpected attack of the Coronavirus (COVID-19) is shaking human society and restructuring the world order now. The COVID-19 has lessened the nature, pace, and scope of the BRI activities due to its impact on global economy, especially the fundamental change in global supply chains (World Economic Forum, 2020). Combined with the US-China trade friction, the prospect of the BRI future looks even dimmer. The COVID-19 pandemic may not lead to the worst scenario from authoritative forecasts, including the collapse of world economy, social and political turmoil in some countries, reshuffling of the world order, and curtail of the global connectivity (Tonchev, 2020), but the PRC certainly will face some short-term impact from the COVID-19. For example, the funding shortfall resulting in the decrease of needed resources in the BRI may cause political and social instability in China, and the demand for infrastructure in the joining countries and regions of the BRI may be severed due to the lack of funding which will weaken Chinese investment. For the long-term impact the COVID-19 definitely will bring about a different BRI, and it may not be more embraced by the rest of the world. However, Tonchev continued, because the BRI is "a symbol of China's emergence as a leading global leader and a big chunk of Xi's legacy", the PRC will find a way to perpetuate the project, like using the "mask diplomacy" strategy to introduce a safe health system to the BRI. As Chinese traditional teaching stipulates that crisis is always a turning point for a better future (wei ji ji shi zhuan ji, 危 机 即 是 转 机), the present unpredictable world situation is providing the PRC an opportunity to face the challenge based on traditional Chinese wisdom, which may possibly reside in the perspective of intercultural communication.

* The original version of this paper was presented at the IAICS 2019 Annual Conference. Brno, Czech Republic.

Acknowledgment

The author would like to thank Professors Ran An, Xiaodong Dai, and Victor Tonn for their valuable opinions for revision of this paper.

References

习近平（2013a）。“习近平在纳扎尔巴耶夫大学的演讲（全文）”。見

http://www. fmprc.gov.cn/mfa_chn//zyxw_602251/t1074151.shtml

习近平（2013b）。“携手建设中国－东盟命运共同体”。見 http://www.xinhuanet.com/world/2013-10/03/c_117591652.htm

习近平（2017a）。“携手推进‘一带一路’建设- 在‘一带一路’国际合作高峰论坛开幕式上的演讲。見：http://www.xinhuanet.com/world/2017-05/14/c_1120969677.htm.

习近平 (2017b). 习近平重要讲话双语实录：在“一带一路”国际合作高峰论坛开幕式上的演讲。见：http://www.catl.org.cn/2017-05/15/content_41501866.htm.

习近平（2017c，12 月 28 日）。“习近平接见 2017 年度驻外使节工作会议与会使节

并发表重要讲话”。新华网。见：http://www.xinhuanet.com/politics/leaders/2017-12/28/c_1122181743.htm.

中华人民共和国和国家发展和改革委员会（2015）。“推动共建丝绸之路经济带和21 世纪海上丝绸之路的愿景与行动”。見：http://www.ndrc.gov.cn/gzdt/201503/t20150328_669091.html

从指责中国走明朝模式看美防长的认识盲区（2018）。见：http://news.dwnews.com/global/news/2018-06-26/60066816.html

安然、刘程、王丽虹（2015）。“孔子学院中方人员跨文化适应能力研究”。北京：中国社会科学出版社。

邝志良（2018）。“‘一带一路’推动全球”。见：http://orientaldaily.on.cc/cnt/finance/20180222/mobile/odn-20180222-0222_00275_001.html

成中英 (1995)。《C 理論：易經管理哲學》。台北：三民书局。

李克強（2015）。“‘推進‘一帶一路’合作建設，加快實施自貿區戰略”。見：http://www.scio.gov.cn/31773/35507/gcyl35511/Document/1529019/1529019.htm.

希文（2017）。“美前总统助理：一带一路关键在沟通”。见：http://global.dwnews.com/news/2017-05-16/59815324.html

何茂春、张冀兵、张雅芃、田斌（2015）。“‘一带一路’战略面临的障碍与对策”。

《新疆师范大学学报：哲学社会科学版》，第 3 期。

时晓莉、张赛（2018，7 月 26 日）。“学界研讨‘一带一路’倡议与跨文化传播”。中国社会科学网。见：http://news.cssn.cn/zx/bwyc/201807/t20180725_4510648. shtml?from=timeline&isappinstalled=0

邵培仁、姚锦云(2018)。“本土之路三十年：华夏传播理论的建构实践（1988–2018）”。《中国传媒报告》，第 3 期，页 4 –18。

张迪 （2018，8 月 1 日）。“中美会战略性对抗并影响一代人吗”？http://news.sina.com.cn/c/2018-08-01/doc-ihhacrce6554416.shtml

张玉佩 （2017）。“导读：文化流动的模式与另类想象”。《中华传播学刊》，第六期，页 3–15。DOI:10.6195/cjcr.2017.31.00

张恒军、吴秀峰 (2019). “一带一路”视域下中华文化认同的内涵、原则和策略”.

《出版发行研究》， 第一期，页 10–15。DOI：CNKI:SUN:CBFX.0.2019-01-003

周公瑾 （2018，July 24）。“ 英媒：中国如何应对一带一路负面评价”。见：http://news.dwnews.com/global/news/2018-07-24/60072849.html

每日头条（2017）。“‘丝绸之路’与‘一带一路’上的文化传播者”。见：https://kk news.cc/zh-tw/culture/68k63vv.html

纽约时报中文网（2017）。“‘一带一路’：中国巨额投资欲重塑全球经济秩序”。见：https://d2tw5djyacg82s.cloudfront.net/business/20170515/china-railway-one-belt-one-road-1-trillion-plan/?utm_source=news-list&utm_medium=email&utm_campaign=newsletter

陈国明（2004a）。“易经八卦与人际关系发展模式”。陈国明（编），“中华传播理论与原则”（页 203–229）。台北，台湾：五南出版社。

陈国明 （2004b）。“和谐与华人沟通行为”。陈国明（编），“中华传播理论与原则”（页 337–362）。台北，台湾：五南出版社。

陈国明（2007）。“跨文化沟通”。鲁曙明（编），“沟通交际学”（页 184–217）。北京：人民大学出版社。

陈国明 （2009）。“死生之是事”。香港：中国学术评论出版社。

陈国明（2011）。“跨文化传播的脉络性”。《傳播研究與實踐》，第 1 卷第 2 期， 頁 13–24 。

陈国明 （2014）。“跨文化学的现状与未来发展”。洪俊浩（编），“传播学新趋势”

（页 582–605）。北京：清华大学出版社。

郑永年（2015）。“中国模式：经验与挑战”。北京：中信出版社。

单波、肖珺（2015）。“文化冲突与跨文化传播”。北京：社会科学文献出版社。 国务院发布《中国制造 2025》（全文）（2015）。见：http://www.gov.cn/ zhengce/content/2015-05/19/content_9784.htm

周山（2014）。“读易随笔”。北京：海豚出版社。

杨晖（2018）。“解码习时代外交思想：百年历史变局下的天下观（二）”。见：http://news.dwnews.com/global/news/2018-07-20/60072229_all.html

姚洋（2011）。“中国模式及其前景”。 见：https://wenku.baidu.com/view/1c91b6170b4e767f5acfcedb.html

施予 (2018) 。“中国一带一路建设项目相继受阻 66 国 234 项遇困境” 。见：http://news.dwnews.com/china/news/2018-07-15/60070860.html

皇金(2018)。从指责中国走明朝模式看美防长的认识盲。见：http://news.dwnews.com/global/news/2018-06-26/60066816.html

姜飞、黄廓（2018）。“论新时代中国特色社会主义核心价值观国际传播的新思路”。《中州学刊》，第 1 期。 页 164–172。

凌云（2018，8 月 2 日）。“中国官媒称不与美全面对抗或是新版韬光养晦”。见：http://news.dwnews.com/china/news/2018-08-02/60074977.html

袁新涛（2014）。“一带一路”建设的国家战略分析”。《理论月刊》，第 11 期，页 5–9。黄涓（2016）。“大机构观与中国道路：孔子学院发展比较研究”。北京：外语教学

与研究出版社。

谢清果、陈昱成（2015）。“‘风草论’：建构中国本土化传播理论的尝试”。《现代传播（中国传媒大学学报）》，第 9 期，页 59–64.

曾仕强 (2005)。“管理大道：中国管理哲学的现代应用”。北京：北京大学。

董明利（2016）。习近平“天下观”的理论渊源、现代诠释和中国方案。《中学政治教学参考：下旬》，第 11 期，页 8–10.

储殷（2018）。“解码习时代外交思想：百年历史变局下的天下观（一）”。见：http://news.dwnews.com/global/news/2018-07-20/60072222_all.html

Adler, N. J. (1980). “Cultural Synergy: The Management of Cross-Cultural Organizations”. In W. W. Burke & L. D. Goodstein (Eds.), *Trends and Issues in OD: Current Theory and Practice* (pp. 163–184). San Diego, CA: University Associates.

Alleyne, M. D. (2009). International Communication Theories. In. S. W. Littlejohn & K. A. Foss (Eds.), *Encyclopedia of Communication Theory* (pp. 537–541). Los Angeles, CA: Sage.

An, R., He, G., & Chen, G. M. (2018). Intercultural Communication Influence of Confucius Institutes: A Yin-Yang Perspective. *China Media Research, 14*(4), 37–45.

Asante, M. (2006). The Rhetoric of Globalization: The Europeanisation of Human Ideas. *Journal of Multicultural Discourses, 1*(2), 152–158.

Asante, M. K. (2007). Communicating Africa: Enabling Centricity for Intercultural Engagement. *China Media Research, 3*(3), 70–75.

Casmir, F. L. (1993). Third-culture Building: A Paradigm Shift for International and Intercultural Communication. In *Communication Yearbook 16* (pp. 407–428). Newbury Park, CA: Sage.

Chen, G. M. (2009a). Beyond the Dichotomy of Communication Studies. *Journal of Asian Communication, 19*(4), 398–411.

Chen, G. M. (2009b). Toward an I Ching Model of Communication. *China Media Research, 5*(3), 72–81.

Chen, G. M. (2010). *A study of Intercultural Communication Competence.* Hong Kong: China Review Academic Publishers.

Chen, G. M. (2012). The Impact of New Media on Intercultural Communication in Global Context. *China Media Research, 8*(2), 1–10.

Chen, G. M. (2013a). Theorizing Intercultural Adaptation from the Perspective of Boundary Game. *China Media Research, 9*(1), 1–10.

Chen, G. M. (2013b). A Zhong Dao Model of Management in Global Context. *Intercultural Communication Studies, 22*(1), 1–8.

Chen, G. M. (2015a). Seeking Common Ground While Accepting Differences Through Tolerance: U.S.-China Intercultural Communication in Global Community. In L. A. Samovar, R. E. Porter, E. R. McDaniel, & C. S. Roy (Eds.), *Intercultural Communication: A Reader* (pp. 465–471). Boston, MA: Cengage Learning.

Chen, G. M. (2015b). Theorizing Global Community as Cultural Home in the New Century. *International Journal of Intercultural Relations, 46*, 73–81.

Chen, G. M. (2017). The Yin and Yang of Conflict Management and Resolution. In X-d. Dai & G. M. Chen (Eds.), *Conflict Management and Intercultural Communication* (pp. 144–154). Oxfordshire, UK: Taylor & Francis.

Chen, G. M., & An, R. (2009). A Chinese Model of Intercultural Leadership Competence. In D. K. Deardorff (Ed.), *The SAGE Handbook of Intercultural Competence* (pp. 196–208). Thousand Oaks, CA: Sage.

Chen, G. M., & Starosta, W. J. (Eds.). (2000). *Communication and Global Society*. New York: Peter Lang.

Chen, G. M., & Starosta, W. J. (2005). *Foundations of Intercultural Communication*. Lanham, MD: University Press of America.

Chen, G. M., & Young, P. (2012). Intercultural Communication Competence. In A. Goodboy & K. Shultz (Eds.), *Introduction to Communication: Translating Scholarship into Meaningful Practice* (pp. 175–188). Dubuque, IA: Kendall-Hunt.

Chen, G. M., & Zhang, K. (2010). New Media and Cultural Identity in the Global Society. In R. Taiwo (Ed.), *Handbook of Research on Discourse Behavior and Digital Communication: Language Structures and Social Interaction* (pp. 801–815). Hershey, PA: Idea Group Inc.

Chen, M.-j. (2002). Transcending Paradox: The Chinese "middle-way" Perspective. *Asian Pacific Journal of Management, 19*, 179–199.

Cohen, A. P. (2000). Introduction: Discriminating Relations – Identity, Boundary and Authenticity. In A. P. Cohen (Ed.), *Signifying Identities: Anthropological Perspectives on Boundaries and Contested Values* (pp. 1–13). New York: Routledge.

Condon, J. C., & Yousef, F. S. (1975). *An Introduction to Intercultural Communication*. New York: Prentice Hall.

Creemers, R. (2015). Never the Twain Shall Meet? Rethinking China's Public Diplomacy Policy. *Chinese Journal of Communication, 8*(3), 306–322.

CSIS. (2021). *Belt Road*. Retrieved from: https://reconnectingasia.csis.org/analysis/entries/traveling-60000km-across-chinas-belt-and-road/.

Dai, X.-d. (2010). Intersubjectivity and Interculturality: A Conceptual Link. *China Media Research, 6*(1), 12–19.

Dai, X-d. (2012). Out of a Dialogical Dilemma: The Construction of Interculturality. In X-d. Dai & S. J. Kulich (Eds.), *Intercultural Adaptation (1): Theoretical Explorations and Empirical Studies* (pp. 97–114). Shanghai: Shanghai Foreign Language Education Press.

Dai, X-d., & Chen, G. M. (2014a). The Construction of National Image in the Media and the Management of Intercultural Conflicts. In R. S. Fortner & P. M. Fackler (Eds.), *International Handbook of Media and Mass Communication Theory* (pp. 708–725). Hoboken, NJ: Wiley-Balckwell.

Dai, X.-d., & Chen, G. M. (Eds.). (2014b). *Intercultural Communication Competence: Conceptualization and Its Development in Cultural Contexts and Interactions*. Newcastle upon Tyne, UK: Cambridge Scholars.

Dai, X.-d., & Chen, G. M. (2017). *Conflict Management and Intercultural Communication: The art of Intercultural Harmony*. New York: Routledge.

Deardorff, D. K. (Ed.). (2009). *The Sage Handbook of Intercultural Competence.* Thousand Oaks, CA: Sage.

Fan, Y. (2002). The National Image of Global Brands. *Journal of Brand Management, 9*(3), 180–192.

Fernandez, J. W. (2000). Peripheral Wisdom. In A. P. Cohen (Ed.), *Signifying Identities: Anthropological Perspectives on Boundaries and Contested Values* (pp. 117–144). New York: Routledge.

Flew, T. (2005). *New Media*. New York: Oxford University Press.

Green Belt and Road Initiative Center. (2020). *Countries of the Belt and Road Initiative.* Retrieve from: https://green-bri.org/countries-of-the-belt-and-road-initiative-bri (BRI).

Gudykunst, W. B. (1987). Cross-Cultural Comparisons. In C. R. Berger & S. H. Chaffee (Eds.), *Handbook of Communication Science* (pp. 847–889). Beverly Hills, CA: Sage.

Gullion, E. (1965). *Public Diplomacy*. Retrieved from: http://publicdiplomacy.wikia.com/wiki/Edmund_Gullion.

Hall, E. T. (1976). *Beyond Culture*. Garden City, NY: Anchor.

HKTDC. （2020.）。"一带一路简要"。见：https://beltandroad.hktdc.com/tc/belt-and-road-basics

Hofstede, G. (1984). *Culture's Consequences*. Beverly Hills, CA: Sage.

Huang, Z. A., & Wang, R. (2020). "Panda engagement" in China's Digital Public Diplomacy. *Asian Journal of Communication, 30*(2) 118–140.

Kluckhohn, C., & Strodbeck, F. (1961). *Variations in Value Orientations.* Evanston, IL: Row, Peterson.

Manheim, J. B., & Albritton, R. B. (1984). Changing National Images: International Public Relations and Media Agenda Setting Source. *The American Political Science Review, 78*(3), 641–65.

Miike, Y. (2006). Non-Western Theory in Western Research? An Asiacentric Agenda for Asian Communication Studies. *Review of Communication*, 6(1/2), 4–31.

Mitchell, M, J. (1986). *International Culture Relations*. London: Allen & Unwin Publishers Ltd. Murray, M. (2011, November). *Constraining Divergent Voices: Western Media Coverage of Protests during the 2008 Beijing Olympic Games.* Paper presented at the Annual Conference of the National Communication Association, New Orleans, Louisiana.

Nye, J. (2006). *Hard Power, Soft Power, and Leadership*. A public seminar at Kennedy School of Government of Harvard University. Retrieved from: https://www.belfercenter.org/event/hard-power-soft-power-and-leadership.

Nye, J. (2008). Public Diplomacy and Soft Power. *Annals of the American Academy of Political and Social Science, 616*(1), 94–109.

Oberg, K. (1954). *Culture Shock*. Panel discussion at the Midwest Regional Meeting of the Institute of International Education in Chicago, November 28, 1951. Retrieved from: https://citeseerx.ist.psu.edu/document?repid=rep1&type=pdf&doi=c787fddd7e1557f100b9703a41f6f5ae2dac0412

Orbe, M. P. (1998). *Constructing Co-Cultural Theory*. Thousand Oaks, CA: Sage.

Overholt, W. H. (2015). *One Belt, One Road, One Pivot*. Retrieved from: https://globalasia.org/article/one•belt•one•road•one•pivot/.

Page, J., & Shah, S. (2018, July 22). China's Global Building Spree Runs into Trouble in Pakistan. *The Wall Street Journal*. Retrieved from: https://www.wsj.com/articles/chinas-global-building-spree-runs-into-trouble-in-pakistan-1532280460.

Park, R. E. (1928). Human Migration and the Marginal Man. *American Journal of Sociology, 33*(6), 881–893.

Perdinand, P. (2016). Westward Ho – The China Dream and "one belt, one road": Chinese Foreign Policy under Xi Jinping. *International Affairs, 92*(4), 941–957.

Rich, A. (1974). *Interracial Communication*. New York: Harper & Row.

Rogers, E. M. (1999). Georg Simmel's Concept of the Stranger and Intercultural Communication Research. *Communication Theory, 9*(1), 58–74.

Schuman, M. (2018, July 21). Xi Needs a Confucian Foreign Policy. *Bloomberg Opinion*. Retrieved from: https://www.bloomberg.com/view/articles/2018-07-21/xi-needs-a-confucian-foreign-policy.

Schutz, W. (1966). *The Interpersonal Underworld*. Palo Alto, CA: Science and Behavior Books.

Schwartz, S. H. (1992). 'Universals in the Content and Structure of Values: Theory and Empirical Tests in 20 Countries'. In M. Zanna (Ed.), *Advances in Experimental Social Psychology* (Vol. 25., pp. 1–65). New York: Academic Press.

Shambaugh, D. (2007, January). China's Propaganda System: Institutions, Processes and Efficacy. *The China Journal, 57*, 25–58.

Shils, E. (1975). *Center and Periphery: Essays in Macrosociology*. Chicago, IL: University of Chicago Press.

Sorrells, K. (2013). *Intercultural Communication: Globalization and Social Justice*. Thousand Oaks, CA: Sage.

Starosta, W. J., & Chen, G. M. (2003). "Ferment," an Ethic of Caring, and the Corrective Power of Dialogue. *International and Intercultural Communication Annual, 26*, 3–23.

Stephens, O. (1955). *Facts to a Candid World*. Stanford, CA: Stanford University Press.

Straubhaar, J. D. (1991). Beyond Media Imperialism: Asymmetrical Interdependence and Cultural Proximity. *Critical Studies in Mass Communication, 8*(1), 39–59.

Swine, M. D. (2015). Chinese Views and Commentary on the "one belt, one road" Initiative. *China Leadership Monitor, 47* (Summer), 1–16.

Syed, N. A. (2010). The Effect of Beijing 2008 on China's Image in the United States: A Study of US Media and Polls. *The International Journal of the History of Sport, 27*(16–18), 2863–2892.

Thu, H. L. (2018, July 24). *China's Aggression Is Starting to Backfire*. Retrieved from: https://www.yahoo.com/news/china-apos-aggression-starting-backfire-235200989.html

Tian, D.-X., & Deng, L.-J. (2018). *Leadership Roles of Peng Liyuan as China's First Lady. China Media Research, 14*(3), 8–20.

Tonchev, P. (2020). *The Belt and Road after COVID-19*. Retrieved from: https://thediplomat.com/2020/04/the-belt-and-road-after-covid-19/.

Tuch, H. N. (1990). *Communicating with the World: The U.S. Public Diplomacy Overseas*. New York: St. Martin's Press.

Winter, T. (2016, March 29). One Belt, One Road, One Heritage: Cultural Diplomacy and the Silk Road. *The Diplomat*. Retrieved from: http://thediplomat.com/2016/03/one-belt-one-road-one-heritage-cultural-diplomacy-and-the-silk-road/.

World Economic Forum. (2020). *How Will COVID-19 Affect China's Belt and Road Initiative?* Retrieved from: https://www.weforum.org/agenda/2020/05/covid-19-coronavirus-disrupt-chinas-bri/.

Xiuhanet. (2021). *The Belt and Road Initiative Map*. Retrieved from: http://www.xinhuanet.com/fortune/cjzthgjj/104.htm.

Zhao, Y. (2013). China's Quest for Soft Power: Imperatives, Impediments and Irreconcilable Tensions? *Javnost-The Public, 20*(4), 17–30.

Part III The Meaning of Messages

Introduction to Risky Business: What You Lose and What You Gain in Translation

By Barbara Lewandowska-Tomaszczyk

The next text takes a closer look at translations. It is pointed out that translations from one language to another often do not transfer identical meanings due to linguistic and cultural differences. Since a transfer of identical meaning is often not possible, a broader description is often necessary when translating from one language to another. The use of equivalents can be helpful, but sometimes such equivalents do not exist in the other language. This chapter, thus, raises the reader's awareness to the (potential) problems associated with translations, i.e. that it is often not possible to translate the exact meaning from one text to another due to variations in the language. This is important because many people assume that the translated text holds and conveys the same meaning from the Source Language to the Target Language. But as Barbara Lewandowska-Tomaszczyk points out, this is often not possible. The chapter contains many examples which illustrate this point.

The chapter is important because in today's global world most of the correspondence is carried out in English. This exchange can be between native speakers of different dialects of English, native speakers of English and non-native speakers, or between non-native speakers. It can be assumed that most interlocutors will assign English messages a meaning that is typical for their native language or dialect. Consequently, these interlocutors will assume meaning when in actual fact they do not. While generally, it is not necessary to have a hundred percent convergence in meaning in order to communicate with one another, there can be situations where a greater degree of convergence in meaning is needed – such as, for example, during a legal dispute. For example, most German sales reps will probably assume that a *sales contract* is equivalent to a German *Kaufvertrag* because that is the standard translation. And assuming that a *sales contract* is a *Kaufvertrag*, they will transfer the meaning that is typically associated with a *Kaufvertrag* also to a *sales contract*. This is, though, a faulty assumption since a *sales contract* is governed by the legal principle of consideration, i.e. an equivalent value needs to be exchanged for the contract to be enforceable, which does not exist in German contract law. If there are no legal disputes, this difference will probably not be relevant. But it would be decisive if there is a dispute as to whether the contract is enforceable or not. That is why readers ought to take a closer look at this chapter to become aware of potential pitfalls associated with translations.

Michael B. Hinner

Barbara Lewandowska-Tomaszczyk is full Professor Dr habil. in Linguistics at the Department of Language and Communication at the State University of Applied Sciences in Konin (Poland), formerly at the University of Lodz. Her research focuses on cognitive semantics and pragmatics of language contrasts, corpus linguistics and their applications in translation, media studies, and incivility in online discourse.

Barbara Lewandowska-Tomaszczyk

Risky Business: What You Lose and What You Gain in Translation

Translation and Its Types

The word *translation* is related, by its historical origin, to the Latin sense *"carried across"*. Translation is thus broadly defined as *transfer* of meaning from one language, called a Source Language (SL), into another, dubbed a Target Language (TL). In this context, crucial issues both in translation theories and in day-to-day translation practice are the interpretation of what is meant by *meaning* as well as the clarification of the concept of *transfer* itself. What is also needed is shedding some light on the question why translation can be considered a risky business and what can be lost and what can be gained in the process of translation.

The term *translation* is a general term which refers to a number of different translation types. The main present-day division runs along different lines such as spoken translation – referred to as *interpreting*, written translation, *audio-visual* translation, and a number of other – mostly evolving – disciplines of translation such as *community translation*, i.e., translation done by community members in social and urgent contexts, irrespective of whether the individuals performing the translation tasks are professional translators or not. Another type of a new professional activity involving translation is *audio description* (also *audiodescription*), defined as *the verbal depiction of key visual elements in media and live productions.* In other words, it is a spoken description of the characters and actions presented on the screen, including translation of visual language messages, by the translator – audio descriptor – for the sake of a blind audience. There are also other translation types, such as the border case between spoken and written kinds (e.g., translation of the text which was first written and then delivered as a spoken action, i.e., written-to-spoken translation), *conference* and *simultaneous* translation types of spoken language, and a rich typology of translational activities connected with subtypes of the main categories. Such translation acts as e.g., dubbing, subtitling, also *surtitling* – located above the screen, as in theatre performances – are the most frequent categories of audio-visual translation.

Still another type of translation service is related to *localization*, that is the adaptation of a product or service, and in our case – messages adapted to meet the needs of a particular language and culture, of the national, regional, or professional character as e.g., in the case of advertisements, which should be *localized*, i.e., adjusted both linguistically and visually to meet the expectations of a particular population, who is its addressee.

Another, separate, domain of translational activities, both theoretically and practically oriented, is *Machine Translation* (MT) and, connected with it, *Computer-Aided Translation* (CAT). MT is a computer-performed, automatic translation from one language into another. Such systems as Google Translate, are examples of automatic translation systems and in this case it is a multilingual neural machine translation service developed by Google, to translate different types of text, and websites from one language into another.

Depending on the type of translational activities – spoken, written, simultaneous, etc., as well as the *context*, *domain* and *text* and *style* types to be translated (official and formal versus casual talk, then *medical*, *legal*, etc., versus e.g., *literary* translation), the categories of translational strategic activities, are used in a different scale and in different proportions.

What Are the Problems with Translation?

Although all human beings use language for communication and languages possess some universal properties, they do not have *identical* systems. They all have many meanings attached to one linguistic form (*polysemy*), such as e.g., different senses of the form *expire* in English "coming to the end of a document validity" on the one hand and "die" on the other, but these forms are different in different languages and they naturally involve entirely distinct sets of words. Then, obviously, what in one language is called one name e.g., *dog* in English, may typically bear a different label for the same object in another langugge such as *chien* in French. Thirdly, there are forms in common across cultures and languages but they often are associated with different connotations, which open up mental spaces for associations distinct or entirely unrecognizable in another language e.g., the form *shaman*, originally from the Tungusic languages, denoting a person who is believed to interact with spirits in states of altered consciousness, which can have either positive or negative connotations in world languages and cultures.

Traps Within Words: One Word form with More Meanings (*Polysemy*)

Some forms in language have more than one meaning attached to the same form. A person translating from English as a Source Language (SL) to any other language (Target Language – TL), has to recognize which of these meanings in the original utterance conveys a correct sense in a given context. It does make a lot of difference, for instance, whether you will be talking in the TL about your own *body chest*, i.e., an upper part of your torso, or else of a *small chest* sitting on the shelf in your studio, or else a *big wooden chest* with lots of your clothing items inside, your worn-out slippers and piles of unread books. Another English word such as *cup* too displays a number of different, though related senses, e.g., *a tea cup*, *FIFA World Cup*, or else a *bra cup*. Each of these meanings is likely to have a different name in the target language one translates it to.

Different Words with Similar Meanings (*Synonymy*)

Different words on the other hand can be recognized to have similar meanings, i.e., they show a *synonymy* relation. In fact, according to one of the synonymy tests such words have to be *sufficiently similar* to allow their substitution in the same text. The similarity is perceived and conceived by language users taking various criteria into consideration (Lewandowska-Tomaszczyk, 2010) such as perceptual, functional, axiological, ideological, inferential (logical), etc. properties. Inferentially, speakers can refer to metonymic (when a part of an object is used to talk about the whole object or vice versa), metaphorical, etc. properties and intensify some aspects and weaken others in a different language system.

The criterion of substitution, substitution *salva veritate* as some philosophers would call this, is difficult, or even impossible in a natural language to achieve. If some words were *fully* substitutable for others, one would not need them in the language system for a rational reason, the principle familiar from Zipf's well-known *least effort law* (1949). Following this line of reasoning we could propose that some words tend to be substitutable for others in some contexts if they belong to the same *conceptual cluster*, or are located across different concepts within the cluster, although they invariably present somewhat different aspects and properties of seemingly the same meanings (Lewandowska-Tomaszczyk, 2017). Below in (1), a *clustering network* presents an exemplary instance of the multiple *polysemous* lexical form *train*, generated from the language collections of the British National Corpus. Each of the polysemous forms in turn, contains a few clusters of the *synonymous* type. The similar – but not identiccal – form *train*, come historically from Old French *train*, originally from Latin *trahere* "pull, draw", which developed in time signifying first "trailing part of a robe" and "retinue"; the latter gave rise to "a line of travelling people or vehicles", and later to "a connected series of things". The early verb sense "cause a plant to grow in a desired shape" was the basis of the further extended meanings of instruct and instruction[1].

1 https://languages.oup.com/google-dictionary-en/

What can thus be observed is that the concepts such as *train* will be a part of a whole cluster of senses, with a strong position of the notion of *station*, on the one hand but also *subway*, and *bus*, with the foregrounded concept of *rail*, on the other. *Train* is also polysemously linked to *education* and *drill* (training) as was discussed in the above paragraph, the latter, again polysemously, associated both with *practice*, but also, again polysemously (metonymically), with physical drilling with a tool, where the associated item *oil* appears (see Lewandowska-Tomaszczyk, 2007 for a typology of polysemy). The presented cluster of *train* is characteristic for English but not necessarily for other languages. For such radial structures as this one though, the *closest members* can be represented, in which degrees of semantic similarity can be calculated and defined with numerical

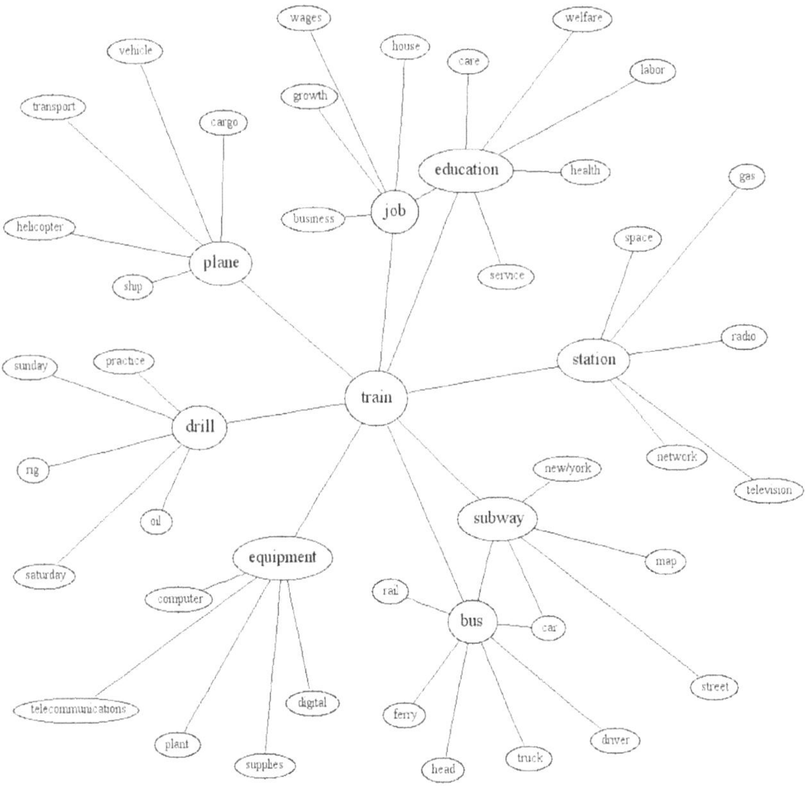

Figure 1: Infomap *Train* Cluster

Retrieved from: http://www-csli.stanford.edu/semlab-hold/infomap.h8tml Latent Semantic Analysis.

values. Some of these words, from the same clusetrs and close in their networked meanings, are also selected as convenient equivalents in translated texts.

One of the symptoms of the cluster item similarity is that language users tend to replace one such word for another in their interaction as e.g., in the case of the Verb *train*: *The teacher* ***practices*** *spelling with the learners – The teacher* ***drills*** *the learners in spelling.* It has to be emphasized that such forms from this and other clusters (*practice* for *drill*, *job* for *business*, *labour* for *service*), are not synonyms in the strict sense, but they can function as *practical approximations* in the *sensu lato* in authentic language contexts. Such uses are typical of translation in which looser TL equivalents from a repertory of close concepts are selected to render a SL sense.

It goes without saying that in some *restricted-domain* contexts such as medicine, law, engineering, etc., we certainly make translated meanings more precise, while in some others one can intentionally – as in literary translation, or unintentionally – particularly in heavily culture-bound tests, one leaves them more approximate and uses conceptually neighbouring concepts from the pool of closest senses.

The problem with the equivalents to these different language items which have no direct equivalents in other languages is that there is no one lexical item but rather *a whole set of words* which can usually have distinct forms, of different origin, having only part of the overlapping meanings between the words in the set, which are candidates to be used in translated texts. This certainly causes translational problems, particularly when, for example in jokes as in the one in which on a rainy day a teacher comes to the classroom wearing sunglasses and a student asks him: '- Why are you wearing sunglasses? It's such a gloomy day' and the teacher answers: "Because you're so *bright*"[2]. This is certainly a play on the polysemous word *bright* – between the sense of *shining*, which is opposite (called *antonym*) to "rainy" and "gloomy", and the other sense – its *metaphoric* extension – which refers as in this case, to *talented*, *intelligent*, *quick-witted* persons. This joke is sometimes difficult and problematic to convey in another language, one which would include a similar – linguistically expressed – connection between the shining light and mental talents[3].

2 based on Nerlich (1998), who also quotes another polysemy-based joke, explotig the meanings of the word 'hardest' as 'solid/rigid' and 'diffcult to learn/acquire' in English: 'What's the hardest thing when learning to ride a bike? – The road'.

3 More details on polysemy and prototypes see Lewandowska-Tomaszczyk (2007).

Classical polysemy, understood in this way, should be distinguished from what is usually known as *vagueness*, where a word is unmarked for a certain category or else it is complex in meaning, difficult to define. Such cases will be discussed in further sections.

Another class representing related senses involves monocentric conceptual categories such as e.g. *a bird*, which however embrace all – distinct – varieties of birds, from most central, most schematic *prototypes* (Rosch, 1983) such as sparrow or robin, through eagles and owls, to peripheral, at least in European cultures, category exemplars such as penguins or ostriches. That would mean that if the language user from a culture outside Europe hears generally about *birds* in England or Germany s/he does not necessarily activate in his/her mind the same prototype of bird as that in non-European locations, but might rather think of an ostrich or penguin, category members (proto)typical for their contexts and surroundings (Lakoff, 1987).

Different Syntactic Associations in Different Languages

In the first paragraph the phrase *a small chest sitting on the shelf in your studio* was quoted, in which a *position* of the small chest on the shelf was indicated. In English, objects can *sit* – like humans or animals – on other objects which support them, while some flat things might *lie* on them. This is not necessarily the case with other languages – in some of them objects *lie* or *stand* on shelves or on tables. Sitting is typically associated in English with a longer duration during which the object was placed in a given location and not touched since then as in (2–5) below.

Moreover, we can also say in English " 'The book is *standing* on the shelf' provided there is a clear distinction on which edge the book is positioned but it can be either sitting, lying, or standing (the latter implies an upright position of the object), similarly to a human being acquiring either a lying, sitting or standing position. All these options depend both of the overall shape and types of the posture a person, animal or object can prototypically acquire. These typical features or properties associated with particular activities and behaviour can be considered parts of what referred to by James Gibson (1966, 1975) as object *affordances*. In such languages as Polish the book on the shelf the book is lying or standing. It can be sitting in rather humorous contexts. When the objects are put one next to the other on the shelf, the English speaker can also use the, figuratively coloured, verb *line up*, evoking an image of a line row, while in Polish this effect cannot be exactly re-created in word-to-word translation but rather general equivalents *znajdują się* are used, corresponding to the English *there is /there are* phrases, or a more descriptive option *lined up – stoją w linii* or *obok* "stand in line" or "stand near" can also be proposed in Polish. The Polish equivalent *odłożony* "put aside" in (5) indicates a longer duration connected with this position, which is also present in the metaphoric English *sit* in such contexts.

(2) in supermarkets where numerous bottles with the same contents *are lined up on a shelf.*

(3) **English**	**Polish**
[The products] may *sit together* on the shelf	Różne produkty mogą *stać koło siebie* na półce

(4)

English	**Polish**
in supermarkets where numerous bottles with the same contents *are lined up* on a shelf.	w supermarketach, gdzie na jednej półce *znajduje się obok siebie* duża liczba butelek z tą samą zawartością.

(5)

English	**Polish**
Moreover, scenarios are not very useful if they *sit* on a shelf.	Co więcej, scenariusz *odłożony* na półkę nie na wiele się przydaje.

Specialized Language Translation – Terms and Ontologies

Specialized language translation posits still another kind of dilemma referring to the position of *terms* and *set phrases* in language for specific purposes, used in restricted domains.

Terminology deals with *specialized terms* in particular science fields in which such as words and set phrases (*collocations*) are used, in philosophy, physics, sociology, mathematics, linguistics or law, or else in practical human activities e.g., building a house, cooking a meal, producing wine or else painting or literature.

Terminology involves *term identification*, their multiple related meanings, relations between them (Lewandowska-Tomaszczyk, 2008), and their *equivalence* for translation purposes.

Each restricted domain of human activity is associated with its own *ontology*, i.e., a hierarchical system of terms representing a given part of the outside reality, such as e.g., contract law or nuclear physics. Contemporary ontologies involved in computer-based conceptual modelling are in the majority of cases domain-specific taxonomies of terms (see Lewandowska-Tomaszczyk, 2003), as e.g., generally, all educational system ontologies might include the following levels labelled by corresponding terms: *nursery*, *kindergarden*, *primary school*, *middle* or *secondary* school, *high* school, [profiled: *general* vs. *vocational*], *college*, *high vocational school / university / academy / university.*

The British English ontological system for educational domain is different, as for a number of others domains (e.g. administrative system, law, etc.), from those in other schooling systems, e.g., the British schooling system includes *grammar schools*, i.e., state secondary schools that select their pupils by means of an examination taken by children at age 11, known as the "11-plus". There are also *public schools* there. Such schools are rather elitist now and the name "public" is only of historical value in the sense that such schools used to be open to pupils irrespective of their background and location. Thus, a literal translation of the form *public* in *English public schools* might not be an adequate option in other languages.

Another example, concerning the *administrative structure* of the country, is equally troublesome. The translator can either select the closest possible TL level of (administrative unit) equivalence for his/her purposes e.g., Pol. *województwo* "county/shire, etc.", s/he resorts to a higher, more general unit "region", can coin a calque "voivodship" or retain the original Polish form as a loan-word "województwo", most often with an adequate definition or explanation e.g., "the chief unit in the territorial division in Poland for administrative, judicial and political purposes" or "the largest local government unit in Poland".

Words in general language frequently carry either distinct or modified senses when contrasted with *terms*. Compare the word *mass*, which is associated with a property of weight in ordinary English, while it has no necessary association with weight in physics, where *mass* is a relation to acceleration while the property of weight might be inferred (cf. Frawley, 1992). The translation of a text with a specialized lexicon then should retain in the TL text both the universally acknowledged terms and collocations of a particular domain and, whenever possible, the background knowledge structure of the text in the SL.

Translation errors in such domains are most striking and considered unacceptable. Durán Muńoz (2012) analyses tourist texts (brochures, tourist guides, menus, etc.), in which irritating spelling, collocational, syntactic and terminological mistakes are identified such as quoted by the author: *Eine der beliebtesten Modalitäten ist das *Besteigen vonsteilen Felsen* (*Bergsteigen*) and **Risokoliebhaber* (*Risikoliebhaber*). Among different materials with the information on various tourist activities Durán Muńoz identifies the following erroneous items, to quote a few: **Fisherei* is used instead of *Angeln* in German to translate *sport fishing* (English) or *pesca deportiva* (in Spanish). Along the same lines, *Fischerei* is misused in this context as it is wrongly employed to refer to a sport or tourist activity in the the place of the correct sense *Angeln*. **Freestyle-Klettern* in German used as an equivalent of *free climbing* in English misuses the equipment the climber uses for the style. **Swimm* instead of *diven* is another case of mistranslation.

To reassume, word meanings in language then cannot be stored in crisp, impenetrable compartments. Rather, they can be regarded as a conceptual map or networks of interrelated nodes, which correspond to individual vocabulary items of the language and imply their syntax (Langacker, 1987, 1991). The boundaries between the levels, or types of meaning, are not always stable or clear-cut but, taken together, they are responsible for the total effect of linguistic communication. Therefore, one needs to have a look at those different types of problem areas and see how translators attempt to solve them.

A practical piece of advice for the novice translator would be to consult authentic language materials. If a dictionary is used, compiled on the basis of large, systematic collections of authentic language, *language corpora*, particularly domain-restricted and specialized ones, it is likely to provide reliable language materials and information on their use. For general language worth consulting are the English resources, e.g., *British National Corpus* (BNC), *Corpus of Contemporary American* (COCA), to mention just a couple, but there are numerous others – of a number of languages freely available online. Some other resources can be used to automatically generate example-based translational equivalents from larger stretches of professionally translated Texts not to mention large Translation Memories to store translated texts.

A certain problem related to printed dictionaries and encyclopaedic thesauri (concept-based lists of words) is that they cannot afford comprising all those varied instances of distinct forms or uses, while the large language corpora (now also multimodal – verbal and visual – collections Lewandowska-Tomaszczyk, 2003) include both the most frequent as well as less frequent forms in fuller contexts. However, to use all of these reference materials to the user's advantage, one needs first to acquire a sufficient degree of the Target Language competence and TL sensitivity in order to avoid an undiscriminating use of the resources, which might lead to gross translation errors or inadequacies.

Translation of Historical Texts – Words Change in Time

Translation of historical texts is particularly challenging due to language and meaning changes. The historical sense of e.g., English *nice*[4] was close to "foolish", " silly", " ignorant" or "cowardly", later to come to mean "strange", "rare" and "reserved", replaced later by the meanings "agreeable", delightful, followed by "kind", "thoughtful", up to the present-day entirely positive sense. Another such well-known example is the history of the word *toilet* in English[5]. In the 16th century it used to refer to a kind of cloth, a diminutive form of French "toile" (linen cloth) and was later used in English to refer to a piece of cloth put on shoulders during hairdressing. Later it became *a cloth for use on dressing tables*, which stared to refer to *the items* on the dressing table (*toiletries*). Then it became *the dressing table* itself, followed by the shift of meaning towards the *act* of dressing and, further on, embraced the act of receiving *visitors* while dressing, eventually the dressing *room* itself, followed by any kind of *private room* near a bedroom, then a room used *lavatorially*, and finally the *lavatory* (from Latin *lavare* "to wash" itself.) This meaning development can explain why *toilet water* in English means either a type of perfume or else water in a toilet. In the present day use, the words *restroom* or *bathroom* are generally used in the basic sense of *lavatory*. Obviously translators need to be aware of such historical changes and use in the texts they render into another language as e.g., in the 17th century text, in which the author wrote: "The ordinary citizens Wives and Daughters wear a kind of *Toilet* on their Heads"[6], where *toilet* refers to a type of cloth mentioned above.

Connected with the above example of *toilet* of meaning change and the following replacements (dubbed *euphemisms*) is also a question of so-called *taboo words* which are words and expressions avoided in public discourse. The word "bathroom" replacing previous "toilet" is one such example, others would include e.g., cases when they are considered e.g., politically incorrect as e.g., the forms "handicapped" or a "person with disabilities", euphemistically referred to as "persons having special needs" in present-day discourse.

Meanings Specific to One Language and Culture

Meanings of words, phrases and utterances are all immersed in particular and situational contexts from which they take their more definite senses, scope, colouring, and enrichment.

---

4 https://languages.oup.com/google-dictionary-en/

5 https://www.merriam-webster.com/words-at-play/word-history-of-toilet

6 https://public.oed.com/blog/march-2014-update-release-notes-toilet/

There are also numerous cases in which meanings present in one culture are simply absent in another one. The Japanese concept of *amae* 甘え (the lexical form borrowed from Greek) is related to indulgent dependency, a particular bond, based on servile dependency between mother and child, which, as a phenomenon, is less typical of the majority of Anglo-Saxon cultures – British or American (Smith & Nomi, 2000). Another concept of this kind, current in Welsh is the notion of *hiraeth*, denoting a longing for home, homesickness tinged with sadness and grief, in the literal translation meaning 'long gone'[7]. Such and other similar words lack fully-fledged equivalents in other linguistic and cultural systems and need to be translated either descriptively, in terms of approximate forms, or by means of clusters of semantically neighbouring notions.

One such instance of rather culture-specific, liquid and fuzzy concepts difficult to grasp by non-native speakers is the German *Gemütlichkeit*, meticulously analysed in a recent study by Petrov and Mizin (2021). The authors perceive the meaning of *Gemütlichkeit* in terms of what is called here a conceptual *cluster*, combined with *Sicherheit*, *Zuverlässigkeit* and *Geborgenheit*, which they consider "a unique 'safety-cosiness quartet' " of the German-speaking communities value system. Those, together with the concept *Ordnung*, is, as claimed in the study, opposed to the existential fear – *Angst*. The *Gemütlichkeit* / *gemütlich* referring to a pleasant evening or walk, and connected with *Feierabend* runs opposite to the periods of gloom and gloomy weather as *ungemütlich* [uncosy].

It is next to impossible to find complete equivalents of the presented concept in other languages and cultures, but the cluster members identification approach might be an effective strategy in translation. The form *Gemütlichkeit*, derived from *Gemüt* (nature, soul, character), can be analysed into a number of cluster concepts, quoted extensively below (Mizin & Petrov, p. 38), which might be proposed to possess a more universal characterization:

(6) 1 'comfort', e.g., Das ist ein heller, schmaler Raum, der mit Sofas und Lounge-Liegen urbane Gemütlichkeit ausstrahlt [This is a cheerful, narrow room which radiates urban cosiness by its sofas and arm-chairs];

2 'peace of mind', e.g., Als ich das gläserne Dampfbad im Wellness-Bereich dann doch finde, bin ich erleichtert über die Gemütlichkeit [When I do find a steam sauna in a spa salon I feel better because of the feeling of cosiness];

3 'social comfort', e.g., Gemütlichkeit bedeutet für mich, niemanden sehen zu müssen [For me "Gemütlichkeit" means absence of necessity to see somebody];

7 https://sociology.lightningpath.org/ejs-archives/vol005.001/smith-nomi.html

4 'amity / friendliness', e.g., Hauptgrund seien soziale Aspekte wie Geselligkeit und Gemütlichkeit – sowohl in Familien als auch beim Spieleabend mit Freunden [The main reasons are such social factors as friendliness and cosiness – both in the family circle and while playing with friends in the evening];

5 'physical and mental relaxation', e.g., Gemütlichkeit: Endlich wieder Sofa-Zeit! [Cosiness: sofa-time again at last!];

6 'mental cosiness', e.g., Drinnen verbreiten warme Farben mit viel Holz eine konservative Gemütlichkeit [Inside warm colours together with rich wood decoration create conservative (traditional) cosiness];

7 'mental solace', e.g., Als ich mich auf diese Geschichte vorbereitete, lag ich an einem See in Brandenburg und wollte in aller Gemütlichkeit die Einführung in die Gender Studies von Franziska Schößler lesen [When I was preparing for this event I was lying on a lakeshore in Brandenburg and wanted to read the introduction to gender studies by Franziska Schößler in the atmosphere of utmost cosiness].

To re-create the meaning of the analysed concept in other languages then, translators resort to one or many of the cluster concepts identified above to *approximate* its sense to the speakers. Moreover, Mizin and Petrov indicate some of the modifications of the German senses in their enriched forms in dialects of German, e.g., in Swiss German and oppose them to similar *Gemütlichkeit* types in other Germanic languages:

(7) 9 Hier muss die schweizerische Gemütlichkeit mit asiatischer Eleganz zusammenfinden [Here the Swiss cosiness, the so called " Gemütlichkeit", should be combined with the Oriental elegance].

10 Es sind noch knapp zweihundert Kilometer bis zur Grenze, hinter der hygge wieder "Gemütlichkeit" heißt und man dabei an Eichenschrankwände denkt, an Kupferteller, den röhrenden Hirsch an der Wand und den Tatort mit Jan Josef Liefers [Some 200 kilometres to the border after which *hygge* (Danish cosiness) will be again called "Gemütlichkeit" (German cosiness) and one will think about an oak wall unit, about a copper plate, a belling deer on the wall and about a series "Crime Scene" with Jan Josef Liefers].

Lexical Gaps in One or in More Languages

Connected with the previous sections are lexical cases which display parts of a regular pattern in their own language but one of the structurally expected elements is missing. In English and in many other languages there are words for a body of a dead human being (*corpse*). Another name is used for a body of a dead animal (*carcass*), but there is no word for a dead plant. Such empty slots as the one there are labelled *lexical gaps*.

Furthermore, one concept and its lexical label as well as its positive or negative counterpart can be present in one language but not in the other. In such cases the language system exerts some semantic pressure on the existing word(s). In Polish there is one word for more positive pride – *duma*, and another – for negative pride (hubris) – *pycha*. However, in English there is one label *pride,* similarly to German *Stolz,* which cover both aspects. In Polish the relevant name for one of the Seven Deadly Sins – *Sieben Hauptsünden* (Pol. *Siedem Grzechów Głównych*) is precisely *pycha* "negative, excessive pride", while the English equivalent in the same text remains *pride*, containing a fully negative polarity of pride in this case. The fact that pride in Polish possesses two manifestations – one more, and the other – less positive, makes the distinction between the two types of emotion more salient (Lewandowska-Tomaszczyk & Wilson, 2017). Experienced translators are obviously aware of such meaning indeterminacy so they use in their translation of Polish *pycha* one of the English negative cluster neighbours of *pride* e.g., *conceit*, *ambition* or *arrogance* to communicate the entirely negative sense as an equivalent of (Lewandowska-Tomaszczyk &Wilson, 2017):

(8) Pol. Nienasycona *pycha* władców > Eng. unmeasurable *ambition* of princes
Pol. A *pycha* równała ich z obrazem Boga > Eng. but in *arrogance* they equated themselves with God's image.

In other cases of language gaps there are instances in which one language does not have an equivalent term as the other one on the same taxonomic level, as e.g., in English there is the general verb "to go", which does not have a direct equivalent on the same level of generality in Polish and needs to be rendered either as *iść* "walk" or *jechać* "move using a vehicle" in regular contexts. This *displacement of senses* (Lewandowska-Tomaszczyk, 2010) goes even deeper in the taxonomy as can be presented in the schema below:

(9) **Displacement of senses**

Eng. go (to school)
    Pol. iść/chodzić – [
        Eng. walk –[Pol.
        spacerować
  Eng. go – [
    Eng. go (by bus)
      Pol. jechać/jeździć – [
        Eng. drive –[Pol.
          prowadzić
            samochód
        ride

Language-Specific Division of the World

Translators always risk importing inappropriate idiom and usage into the target-language translation. Few idiomatic expressions will have an exact counterpart in the Target Language. They are typically rendered as language-specific idioms e. g., The Polish equivalents of the English greeting *How are you?* might be *Co słychać?* lit. "What to hear?", *Jak się masz*? lit. "How are you having yourself"?, which, translated literally, sound nonsensical. The North Chinese greeting is a literal equivalent to English *Have you eaten today?* [*chifanle meiyou*] rather than *Are you well?* [*ni hao?*]. Such pragmatic formulae are often useful to uncover cultural-historical layers of particular language use.

The pragmatically oriented cultural perspectives discussed above can also be reflected in a distinct conceptual-semantic portrayal of language-specific divisions of outside reality. In the Tzeltal language[8] rabbits belong together with squirrels in the categorization system. On the other hand, the cultural specificity of their system adopts the division of some everyday activities into a much higher number of minutely nuanced types such as e.g., the Tzeltal equivalents of Eng. *carry* are almost uncountable: *jelup'in* "to carry across the shoulders", *nol* "to carry in the palm of the hand", *chup* "to carry in a pocket or pouch", *chuy* "to carry in a bag", *lats'* "to carry under the arm", *pach* "to carry on the head", *toy* "to carry aloft", *yom* "to carry different items together", *lut'* "to carry with tongs", *pet* "to carry in the arms", *cats'* "to carry between one's teeth", *lup* "to carry on a spoon", *lat'* "to carry in a container", *cuch* "to carry on the back". Such distinctions are not surprising as, even among European language, English distinguishes between *strike* performed by foot/leg as *kick* and that by fist/hand as *punch*, while the French use – one of these only, accompanied by a descriptive phrase: *donner un coup de pied* "to strike with a foot' *donner un coup de poing* "to strike with the fist'.

Other Translational Dilemmas

There are also social or ideological choices the author or its translator make. The case of distinct evaluative marking – positive or negative – on such concepts as *liberal democracy* or *patriotism* (Lewandowska-Tomaszczyk, 2012) are some of such examples. Distinctions in such *axiological* markedness are the attention areas in translation, as in the case of the concept of *whistleblower* 'a person, who informs about something to stop it', 'a person who reveals wrongdoings

8 The examples quoted in this section have been discussed in Lewandowska-Tomaszczyk (2004).

to official bodies', which can bear different – positive or negative – marking, depending both on national as well as on social and other types of value systems represented both by the original author and the translator. A somewhat similar problem is observed in cases when the translator wants to reveal or even impose, sometimes by means of extended footnotes, often unrelated to the main topic of the translated work, their own attitudes and ideology, which can be considered an infringement of the code of good practice in this profession.

Grammatical differences across languages too, frequently emphasized by cultural differences, are also one of the main causes of the reconceptualization of the original meanings. Thus, there are distinctions in the construal of the world as expressed in terms of e.g., distinct conceptualizations based on different structures to convey similar meanings such as e.g., the object and infinitive construction 'I'd like *her to come* earlier' in English, as opposed to those languages such as Russian or Polish, which use a more sentential way to express this meaning *Я бы хотел, чтобы она пришла* 'I'd like so that (expressing desire) she came (Subjunctive – expressing not real – but projected future)'. Other instances can be connected with word grammar as e.g., gender. Although nouns in English do not take feminine or masculine gender in grammar, *death* is often metaphorically represented in terms of a male figure in English and other Germanic languages rather than as a female e.g., in the song "*Death* and All *His* Friends" performed by British rock band Coldplay, rather than as a female as in the Polish, or generally Slavic, literary and artistic representations.

Another type of language contrast which has a significant bearing on translation are language differences between a *distinct division of the world*, objects, and activities into parts. Both in the English and Polish COOKING domain, we distinguish a range of different types of food preparation: *grilling, roasting, broiling, barbecue, frying, boiling*, etc. However, the Polish general *gotować* is not one superordinate equivalent with a unique *cook* sense. It is polysemous between *cooking* and *boiling* as in e.g., 'to cook dinner' – *(u)gotować obiad*, 'to boil water' – *(za)gotować wodę*, etc. Moreover, some of the most recent cooking styles in Polish are dubbed after the Anglo-Saxon ones and use their names as loanwords: Eng. *grill, to grill, grilled* Pol. *grill/gril/gryl, grylować, grylowany* (and their orthographic variants). The form *barbecue* on the other hand, though used as a verb in English, is taken mostly to mean food, a meal or an event in Polish as in *robić barbecue* lit.'to make barbecued meat or meal' or 'to have a barbecue party'.

The unintended mistakes which might occur in translation are mistranslations related to the presence of so-called *false friends* or, as some call them, *treacherous twins*, from – originally in French – *faux amis*, or *belles infidèles*, English *the beautiful unfaithful.* Examples of German false friends to the English words, which have different meanings but similar spelling in these languages comprise e.g., Eng. *bald* "having no hair" – German false friend *bald* "soon", Eng. *actual* "existing in fact, real" – German false friend *aktuell* 'up to date' and numerous others.

Cultural and Situational Contexts Shed New Light on Meaning

The concept of culture has been invoked a few times in this chapter. The constitutive properties of culture can be proposed to involve *patterning*, i.e. presence of repeated structure, *shareability*, *learnability*, *cultural transmission* (also generational) in terms of symbols and signs, cultural imagery and its *embodiments* in human achievement in thought and in artifacts (Lewandowska-Tomaszczyk, 2015).

The word *house* in English is frequently translated as the Greek *oikos* and the Papua New Guinea word *numuno* (Lewandowska-Tomaszczyk, 2004). Although they look like perfect equivalents, in actual fact they show a number of differences – in the shape of the buildings, kinds of roofs – a ridge roof in a typical English house, a flat roof in *oikos*, a round thatched roof in *numuno.* They also perform distinct auxiliary functions – the housetop can be regularly used for praying in some cultures but not in English. These words are thus contrastive in some translational contexts, even though the central meaning component is the same.

The strategies of lexis translation proposed by translation specialist Mona Baker (1992) comprise translation by a superordinate category *(e.g., to shampoo* by *to wash),* translation by a more neutral word *(a prick* by *a bloke),* translation by culture-specific equivalents *(a pint* by *a litre),* translation by loan words *(service* as *service/servis/serwis* etc.), optionally followed by an explanation, or as translation by a paraphrase or neologisms e.g., in the Dutch words *ansjovis* ("anchovy"), the second part was modified to resemble *vis* ("fish"), although the word originates in Spanish *anchova.*[9]

Language and culture go hand in hand and this matters in translation. Disregarding this principle can bring about deplorable consequences not only in translation but also in real life. Such a case[10] can be seen in a story quoted by linguists Marko Dragojevic and colleagues about a cafe in an area of Bosnia

9 https://en.wikipedia.org/wiki/Phono-semantic_matching#German

10 The two cases referred to in this section are quoted from ***Polite to a fault*** Language wars: the 19 greatest linguistic spats of all time | Language | The Guardian

and Herzegovina controlled by Croatians during the 1992–95 war. "On its menu, the cafe offered its customers coffee at three different prices, depending on which pronunciation customers used to order the item. *Kava*, indexing a Croatian, and by extension, Catholic identity, was sold for the modest price of 1 Deutsche Mark. *Kafa*, indexing a Serbian and Orthodox Christian identity, was not available for sale. Finally, *kahva*, indexing a Bosnian Muslim identity, cost the customer a 'bullet in the forehead' ".

Translation mistakes and inadequacies can also bring about undesired, often entirely opposite, consequences to the ones intended by the SL speaker. In 1969 when US president Richard Nixon met with the Japanese Prime Minister Eisaku Satō in the White House, they were discussing the final fate of the Okinawa Islands. Nixon was trying to make a deal about this, combining it with trading textile imports. According to the New York Times, "Mr Sato replied as he looked ceilingward, *Zensho shimasu*. Literally, the phrase means: 'I will do my best,' and that's how the interpreter translated it. What it really means to most Japanese is: 'No way.' When the Japanese government did precisely nothing, Nixon was furious, branding Sato a liar."

Another case involving the same sides – USA and Japan – and a similar linguistic expressiveness difference between these cultures, involves the WWII supposed translation mistake, which, as some sources quote, was the direct cause of the Hiroshima bombing. The purported erroneous interpreting of the Japanese answer *Mokusatsu* as one – rather impolite and condescending – of its possible English counterparts, is reported to be the cause of the bombing. Here though, in the most recent analysis of this case, the author Boris Naimushin (2021, p. 95) takes an opposite view and, not denying the linguistic and translational facts – proposes that this interpretation serves the sole purpose of switching "the focus of the problem from politics into linguistics".

Nevertheless, such and similar cases show that there is no doubt that languages are part of culture and this combination can be decisive in communication and miscommunication. This theme is prevailing in a number of studies of language use, e.g., degrees of reserve or explicitness shown in language, politeness strategies, emotion expression and the like.

Some of the properties of more expressive cultures like that of the American – as opposed to say – the British culture are, inert alia (Lewandowska-Tomaszczyk and Wilson 2021) the use of richer and less ambiguous lexis, general verbosity, the use of more frequent intensive modifiers, a lower frequency of hesitation markers (such as e.g., *rather* – frequent in British English), a higher number of repetitions. These traces are also connected with different politeness types (Brown & Levinson, 1987) which, like e.g., in the majority of Southern cultures – is called "positive politeness" and emphasizes expressiveness, as against Japanese or British "negative politeness" which is linked, to put it briefly, with the principle "do not interfere, do not impose your opinion on others". And this might have been part of the Japanese misunderstanding. On the other hand, it is precisely the interpreter's job to be aware of such cultural nuances and react accordingly.

Literature – Multiple Translations of the Same Text

One of the special aspects of meaning are the *aesthetic aspects,* interesting in general language and particularly in the language of literature, predominantly poetry. The aesthetic aspects of language and discourse are evident mostly in the *form* of expression, although this form is not a meaningless or less important part of overall meaning. Contrary to the general conviction that the *same* message can be communicated in *different forms,* I want to argue that any time the speaker changes the form, the message is – to varying degrees – modified as well.

The linguistic *form of words* can be traced in such onomatopaeic (i.e., sound-imitating) words, which present a degree of general conventionalization, as e.g., Kazakh көкек [kökek], Polish *kukułka*, German *Kuckuck* and a similar form – *cuckoo* in English. Such words clearly possess sound-imitating effects but even such forms are not fully identical across languages and are subject to language-bound conventionalization rules as in the English *tap-tap* and Polish *puk puk*, Polish *hau hau* corresponding to the English *bow-wow.*

It is precisely the *form*, and the aesthetic level of meanings that are the salient property of translation of literary texts, most demanding on the one hand but also offering the largest area for translator creativity and leaving her/him more space for individual selection of existing options and of coining new, unattested unrecordeed, language forms.

By way of example consider the two translations of the well-known English novel by J.J.R. Tolkien *The Lord of the Rings*, rendered first into German by Margaret Carroux in 1969–70 and, more recently by Wolfgang Klege[11]. Tolkien himself, with his partly German family background and, first of all, thoroughly familiar with the German language and culture, endorsed the use of e.g., the form *Gouw* in the Dutch translation. The word refers to an area corresponding to the land of meadow in the novel, and Tolkien recommended the corresponding German form *Gau* as the best suited German equivalent of this concept. However, Carroux chose the – apparently previously unattested – German *Auenland* to

11 see: https://en.wikipedia.org/wiki/Translations_of_The_Lord_of_the_Rings#German

name the *meadow-land* instead, probably because of undesired connotations of the former with the times of WWII.

At the same time, the translator chose some *literal* rendering of some of the proper names in *Der Herr der Ringe,* the title she gave to her version of the novel. The English name *Baggins* was rendered as *Beutlin* (*Beutel* Eng. 'bag'), while on the other hand the translator's creativity is recorded in the translation of the proper name *Shelob*, (Eng. *she* and *lob* – dialectal for *spider*), which was rendered by Carroux as *Kankra* – though unrelated to the original English form – retaining a dialectal flavour by an artificial feminine form from the dialectal German *Kanker.* The German *Kanker* refers to "opiliones, an order of arachnids in zoology" (i.e., related to cancer on the one hand and having direct relevance to spiders on the other, as seen in its colloquial English equivalent *daddy-longlegs*).

A new German translation of *The Lord of the Rings* by Wolfgang Krege is a modernized version and n an interesting point is that the word *Lord* in the title was translated as *Herr* by Carroux, and as *Chef in* Krege's version, though he changed to *Herr* in the following editions of the novel[12] The use of *Herr* and *Chef* are examples of *domestication of* the English *Lord,* while e.g., the Thai translation of the title as ลอร์ดออฟเดอะริงส์ [Lxr̒d xxf dexa rings̄̒] in which the title *lord* is retained is an instance of foreignization. The foreignization strategy is also evident in all translation versions of the *Harry Potter* name in world languages, possibly to keep the more exotic element for non-native readers, unlike e.g., *Winnie-the-Pooh,* whose name has been most frequently domesticated to ensure higher intelligibility to the younger audience.

Domestication can be achieved either by translating morpheme for morpheme, as was the case with rendering of proper names described above, by substituting native-for-foreign measurement, temperature, etc. systems, even though in the same paragraph, domestication and foreignization strategies can appear side by side. The "foreign accent" is weakened this way, but not entirely lost.

Coming back to Tolkien's stories the family name *Chubbs* which appears in the original was domesticated into German *Pausbacken* "chubby cheeks", while in the two translated versions of this novel into Polish the domesticated equivalents explore the resemblance of either a phonetic (sound) resemblance in calling the family *Czubowie* lit. "tops/crests", or else in a semantic (meaning) type rendering them as *Pyzowie*, from the Pol. word *pyza* [regional dumpling], denoting larger round dumplings.

Particular attention needed in literature – and especially – poetry, is paid to new words – neologisms – invented and used by the authors and in the attempts at rendering them in other languages. A good example here is the poem *Jabberwocky*, published in the novel *Alice in Wonderland* authored by Lewis Carroll. The first excerpt is the original text, followed by three different translations into German, and the last one – for the sake of contrast – is an Italian translation of the same part of the poem:

(10) **Jabberwocky**[13]

Lewis Carroll (Charles Lutwidge Dodgson)

'Twas brillig, and the slithy toves
Did gyre and gimble in the wabe;

---

12 http://tolkiengateway.net/wiki/Translated_names

13 The original and the quoted translations are retrieved from http://www76.pair.com/keithlim/jabberwocky/poem/jabberwocky.html

All mimsy were the borogoves,
And the mome raths outgrabe'.
"Beware the Jabberwock, my son!
The jaws that bite, the claws that catch!
Beware the Jubjub bird, and shun
The frumious Bandersnatch!"

(11) **Der Jammerwoch**

Robert Scott

Es brillig war. Die schlichte Toven Wirrten und wimmelten in Waben;Und aller-mümsige BurggovenDie mohmen Räth' ausgraben.
»Bewahre doch vor Jammerwoch!Die Zähne knirschen, Krallen kratzen! Bewahr' vor Jubjub-Vogel, vorFrumi
ösen Banderschntzchen!«

(12) **Brabbelback**

Lieselotte & Martin Remane

Es sunnte Gold, und Molch und Lurchkrawallten 'rum im grünen Kreis,
den Flattrings ging es durch und durch,
sie quiepsten wie die Quiekedeis.
»Nimm dich in acht vorm Brabbelback,mein Sohn! Er beißt, wenn er dich packt.
Reiß aus, reiß aus vorm Sabbelschnack,vorm Jubjub, der dich zwickt und zwackt!«

(13) **Der Zipferlake**

Christian Enzensberger

Verdaustig war's, und glaße Wieben
rotterten gorkicht im Gemank.
Gar elump war der Pluckerwank,
und die gabben Schweisel frieben.
»Hab acht vorm Zipferlak, mein Kind!Sein Maul ist beiß, sein Griff ist bohr.
Vorm Fliegelflagel sieh dich vor,dem mampfen Schnatterrind.«

(14) **Italian**

Il Ciarlestrone

Adriana Crespi

Era brillosto, e gli alacridi tossisucchiellavano scabbi nel pantúle:Méstili eran tutti i paparossi,
e strombavan musando i tartarocchi.
«Attento al Ciarlestrone, figlio mio!
Fauci che azzannano, fauci che ti artigliano,
attento all'uccel Giuggio e attento ancoraAl fumibondo chiappabana!»

The differences in the sound perception, underlying meanings, length of stanzas, and types of rhyming are obvious components of distinct aesthetic effects of these versions. They obviously show most similarities among the three German texts, their structural and lexical likeness to the English original and the strongest interpretative differences in the Italian translation, with its soft vocalic endings of the stanzas as well as milder rhyme effects.

Language and Reality[14]

Exercises such as those in the previous sections show that language is not directly linked with the extralinguistic world. There is a relation between the two via the process of *mental imagery construction* (cf. Fauconnier & Turner, 1996), which combines both linguistic and encyclopaedic knowledge, speakers' intentions, their expectations and preferences. In such a model, both linguistic context including the language used, a wide situational context with the participants of the translation process, their psychological and emotional states, needs, expectations as well as social positions and ranks, belong to a set conditions that may shape the overall scene. Such a scene and its conditioning, reflected in our minds are referred to as *conceptualizations* of the outside reality, constrained by diverse language *conventions*, typical of a given language system.

Language users perceive and structure their experiences in different ways of their own choice and, as a result, convey an individual portrayal of what they want to communicate and how they present the message, certainly within conventions referring to the sounds, words, and grammar of a particular language. In other words, they communicate an individual *construal of the world* (cf. Langacker, 1987, pp. 487–488).

The fundamental assumption of the approach presented in this chapter is that the meaning of any linguistic unit is *not* an *objective structure of a conceived* situation, but resides also in the *way* the content is construed and portrayed in a given language.

All in all, each language user has the potential to convey an individual *portayal* of the content s/he wants to communicate, an individual *construal of the world* (cf. Langacker, 1987, pp. 487–488). The fundamental assumption of this approach is that the meaning of any linguistic unit is *not* an *objective structure of a conceived* situation, its conceptual content alone, but resides also in the way

14 A discussion of meaning and translation discussed in this chapter relies on Lewandowska-Tomaszczyk 2010, and 2015.

the content is construed and portrayed. The way one does this is in large part impressed by a given language system, but in others – it depends on the speaker, addressee, and to a certain extent – context of communication.

What Is Meaning Then?

What is meaning of a message then, how do we understand meaning, where can meaning be localized? Out of a number of distinct philosophical stands put forward in different historical times, we might present here a proposal that linguistic meanings are in fact *stimulators* to activate a mental image. They are *instructions* (cf. Seuren, 1985; Lewandowska-Tomaszczyk, 1996) to build *mental models* of people, objects, activities or events, making reference to those entities stored in our memory and tailor them to current contexts. For instance, the meaning of the word *furniture* is a stimulator to activate a mental model of a rather generalized set of schematically portrayed articles that are used to make a room or building suitable for living or working. The most salient, prototypical, members of *table, chair* or *bed*, are of a less schematic character that the superordinate *furniture.* In a particular situation we make these meanings more specific, such as *this armchair, a large oval table*, or *a twin bed.*

Some words, phrases, or grammatical forms such as e.g., *John might arrive tomorrow* encourage creating mental images of a *possibility* type ('It is possible that John will arrive tomorrow') or in another example e.g., the English form *infotainment* triggers the integrated, blended sense, combining two mental spaces (Turner & Fauconnier, 1995) of broadcast material aiming to be *both* entertaining and informative or making reference to products, appliances that than provide both information and entertainment. This last example is particularly telling for the purposes of translation discussion – as it is precisely such cases, among many others, that are subject to language-specific ways of forming new words in some languages, though not in others. If one wants to translate such words into other languages, diverse strategies of rendering them can be used such as e.g., in this specialized English phrase *in-car infotainment system*, which is defined as a combination of vehicle systems which are used to deliver entertainment and information to the driver and the passengers through audio/ video interfaces, control elements like touch screen displays, button panel, voice commands, etc..[15], its French equivalent compound form can be proposed

15 https://www.google.com/search?q=in-car+infotainment+system+definition&oq=in-car+infotainment+system+definition&aqs=chrome..69i57j33i22i29i30l3.15075j0j4&sourceid=chrome&ie=UTF-

such as e.g., *nouveau système d'info-divertissement* or one might simply resort to borrowing the English form into French as in the phrase *systèmes d'infotainment*, while in Polish, apart from the borrowing option, a more descriptive, analytically transparent form, is used *samochodowy system informacyjno-rozrywkowy* in the literal sense of "car information-entertainment system".

Are Languages Inter-Translatable? Relativity Hypothesis

American linguists of the first half of the 20th century, Benjamin Lee Whorf (1956) and Edward Sapir proposed what is called a Relativity Hypothesis, or a thesis of conceptual determinism, which in its strong version, implies that language predetermines our way of thinking and our vision of the world. The conclusion from this thesis is that faithful translation is not possible. Philosopher Willard Van Orman Quine (1964) proposed a *Radical Untranslatability Hypothesis*, in which he proclaimed the impossibility of translation, and that of communication at the same time. Quine based his argument on a thought experiment. He proposed that if a speaker of an imaginary, unknown, language nobody from another culture is familiar with, says e.g., *Gavagai!*, even looking at or pointing at a rabbit running in front of them, nobody from another culture might identify the meaning of what he said. He might have uttered any phrase or sentence at that moment e.g., "Oh, rabbit!" or "What a nice fur!" or "I hate these animals!", "What a lovely creature!" or even 'What a lovely day we're having, aren't we!'. The counterargument to Quine's claim might emphasize human willingness to communicate and to pursue joint, common tasks by making an effort toward satisfying outcomes, also as far as verbal understanding is concerned.

The weak version of the Sapir-Whorf's hypothesis proposes that language expresses our vision of the world. This less radical stance is also shared as a point of reasoning in the present study. We agree that full equivalence between languages is not attainable, and yet, humans are reasonable beings and are capable of making intelligent guesses. Hence, the moment we want to communicate and start cooperating on a task, then, based on the common contexts, common human properties and possible values, we find a possibility to align our own Source Language meanings with *approximate, closest possible, meanings* in the Target Language (Lewandowska-Tomaszczyk, 2010).

Meaning Re-Conceptualization in Translation

To res-asssume, translation cannot be considered a "transfer" of the *same meaning* from a Target to a Source language. The meanings in each of the languages, be it French, German, English, or Chinese are not *the same*, they are shaped by the language-specific rules of grammar, word-formation, etc., which leads to somewhat different mental activation of concepts and *conceptualizations* of the whole scenes and events in the minds of users of particular languages. Thus, rather than being transfer of meanings, translation is better regarded as a dynamic set of *re-conceptualization* of an original SL message expressed in TL terms and understood, interpreted, and stored in memory as somewhat different mental images.

Reconceptualization is not a simple one-act process. Originating with a SL author, the message is accepted and re-conceptualized by SL recipients, each with an individual life experience, different background knowledge, in a number of possible contexts. The translator is the third of the SL users and at the same time, an originator of a new reconceptualized – TL – version. The *construal* of scenes portrayed in the TL text is performed in terms of the the blending between the SL and TL concepts and the principles of L grammar and its style conventions. However, even here, one can recognize the "linguistic fingerprints" of the SL, which leaves its traced in a TL text (Porter et al. in press; Venuti, 2017).

Conclusions: Losses and Gains in Translation

From the above discussion we can conclude that *approximative communication*, Gestalt in nature, aims either at best approximation possible under given conditions or at more-or-less communication. The speaker can also choose an approximative form for rhetorical and emotive purposes, to impress the audience, surprise them, etc., or for connative reasons, to persuade the audience or impose an ideology. This frequently takes place in the trading scenario in the case of advertisements. The common technique is understatement and the use of information selectively (*We sell the best beer*).

In some other contexts language is produced automatically in chunks, predominantly in spoken discourse, with weaker control by the Speaker, so the outcomes are certain conventional routines (e.g. *I'm sorry*), not necessarily in one-to-one correspondence with the nuances of relevant intentions.

Linguistic modification phrases can have a fairly wide scope of reference, e.g. the nominal phrase *red pencil* can refer to the pencil surface, pencil graphite part or both (see Langacker's, 1993 *active zones* or *reference points*). The phrase is underdetermined outside the context even though it refers to a fairly steady element in our surrounding. Other lexical combinations are subject to even more varied possible interpretations, which is one of the sources of semantic approximation.

Thus, we build meanings in the interaction, while inter-langual equivalence is dynamic, as first identified by Eugene Nida as early as 1964, while in the literal sense equi-valece – being of equal worth, is in fact a *dynamic* blend, a vector of *culture* and mental *construal* of different types, expressed in language. Langacker (1987, p. 52) proposes that language is a set of structures graded with reference to their prototypicality and entrenchment. In other words, the farther a structure is from the prototype, the less likely it will function as part of a convention in the linguistic system. Prototypicality connected with the basic categorization level, the earliest to acquire and the easiest to recall, involves various category members in different conceptual and linguistic systems. The prototypical tree or bird, talking of natural kind objects, vehicle or food, to mention artefacts, can be diverse in different cultures.

Communication among people from different linguistic and cultural backgrounds involves both a combination of independent linguistic and cultural inputs and links between the two cultural concepts as well as a development of new categories, a result of *blending* – putting together – of distinct classes of items, originating from different cultural and linguistic patterns of trans-cultural nature, which do not represent two input systems (Source Culture and Target Culture) but rather a *third quality*, a new one, emerging at the points of contact between the two cultures and the individuals who represent them (Fauconnier, 1985).

An ideal translation should contain the same number of possible interpretations, even faulty or erroneous at places, as the original text. Günther Kandler describes such an ideal translation as one that "allows of exactly the same breadth of interpretation (and even misinterpretation) as the original." (Kandler in Carey & Jumpelt, 1963, p. 294.) As can be seen from the present analysis, this is an idealistic and futile expectation. Languages offer an interpretive multiplicity, which has its origin in different aspects of world languages. The translator then faces a dilemma and the question asked by Alice is always valid:

- 'When *I* use a word' Humpty Dumpty said, in a rather scornful tone, 'it means just
  what I choose it to mean – neither more nor less'.
- 'The question is', said Alice, 'whether you *can* make words mean so many different things'.
- 'The question is', said Humpty Dumpty, 'which is to be the master – that's all'. (Carroll, 1965 [1871], p. 269).

References

Baker, M. (1992). *In Other Words: A Coursebook on Translation*. London: Routledge.

Brown, P., & Levinson, S. C. (1987). *Politeness: Some Universals in Language Usage*. Cambridge: Cambridge University Press.

Carroll, L. (1965) [1865]. *Alice Adventures in Wonderland*. Signet Classics (Penguin Group).

Carroll, L. (1965) [1871]. *Through the Looking Glass and What Alice Found There*. Signet Classics (Penguin Group).

Durán Muńoz, I. (2012). Analysing Common Mistakes in Translations of Tourist Texts (Spanish, English and German). *On Omáze in, 26*(2012/2), 335–349.

Fauconnier, G. 1985. *Mental Spaces*. Cambridge, MA: MIT Press.

Fauconnier, G. & Turne, M. (1996). Blending as a Central Process of Grammar. In A. Goldberg (Ed.) *Conceptual Structure, Discourse, and Language* (pp. 113–129). Cambridge, UK: Cambridge University Press.

Frawley, W. (1992). Semantics, Sublanguage, and the Translation of Specialized Lexicon. In B. Lewandowska-Tomaszczyk & M. Thelen (Eds.), *Tanslation and Meaning* (pp. 321–332). Part 2. Maastricht.

Gibson, J. J. (1966). *The Senses Considered as Perceptual Systems*. London: Allen and Unwin.

Gibson, J. J. (1975). Affordances and Behavior. In E. S. Reed & R. Jones (Eds.), *Reasons for Realism: Selected Essays of James J. Gibson* (pp. 410–411). Hillsdale, NJ: Lawrence Erlbaum.

Kandler, G. (1963). On the Problem of Quality in Translation: Basic Considerations. In: E. Carey & J. W. Rumpelt (Eds.), *Quality in Translation. Proceedings of the IIIrd congress of the International Federation of Translators (FIT)* (pp. 291–298). Bad Godesberg, 1959. London/New York: Pergamon Press.

Lakoff, G. (1987). *Women, Fire and Dangerous Thing: What Categories Reveal about the Mind*. Chicago: Chicago University Press.

Langacker, R. W. (1987). *Foundations of Cognitive Grammar* (Vol. 1). Stanford: Stanford University Press.

Langacker, R. W. (1991). *Foundations of Cognitive Grammar, Vol. 2: Descriptive Application*. Stanford, CA: Stanford University Press.

Langacker, R. W. (1993). Reference-Point Constructions. *Cognitive Linguistics, 4, 1*–38. http://dx.doi.org/10.1515/cogl.1993.4.1.1

Lewandowska-Tomaszczyk, B. (1996). *Depth of Negation – A Cognitive=Semntic Study*. Lodz: Lodz University Press.

Lewandowska-Tomaszczyk, B. (2003). Ontologies and Language Corpora. In B. Lewandowska-Tomaszczyk (Ed.), *PALC 2001: Practical Applications in Language Corpora* (pp. 11–32). Frankfurt a. Main: Peter Lang.

Lewandowska-Tomaszczyk, B. (2004). Lexical Problems of Translation. In Armin Paul Frank, Norbert Greiner, Theo Hermans, Haral Kittel, Werner Koller, José Lambert & Fritz Paul (Eds.), *Art. 48. Vol. 1. An International Encyclopaedia of Translation Studies* (3 Vols, pp. 455–465). Berlin: Mouton de Gryuter.

Lewandowska-Tomaszczyk, B. (2007). Polysemy, Prototypes and Radial Categories. In Dirk Geeraerts & Hubert Cuyckens (Eds.), *Handbook of Cognitive Linguistics* (pp. 139–169). Oxford: Oxford University Press.

Lewandowska-Tomaszczyk, B. (2008). On the Cross-Language Relationship in Lexicology and Terminology. In B. Lewandowska-Tomaszczyk and M. Thelen (Eds.), *Translation and Meaning* (pp. 297–307). Part 8. Maastricht: Zuyd University.

Lewandowska-Tomaszczyk, B. (2010). Re-conceptualization and the Emergence of Discourse Meaning as a Theory of Translation. In B. Lewandowska-Tomaszczyk & M. Thelen (Eds.) *Meaning in Translation* (pp. 105–148.). Frankfurt a. Main: Peter Lang.

Lewandowska-Tomaszczyk, B. (2012). Approximative Spaces and the Tolerance Threshold in Communication. *International Journal of Cognitive Linguistics, 2*(2), 2–19.

Lewandowska-Tomaszczyk, B. (2015). Equivalence. In L. Bogucki, S. Goźdz-Roszkowski, & P. Stalmaszczyk (Eds.), *Ways to Translation* (pp. 11–54). Lodz: Lodz University Press.

Lewandowska-Tomaszczyk, B. (2017). Cluster Equivalence, General Language, and Language for Specific Purposes. In M. Grygiel (Ed.), *Cognitive Approaches to Specialist Language* (pp. 384–418). Newcastle upon Tyne: Cambridge Scholars Publishing.

Lewandowska-Tomaszczyk, B., & Wilson, P. A. (2017). Pride in British English and Polish: A Cultural Linguistic Perspective. In Farzad Sharifian (Ed.), *Advances in Cultural Linguistics* (pp. 247–288). Singapore: Springer Nature Pte Ltd.

Lewandowska-Tomaszczyk, B., & Wilson, P. A. (2021). Expressive and Reserved Cultural Linguistic Schemas: British and American Pride Clusters. In Marzieh Sadeghpour & Farzad Sharifian (Eds.), *Cultural Linguistics and World Englishes* (pp. 261–293). Berlin: Springer.

Naimushin, B. (2021). Hiroshima, Mokusatsu and Alleged Mistranslations. *English Studies at NBU, 7*(1), 87–96. https://doi.org/10.33919/esnbu.21.1.6.

Nida, E. (1964). *Toward a Science of Translating: With Special Reference to Principles and Procedures Involved in Bible Translating*. Leiden: Brill.

Petrov, O., & Mizin, K. (2021). Emotional State Gemütlichkeit in Cross-Cultural Perspective: Corpus-based Approach. *Studies about Languages / Kalbų Studijos, 38*, 43–60. https://doi.org/10.5755/j01.sal.1.38.26581.

Porter, J. D., Ilchuk, Y., & Dombrowski, Q. (2021). Linguistic Fingerprints on Translation's Lens. *Journal of Data Mining and Digital Humanities*. Retrieved from: http://jdmdh.episciences.org ISSN 2416-5999.

Quine, W. V. (1964). Meaning and Translation. In J. A. Fodor & J. J. Katz (Eds), *The Structure of Language: Readings in the Philosophy of Language* (pp. 460–478). Englewood Cliffs, NJ: Prentice-Hall.

Rosch, E. (1983). Prototype Classification and Logical Classification: The Two Systems. In E. Scholnick (Ed.), *New Trends in Cognitive Representation: Challenges to Piaget's Theory* (pp. 73–86). Hillsdale, NJ: Lawrence Erlbaum Associates.

Seuren, P. A. M. (1985). *Discourse Semantics*. Oxford: Blackwell.

Smith, H. W., & Nomi, T. (2000). Is Amae the Key to Understanding Japanese Culture? *Electronic Journal of Sociology*. ISSN: 1198 3655. Retrieved from: https://sociology.lightningpath.org/ejs-archives/vol005.001/smith-nomi.html

Tolkien, J. R. R. (1994). *The Lord of the Rings*. Boston/New York: Houghton Mifflin Company. Translated into German 1969–1970. Der Herr der Ringe Margaret Carroux and Ebba-Margareta von Freymann (poems). By Wolfgang Krege (2000). Stuttgart: Klett-Cotta. Translated into Polish by Jerzy Łoziński Bractwo Pierścienia 1996. Poznań: Zysk i S-ka. tr. by Marta Skibniewska 2001 Drużyna Pierścienia Warszawa: MUZA S.A.

Turner, M., & Fauconnier, G. 1995. Conceptual Integration and Formal Expression. *Metaphor & Symbolic Activity, 10*(3), 183–204.

Venuti, L. (2017). *The Translator's Invisibility: A History of Translation*. New York: Routledge.

Whorf, B. L. (1956). *Language, Thought and Reality* (J. B. Carroll, Ed.). New York: Wiley.

Introduction to Natural Resources and Communication: When the Rhetorical Tradition Confronts the Real Economy

By Craig Frayne

The next chapter examines how communication and linguistics influence natural resource projects and what needs to be considered in understanding the different perspectives of the interactors. It is pointed out that while natural resource and environmental management research focuses on stakeholders, the culture of the various stakeholders is, though, often ignored. Stakeholders refer to the various interest groups affected by projects and policies associated with natural resources and conservation. Stakeholder analysis, thus, focuses on the (power) relationships between the various stakeholders. Frayne argues that one needs to also consider the cultural ties to the landscape and how these are then reflected in the rhetoric of people involved in the management of the natural resources and conservation. A focus only on the stakeholders fails to address the complexity and richness of culture and communication. Since human communication is complex, it is necessary to examine it from various perspectives; these include various levels ranging from the larger ecological environment to such cultural aspects as values and worldviews all the way to cognitive frames and mental representations of individuals. How this works is illustrated with the analysis of specific examples. This analysis reveals that discourse consists of multiple culturally embedded language games. However, humans have a need to reduce and simplify complex issues in order to comprehend them which can result in simplifications similar to stereotypes. And finally, it is pointed out that intercultural competence is needed to communicate successfully and appropriately which involves cognitive complexity. This cognitive complexity needs to include the ability to navigate shifting contexts, distinguish different levels (ecological, cultural, socio-economic, cognitive), and integrate them in practice. The chapter, thus, offers insights into the communicative and cultural aspects that need to be considered when examining the discourse associated with the management of natural resources and conservation.

Michael B. Hinner

Craig Frayne is an independent researcher and writer based in Canada. He has worked professionally in environmental as well as development communication roles with businesses, citizens groups, and NGOs in Europe, Canada, and Latin America. Following graduate studies in engineering and natural sciences, he completed a doctoral dissertation "Language Games and Nature", which looked at intercultural communication in the context of natural resource debates.

Craig Frayne

Natural Resources and Communication: When the Rhetorical Tradition Confronts the Real Economy

The backdrop to a discussion of natural resources will be familiar to many readers in a business or policy audience. The global economy is fuelled by increasing amounts of finite resources. Trillions of dollars will need to be invested in the coming years to simply meet UN Development Goals (UNCTAD, 2014). The amount of minerals, ores, fossil fuels, and biomass consumed globally is projected to triple by 2050 (National Intelligence Council, 2013). Added to this are fiscal stimulus packages, climate targets, and associated green technology mandates projected to drive demand for strategic minerals (Jones et al., 2020). At the time of writing (October 2021), food and energy inflation are at levels not seen in decades and supply chain disruptions are a reminder of the interconnectedness of the global material metabolism.

This chapter draws attention to what is perhaps a less familiar dimension of resource economics. We'll consider how raw material – the most tangible of economic concepts – intersects with the more symbolic realms of human language and communication. It is at this dichotomous intersection where the global economic engine is prone to run up against different interests, values, and conceptions of how the system itself functions (or ought to). The consequence can be crises for businesses, households, and entire economies. Historically, state legal and executive apparatuses have acted to bring these crises to a resolution. Whether this has led to sustainable, just, and desirable outcomes is another discussion.

This chapter explores how communication and linguistics can help us understand the dynamics of the natural resource projects. My research has analyzed intercultural and intergroup communication dynamics of energy and waste infrastructure projects, mining, as well as themes of the bio-economy like genetically modified seed (Frayne, 2021a). Here, I'll outline what I see as problematic aspects of common approaches among organizations and businesses. In practice, these approaches often fall under the rubric of stakeholder or strategic communication. In theory, I argue, they are rooted in the rhetorical tradition which views communication as the practical art of influencing outcomes (Craig,

1999, p. 135). For counter-consideration, a proposed methodology is outlined with examples and insights for professional settings.

Beyond Stakeholders

The term *stakeholder* has become common in natural resource and environmental management. Stakeholders are identified as distinctive interest groups that are affected by projects and policies related to natural resources and conservation (Reed et al., 2009). While there is no cross-cutting definition of what constitutes a stakeholder in a given situation (Billgren & Holmén, 2008), cultural identity is, no doubt, a key factor. Insights from intercultural communication are pertinent when stakeholders consist of people from different cultures, which is practically an inevitability in the modern world.

Stakeholder analysis has roots in policy and business management; the former being concerned with power and influence in the policy process, the latter with threats and opportunities that could affect the success of the firm (Varvasovszky, 2000). In many sectors, notably natural resources, stakeholder analysis has included systematic relationship mapping and charting the interest/influence of different actors (e.g., Lindenberg & Crosby, 1981). Such approaches can be described as instrumental or means-ends, in that they are intended to influence and achieve desired outcomes. Even studies with an intercultural focus could be described in this light such as, for instance, Wang, Ni, and De la Flor (2014) who use an intercultural competence model to assess public relations management in the Peruvian mining industry. By contrast, normative approaches are also found in natural resource and environmental management literature, often under the banner of stakeholder participation or communication. Normative approaches employ notions of justice, democracy, or morality to assess legitimacy among stakeholders (Reed et al., 2009). Such approaches might stress stakeholder participation, equity, and involvement of marginalized groups in decision making processes (Johnson et al., 2004).

My research proposes a move beyond the notion of stakeholders, towards more in-depth understandings of communication itself. This is not to suggest there are not merits to stakeholder analysis as a discipline and practice. However, stakeholder approaches can be problematic when it comes to the nuances of the debates and the outcomes beyond financial interests of organizations. The very definition of a stakeholder as anyone affected by a decision (Freeman, 1983) is problematic if, in practice, stakeholder communication is restricted to individuals and groups deemed to have enough relative influence to warrant consideration by proponents or regulators. The idea of stakeholder groups is also problematic from a conceptual, intercultural standpoint. The natural world is a source of cultural identity. People with historical, cultural, and spiritual relationships to landscapes and lifeforms are more than stakeholders to be considered alongside institutions, corporate entities, and others whose interests are often material and bureaucratic. A cultural relationship to the natural world is one of dwelling, care, and meaning.

While the shortcomings are most evident with respect to instrumental approaches, it is also borne out of inadequacies in normative frameworks. Normative stakeholder communication theory is often premised on Habermas' (1984) communicative rationality, which aims for rational agreement through dialogue to establish shared understanding and consensus. This aim is underpinned by the premise that transparent and clear language, as opposed to force or manipulation, can generate consensus. This aim may seem amenable to intercultural understanding but the issue here, as Czobor-Lupp (2008) points out, is the assumption of linguistic clarity, transparency, and rationality. Language can, of course, be all those things. However, language – particularly when imbued with cultural meanings – is also aesthetic, rhetorical, and metaphorical. As Lakoff (2010) claims, the Enlightenment ideal of language and reason is often a barrier to understanding why people hold certain views towards environmental issues.

To summarize, stakeholder approaches fail to address the complexity and depth of human cultures and communication. Strategic communication, rooted in a rhetorical art of achieving desired outcomes, is often inauthentic and culturally dismissive. Similarly, appeals to dialogue and reason often fail to account for the complexity of human languages and forms of life.

Multilevel Discourse Analysis

The shortcomings outlined above point to the challenge in conceptualizing human languages and cultures. I often cite Sluga's (2011) discussion of the Austrian-British philosopher Ludwig Wittgenstein to refer to languages, cultures, and communication as hyper-complexities. It is unsurprising that intercultural communication is a field of "theoretical turbulence" (Poutiainen, 2014). Over several decades, the discipline has spanned microcultural and metalinguistic elements of communication as well as the macrocontext of social and economic systems (Leeds-Hurwitz, 2013; Moon, 2011). More recently, in line with the Zeitgeist, an ecological turn (Kinefuchi, 2018) proposes to take the macro a step further, beyond the traditional scope of the field.

To be sure, simply stating that something is complex is not helpful, particularly for a business or policy audience. However, as with social sciences like economics, it's important to be aware of situations where methodologies and models are, at best, partial representations. As with economics, there are real, often harsh, implications for failing to acknowledge that we don't have the whole picture.

In the face of the conceptual challenges, my research aims to survey the landscape of human communication through a holistic framework called multilevel discourse analysis. Discourse here refers to communication in the broadest sense: ordinary spoken/written language as well nonverbals, signs, and symbols. By distinguishing communication according to levels (ecological, cultural, socio-economic, and cognitive) we can gain insight into the many variables and contexts that lead to misunderstandings. The levels cascade in a top-down manner from macro to micro, and are summarized as follows:

- *Ecological.* Discourse about nature and the more-than-human world. This includes discourse that concerns ecology in a scientific sense, the geographic and cyber-physical situatedness of communication, as well as human subjective experiences of environments [*Umwelten*].
- *Cultural.* Expressions of identity, values, and worldviews; people commenting about who they are, either directly or indirectly.
- *Socio-Economic.* Discourse related to economics, institutions, and power relations. Notably, aspects of social existence that do not express cultural identity.
- *Cognitive.* Mental representations and cognitive frames as reflected in communication. This level draws on concepts from cognitive linguistics as well as nonverbal communication.

To distinguish levels in this way is, necessarily, a simplification. In practice, these factors blend and there are not clear dividing lines between them. Ecological discourse is often cultural, the cultural and social realms are overlapping, and so on. Likewise, insights from cognitive linguistics do not apply to a subset of communication, they are features of communication itself. Nonetheless, segmenting communication in this way can help one view an otherwise unsurveyable landscape.

Methodological challenges are the data requirements and wide scope of analysis. In practice, the methodology utilizes corpus linguistics and to obtain and analyze large, representative data sets.[1] Computational methods can help gain insights that would be impossible through human analysis alone (Hunston, 2002). Ideally, the methodology would combine the emic depth of ethnographic fieldwork and interviews with the breadth and generality possible with large and varied corpora.

1 In linguistics, a corpus is a collection of machine-readable texts stored in an electronic database (Baker, 2006).

Examples

Verbal Communication about a Gas Pipeline

The first example is an analysis of verbal communication surrounding the Dakota Access Pipeline (DAP).[2] Using a web-corpus, I collected hundreds of text quotations from statements made by individuals in the context of the 2016 protests and gatherings on Standing Rock Sioux territory bordering North and South Dakota. In these quotes, culture – specifically indigenous identity – was central. However, culture was bound up with political and economic relations as well as the common (and understandable) tendency to view a pipeline primarily as a scientific and engineering problem. The multilevel framework was used to integrate disparate aspects of the debate.

Quotes were first categorized based on whether they represented the pro- and anti-pipeline side of the debate. These statements were then identified as expressing ecological, cultural, socio-economic themes. Cognitive analysis looked to categorizations, connotations, and conceptual schemas implicit in statements.

Notable in the ecological level of analysis was the framing of natural resources. Project proponents often spoke of the physical environment as something that can be managed and controlled, both through technology and the legal framework. Statements had the effect of conveying an impression of competence and control with respect to the built, physical environment. Proponents also made the case for the pipeline as needed infrastructure for economic growth and energy security. At both the ecological and socio-economic levels, there was an implicit "back-and-forth" legitimacy exchange between pro- and anti- sides. Whereas proponents aimed to establish and uphold legitimacy over resources and infrastructure, opponents challenged that legitimacy. Points of contention encompassed water quality concerns, health risks, global climate, economic inequality, and the role of executive and judicial branches vis à vis protestors and the corporate entity. The cognitive level revealed how this exchange became polarized. Analysis drawing on cognitive linguistic concepts of radial categories and idealized cognitive models (Lakoff, 1987) showed how stereotyping, in/out group identification, and othering was at play to create negative associations with protestors, with the effect of placing certain actors beyond the pale.

---

2 Data and more detailed discussion can be found in *Demarcating Cultural Expressions in the Dakota Access Pipeline Debate* (Frayne, 2021b)

Interestingly, there was a sense in which cultural statements stood apart from the legitimacy exchange described above. Cultural expressions – often referring to holistic relationships between people, culture, nature, and the economy – operated in an entirely different frame of meaning from that of the proponent/opponent poles. Language was often symbolic, connotative, and metaphorical. Rather than intercultural misunderstanding between sides of the debate, there was an evading of the culture altogether. In other words, rather than communication or dialogue in the framework of cultural meanings, there was a tendency to reduce or strip away cultural identity and context. Cultural discourse in this case, might be conceived as a turning away from the language of social/institutional power structures. On the part of opponents, one might claim lost of trust and legitimacy in the discursive space is countered by assertions of shared identity and experience. On the part of proponents, decontextualizing might be seen (deliberately or otherwise) as a way of managing the discourse. Keeping the subject bound within the expertise of certain groups (e.g., institutions, professional communities, corporations) helps maintain legitimacy and authority of those groups.

This analysis gives insight into how to reconcile critical and interpretive approaches to communication. On the one hand, there is a need for hard-edged critical analysis of socio-economic factors like financial and legal relations; on the other, is a need to account for elusive cultural meanings and perspectives of unique, diverse groups and individuals. In this example, a multilevel discourse approach helped distinguish the blurred line between political/economic and culture dimensions of these debates.

Nonverbals in Mining Debates

The second example discusses nonverbal analysis of mining discourse. While many insights can be gained from textual analysis. Nonverbals can be analyzed with multimodal communication, which draws from the textual as well as aural, linguistic, spatial, and visual capacities or modes (Murray, 2013). Prior to discussing the example, it will be helpful to outline of why nonverbals are essential to meaning and communication:

- Human cognition is mostly (some research has claimed 98 %) unconscious and is inseparable from emotion. Moreover, cognition is embodied, meaning ideas, language, and even thought are mediated by the body (Lakoff, 2010).
- Human needs, emotions, and intentions are processed by the limbic brain. Nonverbal communication, in particular body language is, to a large extent,

the expression of unconscious limbic processing (Lamendella, 1977). Gestures are expressions of embodied cognition (Kinsbourne, 2006).
- In contrast to largely unconscious nonverbal communication, verbal language is more consciously driven and concentrated in the frontal lobe of the brain, which is responsible for thinking, planning, and judgment.

Nonverbals often occur without our conscious awareness and, thus, are explicable in terms of the limbic system. Involuntary facial expressions, for instance, originate in the subcortical areas of the brain (Matsumoto & Hwang, 2013). There is also evidence that head movements encode emotional intent (Livingstone & Palmer, 2016).

To capture this often-overlooked dimension of communication, I collected eight hours of audio and video recordings representing different perspectives on various mining operations and proposed developments. These included interviews, documentaries, recordings of "town hall" type meetings. Timestamps of interest (points in the recording with distinctive and pronounced non-verbal expression) were then annotated and analyzed. Segments were categorized based on ecological, cultural, and socio-economic subject matter. (The cognitive level was not isolated since all the nonverbal analyses centre on cognition.)

The observed trends in facial expressions and gestures suggested that different cognitive responses were exhibited at different levels of discourse. The ecological level exhibited more verbal and spatial reasoning and did not appear to trigger emotional responses. In other words, the "fight or flight" emotional responses of limbic system and subcortical areas of the brain were being mediated. In contrast, speakers at the ecological level generally showed less facial expression. Gestures were predominantly iconic and depicted physical/spatial processes. Compared to the other levels of analysis, intonation and stress was less pronounced. Speakers at the cultural level displayed more power and confidence gestures, including pointing (to add emphasis), thumb displays, and fist pumping. Gestures were more metaphoric than was the case in the ecological level, depicting abstract concepts such as God, culture, identity, and fighting back. Contempt and agitation were displayed, at one point by a contempt expression (raised side of mouth) as well as the backwards thumb gesture on another occasion. The socio-economic level displayed a high degree of emotion, often expressed in the eyes. Universal facial expressions of fear and sadness could be seen in speakers and listeners. Gestures also indicated hopelessness and innocence, such as the palm open "pleading" gesture as well as the shoulder shrug.

The consequence is that the ability to read nuanced, face-to-face, non-verbal communication matters a great deal in the context of these projects. Engaging and mobilizing people will depend on framing issues in a way that speaks to their implicit, unconscious attitudes. Along similar lines, Lakoff (2010) discussed cognitive linguistic aspects of environmental communication, stressing the importance of discussing environmental issues in terms of moral values; the efficacy of stories and narratives as opposed to statistics and bland facts; the necessity to address everyday concerns and avoid technical jargon (79–80). Based on observations from the nonverbal analysis of mining debates, the point about moral values could emphasize cultural identity and worldviews. Also, on the point "everyday concerns", one might stress the importance of framing issues in terms of economic livelihoods.

Implications

To be sure, researching these topics is different dealing with them in the field, workplace, or community life. In practice, challenges of conceptualize languages and cultures are eclipsed by our limited perspectives within organizational and situational constraints. The method and examples outlined in this chapter is how I approached the challenge from a research perspective, but this does not necessarily translate directly into applied methodology or industry best practices. That said, some considerations can be helpful.

First is recognizing when legal/rationalistic or rhetorical communication is being used in settings where others are employing cultural meanings. The pipeline example suggests that rather than taking a view of intercultural misunderstanding as incompatibility between different cultural communities (Ting-Toomey & Oetzel, 2001), it may be more appropriate (at least in some cases) to view the misunderstanding in terms of whether the cultural dynamics are even being taken into account. To put it another way, discourse consists of multiple culturally embedded language games, but there is a tendency to reduce, simplify, and decontextualize. This tendency is perhaps a manifestation of bias or mental shortcuts the human brain uses to reduce complexity (Tversky & Kahneman, 1974). Uncertainty leads to the stress response in humans (De Berker et al., 2016) so it is natural to seek more secure conceptual ground by replacing ambiguous concepts (like culture) with clear and distinct frameworks (like law or empirical science). Cognitively, this categorization functions similar to stereotype, where information is simplified in order to make sense of an otherwise too complex world (Tajfel, 1981). While this simplification may be inevitable, being aware of it will add depth to communicative practice.

Another consideration has to do with the public sphere in which communication occurs. The pipeline case, as well as many other citizen mobilizations, draws attention to the forums and spaces for communication in the modern world. These spaces are many and are rapidly evolving due to technology. At the same time, one could argue that spaces for free, authentic, 'in the flesh' communication are under threat by private, institutional interests. Citizen environmental movements, as well as more spontaneous disruptions to the resource engine of the economy, might be seen as openings of a public sphere whose official channels (e.g., media, political process, etc.) have been closed off. These openings often take place on the periphery, outside formal centres of power, in places where narratives of progress are more likely to clash with material and historical realities. By viewing natural resource communication through a civic and historical (as opposed to a strictly economic) lens, we can gain a better understanding of context and significance.

A final consideration has to do with intercultural competency. One aspect of intercultural competence is cognitive complexity, which has been identified as important in avoiding stereotypes and being perceptive to subtleties in communication. While these aspects certainly apply to the present discussion, there are other dimensions of cognitive complexity when it comes to natural resource communication. While cognitive complexity often refers to perceptual and communicative skills (e.g., perceiving nuanced differences), there is also need for complexity in terms of abstract mental structures and frames. Cognitive complexity might be elaborated as an ability to navigate shifting contexts, distinguish different levels (ecological, cultural, socio-economic, cognitive), and integrate them in practice.

References

Baker, P. (2006). *Using Corpora in Discourse Analysis*. London, New York: Continuum.

Billgren, C., & Holmén, H. (2008). Approaching Reality: Comparing Stakeholder Analysis and Cultural Theory in the Context of Natural Resource Management. *Land Use Policy*, *25*(4), 550–562. https://doi.org/10.1016/j.landusepol.2007.11.004

Craig, R. T. (1999). Communication Theory as a Field. *Communication Theory*, *9*(2), 119–161. https://doi.org/10.1111/j.1468-2885.1999.tb00355.x.

Czobor-Lupp, M. (2008). Communicative Reason and Intercultural Understanding: A Critical Discussion of Habermas. *European Journal of Political Theory*, *7*(4), 430–448. https://doi.org/10.1177/147488510809405

De Berker, A. O., Rutledge, R. B., Mathys, C., Marshall, L., Cross, G. F., Dolan, R. J., & Bestmann, S. (2016). Computations of Uncertainty Mediate Acute

Stress Responses in Humans. *Nature Communications*, *7*, 1–11. https://doi.org/10.1038/ncomms10996.

Frayne, C. (2021a). Corpus-based Analysis of Genetically Modified Seed Discourse. *Discourse & Society*, 33(2), 175–19232.

Frayne, C. (2021b). Demarcating Cultural Expressions in the Dakota Access Pipeline Debate. *International Journal of Language and Culture (in Review)*.

Freeman, R. E. (1983). *Strategic Management: A Stakeholder Approach*. New York: Cambridge University Press.

Habermas, J. (1984). *The Theory of Communicative Action, Vol. 1: Reason and the Rationalization of Society*. Boston: Beacon Press.

Hunston, S. (2002). *Corpora in Applied Linguistics*. Cambridge: Cambridge University Press.

Johnson, N., Lilja, N., Ashby, J. A., & Garcia, J. A. (2004). The Practice of Participatory Research and Gender Analysis in Natural Resource Management. *Natural Resources Forum*, *28*(3), 189–200. https://doi.org/10.1111/j.1477-8947.2004.00088.x.

Kinefuchi, E. (2018). Critical discourse analysis and an ecological turn in intercultural communication. *Review of Communication: Critical Discourse Studies and/in Communication: Theories, Methodologies, and Pedagogies at the Intersections (special issue)*. *18*(3), 212–230. doi: 10.1080/15358593.2018.1479882

Kinsbourne, M. (2006). Gestures as Embodied Cognition: A Neurodevelopmental Interpretation. *Gesture*, *6*(2), 205–214.

Lakoff, G. (1987). *Women, Fire, and Dangerous Things*. Chicago: University of Chicago.

Lakoff, G. (2010). Why It Matters How We Frame the Environment. *Environmental Communication*, *4*(1), 70–81. https://doi.org/10.1080/17524030903529749.

Lamendella, J. T. (1977). The Limbic System in Human Communication (pp. 157–222). https://doi.org/10.1016/B978-0-12-746303-2.50010-5.

Leeds-Hurwitz, W. (2013). Notes in the History of Intercultural Communication: The Foreign Service Institute and the Mandate for Intercultural Training. In M. K. Asante, Y. Miike, & J. Yin (Eds.), *The Global Intercultural Communication Reader* (2nd ed., pp. 17–34). New York: Routledge. Retrieved from: https://doi.org/10.1080/00335639009383919.

Lindenberg, M. M., & Crosby, B. L. (1981). *Managing Development: The Political Dimension*. West Hartford, CT: Kumarian Press.

Livingstone, S., & Palmer, C. (2016). Head Movements Encode Emotions During Speech and Song. *Emotion* (Vol. 16). https://doi.org/10.1037/emo0000106.

Matsumoto, D., & Hwang, H. S. (2013). Facial Expressions. In D. Matsumoto, M. G. Frank, & H. S. Hwang (Eds.), *Nonverbal Communication: Science and Applications*. Los Angeles: Sage.

Moon, D. G. (2011). Critical Reflections on Culture and Critical Intercultural Communication. In *The Handbook of Critical Intercultural Communication* (pp. 34–52). https://doi.org/10.1002/9781444390681.ch3.

Murray, J. (2013). Composing Multimodality. In C. Lutkewitte (Ed.), *Multimodal Composition: A Critical Sourcebook*. Boston: Bedford/St. Martin's.

National Intelligence Council. (2013). Natural Resources in 2020, 2030, and 2040: Implications for the United States. *National Intelligence Council Report* (Vol. 05). Retrieved from: https://www.dni.gov/files/documents/NICR.

Poutiainen, S. (2014). Introduction. In *Theoretical Turbulence in Intercultural Communication Studies*. Newcastle upon Tyne: Cambridge Scholars Publishing.

Reed, M. S., Graves, A., Dandy, N., Posthumus, H., Hubacek, K., Morris, J., … Stringer, L. C. (2009). Who's in and Why? A Typology of Stakeholder Analysis Methods for Natural Resource Management. *Journal of Environmental Management*, *90*(5), 1933–1949. https://doi.org/10.1016/j.jenvman.2009.01.001.

Sluga, H. (2011). *Wittgenstein*. Oxford: Wiley-Blackwell.

Tajfel, H. (1981). Social Stereotypes and Social Groups. In J. C. Turner & H. Giles (Eds.), *Intergroup Behaviour* (pp. 144–167). Oxford, UK: Blackwell.

Ting-Toomey, S., & Oetzel, J. G. (2001). *Managing Intercultural Conflict Effectively*. Thousand Oaks, CA: Sage.

Tversky, A., & Kahneman, D. (1974). Judgment under Uncertainty: Heuristics and Biases. *Science*, *185*(4157), 1124–1131.

UNCTAD. (2014). *World Investment Report*. Geneva. Retrieved from: https://unctad.org/en/PublicationsLibrary/wir2014_en.pdf.

Varvasovszky, Z. (2000). Stakeholder Analysis: A Review. *Health Planning and Policy*, *15*(3), 239–246.

Wang, Q., Ni, L., & De la Flor, M. (2014). An Intercultural Competence Model of Strategic Public Relations Management in the Peru Mining Industry Context. *Journal of Public Relations Research*, *26*(1), 1–22. https://doi.org/10.1080/1062726X.2013.795864.

Introduction to The Long Arm of the Legal Metaphor: Pragmatics and Legal Discourse

By Douglas Ponton

The next chapter takes a closer look at discourse analysis (i.e. how meaning is constructed in texts) and pragmatics (i.e. how situational factors influence discourse). It is pointed out that words have more than just a denotational meaning, i.e. a literal meaning, but instead multiple meanings depending on the actual situation. Ponton also notes that competent communicators take this into consideration when formulating their messages. Messages are often not formulated very clearly; in part due to allusions. It is often assumed that one's counterpart is aware of this and understands what is alluded to by the other person. In this particular text, Ponton examines legal metaphors which play a central role in legal discourse. Metaphors are essentially words used in place of other words so that the meaning of metaphors are not the literal meaning of the words used as a metaphor. By analyzing legal metaphors, it is possible to show how metaphors function and how an understanding of these metaphors is central to understanding the intended meaning of messages.

From these examples, it should be clear that metaphors often play an important role in communication. That is why it is important to understand the principles at work here in order to get a clearer idea of the actual intended meaning. Since business is essentially all about communication, this chapter might serve as an example of how pragmatics can be helpful in understanding meaning beyond the denotative meaning of messages. While this might create problems in one's own native language when communicating about topics and contents one is not familiar with, it should become clear and apparent how metaphors can easily lead to misunderstandings in an intercultural context that also involves a language other than one's own native language(s). Due care should thus be taken when communicating in other languages or about topics one is not familiar with because misunderstandings could easily occur.

Michael B. Hinner

Douglas Mark Ponton has lived in Sicily for twenty years, and is Associate Professor of English Language and Translation at the Department of Political and Social Sciences, University of Catania. His research interests include political discourse analysis, ecolinguistics, discourse in interaction, applied linguistics, pragmatics, corpus linguistics and critical discourse studies. He has held teaching and research positions at the universities of Catania, Messina and Pisa. His most recent research projects concern representations of Russia in western media, the Montalbano effect on tourism in Sicily, processes of late industrialism and ecological questions in South-Eastern Sicily, and Sicilian dialect theatre. His main publications are *For Arguments Sake: speaker evaluation in modern political discourse* (2011), and most recently *Understanding Political Persuasion: Linguistic and Rhetorical Analysis* (2019). As well as politics, his research deals with a variety of social topics, including legal metaphor and crime, the discourse of mediation, migration, cross-cultural politeness, folk traditions including proverbs and, last but not least, the Blues. He is on the editorial board of the Russian Journal of Linguistics, and is linguistic consultant for Vernon Press. He is peer reviewer for numerous national and international journals.

In free time he enjoys playing music and singing songs from the sixties, is a keen chess player, and also likes exploring the countryside and seascapes of Sicily. He is a member of several local associations including Legambiente, and participates in their environmental activities.

Douglas Ponton

The Long Arm of the Legal Metaphor: Pragmatics and Legal Discourse

Introduction – Discourse Analysis and Pragmatics

In recent years there has been widespread interest, across the social sciences, in the role of language, so that discourse analysis is no longer the exclusive terrain of linguists but is practised in fields like Sociology, Economics, History, Philosophy, Geography, etc., and this phenomenon is even found in hard sciences such as Maths, Physics and Chemistry.[1] The trend is partly explained by the increased sophistication of teaching methodologies in modern times, but it is not confined to questions of classroom communication or the dissemination of research. Rather, there is a growing sense that to study Economics, for example, means to imbibe a way of looking at the world, of representing things and talking about them, which is unique to the subject. The lexis of Economics contains mysterious terms for the uninitiated – *economies of scale, marginal utility, satisficing, scarcity, supply and demand* – each of which needs to be unpacked and absorbed before the student can acquire the mindset of the economist. Many of these terms, moreover, have been bones of contention among conflicting schools. To really master the "discourse" of Economics is to have a clear picture of how the theoretical debate has clarified the issues for which these terms are verbal proxies, how thinkers have used these tokens to develop their arguments, many of which will still be contested today (Salvi & Incelli, 1999).

Discourse analysis is a very general term for approaches that focus on how meanings are constructed in texts. Another influential approach to these issues is known as "pragmatics" (Leech, 2016) which will be explored in more depth in this chapter. Pragmatics asks what is going on when someone says something; it recognises the importance of situational factors in understanding discourse. It also understands the fluidity of language; that words can have, not just "two meanings", as in the Led Zeppelin song, but many, according to the context they are uttered in. Consider the phrase 'it's hot in here'. If we are standing in a

1 For more details of discourse analysis applied to research in Social Sciences generally, see Taylor, 2013. For applications to specific fields see, e.g. Hjelm, 2013 (Sociology), Samuels, 1990 (Economics), Doran, 2018 (Physics), etc.

greenhouse, the phrase might signify that the speaker thinks that conditions are ideal for growing cucumbers. If mother and daughter are standing in a stuffy museum, the intended meaning might be: "take off your jumper". Or, if one office-worker says it to another, they might mean: "please open the window". Let us think about the first example in a little more depth. If the speaker's intended meaning was: "Look, conditions here are ideal for growing cucumbers, *you should plant some*", then why didn't they just say so? It seems that expert language users prefer not to spell everything out in words of one syllable, but rather presume an equal level of competence in their hearers, and speak allusively, trusting that their meaning will get across.[2]

Pragmatics, then, is concerned with *meanings*, and hopefully the above will have shown that meaning is not confined to what linguists call the "denotational" or literal, surface meaning of words and their combinations. What is relevant is what the words mean in context (Van Dijk, 2008), and in our discussion so far, the context may also be determined by the specifics of the academic field: "demand" means one thing (or rather, many things!) to an economist, but something very different in everyday conversation.

The study that follows explores some of these issues in the field of the law, another area where there is a growing interest in discourse analysis (Shuy, 2006, 2015). Legal English, or "legaleze", is notorious for its use of tangled language, but there are usually good reasons for the complexity of definitions such as that of 'to steal':

> the wrongful or willful taking of money or property belonging to someone else with intent to deprive the owner of its use or benefit either temporarily or permanently.

To the layman, this may seem unnecessarily contorted or tautological; however, on closer examination, it is evident that the formula precludes a person accused of theft excusing themselves on the grounds that they intended only to borrow

2 This can be taken further. In the case of the cucumber example, we would have to presume that the two participants had some special 'cucumber related' thinking going on; perhaps they had just been discussing cucumbers, or A knew that B had a special love of cucumbers. Otherwise it is unlikely that the hearer could guess the intended meaning correctly. In the museum case, we might want to ask how it is that the child knows her mother wishes her to remove her jumper, rather than some other item of clothing such as her gloves, scarf or hat? A pragmatic perspective is one that considers all the real-world factors that are seen as relevant to the construction of situated meanings in text or conversation.

the item. It also rules out abstract thefts, making sure that 'he stole my heart' remains a metaphor and not a possible criminal offence.

Metaphor in Legal Discourse

In this chapter, the focus is on the role of metaphor in legal discourse. I suggest that metaphor is not simply a decorative resource, whose function is to put some sugar on otherwise dry legal language, but rather represents a basic tool through which the business of law is carried on; without which, indeed, the practise of law may not be possible, or at least, would look very different.

Metaphor is frequently used by the general public to think about the law (Hibbitts, 1994), in phrases like "*the Old Bill, to come up before the beak, to do porridge, to be in stir, in the nick*", etc. When "the long arm of the law" is mentioned, for example, it refers to the quasi-omnipresence of legal officers, their ability to track down wrongdoers and bring them to trial.[3] In "Hurricane", his celebrated 1975 song about in/justice, Bob Dylan said he was ashamed 'to live in a land where justice is a game', a common metaphor. Metaphors can be descriptive, but they can also engage in covert processes of argumentation, as in this example. A "game" might seem an appropriate descriptive metaphor for the process of trial, where the accused has a chance of "winning' – being acquitted, or "losing", being condemned, according to the way the trial goes. However, just as a sporting contest can be rigged, so too a trial can be deeply unfair if the evidence is faked, if witnesses perjure themselves, if judges are biased, and so on. Dylan's metaphor appeals to a notion that his listeners will mostly share, that a trial *ought to be* fair, it ought not to be a game – or at least, if it is a game, it should be played fairly, according to the rules.

Similarly, when Hamlet, in his 'to be or not to be' solliloquy, mentions "the law's delay" as one factor providing possible motives for suicide, the metaphor, which pictures the law as a long-awaited event, is implicitly critical of the justice system – it would be good to have quicker redress to legal wrongs.

The word metaphor comes from the greek *μεταφορά*: μετά, "with, by, across", and φέρω, "to carry", "to bring", so metaphor means 'to get one's meaning across'. Legal metaphors, though, are not just ways which non-specialists think about the law; on the contrary, they play a central role in legal discourse itself, at the level of legislation in law-making, and in the courtroom scenarios in which the laws are

3 For more on metaphors as a fundamental resource of legal discourse generally, there are many recent studies (Smith, 2007; Houbert, 2008; Morra, 2010; Richardson, 2014; etc.).

applied. Indeed, it has been suggested that legal reasoning is itself metaphorical (Philippopoulos-Mihalopoulos, 2016). As Bosmajian (1992, p. 1) says:

> At all levels metaphors, metonymies, personifications, and other tropes appearing in court opinions have attained permanence, have become institutionalized and relied upon as principles, standards, doctrines, and premises in arriving at judicial judgments.

Dramatic metaphors are frequently used in courtroom harangues, with the aim of persuading the jury to find for or against the plaintiff:

> If, after this evidence you are prepared to convict my client, the sword of justice will surely fall from its sheath (Simpson, 1963, pp. 120–121)

But they are also found to be central in the processes in which the law itself is discussed among specialists, debated over and legislated; in other words, they are fundamental in the law's understanding of itself, as this unfolds across time (Klinck, 1992, in Richardson, 2014).

In this chapter, I provide some linguistic tools and concepts for the exploration of these issues, and apply them in courtroom data from the US Supreme Court. Other illustrative metaphors are taken from other sources, mainly the Cambridge Law Journal. The aim is to show how such linguistic analysis can shed light on what are generally viewed as opaque discursive matters, and that metaphor is not just a decorative feature of legal language, but rather a central resource in the construction of legal meanings; indeed, of the law itself.

More about Metaphor

Aristotle thought of metaphor as a compressed form of analogy, which gave aesthetic pleasure because of its "clarity and sweetness and strangeness" (Aristotle, 2007, p. 200). He saw it, at least partly, as a means of conceptualising the unfamiliar in terms of the familiar (Kirby, 1997, pp. 541–2). For example, he gives an illustration from Pericles, who compares the deaths in battle of many young Athenians to the absence of Spring from the year (Aristotle, 2007, p. 71). Here, what is unfamiliar, the catastrophic loss in the community of so many young men, is expressed by implicit analogy with something more familiar; the recurrence of Spring. In this perspective, Aristotle emphasises the poetic function of metaphor; it is an artistic way of coming to terms with the unknown, or with disturbing aspects of experience.

Many metaphors, known as "dead metaphors", have become so common that their original metaphorical nature is simply "invisible"; we speak of time passing, of someone bitching, of falling in love, and so on, without realising we are using metaphor. Some examples from legal discourse in the Cambridge Law Journal:

2018 (77: 1) The rule has *deep roots*.
2018 (77: 1) the most *adventurous steps* were taken
2018 (77: 1) This new enforcement tool was added to the UK prosecutors' *armoury* by the Crime and Courts Act 2013

Seemingly dead metaphors "may potentially be activated during language use (Müller, 2008, p. 6), and each of these examples, in the context of a legal report, can be seen as endowed with dialogical potential. For example, to describe a rule as having 'deep roots' is to evoke an image of a sturdy, seasoned tree, perhaps – in other words, the rule in question is part of a consolidated system, worthy of respect – arguably, it should not be interfered with or lightly reformed.

One influential modern perspective, from Cognitive Linguistics (Lakoff & Johnson, 2003), relegates the aesthetic/pleasurable dimensions of metaphor, probably key for Aristotle, to a secondary position. From being seen as just another among many rhetorical devices, a central role is claimed for metaphor in human language development, in cognition, in the evolution and structuring of human thought (Lakoff & Johnson, 2003, p. 202). The definition of metaphor proposed is very simple: "understanding and experiencing one kind of thing in terms of another" (Lakoff & Johnson, 2003, p. 5). They outline a series of "conceptual metaphors", such as UP IS GOOD, and DOWN IS BAD, which, psychically imprinted in earliest childhood, support our adult cognitive processes and find expression in everyday speech (e.g. to feel "over the moon", "on a high", "on cloud nine", etc.; or alternatively, "down in the dumps", "beneath the underdog", "depressed", etc.).[4] Extending this perspective into legal discourse, a fairly common conceptual metaphor is THE LAW IS A BUILDING. The following example, from the Cambridge Law Journal, refers to this underlying conceptual pattern:

1. The theoretical and historical fragility of the doctrine of benefit and burden is exposed, thus *buttressing* the case for reform (2018. 77: 1)

4 The theory has been criticised on several counts (Ritchie, 2006). For my part, there are two possible issues; firstly, it is not easy to understand how the underlying 'conceptual metaphors' are identified by the analyst. Some are described by Lakoff and Johnson, but they do not lay out ground rules for identifying these metaphors in fresh data. Secondly, it is difficult to apply the theory to each and every metaphor one encounters in real life discourse. This is not the place to explore these limitations in more detail; what I retain from their account is the definition that views metaphor as thinking about, or experiencing, something in terms of something else. Also, the sense, not altogether absent from other theories of metaphor, that there is something fundamental about metaphor in human thought processes.

We are concerned here with the tendency to conceive of legal arguments as buildings (*to construct an argument, to lay the foundations, to demolish, knock down,* etc.). This example illustrates a perspective emphasised in this chapter, the *dialogical potential* of metaphor (White, 2003; Kecskes, 2016; Bondi, 2018). Such a theoretical angle focuses on the speaker or writer's interaction with their intended audience (Wong, 2005), who may or may not be present during the discourse, as they engage with a range of opinions, anticipate issues, refute imaginary objections, and so on. The perspective is a relevant one for considering many genres of academic discourse, and the law is no exception.

The Cambridge Law Journal is a forum for the discussion of current cases, in which legal specialists engage with one another, and the case reports frequently advance direct or implicit commentaries on the sentences and legislation involved; in the example just given, the writer argues for the reform of a legal doctrine. The metaphor is central when we consider the fragment's dialogical force. Lakoff and Johnson account for this effect in terms of our life experience, especially our bodily perceptions: when we hear of a fragile structure that needs "buttressing", we have an automatic, hard-wired response that says "*do something about it*", "*shore it up*". It is possible to say the same thing without metaphor:

> The theoretical and historical fragility of the doctrine of benefit and burden is exposed, thus strengthening the case for reform

But the persuasive force of this is noticeably weaker.

As an example of this chapter's perspective on legal metaphor, consider the "fruit of the poisonous tree" metaphor, which was first used in Nardone v. United States in 1939. This refers to what is more prosaically termed the "exclusionary rule", which specifies that evidence which is obtained illegally may not be admitted during a trial. The online legal dictionary (Farlex, 2008) gives a detailed account of the evolution of this metaphor, and some examples that make its meaning clear. For example, if police stop a driver for a minor traffic offence and then discover drugs in the car, those drugs, which were found because police conducted an illegal search, may not be considered at trial. Supposing that the police, having found the drugs, request a search warrant for the driver's house, and in the search discover a stolen lawnmower. The lawnmower too, would not be considered because, although the search this time was legal, it was only found on the basis of knowledge gained from the first illegal search. As Farlex puts it:

> The fruit of this poisonous tree is evidence later discovered because of knowledge gained from the first illegal search, arrest, or interrogation. The poisonous tree and the fruit are both excluded from a criminal trial.

In this example, the drugs are the "poisonous tree", and the lawnmower, the "fruit". The whole complex business of what evidence is to be admitted or excluded at trial and why, is summed up in what becomes generally known as "the poisonous tree doctrine", which becomes an established part of US law.

The metaphor provides a convenient shorthand, and is a punchier, more colourful way of talking about legal niceties than literal alternatives. But more than this; it encapsulates axiological meanings, conceptions of justice and social theories, engages with social actors and human processes on a number of levels. Arguably, we need to look for the significance of the metaphor in a web of associations: the "tree" that is the justice system has its roots in the soil of America, with its proud founding fathers, its republican principles and constitutional guarantees. It is not producing the looked-for fruit of fairness for all, but something that is poisonous, toxic, corrupt. Because of such social resonance, use of this metaphor has a tremendous pragmatic force. That is to say, there is a strong sense, enfolded within the metaphor itself, that it is *morally right* not to admit such evidence.

More about Pragmatics

As has been said, above, pragmatics focuses on the power, and at times, on the ambiguity of language, in construing meanings. There is a clear distinction between the denotational meaning of a word on a page and its actual meaning in any real-life context. For example, we know the meaning of each word in the sentence: "Can you pass the salt?" However, we would be surprised if someone responded to the request: "Yes. I'm perfectly able to pass the salt", without passing it (Groefsema, 1992). Pragmatics focuses on explaining the reasons for our surprise, which centre on the misunderstanding between speaker (S) and hearer of S's intended meaning, which was to use language to *request* a certain action. The hearer, instead, "heard" the sentence as an enquiry about their ability, actually a perfectly accurate understanding based on the semantics of the modal verb "can". In the same way, we know that a parent who tells their child: "Your room is a pigsty" is not offering a detached description, but rather requiring them to tidy it up.

Speech act theory, an important branch of pragmatics, describes other types of situation where language is used to 'do' things (Austin, 1975), performing actions like *apologising, promising, complaining, ordering, booking, urging, persuading, warning*, and so on (Searle, 2010). In order to understand what language is being used to do, it is necessary to consider the context as well as the words. One branch of early pragmatics looked at a certain type of utterance known as "performatives" (Searle, ibid), where to make a statement is literally to do something, as in:

1. I now pronounce you man and wife
2. I name this ship the Queen Elizabeth
3. You're fired!

In each case, our world knowledge fills in the missing context details, which include necessary participants (a clergyman, a local dignitary, a boss) and social features (a church, a port, a workplace). Some aspects of this social background are *necessary* in order for the discourse to have any meaning whatsoever – for (3) to have meaning it is necessary that S has the authority to dismiss H, that they are in an employer/employee relation, and so on.

In each case, to bring the discussion back to the legal context, there are legal consequences for each of these utterances; the couple are now legally married, the ship has been named, and an employee has been dismissed.

These same considerations apply to the following well-known utterance, used to perform the action of *swearing in* a witness:

> I swear by Almighty God that the evidence which I shall give shall be the truth, the whole truth and nothing but the truth

Without the specifics of a courtroom setting, these words are meaningless and, in fact, never used, except perhaps for humorous purposes.[5]

In landmark research for what became "forensic linguistics", Malcolm Coulthard discusses the 1953 Derek Bentley case, where the decisive evidence turned on considerations of this kind (Coulthard, 1993, 1996). Bentley had been involved in an armed robbery. The police arrived, and Bentley, from the roof, called out to a 16 year-old member of the gang below: "Let him have it, Chris!", whereupon the boy fatally shot an officer. At the trial, Bentley claimed that his meaning had not been "shoot him" but rather, "give him the weapon", but he was

5 Performatives occur in all kinds of contexts. Chess players of all nationalities, for example, will know that the rule for adjusting a piece during play is to pronounce the French words 'j'adoube' (I adjust) while adjusting the piece in question. A discussion between two grandmasters, of the confusion sown when players deviate from the formula and instead use the apparently more comprehensible English version ('I adjust') is illuminating, from a pragmatic perspective: https://www.youtube.com/watch?v=7hPMsHzLwes&t=4203s, at 1: 50. 18. Though the denotational meaning in each case is exactly the same, it is a question whether use of the English version is even acceptable, from the normative perspective, or whether the only linguistic formula that can correctly be said to perform the action is the French one.

not believed, and was executed. Here, both the surface meaning of the words used, as well as the pragmatic, situated meaning, are ambiguous – either could have been S's intended meaning, and the trial hinged on this fact.

A pragmatic perspective, then, focuses on words as they are used in specific contexts, to create and communicate meanings. The Bentley case is a vivid example of the centrality of words and their situated meanings in legal discourse, but similar linguistic controversies feature in the proceedings of many trials, even of the routine kind.

Data: From the Proceedings of the US Supreme Court

In other research on this topic (Ponton & Canepa, forthcoming), I have explored legal metaphor in written discourse. This chapter, instead, focuses on metaphor in spoken discourse, the archetypal context in which "forensic rhetoric", one of three types of rhetoric identified by Aristotle, occurs (Furley & Nehamas, 2015; O'Connell, 2017). In this, language is used to convey information about cases, frame events and, in reaching a verdict, to bring about a specific real-world outcome. Authentic courtroom data, frequently covered by legal restrictions, is hard to come by; fortunately, the US Supreme Court provides a state of the art site with full transcripts of legal proceedings. Each text is accompanied by recordings, so that it would also be possible to focus on oral discourse features such as voice quality or intonation. For each case, the site includes a syllabus or outline, and opinions of members of the court. In this study I deal with the metaphors in one case, Tapia vs. the United States, April 18, 2011.[6] Having read through some of the transcripts, I selected the Tapia case as a representative sample. The intention is not to focus on discourse that, for whatever reason, is especially rich in metaphor, but rather to take a case more or less at random, observe the linguistic behaviour of these legal practitioners engaged in their daily professional lives and note the use they make of metaphor.

The debate, however, does open with a striking exemplification of the perspective on legal metaphor outlined above:

> JUSTICE KENNEDY: You have, in effect, a one-way ratchet. If the judge really thinks rehabilitation is a - a - a primary or an important component of the sentence, then it reduces the prison term. It could never increase it.

To understand this, let us consider some details of the case. Tapia, a heroin addict, had been convicted of smuggling unauthorized aliens into the United States. The

6 Oyez. Online at: https://www.oyez.org/cases/2010/10-5400, last visit 11/07/2021.

District Court imposed a 51-month prison term, reasoning that she should serve that long in order to qualify for and complete the Bureau of Prisons' Residential Drug Abuse Programme. However, it was objected to the Supreme Court that, under the provisions of US Code 3582, "imprisonment is not an appropriate means of promoting correction and rehabilitation". These provisions were introduced in 1984, as various participants claim during the hearing, against a backdrop of widespread dissatisfaction with the notion that it was possible to rehabilitate prisoners by making them participate in such programmes. It was felt that, instead, these programmes should be undertaken outside prison in the local community. So, while previously it had been the practise if there was, say, a 500 hour rehab programme in a certain prison for a judge to *increase* a sentence in order that the detainee participate in it, this was no longer possible. As Kennedy says here, judges should instead *reduce* prison terms to arrive at a workable solution that considers the needs of rehabilitation and punishment separately, rather than trying to combine the two.

Thus, Justice Kennedy's metaphor, the "one-way ratchet", serves several purposes: firstly, it contextualises the Tapia case, recalling significant legal details that have a bearing on the court's deliberations. "This is another case", he is saying, "where prison terms can only move in one direction, i.e., *downwards*". To a degree, opening the debate with this metaphor also represents a significant *move*[7] in laying out the terrain to be covered, which will centre on whether the Tapia case is, or is not, a case of this kind. If the debate should decide this question in the affermative, the metaphor also has a bearing on the court's final decision. As already mentioned, in sentencing Tapia, the District Court did lengthen her sentence explicitly to let her participate in a rehab programme, and the Supreme Court therefore has no option other than to find for the appellant.

In the next section the findings are discussed.

7 Move analysis (Swales 1981) is a topdown approach to analyzing the discourse structure of texts; the text is described as a sequence of 'moves', where each move represents a stretch of text expressing a particular communicative (that is, semantic) function (from Upton & Cohen, 2009: 4).

Findings: The Supreme Court Metaphors

Table 1: Below, Shows the Metaphors Identified in the Debate[8]

	Page: Lines	Metaphor	Source / Target
1	5: 24–5	Intended *to smooth the transition* from prison to true liberty	Polishing / Release from prison
2	6: 1	(supervised release) is specifically a *rehabilitative vehicle*	A vehicle / release from prison
3	6: 4–5	3582, by its terms, simply doesn't *govern* a revocation of supervised release	A governer / a legal act
4	6: 11–13	isn't punishment and rehabilitation often *flip sides* of each other?	A coin / punishment and rehab
5	6: 17	*escalating series* of serious offenses	An escalator / Offences
6	6: 18	Logically, she has *to be put away*	s.thing you put in a cupboard / a prisoner
7	8: 12	plus 5 months for *the bail jump*	Bail / A hay bale (?)
8	8: 22–23	she was really *going down the wrong road* here.	A road / moral choices
9	8: 24	She gets involved in *alien* smuggling	Aliens / migrants

(*Continued*)

8 I have tried to note every metaphor, omitting occasional cases of repetition, as in 'to give weight' to. However, there are methodological issues here, connected with the definition and identification of what is seen to constitute a metaphor. Many words that are clearly metaphorical in origin have passed into the language under the new meaning, and are known as 'conventional', sometimes 'dead' metaphors. For example, the word 'provision', whose original meaning arguably concerns providing food for the family, has been applied to the stipulations of a legal act. I have been guided in selecting, or omitting, these conventional metaphors, by considerations of the likely dialogical impact in each case.

Table 1: Continued

	Page: Lines	Metaphor	Source / Target
10	9: 24–25	So now we want some *talismanic* words where the judge says what I said	Magic spell / legal sentence
11	11: 18–19	if you have *to go away* for 3 years, you will appreciate	A journey / prison
12	20: 15–16	we're *inside the district court's head*	Head / thoughts
13	21: 21–24	sentencing courts will *follow that map.*	A map / Legal guidelines
14	25: 10–11	danger *can't be abated* without a drug treatment program	A storm / social unrest
15	28: 15–16	this Act *stripped judges* of the power to do this	Clothing / legal powers
16	29: 25	That is a *forward-looking* matter.	Space / Time
17	30: 20–21	the Act meant to *disable* judges from doing this.	Dis/ability / legal powers
18	32: 10–11	everyone can be rehabilitated simply by *throwing them in prison*	Throwing / imprisoning
19	32: 20–21	you can't keep someone in jail *tied to* completion of programs	s. thing tied to another / a commitment
20	36: 24–25	the ordinary appellate review that this Court has *fleshed out* in Rita, Gall, and Kimbrough.	The body / legal details
21	37: 1–2	the judge can give it *a fair amount of weight*	Weight / consideration
22	37: 13	the *thicket* of issues	A forest / legal issues
23	37: 15–16	*disentangling sentences* that are otherwise reasonable,	String / legal sentences
24	37: 27	away from his criminal associates, away from his *pattern* of life	Pattern / lifestyle
25	38: 1–2	We've been down *that road.*	A road / a course of action

Table 1: Continued

	Page: Lines	Metaphor	Source / Target
26	38: 10–11	wouldn't your proposal lead to *unevenness* in sentencing?	A surface / fairness
27	38: 39	this *swings* from one judge to another	A pendulum / changing policies
28	40: 8–9	allows appellate courts to *harmonize* what they're doing.	Music / court decisions
29	40: 22–23	only a *couple of places* in the Sentencing Reform Act	Places / points in documents
30	41: 4	It *skips over* retribution	Skipping /omitting
31	42: 20	we do have *a fallback* argument	A person falling (safely) / an argument
32	43: 10–11	The judge is *balancing* three or four factors; it's *in the mix*	1) a circus performer / a judge; 2) a mixer / process of deliberation
33	45: 18	Judges can *prescribe* it?	Medicine / legal actions

It will be noticed that many of these metaphors are of the conventional, or "dead" variety alluded to above; through repeated use they have become somewhat empty of any special rhetorical force, and they are used as "ordinary language", i.e., people don't necessarily realise they are using a metaphor: *the flip side, forward-looking, in the mix*, etc. However, I suggest, even such metaphors may have an argumentative, or dialogic potential. For example, "the flip side" is used here to advance a particular view:

> isn't punishment and rehabilitation often flip sides of each other? (p. 7, l. 12)

By using this metaphor, which figures punishment and rehabilitation as the two sides of a coin, Justice Sotomayor advances a covert argumentative position, i.e. that to punish by imprisonment *is* to rehabilitate; the two things are intimately connected. At times such metaphors index socio-cultural background factors that are potentially controversial:

> She gets involved in alien smuggling (p. 9, l.24)

Reference to immigrants as aliens has been discursive practise in the US for more than 200 years (Ackerman, 2014); recently, California removed the term from its Labour Code because of its derogatory associations (Diep, 2015). The term is made more weighty in this context by its occurence in conjuction with "smuggling", a negatively judged activity, and by the judge's reference to the plaintiff's "troubled past" (l.23–24), and his explicit negative evaluative comment, "which is very serious" (l. 25).[9]

The actors in this trial are the Chief Justice, John G. Roberts and eight associate judges, as well as Reuben Cahn for the petitioner, Matthew Roberts for the *vacatur*[10], and Stephanos Bibas the *amicus curiae*[11]. In the following discussion I analyse some of the metaphors, linking them to their role within the argumentative structures that emerge within the case.

In considering the discursive terrain covered during this debate a useful tool, that features in Wodak's Discourse-Historical method (Wodak & Meyer, 2001), is that of *topoi* (singular, *topos*) a term from argumentation theory that refers to the thematic content, viewing topoi as "reservoirs of generalised key ideas" (Richardson, 2004, p. 230).[12] One key *topos* in this debate, for example, is the notion that imprisonment is/is not rehabilitative. It will be found that this notion forms the backdrop for a significant part of the discussion, a theme that recurs throughout, surfacing at different points; it constitutes a focus for implicit and explicit argumentation. This particular topos emerges from intense debate in society at large concerning the issues; it is not simply an abstract "idea" but rather sums up an aspect of the lived experiences of many Americans involved in the penal system. The topos occurs right at the beginning, in Cahn's opening presentation:

> Congress intended that defendants should no longer be sent to prison for purposes of rehabilitation (p. 3, 4)

A list of the topoi found during the debate provides an overview of the argumentative terrain, and will be useful preparation for an exploration of the

9 Arguably, the semantics of 'alien' in this context have altered greatly since its original use; today it is hard not to think of extra-terrestrial associations; immigrants are effectively dehumanised by the term in both senses.

10 He backs up Cahn, arguing that the judgement in the Tapias District Court case should be 'set aside'.

11 A consulting figure who assists the court by offering expert opinions.

12 See (Žagar, 2010) for a critical appraisal of *topoi* as used in Discourse Historical research. The author suggests that, rather than encapsulating a specific technical sense, the term reflects a common approach to texts within literary criticism and everyday usage generally, i.e. the identification of themes, its original sense in Aristotelian rhetorical studies.

role of metaphors in such discourse. Identification of topoi is carried out on the basis of a close reading and assessment of the semantic landscape.[13]

Table 2: Topoi in the Debate

Topos	**Instantiation**	**Page/line**
Incarceration as Rehabilitation	a need for rehabilitation can push the judge [..] into moving the individual either out of an incarceration sentence into probation	4.12–15
Link Between Addiction and Criminality	Without drug treatment, we can't deter her [..] this crime, given her background, deserves this kind of sentence	7. 21–23
Motivations for Sentencing	the issue here is what was the judge's primary purpose?	10.19
Decree N. 3582	that is a violation of 3582	10.23
Lengthening Sentences to Get Prisoners into Programmes	It couldn't be clearer that he's computing the length of the sentence on the basis of what correctional treatment will be received	12.5–7
The One-Way Ratchet	Justice Kennedy's question at the start about the one-way ratchet?	14.13–14
Practical Legal Realities	whenever the presentencing report says the person has a drug problem and there's a one-and-a-half-year drug program in the prison, he sentences those people to one and a half years? Regularly.	20.14–18

Rather than an in-depth analysis of each metaphor (or each topos), which space considerations prohibit, let us look at the dialogical role played by some of the metaphors in these samples of courtroom dialogue.

Incarceration as Rehabilitation

This topos occurs at the outset of the exchanges, and recurs throughout the ongoing dialogue. Here, the notion arises in discussing the practice of "supervised release", a period of post-confinement, in-community monitoring which forms a part of the sentences of many US criminals (Berman, 2021). In

13 In the paper just mentioned, Žagar (2010) claims that Wodak and other proponents of the Discourse-Historical method provide insufficient accounts of the means by which *topoi* in a text are to be identified, as well as other technical critiques. I hope that my account, above, adequately addresses this critique.

the first extract from proceedings we hear Mr Reuben Cahn, for the appellant, answering questions from one of the panel of judges:

> JUSTICE GINSBURG: But it is strange, isn't it, that they [judges in District Courts] can take rehabilitation into account for the supervised release. I mean, that – that's a provision, isn't it? As far as supervised release is concerned, the judge can take account of rehabilitation in setting the length of the term, but can't do that for the prison time.
>
> MR. CAHN: Well, certainly with regard to supervised release, we think, as far as setting the term of supervised release, the judge is required to take rehabilitation concerns into account, and that's because supervised release is intended to smooth the transition from prison to true liberty and is specifically a rehabilitative vehicle.

Cahn's response uses two metaphors whose dialogical impact is to emphasise the desirability and effectiveness of this legal instrument. Under supervised release, in fact, a number of measures that might assist the prisoner with their attempt to re-adapt to normal life are envisaged, such as drug treatment, mental health counseling, and housing and employment assistance (see Berman, op. cit). The first conceptualises supervised release as a "path/road", the second as a "vehicle". Rhetorically, the picture involved in these two metaphors is as follows:

Table 3: Supervised Release is a Path/Road

Target	Source	Pragmatic meaning	Comment
Supervised release	Path / Road	Heightens the attractiveness of SR, its functionality and effectiveness	The metaphor nestles comfortably within an overarching metaphorical conception of the law as 'a roadmap'

Interpretation of the source of this first metaphor, as a path or road, is assisted by the second with its explicit reference to a "vehicle". Paths can be smooth and hence easy to travel down or difficult, full of obstacles. In passing, we should note the presence of another metaphorical nuance: the process of "release" is conceived of in terms of a journey *from* one place, "prison", *to* another, which is labelled "true liberty".[14] Within this discourse are enfolded attitudes to the

14 There are overtones, in this typically Anglo-Saxon conceptualisation of justice, of the discourse of one of the key works of popular Puritan theology, Bunyan's 'Pilgrim's Progress', which metaphorically conceives of the hero's journey from his hometown, the 'City of Destruction', or this world, to the 'Celestial City', heaven. Like the biblical precepts followed by Pilgrim, human law may serve as a 'map' (Schmidtz, 2006) by means of which men navigate the social world.

justice system that emerge, on a little unpacking; it is worthwhile to make this effort because we may better appreciate the real nature of this discussion, which essentially relate to the aims and ideals of the US justice system itself. Thus, imprisonment is not simply depriving someone of their liberty; rather, it is part of a process (or better, a stage of a *journey*) that will terminate in the prisoner's re-admission into the normal life of a local community. Cahn does not simply speak of the prisoner moving from "prison" to 'liberty', but significantly adds the pre-modifying adjective 'true' to the latter noun. The prisoner is not automatically free, in other words, once their sentence has been served; rather, the process or journey is only completed once they have successfully resolved all their criminal issues and become reintegrated into the productive life of the nation as a whole.

The vehicle metaphor carries these implicit meanings forward, adding to them the idea of efficiency, since a vehicle is clearly the most efficient way of getting from one place to another. Once again, we notice the conceptualisation of social life as a neighbourhood, perhaps, for which the justice system provides maps (Schmidtz, 2006).

Table 4: Supervised Release Is a Vehicle

Target	Source	Pragmatic meaning	Comment
Supervised release	A vehicle	Heightens the attractiveness of SR, its functionality and effectiveness	Underlines the journey motif, as well as the "background metaphor" of the justice system as a neighbourhood, laws as "roadmaps", and so on

This discussion, arguably, is more incisive to the extent that we remember the overall rhetorical goal of Mr Cahn, which is to convince the court that they should uphold his client's appeal. Supervised release, it is argued here and elsewhere in the transcript, is the appropriate support for the rehabilitative purposes of penal punishment. This contrasts with the approach taken by the District Court in question, which had been to give Ms Tapia a longer sentence so that it would be possible for her to participate in rehabilitative drug programmes while in prison.

Against this background, Justice Sotomayor's comments, also expressed by means of a metaphor, need to be interpreted:

> JUSTICE SOTOMAYOR: Counsel, aren't – isn't punishment and rehabilitation often flip sides of each other? If you read what the judge said here, his comment was this man – or this woman, I'm sorry, has been involved in a series – escalating series of serious

offenses. Logically, she has to be put away for a long time unless she gets rehabilitation because there's going to be no deterrence otherwise.

Table 5: Punishment and Rehabilitation Are Two Sides of a Coin

Target	Source	Pragmatic meaning	Comment
Punishment and rehabilitation	A coin	To punish is often to rehabilitate	Introduces the notion of "deterrence"

Justice Sotomayor galigns with the voices in this debate defending the District Court's original decision, i.e. to give Tapia a longer sentence so that she could participate in prison rehabilitation programmes. The force of the metaphor, crucially, is moderated by the adverb "often", so that the speaker is not arguing that punishment, *in itself*, is rehabilitative, but that it may have been in this case.[15] However, from a rhetorical perspective, the persuasive force of this metaphor is significantly undermined by this nuance, as well as by Sotomayor's hesitancy, a grammatical slip and the fact that he does not assert the relation positively, but rather puts the proposition in a rhetorical question to his interlocutor. He also goes off topic, suggesting that the long sentence may not have been motivated by considerations of rehabilitation, but rather for reasons of deterrent. All of these factors weaken the rhetorical force of the metaphor, so that it appears more of a random observation than a pointed one. The metaphor claims that, in certain cases, punishment and rehabilitation may be closely – inextricably – linked, so that it is impossible to have one without the other. But it lacks force here, because no information is provided that would allow listeners to appreciate in what circumstances this connection does arise, nor does the speaker advance a claim that it has arisen in the case before the court.

15 In point of fact, none of the justices, including Sotomayor, argue the strong case for punishment as rehabilitation. The connection between a longer sentence and rehabilitation, it is established, depends on the fact that detainees can participate in specific rehabilitative programmes whilst inside. As we saw above, Cahn opens his argument by citing decree n. 3852, where Congress, he says, "recognize that imprisonment is not an appropriate means of promoting correction and rehabilitation" (pp. 3, 11–13).

The One-Way Ratchet

Each of the several topoi identified could be analysed in the same way, to assess the role of the metaphors within the specific argumentation, but as space is limited we shall briefly return to what has been identified above as a key metaphor, the one-way ratchet with which Justice Kennedy begins his response to Cahn's first statement:

> JUSTICE KENNEDY: You have, in effect, a one-way ratchet. If the judge really thinks rehabilitation is a - a - a primary or an important component of the sentence, then it reduces the prison term. It could never increase it. So you have a one-way ratchet (pp. 4, 4–9)

As Wikipedia tells us, a ratchet is 'a mechanical device that allows continuous linear or rotary motion in only one direction while preventing motion in the opposite direction'. Kennedy's metaphor, therefore, is crucial in framing the ensuing legal discussion. Effectively, in order to argue that the District Court had been correct in their decision – to find against the plaintiff – this argumentative frame must somehow be defeated. It must be argued, for instance, that for some reason this does not apply to the Tapia case; there might be exceptions, other reasons for increasing the sentence, and so on. Equally, the metaphor provides Cahn with a clear argumentative strategy – he must only be sure that the judge in question did increase the sentence for reasons linked to rehabilitation, provide some details of the legal framework (decree 3852), and he has a watertight case.

In fact, Cahn's response immediately expands on Kennedy's metaphor, referring to specific legal details of decree 3852:

> MR. CAHN: Yes, Your Honor. I believe that that's correct, that the – that the way in which the statute is set up, the logic of 3582 is that a need for rehabilitation can push the judge, the sentencing judge, into moving the individual either out of an incarceration sentence into probation or lower the sentence to get that individual into supervisory release where rehabilitation current – concerns are properly addressed under the statute (pp. 4, 10–18)

It is not possible to cover here all the twists and turns of the lengthy debate. In the first part, the one-way ratchet metaphor, as described here, is a relevant topos which orients many statements. As one example, consider this contribution from Justice Scalia:

> JUSTICE SCALIA: The judge did say, didn't he – this is on page 27 of the Joint Appendix – "the sentence has to be sufficient to provide needed correctional treatment, and here I think the needed correctional treatment is the 500-hour drug program." It couldn't be clearer that he's computing the length of the sentence on the basis of what correctional

> treatment will be received. It "has to be sufficient to provide needed correctional treatment." (pp. 12, 1–8)

In terms of the one-way ratchet argumentative frame, the force of this contribution is to underline the fact that the District Court judge did indeed increase Tapia's sentence in order that she should be able to participate in the prison rehabilitation programme. In effect, Scalia's sentence provides backing (Toulmin, 2003) for the claim in an implicit (though uncomplicated) argumentative structure:

> Since: decree 3852 says that judges may not increase sentences for purposes of rehabilitation but only reduce them (the one-way ratchet);

And Since: In this case the District Court did increase the sentence for just this purpose;

Therefore: The plaintiff's case should be upheld

This implicit argumentative structure underlies the entire proceedings. It is never spelled out, but all parties recognise it and, as has been said before, its rhetorical force is enjoined by the one-way ratchet metaphor with which the case is presented. As final proof of the metaphor's relevance in the debate, it is noticeable that, as Cahn gives way to his counterpart, Roberts for the vacatur, it immediately re-surfaces:

> JUSTICE KAGAN: Mr. Roberts, could I take you back to Justice Kennedy's question at the start about the one-way ratchet? What's the government's theory about what Congress might have been thinking when it said you can't think about rehabilitation to sentence or to lengthen a sentence, but you can think about rehabilitation to make a decision not to sentence or to shorten a sentence?

In other words, the discussion is now passing from the specifics of the Tapia case to the realms of speculation about Congress's motives, in order, perhaps, to find a possible loophole or exception that may counteract the force of the one-way ratchet metaphor.

Conclusion

From the above discussion it will, I hope, be clear that metaphor plays a significant role in legal discourse, though naturally any conclusions that may be advanced would require the corroboration of numerically oriented studies. I feel that the Tapia case discussed in detail above is fairly representative of discursive behaviour found in many legal contexts, but this cannot be more than a general idea at present. Here I would just like to offer a few discursive considerations by way of summing up the point so far reached by this research.

Firstly, what is striking is the way that the "one-way ratchet" metaphor is impressed upon this debate, so that it really constrains the course of proceedings. But it is important to take a step beyond the words, and consider the processes involved in their selection. Let us imagine Justice Kennedy preparing his address, pondering the Tapia case, assessing the legal frameworks, when it occurs to him that 'a one-way ratchet' might be a useful way of saying that, if a judge wants to include hours for rehabilitation in their sentence, they may not increase the sentence but must instead reduce it. In other words, following in the consolidated tradition of metaphorical thinking in the legal profession described above (see also Ponton & Canepa, forthcoming), Justice Kennedy has hit upon an apt metaphor that encapsulates the specifics of the legal case in hand. Moreover we observe, in the debate, how the metaphor is wielded by other participants, it becomes a way of thinking about these complex legal realities, is incorporated into the debate, and finally plays a role in shaping the outcome.

It is a metaphor that rests, in its turn, on another metaphor, on what Lakoff & Johnson (2003) would term a "conceptual metaphor": THE LAW IS A TOOL. This metaphor is one way in which legal practitioners conceive of what they do.

From this perspective it is also worth underlining the point made above concerning the way that metaphor may afford glimpses of underlying conceptions, beliefs, ideologies. We *shouldn't* simply view "freedom" as a state of non-detention. We *should* think of imprisonment as the beginning of a path back to "true" liberty.

To continue in this vein: a focus on metaphor allows us to perceive, for instance, that the law may be thought of as a "map" to navigate humans through the social world, which is not some Panglossian paradise, but rather a dangerous neighbourhood where some people do not respect basic norms of social behaviour.

In sum, metaphor is more than a simple rhetorical tool that, by delighting jurors, helps persuade them of the counsel's point of view. It is a part of the law itself – to put it metaphorically, a part of the fabric of the law, a means through which the law is conceptualised and carried out. Justice Kennedy may not have been the inventor of the "one-way ratchet" metaphor; he may have borrowed it from some other source. But it is certain that this case will not be its sole outing; rather, it will be re-used whenever another opportunity arises, and so most likely pass into the discursive traditions of US justice.

References

Ackerman, E. (2014). “What Part of Illegal Don’t You Understand?”: Bureaucracy and Civil Society in the Shaping of Illegality. *Ethnic and Racial Studies, 37*(2), 181–203. https://doi.org/10.1080/01419870.2012.705008.

Aristotle. (2007). *On Rhetoric: A Theory of Civic Discourse* (2nd ed.). (G. A. Kennedy, Trans.). New York, NY: Oxford University Press.

Austin, J. L. (1975). *How to Do Things with Words* (2d ed.). Oxford [Eng.]: Clarendon Press.

Berman, R. M. (2021). The Regulatory Review. *Federal Court Involvement in Supervised Release*. Retrieved August 12, 2021, from: https://www.theregreview.org/2021/06/28/berman-federal-court-involvement-supervised-release/.

Bondi, M. (2018). Dialogicity in Written Language Use: Variation across Expert Action Games. In E. Weigand & I. Kecskes (Eds.), *Dialogue Studies* (Vol. 31, pp. 137–70). Amsterdam: John Benjamins Publishing Company.

Bosmajian, H. A. (1992). *Metaphor and Reason in Judicial Opinions*. Carbondale: Southern Illinois University Press.

Coulthard, R. M. (1993). Beginning the Study of Forensic Texts: Corpus, Concordance, Collocation. In M. Hoey (Ed.), *Data Description Discourse* (pp. 86–97). London: HarperCollins.

Coulthard, M. (1996). ...and then... Language description and author attribution. *Forensic Linguistics*: the *International Journal* of *Speech*, *Language* and the *Law* *4*, 252–261.

Diep, F. (2015). ‘Why Did We Ever Call Undocumente Immigrants “Aliens”?’. *PAC. Standard* (Aug. 12, 2015). Retrieved from: https://psmag.com/news/the-world-outside-of-america-is-basically-outer-space-right

Doran, Y. J. (2018). *The Discourse of Physics: Building Knowledge through Language, Mathematics and Image*. New York, London: Routledge.

Farlex. (2008). The Fruit of the Poisonous Tree. *The Free Dictionary*. Retrieved July 9, 2021, from: https://legal-dictionary.thefreedictionary.com/Fruit+of+a+poisonous+tree.

Furley, D. J., & Nehamas, A. (2015). *Aristotle’s ‘Rhetoric’: Philosophical Essays*. Princeton: Princeton University Press.

Groefsema, M. (1992). “Can You Pass the Salt?”: A Short-Circuited Implicature? *Lingua, 87*(1–2), 103–35. https://doi.org/10.1016/0024-3841(92)90028-H.

Hibbitts, B. J. (1994). Making Sense of Metaphors: Visuality, Aurality and the Reconfiguration of American Legal Discourse. *Cardozo Law Review, 16*, 229–350.

Hjelm, T. (2013). Empowering Discourse: Discourse Analysis as Method and Practice in the Sociology Classroom. *Teaching in Higher Education, 18*(8), 871–82. https://doi.org/10.1080/13562517.2013.795940.

Houbert, F. (2008). caught in the Web of the Law. *Le traducteur juridique face à la métaphore,* 1–15. http://www.initerm.net/post/2011/05/18/Les-metaphores-juridiques

Kecskes. (2016). A Dialogic Approach to Pragmatics. *Russian Journal of Linguistics, 20*(4), 26–42. https://doi.org/10.22363/2312-9182-2016-20-4-26-42.

Kirby, J. T. (1997). Aristotle on Metaphor. *The American Journal of Philology, 118*(4), 517–554.

Klinck, D.R. (19992). *The Word of the Law: Approaches to Legal Discourse.* Ottawa: Carleton University Press.

Lakoff, G., & Johnson, M. (2003). *Metaphors We Live By.* Chicago: University of Chicago Press.

Leech, G. (2016). *Principles of Pragmatics* (1st ed.). London: Routledge.

Morra, L. (2010). New Models for Language Understanding and the Cognitive Approach to Legal Metaphors. *International Journal for the Semiotics of Law - Revue Internationale de Sémiotique Juridique 23 (4),* 387–405.

O'Connell, P. A. (2017). *The Rhetoric of Seeing in Attic Forensic Oratory* (1st ed.). Austin: University of Texas Press.

Philippopoulos-Mihalopoulos, A. (2016). Flesh of the Law: Material Legal Metaphors. *Journal of Law and Society, 43*(1), 45–65. http://www.jstor.org/stable/43862465

Richardson, J. (2004). *(Mis)Representing Islam: The Racism and Rhetoric of British Broadsheet Newspapers* (Vol. 9.). Amsterdam: John Benjamins Publishing Company.

Ritchie, L. D. (2006). *Context and Connection in Metaphor.* London, UK: Palgrave Macmillan.

Salvi, R., & Incelli, E. (1999). *The Language of Economics: A Theoretical and Pragmatical Approach.* Roma: CISU.

Samuels, W. J. (1990). *Economics As Discourse: An Analysis of the Language of Economists.* Dordrecht: Springer Netherlands.

Schmidtz, D. (2006). *Elements of Justice.* Cambridge, New York: Cambridge University Press.

Searle, J. R. (2010). *Expression and Meaning: Studies in the Theory of Speech Acts.* Nachdr. Cambridge: Cambridge University Press.

Shuy, R. W. (2006). *Linguistics in the Courtroom: A Practical Guide.* Oxford, New York: Oxford University Press.

Shuy, R. W. (2015). Discourse Analysis in the Legal Context. In D. Tannen, H. E. Hamilton, & D. Schiffrin (Eds.), *The Handbook of Discourse Analysis* (pp. 822–40). Hoboken, NJ, USA: John Wiley & Sons, Inc.

Simpson, Sir J. (1963). The Old Bailey. *Medico-Legal Journal, 31*(3), 114–25. https://doi.org/10.1177/002581726303100302.

Smith, M.R. (2007). Levels of Metaphor in Persuasive Legal Writing. *Mercer Law Review 58*, 919–947.

Swales, J. M. (1981). *Aspects of Article Introductions.* Birmingham, England: Language Studies Unit, University of Aston in Birmingham.

Taylor, S. (2013). *What Is Discourse Analysis?* London, England: Bloomsbury Academic.

Toulmin, S. E. (2003). *The Uses of Argument.* Cambridge, UK: Cambridge University Press.

Upton, T. A., & Cohen, M. A. (2009). An Approach to Corpus-Based Discourse Analysis: The Move Analysis as Example. *Discourse Studies, 11*(5), 585–605. https://doi.org/10.1177/1461445609341006.

Van Dijk, T. (2008). Context Theory and The Foundation of Pragmatics. Plenary Lecture Congress of the Pragmatics Society of Japan. *Studies in Pragmatics, 10*, 1–13.

White, P. R. R. (2003). Beyond Modality and Hedging: A Dialogic View of the Language of Intersubjective Stance. *Text – Interdisciplinary Journal for the Study of Discourse, 23*(2). https://doi.org/10.1515/text.2003.011.

Wodak, R., & Meyer, M. (2001). *Methods of Critical Discourse Analysis.* 6 Bonhill Street, London EC2A 4PU: SAGE Publications, Ltd.

Wong, A. T. Y. (2005). 'Writers' Mental Representations of the Intended Audience and of the Rhetorical Purpose for Writing and the Strategies That They Employed When They Composed'. *System, 33*(1), 29–47. https://doi.org/10.1016/j.system.2004.06.009.

Žagar, I. (2010). Topoi in Critical Discourse Analysis. *Lodz Papers in Pragmatics, 6*(1). https://doi.org/10.2478/v10016-010-0002-1.

Introduction to "Pardon My French" or What It Means to Be a Good Communicator in France

By Noémie Hermeking

The next chapter examines intercultural communication competence in general and French culture in particular from an anthropological perspective. In order to be do so, it is necessary to have the necessary language skills and cultural fluency as well as the ability to self-reflect because one's own ethnocentrism can distort reality. Hermeking points out that fables can be a great tool to help explain French culture because they provide insights into habits, customs, beliefs, and normative behavior. Reading and analyzing fables can be helpful in understanding the indirect, high context communication style typically used by natives of French culture. Such analysis includes self-reflection and attempting to understand the messages from the perspective of others – important aspects of intercultural communication competence because it helps overcome ethnocentrism. Obviously, one could use similar examples from literature to provide insights also into other cultures; after all, literature is a cultural artifact. At the same time, works of literature also describe sociofacts (i.e. the behavioral habits, norms, and customs of a culture), and they provide clues as to the mentifacts (i.e. beliefs and preferred cognitive or thinking styles) of a culture. This is critically important in the world of business because this knowledge can help avoid misunderstandings by preparing one for potentially hidden or indirect messages that typically accompany verbal messages – in other words, one needs to be able to read in-between the lines. And here, literature can be one's guide. Please insert below text:

Michael B. Hinner

Noémie Hermeking holds a Ph.D. in sociocultural anthropology from Indiana University in Bloomington, USA and an M.A. in social anthropology and ethnology from l´École des hautes études en sciences sociales (EHESS) in Paris. She has done extensive research with Indigenous communities both in Canada and the USA. Her research interest lie primarily within the fields of intercultural education and communication, educational equity, Indigenous studies and research ethics. Currently, she is a research assistant at the Coburg University of Applied Sciences for the EU-project Parh2Integrity and a senior project leader for the foundation Kick ins Leben, Munich. She is also a lecturer at various universities and colleges and works as an intercultural trainer. She has been a member of INIEDA (International Network for Intercultural Education Activities) since 2014.

Noémie Hermeking

“Pardon My French” or What It Means to Be a Good Communicator in France

Introduction

Having great intercultural communication skills is simply not enough to be considered a convincing communicator across cultures. This article explores what it means to be an effective communicator in France. Because communication and culture are so intertwined, I will focus specifically on French culture and language and provide a detailed analysis of an example I use in my intercultural workshops to prepare businesses that would like to work in France. The purpose of this example is to unravel the hidden meanings of intercultural communication, often disguised for outsiders and people unfamiliar with the French context. Being half-French/half-German, having studied, worked in both countries, plus applying my anthropological perspective of comprehending cultures from within, will strengthen my point.

Understanding Culture

“The scholarly study of language (linguistics) is largely separate from the study of culture (anthropology)” (Shaules, 2019, p. 9).

To communicate effectively across cultures, it is fundamental to have a firm grasp of one´s own cultural lens. As the American anthropologist Edward T. Hall eloquently noted, “Culture hides much more than it reveals, and strangely enough what it hides, it hides most effectively from its own participants” (1959, p. 39). Gaining a deeper understanding on cultural silences and how culture is constructed, while simultaneously becoming aware of one’s own ethnocentrism, biases, and the impact these elements have on our cultural self, is a crucial step to understand other cultures. For Hall, only by having an adequate knowledge about the self and one’s “built-in blinders”, (1976, p. 220), can one have the ability to understand the “Other”[1].

1 For a critique of “othering”, also within the field of anthropology, refer to Marcus and Fisher (1986).

Anthropologists Alfred Kroeber and Clyde Kluckhohn, who collected more than 160 different definitions of culture, concluded that "culture consists of patterns … of … behavior acquired and transmitted by symbols, constituting the distinctive achievement of human groups, including their embodiments in artifacts; the essential core of culture consists of traditional, … historical … ideas and especially their attached values; culture systems may, on the one hand, be considered as products of action, on the other as conditioning elements of further action" (1952, p. 181). Even while definitions of culture change over time, I will build on Andrew Cohen's idea of how our world can be meaningful in any and multiple contexts. Cohen argued "Culture, in this view, is the means by which we make meaning, and with which we make the world meaningful to ourselves, and ourselves meaningful to the world" (1993, p. 196). From an anthropological perspective, culture is not static, but is always reinventing itself. I understand culture as various puzzle pieces that only together make a whole. By applying this dynamism to intercultural interaction, it becomes clear that meaning-making is context-situated and negotiated (Bjerregaard et al., 2009) and we ourselves are active creators/shapers of culture.

Scholars from various fields have tried to develop taxonomies to compare (business) cultures/cross-cultural management (CCM), its norms, its beliefs and its practices with one another to understand intercultural communication (Hall, 1959, 1976; Hamden-Turner & Trompenaars, 1997; Hofstede, 1997; Kluckhohn, F. R. & Strodtbeck, 1961; Schwartz, 2006; Thomas, 1993). From a contemporary anthropological perspective, there are certain limitations to these frameworks, as cultures cannot be compartmentalized. Bjerregaard et al. critiqued these models that hold onto an outdated view of culture relinquished in the field of anthropology in the 1960s in the following way (2009, p. 211): "The functionalist perspective has led to an unproductive understanding of culture and acculturation where potential for disagreement, antagonism, power relations and conflict are never dealt with, where social and political overtones are squelched, and where sensitivities relating to hierarchical positioning and power differentials across partisan interests are habitually overlooked" (2009, p. 208). Moreover, holism and multi-perspectivity as the hallmarks of anthropology reaffirm the need to look at cultures intertwined with various components. Cultures cannot be considered within a vacuum by nihilating the importance of cultural context (Helman, 2007, p. 7), speaking against a fixed and static understanding of (business) cultures. Furthermore, one should keep in mind that regardless of the intercultural interaction, it is not just culture, but also the context (for example, the power asymmetries and status) and individuals which add to the complexity of the situation. Therefore, culture and intercultural situations should be interpreted, never as a single story, but as multiple contours and in its versatility. Nevertheless, these cultural taxonomies allow for a preliminary understanding to describe cultural landscapes in which to apply these insights to intercultural interactions.

Importance of (Applied) Anthropology

'It may be held that it is laudable for an anthropologist to investigate practical problems. Possibly it is, but if he does so, he must realize that he is no longer acting within the anthropological field but in the non-scientific field of administration.' (Evans-Pritchard, 1946, p. 93)

Anthropology is the study of humankind. The relevance of applied anthropology to solve contemporary issues and problems has grown over the years since Evans Pritchard shared his perspective on the matter. While ethnographic fieldwork used to be conducted with local communities in "exotic" places, it has now become geographically unbound, even used as a tool in the digital world to understand user experiences. Taking from Davis' (2021) words on building a more equitable society: "Anthropology is the antidote to nativism, the enemy of hate, a vaccine of understanding, tolerance and compassion that silences the rhetoric of demagogues… "(para. 19). Eighty-six years before Davis, Margaret Mead, a pioneer anthropologist, wrote in 1935: "Anthropology demands the open- mindedness with which one must look and listen, … " (1935, p. ix). Beside the receptiveness that both Davis and Mead are advocating for, I think that current anthropologist also have to be aware and act upon their unconscious biases for real societal change to take place.

In this line of thought, I will use the term "applied anthropology" within these manifold definitions to refer to the knowledge, skills, and methods that present-day anthropologists put into practice to solve societal challenges and problems. This anthropological lens has much to offer to contemporary settings by "defining our common humanity and celebrating diversity" (Tett, 2021, p. 233). Intercultural trainings are invaluable for initiating a change of perspective by putting oneself in the other person´s shoes. Anthropologists can provide valuable insights into developing intercultural (competence) workshops since they, themselves, have felt what it was like to be an outsider, the "Other", while conducting ethnographic research (fieldwork) in foreign settings. At the same time, the feeling of "Otherness" is a reminder to remain humble and not, as a Native American respondent once said to me, to "walk around as a peacock." Furthermore, the anthropological lens can help businesses to keep an open mind when working with other cultures. There is no "right" or "wrong" approach, but in other cultures it might just be "different to our own" perspective.

Intercultural Competence, Hence Fluency

"The question is not how to get rid of differences in this world, but how to better cope/live with them" (Mall, 2014, p. 29).

Considering demographic, economic, technological, and societal changes, intercultural competence has become a key concept for the global reality of the 21st century. "Intercultural competence is an opportunity to learn to live and engage in an ever-changing world" (Waldhubel, 2014, p. 147), while "defusing conflicts and setting the foundations of peaceful coexistence" (UNESCO, 2013, p. 6). To communicate effectively across cultures, language skills and intercultural fluency are prerequisites that allow new synergies to flourish. Milton Bennett has defined this process of becoming interculturally competent as "different developmental stages of sensitivity", starting with awareness to self-reflection and finally progressing to understanding (2001). This means that it is of utmost importance to get out of one's cultural comfort zone for this learning to take place.

Being interculturally competent, and hence being able to communicate across cultures effectively, means to be aware of one's ethnocentrism. Gudykunst and Nishida (1994) have argued that one cannot avoid ethnocentrism. Still, being aware of your ethnocentric views and being able to critically reflect upon them is necessary if you do not want to make false assumptions about your interlocutor. At the same time, becoming interculturally fluent is a lifelong process and intercultural misunderstandings cannot always be avoided, but can be lessened with a solid grasp of your own and other people's culture.

High- and Low-Context Communication

The terms high-context and low-context communication explain differences in communication styles between cultural groups. Edward T. Hall coined the term "low and high-context communication" in 1976 in his publication "Beyond Culture" to compare high- and low-context communication styles, interpreting the value cultures place on indirect and direct communication. Hall often exemplified the difference between these two communication styles by using the analogy of marriage. "Newlyweds need to state their message explicitly and repeat them frequently to ensure they are received accurately," (Meyer, 2014, p. 41) but over the years they might be able to understand each other without even talking explicitly to each other anymore, because they are so familiar with this context.

To better illustrate my point about French culture and language, I will compare it to their German counterparts where needed.[2] French, a Romance language, and German, one of the Indo-European languages, have different communication styles. The German communication style tends to be rather direct and precise, leaving little room for interpretation, an example of low communication. What is said in German is usually meant that way, basically *Klartext reden* (plain/straight talking). Telling a friend, we should get together next week usually means that this is really intended to occur. However, this is not the case in France. In France, people in general tend to be quite indirect when they talk, often talking with an underlying meaning. You must be able to read between the lines, grasp the unspoken silences and simultaneously understand the context of the conversation to understand the high-context communication style of French people. Of course, this can lead to some intercultural misunderstandings, when a German person does not understand what the French counterpart is implicitly trying to tell him/her.

For example, in Germany when you want the bus to stop, you hit the button and it says: "Bus stopt" (the bus stops). You know the bus will stop. In French it is "Arrêt demandé." (A request to stop has been made). From a German perspective you are not sure if the bus will come to a stop or not, but of course, a person socialized in France understands the underlying message.

Nevertheless, a culture is never completely high or low communication. Compared to German the French communication style is not always indirect. As an example one needs to be aware when receiving negative feedback even French people tend to be more direct in this situation and do not use "downgrader" words that lessen the criticism (Meyer, 2016, 2014), reminding ourselves that we have all been socialized and conditioned in our way of communicating.

Being a Good Communicator in France

The French language played an important role in unifying the country after the French Revolution. Regional languages were forbidden, and French was the official language to be used thereafter. Various policies have been developed over the years for French-only use. For example, it was only in 1989 that the Pasteur Institute announced that it would start publishing in English to gain a bigger

2 I have been socialized in these two cultures myself, have lived, studied and worked in these two cultures/countries, which I call home(s).

readership[3]. Master's degree classes at the university level are often still held in French, in contrast to other European countries. This suggests once again the tendency of French institutions to preserve the native language. Even during my intercultural workshops, I always tell participants, particularly in France, that speaking the local language, even if it is just a few words, can be useful while simultaneously being a door opener. Being a good communicator in France means to talk persuasively, skillfully and in a sophisticated manner by coining some "culture générale" knowledge (general culture[4]). For example, combining this culture générale with the implicit communication style au *2ème degré* (second-degree message), I have devised a strategy using fables of La Fontaine, which I often employ during my intercultural workshops to prepare participants for French culture and hence to be better communicators.

Fables

Fables are great carriers of cultural messages. These stories reveal habits, customs, beliefs, and normative behavior of any cultural group. They might be used simply for entertainment, but they may also be employed as tools to teach educational lessons. Fables mesmerize both young and adults, because they are relatable to all at a personal level. These stories and their meanings are deeply ingrained/part of our habitus in what make us "human".

Beside the fact that fables and stories in general are carriers of cultural meanings, La Fontaine offers a great example of second-degree messages through his literary style. La Fontaine was not the only writer to use stories for political ends, as Marina Webster exemplifies through literature written by women in the 17th century. Renée J. Kohn wrote specifically about the second degree of La Fontaine's poetry as exemplified in his work *Adonis* in the following words:

> *La Fontaine réussit en poésie ce que Poussin fit en peinture, une sorte d'idéalisation vraie de la mythologie; ce que le peintre atteint grâce à la pure beauté des paysages et des corps, le poète le recrée par la puissance de la rêverie, et la lancinante douceur de sentiments*

3 Asuncion-Lande, N. (1998). English as the dominant Language for Intercultural communication: Prospects for the next century (p. 73). In K. S. Sitaram & M. H. Prosser (Eds.) Civic Discourse: Multiculturalism, Cultural Diversity, and Global Communication (pp. 67–82). Stamford, CT: Ablex.

4 The "general culture" I am referring to might be compared to the German word *Bildung*, as it was perceived by Johann Wolfgang von Goethe in the 18th century. His literature is still part of German classics today and part of the educational curriculum.

> *simples, bonheur de l'amour, tristesse de l'absence et de la mort. Ce que la lumière est aux paysages de Poussin, l'art extrême de l'expression l'est à l'Adonis* (Kohn, 1956, p. 81).
> La Fontaine achieves in poetry what Poussin did in painting: a sort of true idealization of mythology. What the painter achieves due to pure beauty of landscapes and bodies, the poet recreated by the power of reverie, and the haunting sweetness of simple feelings, happiness of love, sadness of absence and death. What light is to Poussin's landscapes, the extreme art of expression is to Adonis (my translation).

Even though La Fontaine celebrated his 400th anniversary in July 2021, his literature is remains part of the French curriculum today. School children learn and recite some of these fables, such as "The ant and the cricket/grasshopper", "The fox and the crow", and "The tortoise and the hare". La Fontaine was inspired by Aesop's Greek lyrics that date back to the 7th century B.C. To this day, the fables are used in cartoons, performed at the theatre, included in exhibitions, represented in monuments and paintings, or used as metaphors for politics and daily life.

Since 1848, the year of the first presidential election in France, French presidential candidates

have been caricaturized in the media (Doizy& Dupuy, 2016), a "tradition" that has carried on to the present day. Some politicians, such as Nicolas Sarkozy, François Hollande and Ségolène Royal, were represented by the animals of La Fontaine's fables. Recently President Emmanuel Macron hoped all French school children would be awakened to French literature, just as he was by his grandmother through the fables of La Fontaine (Pantel, 2021). Indeed, La Fontaine´s work is still carefully passed on through generations, not only at school but also through other mediums.

Because many French people can recite some of these verses in the fables, people in France can give the sense that they are "cultured" by this simple act. La Fontaine's literary language helps readers to become familiar with French culture and its underlying critique on society and politics, while exemplifying human vices and their moral consequences.[5] Consequently, La Fontaine"s writings serve to "please and instruct" children and adults alike (Tiefenbrun, 1981, p. 50), adding humor and wit as necessary ingredients. The works of La Fontaine, like those of Molière or Racine, are pillars of French literature. They are classics and part of the French patrimony.

Some of La Fontaine´s writings were specifically addressed to the Dauphin, the son of Louis XIV and Marie- Thérèse, even dedicating his fables to the prince

---

5 In *L'homme et la couleuvre*, the cow accuses humans of reducing its status to a sole nurturer, only benefiting humans.

(La Fontaine, 1991, p. 3–4). The protagonists of his fables are neither fully animals nor humans. By giving the animals a humanlike character, La Fontaine is able to hide second-degree messages. The use of animals as metaphors is a choice that La Fontaine explained in the following terms:

> "*Les propriétés des animaux et leurs divers caractères y sont exprimés ; par conséquent les nôtres aussi, puisque nous sommes l'abrégé de ce qu'il y a de bon et de mauvais dans les créatures irraisonnables.*" (La Fontaine, 1991, pp. 3–4).
> "The attributes of animals and their various characters are expressed therein; therefore, ours too, since we are the abbreviation of what is good and bad in unreasonable creatures" (my translation).

Even when La Fontaine used animals as main protagonists in his stories, he did so without overly criticizing the authority of the establishment, specifically the reign of King Louis XIV. His ability to manipulate language without the dangers of retaliation exemplifies a body of works representative of high-context communication. La Fontaine also used wordplay and metaphors to force the reader to look for the underlying messages, to read in-between the lines (Tiefenbrun, 1981, p. 52)

La Fontaine wrote much of his work during the 17th century, a historical moment when all the literature published in France could be sanctioned by the royal library. Sanctions could end the career of any artist. Acting against the king´s favor could lead to sanctions, and even imprisonment, such was the fate of Nicolas Fouquet, a friend of La Fontaine. By using animalesque characters (often anthropomorphic) and giving them a human voice, La Fontaine could not be accused of criticizing either society or, most importantly, the king and/or the Catholic Church. "*Tout parle en mon ouvrage, même les poisons.*" "Everything speaks in my work, even the fish." (La Fontaine, 1991, p. 29).

His choice of animals was deliberate. In several legends, the lion, the king of the animal world, is superior to all the other animals and is the ruler of the animal society. Once again, this is an allusion to Louis XIV, who is superior to the rest of society, even though La Fontaine often questioned his position as monarch in his stories.[6]

To further illustrate the high-context communication of French language and culture, I will use the poem about the ant and the grasshopper/cricket to illustrate the manifold interpretations that are hidden under the surface.

---

6 During the Monarchy in Germany in the 18th century, theater plays used such loopholes to partially criticize authority as the program of the Anhaltisches Theater in Dessau testifies. For more information read Moritz von Prosky´s publication (1894) *Das Herzogliche Hoftheater zu Dessau: in seinen Anfängen bis zur Gegenwart.* Dessau: Baumann.

"A grasshopper gay
Sang the summer away,
And found herself poor
By the winter's first roar.
Of meat or of bread, Not a morsel she had!
So a begging she went,
To her neighbour the ant,
For the loan of some wheat,
Which would serve her to eat,
Till the season came round.
"I will pay you," she saith,
"On an animal's faith,
Double weight in the pound
Ere the harvest be bound."
The ant is a friend
(And here she might mend)
Little given to lend.
"How spent you the summer?"
Quoth she, looking shame
At the borrowing dame.
"Night and day to each comer
I sang, if you please."
"You sang! I'm at ease;
For 'tis plain at a glance,
Now, ma'am, you must dance." [7]

Different interpretations, and hence "multi-level messages," are possible due to the "artistic indirectness of metaphoric language" used by La Fontaine (Tiefenbrun, 1981, p. 60). The two animal characters are used as metaphors for human behavior. Is it more important to live in the present moment or in anticipation of the future, be an egoist or reckless? This might be seen as a first-degree message; a situated context is not needed for interpretation.

Considering the times in which the fables were written, various underlying messages are possible too. Erin Meyer has argued that the second-degree message here was a subtle way to tell "Louis XIV that he was spending too much money on rerouting the Eure River to supply water to the Versailles fountains." (Meyer, 2016, p. 38). La Fontaine was not the only writer to criticize the king's spending. According to Marina Warner, "Starlight" by Henriette-Julie de Murat also alluded to "Louis XIV's ruinous wars and the cult of military might" (1996,

7 La Fontaine, J. *Fables of La Fontaine*, translated from the French by Elizur Wright. Fourth edition, (1856), book 1, fable 1, pp. 47–48, 2. Boston: Sanborn, Carter and Bazin.

p. 12). The opera "The Marriage of Figaro" by Pierre Beaumarchés and other artists aimed, through political satire, to draw attention to social inequalities.

La Fontaine might have been identifying with the cricket himself, since he could be considered an "artist" like the cricket and, as Boris Dondé indicated, La Fontaine was not the greatest example of caution himself, having spent all his family fortune (2021, p. 28). In addition, Dondé continues his reasoning by exemplifying the ambiguity of this fable, taking neither the side of the cricket nor that of the ant. Even though the cricket says it will pay the ant back before August, with interest, one wonders how that would be possible before harvest time. At the same time, considering the social context of the time, certain moral lessons were also introduced. For example, the Church forbade lending to others and receiving interest/benefits in return (Dondé, 2021, p. 28). This may have been the reason why the ant was not "someone who lends". Furthermore, since this poem has an open ending without the traditional moral, the reader is free to choose her/his own interpretation. With various layers of meaning, it becomes clear that context is needed to make sense of what the intended, and sometimes ambiguous, meaning.

Intercultural Workshop

In my workshop, individuals come with their own preconceived notions about communication and culture. They believe by speaking truthfully about each other ´s culture is a linear path for mutual understanding. Because language and culture are complex systems that do not reflect a linear path, I use the work of La Fontaine to show how context in intercultural communications is key. Additionally, the work of La Fontaine allows me to demonstrate the logic of French culture and historical importance for French people today. Participants read the fable of the ant and the cricket. After some linear thinking is expressed, I show the importance of the sociocultural context when the fables were first written to dive beneath the surface for a deeper understanding. In a second step, I ask participants to go back and forth in low and high communication style, by expressing a message directly and in an indirect manner. Attendees experience a real challenge in juggling these two styles, making it clear how everyone has been conditioned in a particular communicative style. At this point the relevance of a change of perspective and realizing everyone´s ethnocentrism is usually achieved. In a third step, I then invite participants to transfer this newly gained knowledge to today´s French business world and its second-degree messages. Consequently, an outsider to French communication, will be aware that what was said is not always what was meant precisely, and will then be able to look for these hidden messages.

Conclusion

Resonating on a personal and societal level, La Fontaine´s literature remains as popular as it was 400 years ago, representing a national icon surviving turbulent times. Drawing on La Fontaine´s communicative style, while referencing French culture, fables are a great resource for an intercultural workshop. La Fontaine's work can be understood as a mirror that invites the reader to reflect on the self and the other. Its position away from the self serves to keep the necessary distance and to adjust it over time. The works of La Fontaine compel us to evaluate the usefulness of his work through the lens of applied anthropology. Together, they contribute to one's perspective for more meaningful intercultural understanding and communication.

To be willing and open to consider different communication styles is a starting point for cultures approaching each other- just like the desire to seek mutual understanding. Seeing the unspoken silences, thus understanding the particularity of this French communication style, will facilitate the process of becoming a good communicator in France. La Fontaine reminds us to be humble: "Just because you have seen a lot, does not mean that you retained a lot."("*Quiconque a beaucoup vu/ peut avoir beaucoup retenu.*" (Tiefenbrun, 1981, p. 52). This may be another quotation you might want to use to impress your French counterpart. *Pourquoi pas*? (Why not?)

References

Asuncion-Lande, N. (1998). English as the dominant Language for Intercultural communication: Prospects for the next century (p. 73). In K. S. Sitaram & M. H. Prosser (Eds.) *Civic Discourse: Multiculturalism, Cultural Diversity, and Global Communication* (pp. 67–82). Stamford, CT: Ablex.

Bennet, M. (2001). *Intercultural Competence for Global Leadership*. Retrieved September 07, 2021, from: http://www.idrinstitute.org/allegati/IDRI_t_Pubblicazioni/4/FILE_Documento.pdf.

Bjerregaard, T., Lauring, J., & Klitmøller, A. (2009). A Critical Analysis of Intercultural Communication Research in Cross-Cultural Management Introducing Newer Developments in Anthropology. *Critical Perspectives on International Business*, 5(3), 207–228. https://doi.org/10.1108/17422040910974695.

Cohen, A. P. (1993). Culture as Identity: An Anthropologist's View. *New Literary History, 24*(1), 195–209. https://doi.org/10.2307/469278

Davis, W. (2021). Why Anthropology Matters. Retrieved from: https://www.scientificamerican.com/article/why-anthropology-matters/.

Doizy, G., & Dupuy, P. (2016). De 1848 à nos jours : le président de la République face à son double caricatural cahiers d histoires. *Revue d Histories Critiques,* 106, 132.

Dondé, B. (2021). La Cigale et la Fourmi. Critique de l´insouciance ou de l´égoïsme?. *La Fontaine. Les dessous des « Fables »* (p. 28). Paris: Le Point Références.

Evans-Pritschard, E. (1946). *Applied Anthropology. Africa, 16*(2), 92–98.

Gudykunst, W. B., & Nishida, T. (1994). *Bridging Japanese/North American Differences*. Thousand Oaks, CA: Sage.

Hall, E. T (1959). *The Silent Language*. New York: Anchor Books Doubleday.

Hall, E. T. (1976). *Beyond Culture*. New York: Anchor Books Doubleday.

Hamden-Turner, C., & Trompenaars, F. (1997). Response to Geert Hofstede. *International Journal of Intercultural Relations, 21*(1), 149–159.

Helman, C. (2007). *Culture, Health and Illness*. Amsterdam: Elsevier Science.

Hofstede, G. (1997). *Cultures and Organizations: Software of the Mind*. New York: McGraw Hill.

Kluckhohn, F. R., & Strodtbeck, F. L. (1961). *Variations in Value Orientations*. Evanston, IL: Row Peterson.

Kohn, R. J. (1956). Réflexions sur l'Adonis de La Fontaine. *The Romanic Review, 47*(2).

Kroeber, A. L., & Kluckhohn, C. (1952). *Culture: A Critical Review of Concepts and Definitions*. Cambridge, MA: Peabody Museum.

La Fontaine, J. (1856). *Fables of La Fontaine*, translated from the French by Elizur Wright (4th ed.), book 1, fable 1, 47–48, 2. Boston: Sanborn, Carter, and Bazin.

La Fontaine, J. de. (1991). *Fables contes et nouvelles, Oeuvres complètes, t. I. Collection « Bibliothèque de la Pléiade »*. Paris: Gallimard.

Mall, R. A. (2014). Die Frage ist nicht, wie man Differenzen aus der Welt schafft, sondern wie man mit ihnen umgeht. Betrachtungen aus interkultureller Sicht. In A. Moosmüller & J. Möller-Kiero (Eds.), *Interkulturalität und kulturelle Diversität* (pp. 29–45). Münster: Waxmann.

Marcus, G. E., & Fischer, M. M. J. (1986). *Anthropology as Cultural Critique: An Experimental Moment in the Human Sciences*. Chicago, IL: University of Chicago Press.

Mead, M. 1935 (1977). *Sex and Temperament in Three Primitives Societies.* London: Henley, Routledge & Kegan Paul.

Meyer, E. (2014). How To Say "This Is Crap". In *Different Cultures, Harvard Business Review.* Retrieved September19, 2021, from: https://hbr.org/2014/02/how-to-say-this-is-crap-in-different-cultures.

Meyer, E. (2016). *The Culture Map: Decoding How People Think, Lead, and Get Things Done Across Cultures.* New York, NY: Public Affairs.

Pantel, N. (2021). *Wie die Unschuld auf dem Lande*, SZ, 17. June 2021. Retrieved September 01, 2021, from: https://www.sueddeutsche.de/politik/macron-frankreich-tour-wahlkampf-1.5325052

Schwartz, S. H. (2006). A Theory of Cultural Value Orientations: Explication and Applications. *Comparative Sociology, 5*(2–3), 137–182.

Shaules, J. (2019). *Language, Culture, and the Embodied Mind A Developmental Model of Linguaculture Learning.* Springer.

Tett, G. (2021). *Anthro-Vision. How Anthropology Can Explain Business and Life.* London: Penguin Books.

Thomas, A. (1993). *Kulturvergleichende Psychologie. Eine Einführung.* Göttingen: Hogrefe Verlag.

Tiefenbrun, S. (1981). The Art and Artistry of Teaching in the Fables of La Fontaine. *L'Esprit Créateur*, Winter 1981, *21*(4).

Unesco. (2013). *Intercultural Competences: A Conceptual and Operational Framework.* Retrieved September 01, 2021, from: https://en.unesco.org/interculturaldialogue/resources/132.

Waldhubel, N. (2014). Where Are You From? – or the Importance of Intercultural Competence for Identity Construction. *Lodz Papers in Pragmatics, 10*(1), 147–161.Versita: De Gruyter Mouton.

Warner, W. (1996). *Wonder Tales: Six Stories of Enchantment.* London: Chatto & Windus Ltd.

Introduction to Conversational Device of Formulation: Facilitating Exchange in Intercultural Settings

By Ling Chen

The following chapter examines formulations within the context of intercultural dialog. Simply put, formulations include the rewording of previous messages to confirm whether the meaning of the message has been properly understood or not. Formulations are used among native speakers to ensure that they have understood one another as well as among non-native speakers and native speakers or non-native speakers and other non-native speakers. It is, though, pointed out that native speakers often use formulation for more abstract summaries and commentaries whereas non-native speakers use formulations to verify the intended meaning of messages on a more pragmatic level than a semantic level. Ensuring that the intended message has been properly understood is important because, to some extent, it also encourages frame convergence which tends to reduce misunderstandings and avoid possible conflicts arising out of these misunderstandings. Deliberately incorporating formulations into one's conversation with others in an intercultural context is, thus, a useful tool which helps reduce potential misunderstandings. After all, there are many situations in the world of business that involve the interaction of native speakers and non-native speakers or non-native speakers with other non-native speakers. Situations that have the potential for misunderstandings, whether it be between members of a diverse workforce, between representatives of two different companies, or between company representatives and customers. Consequently, the insights and concepts discussed in this chapter can be very informative and helpful because communication makes business possible, but could also hinder it. Consequently, it is essential to avoid potential misunderstandings, and this chapters shows how that may be accomplished.

Michael B. Hinner

Ling Chen (PhD, Ohio State Univ.) is Professor Emeritus, the School of Communication, Hong Kong Baptist University.

Her areas of interest include Chinese Communication, Communication Competence, Intercultural Communication, Language and Social Interaction, and Organizational Communication. Interests in the role of culture in communication in different social contexts at various level of interaction and in intercultural encounters have been center of her research and scholarship. She has published 3 books and over 70 articles in books or academic journals, from research on such topics as verbal adaptive strategies in native-nonnative speaker interaction, managerial communication in Chinese business organizations, friendship dialectics among Chinese in Hong Kong, cultural learning of sojourners, cultural identity as a production in process, Chinese traditional value orientations, argumentative tendency of Chinese and Japanese. Her latest works are on host community acculturation orientations and ethnic minority communication.

Aside from professional association services, e.g., as Intercultural Communication Division Chair of the International Communication Association, President of the Association for Chinese Communication Studies and Vice-President of China's Association for Intercultural Communication Studies, Chen was Editor of *Management Communication Quarterly*, Associate Editor of *Communication Theory*. She served on the editorial board of a few international journals, e.g., *Communication Studies, Discourse and Communication, Howard Journal of Communications, Human Communication Research, Human Technology: An Interdisciplinary Journal on Humans in ICT Environments, Journal of Communication, Journal of Intercultural Communication Research, Journal of International and Intercultural Communication,* and *Management Communication Quarterly,* and continues on these: *Chinese Journal of Communication, Journal of Applied Communication Research.*

Ling Chen

Conversational Device of Formulation: Facilitating Exchange in Intercultural Settings

In an everyday conversation, participants' orientation toward each other and toward a mutually agreeable cause of interaction is accomplished in their communicative acts, typically in conversational moves (Stokes & Hewitt, 1976). Maintained with regular understanding check of various forms, mutual orientation in conversation enables co-participants to get a hold of the current state of conversation with a more or less shared understanding of the preceding talk as well as the conversation situation. Participants present to each other what they mean and/or what they mean to do by their talk. Understanding checks mark the specific points perceivably in need of clarification or elaboration, thus also render visible the negotiable, adaptable, and coordinated nature of the seemingly smooth-flowing conversation that usually appears effortless and unproblematic. Conversational devices such as formulations, frequently functioning as understanding check, are of interest because these devices demonstrate the on-going nature of the process in which co-participants of a conversation manage to understand each other and make sense of the situation. Formulations comment on part of the talk to secure an appropriate understanding of the conversation as social actions. This device for talk presents to conversation co-participants verbal clues as to which direction the conversation may be going and how/how well the conversation partners may have understood each other in terms of what they have made of the situation at hand. As verbal messages that explicitly or implicitly comment on the content and point to participants' social relationship or communication intent, formulations are instances of metacommunication that is an integral property of communication (e.g., Leeds-Hurwitz, 1989). This meta-communicative devise may be taken up to facilitate the conversation when there appears to have understanding issues and smooth out the process.

In this paper, we first review and follow development of works on this topic. The paper then examines and compares the use of formulations in two types of situation: interactions between two native speakers and that between a native and a nonnative speaker, the latter being common in intercultural interactions. From a broader perspective of social construction of reality and informed by the speech act theory, we discuss how such particular intra- and intercultural conversation settings may be defined or constructed in conversational moves such as formulations. A detailed comparison between the two settings is presented for illustration. On base of the discussion the paper last explores possible use of formulation to facilitate intercultural communication where participants are unfamiliar with each other's interactional rules or language use.

Formulations

A property of natural language is such that people can, and recognize that they do as they may easily, mean "differently than what they can say in so many words" (Garfinkel & Sacks, 1970, p. 362). Conversational formulations provide participants a way to demonstrate or achieve understanding by saying-in-so-many-words-what-we-are-doing (Garfinkel & Sacks, 1970) among alternatives. Formulations are meta-communicative by definition, referring back and forward to previous and following utterances. Co-participants explicitly or implicitly talk about the conversation (or part of) they are carrying out at the moment, as a way to specify or clarify their intended meaning. How formulations, as the talk about talk, explicate or characterize what participants are talking about is yet another matter. Formulation may not only facilitating talk but may aid construction of interaction situation for mutual understanding, so much so that formulations are referred to as "a valuable interactional resource" (Nakamura, 2010).

Developed from sociological conversational analysis in the 1970s, past decades or so have seen attention on role and use of formulation as a conversational device in fields as diverse as education (e.g., Nakamura, 2010), business (e.g., Clifton, 2006; Franco & Nielsen, 2018; Mansson, 2015), health care (e.g., Beach & Dixson, 2001), counselling/therapy (e.g., Antaki, 2008; Weiste, 2016), and mental-health peer-support phone talk (Pudlinski, 2019), even in online chat counselling (Stommel & van der Houwen, 2013). Researchers have shown formulations to be quite versatile and function in a variety of ways, all this in an auxiliary role extending from the understanding check.

Barnes (2007) for example notes its use for closing the business-at-hand and moving on to the next topic. Franco & Nielsen (2018) identify some formulations used to encourage reflection and some others for facilitating action. Among conversation devices, formulations in particular are found to facilitate main tasks at hand through talk (Drew, 2003) and be contextually specific. There are occasions when formulations are employed to articulate the unsaid, what perceived to be a remark a speaker could have said but has not done so in so much words (Bolden, 2010). Along the same line, the interest at this point for us, too, is what formulations may accomplish for conversation co-participants and particularly how it is accomplished in conversation, to be discussed next.

An instance of formulation occurs anaphorically to offer a summary, an interpretation of what has been said, or an interpretation of what is implied in what has been said. In doing so, formulations preserve the important information from the previous utterances and leave out, or delete, the unimportant; sometimes transform the original information (or part of) by extending it in logically or pragmatically. The three central properties of preservation, deletion and transformation serve as a basis for a distinction between two basic forms of conversational formulation: gist and upshots (Heritage & Watson, 1979).

Co-participants formulate the gist of utterances in the preceding talk mainly through preservation and deletion, by way of a summery or a paraphrase. Basically re-presenting the original information with different wording, such formulations often serve to clarify and to demonstrate a speaker's understanding of the talk so far, and to indicate to the conversation partner that the speaker is or intends to be in touch with what is going on in the conversation.

Example 1 (from Heritage & Watson, 1979: 134; G=group therapy member; Dr=therapist)[1]

1 G: =Which I don't like leavin it in company with people around
2 me (.05) cos I always have that feeling that their sayin
3 oh well (1.0) he:s just a () pickin it
4 – > Dr: So what you'r saying is that you'r self conscious
5 G: Uhm

The upshot is formulated on the base of the gist, as its logical or pragmatic extension. An upshot presupposes an un-explicated version of gist, which follows from an interpretation of the relevant utterance(s) represented by the gist. In response to a perceived perlocutionary intent, which is potentially infinitely numerous (Levinson, 1983), of the relevant talk, upshots involve extensive sense-making and meaning transformation. Rather than simply preserve the original information, upshots are formulated to elaborate and expand on what is said. Upshots pick out what is probably meant but not explicitly said in so many words.

Example 2 (from Heritage & Watson, 1979, p. 135; C=caller; S=a crisis center staff member)

1 Line numbers are specified for ease of explanation. They do not correspond to those in the original transcripts.

1	C:	now a: red 100 came for her and I think she phoned you before it
2		came, would you have any record – of it you know?
3	S:	er well I'm sorry but we just can't divulge any information at all
4 ->	C:	you can't do anything
5	S:	I'm sorry I can't no
	(...)	

As part of conversational organization, understanding checks by way of formulation are routinely accomplished in adjacency pair involving both co-participants in alternating turns[2]. A formulation from one person as the first pair part is usually followed by dis-/confirmation, or decision following Heritage & Watson (1979), from the other in the next turn. Whereas confirmation is massively preferred (Pomerantz, 1984), disconfirmation is also common albeit often presented as a qualified confirmation (e.g., "Yeah, but ...;" "Well, actually," etc.). The decision, the second pair part that joins in the understanding check, frequently determines the direction of the conversation from there on, depending on whether it is confirmation or disconfirmation.

Native-Native Speakers and Native-Nonnative Speaker Conversations

A most common subset of intercultural interaction is conversations involving a native speaker (NS) and a nonnative speaker (NNS). Such conversation is characterized by co-participants' largely lack of a shared background, which is associated with a common native language, its use, and related sociocultural rules of interaction. For co-participants, this lack of shared language-use experience not only gives rise to a greater possibility for misunderstanding or non-understanding, compared to the conversation between two NSs (e.g., Gass & Varonis, 1985), but also puts constraints on available options for remedy. On the other hand, co-participants of NS-NNS conversation do, just as NS-NS co-participants, share a same interaction context and some proficiency of

2 Formulations may also be of ones' own talk as a "news deliverer" (see Heritage and Watson, 1979), which have a different structural organization, but are not examined here.

the language used in the interaction as a common ground. They also ordinarily share the Cooperative Principle (Grice, 1975) in conversation. We thus assume that, aside from the *a priori* shared language-related knowledge base or the relative lack of it, all conversations also contribute to, as well as build on, a common ground in the ongoing talk. Conversation thus is an activity in the making through coordinated contributions of co-participants (Schegloff, 1982). The degree to which there is shared background or knowledge at the outset between co-participants is manifested in their conversation moves and messages that influence the progress of and shape the organization of conversation. A comparative examination of these two settings enables us to understand conversation in alternative terms as a dynamic as well as a reflexive process, regardless of or in spite of whom participants are[3]. We may see the conversation moves co-participants make and the way each move constrains subsequent acts. Every move limits the choice of alternative acts and frames the context in which these acts occur. NS-NNS and NS-NS interaction settings are, in this sense, defined by conversation moves in empirical terms instead of theoretical ones based *a priori* on the language status of participants.

Formulations in Two Interaction Settings

This section examines instances of formulations in actual occurrence of talk-in-interaction conversations between NSs and between a NS and a NNS[4]. With the aid of the talk preceding or following each instance, comparisons are made between the two groups, in terms of functional and structural aspects of the talk, to describe conversation co-participants' understanding check as part of the displayed sense making.

In NS-NS Conversations. These extracts are from conversations between two NSs.

---

3 In this sense, the navigation process of NS-NNS conversations would be informative of intercultural communication in general, whether or not conversation includes a NNS participant.

4 Conversation transcripts are of initial interactions (a) between two Americans and (b) between an American and a non-American nonnative-speaker partner. These are conversations taking place in a lab, whereby two previously unacquainted individuals were brought together to talk and get to know each other in a private room. This arrangement allowed for a relatively uniform interaction setting and also solicited a very close-to-real-life conversation. All co-participants were students from a large Midwestern US university; NNSs were from East-Asian countries.

Extract <1>, (PJTII, 3.1, p. 3)[5]

1	A:	(…) Once I tried to get an internship in WCNI, and I got beat out by an OU person
2		because he wanted full-time and I only wanted part-time=
3	B:	=Uh hun=
4	A:	=So I no longer listen to WNCI, as they turned me down. I can't do that. ((laugh))
5 – >	B:	Opted out.
6	A:	That's right. I was a (demon) ((laugh))

In line 5, speaker B advances a version of his understanding of speaker A's self-disclosure whereby B initiates an understanding check. A's "no longer listen(ing) to" (line 4) that radio station WCNI is summarized in "opt(ing) out," as an action out of deliberate choice. The formulation makes more explicit A's ambiguously expressed intention of "won't do," which is a reading of "can't do," by adding the element of intent to the reported behavior of "no longer listen(ing) to." This interpretation is immediately confirmed (line 6) by A, who joins in the effort of sense management and adds an assessment of the behavior in question as that of a "demon". At this particular point, the two co-participants appear to be in agreement, with an achieved understanding of this specific stretch of talk.

Extract <2>, (AAII.10.20, p. 2)

1	A:	I know. So what, what do you like to do in your spare time?
2	B:	I don't know, I mean, me and my friends get together, we just do – anything, [I mean
3	A:	[Ehm.=
4	B:	=movies, parties.
5– >	A:	Just hanging out.
6	B:	Yeah. ((laugh)) – And you, how about you?

5 'A,' 'B' are randomly assigned for alternating speakers in each excerpt. 'N' is used to identify the non-native speaker.

Speaker A summarizes (line 5) what speaker B says she does at leisure time. All activities and more, unspecified, are generalized into a broader categorization of "just hanging out." This presentation of the gist with a slang not only displays A's understanding of B's account of spare time activity. It also imparts an understanding of the emotional connotation: B simply passing time with friends as companion and not necessarily doing anything in particular. B confirms this, slightly transformed, interpretation both verbally and nonverbally. As a signal of acknowledging feeling understood, B's laughter serves to reinforce the verbal confirmation. The two are aligned so far, and their talk continues.

Extract <3>, (AAII.10.20, p. 3)

1	A:	So do you have friends in OU?
2	B:	Ehun. I was supposed to go there.
3	A:	Oh, were you?
4	B:	Yeah. – Bags are packed and everything, but ((laugh))=
5– >	A:	=Didn't decide to go, eh?
6	B:	Well, I had a full ride here and – I had a=
7	A:	=Really?
8	B:	Well, my freshman year. ((laugh))
9	A:	Wow. Academic?
10	B:	Yeah. Well no. I had like academics and other grants, and – stuff like that. Just a
11		bunch of stuff. But then after that, the money sort of just slowly started to go
12		away. ((laugh))
13– >	A:	Yeah, yeah. Ohio University is – a lot more expensive than this.
14	B:	Yeah. See I was going to do the monthly payment plan, but it's still too much.
15	A:	Ehun.
16	B:	So I said forget it ((laugh)) like forget it.
17– >	A:	Yeah. Then if you take out a bank loan, you end up paying for it – twenty years
18		after you graduate.

19– >	B:	Yeah, I know. Let's just say you get a job.
20	A:	Yeah. Yep. – So are you worrying about not getting a job after you graduate?

In this extract, we see four formulations in close proximity. In this case it happens to demonstrate a gradual achievement between the co-participants of a better understanding as the conversation unfolds to develop a topic at hand. Speaker A first presents (line 5) a formulation of B's unfinished utterance about not going to OU (line 4), which is reported not in so many words but in the manner the utterance is produced. She hints at her would-have-been association with OU with "supposed to go," implying its nonrealization. She then proceeds with a vivid depiction of a scene of leaving, "bags are packed and everything," only leading to a disjunctive "but" followed by laughers. This manner of talk suggests a sense of mischief or irony. At least, it seems it is the way A understood it, who thus formulates a probable end of story that B did not go and that it was a voluntary decision. This interpretation, however, is only accepted with qualification by B in line 6, who seems to read into A's remark (about the decision of not going) a reference to a (less than desirable) financial state. In this first round of understanding check through formulation, B's response indirectly confirms that she did not go to OU. She acknowledges that financial consideration was the reason for the decision of not going but expresses reservation for one possible aspect of A's formulation – the actual time frame, as B had a "full ride" to begin with. This move introduces the subject of money into the talk about going to OU. In a few turns, B links the talk back to the initial discussion, explaining the reason for not going to OU that she was running out of money. A then formulates (line 13) a conclusion of what speaker B has said, that OU is very expensive. This upshot from A presents an adjustment of position to accommodate the fact that B did have financial means for an education, by pointing out that OU is beyond average means. This second round of understanding check ends with B's confirmation, who produces further evidence (line 14) to support A's formulation, that even monthly payment is too much of a burden. Having established understanding so far, A proceeds with a third formulation, on her next full turn (line 17), that even a bank loan wouldn't help much since one will "end up paying for it twenty years" later. A's remark not only interprets but expands on what B says. This formulation also receives confirmation from B, who in turn produces a formulation of her own, developing the topic further on the base of A's remark, that the ability of "paying for" the loan is contingent upon one getting a job. B's this formulation also meets with a confirmation by A in the following turn. All these formulated scenarios preserve the original information of not going to OU due to insufficient financial means and also explore a variety of extended meanings evolved from it.

Extract <4>, (AAII, 2.12, p. 9)

1	B:	Really. Our house is full of antique. I used to hate them, b'cause they are like – they
2		are old and (they used) to build dirt. (…) Now I've grown up, I much appreciate
3		them. You don't ever have to change=you know, people in my house, they have
4		to get new furniture (and). If you have modern furniture, modern goes out, and
5		antique doesn't. (.3) I like that.
6– >	A:	Plus you can always sell antique, if you don't like them. You can trade out, trade
7		over, whatever, if you want to change style. You can't sell something from
8		Glick's for five years.
		((both laugh))
9	B:	That's so true. That's funny.

A's formulation in line 6 is presented on the base of the gist of B's remarks – the advantage of owning antics, displaying an understanding of the talk while contributing to it with further related information, that antique are valuable. The sentiment is shared, as is the message, that antics are appreciated for their monetary, exchangeable, as well as aesthetic, values. Both the message and sentiment are mutually understood and acknowledged in their laughers after line 8, followed by B's verbal confirmation with emphasis – "so true," to express her being positive about this.

As illustrated above, formulations examined here are often used to summarize previous utterance(s) from the other participant. It also serves to offer one's interpretation of what the partner has said explicitly or implicitly. A formulation presents an effort for accurate understanding of the partner's intended meaning, by seeking confirmation of one's interpretation. The interpretation is explicitly about the other's message and implicitly about the flow of the conversation. It suggests an interest in the interaction and a respect for the partner. It also indirectly points to a potentially fruitful area for the conversation to develop into. All these functions of formulations benefit the interactional relationship. Understanding achieved in this manner represents a smooth and synchronized conversational occasion.

In NS-NNS Conversation. We will now examine formulations in conversations with a non-native speaker from a non-American culture.

Extract <5>, (AFII.16.36, p. 4)

1	A:	…I have been a secretary for ten years now.
2	N:	Oh, right. Secretary should be interesting.
3	A:	You think? No, no. You do everything, with little gratification and appreciation
4		and – low pay.
5	N:	It that a company=is it a big company?
6	A:	No, it's a bank, Huntington Bank.
7	N:	Oh, ok.=
8	A:	=A corporation, I worked for the corporation, but.
9	N:	No? ((laugh))
10	A:	No. (.4) But it is a good paying job, until I get out of school. So.
11– >	N:	Ok. So you are not pretty satisfied? ((laugh))
12	A:	Enhun. I have been a secretary for like ten years and I never
13		have been satisfied, so that's why now I need to do something that's more
14		challenging.

In this case, speaker N seems to be unsure of what speaker A says thus responding with a question "No?" Perhaps, N is a little puzzled by A's position on her job as a secretary: that it is uninteresting, thankless, and low pay, yet staying at the job for a long time. A's explanation about it as a good paying job clarifies it a little for N, who then tentatively offers a formulation of what she understands (line 11). Tentative as seen in the way it is presented, as a question. N's earlier incorrect assessment (line 2) rejected by A (line 3) also makes it likely that N is more cautious later on. The uncertainty is also suggested by the use of conjunction "so," which is to ensure that the remark is taken as N's understanding of the immediately previous message of A. This formulation is a rephrasing of the basic information in, thus consistent to and preserving the gist of, A's original remark. This time A accepts N's formulation as an appropriate understanding and follows up with further explication of her own position on this matter.

Extract <6>, (AAII.3.13-AF, p. 1)

1	A:	I'm I'm a sophomore.
2	N:	Sophomore. Any major?
3	A:	Well, I was an economics major, but er – they told me I had to be in school for real
4		long time – to get – a job with that.
5	N:	Oh. Economics.
6	A:	Yeah. It is=it was. I didn't have too much trouble with it. It's kind of like boring
7		though.
8	N:	((laugh))
9	A:	It's it was not for me. I don't know what I'm going to do. Don't have any ideas
10		really.
11–>	N:	So you don't want to take, not in any one of the majors in undergraduate.
12	A:	Well, I've taken, I am a minor in economics, and I just since I have taken as much
		as I have already, and er I don't really – I don't think I'm going to major in it though,
		I so I might just as well to be minor in it. What the heck!
		((Both laugh))
		(…)

In extract 1.6, speaker N doesn't seem to have doubt about what A says, and yet advances a formulation, also preceded with conjunction "so," to paraphrase A's remarks for checking. The formulation is indirectly disconfirmed. A corrects N by pointing out that he is an economics minor, meaning not "not wanting to take" and not "not in any one of the majors." N's formulation preserves the wrong information, or simply misses the right information, i.e., A's (unspecified) reluctance to be a student without major. This sentiment is not explicitly expressed but subtly displayed in A's reply to N's inquiry of his major (line 3). The reply opens with a hedging "well" to introduce his ex-major and an explanation of the reason of it being "ex," without explicit about the current status of having no major. N understands the face value of the verbal content but not the message conveyed in the manner of content presentation, while A continues to offer reasoning of having economics as a minor.

Extract <7>, (AFII.3.33, p. 6)

1	N:	No, () you guys are so young compared to us. We wasted a lot like in high
2		school. Our high school is two years longer you guys'. We need to go after high
3		school – we have to go through (pre-) for two years – before I come here.
4		Say in our country, I need to (pre-) two years, I need to go to college for four
5		years.
		(.4)
6– >	A:	So you are not a freshman now?
7	N:	I am a senior and graduating.
8	A:	You are graduating?
9	N:	Yeah.
10– >	A:	So the first two years you are in Malaysia=
11	N:	=in Malaysia.
12	A:	then transfer=
13	N:	=Yeah, transfer to here.
14	A:	OK. It is not bad at all. It is not bad at all. (

The first formulation from speaker A's (line 6) is a summary of N's preceding remarks. The second formulation (line 10) is a part-paraphrase and part-summary of what speaker N says. Both formulations are confirmed, while both are preceded by conjunction "so" to ensure a cohesive reading. The two formulations are produced back to back sandwiching a repetition of the other's message, none of which really develop the conversation topically. These formulations simply recycle the presented content message in different wordings. Use of "so," together with formulations put forward in this way, serves to indicate A's interest in proper understanding as well as a degree of uncertainty about such an understanding of N. N seems to sense this uncertainty, and is quick to confirm (line 11, 13) to ensure A of his correct reading of what she is saying and they are discussing.

Extract <8>, (AFI.5.25, p. 2)

1	A:	(…) So, what is you boyfriend or – what are you majoring in?
2	N:	Er me?
3	A:	[Ehum
4	N:	[I am trying to major in nursing.
5	A:	Really? My best friend is in nursing.
6	N:	Really?
7	A:	Yeah.
8	N:	But – actually I was in nursing in my country. I came here to – a:h attend the test
9		(and tested) and get my Bachelor degree from OSU.
		(.4)
10	A:	Is it ehm is our nursing program more advanced or is it the same?
11	N:	Oh. – Not really the same. But – eh I have learned so many things here, a:nd -
12		but generally speaking you can say that's the same.
13	A:	Are they?
14	B:	Yeah.
15– >	A:	So you could've learned the same thing back home or ()
16	B:	Ehun. – Some ideas just – are newer than I my home, newer than I have, how to
17		care for patients, and ehm the technical maybe you can say, it is newer. It is new
18		for me. (…)

A's formulation in line 15 is also a rephrasing of N's remark led by "so," which is interesting in the immediate context of the conversation. N first does not quite follow what is asked of her (line 2). She then reverses herself twice in the stretch of talk that follows. In line 8, that she is "trying to major in nursing" but "actually was in nursing" in her own country, and in line 11–12, that the nursing program is "not really the same" but is "generally the same" for two countries. To this last part, A follows up with a direct question (line 13) for confirmation, gets it, and follows up with the formulation in the next turn. Speaker A displays her effort to ensure a proper understanding of N – the question may well be an unsuccessful attempt to solicit more input from N. N confirms the formulation from A that the nursing program is the same in two countries, then, again, proceeds to elaborate that there is something more recently developed or "newer" in the U.S. programs. This last remark is somewhat inconsistent to what is just confirmed that one would learn the same thing back home as in the US.

Overall then, we can see there are differences between NS-NNS conversations and NS-NS conversation in exact use of formulations regarding the depth of understanding. While all formulations interpret and summarize what has been going on so far in conversation, (a) those in <1> to <4>, from conversations between two NSs, depart from original expressions to render a version of current speaker's own understanding of what the other has communicated up till that point. In contrast, (b) formulations in <5> to <8>, from conversations between a native and a nonnative speaker, are mostly slight rewording of what the other has said, sticking to the original content more rather than less.

Formulations in the NS-NS conversations are mostly confirmed, reflecting the relative accuracy in understanding not just the literal meanings but also the implied meanings. Formulations in these conversations are offered with greater certainty as well on the part of the speaker. Co-participants in NS-NS interaction exchange ideas and negotiate meanings more on the pragmatic level and less on the semantic level. Formulations occur to facilitate in-depth, more elaborate development of topics and exchange of co-paticipants' viewpoints and feelings on the topics. Formulations help constitute the context of a relative easy or smooth interaction semantically that is NS-NS conversation. The context becomes part of shared information for the co-participants to feed-forward into their ongoing exchanges.

Formulations in NS-NNS conversation have a tone of expression that is less certain, as seen from the use of conjecture "so" in several cases, indicating an effort to make structural connection to what the other says. Addition of "so" in these examples builds in an expressed expectation of confirmation or at least a direct response. This somehow strengthens the already existing constraints of formulation-decision adjacency pair, making it markedly inappropriate if the other does not respond to it in the next turn. Formulations in NS-NNS conversations encode the speaker's plead for and offer of more cooperation from the partner and contribute more to semantic level understanding. Whereas mutual understanding is achieved with help of formulations, it is agreement on meaning at a factual, or literal, level with respect to what has been communicated verbally. Connoative and implicative meanings are present and available, but are often missed, neglected, misunderstood, or simply ignored by co-participants. This kind of contextualization is a message in itself for co-participants to adjust their subsequent moves and understandings accordingly.

Intercultural Interaction by Way of Formulations in Talk

Proper understandings being the point for communication, understanding checks are indispensable, which guide co-participants to make necessary adjustments so as to get their messages across and to interpret properly the messages they receive. Formulations for understanding check comment implicitly or explicitly on one's own talk and on the talk of the other so as to secure and display co-participants' understanding of one another. Through formulations, co-participants reveal their intent and perceptions about the on-going in conversation. The examination of formulations above identifies similarity as well as difference in conversations in the NS-NS and NS-NNS settings. One can see that conversation co-participants routinely engage in understanding checks by way of formulations, whether the talk is between two native speakers or between a native speaker and a non-native speaker. The similarity is seen in exhibited functional acts and in structural sequence. This observation suggests probable culture-general nature of these devices, a topic awaiting future investigations into other than English conversations. For the interest here, we see use of formulation (in the two basic forms) helps conversation participants make sense of their talk, ensure mutual understanding, so as proceed with the interaction.

On the other hand, there are pragmatic differences in use of formulations in the two types of conversation, with respect to the kind of understanding involved. Uses of formulations reveal co-participants' mutual adjustment to somewhat differ for gaining proper understanding of what is said: simple comprehension as well as interpretation of the intended meaning. In NS-NS conversations formulations frequently go beyond the surface meaning of the remark to seek clarification and move to understand possible implicature, presupposition, and the like. Formulations there also draw on pragmatic considerations and emotional connotations; therefore may tend to bear more on individual identity and conversation relationship negotiation. In conversations with a non-native speaker, formulations tend to attend to the comprehension of literal meaning, showing co-participants making efforts to make sure they understand the message content of what the other is telling them. This particular use reflects and contextualizes the interaction as an unaccustomed one and somewhat difficult, which demands greater effort of meaning negotiation at a relatively basic, surface content level. It exhibits the mutual unfamiliarity between NS-NNS co-participants – including of each other's conversation routine and flow, their displayed awareness of this fact, and their willing cooperation to cope with it.

Contextual features of the conversation such as shared knowledge and mutual familiarity may be occasioned and established in and through concerted accomplishment of the social order of talk with conversation devices such as formulations. In this sense, co-participants being native or nonnative speakers of a particular language become less useful information for understanding of NSs or NS-NNS interactions. More informative are conversational moves, such as formulation, that co-participants make in response to their understanding of their own and their partner's moves and messages in interaction, identifying the actual point in need of attention and do more work there to get it right. The same would be conceivably applicable to intercultural interaction in general due to participants' similarly greater mutual unfamiliarity. Whereas more studies are needed for insight into other conversation devices reflective and constitutive of conversations between persons of various language and cultural backgrounds, what we have learned about formulation may be of some value to help enhance intercultural communication and facilitate verbal interactions.

We now turn to formulations' potential benefit to intercultural participants of a conversation. The primary function of formulations, understanding check as seen in gist and upshot, is fundamental to any communication to proceed. Also, in contrast to clarification request or direct questions about the content, which may achieve the same result in direct and straightforward manners, formulations are not so direct or blunt, and place the burden on the speaking party. Rather than encumbering the conversation partner with the responsibility to make things clear, formulation makers cooperatively take it on in seeking dis-/confirmation of their own understanding. This move not only indicates their cooperation and respect, but also shifts the focus away from (possible) language issues, which could make the partner self-conscious and the exchange harder. All these advantages of formulations, especially a keen awareness of them, would likely encourage proactive utilization of formulations and thus increases the chance of successful verbal exchanges. To this end, intercultural communicators may be trained for greater awareness to cultivate mindfulness in this regard.

They may become quick to initiate formulations and do that often, especially at points of even slightest possible content ambiguity and uncertainty. Ambiguity and uncertainly about the content tend to be common occurrence in an intercultural situation that participants usually can perceive, yet often are at a loss as to how to deal with it without drawing attention to language issues or implying inadequacy on part of the other participant. Conversational formulation may offer a way out of this fix to get the talk back on track and move along. In such situations, providing a gist of what the other has just conveyed would be a good choice. It would fit naturally in the conversation flow, reassuring their attentiveness as well as sincerity. Moreover, a gist provides the partner with a chance to reiterate or clarify with confirmation or disconfirmation, and then correction if needed. This way, mutual understanding of the content by the point is established and the talk may continue seamlessly. On the other hand, an upshot would be the formulation of choice if one is somewhat certain of what the other has said, yet would like to go further to extend the point. One may proceed on that base by way of an understanding check while also sharing one's view on the matter at hand to increase mutual understanding and somewhat further develop the common ground.

To conclude, conversation being a rule-governed, coordinated communicative activity, tactical moves of formulations are similar in function and structural sequence in most talks, whereas pragmatic differences are seen in their use in different context. Formulations reflect and help define intercultural conversation, especially those with NS and NNS participation, as ones that are carried out and constructed by co-participants somewhat differently than usual. Furthermore, intercultural interaction participants may and often employ formulations to not only engage in understanding check, but to signal their cooperative intent, ensure smooth exchange, and contribute to the talk at hand. Intercultural trainings may include and increase utilization of formulations in communication for better content understanding and successful interaction.

References

Antaki, C. (2008). Formulations in Psychotherapy. *Discourse Studies*, *7*(6), 627–647. https://doi.org/10.1017/CBO9780511490002.003.

Barnes, R. (2007). Formulations and the Facilitation of Common Agreement in Meetings Talk. *Text & Talk*, *27*(3), 273–296. https://doi.org/10.1515/TEXT. health appraisal 2007.011.

Beach, W., & Dixson, C. N. (2001). Revealing Moments: Formulating Understandings of Adverse Experiences in a Interview. *Social Science and Medicin*, *52*(1), 25–44. https://doi.org/10.1016/S0277-9536(00)00118-0.

Bolden, G. B. (2010). 'Articulating the unsaid' Via and-Prefaced Formulations of Others' Talk. *Discourse Studies*, *12*, 5–32. https://doi.org/10.1177/1461445609346770.

Clifton, J. (2006). A Conversation Analytical Approach to Business Communication: The Case of Leadership. *The Journal of Business Communication*, 43(3), 202–219.

Drew, P. (2003). Comparative Analysis of Talk-In-Interaction Indifferent Institutional Settings: A Sketch. In P. J. Glenn, C. D. LeBaron, & J. Mandelbaum (Eds.), *Studies in Language and Social Interaction: In Honour of Robert Hopper* (pp. 293–308). Mahwah, NJ: Erlbaum.

Franco, L. A., & Nielsen, M. F. (2018). Examining Group Facilitation in Situ: The Use of Formulations in Facilitation Practice. *Group Decision Negotiation*, 27, 735–756. https://doi.org/10.1007/s10726-018-9577-7

Garfinkel, H., & Sacks, H. (1970). On Formal Structures of Practical Actions. In J. C. McKinney & A. Tiryakian (Eds.), *Theoreticalsociology Perspectives and Developments* (pp. 337–366). New York, NY: Appleton-Centruary-Crofts.

Gass, S., & Varonis, E. M. (1985). Variation in Native Speaker Speech Modification to Nonnative Speakers. *Studies in Second Language Acquisition*, 7, 37–58.

Grice, H. P. (1975). Logic and Conversation. In P. Cole & J. Morgan (Eds.), *Syntax and Semantics* (pp. 41–58). New York, NY: Academic Press.

Heritage, J., & Watson, R. (1979). Formulations as Conversational Objects. In G. Psathas (Ed.), *Everyday Language: Studies in Ethnomethodology* (pp. 123–161). New York: Irvington.

Leeds-Hurwitz, W. (1989). *Communication in Everyday Life: A Social Interpretation*. Norwood, NJ: Ablex.

Levinson, S. C. (1983). *Pragmatics*. Cambridge: Cambridge University Press.

Mansson, L. (2015). Pre-Closing Formulations in Meeting Talk: A Study of a Cross-Functional Team Meeting at Ericsson in Sweden. Södertörn University, Sweden (Bachelor Thesis). Retrieved from: http://urn.kb.se/resolve?urn=urn:nbn:se:sh:diva-27797.

Nakamura, I. (2010). Formulation as Evidence of Understanding in Teacher–Student Talk. *ELT Journal*, *64*(2), 125–134. https://doi.org/10.1093/elt/ccp050.

Pomerantz, A. (1984). Agreeing and Disagreeing with Assessments: Some Features of Preferred/Dispreferred Turn Shapes. In J. M. Atkinson & J. Heritage (Eds.), *Structures of Social Action: Studies in Conversation Analysis* (pp. 57–101). Cambridge: Cambridge University Press.

Pudlinski, C. (2019). Formulating Another's Report of Troubles in Peer Support. *Communication and Medicine*, *16*(1), 67–80. https://doi.org/10.1558/cam.41613.

Schegloff, E. A. (1982). Discourse as an Interaction Achievement: Some Uses of "uh huh" and Other Things That Come between Sentences. In D. Tannen (Ed.) *Georgetown University Roundtable on Language and Linguistics 1981.*

Analyzing Discourse: Text and Talk (pp. 71–91). Washington, DC: Georgetown University Press.

Stokes, R., & Hewitt, J. P. (1976). Aligning Actions. *American Sociological Review, 41*, 838–849.

Stommel, W., & van der Houwen, F. (2013). Formulations in 'Trouble' Chat Sessions. *Language@Internet, 10*, article 3. Retrieved from: https://nbn-resolving.org/urn:nbn:de:0009-7-36966.

Weiste, E. (2016). Formulations in Occupational Therapy: Managing Talk about Psychiatric Outpatients' Emotional States. *Journal of Pragmatics, 105*, 59–73. https://doi.org/10.1016/j.pragma.2016.08.007.

Introduction to Is It Habitual or Innovative? A Study of Communicative Interactions of Expatriates in an International Joint-Venture

By Juana Du and Zhenyi Li

The chapter examines the use of language in an international work environment to determine if and how language is used to foster better relationships at the workplace. It is pointed out that English has become the *lingua franca* global corporations. But mere fluency in English may not be enough. Instead, it is noted that relationship building is an important factor as well. Relationships may be built around specific rituals or ceremonies that involve all actors. It is further noted that attempts to learn the host language, even if it is quite rudimentary, can encourage and strengthen relationships. So language can be used to build relationships, but such relationship building requires more than just the exchange of words. Other social activities are also needed during which the interactors communicate with one another. Businesses may take note of this and consider offering activities that encourage social interaction beyond the work at hand. And companies ought to encourage learning the host language because these undertakings encourage relationships as well.

The chapter also points out that familiarity and use of the corporate internal jargon and acronyms is helpful in establishing relationships. When newcomers are unfamiliar with the corporate jargon and acronyms, they often feel left out. So in order to foster a stronger identification with the respective company, it is also necessary to familiarize new employees with the corporate jargon and acronyms. Quite often, though, this is forgotten when preparing staff members for an overseas assignment. These are important insights that can help improve the relationships at the workplace; especially with a diverse workforce.

Michael B. Hinner

Juana Du is an associate professor in the school of Communication and Culture at Royal Roads University, Victoria, BC, Canada. Her research interests include improving intercultural communication in a globalized world, cross-cultural adaptation of international students, expatriate training and relocation, organizational diversity and culture, organizational learning and knowledge management, and subsidiaries of multinational enterprises and innovation.

Dr. Du was a post-doctorate researcher at the Polytechnic Institute of New York University, and a visiting scholar at Techinische Universitat Bergakademie Freiberg in Germany and at Ohio University in the U.S. She has presented at many international academic conferences, and published numerous book chapters and journal articles. Recently Dr. Du has published at the *Journal of International Management, Journal of World Business, Asia Pacific Journal of Management, Oxford Bibliography* and served as a journal reviewer for several journals. Dr. Du is an elected division officer of the International Communication Association (ICA, 2017 to 2020), and Caucus Chair of Academy of Management (AOM 2020). She has won numerous academic awards including Best Student Paper of Intercultural Communication Division of International Communication Association, Germany's DAAD Scholarship of Young Academics, the Award of Scholarship of LEWI, Hong Kong, and Asia Pacific Foundation Policy Research Grant (innovation, Canada).

Zhenyi Li is a Professor teaching intercultural communication at Royal Roads University, Victoria, BC, Canada. His research focuses on solutions for health care, marketing, education, and organizational development when cultural differences cause confusion, misunderstanding, and mistrust. He has published one book, edited three conference proceedings, authored more than 20 journal articles and book chapters, and presented in more than 100 conferences. Dr. Li received Kelly Outstanding Teaching Award from Royal Roads University, Silver Quill Award from Canadian Physiotherapy Association, and Innovation in International Education Award from Canadian Bureau for International Education, Best Trainer of the Year Award from International Research Institute. Dr. Li has been executive member in Society of Intercultural Education, Training and Research (SIETAR) in British Columbia and Europe. He serves as consultant for provincial ministries and health authorities in British Columbia, City of Richmond (BC), and many organizations.

Juana Du and Zhenyi Li

Is It Habitual or Innovative? A Study of Communicative Interactions of Expatriates in an International Joint-Venture

Introduction

There is a burgeoning attention on intercultural communication experiences of expatriate managers when encountering foreign cultures (Harzing & Feely, 2008; Brannen et al., 2014). Researchers have emphasized on how expatriate managers can better navigate in their host culture for effective intercultural communication. While most empirical studies have emphasized communication competence and referred language as an ancillary variable (Peltokorpi, 2007; Bhaskar-Shrinivas et al., 2005), researchers called for studies to examine the key role of language in intercultural communication and adjustment of international sojourners (Mughan, 2015). In particular, much research has contested the over-simplification that English proficiency is the key to improve communication competence and to solve all communication problems, thus attributing this to the ubiquitous presence of English as a lingua franca in global business (Barner-Rasmussen & Aarnio, 2011; Piekkari et al., 2005). Researchers have also called for more comprehensive understanding of the use of language in multinational corporations, considering the complex landscape of global business and multilingual organizations (Steyaert et al., 2011; Maclean, 2006).

Research on intercultural communication of expatriates has traditionally focused communication competence, and regarded improving communication competence as an effective approach to enhance intercultural communication of managers in multinational organizations, in order to enhance job performance. Interestingly, while this line of work covers many areas of communication capabilities, the issue of English proficiency level has been emphasized to advocate for language training (e.g. English in particular) (Aryee 1997; Chen et al., 2006; Harzing & Feely 2008; Puck et al., 2008; Welch & Welch, 2008). While acknowledging the direct impact of communication competence on job performance, there is an increasing scholarly interest in the sociocultural context where those communication and interactions take place. Following this line of inquiry, researchers argue that contextualization is to be considered, in order to develop a comprehensive understanding of intercultural communication experiences of expatriate managers (Wang et al., 2017). Besides the socio-cultural context where those communication activities are embedded, it is imperative to consider the complexity of corporate context, which is usually constitutive of corporate values, norms, communication protocols, practices and employee behaviors.

In the current study, we map a very complex environment of intercultural communication of expatriate managers from China who are working in an international joint-venture (IJVs) at Abu Dhabi, the United Arab Emirates. Expatriate managers from China have to cope with the challenges of English proficiency as English is the corporate lingual franca in the studied multinational corporation. Furthermore, they are also facing the linguistic and cultural challenges to communicate with co-workers in the host country where Arabic is the official language. The complexity and foreignness of the host language and culture, adds another layer of richness to the studied context, in order to understand the intercultural communication experiences and language coping strategies of expatriate managers. We delineate a multi-layer context where intercultural communication activities take place between Chinese expatriates and local employees. The impact of corporate communication contexts which largely impact intercultural communication activities on a daily basis are highlighted, in order to understand the dynamic of languages in a complex scenario of multinational settings.

This study examines intercultural communication experiences of expatriate managers in a multinational organization. We emphasize the role of language in intercultural communication experiences, by considering the multi-layer complexity of communication actions in a multinational organization. Drown upon the framework of Mediated Discourse Analysis (MDA) (Scollon, 1998, 1999, 2001, 2002), we examine communication actions and experiences of expatriate managers, through the analysis of language (discourse, texts) as meditational means for the mediated actions. In particular, we discuss the language coping strategies of expatriate managers to adjust during their intercultural interactions in the context of multinational corporations. We have identified several communicative actions of expatriate managers to interact with local co-workers within the multinational corporate environment, which mirrors the multilayer complexity of sociocultural and corporate communication contexts. We argue that, through a lens of nexus of practice, expatriate managers have navigated the linguistic and cultural boundaries adopting language coping strategies. We conducted 40 in-depth interviews with expatriate managers working in the studied international joint-venture (IJVs) in Abu Dhabi, the United Arab Emirates.

The current research contributes to the literature on intercultural interactions and adjustment, particularly to our understandings of intercultural practices and language coping strategies of expatriate managers in international joint-ventures. First, our research contributes to theoretical discussions on Mediated Discourse Analysis (MDA), and suggests the need to incorporate multilayer complexity of corporate communication contexts. The research findings also contribute to the literature of intercultural interactions and adjustment of expatriate managers, and highlight the importance of social interactions during intercultural adjustment from a lens of nexus of practice. Lastly, our research provides important empirical insights to theory development around language use and multilingual landscape in multinational enterprises, as previous researchers call for a more advanced theoretical understanding.

Theoretical Framework and Research Questions

The framework of mediated discourse analysis (MDA) developed by Ron Scollon and his colleagues, regards the analysis of language (e.g. discourse, texts) as meditational means for the mediated actions. According to Scollon (2001a), MDA framework includes six central components: mediated action, site of engagement, mediated means, practice and meditational means, nexus of practice, and community of practice. It provides a new perspective to examine intercultural practices and actions with an emphasis on social interactions.

Mediational Means and Nexus of Practice

According to Scollon (2001a), a mediated action is an action taken by social actors with mediated means (e.g. material objects that results in a product such as artifact or performance). As social practices rarely occur in isolation, any communication activity often combines several mediated actions. Every mediated action is taken in a site of engagement, where a site of engagement is not simply a physical place, but a window that opens the possibility for the mediated action to occur (Norris, 2009). Mediational means (Wertsch, 1991) are the basis of MDA which represents an abstract way of making meaning through participation in a set of social practices (e.g. writing, drawing, playing, interacting, etc.) with material instruments (e.g. papers, notebooks, pencils, etc.) to construct messages. Hence, a mediational means always expresses certain identities and group membership, as it is associated with a set of shared social practices with specific meaning attached. The idea of mediational means resonates with Scollon's perspective on culture which is regarded as "a very loose collection of meditational means organized into much smaller discourses to which all persons have accesses to" (Scollon, 1996a, 1996b, p. 10). Scollon advocated that culture would be better conceived as an imagined community (Anderson, 1991), and called for a focus to be placed on social action as an observable unit of analysis.

The MDA framework regards language as mediational means, and advances understandings of intercultural interactions by highlighting the importance of social actions. Through mediational means (e.g. language), social actors transform mediated actions into social practices. By continual engagement in social actions people are usually partially aware of nearly automatic practices as it accumulates as part of a set of internalized dispositions that makes up habitus (Bourdieu, 1977). Scollon (2002) developed the concept of "nexus of practice" which links individuals through a social action, e.g., buying a cup of coffee, rather than any fixed social relationship, e.g., kinship. The idea of "nexus of practice" emphasizes the linkage to social action and does not presume that individuals share a set of practices. For instance, buying coffee is a different social practice from making and selling coffee that may link to group identities and memberships. People engage in daily activities which signal cumulative social practices and cultural values embedded in group habitus, and those are often not noticed by social actors. Interactions of valued and expected practices from nexus of practice (Scollon, 2001a, 2001b) produces naturalized ways of "doing and being" that signal our membership to certain groups or discourses (Gee, 2005).

Scollon (2002) further highlights the importance of temporal framing of a social action in a particular sociocultural context as an interaction can make a tremendous difference in the framework of defining "what is going on". As there is often a certain timeframe for appropriation for meditational means, e.g. the persons who use those languages as mediational means in an interaction may have a history, the circumference of the interaction could appear quite different if one expands or changes the timeframe (Scollon, 2001a, 2001b; de Saint-Georges, 2005). While this perspective certainly highlights both parties in the intercultural interactions, it leads to a very important meta-analytic question and lends ambiguity to answer the question "who is framing or defining what is going on and how?" (Burke, 1969). Scollon and Scollon (1995) argues that the intercultural quality is not the most important factor for understanding what is going on in most interactions, where this perspective incorporates Burke's pentad of motives (Burke, 1969). Burke argues that there are in fact many ways in which one can interpret the origin and trajectory of an action.

Scollon further distinguishes between social practices and social actions through MDA analyses. Scollon (2001b) argues that practices are these recurring actions that are usually learned by participating in the everyday social life within a specific community. Thus, Scollon defines a practice as "a historical accumulation within the habitus/historical body of the social actor of mediated actions taken over his or her life (experience) which are recognizable to other social actors as 'the same' social action" (2001b, p.149).

The Idea of MDA and Discourse in Context

Scollon (1996a) highlights the important idea of "discourse" in MDA, and asked the question of what is the role of discourse in those actions? By whom is it produced, why is it used, and what motives are behind it? This approach emphasizes texts as how they could be used to mediate the real-time actions in social interactions, rather than the meaning of texts. It further distinguishes the possible linkage between language and discourse, as "the language we use, must always be borrowed from *some* discourse which is located in time, history, and society, and our listeners hear not only meaning but also the time, history, and society from which we have borrowed our language." (Scollon, 1996a, p. 10). For instance, the use of languages from a certain discourse usually reminds people the historical and social context once the discourse has enacted in.

Discourse not only includes written and spoken texts, but also the broader social and historical discourses (Gee, 1996) embodied in the context, in people's beliefs, in objects and artifacts, which usually reflects a set of attitudes, beliefs, representations, etc. Researchers further question that as discourse stands as an autonomous component of the nexus, could the historical body and institutionalized social relation be included as parts of discourse cycles (Lou, 2009).

As MDA builds directly on the Mediated Action (MA) framework (Wertsch, 1998), it brings an ethnographic understanding of the idea of "sites of engagement" in which action takes place, including the range of semiotic and material tools that intersect in action (de Saint-Georges & O'Connor, 2014). MDA framework focuses not exclusively on individual actors, nor on social groups or institutions, nor on mediational means, but rather on the "nexus of practice", where those elements intersect and are brought into engagement (Scollon, 2005, p. 20). In this sense, researchers following the MDA framework are not usually starting their inquiries with theoretical questions, but rather by tackling real-life problem or social issues (Scollon, 2005). Following this line of inquiry, MDA analysis also emphasizes interdisciplinarity, and is regarded as a form of "meta-methodology" which aggregates a variety of perspectives, e.g. interactional sociolinguistics, linguistic anthropology, critical discourse analysis, social semiotics, cultural psychology, etc.

Dawn upon the framework of MDA, this research examines the intercultural practices of expatriate managers in multinational organization settings. By identifying and looking into several mediated actions of expatriate managers, it explains how those communicative actions are developed and shared in the intercultural/ organizational contexts. It looks into the dynamic of language and proposes the question that whether those communicative actions are habitual or innovative, intentional or accidental? This research examines the language coping strategies that expatriate managers adopt to navigate through cultural and linguistic boundaries through a lens of nexus of practice. The findings have important theoretical and practical implications.

Method

Study Site

The interviewed managers are working at the site of an international joint-venture between a Chinese company and a UAE company. The joint-venture was established since 2012, and the Chinese company is one of the most important international partners and holds a major portion of the share. The UAE company is a well-established national company in the energy industry and has a long history of collaborating with international partners. English is the lingua franca of the company where most employees speak fluent English. The company employs people from a wide variety of cultural and linguistic backgrounds, and expatriate managers with technology expertise who have played important roles in the growth of the company. Workplace diversity has been written into the company value, to encourage expatriate managers to perform well in the company. The Chinese partners brought in more than 100 engineers and managers who are employed by a national Chinese company. Those Chinese managers are often on three to five year overseas assignments working at Abu Dhabi, according to the corporate human resource policy. Senior Chinese managers usually stay longer in Abu Dhabi depending on their positions and tenures. All Chinese expatriates speak fluent English and have received short term language and cultural training before they departed from China. Those Chinese managers usually take annual vacation back to the headquarter in China as most of their family members are still in China.

Data Collection

To gain a deep understanding of the communication experiences of expatriate managers, we conducted semi-structured in-depth interviews. In total, 41 Chinese managers who are working in the joint-venture in the Abu Dhabi were interviewed between June to August, 2021. With the support of the human resources department, participants were invited on a voluntary basis and all signed to agree to participate in this project. All interviewed managers were between 31 to 63 years of age, with 4 female managers and 37 male managers. The overall work experiences of managers ranged from 2 years to 41 years, where 17 individuals of the sample had previous experiences working in a third country before arriving in Abu Dhabi from China. The gender distribution of the study sample is consistent with the gender reality in the studied corporation (e.g. around 90 % of Chinese expatriate managers are males). Interviewed managers varied on a wide range of working job positions, including manufacturing, site supervising, process management, quality control, project management, procurement, safety and risk management, etc. Among those managers, 7 of them received doctoral degrees, 23 of them had masters' degrees, 8 of them had bachelors' degrees and 3 of them received college diplomas. In terms of their linguistic backgrounds, as they came from different regions of China, Mandarin is regarded as the corporate language in the headquarters of their Chinese company in Beijing, although many of them also speak different Chinese dialects. English is the lingua franca in the joint-venture in Abu Dhabi, and all Chinese managers speak English as their second language. Several managers also speak other languages such as Arabic, Spanish, etc.

The interviews last from 57 mins to 95 minutes. All of the interviews were conducted via Zoom due to the lockdown of COVID-19, and were recorded with consent by the interviewees. The process for conducting interviews was designed taking into account practical suggestions from Bauer and Gaskell (2000). In the initial phase, the researchers disclose the purpose of research project to the interviewees, and ensure them full confidentiality and anonymity. The interviewer gathers background information such as demographic information (e.g. age, gender), educational and professional background, and previous work and intercultural experiences. Collected information helps the interviewer interpret the interviewee's communication experiences and stories. The interviewees were asked a series of detailed and open-ended questions, such as "Can you think of something particularly surprising/ frustrating/ difficult/ positive/ thought-provoking/challenging about your communication experiences with your local peers?" "How do you deal with those particular situations?" "What do you feel about those communication experiences?" "Are you satisfied with your communication experiences and why", etc. Recordings of the interview were all transcribed via a computer software, which generated about 1200 pages of transcripts. The interviews were conducted in Mandarin, the mother tongue of the interviewed managers, as a friendly manner to invite and encourage interviewees to tell their experiences openly with the language they are most familiar with. The interview transcripts were then translated into English.

Due to the impact of COVID-19 in the workplace at Abu Dhabi (e.g. work has been moved to online to a large extent), researchers were not able to use participatory observation methods to collect information about the working environment. Instead, interviewees were asked to describe their perceptions and experiences of the workplace. Organizational documents were also collected with support of the Human Resources office, including brochures, manuals, videos and other corporate materials. Those materials provided supplemental data to understand the organizational context and practices related to daily intercultural communication and interactions.

Data Analysis

We analyzed the interviewed data following the inductive and abductive steps (Dubois & Gadde, 2002). This systematic combining of inductive and abductive approaches allows the researchers to generate theoretical insights from the process of analyzing empirical data, based on modifying existing frameworks (Dubois & Gadde, 2002). Following this data analysis process, we coded data and identified the first order themes, and then generate the second order themes by combing and reducing theme categories. In the next step, we take the abductive approach to iteratively matched all of the identified themes against the theoretical bases (Ketokivi & Mantere, 2010). By doing so, insights generated from empirical data and theoretical framework evolve simultaneously. The researchers introduced the third order themes by comparing between the emerging themes from the data and theoretical constructs. Researchers used the software MAXQDA in the data analysis process to support data categorization and virtualization.

Results

A. "It is all about relationships!" Are those communication actions habitual or innovative?

Several communicative actions of expatriate managers were emerged from the specific cultural context of our study. For instance, one expatriate manager described a case scenario as following:

> *"I just came back from my annual vacation in Beijing, China. I brought several Chinese tea boxes as gifts for my co-workers who working on the same team. It is a real surprise to see how this friendly gesture was welcomed by my Arab co-workers. When I explained the tea ceremony as a Chinese traditional cultural ritual, my co-worker – an Arab manager was keen in hearing more and kept asking questions. We ended up discussing about how to make tea using the coffee pot while we were both standing at the coffee corner during work break. Then the next day, before our meeting started, that Arab manager said hello to me first when he saw me and also made a quick comment about how Chinese government was successful in controlling the infected covid-19 cases, which surprized me a lot when comparing with his previous attitudes and negative comments at another team meeting. He seems much friendlier than before, and we even went to the pub together after work occasionally. Later, bringing team members cultural gifts once returned from vacations in China gradually became a cultural habit for our team." (Interviewee 10, male)*

This interviewed manager described a scenario where he sent a gift as a friendly gesture, which received very positive and unexpected response from his Arab co-workers. In this case, sending a gift as mediated action by a Chinese manager (as a social actor) happens at a single time, and has been transformed into social practices that are shared by other co-workers on the team. Social meanings (e.g. making friends) was gradually attached to this action, considering that building relationship is a relational feature valued by both Chinese and Arab culture to a large extent. In this sense, the sociocultural context where this mediated action embedded provides possibilities for shared understanding and interpretations. Furthermore, considering the particular societal and temporal context where this conversation and interaction takes place, e.g. the widespread of Covid-19, alongside with the various approaches to develop different national governance and health policies which have impacted public' social and cultural perceptions towards a certain cultural/ ethnic group, it offers an opportunity for social actors to construct mediational meanings (e.g. making friends) through mediated actions (e.g. sending gifts in this case). This sociocultural meaning is particularly relevant and important for team members on the same team, including Arabic managers and Chinese managers, as it has been naturalized as a way of "doing and being" through cumulative social practices. It links team members to a "nexus of practice" and develops a team cultural habit to bridge existing gaps among team members due to different levels of cultural and linguistic competence.

B. "Expertise and respect!" Are those communication actions intentional or accidental?

One of the interviewed managers described a very interesting scenario which further elaborates the important role of social interactions among Chinese expatriate managers and the local Arab managers.

> *"Most Chinese managers here can speak fluent English, although with different proficiency levels. Only few of us learn Arabic because it is very difficult. Additionally, we are here on international assignments and will either return to China or go to another country after 3 years, so there is no need to learn Arab. Some of my colleagues got married and have kids born at Abu Dhabi, but they wouldn't let their kids learn Arabic. It is simply not that useful. There was a time I had to attend a meeting during Ramandan (Muslim holiday). It is quite common for Arab managers to greet each other by saying " Eid Mubarak"* (عيد مبارك in Arabic), *I followed this cultural greeting ritual and my Arab manager asked me if I was learning Arabic. I smiled and replied "I would love to". He appears to be really pleased to hear this and we had a very good meeting that day. So I started to follow those local cultural manners, and can now only say a few words with strong accent." (Interviewee 17, male)*

By looking into this communication scenario, it is quite fascinating to see how language (e.g. the Arabic greeting words in this case) as mediational means leads to a "nexus of practice". By saying "Eid Mubarak" (عيد مبارك in Arabic), it links individual managers across different cultural and social groups. Despite the fact that most managers find it difficult to learn Arabic or not holding a positive attitude toward learning Arabic, those a few word expressions in Arabic actually serve as mediational means to transform one occasional practice (e.g. greeting colleagues in Arabic language at the beginning of team meetings) to social practices with clear intentions on a continuous basis. In this sense, the meaning of respect in local culture has been well conveyed from the message sender to receivers. This is described as shared social practices by Chinese managers, which serves as a coping strategy to deal with challenges of learning the host language (e.g. Arabic), which shows their positive attitudes towards the host language. As a result, the linguistic inefficiency was overcome during social interactions. By continuing engaging in social actions that people firstly were only partially aware of, or even unaware of, people develop group habitus which are based on shared values and expectations, and form a nexus of practice which signals memberships and groups discourses (e.g. we all respect and are willing to learn the local culture and the host language). It is also worthwhile to notice although English as lingua franca accepted by the international employees in this joint-venture, the expectations to communicate (to some extent) in the host language still signals one's communication competence to a large extent, and impact expatriate job performances to a larger extent. Therefore, as a coping strategy to adjust to the host culture, expatriate managers openly expressed and demonstrated their willingness and competence to learn and speak Arabic in those formal corporate settings, e.g. team meetings. Actually, this social practice has also become popular and accepted by most international managers, and the use of it extends beyond the time of Ramandan to time of other local cultural festivals, even regular time. It became a communication habit shared by international managers, which also contributed to the diverse organizational climate, as diversity has been written to core values of this multinational corporation. By noticing those expressions and words in Arabic at different occasions in the corporate life, it offers crucial and practical insights to further looking into the multilingual landscape of MNEs in present time.

C. Acronym names and corporate language

Besides the cultural and linguistic difficulties in the host culture, several interviewees also mentioned about "acronym names" as a challenge during intercultural actions while they adjust to the corporate communication settings in the host culture. A manager described her experiences below as:

> *"During the first couple of months, it is not English per say that makes the conversation difficult, rather it is about those acronym names used in the joint-venture. I didn't realize there were so many acronym names expressed during daily communication, such as acronym names of corporate structures and units, locations and cultural rituals, etc. Acronym names related to technological terms are the easiest ones to understand, usually it is those about corporate units and structures that are most difficult to learn. Even though it is really a very trivial thing, more than once has it made me feel like I do not really belong to this new company." (Interview 23, female)*

Acronym names are usually rooted and generated in a particular cultural or institutional context, so it is quite understandable that new members find it challenging to comprehend it. The language of acronym names adds another layer of complexity to those cultural and linguistic challenges for expatriate managers to cope with. As described by one of the interviewed managers, corporate acronym names, e.g. related to corporate structure, working units, special expressions of working procedures, are most difficult to learn, as those require individuals to situate themselves in a good amount of corporate knowledge and corporate history background. Acronym names are usually part of organizational knowledge which could embody those core corporate values and assumptions. Individuals who have identified more core corporate values and corporate history will be more likely to use acronym names often during their daily communication and interactions with co-workers. In this sense, good comprehension and use of acronym names usually signal individual employees' identification with their organizations to a larger extent. On the one hand, people may feel a higher level of belonging with their corporations once they are familiar with communicating with their co-workers using those acronym names. In this sense, acronym names as mediational means connect expatriate managers who share similar communication practices via a nexus of practices; On the other hand, acronym names could draw organizational boundaries between those seasoned local managers who have years of experiences within the organization (e.g. mostly are Arab managers in this case), and those who are new to the organizational history and context (e.g. Chinese expatriate managers who find it challenging to comprehend). Even in some situations, members who don't master this special corporate language, or feel reluctant to use and practise this corporate language system, might position themselves differently during communicative interactions. In some occasions, the use of acronym names – a part of corporate language system could impact the dynamics of communicative interactions, and those who don't adopt might be treated by their co-workers differently during communicative actions. For instance, as expressed by the following interviewee:

> *"There was a time that I have been told by my supervisor about the special meaning of a corporate structure term, however, I didn't really remember at that moment. So the next time, I still use the full name instead of the acronym names during our team meetings. Somehow I felt that this was interpreted by my local co-workers as reluctantcy to adopt acronym names and as a result they doubt about my intention. It is simply because I didn't remember. Once I realize this, I paid more attention to those acronym names and use them more intentionally while I communicate with my local co-workers." (Interviewee 36, male)*

In the above scenario, it is quite fascinating to notice the mediational means co-created by organizational members through mediated actions (e.g. adapting acronym names within the organizational context). Those mediational meanings are co-created and shared by organizational members through daily interactions within the organizational cultural and historical context. Expatriate managers engaging in those communication actions by using acronym names intentionally or unintentionally, became cumulative social practices within the organizational life. It is worth discussing that the creation of acronym names has been situated in a specific time and place within the landscape of organizational development, so managers hear not only meaning of those acronym names, but also the time and history from which those acronym names are created. In that sense, expectations of adopting acronym names among organizational members, are related to the corporate values and could contribute to the construction of organizational reality. The adoption of acronym names could signal the level of organizational membership and organizational identity to a large extent. Individual actors (e.g. managers), institutions (e.g. corporations), mediational means (e.g. acronym names and a possible corporate language dictionary) are all brought together into the site of engagement through the nexus of practice. It affirmed the notion that MDA framework focuses not exclusively on individual actors, nor on social groups or institutions, nor on mediational means, but rather on the nexus of practice.

Conclusion and Discussion

This research examined intercultural communication experiences of expatriate managers in an international joint-venture in Abu Dhabi, the United Arab Emirates. It extends the discussion on MDA analysis of language as mediational means in social interaction suggests the need to incorporate multilayer complexity of corporate and intercultural contexts. The research results provide abundant empirical evidence to explain the dynamics of language in intercultural encounters in a complex multinational corporate setting, and how language coping strategies have been developed from accumulative social practices both internationally and accidently. The research findings also contribute to the literature of intercultural interaction and adjustment of expatriate managers, and highlight the importance of social interactions during intercultural adjustment. Last but not the least, the research results contribute to the understandings of multilingual landscape of multinational corporations and call for further studies to understand the role of language in multilingual organizations.

MDA and Nexus of Practices

Multinational corporations are situated with intercultural communication actions supported by powerful discursive regimes. Mediated communication actions, occur in social space situated in a particular time and place. By looking into communication experiences and coping strategies of expatriate managers in this current study, we extend the discussions of MDA framework to incorporate an institutional perspective (e.g. corporate settings), and explain how corporate language (e.g. acronym names) could impact social interactions among managers. We highlight the important role of social interaction through which expatriate managers developed different coping strategies to cope with the multi-layer complexity in communicating with co-workers in multinational corporations, and adjust to the host culture. Rather than improving English proficiency, expatriate managers have navigated through the linguistic and cultural challenges by adopting copying strategies through social interactions. Those mediated communication actions through language as mediational means became accumulative social practices within the organizational context

(Scollon, 2005). Particularly, it is interesting to find how the complex cultural elements (e.g. both at individual and organizational level) interweave into the intercultural contexts where those communication actions take place. This contributed to the current discussions that incorporating institutionalized social relation and related language could advance our understanding of discourse, that stand as an autonomous component of the nexus of practice (Lou, 2009). Future studies should investigate different institutional and organizational contexts and examine how an integration of institutional perspective could contribute to further understanding of the role of language based on MDA analysis.

Language Coping Strategies and Intercultural Adjustment

Studies on intercultural adjustment of expatriate managers have been emphasized host language proficiency (e.g. particularly about English proficiency in English-speaking countries), and regarded host language proficiency as one of the most important factors that impact intercultural interactions and adjustment (Black & Mendenhall, 1990; Selmer & Lauring, 2011; Selmer, 2006). Our results contribute to current understanding of intercultural communication experiences of expatriates by offering empirical insights into the dynamic process of language during intercultural interactions. By examining language coping strategies of expatriate managers, we support the notion that rather than language proficiency itself, how language copying strategies have been developed from intercultural communication settings through social interaction, plays a crucial role in intercultural adjustment experiences of expatriate managers. Within an emphasis on mediated actions following the framework of MDA, our research findings provide a novel perspective on examining intercultural communication copying strategies of expatriate managers working in an international joint-venture. We map a complex organizational environment of social interactions and intercultural communication in this study, and offer in-depth understanding of the dynamics of nexus of practices of social actors and mediated actions, where mediational means are brought together through culturally bounded social interactions within the organizational context. We call for further studies to examine the dynamics of social interactions between expatriate managers and different co-worker groups, considering the possible impact of their cultural and linguistic backgrounds and capacities.

The Role of Language and Multilingual Organizations

Researchers have examined English as a *lingua franca* in global businesses, and contested the over-simplification that English competence can solve all communication problems (Barner-Rasmussen & Aarnio, 2011; Boussebaa et al., 2014; Sanden, 2016). Our results contribute to the literature on language in multinational corporations, and advance the understanding of the role of language by looking into the dynamics of English in social interactions in corporate settings. We extend the discussions to incorporate the perspective of corporate language with an emphasis on use of acronym names, which is particularly relevant in the current study of international joint-ventures. By highlighting the nexus of practices around acronym names, we elaborate the social practices around the use of corporate language within an institutional context (e.g. multinational corporation in this study). Furthermore, studies should investigate different aspects of the use of corporate language by managers (e.g. words, including languages and terminologies, visuals, etc.), in order to advance understanding of the role of different types of languages in multinational organizations. As the current study examines a corporate environment where English is the *lingual franca*, we also call for studies to further look into use of other languages or multilingual practices in global businesses.

Implication for Practices and Limitations

Besides theoretical contributions, this research has several important practical implications. First, we suggest that multinational corporations actively design cultural and language training strategies and programs to prepare expatriate managers for effective intercultural communication and adjustment. This resonates with the initiatives of the Chinese government to develop language training programs for managers to learn foreign languages under the Belt and Road Initiative (BRI) since 2013.Comparing with the most common approach with an emphasis on foreign language (e.g. English) and culture training, we advocate human resources managers to explore innovative methods with an emphasis on social interactions and simulations. Second, the research results identified several language-related coping strategies of expatriate managers to adjust during intercultural interactions. We suggest international managers should be more aware of the social and cultural context of their international assignments, and develop language coping strategies as a supplementary method to advance communication competence. Last but not the least, the results of this study offer important insights for multinational corporations to understand the role of language and to develop appropriate language policies to support effective intercultural communication at workplace. Multinational corporations should also develop a comprehensive understanding of language, including words, visuals, and other forms of expressions, as an important way to embrace corporate values and advance “linguascape” of multilingual organizations.

There are several limitations identified in the current study. First, we mainly conducted interviews of expatriate managers working in an international joint-venture in the oil industry to conduct a scenario analysis. Future studies should further investigate on how expatriate managers’ working experiences in different types of organizations and industries considering the specific industrial and institutional environment. Second, since the outbreak of COVID-19 during the spring of 2020, some interactions and work in organizations were moved from a face-to-face to an online environment. Although this transition may have impacted expatriate managers’ working and social experiences, we did not emphasize this in the current study. Future studies should provide more insight on how managers’ social and communication experiences have changed after the global pandemic outbreak. Third, in the current study, we mainly consider the unique culture features and similarities between Chinese and Arab cultures where the results developed are sensitive to specific cultural contexts. It could be interesting to further examine other cultural contexts and the possible implications for expatriate managers to develop language coping strategies during intercultural interactions.

Conclusion

This research captures intercultural communication experiences and language coping strategies of Chinese expatriates working in an international joint-venture in Abu Dhabi, the United Arab Emirates. Looking into the dynamics of language in multinational corporate settings, this research offers us a fresh perspective to prepare expatriate managers for effective intercultural communication and adjustment. Particularly, understanding the importance of social interactions during intercultural communication following the MDA framework, could advance our understanding of communicative actions through a lens of nexus of practice. Considering the growing linguascape of multinational organizations in today’s world, creativity is needed to understand and develop corporate language policies supporting effective and appropriate interactions and performances in global businesses.

References

Anderson, B. (1991). *Imagined Communities: Reflections on the Origin and Spread of Nationalism.* London: Verso.

Aryee, S. (1997). Selection and Training of Expatriate Employees. In N. Anderson & P. Herriot (Eds.), *Handbook of Selection and Appraisal*. London: Wiley.

Barner-Rasmussen, W., & Aarnio, C. (2011). Shifting the Faultlines of Language: A Quantitative Functional Level Exploration of Language Use in MNC Subsidiaries. *Journal of World Business*, *46*(3), 288–295.

Bauer, M. W., & Gaskell, G. (2000). *Qualitative Researching with Text, Image and Sound: A Practical Handbook*. London: SAGE.

Bhaskar-Shrinivas, P., Harrison, D. A., Shaffer, M. A., & Luk, D. M. (2005). Input-Based and Time-Based Models of International Adjustment: Meta-Analytic Evidence and Theoretical Extensions. *Academy of Management Journal*, *48*(2), 257–281.

Black, J. S., & Mendenhall, M. (1990). Cross-cultural Training Effectiveness: A Review and Theoretical Framework. *Academy of Management Review*, *15*, 113–36.

Bourdieu, P. (1977). *Outline of a Theory of Practice*. Cambridge: Cambridge University Press.

Boussebaa, M., Sinha, S., & Gabriel, Y. (2014). Englishization in Offshore Call Centers: A Postcolonial Perspective. *Journal of International Business Studies*, *45*(9), 1152–1169.

Brannen, M. Y., Piekkari, R., & Tietze, S. (2014). The Multifaceted Role of Language in International Business: Unpacking the Forms, Functions and Features of a Critical Challenge to MNC Theory and Performance. *Journal of International Business Studies*, *45*(5), 495–507.

Burke, K. 1969. *A Grammar of Motives*. Englewood Cliffs, N.J.: Prentice Hall.

Chen, S., Geluykens, R., & Choi, C. (2006). The Importance of Language in Global Teams: A Linguistic Perspective. *Management International Review*, *46*(6), 679–695.

de Saint-Georges. (2005). From Anticipation to Performance: Sites of Engagement as Process. In S. Norris & R. H. (Eds.), *Discourse in Action: Introduction to Mediated Discourse Analysis*. London: Routledge.

de Saint-Georges, I., & O'Connor, K. (2014). Mediated Action and Mediated Discourse Analysis: Studying Learning and Becoming at the Nexus of Practice. In Joseph L. Polman, Eleni A. Kyza, D. Kevin O'Neill, Iris Tabak, William R. Penuel, A. Susan Jurow, Kevin O'Connor, Tiffany Lee, and Laura D'Amico (Eds.), *Learning and Becoming in Practice: The International Conference of the Learning Sciences (ICLS)* (Vol. 3, pp. 1692–1696). Colorado, CO: International Society of the Learning Sciences.

Dubois, A., & Gadde, L.-E. (2002). Systematic Combining: An Abductive Approach to Case Research. *Journal of Business Research*, *55*(7), 553.

Gee, J. P. (1996). *Social Linguistics and Literacies: Ideology in Discourses*. London: Routledge Falmer.

Gee, J. P. (2005). *An Introduction to Discourse Analysis: Theory and Method*. London: Routledge.

Harzing, A. W., & Feely, A. J. (2008). The Language Barrier and Its Implications for HQ-Subsidiary Relationships. *Cross Cultural Management: An International Journal, 15*(1), 49–60.

Ketokivi, M., & Mantere, S. (2010). Two Strategies for Inductive Reasoning in Organizational Research. *Academy of Management Review, 35*, 315–333.

Lou, J. J. (2009). How to Do Discourse Analysis: Reflection on Nexus Analysis: Discourse and the Emerging Internet. In J. J. Lou & Inge, S (Eds.), *Special Issue of eVox: Georgetown Working Papers in Language, Discourse & Society in Honor of Ron Scollon* (pp. 50–53). Georgetown University Press.

Maclean, D. (2006). Beyond English: Transnational Corporations and the Strategic Management of Language in a Complex Multilingual Business Environment. *Management Decision. 44*(10), 1377–1390.

Mughan, T. (2015). Introduction: Language and Languages – Moving from the Periphery to the Core. In N. Holden, S. Michailova, & S. Tietze (Eds.), *The Routledge Companion to Cross-Cultural Management* (pp. 79–84). New York: Routledge.

Norris, S. (2009). Mediated Discourse and Social Interaction: A Reflection. In J.J. Lou & S. Inge (Eds.), *Special Issue of eVox: Georgetown Working Papers in Language, Discourse & Society in Honor of Ron Scollon* (pp. 32–34). Georgetown University Press.

Peltokorpi, V. (2007). Intercultural Communication Patterns and Tactics: Nordic Expatriates in Japan. *International Business Review, 16*(1), 68–82.

Piekkari, R., Vaara, E., Tienari, J., & Säntti, R. (2005). Integration or Disintegration? Human Resource Implications of the Common Corporate Language Decision in a Cross-Border Merger. *International Journal of Human Resource Management, 16*(3), 330–344.

Puck, J. F., Holtbrügge, D., & Rausch, E.-M. (2008). Determinants and Consequences of Expatriate Adjustment: A Review of Concepts and Empirical Studies. In D. Holtbrügge (Ed.), *Cultural Adjustment. Theoretical Concepts and Empirical Studies* (pp. 9–32). München: Rainer Hampp Verlag.

Sanden, G. R. (2016). Language: The Sharpest Tool in the Business Strategy Toolbox. *Corporate Communications: An International Journal, 21*(3), 274–288.

Scollon, R. (1996a). *A Mediational View of Intercultural Communication*. Lecture first presented to the School of Linguistics, Macquarie University,

Sydney, Australia, 8 October, 1996, Department of Linguistics and Applied Linguistics, Melbourne University, Melbourne Australia, 9 October 1996 and at the English Department, Guangdong Foreign Studies University, Guangzhou, PRC, 18 October 1996.

Scollon, R. (1996b). Discourse Identity, Social Identity, and Confusion in Intercultural Communication. *Intercultural Communication Studies, VI*(1).

Scollon, R. (1998). *Mediated Discourse as Social Interaction*. London: Longman.

Scollon, R. (1999). Mediated Discourse and Social Interaction. *Research on Language and Social Interaction, 32*(1, 2), 149–54.

Scollon, R. (2001a). *Mediated Discourse: The Nexus of Practice*. London: Routledge.

Scollon, R. (2001b). Action and Text: Toward an Integrated Understanding of the Place of Text in Social (Inter)action. In R. Wodak & M. Meyer (Eds.), *Methods of Critical Discourse Analysis*. London: Sage.

Scollon, R. (2002). *Nexus Analysis: Toward an Ethnography of Motives*, paper presented at the Martin Spector Lecture in Applied Linguistics, Center for Language Acquisition, Pennsylvania State University, October 2002.

Scollon, R. (2005). The Rhythmic Integration of Action and Discourse: Work, the Body and the Earth. In S. Norris & R. H. Jones (Eds.), *Discourse in Action: Introduction to Mediated Discourse Analysis* (pp. 20–31). London: Routledge.

Scollon, R., & Scollon, S. W. (1995). *Intercultural Communication: A Discourse Approach*. Cambridge, MA: Basil Blackwell.

Selmer, J. (2006). Language Ability and Adjustment: Western Expatriates in China. *Thunderbird International Business Review, 48*(3), 347–368.

Selmer, J., & Lauring, J. (2011). Expatriate Academics: Job Factors and Work Outcomes. *International Journal of Manpower, 32*(2).

Steyaert, C., Ostendorp, A., & Gaibrois, C. (2011). Multilingual Organizations as 'linguascapes': Negotiating the Position of English through Discursive Practices. *Journal of World Business, 46*(3), 270–278.

Wang, D., Fan, D., Freeman, S., & Zhu, C. J. (2017). Exploring Cross-Cultural Skills for Expatriate Managers from Chinese Multinationals: Congruence and Contextualization. *Asia Pacific Journal of Management, 34*(1), 123–146.

Welch, D. E., & Welch, L. S. (2008). The Importance of Language in International Knowledge Transfer. *Management International Review, 48*, 339–360.

Wertsch, J. W. (1991). *Voices of the Mind: A Sociocultural Approach to Mediated Action*. Cambridge, MA: Harvard University Press.

Wertsch, J. V. (1998). *Mind as Action*. Oxford University Press.

Part IV Communication at the Workplace

Introduction to More Than One Way to Influence: Organizational Members' Upward Voice in U.S., China, and South Korea

By Xiaowei Shi and Yang Soo Kim

The next chapter points out that today most people can no longer work their entire work life for one and the same employer. Instead, employees must be able to mobilize their acquired knowledge and adapt it to new work environments. At the same time, employees have to undertake proactive measures to enhance their job security. That is why this chapter examines the upward communication of employees. Such communication includes both upward influence and impression management. Shi and Kim present a study they conducted to determine what influence such communication has on organizational members in general and whether culture has a specific impact as well. Upward influence can be considered face threatening as a result of the hierarchical structure; for example, when offering constructive suggestions because they might be considered criticism of a supervisor's decision. Impression management, in turn, refers to the actions and communication undertaken by subordinates to influence how they are seen by others at the work place. The study examines the role of culture (China, South Korea, and the United States) and also gender within this context of upward communication. It revealed that culture does have an impact on the communication; in particular power distance (Hofstede) and assertiveness (GLOBE Study). It was discovered that employees from all three cultures prefer a combination of rational persuasion and impression management. But it was also shown that Chinese employees, for example, prefer to combine reasoning with very ingratiating expressions while South Korean employees combine rational persuasion with negative impression strategies. Surprisingly, the gender of the supervise did not play a significant role. Employees from all three cultures indicated that the affective state of feeling comfortable in talking with their supervisors is very important. That is why companies ought to foster an environment of trust that encourages upward communication because such a positive environment promotes better motivation for work. In other words, companies should encourage communication at the workplace so that employees are willing to openly communicate with their supervisors. These are important insights and reinforce the general assumption that good communication is good for companies.

Michael B. Hinner

Xiaowei Shi earned her Ph.D. in communication from Purdue University in 2009. She is currently Associate Professor in the Department of Communication Studies at Middle Tennessee State University. Her research and teaching focus on influence processes and supportive message production in the contexts of professional and close relationships. Her research findings have been cited over 200 times in peer publications and have earned her four "Top-Paper" Awards from the National Communication Association's Annual Conventions.

Yang Soo Kim is professor in the Department of Communication Studies at Middle Tennessee State University. He earned his Ph.D. degree in Communication at the University of Oklahoma in 2003. As a former expatriate manager, his research focuses on global competence and cross-cultural adaptation among international managers and international students. He has co-authored a book titled "Global Business and Understanding Indonesian Culture" published internationally. Most recent article regarding Adaptive Personality, Communication Competence and Psychological Health among Korean Expatriates in India appeared in the *Journal of Intercultural Communication.*

Xiaowei Shi and Yang Soo Kim

More Than One Way to Influence: Organizational Members' Upward Voice in U.S., China, and South Korea

In today's new career climate, organizational members are no longer entitled to lifelong employment. Rather, a career path is "defined structurally as a series of work contracts over the course of a lifetime" (Buzzanell, 2000, p. 210). Under such new career thinking, organizational individuals face the challenge to mobilize their accumulated learning and to adapt to new work dynamics, while taking proactive actions to enhance job security (Waldron, 1999; Ślebarska et al., 2019). Regarding proactive actions for career enhancement, upward influence behavior has received researchers' attention for more than three decades (Botero & Van Dyne, 2009; Fairhurst, 2007; Kipnis et al., 1980; Shim & Lee, 2001; Shi & Wilson, 2010; Waldron et al., 1993). Upward influence refers to the persuasive attempt initiated by an employee when he or she talks to one's work supervisor on work related issues. Such behavior is purposeful and proactive presumably because it helps portray oneself as a concerned organizational citizen and helps one gain access to organizational decision-making process.

Departing from traditional rationality-based study, the current research suggests that upward voice should be studied as a dual-action communication phenomenon, which involves both persuasion and impression management. By doing so, employees not only impact work processes but also shape the way in which they are perceived by their leaders (Clarke, Alshenalfi, & Garavan, 2019a, 2019b; Bolino et al., 2006). Against the backdrop of upward influence as a dual-action endeavor, the present study explores whether cultural backgrounds affect employees' upward influence behavior. Although we know that organizational influence behavior is rarely universal, the nuanced differences in how cultural backgrounds influence employees' communicative choices remain unclear.

Our beliefs of whether reasoning power will result in compliance-gaining may vary from culture to culture (Hofstede, 1983). What counts as effective reasoning, appropriate expressions of ingratiation, or showing disapproval at workplace may vary depending on specific cultural context (Janosik, 1987). For example, despite their common collectivism culture norms, Chinese and South Korean employees may demonstrate distinct communication strategies when they talk to a manager or to someone who possesses higher positional power in the organizational hierarchy (Hofstede, 1983).

To further elaborate the basis for the present research, we first lay out a theoretical framework and review key concepts in upward influence and impression management. We then introduce a research study examining variations in upward communication among American, South Korean, and Chinese employees. Research questions and hypotheses are raised next. Finally, implications of a cultural-specific approach to understanding organizational influence are discussed.

Upward Influence

This study adopts a situational-assessment-to-message-choice framework to analyze upward influence (Shi & Wilson, 2017). While situational assessments are cognitive processes, communicative actions exist "in the world" (Dillard, 2004, p. 185). Upward influence refers to the phenomenon where a subordinate deliberately selects tactics to influence a more powerful target (typically the supervisor), aiming at changing the target's attitude or behavior for personal or organizational objectives (Waldron, 1999). For instance, upward influence interactions may occur when a subordinate wants to ask one's supervisor for work reassignment or to offer advice on how to improve work operations. Upward influence can involve personal and organizational primary goals. For example, asking for a salary raise is a personal goal, while suggesting a new work operation is a larger organizational goal. The present study focuses on organizational goal-oriented upward communication. Such a behavior is also called "voice," in which employees respond to a dissatisfaction and make constructive suggestions for change intended for organizational benefits (Botero & Van Dyne, 2009; Hirschman, 1970; LePine & Van Dyne, 1998).

One distinct feature of upward influence is that it is potentially face-threatening due to the hierarchical nature between a subordinate and a supervisor. Brown and Levinson (1978) explained that people universally have face concerns. Face is a person's public self-image and something that is "emotionally invested… can be lost, maintained, enhanced, and must be constantly attended to in interaction" (p. 61). By telling the other party what to do, upward influence can threaten the target's (the supervisor) desired self-image as a competent and autonomous leader. It also threats his or her own positive face (e.g., appearing to think she or he "knows it all").

While attempting to be persuasive, an employee might also want to avoid appearing overly critical or demanding of the boss. Pertaining to the current context that employees propose a new change in work, expressions of disapproval may be part of the conversation. Disapproval behavior includes expressing unfavorable judgments and placing responsibility for the errors, mistakes, neglect, or the like, on someone or something (Wilson, 1990). There are fine lines between what constitutes constructive suggestion (i.e., problem-solving) and what constitutes criticism over a leader's decision. Bolino et al. (2016) suggested that people react negatively to those who use such a tactic.

Situational Assessment: Power Distance and Affective Arousal

To manage face threats inherent in persuasion, interpersonal influence theories suggest that there are two situational assessments that are relevant to an upward influence context: (1) power distance and (2) affective arousal. As a cultural variation factor, power distance refers to an individual's perception regarding the degree of power associated with a supervisor over a subordinate (Hofstede, 1980; Lee et al., 2000). In upward voice research, it is conceptually similar to Davison et al.'s (2017) definition of deference in relationship assessment. Based on their study of sales professionals in a Hong Kong telecommunication company, deference to supervisor inhibits employees' willingness to talk to their supervisor when employees experience a low level of control over their job (e.g., newcomers). Similarly, Botero and Van Dyne (2009) found the power distance has a negative association with voice behavior for both U.S. and Colombia employees.

Arousal assessment refers to affective state evaluations (Dillard, 1990), in which employees are concerned with whether they feel comfortable or confident in pursuing certain endeavors. The implicit face concerns give rise to arousal assessment, in which subordinates evaluate situational constraints in terms of whether one should approach or avoid an upward influence attempt (Dillard, 1990; Wilson, 2002). For example, if a subordinate perceives that the potential costs in terms of damage to the relationship or feelings of anxiety are considerable, he or she might simply withdraw from an influence attempt.

Persuasion and Impression Management Strategies

While upward influence is primarily considered as an attempt to engage in work problem- solving, the present research proposes that such a behavior involves purposeful impression management (see Bolino et al., 2016). Researchers have long noted that influence has a broader set of behaviors, which includes not only rationality but also impression management (Kipnis et al., 1980; Yukl & Falbe,

1990). While attempting to voice one's concern on work issues, organizational members also aim to portray oneself as a dedicated colleague and, hence, influence the supervisors' impressions and preferences (Bolino et al., 2006; Huang et al.,2013). Indeed, Falbe and Yukl (1992) reported that upward influence is more effective when reasoning is used in combination with soft tactics such as consultation or ingratiation.

Impression management refers to the behaviors that employees use to shape how they are seen by others at work (Bolino et al., 2016), such as being seen as likeable, dedicated, committed, competent (Bozeman & Kacmar, 1997; Bolino et al., 2008). Among the various impression management tactics, ingratiation tactics are commonly used in supervisor-focused impression management behavior (Wayne & Ferris, 1990). By definition, ingratiation refers to the behavior employees use to engage in favor rendering, opinion conformity, and other forms of activities that are targeted toward superiors in order to be seen as likeable (Wayne & Ferris, 1990; Bolino et al., 2008). Ingratiation behavior is strategic and rewarding in the long run. Prior research suggests a positive association between effective impression management and hiring decisions as well as with performance evaluations (Chen et al., 2008).

Hypotheses and Research Questions

Based on this line of reasoning, the first set of hypotheses is formulated on the relationships between perceived power distance and influence message features (i.e., reasoning, disapproval expressions, and ingratiation expressions). Researchers found that providing rationality during communication serves as one of the most frequently used upward influence strategies across cultures (Shi & Wilson, 2010). That is, a subordinate focuses primarily on analyzing the helpfulness, relevance, and legitimacy of a proposed action. As perceived power distance increases between a subordinate and supervisor, it is expected that individuals may be more likely to focus on the reasoning aspects of influence messages to justify their requests. They may be less willing to confront their supervisors with disapproval tactics. They may express a higher degree of ingratiation in order to generate liking.

H1: Employees' perceived power distance relates positively to their use of rationality in upward influence messages.

H2: Employees' perceived power distance relates negatively to disapproval expressions in upward influence messages.

H3: Employees' perceived power distance relates positively to their use of ingratiation in upward influence messages.

With regard to the affective state assessment, feeling comfortable talking with a supervisor may give rise to reasoning elaborations as well as incorporation of disapproval expression. It is speculated that employees may feel more carefree to express dissatisfactions. The feeling of comfortableness may also give rise to ingratiation behavior, such that employees are more prone to portray themselves as likeable and friendly. As such, the second set of hypotheses is raised:

H4: Employees' affective state assessment (e.g., feeling comfortable) relates positively to their use of reasoning when they imagine interacting with their supervisor.

H5: Employees' affective state assessment (e.g., feeling comfortable) relates positively to their use of disapproval expressions when they imagine interacting with their supervisor.

H6: Employees' affective state assessment (e.g., feeling comfortable) relates positively to their use of ingratiation when they imagine interacting with their supervisor.

Individuals' cultural beliefs (e.g., power distance) explain their upward influence behavior (Brockner, 2003). A culture-in-context approach (Janosik, 1987) suggests that individual differences, cultural values, and the social context all influence social interaction processes and outcomes. As such, the present research proposes that organizational upward influence research needs to pay attention to behavioral preferences and patterns based on cultural contexts. In particular, there are two types of cultural factors that deserve our attention: (1) employees' primary culture and (2) employees' gender role.

Tinsley and Pillutla (1999) argued that national culture provides an environmental context that makes people within that culture prone to use certain influence strategies over others. Trying to get one's way can be seen as assertive or aggressive depending on cultural meanings associated with that behavior. For example, Shim and Lee (2001) found that South Korean R & D project managers seldom use ingratiation tactics because such tactics are viewed as ineffective and manipulative. Instead, they prefer to use direct, firm communication styles (e.g., assertiveness), which are seen as favorable responses in their culture. In contrast, Chinese employees are highly concerned about preserving a peaceful relationship among participants in conflict (Kirkbride et al., 1991). Further, expressing interpersonal warmth is considered as a useful means for Chinese employees to manage conflicts (Tjosvold et al., 2000). Similarly, Shi and Wilson (2010) found that Chinese employees valued a communication clarity goal more than an effectiveness goal when engaging in upward influence. This line of literature gives rises to the following research question:

RQ1: Do employees from China, U.S., and South Korea demonstrate culturally specific patterns in upward influence strategies? If so, how should each of them be described?

Despite the increasing number of female employees present in the work force, researchers have found that organizational members still show a strong tendency to associate a leader with a male image (see Koenig, Eagly, Mitchell, and Ristikari's meta-analysis, 2011). Such a gender-related view of "leaders are men" creates challenges for female leaders in today's organizational life. While employees are aware of their face threatening acts, they do not honor male and female supervisor's face needs the same way in upward influence.

According to status characteristics theory (Berger & Fisek, 2006), during the goal formation process in social interactions, an actor will identify a socially significant characteristic in the target (e.g., gender, race, and occupational position) and use that cue to make differential status evaluations of the target. Individuals then enact certain behaviors toward the target consistent with their perception. This line of literature gives rise to the following research question.

RQ2: In addition to national cultural influence, does a supervisor's gender role (male vs. female) impact how employees engage in upward influence?

Method

Participants

We collected data in the U.S. (southeast region), South Korea (city of Seoul), and China (city of Changchun). After receiving IRB approval from the authors' institutions, the authors contacted a number of organizations through their friends' and relatives' social network in China and South Korea. If employees agreed to participate on a voluntary basis, they were given a survey questionnaire in hard copy or a Qualtrics online survey link upon their request. If the surveys were completed in a hard copy, then completed questionnaires were either mailed to the authors or collected by the authors.

For the U.S. participants, they were recruited using two methods, including (1) recruitment flyers with tear sheets containing the survey website information and (2) communication course websites, in which the authors were the instructors. The online survey website is operated by Qualtrics. The survey link is a reusable link that can be pasted into emails or onto a website. The survey link is unable to track identifying information of respondents.

On the front page of the survey, participants were told that "*the purpose of this study is to gain insight about how you would do or say to a supervisor on a work issue if you are recently hired by the company as a new employee.*"

To qualify for this research, participants were told that they need to meet two inclusion criteria: (a) having at least 1 year work experience at a full-time paid job position and (b) having a supervisor to whom one directly reports. If a college student does not meet these criteria, he or she can recruit another qualified individual to participate and still receive the same amount of extra credit. As a result, total of 413 qualified participants completed the survey, including 132 Americans, 111 Chinese, and 170 South Korean professionals.

For the 132 American employees (98 female, 34 male; $M_{age} = 27.8$, $SD = 10.4$), the majority of them have more than 2 years of work experience (75 %), whereas about 25 % of them have 1–2 years of work experience on various job positions (service, sales, clerical construction, factories). Participants represented a diverse ethnic background, including 66.7 % Caucasian, 20.5 % African American, 3 % Hispanic, 2.3 % Asian, and 7.6 % unidentified.

For the 111 Chinese employees (85 female, 26 male; $M_{age} = 34.2$, $SD = 6.2$), the majority are in their 30s or 40s (66 %). Almost all participants have more than 2 years of work experience (99 %). Based on their reports, the organizations they work for include factories, banks, restaurants, schools, and government offices of the city.

For the 170 South Korean employees (84 female, 106 male; $M_{age} = 38.7$, $SD = 9.8$), the majority are in their 30s or 40s (71 %). The majority of them have more than 2 years of work experience (82 %). Based on their reports, the organizations they worked for include banks, electronic companies, and public corporations.

Procedures

An original version of the questionnaire was initially developed in English. The English questionnaire was translated into Chinese language by the first author and Korean language by the second author. Next, the Chinese and Korean versions were verified by two native speakers to confirm translation accuracy.

Once participants start the survey, they were reminded of the voluntary nature of their participation and the purpose of the study. Next, participants read a scenario, which describes a new employee (referred as "You") has noticed a work problem. In the scenario, it asks participants to imagine what they would do if they recently joined the company as a new employee. This design allows employees to focus on upward influence without any local knowledge about the organization. As newcomers have not fully emerged in a specific organizational culture, their responses may largely reflect their cultural beliefs on how to enact appropriate upward influence. Furthermore, research noted that newcomers tend to experience uncertainties about lack of control over work resources; hence, they are motivated to engage in proactive behavior in information-and-feedback seeking, relationship building, and work-related influence (Ashford & Black, 1996; Davidson et al., 2017; Ślebarska et al., 2019). The scenario started as the following:

> "Suppose you were recently hired by J & M for your experience and expertise in testing a certain product. Your supervisor (Bob) and co-workers were friendly and excited about getting you familiar with the work procedure. You feel you have learned a lot. But at the same time, you have noticed some inefficiency in the current testing method…"

After describing in detail what the work problem is about and how the employee can help improve it, the scenario continues with concerns of impression management.

> "…..you don't want to make Bob and your colleagues (coworkers) feel that you are introducing some big changes to the whole system configuration or give them the impression that you are showing off or know it all."

Finally, the scenario describes the supervisor-subordinate relationship.

> "Bob is a fair supervisor. But your relationship with him does not go beyond the formal employment contract. Bob does not seek out your opinion very often. Now with all these concerns and suggestions, you decide to talk to him."

In this survey, there were two versions of the scenario: a female vs a male supervisor. About half of participants received a "male supervisor version" about to talk to "Bob," who was referred as "him"; whereas the other half were about to talk to "Barb," who was referred as "her." In the Chinse and Korean versions, the female and male supervisors' names were translated into a common male or female name in their culture, respectively.

All participants received the same information except that some participants were told that they were about to talk to a female supervisor, whereas others were about to talk to a male supervisor. Each participant read only one version that was randomly assigned by the Qualtrics system or by the author if a participant preferred a printed version.

After reading the scenario, all participants were asked to write down their actual messages. The procedure was intended to prompt participants to respond to the following situational assessment scale and message quality assessment scale. Finally, participants completed a demographic questionnaire, and other measures that did not particularly pertain to the current research questions.

Instrumentation

Power Distance Assessment. Adapted from Nesler et al.'s (1999) measure of social global power in the workplace, two items measured perceived power distance (Cronbach's α = .60), including "In general, I think Bob has __ (1= less power over me, 3 = equal power with me, 5 = more power over me)" and "As my work supervisor, I think he can influence me to work harder in my work (1= strongly disagree, 3 = neutral, 5 = strongly agree)." These two items were averaged to create an index of power distance assessment with higher scores indicating a higher perceived power inequality between the supervisor and the subordinate, $M = 4.04$, $SD = .78$. Note that mean and SD are based on the entire sample in this and the following reports.

Affective State Assessment. Adapted from Dillard et al. (1989), three items were used to measure perceived arousal level (affective state) when talking to a supervisor (Cronbach's α = .67), including "In general, while I am meeting with Bob, I feel my relationship with him is ___ (1= very close, 3 = neutral, 5 = very distant; item was reverse coded)," "In general, while I am meeting with Bob, I feel ___ (1= not at all threatened, 3 = neutral, 5 = very much threatened; item was reverse coded)," and "In general, while I am meeting with Bob, I feel ___ (1= not at all comfortable, 3 = neutral, 5 = very much comfortable)." These three items were averaged to create an index of affective assessment with higher scores indicating a higher level of comfort in communication, $M = 3.18$, $SD = .72$.

Reasoning. Participants were told to think again about the message they just wrote and evaluate their message quality. Message reasoning is adapted from Lim and Bowers (1991) on a five-point scale (1 = *strongly disagree*, 5 = *strongly agree*). The reasoning scale has two items: "to explore possibilities for her (him) to consider," and "to suggest ways to make our work even better" (α =.60). $M = 4.1$, $SD = .75$.

Disapproval Expression. As there is no existing measure, the authors created two items to tap into the dimensions of displaying criticism and dissatisfaction toward a work situation, including "To express my disapproval of the current situation" and "To demand what I wanted forcefully" (1 = *strongly disagree*, 5 = *strongly agree*), α =.54, M=2.7, $SD = .94$.

Ingratiation. Ingratiation measure examines how employees use other enhancement expressions, such as praise and opinion conformity, or highlight certain qualities of the supervisor so that the target may see the actor as likeable (Bolino et al., 2016). Two items were selected from Bolino and Turnley's (1999) ingratiation scale. They are slightly modified in the current study, including "To let her know that I appreciate her leadership approach" and "To show him that

I care about our work relationship" (1 = *strongly disagree*, 5 = *strongly agree*), α = .71, *M* = 3.7, *SD* = .93.

Results

Means, standard deviations, and zero-order correlations for the independent and dependent variables for the entire sample are shown in Table 1.

Table 1: Means (SD) and Correlations Between Situational Assessment Factors and Message Features

	1	2	3	4	5
1. Affective State Assess		.08	.20***	.34***	-.02
2. Power Distance Assess		1	.32***	-.04	.10*
3. Reasoning			1	.26***	-.03
4. Ingratiation				1	-.06
5. Disapproval					1
Mean	3.18	4.04	4.08	3.74	2.67
(SD)	(.72)	(.78)	(.75)	(.93)	(.94)

***$p < .001$, **$p < .01$, *$p < .05$.

In terms of message features, employees' upward influence messages were found to be relatively high in rational persuasion (*M* =4.08, *SD* =.75) and ingratiation (*M* =3.74, *SD*=.93), close to the mid-point in disapproval expression (*M* = 2.67, *SD*=.94) on a 5-point scale. On average, participants reported a relatively high power distance, *M* = 4.04, *SD*= .78; South Korean employees reported a higher degree of perceived power distance than American and Chinese employees (*M* = 4.37 vs. 4.10 vs. 3.48), *F* (2, 410) = 55.45, *p*= .000. Participants reported close to mid-point in affective state (e.g., feeling comfortable in communication), *M* = 3.08, *SD*= .72; Chinese employees reported a higher level of affective state than American and South Korean employees (M = 3.35 vs. 3.19 vs. 3.06), *F* (2, 410) = 5.40, *p*= .005. With regard to normal distribution of the data, Skewness and Kurtosis scores for the 13 variables are all within the normal range (−1, +1).

Correlations revealed that perceived power distance was strongly and positively associated with the use of rational persuasion in upward influence, *r* = .32, p < .001. *H 1* was supported. Contrary to our prediction, perceived power distance did not have an "inhibiting" effect on employees' display of disapproval. Rather, it had a small but significant positive association with negative impression management, $r = .10$, $p = .046$. *H2* was not supported. Power distance has no significant impact on ingratiation; *H3* was not supported.

Results further revealed that affective state assessment ("feeling comfortable") had a significant positive association with reasoning, hence *H4* is supported. It also had a positive association with use of ingratiation in impression management, $r = .34$, $p < .001$. *H6* was supported. It, however, had no significant impact on expression of disapproval. Hence *H5* was not supported.

Regression analyses further confirmed that affective assessment (feeling comfortable) tends to increase ingratiation expression. Such a pattern is observed in three cultures (see Table 2).

RQ1 investigated whether employees' upward influence communication demonstrated culturally specific patterns. First, a 3 (U.S. vs. China vs. S. Korea) × 2 (male vs. female) factorial ANOVA was conducted on each message dimension, crossing cultural backgrounds and supervisor's gender.

For rational persuasion, cultural background had a main effect, $F(2, 404) = 5.83$, $p = .003$, $\eta^2 = .03$, revealing that U.S. employees reported a significantly higher level of using rationality strategy than Chinese or South Korean employees ($M = 4.26$ vs. 4.01 vs. 3.98), $d = .29$, .45, respectively. There is no supervisor gender effect or interaction effect.

For ingratiation behavior, cultural background also had a significant and strong main effect, $F(2, 404) = 45.03$, $p < .000$, $\eta^2 = .18$, revealing that Chinese employees used significantly more ingratiation tactics than U.S or South Korean employees ($M = 4.37$ vs. 3.54 vs. 3.47), $d = 1.03$, 1.08, respectively. No supervisor gender effect or interaction effect was detected.

For disapproval expressions, both cultural background, $F(2, 402) = 60.66$ $\eta^2 = .23$, and supervisor gender, $F(1, 402) = 14.84$, $\eta^2 = .04$, $ps = .000$, had main effects. Results indicated that South Korean employees used significantly more disapproval tactics than U.S or Chinese employees ($M = 3.21$ vs. 2.30 vs. 2.27), $d = 1.06$, 1.19, respectively.

Results indicated that employees used a higher degree of disapproval toward talking to a male supervisor than a female supervisor, $M = 2.82$ vs. 2.47, $d = .38$. There was no interaction between culture and supervisor gender.

Next, follow-up pairwise comparison analyses were conducted to further explore how different tactics are used in combination within each cultural group. Results revealed that reasoning is the most desirable strategy, followed by ingratiation and disapproval expressions. This pattern is observed for American employees, t's $(131) > 8.91$, $p < .000$, and South Korean employees, t's $(169) > 3.10$, $p < .002$. On the other hand, a different upward influence pattern emerged in Chinese participants' data. They rated ingratiation as their top strategy in upward influence, followed by reasoning. Disapproval is rated as the least favorite (ingratiation $M = 4.37$ vs. reasoning $M = 4.01$ vs. disapproval $M = 2.27$), t's $(110) > 3.84$, $p < .000$.

Taken together, at a group level, American employees differ from other two cultures in using a higher level of rational persuasion. Chinese employees showed a remarkably high degree of using ingratiation impression management. Despite the fact that disapproval expression is the least favored tactics across all three cultures, South Korean employees used it more often in comparison to employees from the other two countries. *RQ1* is addressed. See Figure 1.

Figure 1: Employees' Upward Influence Communication

RQ2 examined whether new employees communicate differently based on a supervisor's gender role. As the above ANOVA analyses revealed, no supervisor gender effect or interaction effect was detected on reasoning and ingratiation, indicating that employees talk to male vs. female supervisors in a similar manner in terms of rational persuasion and ingratiation across three cultures.

On the other hand, however, supervisor's gender had a main effect on disapproval expressions, revealing that employees expressed a higher degree of disapproval toward talking to a male than a female supervisor. Such a pattern manifested in three cultures. *RQ2* is addressed.

Discussion

This study has investigated employees' influence attempts from different cultures. The findings of this study have theoretical and practical implications. It is argued that, even when opportunities exist, sometimes employees still do not want to pursue upward influence due to fear of creating negative impressions in a supervisor's mind. Findings of this study shed new light on tactful influence strategies used by American, Chinese, and South Korean employees.

Theoretical Implications

The present research extends upward influence literature by moving beyond a face threat management framework. Using employees' data from three cultures, this study finds that positive impression management goes hand in hand with persuasion, $r = .26, p < .001$. Put differently, in addition to persuasion, employees across three different cultures reported that they like to use other enhancing tactics to signal appreciation of the leader. Such patterns are largely consistent across the three cultures.

One step further, the present study also offered new evidence supporting the relationship between affective state (e.g., comfort in communication) and employees' voice behavior. When they feel more comfortable talking with a supervisor, their messages tend to exhibit a higher degree of rationality as well as favor-rendering expressions, such as being both rational and friendly. In contrast, perceived power distance can increase rationality of a message but such messages show no relationship-enhancement expressions, such as talking in a plain, matter-of-fact manner.

In addition to the universal patterns on individuals' affective state and message choices, this research provides new evidence on what counts as a "desired" persuasion approach different cultural context. It seems that rational persuasion may not be the only way to influence a supervisor. What counts as a desirable and effective way to influence a supervisor may vary from culture to culture. For example, this research revealed that employees from Chinese culture emphasize positive impressions more than rational persuasion. For South Korean employees, their effort of creating or maintaining desired images in the eye of a supervisor seems to include using disapproval and criticism to express concerns.

A Culture-Centered Perspective

This study finds that a combination of rational persuasion and impression management is considered a desirable approach for upward influence by all three different cultures. On the other hand, there is cultural variation in terms of how rationality is combined with positive vs. negative impression management strategies. For example, Chinese employees pair reasoning with effusive ingratiation expressions. In contrast, South Korean employees complement rational persuasion with a higher level of negative impression strategies.

For Chinese employees, strong ingratiation expressions are prioritized over rational persuasion. This type of behavior could be attributed to Chinese cultural values of power distance and collectivism. According to Hofstede (1980, 1983, 1991), power distance refers to "a measure of the interpersonal power or influence between a superior and a subordinate as perceived by the subordinate" (Hofstede, 1991, p. 71). Individualism/collectivism refers to the degree to which cultures encourage individual needs, wishes, desires, and values in relation to group and collective ones (Hofstede, 1980).

In a higher power distance country like China, employees at a lower rank "feel more comfortable if they were told what to do and what is expected from them" (Lu & Heng, 2009, p. 12). Chinese employees would use non-confronting approaches toward their superiors to avoid challenging them and possibly leading to conflict. Confronting superiors or challenging subordinates can easily harm a good relationship (Lu & Heng, 2009) and trust (Chen et al., 2008). Under the influence of Confucianism based collectivism, Chinese people are "more likely to respect the status quo to keep a harmonious society" (Lu & Heng, 2009). The idea of maintaining harmony is related to preserving face. Face relates to prestige, status, dignity, and respect which plays a dominant and even central role in Chinese social relations and communications (Cardon, 2009). Collectivistic communicators tend to highly emphasize the feelings and face needs of others (Cai et al., 2000; Gudykunst & Matsumoto, 1996). As such, Chinese employees are typically unwilling to give different opinions because this practice is considered as challenging the other person's face, thereby questioning his/her prestige or respect. The fear of losing face and undermining harmony results in the avoidance of conflict and discourages the exchanging of ideas and opinions (Lu & Heng, 2009).

Additionally, collectivism highly values interdependence and conformity within groups and organizations. The collectivistic value of interdependence is clearly reflected in notion of "*quanxi*," which refers to continuous exchange of favors between individuals that facilitates the developing, cultivating, and maintaining of interpersonal relationships (Chen, 1995). *Quanxi* relationships are initiated by higher-ranking managers, which are designed to favor lower-level managers in Chinese organizations (Chen, 1995). Subordinates' dependency on bosses is likely to be high since they are dependent upon them for essential information and resources and approval of work activities (Chen, 1995). Given these cultural values in workplace, Chinese employees tend to adopt ingratiation tactics over any other options in upward influence situations.

On the other hand, for South Korean employees, expressions of disapproval may demonstrate employee loyalty in the eyes of management. For example, it is noteworthy that South Korean employees' use of disapproval expressions is significantly higher than that demonstrated in the other two cultures. As Shim and Lee (2001) indicated, South Korean employees probably tend to perceive ingratiation tactics as inappropriate because it could be seen as ineffective or manipulative in the eyes of their supervisors. Instead, they choose a direct and assertive communication style because it might be perceived more positively by their supervisors. This assertive communication style of South Koreans might be explained from the findings of the GLOBE project. Along with power distance, GLOBE project suggests nine cultural dimensions including assertiveness (House et al., 2004). In this study, South Korea was ranked 21 out of 61 on assertiveness practices, which means, managers were less likely to be offended by an assertive employee's voicing discontent. Relatedly, one study examined South Korean managers' reaction to employees' voicing discontent. The finding of this study indicated that when "trusting" employees object to a company policy aggressively (rather than diplomatically), South Korean managers are likely to attribute the objection to positive motives (i.e., moral concerns) in order for their interests and causes to be heard by their managers (Kim et al., 2009, p. 1014). These findings might provide plausible insight about South Korean employees' choice of disapproval expression in upward influence.

Interestingly, the present research did not detect supervisor's gender effect. Except for disapproval dimension, participants in this study from three different cultures used a similar level of reasoning and ingratiation expressions to either male or female supervisors. Contrary to the speculations that employees may associate male leaders with more respect and honor than to female leaders, results revealed that employees generally treat leaders of either gender group similarly. They showed even a higher degree of disapproval to work situations to male leaders than to female leaders. That part of the finding calls for further research.

Practical Implications

In today's age, many organizational tasks are accomplished at a multinational level for production materials, markets, as well as talents. As such, findings of this research have important practical implications. As discussed previously, there is more than one way to influence others. Some cultures may view ingratiation or disapproval as playing a pivotal role in gaining favorable considerations during an organizational influence process. Failing to recognize cultural variables in influence may result in misunderstanding or wrong judgment in work decisions.

Furthermore, this study chose to use a "newcomer" scenario to solicit employees' input. Organizational entry is the starting point for newcomers to establish their professional identity and participate in decision making in the new workplace. Consistent in three cultures, this study highlighted the important role of the affective state of feeling comfortable in talking with a supervisor. As such, a safe and encouraging environment for upward communication appears to be critical for cultivating organizational citizenship behavior.

Limitations and Directions for Future Research

The present study used a cross-sectional survey method to gather data. It is limited to provide a full understanding of how influence interactions unfold over time. It is also limited to provide a picture of how employees interact in today's multi-cultural organizational environments. Future studies can extend such a design by engaging in cross-cultural comparisons to see how cross-cultural upward influence unfolds. For example, a study might pursue how an American subordinate talks to a Chinese manager, or how a South Korean subordinate talks to an American leader. Such cross-cultural comparisons will allow us to gauge how employees adjust their strategies when an influence target is from a different culture.

Additionally, future research is called for to examine what types of messages are well received by leaders. When we combine reasoning, with ingratiation and expressions of disapproval, will managers from different cultural backgrounds react differently to such messages? Will those messages be interpreted as persuasive in similar or different ways?

In conclusion, the present research examined how employees attempt to influence their work supervisors by focusing on cultural variations. Results demonstrate a culturally unique pattern in terms of the American way, the Chinese way, and the South Korean way to engage in organizational voice. Findings of this research help pave the way for our further exploration of organizational voice in an age of global collaboration.

References

Ashford, S. J., & Black, J. S. (1996). Proactivity During Organizational Entry: The Role of Desire for Control. *Journal of Applied Psychology, 81*(2), 199–214. Retrieved from: https://doi.org/10.1037/0021-9010.81.2.199.

Berger, J., & Fişek, M. H. (2006). Diffuse Status Characteristics and the Spread of Status Value: A Formal Theory. *American Journal of Sociology, 111*(4), 1038–1079.

Bolino, M. C., Kacmar, K. M., Turnley, W. H., & Gilstrap, J. B. (2008). A Multi-Level Review of Impression Management Motives and Behaviors. *Journal of Management, 34*(6), 1080–1109.

Bolino, M., Long, D., & Turnley, W. (2016). Impression Management in Organizations: Critical Questions, Answers, and Areas for Future Research. *Annual Review of Organizational Psychology and Organizational Behavior, 3*, 377–406.

Bolino, M. C., & Turnley, W. H. (1999). Measuring Impression Management in Organizations: A Scale Development Based on the Jones and Pittman Taxonomy. *Organizational Research Methods, 2*(2), 187–206.

Bolino, M. C., Varela, J. A., Bande, B., & Turnley, W. H. (2006). The Impact of Impression-Management Tactics on Supervisor Ratings of Organizational Citizenship Behavior. *Journal of Organizational Behavior: The International Journal of Industrial, Occupational and Organizational Psychology and Behavior, 27*(3), 281–297.

Botero, I. C., & Van Dyne, L. (2009). Employee Voice Behavior: Interactive Effects of LMX and Power Distance in the United States and Colombia. *Management Communication Quarterly, 23*(1), 84–104.

Bozeman, D. P., & Kacmar, K. M. (1997). A Cybernetic Model of Impression Management Processes in Organizations. *Organizational Behavior and Human Decision Processes, 69*(1), 9–30.

Brockner, J. (2003). Unpacking Country Effects: On the Need to Operationalize the Psycho- Logical Determinants of Cross-National Differences. In R. M. Kramer & B. M. Staw (Eds.), *Research in Organizational Behavior* (Vol. 25, pp. 335–369). Greenwich, CT: JAI.

Brown, P., & Levinson, S. C. (1978). Universals in Language Usage: Politeness Phenomena. In *Questions and Politeness: Strategies in Social Interaction* (pp. 56–311). Cambridge: Cambridge University Press.

Buzzanell, P. M. (2000). The Promise and Practice of the New Career and Social Contract: Illusions Exposed and Suggestions for Reform. In P. M. Buzzanell (Ed.), *Rethinking Organizational and Managerial Communication from Feminist Perspectives* (pp. 209–235). Thousand Oaks, CA: Sage.

Cai, D., Wilson, S., & Drake (2000). Culture in the Context of Intercultural Negotiation. *Human Communication Research, 26*(4), 591–617.

Cardon, P. (2009). A Model of Face Practices in Chinese Business Culture: Implications for Western Business Persons. *Thunderbird International Business Review, 51*(1), 19–36.

Chen, M. (1995). *Asian Management Systems: Chinese, Japanese and Korean Styles of Business.* New York: Routledge.

Chen, Y., Wu, J., & Jung, Y. (2008). Cultural Impact on Trust: A Comparison of Virtual Communities in China, Hong Kong, and Taiwan. *Journal of Global Information Technology Management, 11*(1), 28–48.

Clarke, N., Alshenalfi, N., & Garavan, T. (2019a). The Effects of Subordinates' Use of Upward Influence Tactics on Their Supervisors' Job Performance Evaluations in Saudi Arabia: The Significance of Loyalty. *The International Journal of Human Resource Management*, 1–30.

Clarke, N., Alshenalfi, N., & Garavan, T. (2019b). Upward Influence Tactics and Their Effects on Job Performance Ratings and Flexible Working Arrangements: The Mediating Roles of Mutual Recognition Respect and Mutual Appraisal Respect. *Human Resource Management, 58*(4), 397–416.

Davidson, T., Van Dyne, L., & Lin, B. (2017). Too Attached to Speak Up? It Depends: How Supervisor–Subordinate Guanxi and Perceived Job Control Influence Upward Constructive Voice. *Organizational Behavior and Human Decision Processes, 143*, 39–53.

Dillard, J. P. (1990). A Goal-Driven Model of Interpersonal Influence. In J. P. Dillard (Ed.), *Seeking Compliance: The Production of Interpersonal Influence Messages* (pp. 41–56). Scottsdale, ZA: Gorsuch Scarisbrick.

Dillard, J. P. (2004). The goals-plans-action model of interpersonal influence. In J. S. Seiter & R. H. Gass (Eds.), *Perspectives on persuasion, social influence and compliance gaining* (pp. 185–206). Boston: Allyn & Bacon.

Dillard, J. P., Segrin, C., & Harden, J. M. (1989). Primary and Secondary Goals in the Production of Interpersonal Influence Message. *Communication Monographs, 56*, 19–38.

Fairhurst, G. T. (2007). *Discursive Leadership: In Conversation with Leadership Psychology*. Thousand Oaks, CA: Sage.

Falbe, C. M., & Yukl, G. (1992). Consequences for Managers of Using Single Influence Tactics and Combinations of Tactics. *Academy of Management Journal, 35*(3), 638–652.

Gudykunst, W., & Matsumoto, Y. (1996). Cross-Cultural Variability of Communication in Personal Relationships. In W. B. Gudykunst, S. Ting-Toomey, & T. Nishida (Eds.), *Communication in Personal Relationships Across Cultures* (pp. 19–56). London: Sage.

Hirschman, A. O. (1970). *Exit, Voice, and Loyalty: Responses to Decline in Firms, Organizations and States*. Cambridge, MA: Harvard University Press.

Hofstede, G. (1980). *Culture's Consequences: International Differences in Work-Related Values*. Beverly Hills: Sage.

Hofstede, G. (1983). National Cultures in four Dimensions, a Research-Based Theory on Cultural Differences among Nations. *International Studies in Management and Organizations, 14*, 46–74.

Hofstede, G. (1991). *Cultures and Organizations: Software of the Mind*. London: McGraw-Hill.

House, R., Hanges, P., Javidan, M., Dorfman, P., & Gupta, V. (2004). *Culture, Leadership, and Organizations: The GLOBE Study of 62 Societies*. Thousand Oaks, CA: Sage.

Huang, G. H., Zhao, H. H., Niu, X. Y., Ashford, S. J., & Lee, C. (2013). Reducing Job Insecurity and Increasing Performance Ratings: Does Impression Management Matter? *Journal of Applied Psychology, 98*(5), 852.

Janosik, R. J. (1987). Rethinking the Culture-Negotiation Link. *Negotiation Journal, 3*(4), 385–395.

Kim, T., Rosen, B., & Lee, D. (2009). South Korean Managerial Reactions to Voicing Discontent: The Effects of Employee Attitude and Employee Communication Styles. *Journal of Organizational Behavior, 30*, 1001–1018.

Kipnis, D., Schmidt, S. M., & Wilkinson, I. (1980). Intraorganizational Influence Tactics: Explorations in Getting One's Way. *Journal of Applied Psychology, 65*, 440–452.

Kirkbride, P. S., Tang, S. F. Y., & Westwood, R. I. (1991). Chinese Conflict Preferences and Negotiating Behavior: Cultural and Psychological Influences. *Organization Studies, 12*, 365–386.

Koenig, A. M., Eagly, A. H., Mitchell, A. A., & Ristikari, T. (2011). Are Leader Stereotypes Masculine? A Meta-Analysis of Three Research Paradigms. *Psychological Bulletin, 137*(4), 616.

Lee, C., Pillutla, M., & Law, K. S. (2000). Power-Distance, Gender and Organizational Justice. *Journal of Management*, *26*(4), 685–704.

LePine, J. A., & Van Dyne, L. (1998). Predicting Voice Behavior in Work Groups. *Journal of Applied Psychology, 83*(6), 853–868.

Lim, T. S., & Bowers, J. W. (1991). Facework Solidarity, Approbation, and Tact. *Human Communication Research*, *17*(3), 415–450.

Lu, X., & Heng, M. (2009). Cultural Influence on IS Practices in China: A Literature Analysis. *Journal of Global Information Technology Management, 12*, 6–24.

Nesler, M. S., Aguinis, H., Quigley, B. M., Lee, S. J., & Tedeschi, J. T. (1999). The Development and Validation of a Scale Measuring Global Social Power Based on French and Raven's Power Taxonomy. *Journal of Applied Social Psychology*, *29*(4), 750–769.

Shi, X., & Wilson, S. R. (2010). Upward Influence in Contemporary Chinese Organizations: Explicating the Effects of Influence Goal Type and Multiple Goal Importance on Message Reasoning and Politeness. *Management Communication Quarterly*, *24*(4), 579–606.

Shi, X., & Wilson, S. R. (2017). Influence in Organizational Communication. *International Encyclopedia of Organizational Communication*. John Wiley & Sons.

Shim, D., & Lee, M. (2001). Upward Influence Styles of R&D Project Leaders. *IEEE Transactions on Engineering Management*, *48*(4), 394–413.

Ślebarska, K., Soucek, R., & Moser, K. (2019). Increasing Proactive Coping in Organizational Newcomers: Improving Job Adaptation or Rocking the Boat? *Journal of Career Development*, *46*(3), 295–313.

Tinsley, C. H., & Pillutla, M. M. (1999). Negotiating in the United States and Hong Kong. *Journal of International Business Studies*, 29, 711–728.

Tjosvold, D., Leung, K., & Johnson, D. W. (2000). Cooperative and Competitive Conflict in China. In M. Deutsch & P. T. Coleman (Eds.), *The Handbook of Conflict Resolution* (pp. 475–495). San Francisco: Jossey-Bass Publishers.

Waldron, V. R. (1999). Communication Practices of Followers, Members, and Protégés: The Case of Upward Influence Tactics. *Annals of the International Communication Association*, *22*(1), 251–299.

Waldron, V. R., Hunt, M. D., & Dsilva, M. (1993). Towards a Threat Management Model of Upward Communication: A Study of Influence and Maintenance Tactics in the Leader-Member Dyad. *Communication Studies, 44*, 254–270.

Wayne, S. J., & Ferris, G. R. (1990). Influence Tactics, Affect, and Exchange Quality in Supervisor-Subordinate Interactions: A Laboratory Experiment and Field Study. *Journal of Applied Psychology*, *75*(5), 487.

Wilson, S. R. (1990). Development and Test of a Cognitive Rules Model of Interaction Goals. *Communication Monographs, 57*, 81–103.

Wilson, S. R. (2002). *Seeking and Resisting Compliance: Why People Say What They Do When Trying to Influence Others*. Thousand Oaks, CA: Sage.

Yukl, G., & Falbe, C. M. (1990). Influence Tactics and Objectives in Upward, Downward, and Lateral Influence Attempts. *Journal of Applied Psychology, 75*, 132–140.

Table 2: Regression Analysis of Situational Assessment on Message Features across Three Cultures

	U.S. (N = 132)			China (N = 111)			South Korea (N = 170)		
	Ingratiation Impression β	**Disapproval** β	**Reason** β	**Ingratiation Impression** β	**Disapproval** β	**Reason** β	**Ingratiation Impression** β	**Disapproval** β	**Reason** β
Affective State	**.22***	**-.22***	.03	**.24****	-.15	**.27****	**.37*****	**.18***	.10
Power Distance	.07	-.13	**.41*****	**.40*****	**-.23***	**.39*****	-.06	-.05	.09
R^2	.06	.07	.18	.32	.17	.30	.14	.07	.02
F	2.72*	3.27*	9.28***	17.07***	7.07***	15.06***	8.75***	3.94**	1.34

***$p < .001$, **$p < .01$, *$p < .05$

Introduction to What They Say and Do in Chinese Organizations: Examining the Four Aspects of Leader-Member Exchange of the LMX-COMM Model

By Haoyang Chen, Vivian C. Sheer and Tien Ee Dominic Yeo

The chapter examines communication within the context of leadership success within business organizations. In particular, it takes a closer look at widely cited leadership theory, namely the leader-member exchange (LMX) theory, with a particular focus on the role of communication in the leader-member exchange. That is why the study applies Sheeer's LMX-COMM model. The LMX-COMM model focuses on four communicative-behavioural aspects within the leader-member exchange: Work communication exchange, social communication exchange, tangible work exchange, and tangible social exchange. It, thus, addresses the importance of communication within the leader-member exchange – an aspect that is often underrepresented in most of the organizational research despite the fact that leadership cannot function without communication. The study confirmed that communication forms an essential part of the leader-member exchange. It also revealed that in addition to face-to-face communication, social media and instant messaging are used very often in Chinese companies for both work-related communication as well as social communication. Emails and voice calls, in contrast, were used primarily for work communication between supervisors and subordinates. The main reasons why social media and instant messaging were preferred was due to their quick response time and richer information exchange. All told, the study revealed how important communication is in developing, maintaining, and strengthening supervisor-subordinate relationships to facilitate organizational learning. And it revealed how important the social communication exchange is in supervisor-subordinate relationships. After all, open communication is an important element of trust building to ensure better predictability. That is why communication is so important in supervisor-subordinate relationships, and why companies should encourage such communication.

Michael B. Hinner

Haoyang Volun Chen (MPhil, Hong Kong Baptist University) is currently a PhD student at the Faculty of Business and Economics, the University of Hong Kong. His research interests focus on organizational communication, workplace relationships, and moral issues at work. He is the 2020 Top Student Paper Award winner (ICA, OrgComm Division). His work has been published in *Journal of Vocational Behavior* and presented in various communication and management conferences such as the Academy of Management, the Society for Industrial and Organizational Psychology (SIOP), International Communication Association (ICA), and the Association for Education In Journalism and Mass Communication (AEJMC).

Vivian C. Sheer (Ph.D., University of Florida) is a Professor in the Department of Communication Studies, School of Communication, Hong Kong Baptist University. Trained in the empirical tradition of the social sciences, Prof. Sheer employs a variety of methods and measures in her research. She has published works in theory development, measurement assessment, and applied communication. Her applied research areas include organizational communication (e.g., leadership behaviors and workplace interactions) and health communication (e.g., antismoking interventions and AIDS/HIV prevention). The research designs she used include surveys, experiments, focus groups, in-depth interviews, and content analysis. Most of her publications are included in the Social Sciences Citation Index. She has served on six editorial boards of scholarly journals. Currently, she is an editorial board member of *Journal of Communication, Leadership (Sage), and Management Communication Quarterly.*

Tien Ee Dominic Yeo (PhD, University of Cambridge) is an Associate Professor at the Department of Communication Studies, Hong Kong Baptist University where he teaches leadership communication and qualitative communication research. His research examines communication practices and sociocultural phenomena around sexuality, health, and technology with a focus on social media use.

Haoyang Chen, Vivian C. Sheer and Tien Ee Dominic Yeo

What They Say and Do in Chinese Organizations: Examining the Four Aspects of Leader-Member Exchange of the LMX-COMM Model

Introduction

Organizational success requires effective leadership at various management levels. To be effective, managers must exercise their influence via communication and behaviour (Yukl et al., 2013). Although leadership is fundamentally a communication process (Fairhurst, 2010), the role of communication in the leadership process is often inadequately studied in organizational research, as most leadership theories are cognition-based (Junker & van Dick, 2014). Of the few leadership theories that examine communication and interaction, the leader-member exchange (LMX) theory (Dansereau et al., 1975; Dulebohn et al., 2012; Graen & Cashman, 1975) is by far the most widely cited framework (Erdogan & Liden, 2002). Despite the large volume of LMX research, however, very few studies have examined LMX communication or other interaction behaviours (Kelly, 2008), as most focus on LMX relationship quality using the LMX-7 scale (see Martin et al., 2016). Invoking Sheer's (2015) LMX-COMM model, which conceptualizes LMX in terms of four communicative-behavioural aspects, we conducted a thematic analysis of the specific patterns of LMX in Chinese organizations under each of the four aspects of the model (i.e., work communication exchange, social communication exchange, tangible work exchange, and tangible social exchange). In addition, we aimed to address the importance of communication elements in LMX. Given the rapid development in communication technology, we attempted to make a theoretical contribution by addressing the communication channels, largely absent in LMX frameworks, used in the leader-member interaction process.

The context of this study was Chinese organizations not only out of data accessibility and cultural proximity considerations for the authors but more notably because Chinese data are particularly informative for the field of leadership studies. The majority of LMX studies were conducted in individualistic Western contexts (Rockstuhl et al., 2012) even though China has the largest number of organizational members of any single country worldwide.

LMX Theory and the Conceptual Literature

As one of the foremost leadership theories portraying the dyadic relationship between an individual subordinate and a leader, the LMX theory has continued to grow and evolve since its inception over 40 years ago (Bauer & Erdogan, 2015; Erdogan & Liden, 2002). In their seminal work, Dansereau et al. (1975) challenged the notion that subordinates are homogeneous, and that leaders exhibit prescribed behaviours toward them. The attention of leadership scholars was thereby shifted from fixed leadership styles to an individualized dyadic relationship between leaders and subordinates (Bauer & Erdogan, 2015; Omilion-Hodges et al., 2016). In addition, Kelley and Bisel (2014) argued that leadership is better studied through the social exchange and communication of parties within different contexts.

Leader-member exchange was one of the first relational approaches emerging in the field of leadership studies, emphasizing the importance of the unique relationship developed by leaders with each member of their teams and on the outcomes of these relationships (Graen & Uhl-Bien, 1995). Despite four decades of LMX research, however, this approach presents some major inconsistencies (Yu et al., 2018). Furthermore, while some scholars argue that LMX is a relational approach (Lee & Chae, 2017; Le Blanc & González-Romá, 2012), others prefer to define it as behavioural (Levi, 2017; Northouse, 2019).

Leaders tend to exchange more physical resources and allocate more role responsibilities to those with whom they share a closer interpersonal relationship. The exchange quality varies from high to low and can predict different organizational outcomes. For those with high-quality LMX (often in-group members), interactions between leaders and members tend to be closer, and the exchange of tangible or intangible commodities can be more frequent. High-quality LMX can predict better attitudinal (e.g., Erdogan & Enders, 2007), behavioural (e.g., Bauer et al., 2006; Kim et al., 2010), and perceptual outcomes (e.g., Erdogan & Bauer, 2010; Kim & George, 2005). In contrast, low-quality exchanges may result in lower satisfaction levels, less commitment, and worse performance. The purpose of the LMX construct is to measure the exchange and, more importantly, to predict organizational outcomes (Burns & Otte, 1999).

Conceptually, LMX is communicative, entailing two-way, mutual interaction between leaders and members. As a theory rooted in social exchange theory, the LMX construct should portray the *exchange*. However, previous conceptual definitions of LMX missed this essential element and the exchange-related constructs did not directly examine the *exchange*. Despite the enormous amount of data collected, leadership scholars often ignore the role of language, communication, and discursive practices (Kelly, 2008) even though the traditional perspective of LMX advocates the examination of these communication elements. Various definitions of LMX portray leaders' and members' characteristics, and interpersonal relationship attributes – most of which are antecedents to LMX – instead of the actual *exchange*.

Communicative Conceptualization of LMX: LMX-COMM

After the long evolution of LMX, an explicit behavioural conceptualization was introduced in Sheer's (2015) work. LMX involves a two-way communication process in which both leaders and members interact and co-contribute to the relationship. To appropriately portray the LMX construct, behavioural indicators that are observable and measurable should be introduced. In this study, we classify leader-member interactions using Sheer's (2015) four-dimensional LMX-COMM that consists of work communication exchange, social communication exchange, tangible work exchange, and tangible social exchange. *Work communication exchange* refers to the process of leaders and members sharing ideas and giving feedback on organizational policy, tasks, development, rewards, and other work issues. *Social communication exchange* denotes the discussion of non-work issues, including family issues, auxiliary activities, and societal issues. *Tangible work exchange* includes bartering services, compensation, work rewards (such as promotions and development opportunities), commodities, working time, and work tasks for organizational goals. *Social exchanges* are those exchange behaviours that are not directly related to work. Leaders and members exchange favors, gifts, or commodities for interpersonal social purposes. Considering that the robustness of these four dimensions of LMX in portraying leader-member interactions has yet to be determined, the following research question was raised:

RQ1: To what extent do the four dimensions of LMX manifest in Chinese organizations?

Four more research questions were posed to examine the specific themes in each dimension:

RQ2: What are the salient themes for work communication exchange in Chinese organizations?

RQ3: What are the salient themes for social communication exchange in Chinese organizations?

RQ4: What are the salient themes for tangible work exchange in Chinese organizations?

RQ5: What are the salient themes for tangible social exchange in Chinese organizations?

Communication Channels Used in Chinese Organizations

Communication is not possible without media. Communication content do differ according to the channels that transmit it (Lee, 2011; Turner et al., 2010). Logically, the supervisor-subordinate dyad enacts different types of exchange via different channels. In previous LMX studies, scholars often emphasized the LMX construct and its relationship to other constructs (as antecedents, moderators, and outcomes); only a few LMX studies have explored communication channels (e.g., Sin et al., 2009; Turnage & Goodboy, 2016). The extant literature rarely treats LMX as a construct of communication, and less so the communication channels. With the development of digital technologies, the communication patterns, and media use of managers in contemporary organizations have changed (Avolio et al., 2014). In the workplace, the supervisor and the subordinate may communicate with each other through face-to-face and mediated communication channels such as email and social media (Lee, 2010; Turner et al., 2010).

Face-to-face communication, as one of the most frequently adopted communication channels (Smith et al., 2018), enables people to immediately and intimately interact with each other (Begley, 2004). In the workplace, in contrast to face-to-face communication, mediated communication channels convey other forms of information such as texts, files, or pictures. Email is one of the most widely adopted communication channels in organizations (D'Urso & Pierce, 2009), where it has become an integral part of work communication (Turnage & Goodboy, 2016). As a formal communication channel (Braun et al., 2019), email is deemed to be effective for exchanging information (Lee et al., 2005) and an appropriate approach to remote communication (Lee, 2011). Furthermore, social media and instant messaging have enabled employees to communicate on both work- and non-work issues and participate in social activities to foster better interpersonal relationships, while affecting not only the amount of communication but also its outcomes on people's lives (Chu, 2020). While much research has examined the communication channels used in the workplace, the extant LMX literature has not investigated how employees use these channels for work and social communication exchanges. This study, therefore, seeks to ascertain if types of exchange are associated with specific types of communication channels in Chinese organizations through the following research question:

RQ6: What communication channels are used in leader-member work communication and social communication exchanges in Chinese organizations?

Methods

Participants

Small group interviews were conducted to better understand the leader-member interaction behaviours within Chinese organizations. Research ethics approval was obtained from the authors' institutional review board before the commencement of this study. To be eligible for this study, participants must either currently have a direct supervisor or have had one in the prior two months. A total of 11 group interviews were conducted from February 2020 to March 2020, which comprised 33 employees from various types of organizations in 10 cities across China. All participants – 16 men and 17 women – had a direct supervisor and 16 participants had subordinates. Participants were from more than 10 industries that included advertising and public relations, banking and finance, consulting, journalism, government, IT and e-commerce, NGO, real estate, public facilities, telecoms, and transportation. The positions of the participants within their organizations ranged from employees and team members to top management and company executives. Participants' ages ranged between 23 and 50 years, while their supervisors' ages were between 24 and 58 years. Those in a supervisory role reported having between 1 and 52 subordinates.

Procedures

The first author conducted all interviews, which began with open-ended questions to allow participants to recall their daily communications and interactions without imposing a prior framework. Participants were encouraged to describe the interaction processes in detail and to give examples of the communication channels used in the leader-member interaction processes. To ascertain the extent to which the four-dimensional framework manifests in Chinese organizations, they were not guided at this stage to avoid responding based on the LMX-COMM model. As the interview questions in the first part were open-ended, the first author took note of any issues that were uniquely characteristic of Chinese culture. All researchers are of Chinese origin and were mindful of detecting cultural specificity.

Following the open-ended questions, the participants were introduced to the four-faceted LMX model and asked to provide examples, if any, for each dimension of the model. Participants were asked to describe as many leader-member interactions as they could recall. If they had subordinates, they were also asked the equivalent questions in their role as supervisor. Despite prior literature indicating that email is one of the most adopted communication channels in the workplace, emails were not frequently mentioned by participants. To investigate this disjuncture, participants were asked follow-up questions about the reasons for their infrequent use of emails in work communication.

Data Analysis

After all the interviews were completed, the audio recordings were transcribed and entered into the qualitative data analysis software, NVivo. Our data analysis adopted a theoretical thematic analytical approach (Braun & Clarke, 2006) based on the LMX-COMM model. After familiarizing ourselves with the data, we generated an initial coding scheme using four randomly selected interview transcripts. The initial coding process generated 33 behaviours and communication topics including performance discussion and work-related gossip, which were classified according to the four facets of LMX-COMM. Additionally, the communication channels described were coded and six were identified: face-to-face, voice call, email, internal communication applications, WeChat (similar to but with more features than WhatsApp) and WhatsApp. When coding the communication channels, the first author noted the circumstances for using certain channels for later analysis.

Using the 33-theme coding scheme, the first author (in consultation with the second author) coded all 11 interview transcripts. During this process, five additional themes were identified. All 38 themes were reviewed, and similar themes combined. For instance, giving gifts, giving red (money) packets, and treating each other to drinks and meals were combined because they all involved the exchange of commodities with monetary value. At this stage, 27 themes of communication interaction were generated plus one additional channel – Skype, resulting in a total of seven communication channels. After refinements, internal communication applications, Skype, WeChat, and WhatsApp were classified as social media and instant messaging. The scenario of using communication channels for work or social communication was also coded.

During the coding process, we observed that certain behaviours and communication topics were neither mutual nor reciprocated by either party of the leader-member dyad. To ensure consistency and precision in clarifying the LMX construct, we periodically returned to Sheer's (2015) conceptualization of the LMX construct. To qualify as LMX behaviours, and communication needed to be mutual or reciprocal. Specifically, the supervisor and subordinate were both required to engage in communication, physical activities, or the exchange of tangible commodities and services. Nevertheless, one-way interactions could be initiated by either the leader or the member without a specified or expected return – as in helping the subordinate to map out their career plan whereby the subordinate could not reciprocate the behaviour. Five one-way behaviours were observed. As the focus of this study is to identify LMX-COMM themes, one-way behaviours were excluded. In the end, 22 LMX themes were identified and presented.

Findings

Four-Dimensional LMX (RQ1)

In the context of Chinese organizations, all LMX behaviours and topics, including negative topics, were fully accounted for by the four-dimensional framework of LMX-COMM (Sheer, 2015), namely, work communication exchange, social communication exchange, tangible work exchange, and tangible social exchange. No new dimensions emerged.

Work Communication Exchange (RQ2)

The first dimension of LMX-COMM was work communication exchange, including the interactions about information sharing and exchanges of opinion related to work or workplace issues. Work communication exchanges were classified into six themes. Four of the themes were positive or neutral work communication exchange, and two were negative topics in work communication exchange (see Table 1).

Positive or Neutral Work Communication Exchange

Company Future, Policy, and Industry Insight. Supervisors and subordinates discussed the company's future, government policy, and some industry insights with each other as a process of information sharing and learning. This communication content was mentioned frequently by 17 subordinates and 6 supervisors. Whether it was a formal meeting or more casual interactions, supervisors and subordinates often shared ideas or insights, such as "We discussed the position of our company in the whole industry, the development of the industry, and our competitors."

Table 1: Communication Exchange Topics

Work Communication Exchange	$n_{W\ Sup}$	$n_{W\ Sub}$
Positive and neutral topics		
Company future, policy, and industry insight (e.g., company future, development, strategic plans; new government policies; competitors, markets)	17	6
Performance (e.g., performance, problems, and solutions)	26	10
Work re-arrangement (e.g., personal preferences on work adjustment and work tasks; other colleagues' and subordinates' work re-arrangements)	3	1
Work facilities (e.g., discussion of the change of office location; improving work environment, the workplace appearance which is presented to the customers)	15	6
Negative topics		
Personnel change gossip (e.g., company executives' or colleagues' personnel change gossip)	4	2
Work complaint (e.g., other colleagues' poor performance and personalities; supervisors' problems; company structural problems, messy workflow, complicated procedures)	26	3
Social Communication Exchange		
Positive and neutral topics		
Activities (e.g., concerts, sports activities, shows, restaurants, shopping, sales discount)	12	4
Asset management (e.g., real estate purchasing, vehicles, financial investments)	13	3
Families and friends (e.g., children's education, family members' health condition, sweet family time, roommates, relationship with their friends)	18	6
Hobbies (e.g., film, books, TV shows, video games, favorite celebrities)	12	6
Hot social topics (e.g., social news, Covid-19, politics, US-China trade war)	8	2
Negative topics		
Non-work gossip (e.g., gossip related to celebrities or key opinion leaders, other colleagues, higher level supervisors, and company executives)	7	1
Venting about negative events in life (e.g., negative emotions, unpleasant life trivialities, or health problems)	3	-

Note. $n_{w\ Sup}$ denotes number of participants describing interactions with their supervisor. $n_{w\ Sub}$ denotes number of participants describing interactions with their own subordinates.

Performance. Supervisors discussed their subordinates' positive or negative performance and means of improvement. This topic was the most frequently mentioned by 26 subordinates and 10 supervisors. Supervisors sometimes initiated such interactions. They exchanged ideas on performance and gave instructions or solutions to the current conditions. During formal occasions, such as routine performance review meetings, a subordinate's performance was appraised by the supervisor.

Work Re-Arrangement. Work re-arrangement was occasionally mentioned by 3 subordinates and one supervisor through mutual communication process. This theme referred to the discussion between the supervisor and subordinate related to the change of personnel or work arrangement issues. Supervisors asked for ideas from the subordinates about their preferences and ideas on others' or their own positional changes or work content adjustment, such as "Before adjusting my work, we talked about my ideas and my preferences for the work direction and content".

Work Facility. Fifteen subordinates and six supervisors mentioned that they engaged in conversations about the working environment, conditions, and facilities, such as problems with furniture or other facility glitches. The supervisor asked for subordinates' ideas, or alternatively subordinates put forward suggestions to the supervisor – followed by constructive changes to the working environment including "We were planning to move to a new office. So, he asked about where to change and what to prepare for the new venue."

Negative Topics in Work Communication Exchange

Negative topics were not engaged with negative intent or to lead to negative consequences but were potentially negative to anyone in the communication dyad or others. To better understand negative topics, this study distinguished between gossip and complaints in the work communication exchange. Gossip generally denotes the discussion of others' personal experience, life events, or other issues that are not directly related to the gossipers (Kuo et al., 2015). Gossip pertaining to work communication thus involves others' work life matters or work behaviour not directly related to the supervisor or the subordinate. Complaints refers to talking about the supervisor's or subordinate's personal negative experiences and events related to work issues.

Personnel Change Gossip. Supervisors and subordinates exchanged gossip about personnel changes among the executives in their company. Four subordinates and two supervisors reported discussing personnel gossip with their supervisors. They shared the information during chitchat, including "I discuss with my subordinates and talk about the gossip around personnel change, such as who is leaving, or if there will be a new management trainee arriving, or the change of CEO."

Work Complaint. When conducting tasks and routine work, employees often encountered annoying people or problems. Subsequently, they would complain about these issues to express negative feelings and delineate the situation. Twenty-six subordinates and three supervisors mentioned such complaints in the workplace which, it was observed, were quite common. Typically, the complaint included three parts: complaining about colleagues, supervisors, and the company's structural problems, messy workflow, or complicated procedures, such as "I would complain to him [the supervisor] that my own interest was 'touched' [encroached on] by someone else, and he might help me to resolve this issue."

Social Communication Exchange (RQ3)

The second dimension of LMX-COMM is social communication exchange, which indicates mutual communication behaviours relating to non-work issues. Seven themes dimension emerged from the interview data, which were divided into two clusters: (a) positive or neutral social communication exchange, and (b) negative topics in social communication exchange (see Table 1 for a summary).

Positive or Neutral Social Communication Exchange

Activities. This theme denotes the mutual discussion or planning to participate in, or the logistics of joining, an activity. The supervisor and subordinate shared information on activities and provided leads to each other, such as concerts, sports activities, shows, updates on the restaurant, or shopping information. Twelve subordinates and four supervisors mentioned having discussed such activities.

Asset Management. Materialism has been a salient characteristic of Chinese culture – adults making conversations about asset management is quite commonplace (Awanis et al., 2017). Accordingly, interviewees mentioned their discussions on asset management, including real estate, vehicles, or financial investment issues, such as "In purchasing real estate properties, we chatted about which area offered the promise of high returns". This theme was often mentioned by older participants. Thirteen subordinates and three supervisors said that they shared this information in the supervisor-subordinate dyads.

Families and Friends. Eighteen subordinates and six supervisors mentioned frequent conversations about their family members and friends in casual dyadic conversations, including family activities, relationships, children's education, family problems, activities with friends, and social relationships.

Hobbies. Twelve subordinates and six supervisors reported hobby-related topics in dyadic communication, which included travel, films, books, TV shows, video games, and following favorite celebrities, and topics that included involved personal preferences and lifestyle activities.

"Hot" Social Topics. During informal dyadic conversations between supervisors and subordinates, topical social issues were often discussed. They engaged in conversations on – and sometimes debated – political issues, international relations, epidemics, social events, and local news, among others. Eight subordinates and two supervisors reported such topics and said that both parties contributed their viewpoints or new information.

Negative Topics in Social Communication Exchange

Non-Work Gossip. Participants (7 subordinates and 1 supervisor) mentioned that they occasionally shared gossips which was not directly related to work – often related to a particular company executive's personal life or the interesting life experience of an acquaintance – with their supervisor or subordinates, including "We talked about how our Chairman cheated on his wife, and this has been a hot topic on social media."

Venting About Negative Events in Life. Participants mentioned venting or complaining about non-work issues to their supervisor or subordinates, such as their negative life events, romantic relationships, and health conditions, "we often discuss our boyfriend and complain about their problems".

Tangible Work Exchange (RQ4)

Tangible work exchange denotes the exchange of services, compensation, and rewards that are related to work tasks to serve organizational goals (Sheer, 2015). Three tangible work exchange themes emerged from the interview data (see Table 2).

Table 2: Tangible Exchange Behaviours

Tangible Work Exchange	$n_{W\ Sup}$	$n_{W\ Sub}$
Covering workload (e.g., covering the workload for each other, doing the unfinished work for each other)	12	8
Compensatory time-off (e.g., giving time off after working overtime, reducing work amount after intensive workload)	8	3
Work help (e.g., helping to tackle with technical problems, helping to finish the other's work)	28	8
Tangible Social Exchange		
Partaking in after-work drinks and meals (e.g., inviting each other to after-work drinks and meals)	14	7
Attending special occasions (e.g., attending each other's or each other's family members' wedding, baby shower, funeral, graduation, and birthday)	5	2
Participating in leisure activities (e.g., attending entertainment activities together such as concerts, exercise walks, museum visits, karaoke, and gaming)	12	3
Giving gifts and treats (e.g., giving each other small gifts, red packets; treating each other to small snacks, drinks, bubble tea, or meals)	24	10
Helping with personal matters unrelated to work (e.g., helping one another with personal problems and issues, sharing *guanxi* [personal networks], finding a doctor)	12	9
Introducing families and friends (e.g., introducing family members and friends to each other)	9	4

Note. $n_{w\ Sup}$ denotes number of participants describing interactions with their supervisor. $n_{w\ Sub}$ denotes number of participants describing interactions with their own subordinates.

Covering Workload

Twelve subordinates and eight supervisors said they covered the workload for their supervisor or subordinate when the need arose which may be viewed as reciprocity of favors pertaining to work. Some offers were voluntarily extended when one party noticed the need of the other; sometimes the supervisor or the subordinate explicitly requested help, as in the case of a project delay.

Compensatory Time-Off

Eight subordinates and three supervisors mentioned compensatory time-off issues. When subordinates had to work overtime or their working schedule was too intensive, the supervisor occasionally provided time off as a form of compensation or exchange – where one puts in extra work time now in exchange for time off later.

Work Help

In the daily work routine, extending help on work issues between supervisors and subordinates is inevitable, as mentioned by 28 subordinates and 8 supervisors. Extending help, such as "My boss helped in communicating with some suppliers that I did not know", differs from covering each other's workload in that helping entails a limited aspect of a task; by contrast, covering work entails doing the entire work for the individual, such as "My boss bargained a good deal for me." Work help may be exchanged as it is reciprocated later. Such help may be solicited by the subordinate or the supervisor, or proactively extended without an explicit request.

Tangible Social Exchange (RQ5)

The final dimension of LMX-COMM is *tangible social exchange*, which denotes the exchange of tangible commodities, gifts, or favors to facilitate social relationships that do not pertain to work tasks. Six themes of tangible social exchange were frequently mentioned in the interviews.

Partaking in After-Work Drinks or Meals

After-work drinks or meals were commonly mentioned by participants, 14 subordinates and seven supervisors, who reported their experiences of inviting and joining each other for drinks or dinner after work. In the process of engaging in such activities, both parties contributed to the relationship. It is normal for those who have a good relationship with their supervisor or subordinates to have a drink or a meal after work in Chinese organizations.

Attending Special Occasions

In any culture, attending personal events of significance represents interpersonal closeness and social courtesy (Yick & Gupta, 2002). Five subordinates and two supervisors mentioned that they attended each other's or family members' special occasions with their supervisors and subordinates. Commemorations, celebrations, or ceremonies cited in the interviews included weddings, newborn parties, funerals, and graduations. Apart from their attendance at these events, participants would give a red (money) packet or money on the side to signal politeness or best wishes. In Chinese culture, the recipient is normally expected to reciprocate social courtesy by attending special occasions and/or giving a red packet in return.

Participating in Leisure Activities

Twelve subordinates and three supervisors reported engaging in mutual leisure activities, including entertainment, such as watching movies and karaoke, or sports, such as hiking.

Giving Gifts and Treats

Twenty-four subordinates and ten supervisors reported that they had exchanged small gifts or red packets and treated each other to drinks, snacks, or meals. Although these may occur in conjunction with the two earlier mentioned themes – partaking in after-work drinks or meals and attending special occasions – it entails less mutual communication or invitation on the part of the recipient. Moreover, the recipient may not necessarily reciprocate the gift or treat immediately or in an equivalent form such as giving the person some snacks in return for treating them to a meal.

Helping with Personal Matters Unrelated to Work

Several participants mentioned that they had provided (received) a personal favor to (from) their supervisor and subordinates. When encountering problems in their personal lives, it was not uncommon for participants to ask their supervisor or subordinates for help; a favor that they would return in some way later. Typically, these personal favors entailed tapping into the other party's social connections and resources such as locating an acquaintance in hospital or obtaining a discount on one's real estate purchase.

Introducing Families and Friends

The leader-member dyad would introduce their family members and friends to each other. Nine subordinates and four supervisors revealed having had such interactions. These participants highlighted the good relationships with their supervisor or subordinates as the basis for introducing their family members or friends to each other, which typically occurred during a special occasion or leisure activity.

Communication Channels (RQ6)

Four main communication channels were identified: email, face-to-face, voice call, and social media. Face-to-face was the most frequently mentioned communication channel and mentioned by all participants. Social media and instant messaging were the next most frequently cited channels. Only one of the subordinates failed to mention communication via social media. Certain communication channels served more as formal communication tools to support the work between the supervisor and subordinates (work communication), while some channels further served social communication ends (see Table 3).

Table 3: Communication Channels Used

Communication Channels	$n_{w\ Sup}$	$n_{w\ Sup}$
Email (normally used by foreign or joint venture companies) Work communication (e.g., sharing instructions, files, and formal information, mass routine emails; remote communication such as from home or a remote office)	11	3
Face-to-face (used in all organizations) Work Communication (e.g., delivering tasks, giving instructions, making comments, performance review, promotion notifications) Social Communication (e.g., chitchat in office, at lunch, or after work)	33	15
Voice call Work Communication (e.g., delivering work tasks, summoning somebody, informing and discussing emergencies, when working from home/remote offices)	8	3
Social media apps	31	9
Internal social media applications (mostly used in by technology companies)	5	–
Skype (used in multinational companies)	1	1
WeChat (widely used in Mainland Chinese organizations)	27	8
WhatsApp (used in Hong Kong companies)	2	–
Work Communication (e.g., assigning and discussing tasks, giving instructions, sharing files, giving feedback) Social Communication (e.g., chitchats, after-work social communication)		

Note. $n_{w\ Sup}$ denotes number of participants describing interactions with their supervisor. $n_{w\ Sub}$ denotes number of participants describing interactions with their own subordinates.

Emails

Only a third (n = 11) of the interviewed subordinates and three supervisors mentioned that they had used emails for mutual communication as they regarded email as a formal channel. Emails were used by supervisors and subordinates primarily to exchange files, feedback, tasks, notifications, and reminders. Participants also mentioned that email exchanges facilitated communication when individuals were not available or onsite, as when working from home or within a global office. Several participants, however, mentioned that they seldom used email at work or had only started using emails while working from home owing to the Covid-19 pandemic.

Face-to-Face

The most traditional communication channel – in-person or face-to-face communication – was mentioned as a conduit for discussing work-related tasks and issues along with social topics and non-work issues, which occurred both at the workplace or after work. Face-to-face communication was observed to be limited by spatial considerations. Ten subordinates and one supervisor attributed their frequency of in-person communication to their being seated nearby in the office.

Voice Calls

Telephone calls represent a traditional communication channel that has been given a technological update via mobile and smartphone applications. Voice calls via mobile phones and smartphone applications (most notably WeChat) enable individuals to contact each other across different locales, facilitating working remotely and from home. Despite its longstanding status, however, voice calls were the least mentioned communication channel by participants (eight subordinates and three supervisors) and were comprised entirely of work communication exchanges. Participants indicated that they would not interact socially (i.e., engage in social communication exchanges) with their supervisors or subordinates via voice calls. Several participants even reported that they would only make voice calls for urgent matters.

Social Media and Instant Messaging

Social media and instant messaging were the second most frequently mentioned communication channels by 31subordinates and 9 supervisors. Apart from the publicly accessible apps (WeChat, Skype, and WhatsApp), participants reported using internal social media applications developed by their organization. WeChat messaging was the most frequently mentioned application. Owing to differences in social media ecology, only participants based in Hong Kong reported using Skype and WhatsApp to communicate with each other, whereas WeChat was mentioned by participants from all regions, including Hong Kong.

Discussion

The four-dimensional framework appears to be a relatively comprehensive typology for understanding LMX behaviours as no additional dimension that did not already fit into the four dimensions emerged.

Centrality of Communication in Leader-Member Interaction

Communication elements were embedded in the themes of each dimension of the LMX-COMM framework. Even during tangible exchanges, communication enabled activities such as participating in social events and exchanging favors and gifts. Communication facilitated all leader-member interactions in daily work-related issues, social discussions, and even physical activities. For example, according to participants, many discussions occurred during after-work drinks and meals – activities that could not independently occur without communication. Reinforcing prior studies (De Vries et al., 2009), this study underscores the essential role of communication in leadership and leader-member interactions needed for organizations to perform (see Tourish, 2014).

Negative Topics in Communication Exchange

As an incremental contribution to the literature, this study explored several negative topics (e.g., gossip and complaints) that were infrequently discussed in previous LMX studies. Gossip and complaints, which are potentially negative to anyone in the communication dyad and anyone else mentioned in the conversation, were often described in the interviews as "sensitive topics" in the communication process. Complaining about someone regarding work issues was the most frequently mentioned topic, over three-quarters of the interviewed subordinates mentioned such complaints. It was observed that gossip and complaints were often initiated by the supervisor, and the subordinate normally only shared information or ideas after their supervisor did so.

Sometimes, discussing sensitive or negative topics related to others can indicate a socially proximate relationship among the discussants with a certain degree of mutual trust (Ellwardt et al., 2012; Kuo et al., 2018). Several participants indicated that they had a close relationship with their supervisor and co-complained about other colleagues' bad performance. This finding is consistent with Kuo et al.'s (2018) research – one of the few LMX studies on negative topics – that workplace gossip and complaints were positively related to the quality of their exchange relationships.

Conversely, negative gossip may lead to negative service performance (e.g., Ye et al., 2019). In extreme cases, excessive discussions of problems may induce burnout and depression (Boren, 2014; Haggard et al., 2011). As such, discussing negative topics represents ambivalent communication behaviour for individuals or organizations. Given that LMX theory generally specifies direct relationships between LMX and outcomes, the discussion of negative topics poses a challenge to the extant theory on whether it should be categorized as a desirable LMX behaviour.

Leader-Member Communication in Chinese Organizations

The findings in this study demonstrate the applicability of the four-dimensional structure of the LMX-COMM model to Chinese organizations. Overall, all thematic topics of communication behaviours mentioned by participants are fully accounted for by the four facets. Nevertheless, relatively distinctive socio-cultural aspects of leader-member communication in Chinese organizations were observed in the type and frequency of social communication exchange, tangible social exchange, and communication channels used. Inevitably, the types of conversational topics and personal concerns differ across various societies and cultures. For instance, buying a house is a major goal among Chinese people, and it is reflected in their social communication and tangible social exchanges. More noticeably, the exchange of red packets is a well-established cultural practice in Chinese societies and is manifested within the tangible social exchange between supervisors and subordinates. Beyond sociocultural practices, the media ecology of the social system inevitably shapes the communication channel used. The findings in this study point to the less frequent use of emails in Chinese organizations and greater use of social media apps, particularly WeChat.

Communication Channels in Leader-Member Exchange

In previous LMX studies, the study context or the basic assumption was that communication was completed face-to-face, such that the effects of different communication channels on exchange content and outcomes were seldom examined. With the transformation of organizations, virtual teams, remote offices, and working from home are increasingly common (Hoch & Dulebohn, 2017) while mediated communication without face-to-face interaction is a reality. In today's organizations, new technologies have allowed leaders and subordinates to exchange messages anywhere and anytime with the help of mediated communication channels (Braun et al., 2019).

Our findings underscore that social media and instant messaging are commonly used in Chinese organizations, gradually becoming a daily work necessity (in delivering tasks, commenting, and sharing files) and fostering social communication (including small talk and gossip), while conveying immediate responses and information between both sides of the communication dyad. In this vein, participants praised the synchronicity of social media and instant messaging, especially when comparing emails to social media. Owing to the design of social media which encourages social sharing, informal communication tends to dramatically increase. Not surprisingly, participants generally reported using only email and voice calls for work communication between supervisors and subordinates and social media for non-work communication.

The extant literature has routinely identified emails as one of the most frequently mentioned communication channels and treated it as an integral element of their work routine (D'Urso & Pierce, 2009). Only a few participants reported using email as a work communication channel. Several reasons have been identified. First, many participants suggested that they did not know how to craft an email properly, and thus were less willing to use email to communicate. Second, participants seemed to be concerned that emails could become records of formal communication that could "come back to haunt me" if they said something wrong. This was particularly relevant when mutual trust levels were low. Third, participants generally expressed a greater preference for, and a higher comfort level with, informal over formal communication. Given that intensive task-oriented discussions might be needed in work communication, emails as a form of formal communication could be too cumbersome to facilitate efficient dialogues. Lastly, participants pointed to the accessibility and widespread adoption of alternative channels for work communication; most notably, the features of social media and instant messaging – such as text, audio, video, images, and documents – facilitated richer information exchange and thus more than adequately substituted for the work functions of email.

Further Developments in LMX-COMM

Our current findings suggest areas for further developments in the LMX-COMM framework. The extant LMX theories, including LMX-COMM, generally assume that leader-member exchange leads to positive employee and organizational outcomes, and the leader-member dyadic interactions described in those frameworks are either positive, neutral, and rational (as in solving work-related issues or problems), rather than negative behaviours. The negative exchange behaviours reported in our interviews necessitate the consideration of how such behaviours can fit with the LMX-COMM model. One solution is to explicitly define the theoretical scope to improve theoretical congruence (Fawcett, 2005). Bacharach's (1989) classical essay advocates that the explanatory power of a theory stems from clearly defined conditions under which the theory functions. In this case, the LMX-COMM can identify positive, neutral, and rational interactions as LMX-desirable behaviours that lead to positive outcomes. In addition, negative acts can be defined as LMX-adverse behaviours that managers and employees should be trained to avoid. Negative behaviours such as gossip, complaints, and co-rumination have already been studied within organizational communication areas that are independent of the LMX literature. Separating those from LMX-desirable behaviours allows conceptual clarity; otherwise, LMX will be too encompassing to be meaningful in guiding management practices.

The uses of certain types of media or communication channels warrant further development in the LMX-COMM framework. The challenge is to identify (a) whether certain exchange interactions are related to the use of particular media, and (b) how media use can facilitate effective LMX interactions. Because a theory is only as good as its practical application, the recognition of conducive media used for LMX can certainly enhance modern-day management practices.

Implications for Leadership Communication Practice

Our findings can help facilitate leadership training in organizations. Several actionable implications are provided in identifying the type of leader-member communication behaviours under each dimension of LMX-COMM for better employee outcomes. Our findings underscore the importance of information sharing between supervisors and subordinates in facilitating organizational learning. Discussions on the industry, company future, competitor information, or performance directly help employees gain greater insights into the industry and work problems, as well as enabling them to adjust their work appropriately. Beyond work-related communication, social communication exchange – which tends to be underemphasized – can also play a significant role in developing and maintaining supervisor-subordinate relationships. Casual and leisure activities are important unofficial avenues for social communication that connects supervisors and subordinates in off-work settings. In addition, as the exchange of favors is a social norm in Chinese culture, exhibiting and communicating appropriate helping behaviours is an essential ingredient for satisfactory leader-member relationships.

Limitations and Future Research Directions

Owing to the social distancing measures vis-à-vis the Covid-19 pandemic, the interviews in this study were conducted via WeChat rather than in person, and participants were either not currently working or working remotely from home. These circumstances might have affected the salience of certain issues (such as the communication channels used). Although participants were asked to identify the communication channels used during leader-member interactions, we acknowledge that not all themes of leader-member interaction behaviour were explicitly linked to a certain type of communication channel.

While the number of supervisors and subordinates who mentioned each theme was noted, the frequency with which they were mentioned was not measured or compared, thus the themes mentioned most were not automatically regarded as salient within each dimension. The salience of communication behaviours within each LMX-COMM facet should be examined in future research via quantitative designs. Accordingly, the findings in this study, with the identified dimensional themes, can help inform the development of a scale to measure the different facets of LMX-COMM, which in turn can be used in future quantitative studies to test the relationships among LMX, organizational outcomes, and communication channels. Future qualitative research should further investigate how the contextual characteristics of organizational hierarchical culture, communication climate, and industry sector influence LMX-COMM behaviours.

In conclusion, we identify 22 themes of LMX communication interactions that fit well within the four dimensions of LMX-COMM. We further draw attention to the presence of negative topics in LMX and their ambivalent role in employee outcomes. The findings also contribute to a better understanding of how different communication channels were used in leader-member dyads within Chinese organizations. These findings facilitate future theoretical developments in the LMX-COMM conceptual framework.

References

Avolio, B. J., Sosik, J. J., Kahai, S. S., & Baker, B. (2014). E-leadership: Re-examining Transformations in Leadership Source and Transmission. *The Leadership Quarterly 25*, 105–131. Retrieved from: https://doi.org/10.1016/j.leaqua.2013.11.003.

Awanis, S., Schlegelmilch, B.B. & Cui, C.C. (2017). Asia's Materialists: Reconciling Collectivism and Materialism. *Journal of International Business Studies 48,* 964–991. https://doi.org/10.1057/s41267-017-0096-6

Bacharach, S. B. (1989). Organizational Theories: Some Criteria for Evaluation. *The Academy of Management Review, 14*(4), 496–515. https://doi.org/10.2307/258555

Bauer, T. N., & Erdogan, B. (2015). Leader-member Exchange (LMX) Theory: An Introduction and Overview. In T. N. Bauer & B. Erdogan (Eds.), *The Oxford Handbook of Leader-Member Exchange* (pp. 1–10). New York, NY: Oxford University Press.

Bauer, T. N., Erdogan, B., Liden, R. C., & Wayne, S. J. (2006). A Longitudinal Study of the Moderating Role of Extraversion: Leader-member Exchange, Performance, and Turnover During New Executive Development. *Journal of Applied Psychology, 91*, 298–310. Retrieved from: https://doi.org/10.1037/0021-9010.91.2.298.

Begley, K. A. (2004). *Face-to-Face Communication: Making Human Connections in Technology-Driven World.* Boston, MA: Thompson Learning.

Boren, J. P. (2014). The Relationships between Co-rumination, Social Support, Stress, and Burnout among Working Adults. *Management Communication Quarterly, 28*(1), 3–25. Retrieved from: https://doi.org/10.1177/0893318913509283.

Braun, S., Hernandez Bark, A., Kirchner, A., Stegmann, S., & Van Dick, R. (2019). Emails from the Boss – Curse or Blessing? Relations between Communication Channels, Leader Evaluation, and Employees' Attitudes. *International Journal of Business Communication 56*(1), 50–81. Retrieved from: https://doi.org/10.1177/2329488415597516.

Braun, V., & Clarke, V. (2006). Using Thematic Analysis in Psychology. *Qualitative Research in Psychology, 3*(2), 77–101. Retrieved from: https://doi.org/10.1191/1478088706qp063oa.

Burns, J., & Otte, F. (1999). Implications Of Leader-Member Exchange Theory and Research for Human Resource Development Research. *Human Resource Development Quarterly 10*(3), 225–248. https://doi.org/10.1002/hrdq.3920100304.

Chu, T. H. (2020). A Meta-analytic Review of the Relationship between Social Media Use and Employee Outcomes. *Telematics and Informatics, 50*, 101379. Retrieved from: https://doi.org/10.1016/j.tele.2020.101379.

Dansereau, F., Graen, G. B., & Haga, W. J. (1975). A Vertical Dyad Linkage Approach to Leadership Within Formal Organizations: A Longitudinal Investigation of the Role Making Process. *Organizational Behaviour and*

Human Performance, 13, 46–78. Retrieved from: https://doi.org/10.1016/0030-5073(75)90005-7.

Dulebohn, J., Bommer, W., Liden, R. C., Brouer, R., & Ferris, G. (2012). A Meta-Analysis of Antecedents and Consequences of Leader-Member Exchange: Integrating the Past with an Eye Toward the Future. *Journal of Management, 38*(6), 1715–1759. Retrieved from: https://doi.org/10.1177/0149206311415280.

D'Urso, S. C., & Pierce, K. M. (2009). Connected to the Organization: A Survey of Communication Technologies in the Modern Organizational Landscape. *Communication Research Reports, 26*(1), 75–81. https://doi.org/10.1080/08824090802637098.

Ellwardt, L., Wittek, R., & Wielers, R. (2012). Talking about the Boss: Effects of Generalized and Interpersonal Trust on Workplace Gossip. *Group & Organization Management, 37(*4), 521–549. https://doi.org/10.1177/1059601112450607.

Erdogan, B., & Bauer, T. N. (2010). Differentiated Leader–Member Exchanges: The Buffering Role of Justice Climate. *Journal of Applied Psychology, 95*(6), 1104–1120. Retrieved from: https://doi.org/10.1037/a0020578.

Erdogan, B., & Enders, J. (2007). Support from the Top: Supervisors' Perceived Organizational Support as a Moderator of Leader-Member Exchange to Satisfaction and Performance Ratings. *Journal of Applied Psychology, 92*, 321–330. Retrieved from: https://doi.org/10.1037/0021-9010.92.2.321.

Erdogan, B., & Liden, R. C. (2002). Social Exchanges in the Workplace: A Review of Recent Developments and Future Research Directions in Leader-Member Exchange Theory. In L. L. Neider & C. A. Schriesheim (Eds.), *Leadership* (pp. 65–114). Greenwich, CT: Information Age Pressing.

Fairhurst, G. T. (2010). *The Power of Framing: Creating the Language of Leadership*. San Francisco: Jossey-Bass.

Fawcett, J. (2005). Criteria for Evaluation ofTtheory. *Nursing Science Quarterly, 18(2)*, 131–135.

Graen, G. B., & Cashman, J. (1975). A Role-Making Model of Leadership in Formal Organizations: A Development Approach. In J. G. Hunt & L. L. Larson (Eds.), *Leadership Frontiers* (pp. 143–165). Kent, OH: Kent State University Press.

Graen, G. B., & Uhl-Bien, M. (1995). Relationship-Based Approach to Leadership: Development of Leader-Member Exchange (LMX) Theory of Leadership Over 25 Years: Applying a Multi-Level Multi-Domain Perspective. *The Leadership Quarterly, 6*, 219–247. Retrieved from: https://doi.org/10.1016/1048-9843(95)90036-5.

Haggard, D. L., Robert, C., & Rose, A. J. (2011). Co-Rumination in the Workplace: Adjustment Trade-Offs for Men and Women Who Engage in Excessive Discussions of Workplace Problems. *Journal of Business and Psychology, 26*(1), 27–40. Retrieved from: https://doi.org/10.1007/s10869-010-9169-2.

Hoch, J. E., & Dulebohn, J. H. (2017). Team Personality Composition, Emergent Leadership and Shared Leadership in Virtual Teams: A Theoretical Framework. *Human Resource Management Review, 27*(4), 678–693. Retrieved from: https://doi.org/10.1016/j.hrmr.2016.12.012.

Junker, N. M., & van Dick, R. (2014). Implicit Theories in Organizational Settings: A Systematic Review and Research Agenda of Implicit Leadership and Followership Theories. *The Leadership Quarterly, 25*(6), 1154–1173. Retrieved from: https://doi.org/10.1016/j.leaqua.2014.09.002.

Kelley, K. M., & Bisel, R. S. (2014). Leaders' Narrative Sensemaking during LMX Role Negotiations: Explaining How Leaders Make Sense of Who to Trust and When. *The Leadership Quarterly, 25*(3), 433–448. https://doi.org/10.1016/j.leaqua.2013.10.011.

Kelly, S. (2008). Leadership: A Categorical Mistake? *Human Relations, 61*(6), 763–782. Retrieved from: https://doi.org/10.1177/0018726708092403.

Kim, B., & George, R. T. (2005). The Relationship between Leader-Member Exchange (LMX) and Psychological Empowerment: A Quick Casual Restaurant Employee Correlation Study. *Journal of Hospitality & Tourism Research, 29*(4), 468–483. Retrieved from: https://doi.org/10.1177/1096348005276498.

Kim, B., Lee, G., & Carlson, K. D. (2010). An Examination of the Nature of the Relationship between Leader-Member Exchange (LMX) and Turnover Intent at Different Organizational Levels. *International Journal of Hospitality Management, 29*, 591–597. Retrieved from: https://doi.org/10.1016/j.ijhm.2009.10.025.

Kuo, C.-C., Chang, K., Quinton, S., Lu, C.-Y., & Lee, I. (2015) Gossip in the Workplace and the Implications for HR Management: A Study of Gossip and Its Relationship to Employee Cynicism. *The International Journal of Human Resource Management, 26:18*, 2288–2307, doi: 10.1080/09585192.2014.985329

Kuo, C. C., Wu, C.-Y., & Lin, C.-W. (2018). Supervisor Workplace Gossip and Its Impact on Employees. *Journal of Managerial Psychology, 33*(1), 93–105. Retrieved from: https://doi.org/10.1108/jmp-04-2017-0159.

Le Blanc, P. M., & González-Romá, V. (2012). A Team Level Investigation of the Relationship between Leader–Member Exchange (LMX) Differentiation, and Commitment and Performance. *The Leadership Quarterly, 23*(3), 534–544. Retrieved from: https://doi.org/10.1016/j.leaqua.2011.12.006.

Lee, C. E. (2010). Face-to-Face versus Computer-Mediated Communication: Exploring Employees' Preference of Effective Employee Communication Channel. *International Journal for the Advancement of Science & Arts, 1*(2), 38–48.

Lee, C. E. (2011). Computer-mediated Communication and Organisational Communication: The Use of New Communication Technology in the Workplace. *The Journal of the South East Asia Research Center for Communication and Humanities, 3*, 1–12.

Lee, K., & Chae, Y. J. (2017). LMX Differentiation, Diversity, and Group Performance. *Career Development International, 22*(2), 106–123. Retrieved from: https://doi.org/10.1108/cdi-11-2015-0154.

Lee, Y., Kozar, K., & Larsen, K. (2005). Does Avatar Email Improve Communication? *Communications of the ACM, 48*, 91–95. Retrieved from: https://doi.org/10.1145/1101779.1101782.

Levi, D. (2017). *Group Dynamics for Teams*. Thousand Oaks, CA: Sage.

Martin, R., Guillaume, Y., Thomas, G., Lee, A., & Epitropaki, O. (2016). Leader–Member Exchange (LMX) and Performance: A Meta-Analytic Review. *Personnel Psychology 69*(1), 67–121. Retrieved from: https://doi.org/10.1111/peps.12100.

Northouse, P. G. (2019). *Introduction to Leadership: Concepts and Practice*. Thousand Oaks, CA: Sage.

Omilion-Hodges, L. M., Ptacek, J. K., & Zerilli, D. H. (2016). A Comprehensive Review and Communication Research Agenda of the Contextualized Workgroup: The Evolution and Future of Leader-Member Exchange, Coworker Exchange, and Team-Member Exchange. *Annals of the International Communication Association, 40*(1), 343–377. Retrieved from: https://doi.org/10.1080/23808985.2015.11735265.

Rockstuhl, T., Dulebohn, J. H., Ang, S., & Shore, L. M. (2012). Leader–Member Exchange (LMX) and Culture: A Meta-Analysis of Correlates of LMX across 23 Countries. *Journal of Applied Psychology, 97*(6), 1097. https://doi.org/10.1037/a0029978.

Sheer, V. C. (2015). "Exchange lost" in Leader–Member Exchange Theory and Research: A Critique and a Reconceptualization. *Leadership, 11*(2), 213–229. Retrieved from: https://doi.org/10.1177/1742715014530935.

Sin, H. P., Nahrgang, J. D., & Morgeson, F. P. (2009). Understanding Why They Don't See Eye to Eye: An Examination of Leader–Member Exchange (LMX) Agreement. *Journal of Applied Psychology, 94*(4), 1048. Retrieved from: https://doi.org/10.1037/a0014827.

Smith, S. A., Patmos, A., & Pitts, M. J. (2018). Communication and Teleworking: A Study of Communication Channel Satisfaction, Personality, and Job Satisfaction for Teleworking Employees. *International Journal of Business Communication, 55*(1), 44–68. Retrieved from: https://doi.org/10.1177/2329488415589101.

Tourish, D. (2014). Leadership, More or Less? A Processual, Communication Perspective on the Role of Agency in Leadership Theory. *Leadership, 10*(1), 79–98. Retrieved from: https://doi.org/10.1177/1742715013509030.

Turnage, A. K., & Goodboy, A. K. (2016). E-mail and Face-to-Face Organizational Dissent as a Function of Leader-Member Exchange Status. *International Journal of Business Communication, 53*, 271–285. Retrieved from: https://doi.org/10.1177/2329488414525456.

Turner, T., Qvarfordt, P., Biehl, J. T., Golovchinsky, G., & Back, M. (2010, April). Exploring the Workplace Communication Ecology. In *Proceedings of the SIGCHI Conference on Human Factors in Computing Systems* (pp. 841–850). New York, NY: ACM Press.

Ye, Y., Zhu, H., Deng, X., & Mu, Z. (2019). Negative Workplace Gossip and Service Outcomes: An Explanation from Social Identity Theory. *International Journal of Hospitality Management, 82*, 159–168. Retrieved from: https://doi.org/10.1016/j.ijhm.2019.04.020.

Yick, A. G., & Gupta, R. (2002). Chinese Cultural Dimensions of Death, Dying, and Bereavement: Focus Group Findings. *Journal of Cultural Diversity, 9*(2), 32–42.

Yu, A., Matta, F. K., & Cornfield, B. (2018). Is Leader–Member Exchange Differentiation Beneficial or Detrimental for Group Effectiveness? A Meta-Analytic Investigation and Theoretical Integration. *Academy of Management Journal, 61*(3), 1158–1188. Retrieved from: https://doi.org/10.5465/amj.2016.1212.

Yukl, G., Mahsud, R., Hassan, S., & Prussia, G. E. (2013). An Improved Measure of Ethical Leadership. *Journal of Leadership & Organizational Studies, 20*(1), 38–48. Retrieved from: https://doi.org/10.1177/1548051811429352 .

Introduction to Does Sex Stereotyping Explain Perceived Managerial Effectiveness after Communication Style and Leadership Style Are Considered?

By Vivian C. Sheer

The chapter focuses on the interrelationship of the communication styles associated with gender and leadership. Sheer points out while there are numerous studies focusing on the role of women in management positions, little has been published on if and how gender differences influence the communication of corporate leaders. This comes as a surprise since communication assumes a central role in management. That is why her study investigates the role of communication among female leaders to determine perceived managerial effectiveness in organizations in Hong Kong. High assertiveness is often associated with positive leadership because it is associated with task completion while low assertiveness is associated with weakness in leadership. Communication immediacy refers to supportive communication and enhances the motivation at the workplace. While men are generally considered to be more assertive than women, it seems that women use more immediate and supportive cues than men. It seems that stereotyping also plays a prominent role in the perceived effectiveness of male and female leadership because men tend to rate women leaders as less effective than male leaders. Even women often consider males to be more effective leaders than women managers. That is why Sheer invested the interrelationship of the communication style with the leadership style and sex stereotyping to predict the perceived male and female leaders' effectiveness. The study revealed that communication immediacy is more important than assertiveness when it comes to the perceived effectiveness of leaders. Sex stereotyping, though, does not seem to play a significant role. This also indicates that communication skills are an important aspect of leadership and, thus, ought to be considered when educating and training leaders.

Michael B. Hinner

Vivian C. Sheer (Ph.D., University of Florida) is a Professor in the Department of Communication Studies, School of Communication, Hong Kong Baptist University. Trained in the empirical tradition of the social sciences, Prof. Sheer employs a variety of methods and measures in her research. She has published works in theory development, measurement assessment, and applied communication. Her applied research areas include organizational communication (e.g., leadership behaviors and workplace interactions) and health communication (e.g., antismoking interventions and AIDS/HIV prevention). The research designs she used include surveys, experiments, focus groups, in-depth interviews, and content analysis. Most of her publications are included in the Social Sciences Citation Index. She has served on six editorial boards of scholarly journals. Currently, she is an editorial board member of *Journal of Communication, Leadership (Sage), and Management Communication Quarterly.*

Vivian C. Sheer

Does Sex Stereotyping Explain Perceived Managerial Effectiveness after Communication Style and Leadership Style Are Considered?

Effective leadership is a key ingredient in determining organizational success (Salahuddin, 2011). Women's participation in the workforce has resulted in an increase in female managers in organizations, although top female executives remain few compared to top male executives (Grant Thornton, 2016). In China, 64 % of women participated in the labor force in 2014 (International Labour Organization, 2017). In Hong Kong, women occupy 50.8 % of the workforce (Census and Statistics Department of Hong Kong SAR, 2016) and hold over 30 % of management positions across various sectors (Women's Commission, 2019). In particular, Carrie Lam is the first woman to hold the top office of Chief Executive of Hong Kong. Thus, the contemporary concept of organizational leadership inevitably consists of both male and female leaders; gender has emerged as an important factor in understanding leadership (Leitch & Stead, 2016). Although perceptions of leadership as a predominantly masculine activity are beginning to change (Rhee & Sigler, 2015), female and male managers' effectiveness can however be evaluated differently.

Although much research has examined sex stereotyping and managerial effectiveness, the role of communication in the leadership process has received little attention (Sheer, 2015). With the broad keywords of "gender/sex stereotyping" and "leader/manager effectiveness," a recent search via ProQuest of PsychInfo and the ABI/INFORM Collection across the past 50 years yielded only 108 relevant published citations. These studies examined (a) descriptive characteristics of sex stereotypes of managers, (b) the relationships between sex/gender (role) stereotypes and manager attributes such as cognition and personality, (c) sex stereotyping and leadership characteristics and perceptions of managers, and (d) sex stereotyping, women's career development, and gender disparity/discrimination. Surprisingly, no published study investigated sex stereotyping in relationship to managers' communication characteristics and managers' effectiveness. A search of Communication and Mass Media Complete resulted in only two studies that examined sex stereotyping and manager communication behavior (i.e., nonverbal communication in Remland et al., 1983 and conflict management behavior in Gayle, 1991). In the few studies on sex stereotyping, leadership, and managerial effectiveness, the interrelationships among the predictors of managerial effectiveness were not examined (e.g., Crites et al., 2015). Given the central role of communication in leadership from the perspective of organizational communication, the current study was designed to contribute to the literature by examining the interrelationships among communication style, leadership style, and sex stereotyping in terms of their effects on perceived managerial effectiveness in organizations in Hong Kong.

Communication and Leadership

Organizational leadership is the process in which individuals (often managers) influence other people (e.g., subordinates) toward the attainment of defined group or organizational goals (Silva, 2016). Leadership derives not only from the manager's organizational position but through his/her communication with others (Matthew & Gilbert, 2009). Research indicates that communication affects leadership. For example, communication styles exerted a significant influence on leadership outcomes (Fan & Han, 2018; Reinout et al., 2010); managers who were sensitive to communication issues consistently obtained high ratings of leadership effectiveness (Brannon, 2011). Thus, communication plays an important role in leading to managerial effectiveness (Bao, 2009; Kerns, 2016; Marilyn, 2007).

Sex Differences, Communication Style, Leadership Style, and Managerial Effectiveness

The classical social role theory (Eagly, 1987) holds that men and women exhibit differences in their communication and leadership styles due to the gendered socialization process. In that process, men and women acquire culturally specific sex-linked personality and behavioral patterns and employ different communication styles (Mulac et al., 2001). Thus, their leadership effectiveness often differs (Herrera et al., 2013). In the context of sex difference and leadership processes, assertiveness and immediacy, the two gender-salient communication attributes, are frequently examined. Research reveals that male and female managers display differences in communication style. Case (1988), for example, discovered that women managers' communication patterns tended to be personal, facilitative, relational, and integrative, whereas men managers were more likely to be assertive, authoritarian, directive, depersonalized, and commanding.

Communication style can be understood via assertiveness and communication immediacy. ***Assertiveness*** refers to a general tendency or behavior that communicates interpersonal dominance, ascendance, and forcefulness (Dasgupta et al., 2012). Assertive communication enables an individual to act in his/her own best interests without denying or infringing upon the rights of others (Arredondo, 2003). Assertive people have strong intentions for domination and voicing opinions (Williams & Tiedens, 2016). Korsgaard, Roberson, and Rymph (1998) explained that managers' assertive communication involves stating his/her own position directly, clearly, and confidently and using nonverbal behavior to command attention from the listener to voice his/her opinions. Men tend to be more assertive, direct, and succinct, whereas women are less assertive, more indirect, and more elaborate (Popp et al., 2003). Women's less assertive language style encourages the other party to respond and facilitates rapport building but reflects tentativeness, which indicates a lack of authority (Lindsey & Zakahi, 2006). Men are more assertive and opinion-laden (Paustian-Underdahl et al., 2014). Assertiveness helps task completion, but low assertiveness is associated with perceived weakness in leadership, which can negatively affect managerial effectiveness.

Communication immediacy refers to the presence and strength of verbal or nonverbal cues. Nonverbal immediate cues include varied voice inflection, gestures, and postures such as sitting close, nodding, smiling, and being vocally expressive (Richmond & McCroskey, 2000). Verbal immediacy pertains to such attentive verbal behaviors as addressing the other party by his/her name, soliciting responses, using collective pronouns ("we" and "our"), and engaging in frequent conversations (Rocca, 2008). Taken together, immediate cues suggest a liking for and an interest in the other party and communicate personal involvement, whereas non-immediate cues imply otherwise (Burgoon & Hale, 1993). In the workplace, a supervisor's immediacy enhances his/her credibility and increases employees' motivation and sense of empowerment (Kelly et al., 2014). Immediate managers are perceived as interpersonally attractive and are viewed positively by subordinates (Hinkle, 2001). Thus, communication immediacy can enhance managerial effectiveness. Women supervisors, often exhibiting more immediate and supportive cues (Post, 2015), can be effective in management; conversely, male managers tend to be verbally direct and argumentative without much consideration of subordinates' reactions.

Leadership style. Leadership style pertains to a leader's behavioral (communicative or non-communicative) pattern with which he/she influences his/her subordinates to achieve group or organizational goals (2013). According to Leitch and Stead (2016), the most studied leadership style in the context of gender and managerial effectiveness is the autocratic-to-democratic continuum, which was initially proposed by White and Lippitt (1960). The researcher discovered that "participative leadership" was used more frequently to refer to the very same leadership behaviors described earlies as democratic leadership. Thus, the term "participative leadership" is adopted in this paper.

Autocratic leaders create and maintain a clear hierarchy with their subordinates. They tend to enact policy and procedures unilaterally and require their followers to observe the rules. They set the group goals on their own and control and dominate the discussion with followers. They also personally direct the completion of a task without informing their followers (Schoel et al., 2011). Autocratic leaders are likely to engage in assertive communication (Ndubueze & Akanni, 2015). ***Participative leaders*** tend to involve followers in goal setting and emphasize interaction within the group. They encourage involvement and participation in the process of achieving a goal (Cunningham et al., 2015), facilitate discussions with followers, and solicit input in setting policies and procedures. Participative leaders tend to display immediate communication behavior (Eken et al., 2014). Theoretically, participative leadership can enhance the productivity, satisfaction, and commitment of followers. Autocratic leadership is only effective in terms of output but is ineffective in enhancing relationships with followers, who are likely to experience dissatisfaction and low commitment. Sex differences in leadership style appear to parallel sex differences in communication style. For example, female managers tend to exhibit more participative leadership and less autocratic leadership than do their male counterparts (Bellou, 2011; Li et al., 2013). A woman's leadership style is more power sharing and interpersonally oriented, whereas a man's style is authority-based and task-oriented (Eagly et al., 2003; Stepp, 2000).

The literature review thus far has established that managers' communication style constitutes at least part of their leadership style, with sex differences resulting in different communication styles and subsequently leadership styles; different leadership styles lead to differences in managerial effectiveness. However, scholars contend that sex stereotyping, more so than sex difference, contributes to the evaluation of managerial effectiveness (e.g., Cuadrado et al., 2008; Maher, 1997).

Sex Stereotyping and Perceived Managerial Effectiveness

Stereotyping is defined as a general human tendency to categorize others' behaviors to predict the behaviors of others; sex/gender stereotyping, then, is the tendency to generalize an individual's abilities and limitations based on that individual's sex (Eagly & Mladinic, 1989). Such stereotyping sets a society's standards for determining maleness and femaleness (Eagly et al., 2003). Stereotyped male descriptors include aggressive, rational, independent, strong, rough, loud, blunt, insensitive, and competitive, whereas stereotyped descriptors of women include submissive, emotional, dependent, fragile, gentle, quiet, tactful, sensitive, and yielding (Heilman & Eagly, 2008). Sex stereotyping has many important implications in management settings.

Scholars concerned with sex stereotyping (e.g., Cuadrado et al., 2008; Maher, 1997) contend that such stereotyping has a considerable force in shaping people's perceptions of male versus female managers' effectiveness. Leadership is a masculine rather than a feminine concept (Koenig et al., 2011) such that sex stereotyping is said to result in fewer career advancement opportunities, less power, and lower status for women than for men (Eagly & Karau, 2002). Sex stereotyping can result in blind prejudice; for example, women managers' effectiveness is perceived as less than that of men managers regardless of leadership behavior. Research reveals that women's competence was rated lower than that of men (Eagly & Karau, 2002); even female subordinates preferred male managers (Cenkci & Ozcelik, 2015). Men were judged more favorably for the same performance as women (Wang et al., 2013), and male subordinates negatively rated female managers (Preko, 2012). Levels of sex stereotyping often determine an individual's view of managers. Men with a high level of sex stereotyping of women evaluated female leaders as less effective than male leaders (Preko, 2012; Roth et al., 2012). Traditional women, with a high degree of sex stereotyping, rated female managers less effective than did less traditional women (Johnson et al., 2008). Thus, sex stereotyping can result in differentiated evaluations of male and female managers' effectiveness.

Managerial Effectiveness

To reflect different aspects of managerial effectiveness, a multi-dimensional approach was used, and five key aspects were identified. The *first* aspect is performance management, because the manger's primary duty is to maintain and enhance subordinates' performance (Chauhan et al., 2005; Bamel et al., 2013). Managers often delegate responsibilities and provide directions to monitor and control subordinates' performance. The *second* aspect pertains to problem solving (Torres et al., 2015; Ruiz et al., 2013). Problem solving is the process by which managers individually or with others identify problems, generate alternatives, evaluate alternatives, and find solutions. The *third* aspect is planning (Anzengruber et al., 2017; William, 2007), which includes planning the future, adapting to change, planning for goal-achievement, and meeting schedules and deadlines. The *fourth* aspect is information provision (Georgiou, 2006; Smutny et al., 2016). Managers are responsible for relaying decisions from those above, articulating their own ideas, and providing feedback to subordinates. The *last* aspect is relationship management (Chauhan et al., 2005; Bamel et al., 2011, 2013; Torres et al., 2015), which includes initiating relationships, cooperating with others, resolving conflict, and maintaining relationships. Perceived managerial effectiveness in this study refers to subordinate perceptions of their managers' effectiveness on these five aspects.

The current research objective was to examine how three factors (communication style, leadership style, and sex stereotyping) can predict perceived male and female managers' effectiveness. Although the current literature review indicates that each of the three factors predicts perceived managerial effectiveness, little is known concerning how these likely predictors exert relative influences. Differently from the predominantly bivariate analysis between sex stereotyping and manager evaluation, of particular interest in the current study was whether sex stereotyping indeed explained any biased evaluation of managerial effectiveness after communication style and leadership style were considered first. Further, communication style, constitutive of leadership, should be considered ahead of leadership style. Three research questions were posed. The research setting was Hong Kong.

RQ1: Is male managers' effectiveness perceived differently from that of their female counterparts?

RQ2: Does sex stereotyping exert an influence on perceived male managers' effectiveness after communication style and leadership style are considered?

RQ3: Does sex stereotyping influence perceived female managers' effectiveness after communication style and leadership style are considered?

Methodology

Sample and Data Collection

A total of 300 questionnaires with an informed consent were distributed via a snowball method to people who held full-time jobs in organizations in Hong Kong. In the initial stage, 40 respondents were recruited via a university alumni network. These respondents each then distributed 5–10 questionnaires to other full-time employees in their personal networks. The screening question asked whether a respondent had worked for both male and female supervisors in the past two years, and only those who had were asked to proceed with the questionnaire. Of the 217 returned questionnaires, 11 questionnaires were discarded because the respondents had never worked for a female manager. The final sample size was 206. Of all respondents, 52.5 % were male, and 47.5 % were female. The mean age was 29.34 years old, ranging from 18 to 54. Approximately 3.5 % were high-level executives, 38.69 % were middle managers, and 57.9 % were low-level employees. Industry sectors consisted of manufacturing (16.7 %), service (41.7 %), government agencies (11.8 %), private nonprofit organizations (6.46 %), and other (23.5 %). Organizational ownerships were local shareholder-owned companies (34.8 %), Western subsidiaries (24.2 %), Asian subsidiaries (15.7 %), Chinese family enterprises (7.6 %), and nonprofit organizations and government agencies (17.3 %). Respondents recalled an average of 7.1 female managers and 10.7 male managers in their current Hong Kong facilities/organizations. That is, nearly 40 % of the managers were female in respondents' organizations.

Questionnaire

The questionnaire was initially written in English and was translated into Chinese, which was translated back into English. A bilingual communication professor resolved discrepancies. The finalized Chinese version was used for the survey. The questionnaire consisted of four parts. In the first part, respondents were asked to recall a male manager for whom they had worked directly in the past two years. They then rated their male managers' communication style, leadership style, and managerial effectiveness. In the second part, respondents recalled a female manager for whom they had directly worked in the past two years, and then rated her communication style, leadership style, and managerial effectiveness. The third part included sex-stereotyping items. The last part gathered respondents' demographic and organizational information that included respondent sex, age, organizational position, number of male managers, and number of female managers in the organization. To counterbalance possible order effects, one-half of the respondents ranked the male manager first and then ranked the female manger; the other one-half rated the male and the female managers in the reversed order.

Measurement

The reality of surveys given at respondents' own times and venues demands short, efficient measures to ensure that all or at least most of the items are rated (Sheer & Rice, 2017). To develop efficient and valid measures necessary for facilitating field surveys, scale development was conducted prior to the current survey. Modified from existing scales and/or culled from the relevant literature, 4 to 7 preliminary items were constructed for each of the following variables: assertiveness, immediacy, autocratic leadership, participative leadership, male stereotyping, female stereotyping, and the five dimensions of managerial effectiveness. Item content was examined by two management communication experts at the university. In a preliminary analysis of measurement, all of these items were rated and evaluated in an MA-in-Communication class with 26 part-time students, who were employees of different organizations. These students did not participate in the main survey. Their feedback was used to improve the measures used in the survey. To achieve a minimum of .70 for Cronbach's alpha, unreliable items were deleted to form a reliable scale. Significant intercorrelations among different variables ranged from .18 to .68, with an average of .38, indicating relative independence among those variables.

Communication styles consisted of assertiveness and immediacy. Due to the absence of established measures for manager assertiveness and immediacy, items were developed in this study. Specifically, five items were generated for manager assertiveness based on the works of Dasgupta et al. (2012) and Korsgaard, Roberson and Rymph (1998). Five items for manager communication immediacy were created based on the literature review. The rating scale ranged from 1 (never) to 7 (frequently). The reliability (Cronbach's alpha) for the five items for assertiveness was .74 for male managers and .77 for female managers. After the deletion of one item, the remaining 4 items for immediacy had a reliability of .77 for male managers and .76 for female managers. See Table 1 for specific items.

Table 1: Multi-Item Measures

Communication Style
Assertiveness (α = .74 – male manager, α = .77 – female manager)
My manager is direct when speaking with subordinates.
My manager is assertive.
My manager attacks others' ideas when he/she disagrees.
My manager often insists on his own views.
My manager always speaks his mind without hesitation.
Immediacy (α = .77 – male manager, α = .76 – female manager)
My manager uses collective pronouns such as "we" and "us" to make subordinates feel included.
My manager uses gesture such as nodding and postures such as leaning forward to show interest in
talking with subordinates.
My manager gives personal examples to illustrate ideas.
My manager is attentive when listening to subordinates.
Leadership Style
Autocratic (α = .72 – male manager, α = .74 – female manager)
My manager insists that subordinates follow his/her rules.
My manager makes most of the decisions for our work unit.
My manager makes decisions alone without asking for suggestions.
My manager exercises strict discipline over subordinates to accomplish tasks.
My manager is bossy and orders subordinates around.
Participative (α = .77 – male manager, α = .81 – female manager)
My manager encourages work group members to express ideas/suggestions.
My manager listens to my work group's ideas and suggestions.
My manager uses my work group's suggestions to make decisions that affect us.
My manager gives all work group members a chance to voice their opinions.
Male stereotyping (α = .85)
Willing to take risk
Tough personality

(*Continued*)

Table 1: Continued

Depending on own belief
Independent
Aggressive
Dominant
Competitive
Female stereotyping (α = .83)
Sensitive to others' needs
Gentle
Affectionate
Agreeable
Understanding
Sympathetic
Managerial Effectiveness
Planning (α = .84 – male manager, α = .81 – female manager)
Planning the future
Adapting to change
Planning for goal achievement
Organizing and orchestrating events
Meeting schedules and deadlines
Problem solving (α = .75 – male manager, α = .76 – female manager)
Identifying the company's problems
Generating new ideas to address old problems
Finding solutions for problems
Performance management (α = .80 – male manager, α = .76 – female manager)
Delegating responsibilities
Providing directions
Motivating subordinates to work hard
Monitoring and controlling performance
Relationship management (α = .81 – male manager, α = .84 – female manager)
Initiating relationships
Cooperating with others
Maintaining relationships
Resolving conflicts

Table 1: Continued

Information provision (α = .74 – male manager, α = .77 – female manager)
Articulating and disseminating ideas
Keeping others informed
Giving performance feedback

Leadership styles included autocratic and participative styles. For autocratic leadership, four items came from Author's (2013) namesake scale, which had been validated in Chinese contexts, and two items not overlapping with Author's scale were extracted from De Hoogh and Den Hartog (2009)'s autocratic leadership scale because their other four items were similar to Author's items. The Likert rating scale ranged from 1 (never) to 7 (frequently). The deletion of one item resulted in a reliable autocratic leadership scale for both male managers (Cronbach's alpha = .72) and female managers (Cronbach's alpha =.74). For participative leadership, six items were modified from Arnold, Arad, Rhoades, and Drasgow's (2000) participative leadership scale with the same Likert rating scale. A reliability analysis resulted in the deletion of two items, which yielded a reliable measure for both male managers (Cronbach's alpha = .77) and female managers (Cronbach's alpha =.81). See Table 1 for specific items.

Sex stereotyping was measured via seven items for male stereotyping and seven items for female stereotyping. These items were extracted from the short form of the Bem Sex Role Inventory (BSRI) (Bem, 1979) based on three principles: (1) items chosen must be representative of masculinity and femininity respectively; (2) items must not overlap with communication style or leadership style measures; and (3) neutral and positive items were included, and socially undesirable items were excluded (Bem suggested this method to shorten his inventory). Respondents were instructed to rate how often each of the seven descriptors about a man/woman was true. The rating scale ranged from 1 (almost never true) to 7 (always true). The male stereotyping items yielded a reliability of .85, and the six female stereotyping items generated a reliability of .83 after one item was deleted. See Table 1.

Managerial effectiveness entailed five dimensions: planning, problem-solving, performance management, relationship management, and information provision. The researcher closely followed the definitions and explanations of the five dimensions as reviewed and created five items for each dimension. The rating scale was from 1 (very ineffective) to 7 (very effective). After the deletion of one or two items from some of the dimensions to achieve reliabilities of .70 or above for both male and female managers, reliabilities of the five dimensions ranged from .74 to .84 for male managers and .76 to .84 for female managers. See Table 1.

Results

Intercorrelations were computed to provide basic information concerning the relationships among the variables. Communication assertiveness and immediacy exhibited no significant correlation, and neither did autocratic leadership and participative leadership. Male stereotyping and female stereotyping had a correlation of .44. The five aspects of managerial effectiveness ranged from .32 to .67 for male managers and .39 to .76 for female managers. Refer to Table 2 for details.

Table 2: Descriptive Statistics and Intercorrelations

	1	2	3	4	5	6	7	8	9	10
Male Managers										
1. Assertiveness										
2. Immediacy	.12									
3. Autocratic leadership	.43**	.12								
4. Participative leadership	.028	.35**	.01							
5. Planning	.22**	.25**	.20**	.15*						
6. Problem solving	.23**	.37**	.36**	.25**	.64**					
7. Performance management	.14*	.29**	.22**	.13	.62**	.63**				
8. Relationship management	.04	.53**	-.02	.34**	.32**	.34**	.37**			
9. Information provision	.23**	.40**	.28**	.12	.62**	.58**	.67**	.47**		
10. M stereotyping	.23**	.11	.27**	-.07	.28**	.42**	.31**	-.03	.30**	
11. F stereotyping	-.30**	.01	-.30**	.03	-.13	-.30**	-.20**	.06	-.27**	.44**
Female managers										
1. Assertiveness										
2. Immediacy	.06									
3. Autocratic leadership	.46**	.11								
4. Participative leadership	-.18**	.62**	-.18**							
5. Planning	.18*	.43**	.16*	.32**						
6. Problem solving	.21**	.44**	.09	.35**	.76**					
7. Performance management	.14*	.37**	.06	.34**	.53**	.39**				
8. Relationship management	-.18**	.54**	-.20**	.58**	.45**	.40**	.44**			
9. Information provision	.13	.43**	.10	.39**	.54**	.43**	.70**	.44**		
10. M stereotyping	-.13	.34**	-.11	.36**	.22**	.09	.23**	.45**	.31**	
11. F stereotyping	.11	-.37**	.11	-.40**	-.16*	-.07	-.24**	-.50**	-.26**	.44**

*** $p < .001$, ** $p < .01$, * $p < .05$

Manager Sex Differences (RQ1)

Respondents recalled a male manager and a female manager they worked for in the past two years and then rated both managers in terms communication style, leadership style, and managerial effectiveness. Paired *t*-tests revealed that male managers received higher scores on assertiveness, autocratic leadership, participative leadership, planning effectiveness, and performance management effectiveness. Female managers received higher scores on communication immediacy and relationship management effectiveness. See Table 3 for details.

Table 3: Paired t-Tests Comparing Male Managers with Female Managers (N = 206)

Variable	**Male** *M(SD)*	**Female** *M(SD)*	*t*
Comm. assertiveness	4.66 (.63)	4.31 (.77)	5.58***
Comm. Immediacy	4.27 (.77)	4.30 (.94)	-.47 ns
Autocratic leadership	4.56 (.66)	4.37 (.85)	2.71**
Participative leadership	4.22 (.76)	4.11 (.92)	1.31**
Problem-solving effectiveness	4.62 (.98)	4.50 (.90)	1.45 ns
Planning effectiveness	4.85 (.86)	4.64 (.79)	3.12 **
Performance mngt effectiveness	4.72 (.95)	4.58 (.89)	2.04*
Relationship mngt effectiveness	4.01 (.92)	4.49 (.95)	-5.27***
Info. provision effectiveness	4.59 (.89)	4.64 (.89)	-.83 ns

Sex Stereotyping and Perceived Male Managers' Effectiveness (RQ2)

Hierarchical linear regression was used to examine whether sex stereotyping played a role in perceived male managers' effectiveness. For diagnostic purposes in terms of how sex stereotyping might influence different aspects of managerial effectiveness, each aspect was examined as a dependent variable. With *perceived male problem-solving effectiveness* as the dependent variable, communication styles (assertiveness and immediacy) were entered as the first block, followed by leadership styles (autocratic and participative styles) as the second block and sex stereotyping (male stereotyping and female stereotyping) as the third block. Then, for controls, number of male managers and number of female managers were entered at the fourth block, and respondent age, sex, organizational post as the last block. Results indicated that male stereotyping explained an additional 10.1 % of the variance in perceived male problem-solving effectiveness. The final model included immediacy, autocratic leadership, participative leadership, and male stereotyping as the significant predictors of male manager problem-solving effectiveness, explaining 36.1 % of the variance. See Table 4 for hierarchical regression details for all aspects of managerial effectiveness.

Table 4: Hierarchical Regression Analysis of Predictors of Male Managers' Effectiveness

		Managerial Effectiveness			
Dependent variables	**Problem Solving**	**Planning**	**Performance Management**	**Relationship Management**	**Information Provision**
	β	*β*	*β*	*β*	*β*
Block 1: Comm.					
Assertiveness	.20**	.19**	ns	ns	.15*
Immediacy	.34***	.23**	.27***	.55***	.37***
(R^2)	(.167***)	(.10***)	(.085***)	(.30***)	(.174***)
Block 2: Leadership					
Autocratic	.30***[a]	ns	ns	ns	.18*
Participative	.16*	ns	ns	.20**	ns
(ΔR^2)	(.093***)	(ns)	(ns)	(.037**)	(.028*)
Block 3: Sex Stereotyping					
Male stereotyping	.27***	.24**	.23**	ns	.15*
Female stereotyping	ns	ns	ns	ns	ns
(ΔR^2)	(.101***)	(.05**)	(.060**)	(ns)	(.051**)
Block 4: Managers					
# of F managers	ns	ns	ns	ns	ns
# of M managers	ns	ns	ns	ns	ns
(ΔR^2)	(ns)	(ns)	(ns)	(ns)	(ns)
Block 5: Respondent					
Age	ns	ns	ns	ns	ns
Sex	ns	ns	ns	ns	ns
Organizational post	ns	ns	ns	ns	ns
(ΔR^2)	(ns)	(ns)	(ns)	(ns)	(ns)
Final Model	Immediacy .25***	Immediacy .18*	Immediacy .23**	Immediacy .48***	Immediacy .36***
	Autocratic .22**	M stereo .24**	M stereo .23**	Participtv. .20**	M stereo .15*

Table 1: Continued

		Managerial Effectiveness			
	Participtv. .19**				
	M stereo .27***				
R^2	.361***	.152***	.144***	.336***	.253***

*** $p < .001$, ** $p < .01$, * $p < .05$

For *planning*, the same hierarchical regression procedure showed that male stereotyping explained an additional 5 % of the variance. The final model contained immediacy and male stereotyping as the two significant positive predictors of male managers' effectiveness in planning (R^2 =.152). For *performance management*, male stereotyping explained an additional variance of 6 %, with the final model containing immediacy and male stereotyping as the two significant predictors (R^2 =.144). For *relationship management*, sex stereotyping was not significantly associated with this aspect of effectiveness. The final model consisted of immediacy and participative leadership as the two positive predictors (R^2 =.336). For *information provision*, male sex stereotyping explained an additional variance of 5.1 %; the final model consisted of immediacy and male stereotyping as the two positive predictors (R^2 =.253). Numbers of male and female managers in the company and respondent demographics exhibited no significant relationship with any aspect of perceived male managers' effectiveness. Refer to Table 4 for details.

Sex Stereotyping and Perceived Female Managers' Effectiveness (RQ3)

The same procedure of hierarchical linear regression was used for all aspects of female managers' effectiveness. For *problem solving*, sex stereotyping exhibited no significant relationship with that aspect of effectiveness. The final model contained assertiveness, immediacy, and participative leadership (R^2 =.239). Refer to Table 5 for details. For *planning*,

Table 5: Hierarchical Regression Analysis of Predictors of Female Managers' Effectiveness

		Managerial Effectiveness			
Dependent variables	**Problem Solving**	**Planning**	**Performance Management**	**Relationship Management**	**Information Provision**
	β	*β*	*β*	*β*	*β*
Block 1: Comm. Style					
Assertiveness	.19**	.17*	.12*	-.22***	ns
Immediacy	.42***	.40***	.36***	.55***	.42***
(R^2)	(.216***)	(.199***)	(.150***)	(.336***)	(.195***)
Block 2: Leadership Style					
Autocratic	ns	ns	ns	-.17*	ns
Participative	.19*	.19*	.27**	.29***	.27**
(ΔR^2)	(.023*)	(.023*)	(.039*)	(.085***)	(.040**)
Block 3: Sex Stereotyping					
My stereotyping	ns	ns	ns	.15*	.18*
Female stereotyping	ns	ns	ns	.23***	ns
(ΔR^2)	(ns)	(ns)	(ns)	(.082***)	(.007*)
Block 4: Managers					
# of F managers	ns	ns	ns	ns	ns
# of M managers	ns	ns	ns	ns	ns
(ΔR^2)	(ns)	(ns)	(ns)	(ns)	(ns)
Block 5: Respondent					
Age	ns	ns	ns	ns	ns
Sex	ns	-.19**	ns	ns	ns
Organizational post	ns	ns	ns	ns	ns
(ΔR^2)	(ns)	(.031*)	(ns)	(ns)	(ns)
Final Model	Assertive .24**	Assertive .17**	Assertive .17*	Immediacy .30***	Assertive .16*
	Immediacy .30***	Immediacy .24*	Immediacy .19*	Autocratic -.15*	Immediacy .19*
	Participtv. .19*	Participtv. .20*	Participtv. .27**	Participtv. .21**	Participtv. .22*

Table 1: Continued

		Managerial Effectiveness			
		Sex -.19**		M stereo .15*	M stereo .18*
				F stereo .23***	
R^2	.239 ***	.236***	.189***	.503***	.278***

*** $p < .001$, ** $p < .01$, * $p < .05$

sex stereotyping showed no significant association. The final model was comprised of assertiveness, immediacy, and participative leadership – all with a positive β – and respondent sex (β= -.19) (R^2 =.236). Respondent sex was dummy-coded as 0 (female) and 1 (male). A negative β indicated that male respondents, compared with female respondents, were more likely to give female managers lower ratings on planning. For *performance management*, sex stereotyping did not exhibit a significant association. The final model consisted of assertiveness, immediacy, and participative leadership (R^2 =.189). For *relationship management,* both male and female stereotyping had a significant β, explaining an additional variance of 8.2 %. The final model contained immediacy, autocratic leadership, participative leadership, male stereotyping, and female stereotyping (R^2 =.503). For *information provision*, male stereotyping had a β of .18. The final model consisted of assertiveness, immediacy, participative leadership, and male stereotyping (R^2 = .278).

Discussion

The current study was designed to address whether managers' sex made a difference in employees' evaluation of their effectiveness, and if so, whether sex stereotyping influenced that judgment after managers' communication style and leadership style were considered.

Impact of Manager Sex

Paired *t*-tests showed that respondents rated male managers higher on communication assertiveness and autocratic leadership, which was consistent with the gender literature. Surprisingly, male managers also received slightly higher scores on participative leadership, which was supposed to be a female managers' strength. The current data could not offer a direct explanation. Chinese women in management positions often were strong-willed individuals and occasionally exhibited masculine behaviors, which might explain why male and female managers differed only slightly in some of the gender-laden leadership attributes but exhibited no difference on one attribute (i.e., communication immediacy). Concerning managerial effectiveness, female managers appeared to be clearly better in relationship management than did their male counterparts, which is consistent with the gender literature. Male managers were slightly more effective than their female counterparts in planning and performance management; male and female managers did not differ in problem-solving or information provision. Contributors to perceived differences in gender-based managerial effectiveness were analyzed – beginning with communication and leadership.

Communication and Leadership as Predictors of Managerial Effectiveness

Leadership theories emphasize managers' leadership style as the key contributor to their effectiveness (Sheer, 2013; Northouse, 2009; Pounder & Greaves, 2020). Organizational communication scholars (e.g., Sheer, 2015; Fairhurst, 2011) argue that communication constitutes an important part of leadership style, thereby contributing to managerial effectiveness. Indeed, the correlational analysis showed that communication style was related to leadership style for both male and female managers. The hierarchical regression results (in Tables 3 & 4) further indicated that for male managers, communication styles entered as the first block (the most fundamental predictor) explained variances ranging from 8.5 % to 30 % in managerial effectiveness, whereas leadership styles (entered as the second block) added either no significant variance or 2.8 % to 9.3 % of the variances in managerial effectiveness. A similar pattern held for female managers. These findings lend support to the current claim that communication is a large part of leadership.

After all five blocks of variables were entered, the final models for male managers' five aspects of effectiveness all contained communication immediacy, and two models (for problem-solving and relationship management, respectively) additionally contained participative leadership style. For female managers' effectiveness, all five final models included communication immediacy and participative leadership, and four models additionally contained assertiveness. Noticeably, communication styles explained much more variance than leadership styles did in managerial effectiveness for both male and female managers.

Sex Stereotyping and Perceived Managerial Effectiveness

Male stereotyping and female stereotyping were positively correlated at .44. The moderate-low correlation revealed that male and female stereotyping were related but relatively independent constructs. Respondents' own sex was not related to their levels of stereotyping. The relative independence between male and female stereotyping exhibited further evidence that male stereotyping and female stereotyping predicted different aspects of managerial effectiveness. As the final regression models concerning male managers' effectiveness indicated, respondents' male stereotyping positively predicted ratings of male managers' problem-solving, planning, performance management, and information provision effectiveness. For female managers, respondents' male stereotyping and female stereotyping both positively predicted female managers' relationship management effectiveness, but male stereotyping predicted only female managers' information provision effectiveness. Male stereotyping appears to have resulted in a bias in favor of male managers, because male stereotyping explained 5.1 % to 10.1 % of additional variances in employees' ratings of their male managers after communication and leadership were considered.

For female managers, compared with male managers, sex stereotyping played a lesser role and influenced only two aspects of female managers' effectiveness relationship management and information provision. Specifically, male stereotyping and female stereotyping co-contributed to higher ratings of relationship management effectiveness and explained an additional 8.2 % of the variance; male stereotyping positively influenced ratings of information provision but explained only .70 % of additional variance. In general, sex stereotyping did not negatively influence ratings of female managers. On a comparative basis, male stereotyping appeared to have helped ratings of male managers' effectiveness in task-based aspects of managerial effectiveness, whereas female managers did not appear to have the same advantage. This difference might explain why male managers received slightly higher ratings than female managers did in those aspects of management effectiveness. Female managers, however, received some benefit of sex stereotyping in their traditionally strong area – relationship management. Sex stereotyping did not lead to blatantly biased ratings in favor of male managers. Managers' behaviors (particularly communication immediacy and participative leadership) exerted much more influence than sex stereotyping did on employees' ratings of managers' effectiveness.

Theoretical Consideration

Communication styles explained more variance in managerial effectiveness than did leadership style, which lends support to organizational communication scholars who conceptualize communication as a fundamental aspect of leadership. Furthermore, leadership behavior, including both communication style and leadership style, serves as a main basis for employees' evaluation of managers' effectiveness. Leadership training theories can be developed with a focus on communication and behavior attributes that enhance leadership effectiveness. The current findings revealed that communication immediacy and participative leadership facilitated managerial effectiveness. Immediacy and participative leadership can be viewed as a relationship orientation for both men and women in the collectivistic Chinese culture rather than the feminine style as viewed in Western cultures. Future theorizing can examine cultural influence on genderization of leadership.

In the gender and management literature, sex stereotyping was often examined as a uni-dimensional construct as though all sex stereotyping exerts the same effects. The current study revealed that male stereotyping and female stereotyping were relatively independent yet related constructs such that adhering to male stereotypes does not necessarily mean adhering to female stereotypes. Indeed, male and female stereotyping exhibited different predictive power. Male stereotyping was most closely related to task-based aspects of effectiveness among male managers, whereas female stereotyping was unrelated to most of the aspects of managerial effectiveness for male or female managers. Noticeably, male stereotyping exerted more influence than female stereotyping on perceptions of managers' effectiveness. Future theorizing might be required to differentiate male from female stereotyping by considering the possibility of sex stereotyping as a multidimensional construct.

Practical Implications

Although the bias of male stereotyping in favor of male managers still existed in the Hong Kong organizations in the current sample, such bias did not appear to be severe. In fact, employees' ratings of managers were explained mostly by managers' behaviors (communication style and leadership style). Employees' age, sex, organization position, and their experience with number of male managers relative to female managers had little effect on their ratings of managers' effectiveness. Aside from just having elected the first female Chief Executive of the territory, Hong Kong appears to have made progress in sex equality with respect to organizational management positions. For example, respondents reported that women occupied nearly 40 % of management positions in the current sample in Hong Kong, which is greater than the 20.4 % of women members in the world's board seats in 2020 (50/50 Women on Boards, 2021). Hong Kong can continue to make progress to become a world leader in gender equality. Another important implication relates to leadership training.

The current study suggests that training communication immediacy (rather than assertiveness) and participative leadership style (rather than autocratic leadership style) can help to improve managerial effectiveness.

Limitations and Future Research

The present study is limited in its scope of investigation. In addition to assertiveness and immediacy, other leader communication attributes must be investigated to gain an in-depth understanding of effective versus ineffective leadership communication behavior. The same argument holds for extending the scope of investigation from autocratic and participative leadership to other leadership styles. Stereotyping, particularly male stereotyping, was found to exert relatively small effects on perceived managerial effectiveness; however, such effects can become stronger when the sample size is much larger. Thus, claims about the influence of sex stereotyping on organizational management in Hong Kong and other parts of the world must be stablished in future studies that use different, larger samples. Furthermore, the present study did not measure cultural traits and relationships between cultures, and the key variables measured in this study were not established. Thus, to understand how the current findings might be explained by Chinese cultural traits and unique Hong Kong cultural traits, future studies need to investigate such cultural traits in relation to the key variables examined in this study.

References

Anzengruber, J., Goetz, M. A., Nold, H., & Woelfle, M. (2017). Effectiveness of Managerial Capabilities at Different Hierarchical Levels. *Journal of Managerial Psychology*, *32*(2), 134–148. https://doi.org/10.1108/JMP-12-2015-0451.

Arnold, J.A., Arad, S., Rhoades, J.A. and Drasgow, F. (2000) The Empowering Leadership Questionnaire: The Construction and Validation of a New Scale for Measuring Leader Behaviors. *Journal of Organizational Behavior, 21*, 249–269.

Arredondo, L. (2003). *Communicating Effectively*. New Delhi: Tata McGraw-Hill Publishing Company.

Bamel, U. K., Rangnekar, S., Stokes, P., & Rastogi, R. (2013). Organizational Climate and Managerial effectiveness: An Indian Perspective. *International Journal of Organizational Analysis*, *21*(2), 198–218. https://doi.org/10.1108/IJOA-09-2011-0514.

Bamel, U. K., Rangnekar, S., & Rastogi, R. (2011). Managerial Effectiveness in Indian Organisations: Reexamining an Instrument in an Indian Context. *Research and Practice in Human Resource Management*, *19*(1), 69–78.

Bao, C. (2009). Comparison of Public and Private Sector Managerial Effectiveness in China: A Three-Parameter Approach. *Journal of Management Development*, *28*(6), 533–541. https://doi.org/10.1108/02621710910959693.

Bellou, V. (2011). Do Women Followers Prefer a Different Leadership Style Than Men?. *The International Journal of Human Resource Management*, *22*(13), 2818–2833. https://doi.org/10.1080/09585192.2011.599677.

Bem, S. L. (1979). Theory and Measurement of Androgyny: A Reply to the Pedhazur-Tetenbaum and Locksley-Colten Critiques. *Journal of Personality and Social Psychology*, *37*(6), 1047–1054. https://doi.org/10.1037/0022-3514.37.6.1047

Brannon, K. L. (2011). The Effects of Leader Communication Medium and Motivating Language on Perceived Leader Effectiveness (Order No. 3447091). Available from ProQuest Dissertations & Theses A&I. (858095856). Retrieved from: https://search.proquest.com/docview/858095856?accountid=11440.

Burgoon, J. K., & Hale, J. L. (1993). Interpersonal Bonding. In S. Petronio, J. K. Alberts, M. L. Hecht, & J. Buley (Eds.), *Contemporary Perspectives on Interpersonal Communication* (pp. 318–358). Madison, WI: Brown & Benchmark.

Case, S. S. (1988). Cultural Differences, Not Deficiencies: An Analysis of Managerial Women's Language. In S. Rose & L. Larwood. (Eds.), *Women's Careers: Pathways and Pitfalls*, (pp. 41–63). New York: Praeger.

Cenkci, A. T., & Ozcelik, G. (2015). Leadership Styles and Subordinate Work Engagement: The Moderating Impact of Leader Gender. *Global Business and Management Research: An International Journal*, *7*(4), 8–20.

Census and Statistics Department Hong Kong SAR. (2016). *Hong Kong Annual Digest of Statistics*. Retrieved from: http://www.statistics.gov.hk/pub/B10100032016AN16B0100.pdf.

Chauhan, V. S., Dhar, U., & Pathak, R. D. (2005). Factorial Constitution of Managerial Effectiveness: Reexamining an Instrument in Indian Context. *Journal of Managerial Psychology*, *20*(2), 164–177.

Crites, S. N., Dickson, K. E., & Lorenz, A. (2015). Nurturing Gender Stereotypes in the Face of Experience: A Study of Leader Gender, Leadership Style, and Satisfaction. *Journal of Organizational Culture, Communications and Conflict*, *19*(1), 1.

Cuadrado, I., Morales, J. F., & Recio, P. (2008). Women's Access to Managerial Positions: An Experimental Study of Leadership Styles and Gender. *The Spanish Journal of Psychology*, *11*(1), 55–65. https://doi.org/10.1017/S113874160000411X.

Cunningham, J., Salomone, J., & Wielgus, N. (2015). Project Management Leadership Style: A Team Member Perspective. *International Journal of Global Business, 8*(2), 27.

Dasgupta, S. A., Suar, D., & Singh, S. (2012). Impact of Managerial Communication Styles on Employees' Attitudes and Behaviours. *Employee Relations, 35*(2), 173–199. https://doi.org/10.1108/01425451311287862.

De Hoogh, A. H. B., & Den Hartog, D. N. (2009). Neuroticism and Locus of Control as Moderators of the Relationships of Charismatic and Autocratic Leadership with Burnout. *Journal of Applied Psychology, 94*(4), 1058–1067. https://doi.org/10.1037/a0016253

Eagly, A. H. (1987). *Sex Differences in Social Behavior: A Social-Role Interpretation*. Hillsdale, NJ: Lawrence Erlbaum Associates.

Eagly, A. H., Johannesen-Schmidt, M. C., & van Engen, M. L. (2003). Transformational, Transactional, and Laissez-Faire Leadership Styles: A Meta-analysis Comparing Women and Men. *Psychological Bulletin, 129*(4), 569–591. https://doi.org/10.1037/0033-2909.129.4.569.

Eagly, A. H., & Karau, S. J. (2002). Role Congruity Theory of Prejudice toward Female Leaders. *Psychological Review, 109*, 573–598. https://doi.org/10.1037//0033-295X.109.3.573.

Eagly, A. H., & Mladinic, A. (1989). Gender Stereotypes and Attitudes toward Women and Men. *Personality and Social Psychology Bulletin, 15*(4), 543–558. https://doi.org/10.1177/0146167289154008.

Eken, I., Özturgut, O., & Craven, A. E. (2014). Leadership Styles and Cultural Intelligence. *Journal of Leadership, Accountability and Ethics, 11*(3), 154.

Fairhurst, G. T. (2011). *The Power of Framing: Creating the Language of Leadership*. San Francisco: Jossey-Bass.

Fan, H., & Han, B. (2018). How Does Leader-Follower Fit or Misfit in Communication Style Matter for Work Outcomes? *Social Behavior and Personality, 46*(7), 1083–1100. https://doi.org/10.2224/sbp.6925.

Georgiou, I. (2006). Managerial Effectiveness from a System Theoretical Point of View. *Systemic Practice and Action Research, 19*(5), 441. https://doi.org/10.1007/s11213-006-9035-3.

Gayle, B. M. (1991). Sex Equity in Workplace Conflict Management. *Journal of Applied Communication Research, 19*(3), 152–169. https://doi.org/10.1080/00909889109365300.

Grant Thornton. (2016). Insights. Women in Business: Turning Promise into Practice. Retrieved from: https://www.grantthornton.global/en/insights/articles/women-in-business-2016/

Heilman, M., & Eagly, A. H. (2008). Gender Stereotypes Are Alive, Well, and Busy Producing Workplace Discrimination. *Industrial and Organizational Psychology, 1*, 393–398. https://doi.org/10.1111/j.1754-9434.2008.00072.x.

Herrera, R., Duncan, P., Ree, M., & Williams, K. (2013). Diversity as A predictor of leadership effectiveness. *Journal of Diversity Management* (Online), *8*(1), 1–14. https://doi.org/10.19030/jdm.v8i1.7848.

Hinkle, L. (2001). Perceptions of Supervisor Nonverbal Immediacy, Vocalics, and Subordinate Liking. *Communication Research Reports, 18*(2), Issue. 2, 2001. https://doi.org/10.1080/08824090109384790.

International Labour Organization. (2017). Labor Force Participation Rate, Female (% of female population ages 15+) (modeled ILO estimate). Retrieved from: http://data.worldbank.org/indicator/SL.TLF.CACT.FE.ZS.

Johnson, S. K., Murphy, S. E., Zewdie, S., & Reichard, R. J. (2008). The Strong, Sensitive Type: Effects of Gender Stereotypes and Leadership Prototypes on the Evaluation of Male and Female Leaders. *Organizational Behavior and Human Decision Processes, 106*(1), 39–60. https://doi.org/10.1016/j.obhdp.2007.12.002.

Kelly, S., Gatytan, J., MacDonald, P., Collins, R., & Denton, Z. (2014). An Investigation of Student Apprehension: Testing Student Predictions of Classroom Aptitude via Brain Hemisphere Dominance. *Business Teacher Education Journal, 40*, 30–35.

Kerns, C. D. (2016). High-Impact Communicating: A Key Leadership Practice. *The Journal of Applied Business and Economics, 18*(5), 11.

Koenig, A. M., Eagly, A. H., Mitchell, A. A., & Ristikari, T. (2011). Are Leader Stereotypes Masculine? A Meta-Analysis of Three Research Paradigms. *Psychological Bulletin, 137*(4), 616–642. https://doi.org/10.1037/a0023557.

Korsgaard, M. A., Roberson, L., & Rymph, R. D. (1998). What Motivates Fairness? The Role of Subordinate Assertive Behavior on Managers' Interactional Fairness. *Journal of Applied Psychology, 83*(5), 731–744. https://doi.org/10.1037/0021-9010.83.5.731.

Leitch, C., & Stead, V. (2016). Special Issue of Leadership: Gender and Leadership. *Leadership, 12*(1), 127–128. https://doi.org/10.1177/1742715015625415.

Li, C., Bao, L., & Jiang, Q. (2013). Leadership Styles of Entrepreneurial Women in Eastern China: Characteristics and Differences. *Social Behavior and Personality: An International Journal, 41*(3), 421. https://doi.org/10.2224/sbp.2013.41.3.421.

Lindsey, A. E., & Zakahi, W. R. (2006). Perceptions of Men and Women Departing from Conversational Sex-Role Stereotypes. In K. Dindia & D. J. Canary (Eds.), *Sex Differences and Similarities in Communication* (2nd ed., pp. 281–298). Mahwah, NJ: Lawrence Erlbaum.

Maher, K. J. (1997). Gender-related Stereotypes of Transformational and Transactional Leadership. *Sex Roles, 37*, 209–225. https://doi.org/1023/A:1025647811219.

Marilyn, M. F. (2007). *Communication-Centered Approach to Leadership: The Relationship of Interpersonal Communication Competence to Transformational Leadership and Emotional Intelligence.* The University of Texas: Arlington.

Matthew, R. F., & Gilbert, W. F. (2009). *Understanding Leadership Perspectives: Theoretical and Practical Approaches.* New York: Springer-Verlag.

Mulac, A., Bradac, J. J., & Gibbons, P. (2001). Empirical Support for the Gender-as-Culture Hypothesis. *Human Communication Research, 27(1)*, 121–152.

Ndubueze, K. I., & Akanni, A. A. (2015). Leadership Style and Organisational Citizenship Behaviour among Employees of Private Companies in Abia State, Nigeria. *Ife Psychologia, 23*(2), 139.

Northouse, P. (2009). *Leadership: Theory and Practice.* Thousand Oaks, CA: Sage.

Paustian-Underdahl, S. C., Walker, L. S., & Woehr, D. J. (2014). Gender and Perceptions of Leadership Effectiveness: A Meta-analysis of Contextual Moderators. *The Journal of Applied Psychology, 99*(6), 1129–1145. https://doi.org/10.1037/a0036751.

Popp, D., Donovan, R. A., Crawford, M., Marsh, K. L., & Peele, M. (2003). Gender, Race, and Speech Style Stereotypes. *Sex Roles, 48*, 317–325.

Post, C. (2015). When Is Female Leadership an Advantage? Coordination Requirements, Team Cohesion, and Team Interaction Norms. *Journal of Organizational Behavior, 36*(8), 1153–1175. https://doi.org/10.1002/job.2031.

Pounder, P., & Greaves, D. E. (2020). Impassioned Leadership Effectiveness: An Assessment of Leadership Styles of Top Leaders in Caribbean Healthcare Systems. *International Journal of Public Leadership, 16*(2), 125–144. https://doi.org/10.1108/IJPL-01-2019-0001.

Preko, A. (2012). Attitude of Male Employees toward Female Managers in Selected Organizations in Ghana. *Researchers World*, 3(3), 86.

Reinout E. de Vries, Bakker-Pieper, A., & Oostenveld, W. (2010). Leadership = Communication? the Relations of Leaders' Communication Styles with Leadership Styles, Knowledge Sharing and Leadership Outcomes. *Journal of Business and Psychology, 25*(3), 367–380. https://doi.org/10.1007/s10869-009-9140-2.

Remland, M. S., Jacobson, C. M., & Jones, T. S. (1983). Evaluations of Sex-Incongruent Nonverbal Communication for Male and Female Managers. *Women's Studies in Communication, 6*(1), 24–33. https://doi.org/10.1080/07491409.1983.11089649.

Rhee, K. S., & Sigler, T. H. (2015). Untangling the Relationship between Gender and Leadership. *Gender in Management, 30*(2), 109. https://doi.org/10.1108/GM-09-2013-0114.

Richmond, V. P., & McCroskey, J. C. (2000). The Impact of Supervisor and Subordinate Immediacy Are Relational and Organizational Outcomes. *Communication Monographs, 67*(1), 85–95. https://doi.org/10.1080/03637750009376496.

Rocca, K. (2008). Participation in the College Classroom: The Impact of Instructor Immediacy and Verbal Aggression. *Journal of Classroom Interaction, 43*(2), 22–33.

Roth, P. L., Purvis, K. L., & Bobko, P. (2012). A Meta-analysis of Gender Group Differences for Measures of Job Performance in Field Studies. *Journal of Management, 38*(2), 719–739. https://doi.org/10.1177/0149206310374774.

Ruiz, C. E., Wang, J., & Hamlin, R. G. (2013). What Makes Managers Effective in Mexico? *Leadership & Organization Development Journal, 34*(2), 130–146. https://doi.org/10.1108/01437731311321904.

Salahuddin, M. M. (2011). Generational Differences Impact on Leadership Style and Organizational Success. *Journal of Diversity Management, 5*(2). https://doi.org/10.19030/jdm.v5i2.805.

Schoel, C., Bluemke, M., Mueller, P., & Stahlberg, D. (2011). When Autocratic Leaders Become an Option – Uncertainty and Self-Esteem Predict Implicit Leadership Preferences. *Journal of Personality and Social Psychology, 101*(3), 521–540. https://doi.org/10.1037/a0023393.

Sheer, V. C. (2013). In Search of Chinese Paternalistic Leadership: Conflicting Evidence from Samples of Mainland China and Hong Kong's Small Family Businesses. *Management Communication Quarterly, 27*(1), 34–60. https://doi.org/10.1177/0893318912458212.

Sheer, V. C. (2015). "Exchange lost" in Leader-Member Exchange Theory and Research: A Critique and a Reconceptualization. *Leadership, 11*(2), 213–229. https://doi.org/10.1177/1742715014530935.

Sheer, V. C., & Rice, R. E. (2017). Mobile Instant Messaging Use and Social Capital: Direct and Indirect Associations with Employee Outcomes. *Information & Management, 54*(1), 90–102. https://doi.org/10.1016/j. im. 2016. 04. 001.

Silva, A. (2016). What Is Leadership? *Journal of Business Studies Quarterly, 8*(1), 1.

Smutny, P., Prochazka, J., & Vaculik, M. (2016). The Relationship between Managerial Skills and Managerial Effectiveness in a Managerial Simulation Game. *Innovar: Revista De Ciencias Administrativasy Sociales, 26*(62), 11–22. https://doi.org/10.15446/innovar.v26n62.59385.

Stepp, P. L. (2000). *Leadership Styles of Male and Female Research Scientists: Transformational or Transactional?* Unpublished manuscript, Cornell University, Ithaca, NY.

Torres, L. E., Ruiz, C. E., Hamlin, B., & Velez-Calle, A. (2015). Perceived Managerial and Leadership Effectiveness in Colombia. *European Journal of Training and Development*, 39(3), 203–219. https://doi.org/10.1108/EJTD-08-2014-0062.

Wang, A., Chiang, J. T., Tsai, C., Lin, T., & Cheng, B. (2013). Gender Makes the Difference: The Moderating Role of Leader Gender on the Relationship between Leadership Styles and Subordinate Performance. *Organizational Behavior and Human Decision Processes, 122*(2), 101–113. https://doi.org/10.1016/j.obhdp.2013.06.001.

White, R., & Lippitt, R. (1960). *Autocracy and Democracy: An Experimental Inquiry*. New York: Harper & Row.

William, R. P. J. (2007). The Impact of Managerial Leadership in Strategic Direction on Organizational Effectiveness. *Futurics, 31*(1/2), 1.

Williams, M. J., & Tiedens, L. Z. (2016). The Subtle Suspension of Backlash: A Meta-analysis of Penalties for Women's Implicit and Explicit Dominance Behavior. *Psychological Bulletin, 142*(2), 165. https://doi.org/10.1037/bul0000039.

Women's Commission. (2019). *Hong Kong Women in Figures 2019*. Retrieved from: https://www.women.gov.hk/download/research/HK_Women2019_e.pdf.

50/50 Women on Boards. (2021). *Gender Diversity Index*. Retrieved from: https://5050wob.com/wp-content/uploads/2021/02/2020-Gender-Diversity-Index-Report-FINAL.pdf.

Introduction to The Conception of Minoritized Student Activists

By Ee Lin Lee

The next chapter examines critical discourse within the context of a university environment, but the findings can be applied in other contexts as well; for example, within business organizations. Discourse refers to the communication exchange in spoken and written form and reflects the macro-level structures of a society and its ideology. Critical discourse, thus, examines the power structures and relationships of organizations. It is pointed out that where power differences exist, for example in most typical educational as well as business organizations, membering or grouping is created due to the existing power relations. Consequently, those who do not share the dominant beliefs and values are considered to be out-group members and not part of the in-group. The notion of in-group versus out-group thinking is theorized by the Social Identity Theory. The theory postulates that members of in-groups tend to discriminate in favor of in-groups and against out-group members. Lee examines discrimination against minority students. This is done through interviews which are then coded and analyzed. The analysis reveals that the university administration essentially seeks to trouble shoot problems as they appear, but it does not seek to find a solution that could permanently reduce the system-inherent discrimination. In order to do so, it would be necessary to carefully listen to what minority students have to say and not attempt to bring them to internalize the ideology of the administration because that would mean they lose their identity. Companies seeking to benefit from diversity in the workforce should heed the advice given in this chapter. As Lee points out, it is important for organizations to legitimize every member's personhood because such a policy fosters solidarity and permits everyone to belong to the community so that out-groups are avoided.

Michael B. Hinner

Ee Lin Lee (Ph.D., University of New Mexico, 2005) is Professor of Communication Studies at Western Washington University, U.S.A. She is the recipient of the 2018 Womxn of Color Empowerment Faculty Award and the Featured Instructor for the 2018 Innovative Teaching Showcase in Engaging Social Justice at Western Washington University. She teaches in the areas of communication research methods (quantitative and qualitative); advanced communication theory (deconstructing Western perspectives in theory development and offering Asiacentric perspectives), issues in intercultural communication (focusing on language and social interaction involving dialogue and Whiteness studies), intercultural communication (addressing White privilege and racial injustices in culture, language, and communication areas), and international and intercultural education. Her research studies are published in multiple outlets, including *The Journal of Multicultural Discourses, Research on Language and Social Interaction, Health Communication, The Oxford Research Encyclopedia of Communication, International Education, and Sustainability.*

Ee Lin Lee

The Conception of Minoritized Student Activists

The Personhood of Minoritized Student Activists

In response to national and local racial tensions, U.S. university administrations often engage in discourses about diversity, equity, and inclusivity (DEI). However, even with DEI initiatives permeating academic discourses and campus life, the massive waves of identity-based student activism seem to render institutional effort ineffective. Student activists seem adamant and relentless in their quest for justice for voices that are oppressed by university administrations (Byrd et al., 2021; Logan et al., 2017). The traditional studies on student activism, thus, underpin the voices and social struggles of marginalized groups at predominantly White institutions (PWIs) (Anderson, 2019; Quaye & Lange, 2020; Robertson, 2021). In turn, critical diversity scholars decry the implications of university administrations' neoliberalized discourses about DEI (Ahmed, 2012; Urciuoli, 1999, 2016). Such studies bring to light the student activists' perspectives and reveal the imposition of dominant ideologies in institutional discourse (Dixson, 2018; Hoffman & Mitchell, 2016).

As part of the larger scholarly effort, this chapter presents yet another perspective – this time focused on university administrators – in calling for the ethical responsibility of higher education to serve all students equally (e.g., see Anderson, 2019). The chapter is based on a study designed to parse out institutional logic that informs university administrators' inclusion, or lack thereof, of student demands in institutional decision-making for policies and practices. In particular, the study seeks to unpack institutional assumptions of minoritized student activists by examining university administrators' spontaneous responses to student activism during an open forum at a PWI.[1] An understanding of the taken-for-granted beliefs in the administrators' discourse reveals ideologies inscribed in the university structure and, especially, among

1 The word *minorized* refers to the process of experiencing systemic exclusion in the context of education. Minoritized students, thus, are those who are situated in the exclusion that is institutionalized and enveloped in sociopolitical and historical contexts in the wider society (Benitez Jr., 2010; Hoffman & Mitchell, 2016).

the elites who control the academic system (Jackson et al., 2016; Jackson & Seiler, 2018).

Institutional discourses reside in sociopolitical and historical contexts. It is hoped that the interrogation of the administrators' language use will contribute to bridging the gap between the ideal imposed on student activists and their lived experiences (Urciuoli, 2020). The reconceptualization of diversity work at the institution in question and in higher education in general calls for the interrogation of the tacit knowledge of the university administrative system. Therefore, the use of a problem-oriented conceptual framework is necessary for revealing ideologies that are inscribed within the dominant institutional discourse (Zanoni & Janssens, 2015). The critical discourse analysis (CDA) is one such framework that supports the inquiry in this study, which is guided by the following question:

RQ: What institutional assumptions about the personhood of minoritized student activists are revealed through university administrators' spontaneous responses to student activism on DEI matters?

Critical Discourse Analysis

Following the tradition in CDA, this study treats discourse as language use that is contextual. Language – the arbitrary symbolic system that interlocutors use to create meanings – is a construction and representation of the social world (Lee, 2016a). Thus, meanings are not neutral, since they are situated in sociopolitics, histories, and power relations (Machin & Mayr, 2012; Rogers, 2011; Wodak, 2012). Discourses, therefore, are institutionalized practices that reveal the social actors' understanding of themselves and others, and the nuances in their mundane experiences (Wodak, 2012).

CDA scholars contend that discourses – texts, talk, and other semiotic interactions – inherently reflect and reproduce the macro-level structures of the society (Fairclough, 2001; Foucault, 1980). Similarly, discourses are ideological (Fairclough, 2016). Since ideology is a means by which the dominant forces in society exercise power over subjugated groups (Fairclough, 2001), the study of discourses is inseparable from the exploration of power relations. As such, the use of CDA as a conceptual framework in any investigation is problem-oriented. Hence, CDA is also emancipatory, since the exploration of social disparities invokes envisioning ways of living that do not reify the existing oppressive structures (Rogers, 2011).

University Discourse in the Conception of Minoritized Student Activists

Where a power differential exists, the subjugation of the non-majoritarian occurs. The delineation between insiders and outsiders – that is, membering – is shaped by and produces existing power relations. Membering or grouping, then, reveals a group's collective, deeply held beliefs about certain people (Carbaugh, 2007; Philipsen et al., 2005). Ultimately, those who do not share the dominant beliefs and values – that is, the Others – are illegitimized (Philipsen, 1975, 1992). Thus, the norms for interactions and expectations of behaviors are subject to institutional constraints and prevailing ideologies in a social community (Foucault, 1980; Machin & Mayr, 2012; Thornborrow, 2001).

Discourses that legitimize one's personhood (i.e., the self) foster solidarity with ingroups and offer belonging in the community. In the context of education, the emotional connection between students and the learning community, afforded by institutional discourses, is fundamental to students' self-worth and wholistic development (Jackson & Seiler, 2018; Lopez-Bonilla, 2011; Merino et al., 2020). In fact, minoritized students' sense of isolation at PWIs is intensified by their lack of identification with institutional discourse and contributes to their low retention and graduation rates (Desai & Abeita, 2017; Jackson et al., 2016; Logan et al., 2017; Merino et al., 2020). Therefore, the authorship of institutional discourses sets campus agendas, determines the visibility of selected voices, and affects student success (Iverson, 2019).

Student Activism

The long history of student protests covers various issues, ranging from political ideology to increases in tuition fees. However, the 2015 University of Missouri student protests about racial tensions on campus marked a milestone – the sharp increase of transnational identity-based student activism about DEI (Logan et al., 2017; Quaye & Lange, 2020; Robertson, 2021). The activism calls out White racism and, thus, ignites discourses about race across campuses and the nation. Students declare counter-narratives to resist institutional ideological dominance (Logan et al., 2017). They disrupt normalized institutional practices that privilege the elites and grieve institutional inequalities in intersectionality. As a form of civil disobedience, student activism often yields sanctions from university administrations and the larger society (Robertson, 2021).

Minoritized students, already the victims of an educational system that is designed to discriminate and exclude, further bear the brunt of chronic stress associated with activism. In addition to unpaid labor in activism, the students strive to balance or must choose among leadership demands, academic responsibilities, and their personal life circumstances (Vaccaro & Mena, 2011). They fight not only for their civil rights, but also for the betterment of the lives of other oppressed (Hoffman & Mitchell, 2016) and society in general. Since organizations resist change, more often than not university administrations apply bureaucratic maneuvers to curtail student activism, turning the activists' endurance into exhaustion (Anderson, 2019; Quaye & Lange, 2020). Therefore, the lack of institutional reciprocity in meeting minoritized student demands devalues the students' lived experiences and illegitimizes their personhood.

Since higher education is a social engineering project, its governance comes with an ethical responsibility to serve all students and the society without discrimination (Lee, 2018, 2019). Therefore, this study maintains that it is the responsibility of university administrations to break the cycle of historical, systemic violence that the dominant groups perform on the minoritized (Goldstein Hode & Meisenbach, 2017). In keeping with the CDA perspective, the discussion and analysis of the system that privileges the majoritarian must necessarily take a critical perspective (Rogers, 2011). Thus, the exploration of power relations in the university administrators' participation in meaning-making challenges their discourse and assumptions. Nevertheless, this study recognizes that many other factors may impact the power relations between students and administrators and, therefore, does not attempt to critique the entirety of the university administrators' responses to student activism beyond their open forum interaction described in the "Method" section.

Method

Situating the Communicative Event

I audio-recorded and transcribed verbatim a 2.5-hour forum at a small liberal arts PWI. Racial minority students were protesting the university administrations' silence after several racial incidents and vandalism in November 2018. More than 300 activists, mostly minoritized students packed into an auditorium to petition the university administration to sign a formal agreement to meet the students' demands. Gender neutral pseudonyms and pronouns are used for all administrators in this study, and their specific position titles are not mentioned to maintain confidentiality. Quoted utterances are lightly edited for clarity and to enhance readability.

Researcher's Positionality

The use of CDA requires researcher engagement in reflexivity in data analysis and interpretation (Rogers, 2011; Thornborrow, 2001; Zienkowski, 2017). This calls for an acknowledgement of my positionality as a researcher, including my socio-ideological stance on DEI matters. My experience as a scholar of color shapes my exploration of power relations among social actors in the study. Furthermore, my tenure of more than a decade at the PWI has allowed me to observe at close quarters the university's progress on DEI matters. While I participate in various ongoing conversations about DEI at the university (e.g., attending, as an observer, rallies and protests on campus, serving on relevant committees, etc.), I have no direct involvement with student activists or their activism. However, I am attuned to systemic injustices and the ways they harm the subjugated.

Data Analysis and Trustworthiness

I reviewed the transcription in its entirety at multiple points in time to familiarize myself with the forum attendees' questions and responses. I then coded the administrators' responses line-by-line using the *RQ* to guide the inductive identification of main concepts (Glaser, & Strauss, 1967; Lindlof & Taylor, 2019). I reexamined each code independently and in comparison with other codes to create several broader categories. I paid particular attention to the administrators' references to personhood (i.e., the self), using words such as *you, we, you all, students, people, individuals,* and *they*. I also paid close attention to utterances worded in the passive voice and stated without reference to agent (i.e., social actors) (Wodak, 2011). As CDA scholars have argued, the absence of an agent in text reveals voices that are muted (Machin & Mayr, 2012).

During the coding process, I switched back and forth between the data and some critical scholarship of DEI works in higher education. I also engaged in memoing – writing reflective notes (Lindlof & Taylor, 2019) – to develop concepts into themes that intersected with institutional DEI work and the roles of various actors – in particular, minoritized students and minoritized student activists. I repeated the aforementioned process comparing the data against other institutional messages about DEI (*incl.* from campus newsletters, announcements of DEI events, the President's emails to the campus community about diversity issues, etc.). My engagement in multiple rounds of inductive coding separated in time addresses intracoder reliability (Bernard, 2011). To enhance the trustworthiness of the study, I consulted with two scholars who are knowledgeable about diversity studies and solicited their feedback regarding main themes that constitute the findings of the study (Bernard, 2011; Creswell, 2019; Creswell & Poth, 2017).

Findings

The administrators' fundamental assumption about the minoritized student activists as the Other illuminates their inherent views of the activists' knowledge, perceptions, individual rights, and autonomy. The portrayal of the Other – that is, those considered different and therefore illegitimized – is elucidated in the following comment from Aidan, a senior administrator:

> … we've had the conversation with several [minoritized] students, and we've worked it out… we have found other ways to make people satisfied with their experiences … if we can talk to each other about it, we'll find ways to get folks through these programs … we'll look at everything, at the situation with your particular nuance … . Now, I don't know [that] everybody is going to be happy all the time. And, sometimes, it's not going to feel as transparent as it should be.

A close reading of Aidan's *exceptional* solutions for the issues raised by minoritized students suggests an academic system that is not inclusive of all students. His celebration of apparently successful uses of non-normative practices to address grievances of minoritized students alludes to progress in the administration's DEI agendas. However, this seemingly positive development only works to reinforce the dominant group's understanding of the Other by erasing their voices. As Aidan's solution suggests, deviants – that is, minoritized students – are accorded non-normative treatment, but using this tactic to accommodate their differences basically treats their *complaints* with contempt, in essence erasing their voices.

Further, Aidan's treatment of the issues raised indicates a problematization of the Other. It suggests that managing the victims and their dissafection is an effective technique for stamping down unpopular issues on campus – in this case allegations that a tenured professor was allowed to continue teaching despite charges that they racially discriminated against and sexually harassed minoritized students. In Aidan's view, the victims' subjective perceptions and feelings were interfering with their academic progress, hence the need to find temporary solutions that would allow them to complete their coursework. The DEI priority revealed in this case is to get the minoritized students graduated – because doing so supports the university's diversity initiatives in enhancing the recruitment, retention, and graduation of underrepresented students. In fact, the graduation rate of racial minority students enhances the university's standing (Galli & Bahamonde, 2018; Iverson, 2019) and is critiqued in scholarship that problematizes the neoliberalized discourse of diversity (Ahmed, 2012; Iverson, 2019, 2019; Urciuoli, 1999, 2016).

However, what remains unsaid in this situation is more troubling, but instructive. The victims were essentially being asked to endure their traumatic experiences in private, since their protests were dismissed. In fact, Aidan's savior complex – which they view as compassion because it allows the students to graduate – only reinforces the prevailing ideologies. Ultimately, the students' complaints may dissipate by attrition through graduation, but the issues they raise about the existing power structures at the university remain unchanged.

Deficiencies in Knowledge

In sharp contrast to Aidan's take on the students, Morgan's melancholic recount of his unique administrative experience seems carefully designed to endear and connect him emotionally with the forum participants.

> I'm originally from Chicago. What would scare me, if really, may be very little… . If something frightens you, [and] if you don't talk [about it], I don't know. So, we have to be able to talk … . I've been here for thirty one years. And, in that time, I have watched things change… . It wasn't easy for me to be the only black man here …

By divulging his background and hometown – a city where the lives of racial minorities are entrenched in racial segregation, Morgan is able to establish common ground with those who suffer social injustices. This discursive strategy lends credibility to Morgan's address to the activists as it seems to support the activists' approach to dealing with racist threats. Morgan assures the activists that, "What we are doing to protect the safety of students, part of it, is education." Shifting the context of the discussion to higher education – the common factor that ties the actors together – further establishes common interest that provides the university constituents a means to relate to each other.

But hidden in Morgan's narrative is the assumption that the problems of minoritized students and activists are self-inflicted. It is generally assumed that the invisibility of the students and activists and their silence about their experiences on campus can only perpetuate their struggles, because administrators are not alerted to their issues. However, the overarching assumption that the students somehow lack sufficient knowledge allows Morgan and other administrators to shift their focus to education – the process of acquiring knowledge. In other words the administrators assume that the students' fundamental need for education trumps all other issues.

Rather than exchange ideas with the activists about their demands, the administrators at the forum prescribed what they deemed to be *appropriate* knowledge the students needed. They cited various university policies and state laws to show how difficult it was to advance DEI agendas at the university. In so doing, they implied that the students lacked the requisite competence and standing to make demands or tackle those issues. This simple act demonstrated the administrators' elitist understanding of knowledge in the predominantly White academic setting to justify the lack of effort in advancing DEI agendas. In this setting, policies and laws – which are mostly arbitrary and the students have no role in formulating (Moore, 2014) – are considered sacrosanct and therefore the final authority.

While lecturing the students, the administrators offered advice on ways the students should deal with discrimination and harassment. However, the advice seemed just a reinforcement of another administrator, Eli's admonition that "the individual student has resources and a place to go to make that complaint" and should, therefore, not resort to protest. This discursive strategy seemed to support their assumption that the students also lacked sufficient knowledge about campus services and administrative supports that were available to them. It did not, however, consider the possibility that the students' aversion to using those services might point to underlying issues with the system rather than to lack of knowledge about their availability. Thus, knowledge about campus services might be neither a tool for resolving campus safety issues, nor a safety mechanism for students defending themselves against discrimination and sexual harassment.

By focusing on knowledge acquisition – the administration's overarching objective for the students – another administrator, Shannon, missed the chance to genuinely reflect on the students' most pressing concerns at that moment. According to Shannon, "… this type of work isn't going to happen sitting here, sitting on the stage, and all of you sitting over there, you know, this is not a session where … serious decisions about [the] institution can be made." That seemed to please Aidan, who added, "Now, that's an administrative decision … this is something where I think you should direct that to all of us up here. Because that's our jobs." Shannon defended the administration's "baby steps forward" approach and all but dismissed the activists' accusations of institutional inertia in advancing DEI initiatives. Taken together, these comments reveal an administration keen on displaying its superiority and imposing its position on the activists. The administrators imply that the students not only lack the knowledge, but also underestimate the competence needed to advance the DEI agenda.

Perceptual Biases

The administrators' lexical choices during their meeting with the students reveal their unstated value judgement. Their dismissal of the protest is implied rather than explicit, though they openly expressed views that the students were harboring perceptual biases. For example, Shannon emphasized the importance of differentiating between perceptual biases and the truth, thus, "... we heard loud and clear from you ... that racist, homophobic slurs are imminent threats. They feel like threats ..." By suggesting that the students expressed fears – that is, their lived experiences – were just *feelings*, the administrator was essentially diminishing them, the implication being that threats that are projected to occur are not current reality. In fact, feelings vary from person to person and are subjective, so the students' perception may have been their reality (Destin et al., 2012).

Furthermore, Morgan's earlier statement that they were not easily intimidated by the little things implies that the student activists' emotional reactions demonstrated their subjective assessment which, to a large extent, was non-normative. To the administrators' rational minds, however, subjectivity clouds judgement, and so the activists' perceived inability to distinguish between their own perceptual biases and reality (e.g., in terms of campus safety) elicited a rebuke from Shannon, "because it is more an issue of *actual* as well as *perceived* safety ... ."

Although shades in perception vary greatly, the administrators seem to think the activists' perceptions are biased. In their eyes, the students' perceived lack of objectivity constitutes a flaw that needs to be corrected. Thus, responding to the activists' reminder that the student demands dated back 10 years, Morgan retorted, "Things [have] changed." Morgan's comment both questions the students' audacity to protest while implying that their own perception that things have changed is less biased. Moreover, by touting their lengthy tenure at the university, as Morgan did, the administrators are implying that that fact alone is evidence that the system allows even those who deviate from the norm (i.e., deviants) to thrive. Although Morgan tried to use their minority status to come off as sympathetic to the cause of those who experience injustices, Morgan also questioned the activists' reactions to racist threats and their motivation for protesting such injustices so, overall, Morgan's comments demonstrate a certain distrust of the victims.

Rights and Freedom

> I send out something to board members every year to come and talk to me. And, I want you to think about that. How many people have come to talk to me? ... I can reach out,

> and I don't force people … fourteen years that I have been with the student board, I have been available the fourteen years. Thank you.

This statement by Morgan reveals their dismay that the students have failed to "take their own personal initiative to come" and talk to the administrators. It throws the ball back in the activists' court, suggesting that the administration respects the students' autonomy in making their own choices and cannot, therefore, impose on their freedom. Taking the cue, Shannon added, "What I would like to do … certainly you can think about it, or you can make your choice… is to invite a small group to actually work with me on an ongoing basis…" Taken at face value, these allusions to student rights and freedoms imply that the administrators value the students' participation in the democratic place, which may not be the case in each situation, as discussed below.

Non-Imposition

Toward the end of the forum, the activists started shouting their petition and related demands at the administrators, urging them to sign a document formalizing the student demands. Other members of the audience joined in and started booing and chanting "Sign! Sign!" The administrators, however, maintained their composure and, thus, demonstrated their higher power positions. Despite their negative assumptions about the activists' personhood, their statements about individual autonomy set clear expectations that the rights of everyone should be respected. For example, when the activists' demands and actions appeared to violate this expectation, Xander admonished, "Can I try to clarify something? And I want to be straightforward about it, that that feels very challenging to me, to be told 'You must sign this!'"

Xander's rebuke was a reminder to the activists to respect others' autonomy, but also to use their time wisely and not trash their goodwill. The implication was that students do not have institutional authority to formalize university policies, and trying to coerce administrators into acceding to their demands will not help them achieve their goals. Regarding the activists demand that a staff member who made fun of minoritized students' pursuits of DEI-related projects be fired, Xander responded:

> … it is not uncommon at this institution to make decisions about moving people out from within an organization. Particularly when we want to think about promoting and supporting folks… And, he will continue to do that. I think that's a pretty reasonable thing. I also hear and appreciate the question about a national search … . I am taking that to heart and I'm reflecting on that question …

Xander was implying that students' role in this instance was limited to providing information; that the rest should be left up to the administration, which has the sole rights and responsibilities to make the final decision. In short, the staff member would continue in their position based on the traditional practice at the university.

Viewed critically, the administration's right to hire and fire staff in this instance produces and reinforces the dominant system, since practice that is already legitimized does not welcome interrogation or revision. Furthermore, the staff in question – whom the students accused of subjecting minoritized students to racist abuse and stalling their DEI-related projects – continues in their role, further perpetuating the power dominance by leaving intact the system they are challenging. Actually, Xander's response mirrored almost exactly Shannon's perspective on the same issue, suggesting that a common administrative strategy was at play. According to Shannon, "… this [forum] is not a venue for talking about individuals, whether someone should be hired or fired." With those words and citing university policy, Shannon dismissed the students' concerns and essentially put an end to the discussion.

The Need for Proper Guidance

The administrators' statements in the forum suggested that they viewed the activists as not just deficient in knowledge and having perceptual biases, but also lacking good judgment and therefore unable to exercise their rights and freedoms. Their remedy: to provide the students the proper guidance. And who better to do this than the administration, a well-educated and legitimized source of knowledge whose members were once professors and therefore consider themselves familiar with student issues.

However, it was clear that the administrators' interests were not necessarily aligned with those of the students. For instance, while Eli pointed to the availability of campus resources for resolving student issues, it was clear they were safeguarding the interests of the administration rather than advancing the students' interests. The administrators seemed to view the students' reluctance or inability to use the campus resources as an affront, but did not tie it to their own lack of empathy or ignorance about the minoritized students' realities. They were quick to stress that autonomy comes with responsibility and offer to guide the students on how to use their freedom and autonomy to better effect. Morgan, for example, suggested the activists had wasted valuable time organizing the forum instead of preparing for their final examinations:

> First and foremost, keep your eye on the prize. Your first priority is to become a graduate… . So, we stick to we do want to do. To make sure we have your input, but it's not on your shoulders, right? So be able to tell one another who's going to come forward to work in that group and to give us that kind of input.

To the activists, however, the urgency to hold the forum trumped everything else – their well-being, health, final examinations, and even graduation. Their actions were in direct opposition to the advice offered by the administrators who, in turn, suggested that the students' judgment was being negatively influenced by their feelings. After all, their demands were neither new nor emergencies, and their attempts to coerce the administrators into acceding to their demands appeared impulsive and a bow to mob mentality. Shannon explained, "… it's not … just something that the administration and I can wave a wand, and then it can happen. It requires negotiation with the unions. It requires other people on the table to make it happen."

> Morgan, speaking in the same vein, added:
> I can't say I have all the answers. I don't. I know a lot of this. Because, as students, it feels like … I as an administrator have all the answers. In my resume, it doesn't say [that I have all the answers]…. And, in my job description, it doesn't say [that I have all the answers]….

Clearly, Shannon and Morgan were *dumbing down* the explanations about the university's actions on DEI matters so the students could understand them better. However, their condescending display of patience could be viewed as further reinforcing their belief that the students are not knowledgeable enough about the weighty matters of university administration.

Conclusion

In its advertising the PWI in this study touts the university's bold DEI initiatives and successes. The university's commitment to building an inclusive community is supported with DEI plans and activities. While the aggressive pursuit of DEI is admirable, it is clear that much work needs to be done to support the university's growing minoritized student population. As demonstrated in this study, a CDA of the university administrators' discourse during the forum with students reveals the underlying tensions in their engagement in DEI work. Despite the university's commitment and work to implement multiple DEI initiatives, the administrators' responses suggest that minoritized students' struggles still need to be understood and addressed by the university leadership.

The administrators' discourse indicates a divide between the activists and the administrators in the understanding of minoritized students' interests. When confronted with the students' demands, the administrators quickly assume superiority in managing what was essentially an intercultural conflict and cited university policies and laws to reinforce their authority. The administrators repeatedly committed themselves to considering the various student demands, but their seeming readiness to commit could easily be viewed as illegitimizing the activists' personhood. Fundamentally, their act of committing itself was non-committal (Ahmed, 2012) – that is, the administrators did not perform any actions to support the student demands. Instead of genuinely exchanging ideas and meeting (some of) the student demands, they diverted the activists' focus and suggested future meetings in smaller groups. In other words the administrators effectively overruled student activism.

While the use of bureaucratic parries might have seemed necessary in the tension-filled forum, the administrators' refusal to accede to any student demands spells trouble for DEI development at the university. First, the activists' list of demands signaled that all was not well with DEI at the university. Second, the demands themselves were not new, as many had existed for more than 10 years. A reasonable conclusion, then, was that the administration was ignorant or deaf to the kind of injustices the students were demanding. It was not lost on the activists that the composition of the administration was 83 % White. That was a body of privileged Whites who had never experienced any subjugation in their lives. The degree to which they could relate to and understand the struggles of minoritized students was minuscule (e.g., see Davis et al., 2020; Long & Mejia, 2016). Barring a genuine connection or deeper understanding of subjugation, it is debatable whether these particular administrators could invest sufficient efforts in the interests of minoritized students.

In fact, the administrators' assumptions about the minoritized student activists' personhood falls right in line with prevailing dominant While ideologies. In particular, viewing the students as deviant and lesser outsiders essentializes the minoritized personhood and problematizes the lived experiences of the Other (Urciuoli, 2008, 2016). Inviting student visits and soliciting input from them reinforces their hypervisibility as DEI experts based on their marked cultural identities (Desai & Abeita, 2017). On the other hand, promising to consider the student demands only after soliciting their input devalues the students' lived experiences. This gesture reveals the administrators' reinforcement of the status quo in selectively privileging or dismissing student issues according to the administration's agendas. Thus, the absence of institutional reciprocity only intensifies the students' invisibility (Byrd et al., 2021).

The CDA of the administrators' spontaneous discourse uncovers effectively these hidden reinforcements of White ideologies that cannot otherwise be captured by university statistics and the abundance of DEI initiatives. The CDA reveals a clear delineation of power relations and the positions of the protagonists in those relations. The delineation by hierarchy reinforces and reproduces the existing institutional structure, as well as prevailing ideologies (Foucault, 1980). As noted by the administrators, the burden of DEI falls on the administration, not the students. At first glance this sounds like something that would benefit minoritized student interests. However, in the context of the forum in which genuine intercultural dialogue was required, the administrators' actions can be viewed as assertion of authority and exclusion of the marginalized. After all, the administrators' claim of responsibility contradicts their lukewarm reception to student demands and lack of openness to student input.

Moreover, the administrators' non-imposition on the students and seeming respect for their autonomy camouflages a strategic or inadvertent subjugation of the activists. Their claim of preserving university tradition actually betrays their goal of protecting institutional authority at the expense of student rights. For example, asserting that certain matters are non-negotiable (e.g., Xander's assertion of "pretty reasonable" hiring practice) demonstrates a reinforcement of predetermined decisions and actions. From defining roles and responsibilities to citing laws and policies, the administrators reveal their expectations that minoritized students will remain silent and subservient. Their insistence that the students play by the rules (e.g., follow university policies, do not challenge state laws, etc.) does not allow space to dismantle the discriminatory practices or existing power structure. These exclusionary practices, therefore, stifle democratic participation (Moore, 2014).

In fact, the quest to maintain traditional university practices shows that decision-making power remains concentrated in the hands of a few. Working in partnership with students, as advertised by the administrators in the forum, is not implemented sincerely and effectively. Were student input to be incorporated in key decisions, the decades long demands would have been partially met. The administrators' solicitation of student input can, thus, be viewed as a strategy to diffuse student angst. The administration is employing a common bureaucratic tactic for managing student activism: commit to talk to the students, but ensure no follow-up. The hope is that the numerous promises and fruitless discussions will wear out the students and resolve the issues (Byrd et al., 2021; Robertson, 2021).

While the act of listening to – that is, acknowledging – the students may make them feel important and powerful whether or not their input is taken seriously, such deception does not translate to effective leadership on DEI matters. It only appears effective because the students advance academically in cohorts, and once one cohort group is graduated, the next cohort may not have the experience to push through their DEI agenda. Although this may ease the burden on the administrators, they end up missing on valuable interactions and potentially rich learning experiences with the students.

Ironically, the administrators have the power and resources to solve many of the problems raised by the minoritized students if they so wish. For them to continue taxing the students, who are already hampered by academic pursuits, with these burdens is ethically inexcusable. To alleviate the ethical concern of abusing the free labor of students who are fighting for these rights, some suggested in the forum that the minoritized students be compensated financially. However, doing so reinforces White ideologies – specifically, the belief that it is the responsibility of people of color to educate Whites about intercultural matters (also see DiAngelo, 2018).

In fact, the context-free assumption about rights and equality is inherently a problem for a university system that emphasizes democracy. The administrators' contention that students have inalienable rights and freedoms results in a collective administration ignorance and refusal to acknowledge the students' realities. Since students reside in a lower power position in the organizational hierarchy, giving minoritized students equal rights to administrators in this structure would disregard the context embedded in inequities and injustices. While the administrators cannot alter the reality of power differences, they could permit democratic participation by, for example, involving the students in electing university officials. Without effective student representation, administrative decisions on matters that are meant to serve student interests become authoritative, not democratic.

Although the administrators who hold positions of power and make crucial decisions that affect the academic experiences and lives of minoritized students often undergo leadership and administrative training, they get little to no training in DEI matters. It is not surprising that the administrators' mission is to support the vision, mission, values and, above all, ideologies of the university, since the administrators are recruited and retained to work for the university. Therefore, there exists a conflict of interest that interferes with genuine conversations on difficult topics, particularly those concerning intersectionality in the White dominant ideology that permeates PWIs.

As was clear during the forum, the administrators defended themselves and the administration and focused on the activists and their actions, rather than on the issues they raised. Doing so prevented the administrators from engaging in the moment and in the critical conversations that could have enriched their knowledge and understanding about the privileges that the system confers on some but not others (Deetz & Simpson, 2004; Simpson, 2008). However, engaging in those difficult conversations calls for the administrators to reflect honestly about their flaws, boldly confront their own ignorance, and diligently explore options that would serve equally all the people in the institution (Deetz & Simpson, 2004; Lee, 2016b; Yep, 2010). Challenging normative practices and assumptions would help them avoid reproducing and perpetuating the prevailing ideologies, but to fight injustices, the administrators would need to put their self-defense aside and genuinely engage the student activists (Lee, 2016b, 2019).

Further, instead of identifying and fixing the issues within the system, the administrators engaged in tokenism by creating special methods meant to *save* minoritized students from their social struggles at the PWI. The temporary solution example, a favorite of Aidan's, provides a quick way out without addressing the underlying problems in the system. But this is not unique to this PWI. As demonstrated in many transnational DEI works, administrators often resort to temporary solutions when the system does not meet their needs or to quiet down grievances (Byrd et al., 2021).

Once again the use of tokenism here does not help disrupt and dismantle the prevailing ideologies (Desai & Abeita, 2017). For example, the university diversity recruitment plan aims to achieve "critical mass" – the most important and timely pursuit according to Shannon. In this case the concept of *critical mass* is used to create the illusion that minoritized students, as well as faculty and staff, can thrive freely in a community with many others who understand and support them. Unfortunately, the mass itself does not fix the problems with the existing system. Ironically, the most relevant *critical mass* in this case is that of the White faculty, staff, and students who constitute the majority at the institution. Therefore, a more productive solution in this situation would be to change the dominant group's taken-for-granted perspectives: a little correctional education to fix the deficiencies in White folks – for example, their knowledge about and perception of racial reality – could be effective at engaging in genuine intercultural dialogue (Lee, 2016b, 2019).

However, to truly enact change, the change must come from within (Lee, 2016b, 2019). In the context of this chapter, the work must begin with the aforementioned education of the dominant group in higher education. In 2018, approximately 70 % of full-time faculty in degree-granting postsecondary institutions was White (National Center for Education Statistics' Digest of Education Statistics 2019). However, the current system of education does not equip educators with sufficient knowledge and skills to disrupt what is essentially White racism (Hendrix & Wilson, 2014; Starosta, 2010; Yep, 2010). Educators from elementary and secondary schools through tertiary education continue to offer educational experiences that distort the nation's racial reality (e.g., see Dixson, 2018). Thus, the very academic system that is supposed to empower citizens to build a free country is instead feeding a dominant system and ideologies that reinforce White privilege and superiority. It is for this reason that some critical scholars view U.S. higher education as a racist institution that supports White supremacy (e.g., see Lee, 2016b).

Indeed, many current practices in U.S. higher education are among the offenders in promoting and perpetuating the institution's – and the nation's – racist pedigree. For example, much of the curriculum is produced and taught by predominantly White Ph.D. holders, most of whom are full-time professors. While it can be argued that scholars of color contribute a portion to this knowledge creation, it is important to understand that most of them are trained and mentored by predominantly White faculty (Lee, 2016b). It is no stretch of the imagination to expect that the knowledge that is thus created and passed down – the version that is officially sanctioned – is White-washed (Lee, 2016b, 2018). Therefore, the cycle of knowledge creation and dissemination in higher education continues to favor the dominant groups and ideologies, to the detriment of the non-dominant groups. It is no wonder, then, that scholarship that disrupts the normalization of Whiteness, such as in this chapter, while sorely needed as part of empirical knowledge creation, is shunned, scorned, and discriminated against in academia (Chakravartty et al., 2018; Yep, 2010). The circle of reproduction of dominant White ideologies is, thus, maintained and even reinforced.

Instead of merely focusing on diversifying recruitment and promoting fancy intercultural events on campus, serious investment is needed on initiatives to educate the insiders within the dominant system. Through critical cultural consciousness, it is hoped that the administrators' erroneous assumptions about the personhood of minoritized student activists can be corrected and negative actions reversed. As of now, these assumptions of a deficient personhood, coupled with the unsupported expectation that the students have unhindered freedom to exercise their rights and autonomy, continue to punish the victims. The administrators' muting of the voice of the Other, therefore, perpetuates the dominant system that reinforces inequity and allows injustices.

References

Ahmed, S. (2012). *On Being Included: Racism and Diversity in Institutional Life*. New York, NY: Duke University Press.

Anderson, R. K. (2019). Toward Thick Responsiveness: Engaging Identity-Based Student Protest Movements. *The Journal of Higher Education*, *90*(3), 402–426. https://doi.org/10.1080/00221546.2018.1512803.

Benitez Jr., M. (2010). Resituating Culture Centers Within a Social Justice Framework: Is There Room for Examining Whiteness? In L. P. Davis (Ed.), *Culture Centers in Higher Education: Perspectives on Identity, Theory, and Practice.* (pp. 119–134). Sterling, VA: Stylus Publishing.

Bernard, H. R. (2011). *Research Methods in Anthropology: Qualitative and Quantitative Approaches.* Lanham, MD: AltaMira Press.

Byrd, W. C., Luney, L. T., Marie, J., & Sanders, K. N. (2021). Demanding Attention: An Exploration of Institutional Characteristics of Recent Student Demands. *Journal of Diversity in Higher Education, 14*(1), 25–36. https://doi.org/10.1037/dhe0000133.

Carbaugh, D. (2007). Cultural Discourse Analysis: Communication Practices and Intercultural Encounters. *Journal of Intercultural Communication Research, 36*(3), 167–182. https://doi.org/10.1080/17475750701737090.

Chakravartty, P., Kuo, R., Grubbs, V., & McIlwain, C. (2018). #CommunicationSoWhite. *Journal of Communication, 68*(2), 254–266. https://doi.org/10.1093/joc/jqy003.

Creswell, J. W. (2019). *Educational Research: Planning, Conducting, and Evaluating Quantitative and Qualitative Research* (6th ed.). New York, NY: Pearson.

Creswell, J. W., & Poth, C. N. (2017). *Qualitative Inquiry and Research Design: Choosing among Five Approaches* (4th ed.). Los Angeles, CA: Sage.

Davis, S. N., Garner, P. W., Jones, R. M., & Mahatmya, D. (2020). The Role of Perceived Support and Local Culture in Undergraduate Research Mentoring by Underrepresented Minority Faculty Members: Findings from a Multi-Institutional Research Collaboration. *Mentoring & Tutoring for Partnership in Learning, 28*(2), 176–188. https://doi.org/10.1080/13611267.2020.1749347.

Deetz, S., & Simpson, J. (2004). Critical Organizational Dialogue: Open Formation and the Demand of "Otherness." In R. Anderson, L. Baxter, & K. Cissna, *Dialogue: Theorizing Difference in Communication Studies* (pp. 141–158). Thousand Oaks, CA: Sage. https://doi.org/10.4135/9781483328683.n9.

Desai, S. R., & Abeita, A. (2017). Institutional Microaggressions at a Hispanic Serving Institution: A Diné (Navajo) Woman Utilizing Tribal Critical Race Theory through Student Activism. *Equity & Excellence in Education, 50*(3), 275–289. https://doi.org/10.1080/10665684.2017.1336498.

Destin, M., Richman, S., Varner, F., & Mandara, J. (2012). "Feeling" Hierarchy: The Pathway from Subjective Social Status to Achievement. *Journal of Adolescence, 35*(6), 1571–1579. https://doi.org/10.1016/j.adolescence.2012.06.006.

DiAngelo, R. J. (2018). *White Fragility: Why It's So Hard for White People to Talk about Racism.* Boston, MA: Beacon Press.

Dixson, A. (2018). "What's going on?": A Critical Race Theory Perspective on Black Lives Matter and Activism in Education. *Urban Education*, *53*(2), 231–247. https://doi.org/10.1177/0042085917747115.

Fairclough, N. (2001). Critical Discourse Analysis as a Method in Social Scientific Research. In R. Wodak & M. Meyer (Eds.), *Methods of Critical Discourse Analysis* (pp. 121–138). London, UK: Sage. https://doi.org/10.4135/9780857028020.

Fairclough, N. (2016). Dialectical-relational Approach to Critical Discourse Analysis in Social Research. In R. Wodak & M. Meyer (Eds.), *Methods of Critical Discourse Studies*. Thousand Oaks, CA: Sage.

Foucault, M. (1980). *Power/Knowledge: Selected Interviews and Other Writings, 1972–1977*. New York, NY: Pantheon Books.

Galli, D. M., & Bahamonde, R. (2018). Assessing IUPUI's Diversity Scholars Research Program: Lessons Learned. *Scholarship and Practice of Undergraduate Research*, *4*(1), 12–17. https://doi.org/10.18833/spur/1/4/10.

Glaser, B. G., & Strauss, A. L. (1967). *The Discovery of Grounded Theory: Strategies for Qualitative Research*. Chicago, IL: Aldine Publishing.

Goldstein Hode, M., & Meisenbach, R. J. (2017). Reproducing Whiteness Through Diversity: A Critical Discourse Analysis of the Pro-Affirmative Action Amicus Briefs in the Fisher Case. *Journal of Diversity in Higher Education*, *10*(2), 162–180. https://doi.org/10.1037/dhe0000014.

Hendrix, K. G., & Wilson, C. (2014). Virtual Invisibility: Race and Communication Education. *Communication Education*, *63*(4), 405–428. https://doi.org/10.1080/03634523.2014.934852.

Hoffman, G. D., & Mitchell, T. D. (2016). Making Diversity "everyone's business": A Discourse Analysis of Institutional Responses to Student Activism for Equity and Inclusion. *Journal of Diversity in Higher Education*, *9*(3), 277–289. https://doi.org/10.1037/dhe0000037.

Iverson, S. B. (2019). Troubling Diversity: An Intersectional Analysis of Diversity Action Plans at U.S. Flagship Universities. In W. C. Byrd, R. Brunn-Bevel, & S. M. Ovink (Eds.), *Intersectionality and Higher Education: Identity and Inequality on College Campuses* (pp. 242–269). New Brunswick, NJ: Rutgers University Press.

Jackson, M. C., Galvez, G., Landa, I., Buonora, P., & Thoman, D. B. (2016). Science that Matters: The Importance of a Cultural Connection in Underrepresented Students' Science Pursuit. *CBE – Life Sciences Education*, *15*(3), 1–12. https://doi.org/10.1187/cbe.16-01-0067.

Jackson, P. A., & Seiler, G. (2018). I Am Smart Enough to Study Postsecondary Science: A Critical Discourse Analysis of Latecomers' Identity Construction in an Online Forum. *Cultural Studies of Science Education, 13*(3), 761–784. https://doi.org/10.1007/s11422-017-9818-0.

Lee, E. L. (2016a). Language and Culture. In J. Nussbaum (Ed.), *Research Encyclopedia of Communication*. New York, NY: Oxford University Press. https://doi.org/10.1093/acrefore/9780190228613.013.26.

Lee, E. L. (2016b). Intercultural Dialogue in Theory and Practice: A Review. *Journal of Multicultural Discourses, 11*(2), 236–242. https://doi.org/10.1080/17447143.2016.1156686.

Lee, E. L. (2018). *WWU Teaching to Stand Up 2017–18: Engaging Social Justice Video [online video]*. Retrieved from: http://cii.wwu.edu/showcase2017/lee/videos.html.

Lee, E. L. (2019). The Segregation of Foreigners in U.S. Mainstream Classrooms. *Sustainability, 11*(11), 3157. https://doi.org/10.3390/su11113157.

Lindlof, T. R., & Taylor, B. C. (2019). *Qualitative Communication Research Methods* (4th ed.). Thousand Oaks, CA: Sage.

Logan, G., Lightfoot, B. A., & Contreras, A. (2017). Black and Brown Millennial Activism on a PWI Campus in the Era of Trump. *The Journal of Negro Education, 86*(3), 252–268. https://doi.org/10.7709/jnegroeducation.86.3.0252.

Long, L. L., & Mejia, J. A. (2016). Conversations about Diversity: Institutional Barriers for Underrepresented Engineering Students. *Journal of Engineering Education, 105*(2), 211–218. https://doi.org/10.1002/jee.20114.

Lopez-Bonilla, G. (2011). Narratives of Exclusion and the Construction of the Self. In R. Rogers (Ed.), *An Introduction to Critical Discourse Analysis in Education*. (2nd ed., pp. 46–67). New York, NY: Taylor & Francis.

Machin, D., & Mayr, A. (2012). *How to Do Critical Discourse Analysis: A Multimodal Approach*. Los Angeles, CA: Sage.

Merino, Y., Thomas, T., Lightfoot, A., Eng, E., Simán, F., Thatcher, K., & Chapman, M. (2020). "They were just waiting for me to mess up": A Critical Discourse Analysis of Immigrant Latinx Teens' Perceptions of Power Dynamics. *Journal of Community Psychology, 48*(2), 605–622. https://doi.org/10.1002/jcop.22276.

Moore, T. L. (2014). *Community-University Engagement: A Process for Building Democratic Communities: ASHE Higher Education Report, 40:2*. Somerset, NJ: John Wiley & Sons. http://ebookcentral.proquest.com/lib/wwu/detail.action?docID=1683805

National Center for Education Statistics. (2021). *Digestof Education Statistics 2019*. Lanham, MD: Bernan Press.

Philipsen, G. (1975). Speaking "like a man" in Teamsterville: Culture Patterns of Role Enactment in an Urban Neighborhood. *Quarterly Journal of Speech, 61*(1), 13–22. https://doi.org/10.1080/00335637509383264.

Philipsen, G. (1992). *Speaking Culturally: Explorations in Social Communication.* Albany, NY: State University of New York Press.

Philipsen, G., Coutu, L., & Covarrubias, P. (2005). Speech Codes Theory: Restatement, Revisions, and a Response to Criticisms. In W. Gudykunst (Ed.), *Theorizing about Communication and Culture* (pp. 55–68). Thousand Oaks, CA: Sage.

Quaye, S. J., & Lange, A. C. (2020). Pete's Letter: A Student Activist's Message to Campus Administrators. *Journal of Diversity in Higher Education*. https://doi.org/10.1037/dhe0000293.

Robertson, R. (2021). A Critical Race Theory Analysis of Transnational Student Activism, Social Media Counter-Stories, and the Hegemonic Logics of Diversity Work in Higher Education. *International Journal of Qualitative Studies in Education, 0*(0), 1–18. https://doi.org/10.1080/09518398.2021.1885073.

Rogers, R. R. L. (2011). *An Introduction to Critical Discourse Analysis in Education* (2nd ed.). New York, NY: Routledge, Taylor & Francis Group.

Simpson, J. L. (2008). The Color-Blind Double Bind: Whiteness and the (Im) possibility of Dialogue. *Communication Theory, 18*(1), 139–159. https://doi.org/10.1111/j.1468-2885.2007.00317.x.

Starosta, W. J. (2010). Reflections on "race" and Publication in Communication Journals: The Case of the Howard Journal of Communications. *Southern Communication Journal, 75*(2), 176–179. https://doi.org/10.1080/1041794100 3613271.

Thornborrow, J. (2001). *Power Talk: Language and Interaction in Institutional Discourse*. London, UK: Taylor & Francis Group. http://ebookcentral.proqu est.com/lib/wwu/detail.action?docID=2036406

Urciuoli, B. (1999). Producing Multiculturalism in Higher Education: Who's Producing What For Whom? *International Journal of Qualitative Studies in Education, 12*(3), 287–298. https://doi.org/10.1080/095183999236141.

Urciuoli, B. (2008). Skills and Selves in the New Workplace. *American Ethnologist, 35*(2), 211–228.

Urciuoli, B. (2016). Neoliberalizing Markedness: The Interpellation of "diverse" College Students. *HAU: Journal of Ethnographic Theory, 6*(3), 201–221. https://doi.org/10.14318/hau6.3.016.

Urciuoli, B. (2020). Racializing, Ethnicizing, and Diversity Discourses: The Forms May Change But the Pragmatics Stay Remarkably the Same. In H. S.

Alim, A. Reyes, & P. V. Kroskrity (Eds.), *The Oxford Handbook of Language and Race* (pp. 108–130). Oxford: Oxford University Press.

Vaccaro, A., & Mena, J. A. (2011). It's Not Burnout, It's More: Queer College Activists of Color and Mental Health. *Journal of Gay & Lesbian Mental Health, 15*(4), 339–367. https://doi.org/10.1080/19359705.2011.600656.

Wodak, R. (2011). Complex Texts: Analysing, Understanding, Explaining and Interpreting Meanings. *Discourse Studies, 13*(5), 623–633. https://doi.org/10.1177/1461445611412745.

Wodak, R. (2012). Language, Power and Identity. *Language Teaching, 45*(2), 215–233. https://doi.org/10.1017/S0261444811000048.

Yep, G. (2010). *Toward the De-subjugation of Racially Marked Knowledges in Communication*. https://doi.org/10.1080/10417941003613263.

Zanoni, P., & Janssens, M. (2015). The Power of Diversity Discourses at Work: On the Interlocking Nature of Diversities and Occupations. *Organization Studies, 36*(11), 1463–1483. https://doi.org/10.1177/0170840615593584.

Zienkowski, J. (2017). Reflexivity in the Transdisciplinary Field of Critical Discourse Studies. *Palgrave Communications, 3*(1), 17007. https://doi.org/10.1057/palcomms.2017.7.

Introduction to Intersectionality, Inclusion, and Diversity in the Workplace

By Katrina N. Hanna and Robert J. Razzante

The next chapter examines inclusion and diversity at the workplace. This is an important topic that needs to be addressed by many companies. It is pointed out that when people meet, a number of factors converge in assessing the other person. People often form certain opinions of others on the basis of these factors; for example, a White woman from a rural town in the American South might lead to the assumption that she could be closed-minded, naïve, or even less intelligent than most. These assumptions in turn could influence how one communicates with that person. In fact, social identities can determine how one sees oneself and how one interacts with other people.

Hanna and Razzante examine the meeting of diverse employees within the context of intersectionality. Intersectionality refers to the actual meeting of diversity at various levels within a company; namely, at the macro-level (e.g. organizing strategies), the meso-level (e.g. organizational practices), and the micro-level (e.g. discursive actions). Intersectionality is an analytical tool that considers the complex identities of the interactors. It tries to find commonalities through and beyond differences. Case studies are used as examples to illustrate intersectionality at the various levels within organizations. These examples show that diversity and intersectionality are composed of multiple factors that influence the interaction with others. This complexity needs to be acknowledged, otherwise the attempts undertaken to overcome prejudices will not be very effective. But it is also pointed out that these efforts ought to be undertaken to promote diversity because organizations with, for example, white women in senior positons are more socially responsible, provide safer, and higher-quality customer service, and are more profitable. These are important arguments on behalf of more diversity.

Michael B. Hinner

Katrina N. Hanna (PhD, Arizona State University) is an Assistant Professor of Communication Studies at California State University, Long Beach. Her primary areas of research focus on the relationship between rhetoric (via music, educational contexts, and everyday advocacy and action) and power. This research is framed through the assumptions of critical race theory and intersectionality. Her recent publications can be found in *Nonprofit and Volunteer Sector Quarterly* and *Journal of Contemporary Rhetoric*. In addition to her research and teaching, Kat leads an international, three-day mindfulness public speaking training. Created and run through Alan Carroll & Associates, this soft-skills training works with IT young professionals in countries like South Africa, Turkey, Oman, Yemen, and Saudi Arabia, just to name a few. Across research, teaching, and consulting,

Kat's work focuses on the power of language to create our world, shape and define the complex lives we live, and how communication can be used in the service of equity and intersectional approaches to racial justice.

Robert J. Razzante (PhD, Arizona State University) is a Visiting Assistant Professor with the Department of Communication Studies at Western Washington University. Rob seeks to weave together his teaching, research, and community engagement to cultivate resilient people and communities who grow from transformative conflict and collaborative learning. Rob's scholarship centers communication as the process of co-constituting culture, power, and (in)equities and ways for using communication as a catalyst for action research. His most recent work used participatory action research for identifying pathways of co-creating an inclusive workplace with a multi-national healthcare organization. Rob's research has been published in academic journals such as *Communication Theory*, *Journal of International and Intercultural Communication*, and *Communication Studies*. He also facilitates three-day *Mindfulness in Action* workshops for an international training and development organization that seeks to infuse mindfulness with people's soft skills regarding conflict management, public speaking, and active listening. The organization, Alan Carroll & Associates, has worked with IT professionals from Nigeria, Turkey, Greece, Yemen, Oman, Saudi Arabia, Kenya, and South Africa to name a few. Rob brings this international experience into his classes and research to promote the idea of being global citizens.

Katrina N. Hanna and Robert J. Razzante

Intersectionality, Inclusion, and Diversity in the Workplace

When it comes to (re)creating many of the organizations and workplaces we have in the U.S., "inclusion" seems to be a recent hot topic. From blog posts and news stories with titles like, "11 Powerful Ways to Nurture Inclusion at the Workplace," "15 Ways to Improve Diversity and Inclusion in the Workplace," and "6 Steps for Building an Inclusive Workplace," we see how this current trend of businesses being encouraged to address their issues of inequity and exclusion is of interest to many. Common suggestions made in these posts about "how to" create an inclusive workplace include: educating leaders, instilling workplace policies that center the goal of building a diverse workforce, and celebrating diverse people, thoughts, and backgrounds. Although these are great goals to have, we find that much of the evidence provided for why inclusion is needed do not always and consistently address the truly complex issues surrounding equity and inclusion in the workplace.

Our goal with this chapter is to demonstrate how we need to be careful and mindful to not reduce complex people and their equally complex lives into oversimplified policies, practices, and assumptions especially within the context of communication in the workplace. To effectively demonstrate our case, we will begin with an overview of intersectionality, its assumptions and goals. From there we will offer a brief overview of what research exists within communication on issues of equity and inclusion within various organizations. With these two framings of intersectionality and communicative research on equity and inclusion, we unpack three different case studies that demonstrate what intersectionality can bring to macro-level organization issues of pay gaps, meso-level issues of hiring and promotions, and micro-level interactions through microaggressions. Ultimately, each case study notes how issues of equity and inclusion can exist at various levels within an organization all while offering one potential roadmap for creating change through the lens of intersectionality.

What Is Intersectionality?

We have all encountered intersections in our life: intersections at a stoplight or where paths converge on a hiking trail. These intersections exist because it is the meeting of multiple, individual lanes or paths. When people talk about intersectionality in relation to concerns of diversity, inclusion, and equity they take this metaphor of roads or paths converging and apply it to people and our various social identities. In this section of the chapter, we will first address what we mean by social identities and then expand on what is intersectionality.

Social identities are categories and labels we apply to people based on their culture, background, history, and various belief systems. Commonly used and referred to social identities are: race, class, gender, sex, sexual orientation, ethnicity, ability, and religion (see Table 1 for clarification on these social identities).

Table 1: Social Identities

Social Identity	**Definition**	**Examples**	**Please Note!**
Race	A socially constructed term used to determine the treatment of people based on physical characteristics (e.g., skin color, hair texture, facial characteristics). Racial categories have changed over time (e.g., Irish Americans were once not considered "White.").	Black, White, Māori, Native American, and Asian.	Race and ethnicity (see below) are often conflated and even used interchangeably. However, they are two distinct concepts. One way to help distinguish between the two is that racialized terms and assumptions will vary by culture and country while ethnicity is more likely to be consistent across cultures and countries.
Class	In a capitalist economy, a system where people are divided and perceived differently based on their position in relation to property, income, and wealth.	Upper class (or wealthy), middle class, and working class (or poor).	In the U.S., we like to pride ourselves on being a classless society. Yes, compared to other systems, people can and do experience economic mobility in this country. However, this is very rare. Subsequently, we do talk about rich people and poor people differently. Rich people are seen as hardworking, dedicated, and innovative, while some poor people are called lazy or leeches.

Table 1: Continued

Social Identity	Definition	Examples	Please Note!
Gender	A social, cultural, and political term that is a learned concept that will vary across time and contexts.	Cis woman, cis man, trans woman, trans man, nonbinary, and gender queer.	The preface of "cis" means "on the side of." A cis woman is a person who identifies as the sex assigned to them at birth, female. "Trans" means "on the opposite side of." A trans woman was assigned male and therefore a "boy" at birth does not identify with being a man. Studies do confirm that most children have a solid sense of their gender as young as 5 and 6 years-old (regardless of what is assigned to them as infants) and that there might be natural brain development that can result in a trans identity.
Sex	A socially constructed term used to define someone's identity based on genitals, hormones, chromosomes, and brain development/ chemistry.	Male, female, and intersex.	As with race and ethnicity, we tend to conflate sex with gender. Some believe that sex determines gender. For example, if you are assigned "female" at birth you are therefore a woman. However, through the experiences of both intersex (people who do not fall into the tightly labeled binary of male/female) and trans individuals we learn that this "neat" connection or line between sex and gender is not so pre-determined and definitive.

(*Continued*)

Table 1: Continued

Social Identity	Definition	Examples	Please Note!
Sexual Orientation	The identity one carries in relation to what gender, genders, or personality traits they are sexually attracted to.	Gay, asexual, queer, lesbian, heterosexual, pansexual, and bi-sexual.	Please keep in mind that the terms and definitions of various sexual orientations are often changing constantly. The important thing is to not assume one's sexual orientation. In addition, gender does not equate sexual orientation. Refrain from making simple, yet oversimplified assumptions based on how someone dresses, acts, talks, etc. and then what their sexual preferences are.
Ethnicity	Identity rooted in the shared language(s), food and agriculture, and customs (although it can be difficult to distinguish customs as being "ethnic" versus "religious," e.g., Christmas holidays).	African American, Caucasian, Chinese, German, Japanese, Mexican, and Middle Eastern.	This is not always the case, but ethnicity tends to be more specific than race. For example, the broad racial category of "Asian" includes Indian, Japanese, Korean, and Chinese ethnicities – whose cultures are distinct and unique from each other. The same can be said for the racial category of White. There are Jewish, Irish, Finnish, and Mexican individuals who would be considered White due to their appearance. Thus, someone can be a White Mexican. Simply put, race and ethnicity are distinct, but sometimes overlapping concepts.

Table 1: Continued

Social Identity	Definition	Examples	Please Note!
Ability	This identity reflects what resources someone must accomplish a goal or perform daily tasks.	Neurotypical, Autistic, deaf/hard of hearing, blind, able-bodied, neurodivergent, and disabled.	Someone's ability status does not indicate what they can do. Autistic, deaf, and disabled people can and do live the same complex lives that neurotypical and able-bodied people do, all while facing ignorance and overt discrimination from other people and various organizations (e.g., school and work).
Religion	A system of faith and belief or belief and worship of some superhuman being or thought.	Islam, Judaism, Buddhism, Christianity, and atheism.	No religious identification or label is a monolith. There are various interpretations of religious texts and practices of people who might refer to themselves under the same umbrella of "Christian," "Jewish," or "Muslim." Your task is to do your best to not generalize about any given religion.

We refer to these as *social* identities because it is through communication with others that societies and peoples determine the meaning behind each of these labels. Knowing this, we must keep in mind that depending on where you are, some might have a different understanding of these terms. In addition, by knowing someone's social identities we are often handed a theoretical script of how to talk to and think about this person. For example, you might run into a White woman on an elevator and after a brief chat you learn that she grew up in a rural town in the South. Based on this information, you might automatically start making assumptions about her (e.g., she might be closed-minded, she might be naive, or she might even be less intelligent than most) and then you might decide to stop talking to her or what you talk about might change. In short, these social identities matter because we use these labels to both determine our sense of self, but also how we treat and interact with those around us.

Intersectionality begins with these social identities. At its most basic level, intersectionality argues that we are more than just one social identity and you cannot oversimplify someone's experiences into just one of these social identities. I (Kat) am not just a cis woman.

By referring only to my gender, we ignore how other aspects of my identity shape and influence how I move through the world and am perceived and treated by people. In this example, many of my assumptions about "womanhood" and gender were heavily shaped by experiences growing up in rural poverty and attending a Christian evangelical church for most of my young life. Thus, this next visual is a more detailed insight into who I am:

However, it does not quite tell the full picture. These identities do not exist in isolation of each other. Therefore, this final visual image becomes a more comprehensive representation of my experiences as a woman living in the U.S. because it acknowledges the overlapping nature of these identities (and subsequently my experiences):

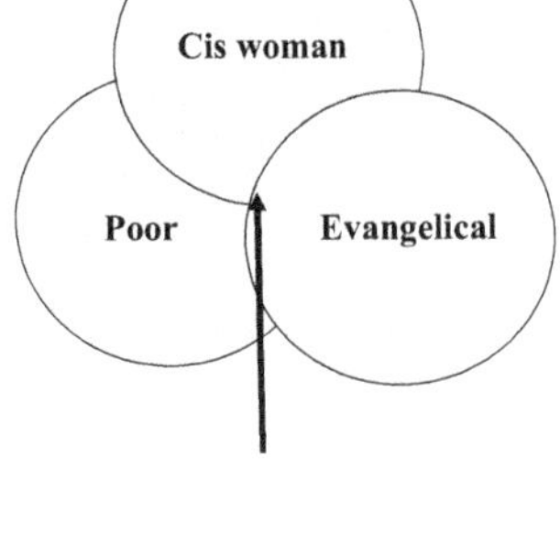

I do not exist in these identities separately but can be found in the center of where all three meet. I could continue to nuance this sense of myself by including other identity markers like race, ability, and sex. Consequently, intersectionality invites us to refrain from oversimplifying people's experiences by forcing them to identify with just one aspect of who they are.

Intersectionality does not stop here. In fact, the goal of intersectionality is not to engage with what is referred to as "pop-bead" approaches to understand someone (Collins & Bilge, 2016). For example, it is not helpful nor fruitful to sit around having everyone listing all their identities (e.g., "Hey folks! I'm Kat, a White, cis woman, who is able-bodied and grew up in Christian churches and rural poverty."). Intersectionality is not an invitation to just state our social identities. We must put those social identities into conversation with the larger society and culture around us. To do so, we must acknowledge that culture and society are not neutral spaces of interaction. All cultures and societies are sites of struggle where a select group of people get to determine the rules, norms, and expectations of the people who live there. In the case of the U.S., we have been built on the experiences of wealthy, land-owning White men; our laws and norms reflected their lived experiences and desires (Hooks, 1984/2015). Those not present when these decisions were made do not get their voices and experiences acknowledged. In other words, they are likely living in a culture and society that does not reflect their own identities and realities.

This struggle with determining whose lives, lifestyles, and customs a given society reflects manifests in what are referred to as ideologies. Ideology is a broad term that can carry many different definitions. For our purposes, ideologies are socially created (not naturally found in the world around us), systematic beliefs, attitudes, and values, that create hierarchies, and offer a "rubric" for how someone is to live their life. For example, living in a democratic society is going to differ from living in an oligarchy and life under feudalism was quite different from our current capitalist landscape. We can find ideologies all around us, even within the social identities noted above (see Table 2)!

Table 2: Ideologies and Social Identities

Social Identity	**Ideology**	**What does it look like?**
Race	Whiteness	Within ideologies of whiteness, we determine which groups of racialized people (their lives, customs, and practices) are to be valued over others. Currently, in the U.S. this means we have a history of laws, policies, and practices that center and privilege white-presenting bodies.
Class	Capitalism	Capitalism is an economic ideology that values competition, individuality, and profits. Within the U.S. capitalism encourages people to "pull themselves up by their bootstraps" and to work hard. If one works hard enough, they will become successful. Thus, capitalism encourages most of us who are not rich to identify with the rich, rather than with those that share our similar economic experiences and backgrounds. Therefore, we like to celebrate the millionaires and demonize those who are most economically insecure.
Gender and Sex	Patriarchy	In its most basic form, patriarchy is the assumption that men should rule and dominate a given society. In addition, this ideology values masculinity and often seeks to demonize femininity. For example, as gender norms have shifted over the centuries, we are more accepting of women taking a big interest in their career (something once only strongly encouraged for men to do), but demonize and critique stay-at-home dads because childcare is considered "women's women" and, therefore, of less value than the type of work we typically expect men to do. Such discourses illustrate the value we place not only on men, but what we deem traditional masculine jobs, activities, and hobbies.

Table 2: Continued

Social Identity	**Ideology**	**What does it look like?**
Sexual Orientation	Heteropatriarchy	Heteropatriarchy is the belief that both heteronormativity and patriarchy work to create norms that celebrate and treat heterosexuality and masculinity as ideal and "natural." Within heteropatriarchy, queer people (anyone who lives outside of being "straight") may experience different kinds of oppression. For example, they might encounter homophobia or outward demonstrations of fear or hatred by individuals, government institutions, and workplaces. A lesbian couple may also experience heterocentrism or the belief that norms of heterosexuality are standard through comments like, "Who is the 'man' and who is the 'woman' in the relationship?" Such comments assume that the only way for a relationship to function is if there is someone performing "traditional" masculine and feminine roles.
Ethnicity	Imperialism and Colonialism	Imperialism occurs when one country or sovereign state actively weakens the political power of another in the name of extending the power and dominion of another country. Colonialism occurs when a country or people partially or completely politically take over another country while exploiting the country's people and resources for economic purposes. The U.S., as we know it today, is the product of colonialism all while continuing imperial practices in places like Puerto Rico and the Middle East. In brief, we can think of colonialism as the practice or act of taking over a different culture and/or nation while imperialism is the belief behind said actions. The important thing is, when colonialism occurs, those overtaking the country or sovereign people (e.g., British settlers in the U.S.) will actively seek to demonize, oppress, and get rid of the native or indigenous people and their customs (e.g., Native peoples of the Americas).

(*Continued*)

Table 1: Continued

Social Identity	Ideology	What does it look like?
Ability	Ableism	Ableism manifests as laws, policies, and social practices that discriminate and create prejudice towards disabled and neuro-atypical people. There are two specific kinds of ableism. Physical ableism is discrimination and prejudice based on someone's physical appearance, while mental ableism is discrimination and prejudice based on someone's cognitive abilities.
Religion	Islam, Protestant, Catholic, and Buddhism, for example.	In the U.S., we are dominated by the assumptions driven by Protestant approaches to Christianity. This manifests in messages that encourage individualism and hard work. In the case of hard work, messages like, "If there is time to lean, there is time to clean," are rooted in Protestant teachings about the evils of idleness and need to be disciplined with one's time.

With intersectionality, the individual (Kat) needs to be understood in relation to these ideologies. Kat is not just a cis woman, who grew up poor and in an evangelical church; she is a product of a patriarchal system that oppresses women and femininity, a capitalist system that values profits over people, and a religion, Christianity, that offers a vast number of interpretations of its religious text that speak to what it means to be a good person, neighbor, and so on. Consequently, while living in the U.S., Kat has likely experienced sexism and classism due to the patriarchal and capitalist beliefs surrounding her, while having the privilege of growing up in an area where many of the same Christian values that were being taught at church were reflected in various laws and rules from the state government to her schools. With intersectionality, I (Kat) can acknowledge and address how I have both experienced oppression (due to my gender and class) while also being privileged because of my religious up-bringing. This both/and of oppression and privilege is key to adopting intersectional thinking into our everyday lives and organizational policies and practices.

Given this background, we come to understand intersectionality as an analytical tool that asks us to consider the complex identities each of us have, in relation to the dominant ideologies in each culture. The goal of intersectionality is not to just list and acknowledge someone's identities. Instead, intersectionality gives us the language to acknowledge the complex, intersecting lives we all live by placing the person in relation to the dominant ideologies in a society and the conflicting oppressions and privileges we all carry because of who we are. To be clear, almost all of us are both privileged in some aspects of our lives and oppressed in others. We invite you to take a few moments and reflect on your own privileges and oppressions based on your society identities.

Consequently, another thing to avoid with intersectionality is what is called "the oppression olympics" (Collins & Bilge, 2016). Many people in this country face oppression across multiple intersections because they are not white, cis-gendered, able-bodied, heterosexual, or a follower of the Christian faith. Take, for example, a trans-Black woman who is neurodivergent. She is going to face oppression through laws, organizational policies and practices, and everyday interactions due to her gender, race, and ability. If she were to engage in a discussion on the prejudices she faces with a white, gay, cis man, she might feel tempted to claim, "Hey! I am more oppressed that you because I face discrimination across *three* of my social identities, not just two." This is not the goal of intersectionality. Intersectionality does not invite us to compete with each other over who is "Most Oppressed." Those conversations rarely go down a productive and constructive path towards creating change and it keeps us from noticing how connected and interrelated we are. Instead of seeing the conversation as a space of competition, the focus instead should be on finding commonalities *through* and *beyond* difference.

The idea of finding commonality through difference embraces the assumptions and goals of intersectional thought and practices. "Commonality" invites us to "incorporate and move beyond sameness, similarity, and difference; commonalities acknowledge and include difference" (Keating, 2013, p. 42). Commonality as a framework specifically asks to adopt a vision for what *could* exist rather than focusing solely on what *is*. In the previous example, getting into a debate about who is "Most Oppressed" forces us to focus only on the current reality for these two people – the conversation won't lead down a path of finding avenues for change. Reimagining the trans-Black, neurodivergent woman and white, gay cis-gendered man's discussion on the prejudices they face through a lens of commonality would invite the two to find what similarities exist in their oppression while looking to craft practices, policies, and laws that could change *both* of their sources of oppression. Sometimes this may look like seeing what similar identities are shared. However, with our example, these two do not share any social identities. Thus, another option of locating commonality is to go beyond their differences to work together to implement organizational changes that address both ableist and homophobic politics and practices. Such actions go beyond an either/or mentality (either we address ableism or homophobia) to acknowledging how a given workplace is oppressive to both people. Ultimately, the spirit of commonality is central to making intersectional changes within our society and our organizations because it both acknowledges difference while asking us to move away from "difference" being the only framework we see each other because of our complex social identities and experiences.

In light of this, experience is central to the assumptions and practices of intersectionality. Earlier forms of intersectional activism, during second wave feminism, for example, advocated that our bodies are a site of knowledge. By thinking about our bodies as vessels that carry knowledge, we challenge that the only kind of "knowing" that exists is what can be taught at a school or in a textbook. Such an argument is important because there is a long history in the U.S. where many people (due to their race, gender, ethnicity, ability, etc.) were actively excluded (and continued to be excluded) from educational spaces, especially higher education (e.g., Apple, 2012). Consequently, arguing, "What I have experienced is knowledge," was (and is) a radical act challenging institutionalized forms of knowledge. The great thing is that we all have knowledge gained through experience! You might have a memory as a child of being told multiple times to not touch a hot stove, but one day you went ahead and touched it. After you experienced that burn, you learned, "Hmm…maybe I shouldn't touch a hot stove." That moment created an embodied, experienced knowledge. In other words, one does not need to read or be lectured on to know what it means or looks like to get your hand burned on a hot stove.

When put into the context of intersectionality, this means that people who experience oppression have the knowledge of that oppression woven into the very fabric of skin: every racist, homophobic, ableist statement or assumption shapes how they move through the world around them. Referred to as "theory of the flesh," the act of treating and honoring experience as knowledge was imperative to the coalition building that women of color did with each other while the Civil Rights Era and second wave of feminism were occurring at the same time in the U.S. (see Anzaldúa, 1987/2012). Simply put "theory of the flesh" argues that the body knows the physical realities of women of color – the concrete or land they grew on, their skin color – come together to create a politics grown out of necessity (Moraga & Anzaldúa, 2015). Centering the body as a vessel of knowledge the intersecting realities of women of color, during the 60s and 70s acknowledges, who were "colored" in the feminist movement ("We only focus on the oppression women face!") and "feminist" in their communities of color ("We only focus on the racism Black people and communities face!"). This meant that women of color, during two major social movements, were asked to leave parts of themselves behind when engaging in either feminist-based activism or activism seeking to change racism.

Therefore, women of color had to create their own spaces of activism that would acknowledge how they experienced the world. They did not just face sexism (as addressed by the feminist movement) nor did they face just racism (as addressed by the Civil Rights movement). Women of color, due to their intersecting social identities of gender *and* race, face sexism and racism simultaneously. In addition, the lived experiences of the individual woman of color were clearly situated in relation to the dominating ideologies of patriarchy and whiteness. The activism of the time sought not to focus on the occasional sexist or racist, but how our places of work, learning, and governing enacted long-stated forms of sexism *and* racism.

In 1989, legal school Kimberlé Crenshaw (who is also credited for coining the term "intersectionality") published research that further demonstrated this overlapping experience of receiving racism and sexism at the same time. She makes her argument by exploring a couple of separate legal cases involving Black women suing their places of work. In these instances, Crenshaw argues how legal discourse confines Black women either to their race or their gender. Consequently, when forced to frame their unique cases of exclusion and oppression at their places of work, through the single lens of race or gender, Black women cannot adequately report on their lived realities; they must either be Black or a woman, but not both, which perpetuates an over-essentializing of identities or the notion that one can be "just" Black or "just" a woman. Moreover, such legal practices perpetuate that a "woman's" experience at work can be read through the experiences of white women and issues of race are to be understood solely in relation to Black men's experiences. Such assumptions and practices cause erasure and make it far more difficult for many historically marginalized people to get the legal (and social) change they deserve because they have overlapping forms of oppression.

A quick, but important note: through this summary of intersectionality, its assumptions, and some of its key concepts, we can see how the call for applying intersectional approaches to issues surrounding equity and inclusion are the product of the lives and work of women of color. We would be remiss as authors to not make this point incredibly clear. To ignore the specific labor and exhaustive efforts done by women of color to fight for equality and change would be a massive disservice to them and their experiences. Does this mean that intersectionality can only be applied to issues of sexism or racism (or patriarchy and whiteness)? Nope! This just means that we are mindful about who created the tool we are using. It also means that we remember to stay away from removing the individual from the surrounding structures and ideologies. Intersectionality requires that we place issues of racism and homophobia into conversation with how whiteness and heteropatriarchy have created a society that values white and straight bodies. It also means that we actively affirm and value personal experiences as knowledge and evidence of oppression. Finally, it also requires that we actively seek to refrain from allowing our differences to keep us from working in coalition together to create more equitable and inclusive places of work.

In the end, intersectionality, through the assumptions of commonalities and lived experiences, asks us to embrace the complexity of our bodies and lives. As summarized by Mari J. Matsuda (1991), an intersectional approach to changing the sources of exclusion and oppression in our everyday lives and organizational practices invites us to ask, "When I see something that looks racist, I ask, 'Where is the patriarchy in this?' When I see something that looks sexist, I ask, 'Where is the heterosexism in this?' When I see something that looks homophobic, I ask, 'Where are the class interests in this?'" (p. 1189). To help you envision what this looks like, we will transition into a summary of research on communication, equity, and inclusion within organizations. From there, we will address three case studies that illustrate how to apply intersectionality into contemporary issues of inclusion and equity within organizations.

Intersectionality and The Workplace

In this chapter, we delineate the focus of our chapter to intersectionality in the context of organizations and the workplaces. Currently, a variety approaches exist to understanding identity and difference in organizational contexts. Critical management studies scholars use the term *gender and diversity* to express relations of power, communication, and identity like gender, race/ethnicity, nationality, sexual orientation, among others (Ashcraft, 2011). Additionally, within communication studies, scholars have taken a feminist approach to examine sex- and gender-relations at work (Acker, 1990; Ashcraft, 2005; Buzzanell, 1994; Parker, 2001). Finally, other scholars use the term *difference* to frame research associated with the social construction of identities, such as race, class, ability, gender, sex, and more (Allen, 1995, 2007, 2014; Ashcraft, 2011; Parker, 2014). Depending on the utility of a term and definition, one might favor one term over others.

By focusing our chapter on intersectionality, we hope to nuance the role intersectional identities play in macro-level organizing strategies, meso-level organizational practices, and micro-level discursive (in)actions. For example, an intersectional lens to identity in the workplace offers spaces to critique macro-level power structures' effect and affect employees and consumers (Steinfeld et al., 2019). Additionally, an intersectional approach to the workplace offers space to understand the meso-level practices that inform the experiences of womxn of color in leadership positions (Sanchez-Hucles & Davis, 2010). With such understanding, organizations can improve working conditions for their employees and remove structural barriers that prevent womxn of color from working their way up the organizational ladder. Finally, intersectionality offers space to understand how intersectional identities are leveraged within micro-level interactions among colleagues, supervisors – supervisees, and employees – consumers (Atewologun et al., 2016; Ferguson, 2018).

In what follows, we take a deeper dive into intersectionality's use as an analytic framework for understanding communication at the macro-, meso-, and micro-levels. We first offer a case regarding the issues of inequity and the discursive messages of the economic worth by critiquing the pay gap. We then explore organizational practices of promotion and how intersectionality provides a framework for eliminating bias-informed practices. Finally, we continue the conversation about biases and prejudice and how an everyday intersectional framework works to hold us accountable when stereotypes inform our micro-level interpersonal (in)action in the workplace.

Case Study #1: Pay Gap

For our first discussion, we are going to briefly talk about issues surrounding pay gaps. This is an important starting point because we notice historical trends of some people being paid less for doing the same work, solely based on one (or more) of their social identities. Most discourse and conversations surrounding the pay gap specify the inequality between how cis men and cis women are paid unequal amounts, for the same kind of work. However, as we will demonstrate in a few paragraphs, our understanding of the gender pay gap invites a much needed intersectional lens because looking at just "cis men" versus "cis women" oversimplifies a more complex reality. To help offer an overview of the realities surrounding the pay gap, we are going to address some common (and often misogynistic) arguments people make to rationalize pay inequities or even argue that women, in general, should be paid less.

One frequent argument made by some individuals is that women are just drawn to jobs that pay less. When we look at women-dominated fields like teaching, registered nurses, and administrative assistants, recent reports show that these three occupations employ 41.9% full-time women and 15.6% full-time men (Institute for Women's Policy Research, 2018). However, this same report found that out of the 20 most common occupations worked in by women,

women still make less than their men counterparts in 18 of those fields. For example, if you are a woman working as a financial manager you are, on average, earning $552 less per week than the men in your same occupation. In another example, when we compare janitors (usually men) to maids and house cleaners (usually women), the men earn 22% more (Miller, 2016). This data illustrates a couple of things. First, as a culture, we do tend to devalue work that we deem more "feminine" because historically "traditional" women's labor (i.e., child raising) offers no physical profit and created an argument that most of women's labor offered no economic productivity (see Folbre, 1991). When women started entering the workforce in greater numbers this same assumption was applied to the work they did: women's workplace labor was not as economically productive as men's. Second, it shows that even within women-dominated fields, the women are going to be paid less than the men they work with.

With this information we need to apply intersectionality to account for how women of color are impacted differently than white women. Data gathered by the U.S. Census Bureau (2018) found that if white men working full-time make $1, then Asian women would make 97 cents to that dollar, white women would make 80 cents, Black women come next with 66 cents to that dollar, and Hispanic women fall into the bottom with 58 cents. You might be curious as to why Asian women (who are coming from a traditionally marginalized and oppressed group of people based on their race and ethnicity) are making, on average, more than white women. There has been plenty of research done to illustrate how discourse of Asians being a "model minority," based on stereotypes that believe Asians are disciplined and hardworking, results in them often getting paid better or being perceived as more successful than other historically marginalized and excluded racial and ethnic groups (e.g., Eguchi & Starosta, 2012; Jin, 2021; Mudambi, 2019; Thorton & Tajima, 2014; Zang, 2010). Especially when many in the U.S. use the perceived collective "success" of Asian Americans post World War II as a racial wedge which minimizes "the role racism plays in the persistent struggles of other racial ethnic/minority groups – especially Black Americans" (Chow, 2017, para. 6). In short, discourses of Asian Americans as a "model minority" seek to create competition between them and other racially/ethnically oppressed and excluded groups all while minimizing the racism and oppression Asians still face in the U.S. Yet this is only one side of the story. These messages also treat the ethnically diverse "Asian" label as a monolith, which is problematic. When we start looking at specific ethnicities in the broad "Asian" category, we see that the highest paid Asians are Chinese Americans and Indian Americans. While other Asian ethnicities, like Thai American and Burmese American women earn anywhere from 50 to 60 cents on the cis white man's dollar (Akhtar, 2019). In the end, paying attention to how race and ethnicity factors into pay inequality offers a more detailed and honest accounting for whose labor is valued more.

A second common argument in support of paying women less states that it is actually women's fault for the pay gap because they don't ask for more money. A recent report does show that 60% of women surveyed have never negotiated their pay with an employer (Leonhardt, 2020). Instead of negotiating with a current job over pay, women are more likely to make the lateral move of quitting their current job to get hired with a new organization, for more money. However, it is important to note that this same survey found that only 48% of men admit to negotiating their salary. A different report conducted by Glassdoor (2016) found that 68% of women accepted the first salary offer at a new job compared to men, at 52 percent. What these numbers show is women are statistically less likely to negotiate their starting salary and to make the request later in their job for a pay raise. The story these numbers do not tell is…why?

Due to our gender norms in the U.S., how we raise girls and boys differently, cis women learn to see negotiation as improper because it makes them seem desperate or "greedy;" while cis men, from a young age, are encouraged to make requests, take up space, and are more actively taught the skills needed to be comfortable negotiating salaries (Sankar, 2017). When we begin to layer other social identities into the conversation, like race, we see that negotiation can be even riskier for a Black or Latina woman because they are often unfairly judged as aggressive or angry, when they might just be passionate; while Asian women are likely to be penalized when they "fail" to be deferential and modest (Larson, 2020, Center for Women and Business). The same report also finds how women with disabilities suffer with lower pay due to receiving a reduced workplace status and structural barriers (i.e., disability accommodations). From this data, we can begin to put together just how difficult it would be for a neurodivergent Latina woman to advocate on her own behalf for a raise. She would likely face resistance due to racial and ethnic stereotypes, sexist notions about how any cis woman should "properly" behave, and a workplace that may not address nor support her disability. This argument does not only ask us to consider how most cis women are culturally raised to not make requests and how others might face additional barriers due to their race and abilities, but to also inquire into the practices of devaluing cis women as they enter once man-dominated occupations we have seen over the decades.

There is some important recent work that shows when cis women begin to enter men-dominated fields, to the point that cis women take over the occupation, the pay declines (Miller, 2016). Here are just a couple of examples: (1) When more cis women started entering the field of recreation (parks or leading camps), the medium hourly wages declined 57 percent; (2) When cis women began entering the field of design at higher rates, the average wage fell 34 percent; and (3) When more cis women became biologists, the average pay fell 18 percent. What does this data demonstrate? We are okay with paying cis women less for the same work cis men do. Yet, when the reverse happens, when cis men begin taking over occupations once dominated by cis women, the pay increases. We can look at computer programming as a great example of this. At the early stages of computer programming, it was seen as a menial role that was appropriate for cis women to complete. When cis men began entering the field at higher rates, the job not only began paying more, but also gained more prestige (Oldenziel, 2001). After dispelling these two common arguments to support or rationalize pay inequity, we want to conclude this section with some guidance on what could be done to make more equitable and inclusive choices.

In the case of pay gap disparities, the goal should not be to either propose "Equal pay for women!" because such campaigns ignore the nuances between the various kinds of women based on other social identities (e.g., White and Asian women make more than Black women do) nor should you attempt a divide-and-conquer approach: "Well, let's focus on paying Black women more and then Latina/Lantix/Hispanic women." What this later approach does is situate equity through a framework of opposition: putting different kinds of women into competition with each other. This kind of win-lose mentality is what has landed us in the pay gap situation we are in now. Thus, the solution to the problem cannot be the same tools that built the problem. As stated so perfectly by Audre Lorde (1984), "The master's tools will never dismantle the master's house (p. 110)." In this argument, Lorde invites the reader to reject how much difference has been used to keep people apart and to hinder equity and inclusion. If we constantly address issues of inequality through a lens of "difference," rather than commonalities, we will only ever bring about temporary change. Our task is to bring about genuine, long-lasting change.

With a tool like intersectionality, we can refrain from broad generalizations (e.g., "all women") while not pitting different kinds of women against each other (e.g., "Asian women should make more than White women"). Intersectionality's focus on complexity and nuance asks for us to make policies and practices at these macro levels that acknowledge difference and the complicated tiers of oppression and privilege. The tool we have most readily to address this directly is language itself. We have the words to speak to complexity. Let's use those words to create policies and practices that reflect the reality of people's lives inside and outside of work. This means sitting with your organization and having an honest conversation about its pay policies and practices and how it treats people differently based on a compilation of their social identities.

Case Study #2: Promotion

Imagine you have been preparing for an important meeting at your job. You spend weeks and hours getting all the necessary data to make a compelling case for the customer. The day arrives for the meeting, and you feel more than prepared. Pausing for a few minutes with your hand resting on the closed conference door, you slightly lower your head, close your eyes, and take a few deep breaths. Pushing the door open, feeling a brief waft of air-conditioned air kiss your cheeks, you put on your best smile and step inside. Taking one of the few remaining seats situated around a large, oval-shaped wooden conference table, you notice not many in the room look like you. You make this observation and tuck it away. You need to be focused.

The meeting begins with the typical pleasantries of any meeting: comments about the weather, current economic realities in the country, and other small talk. Before the meeting takes its shift into the matter at hand, one of the top executives in your organization pivots in his chair, makes eye contact with you, and states, "I don't want to sit down with a woman." He then gathers his materials and leaves. Your heart begins to beat faster, you can feel the nervous thread of sweat forming at your hairline, and you see everyone else in the room is looking at you. Taking a quick stock of your different options, you think to yourself, *My reaction could determine whether or not we keep the customer…I am going to stay. I am going to show my ability to stay calm in high-stress situations.* And you ultimately stay. You not only stay and make an impression on some of the other executives in the company, but you helped keep your company's important customer.

This is a some-what dramatized account of the real experiences of Marshae Mansfield, V.P. and Chief Customer Officer North America at Lenovo. Although many cis woman find themselves slowly moving up the corporate ladder, securing various promotions for themselves, these achievements do not mean they are welcomed with open arms and minds.

While the previous section focused on two common arguments used to perpetuate pay gaps, this section is going to continue the same train of thought by reflecting not on pay, but promotion. To begin, we want to offer a quick insight into some data on the matter. As of 2020, women make up 46.9% of our current workforce and represent 40% of all managerial roles (Marcus, 2020). As we begin to move higher up the corporate ladder, gaps in representation across race and gender widens. A study by Catalyst (2020) did find that cis women in senior management positions increased 29% in 2019, across the globe (a record high), but those rates have not change. When we look at S&P 500 companies, we see only 26.5% of top, senior positions being held by cis woman (Marcus, 2020). A 2019 study by Business Insider offers some more complex data to add some layers. According to their research, the top managerial positions across various organizations are mostly held by cis-white men, at 68 percent. The second most represented group is white women, at 18 percent, followed by men of color at 10 percent, and women of color at 4 percent. What we appreciate about this data is it shows that issues of high-level managerial positions are not just limited to gender. In fact, we see that more cis-white women are in top decision-making positions than men of color.

You have spent decades of your life moving your way up the corporate ladder. You live in a large, vibrant city that has one of the largest percentages of Black college graduates. However, each time you move up the ladder, each step keeps bringing you into a space where fewer and fewer of your colleagues look like you. It gets to the point that by time you have almost reached the top, you are the *only* person with the background and social identities that you carry. You are alone. Not only are you alone, but you watch from the sidelines as the CEO of your company actively and systematically pushes out other people in your organization that occupy a historically marginalized social identity (or identities). In addition, you have spent these years getting slowly promoted as you actively strive to assimilate and integrate yourself into your job's culture. As time goes by, you see how much harder you work than your white counterparts. You live on a constant edge, concerned that any mistake you do make is going to limit your ability to not only move up in the company, but keep your job. You ultimately resign your job when you learn that not only are you alone and treated as the "diversity hire," but that you are getting paid significantly less than what your cis-white men colleagues earn. After bringing up the pay gap to your HR department, you watch in awe and frustration as they lie to your face about the data you have gathered.

These remarks are a compilation of the real-life experiences of Black men and women in their various positions and occupations (Yuan, 2020). Through their lived experiences we get a more detailed, complex, and problematic picture of how difficult it can be to be Black in various organizations. Some of the people interviewed are just one or two Black people in their entire company and yet experience constant messaging from their organization about how important "diversity" is to them. To be clear, how Black women face discrimination at work is going to be different and unique from the challenges Black men face.

Research finds that Black and Latina women face a "double jeopardy" (Berdahl & Moore, 2006). Because they are both women *and* members of a racial and ethnically marginalized group, they experience harassment as women *and* as a Black, Latina, Filipina, Indian, Indigenous individual. In other words, women of color face more workplace harassment and bullying than cis white men, cis white women, and cis men of color. This results in women of color not only getting paid less but limiting how far up an organization's ladder they can climb (Akhtar, 2019).

Finally, these stories also begin to illustrate that inclusion does not simply occur when a company hires someone who is not a cis-heterosexual white man. If these historically marginalized individuals do not feel respected (whether through pay or promotion opportunities) or that they can be themselves at work and have their voices heard, then we know true inclusion has not occurred. To be clear, the issue is not a lack of interest by women of color (especially Black women) wanting to be promoted to higher positions within their organizations. Recent numbers do show that Black women ask for promotions just as frequently as men do (LeanIn & McKinsey & Company, 2019). Yet, for every 100 white men that are promoted to managerial positions, only 58 Black women are promoted. What causes these gaps in promotions? It is not because Black women or other women of color don't work hard (in fact, they often have to work at least twice as hard to get the same recognition that a white woman might) or that they don't want to be promoted. The issue lies within the fabric of a country built around cis-white men and their experiences, practices, and assumptions. These assumptions become woven into the beliefs we have about the "appropriate" corporate culture and hiring/promotion practices. How these assumptions are supported and perpetuated are through the often mundane interactions we have with our colleagues every day. The next case study section will have more to say about these kinds of interactions. Before turning our attention there, let's talk about one way to address issues of promotion and inclusion.

When it comes to seeing real change with issues surrounding promotion, be careful about the assumption that representation fixes issues of discrimination and lack of equity in the workplace. Central to intersectionality's goal is to create tangible, material change. Thus, we must be skeptical about what actual changes are being made. A company may hire a Latina woman CEO, but if the board of directors is still predominantly cis-white men, is that substantial change? Real change comes around when intentional organizational changes that center diverse people and their backgrounds are put into place. This argument is supported with evidence. When we bring more cis women into the highest managerial positions in an organization, those companies become more open to change and face fewer issues because those cis women are less-likely to make risky decisions (Post et al., 2021). If that wasn't enough to convince you, additional research finds that organizations with more cis women in senior positions are more socially responsible, provide safer, and higher-quality customer service, and are more profitable (Byron & Post, 2016; Post & Byron, 2014; Wowak et al., 2020). This is what we mean by allowing diverse thoughts and bodies to manifest in organizational changes: promoting people and allowing them to make substantial changes.

Other reports find that most of the Black women seeking to become a top executive find that they want that position for two reasons: (1) To help create role models for younger Black women and (2) To have a say in the culture of their workplace (Lean In, 2021). This data shows that cis-white women and to a larger extent cis Black women look to use positions of authority, not for personal gain, but for the betterment of the entire company and surrounding culture. When we say inclusion goes beyond a "diversity" hire or promotion, it is ultimately a difference between having someone take a seat at a table versus someone having a seat at the table *and* the space to talk and create positive organizational change.

Micro Level: Microaggressions

As we've explored in this chapter so far, intersectionality is a useful lens to use in the workplace. Here we detail why an understanding of intersectionality is not only useful in relation to larger organizational practices but needed within day-to-day employee interactions. To begin, we offer a story about two childhood friends.

It's a chilly spring afternoon in the city when childhood friends David and Robert walk into a coffee shop to meet a potential business partner. Robert's wearing black sweatpants with a light gray crew neck sweatshirt with a dark green jacket. Dressing for the chilly occasion, David chose to wear a black hoodie himself.

The two young real-estate entrepreneurs in their young 20s chose this centrally located coffee shop for their meeting with a potential business partner to discuss mutual opportunities for conducting business. Coffee shops offer a great ambiance for meeting, talking, working, and relaxing. David and Robert walk in, grab a seat, and enjoy the music while they listen to the murmur of the conversations around them.

Both gentlemen sit on the booth-side of the small circular table meant for one or two people, offering the solo chair to their prospective business partner. As they get settled in, the young men begin planning for their meeting. David and

Robert came from an economically depressed part of town. They rehearse their elevator pitch for how they got into real-estate to begin with: to improve their economically depressed communities.

After some preparation, David wants to use the restroom one last time before their guest arrives. David gets up, goes to use the restroom, however, as he approaches the door, he sees a sign that states "Key required for use. Bathroom for patrons only." Since David and Robert have yet to buy anything, the coffee shop employee not only denies David's access to the bathroom, but also asks him to leave.

Although David wanted to use the restroom, he could do without it considering his main goal is to build a new connection. With the business partner showing up soon, David returns to his seat. As he makes his way back to Robert, David begins to feel animosity, frustration, and anger replacing his optimism, excitement, and mental clarity. After Robert hears what happened, he begins to console David, encouraging him to get rid of that negative energy before their potential partner arrives.

After regaining some sense of clarity, the doors of the coffee shop and both men turn their gazes into the blast of light the now opened doors pour into the room. Instead of their potential partner walking into the coffee shop, it is a group of police officers. It's not unusual for a police officer to be in a coffee shop, but the young entrepreneurs were confused why there were so many! The officers walk up to the counter and begin talking quietly with a coffee shop employee – the same one that denied David access to the restroom. David picks up on this as he sees the employee's eyes guide the officers over to the very booth in which David and Robert are sitting. The officers make their way over, arrest David and Robert, and usher them out of the coffee shop and the potential to establish business with a new partner.

This is the real-life story of Rashon Nelson and Donte Robinson – two Black men being arrested by white police officers in a Starbucks in Philadelphia, Pennsylvania on April 12, 2018. In the story, as it was portrayed here, we intentionally left out race as a key demographic marker in addition to changing the names of the young men. Perhaps you knew this story and your mind automatically jumped to the case of Rashon and Donte. Perhaps this story is new to you, and you began formulating assumptions about the nature of the key characters: Robert, David, the coffee shop employee, the officers. Or even, you had heard of the story, yet it took you a while to catch on.

The process of formulating assumptions – particularly regarding race and class in this story – is a natural process our brains undergo. We often rely upon stereotypes to help us categorize the world around us. Oftentimes, those stereotypes are accompanied by prejudice and biases that categorize and evaluate the nature of one's being. In this story, the coffee shop employee racially and economically profiled Rashon and Donte. However, the operative assumption for the employee was that Black men wearing sweats in a predominantly white coffee shop equals dangerous; a threat needed to be eradicated by authorities. However, removing race from the picture, Robert and David could have been read as two young white hipsters experimenting in real-estate to contribute to the gentrification of economically depressed parts of their city.

This story is a story about interpersonal racial microaggressions that occur in the workplace. A racial microaggression is defined as, "brief and commonplace daily verbal, behavioral, or environmental indignities, whether intentional or unintentional, that communicate hostile, derogatory, or negative racial slights and insults toward people of color" (Sue et al., 2007, p. 271). Microaggressions have also been researched in the context of gender (Capodilupo et al., 2010), education level (Young et al., 2015), and immigration (ShenoyPacker, 2015), to name a few. At its core, a microaggression is a communicative phenomenon rooted in ambiguity, yet serves as a continuous, sustained building block that upholds injustice and inequities (de la Garza, 2020).

In the context of intersectionality studies (Crenshaw, 1989; Collins & Bilge, 2016) and commonalities (Keating, 2013), such ambiguous communication is amplified by the many existing social identities. People's micro-level interactions are heavily informed by the larger societies and norms in which they occur. In this story, the coffee shop employee was making assumptions of Robert and David based on their race and gender performance within a classed area, which are informed by the ideologies of whiteness, capitalism, and normative gender performance. When considered intersectionally, this is a story about discrimination toward Black masculinity and economic status, especially when it appears in predominantly white, affluent contexts. In other words, these men experience a microaggression across three of their social identities, as they were compounded in that moment, together. The barista did not see them as just Black, just men, or just men who were likely not middle-class – they were all three, at once.

As an analytical framework, intersectionality helps disrupt the cognitive shortcuts people make on a daily basis that may contribute to microaggressive behavior. By considering the complex web of social identities, people can begin to question their implicit associations between a social identity marker and the discursive messages that promote prejudice and bias. These discriminatory language-driven shortcuts are based on the way people have been socialized by, and into, whiteness, capitalism, and normative gender performance. Intersectionality, then, becomes a useful, and *needed,* tool to disrupt unjust and discriminatory practices – especially at the micro-level; both inter-and intra-personally. In the end, the existence of microaggressions asks us to consider how our everyday interactions can and do perpetuate exclusion and inequality across all aspects of our lives, including spaces of work.

Concluding Thoughts

We hope that this chapter was able to provide some nuanced and complex understandings to the issues workplaces face when trying to address issues of equity and inclusion. Through the lens of intersectionality, we not only center lived experiences as a vital source of knowledge, but we learn to strive for material, tangible change that reflects the complex lives we all live. Our task to address the complex oppressions and acts of marginalization that many people endure in their workplace must be framed through the lens of commonality rather than difference. When we use "difference" as our guiding framework, all we will see is difference; all we will do is create further competition amongst those most in peril of earning a fair and equitable wage, being promoted into the upper rungs of an organization, and experiencing daily microaggressions that devalue their presence, work, and humanity.

We do not claim to have offered a fully complex and complete layout of the true reality of inequality in spaces of work in the U.S. In fact, an entire multi-part volume would be needed to address all the possible overlaps of various social identities and how they are impacted by issues of workplace inequality and exclusion. What drove our focus here is due, in part, to our own personal commitments to racial justice. That guiding principle can be seen as a bias that influenced what examples and pieces of data we did and did not include in this chapter. However, more importantly, we must return to the ultimate guide to this chapter: intersectionality. Since intersectionality was historically demonstrated by and built on the lives, activism, and sacrifices of predominantly Black women, it is important that our labor here honors their ever-ongoing labor of addressing racism as a primary source of oppression in the U.S. With this in mind, we hope that you begin your own journey of discovering the full complex nature of overlapping social identities and how to cultivate inclusive workplaces. There is a much larger story to tell. We hope you join us in the endeavor to center the complex, to affirm and honor personal experiences, and to locate pathways of commonality in our various spaces of labor and work.

References

Acker, J. (1990). Hierarchies, Jobs, Bodies: A Theory of Gendered Organizations. *Gender & Society*, *4*(2), 139–158. https://doi.org/10.1177/089124390004002002.

Akhtar, A. (2019, December 18). Lower Pay, More Harassment: How Work in America Failed Women of Color in the 2010s. *Business Insider*. Retrieved from: https://www.businessinsider.com/how-work-is-failing-women-of-color-2019-10.

Allen, B. J. (1995). "Diversity" and Organizational Communication. *Journal of Applied Communication Research, 23*(2), 143–155. https://doi.org/10.1080/00909889509365420.

Allen, B. J. (2007). Theorizing Race and Communication. *Communication Monographs, 74*(2), 259–264. https://doi.org/10.1080/03637750701393055.

Allen, B. J. (2014). *Difference Matters: Communicating Social Identity*. Long Grove, IL: Waveland Press.

Anzaldúa, G. (1987/2012). *Borderlands/La Frontera: The New Mestiza* (4th ed.). San Francisco: Aunt Lute Books.

Apple, M. W. (2012). *Education and Power* (2nd ed.). New York: Routledge.

Ashcraft, K. L. (2005). Feminist Organizational Communication Studies: Engaging Gender in Public and Private. In S. May & D. K. Mumby (Eds.), *Engaging Organizational Communication Theory and Research: Multiple Perspectives* (pp. 141–169). Thousand Oaks, CA: Sage.

Ashcraft, K. L. (2011). Knowing Work through the Communication of Difference: A Revised Agenda for Difference Studies. In D. K. Mumby (Ed.), *Reframing Difference in Organizational Communication Studies: Research, Pedagogy, Practice* (pp. 3–29). Thousand Oaks, CA: Sage.

Atewologun, D., Sealy, R., & Vinnicombe, S. (2016). Revealing Intersectional Dynamics in Organizations: Introducing "Intersectional Identity Work." *Gender, Work, and Organization*, *23*(3), 223–247. https://doi.org/10.1111/gwao.12082.

Berdahl, J., & Moore, C. (2006). Workplace Harassment: Double Jeopardy for Minority Women. *The Journal of Applied Psychology*, *91*, 426–436. https://doi.org/10.1037/0021-9010.91.2.426.

Buzzanell, P. M. (1994). Gaining a Voice: Feminist Organizational Communication Theorizing. *Management Communication Quarterly, 7*(4), 339–383. https://doi.org/10.1177/0893318994007004001.

Byron, K., & Post, C. (2016). Women on Boards of Directors and Corporate Social Performance: A Meta-Analysis. *Corporate Governance*, *24*, 428–442. https://doi.org/10.1111/corg.12165.

Capodilupo, C. M., Nadal, K. L., Corman, L., Hamit, S., Lyons, O. B., & Weinberg, A. (2010). The Manifestation of Gender Microaggressions. In D. W. Sue (Ed.), *Microaggressions and Marginality: Manifestation, Dynamics, and Impact* (pp. 193–216). John Wiley & Sons Inc.

Catalyst. (2020, August 11). Women in Management (quick take). *Catalyst*. Retrieved from: https://www.catalyst.org/research/women-in-management/.

Chow, K. (2017, April 19). "Model minority" Myth Used as a Racial Wedge between Asians and Blacks. *NPR*. Retrieved from: https://www.npr.org/sections/codeswitch/2017/04/19/524571669/model-minority-myth-again-used-as-a-racial-wedge-between-asians-and-blacks.

Collins, P. H., & Bilge, S. (2016). *Intersectionality*. Malden, MA: Polity Press.

Crenshaw, K. W. (1989). Demarginalizing the Intersection of Race and Sex: A Black Feminist Critique of Antidiscrimination Doctrine, Feminist Theory, and Antiracist Politics. *University Chicago Legal, 139*, 139–167.

de la Garza, S. A. (2020). Mindful Heresy as Praxis for Change: Responding to Microaggressions as Building Blocks of Hegemony. In Y. F. Niemann, G. Gutiérrez, & C.G. Gonzalez (Eds.), *Presumed Incompetent II: Race, Class, Power, and Resistance of Women in Academia* (pp. 193–203). Logan, UT: Utah State University Press.

Eguchi, S., & Starosta, W. (2012). Negotiating the Model Minority Image: Performative Aspects of College-educated Asian American Professional Men. *Qualitative Research Reports in Communication, 13*, 88–97. https://doi.org/10.1080/17459435.2012.722166.

Ferguson Jr, M. W. (2018). (Re) Negotiating Organizational Socialization: Black Male Scholarship and the Closet. *Management Communication Quarterly, 32*(2), 282–286.

Folbre, N. (1991). The Unproductive Housewife: Her Evolution in Nineteenth-Century Economic Thought. *Signs: Journal of Women in Culture and Society, 16*, 463–484. https://doi.org/10.1086/494679.

Glassdoor. (2016, May 2). 3 in 5 Employees Did Not Negotiate Salary. *Glassdoor*. Retrieved from: https://www.glassdoor.com/blog/3-5-u-s-employees-negotiate-salary/.

Hooks, B. (1984/2015). *Feminist Theory: From Margin to Center*. New York: Routledge.

Institute for Women's Policy Research. (2018). The Gender Wage Gap by Occupation 2018. *Institute for Women's Policy Research*. Retrieved from: https://iwpr.org/iwpr-issues/employment-and-earnings/the-gender-wage-gap-by-occupation-2018/.

Jin, C. H. (2021, May 25). 6 Charts that Dismantle the Trope of Asian Americans as a Model Minority. *NPR*. Retrieved from: https://www.npr.org/2021/05/25/999874296/6-charts-that-dismantle-the-trope-of-asian-americans-as-a-model-minority.

Keating, A. (2013). Beyond Intersectionality: Theorizing Interconnectivity With/in *This Bridge Called My Back: Writings by Radical Women of Color*. In A. L. Keating (Ed.), *Transformation Now!: Toward a Post-Oppositional Politics of Change* (pp. 29–59). Champaign: University of Illinois Press.

Larson, G. G. (2020). Workplace Negotiations, Gender, and Intersectionality. *Center for Women and Business*. Retrieved from: https://bentleydownloads.s3.amazonaws.com/cwb/CWB_Negotiations_Research_Report_Winter_2020.pdf.

Lean In. (2021). Working at the Intersection: What Black Women Are Up Against. *Lean In*. Retrieved from: https://leanin.org/black-women-racism-discrimination-at-work#!.

Lean In & McKinsey & Company. (2019). *Women in the Workplace 2019*. Retrieved from: https://womenintheworkplace.com/.

Leonhardt, M. (2020, January 31). 60% of Women Say They've Never Negotiated Their Salary – and Many Quit Their Job Instead. *CNBC*. Retrieved from: https://www.cnbc.com/2020/01/31/women-more-likely-to-change-jobs-to-get-pay-increase.html.

Lorde, A. (1984). *Sister Outsider: Essays and Speeches*. Berkeley: Crossing Press.

Marcus, B. (2020, March 10). 3 Female Executives Reveal Their Experiences with Gender Bias and What They've Done to Overcome It. *Forbes*. Retrieved from: https://www.forbes.com/sites/bonniemarcus/2020/03/10/3-female-executives-reveal-their-experiences-with-gender-bias-and-what-theyve-done-to-overcome-it/?sh=4dd7932e1239.

Matsuda, M. J. (1991). Beside My Sister, Facing the Enemy: Legal Theory Out of Coalition. *Stanford Law Review*, *43*, 1183–1192. Retrieved from: http://www.jstor.org/stable/1229035?seq=1#page_scan_tab_contents.

Miller, C. C. (2016, March 18). As Women Take over a Male-dominated Field, the Pay Drops. *The New York Times*. Retrieved from: https://www.nytimes.com/2016/03/20/upshot/as-women-take-over-a-male-dominated-field-the-pay-drops.html.

Moraga, C., & Anzaldúa, G. (2015). Entering the Lives of Others: Theory in the Flesh. In C. Moraga & G. Anzaldúa (Eds.), *This Bridge Called My Back: Writings by Radical Women of Color* (4th ed., pp. 19). Albany: SUNY Press.

Mudamib, A. (2019). Racial Satire, Race Talk, and the Model Minority: South Asian Americans Speak Up. *Southern Communication Journal*, *84*, 246–256. https://doi.org/10.1080/1041794X.2019.1639211.

Oldenziel, R. (2001). Man the Maker, Woman the Consumer: The Consumption Junction Revisited. In A.N.H. Creager, E. Lunbeck, L. Schiebinger (Eds.), *Feminism in Twentieth Century Science, Technology, and Medicine* (pp. 128–148). Chicago, IL: University of Chicago Press.

Parker, P. S. (2001). African American Women Executives' Leadership Communication within Dominant-Culture Organizations: (Re) conceptualizing Notions of Collaboration and Instrumentality. *Management Communication Quarterly, 15*(1), 42–82. https://doi.org/10.1177/0893318901151002.

Parker, P. S. (2014). Difference and Organizing. In L. L. Putnam & D. K. Mumby (Eds.), *The SAGE Handbook of Organizational Communication: Advances in Theory, Research, and Methods* (pp. 619–643). Thousand Oaks, CA: Sage.

Post, C., & Byron, K. (2014). Women on Boards and Firm Financial Performance: A Meta-analysis. *Academy of Management Journal, 58*, 1546–1571. https://doi.org/10.5465/amj.2013.0319.

Post, C., Lokshin, B., & Boone, C. (2021, April 6). Research: Adding Women to the C-Suite Changes How Companies Think. *Harvard Business Review*. Retrieved from: https://hbr.org/2021/04/research-adding-women-to-the-c-suite-changes-how-companies-think.

Sánchez-Hucles, J. V., & Davis, D. D. (2010). Women and Women of Color in Leadership: Complexity, Identity, and Intersectionality. *The American Psychologist, 65*(3), 171–181. https://doi.org/10.1037/a0017459.

Sankar, C. (2017, July 13). Why Don't More Women Negotiate? *Forbes*. Retrieved from: https://www.forbes.com/sites/forbescoachescouncil/2017/07/13/why-dont-more-women-negotiate/?sh=393f8822e769.

Steinfield, L., Sanghvi, M., Zayer, L. T., Coleman, C. A., Ourahmoune, N., Harrison, R. L., Hein, W., & Brace-Govan, J. (2019). Transformative Intersectionality: Moving Business towards a Critical Praxis. *Journal of Business Research, 100*, 366–375. https://doi.org/10.1016/j.jbusres.2018.12.031.

Sue, D., Capodilupo, C., Torino, G., Bucceri, J., Holder, A., Nadal, K., & Esquilin, M. (2007). Racial Microaggressions in Everyday Life: Implications for Clinical Practice. *American Psychologist, 62*(4), 271–286. https://doi.org/10.1037/0003-066X.62.4.271.

Thorton, M., & Tajima, A. (2014). A "model" Minority: Japanese Americans as References and Role Models in Black Newspapers, 2000–2010. *Communication & Critical/Cultural Studies, 11*, 139–157. https://doi.org/10.1080/14791420.2014.902086.

Wowak, K. D., Ball, G. P., Post, C., & Ketchen, Jr., D. J. (2020). The Influence of Female Directors on Product Recall Decisions. *Manufacturing & Service Operations Management, 23*, 895–913. https://doi.org/10.1287/msom.2019.0841.

Young, K., Anderson, M., & Stewart, S. (2015). Hierarchical Microaggressions in Higher Education. *Journal of Diversity in Higher Education*, *8*(1), 61.

Yuan, K. (2020, June 16). Working While Black: Stories from Black Corporate America. *Fortune*. Retrieved from: https://fortune.com/longform/working-while-black-in-corporate-america-racism-microaggressions-stories/

Zang, T. (2010). Asian Americans beyond the Model Minority Stereotype: The Nerdy and the Left Out. *Journal of International & Intercultural Communication*, *3*, 20–37. https://doi.org/10.1080/17513050903428109.

Part V Politeness and Emotion at the Workplace

Introduction to (Im)politeness in Computer Mediated Discourse at Work

By Carmen Santamaría-García

The next chapter notes that current research on (im)politeness focuses on both interlocutors whereas in the past it had concentrated either on the speaker or the receiver. With the advent of virtual teams in today's business world, research has also examined the impact of this medium on interpersonal interactions in general and (im)politeness in particular. It is quite apparent that mediated communication is more dependent on linguistic exchanges than more traditional face-to-face communication. However, such other aspects as emoticons, turn-taking strategies, unconventional orthography, or the use of capitalization need to be also considered to fully understand the computer mediated discourse. That is why virtual communication requires more intense communication to compensate for the technological constraints. Interestingly, it seems that most virtual teams, regardless of their cultural background, seek to avoid confrontation in order to preserve a positive atmosphere. However, it is pointed out that conflicts around tasks are not only necessary, but actually desirable for successful realization of the tasks because conflicts can reveal disagreements that the interlocutors had not been aware of or suggest different means of completing tasks. This is an important insight which ought to be kept in mind whenever virtual teams are being created.

It is also pointed out in this chapter that all linguistic aspects need to be considered when analyzing computer mediated discourse, in particular when it comes to comparing different languages, because the author argues one cannot associate the same meaning to messages that are formulated and directed at others in English as one could in Spanish. The meaning of such messages encompasses more than mere words. That is why some messages could be considered polite in one language, but when translated into another language would appear to be impolite. For example, in German the use of the formal second person singular *Sie* would make a request appear to be more polite than the use of the informal second person singular *Du* while in English both pronouns would be translated as *you*. That is why English would use polite "fillers" that are not necessary in German; and if those fillers are translated into German, they would sound superfluous or bombastic. In contrast, the direct translation into English of a German polite request using *Sie* would make that German request appear to be very direct and impolite in English.

Michael B. Hinner

Carmen Santamaría-García, European PhD in Linguistics (Complutense University, Madrid, 2003), has been combining teaching and research as part of the Philosophy and Letters Faculty (Alcalá University) since 1994, holding tenure in English Language and Applied Linguistics since 1997. During these years she has been course designer and teacher of more than 30 courses at degree, master and postgraduate levels in more than 10 programmes in Education, Audiovisual communication, English language and Translation Studies at Alcalá University. She has supervised doctor, master and undergraduate dissertations in the fields of Pragmatics, Discourse Analysis, Translation and Teacher Education in English Language.

Her research interests and teaching fields spread along Applied Linguistics, Communication and Education (Intercultural Pragmatics, Discourse and Conversation Analysis, Translation and Methodology of the English Language and Education) at both undergraduate and postgraduate levels. These are also the areas covered in her publications, together with corpus linguistics and computer-mediated communication, with more than forty articles and chapters in international academic journals and books.

Some of her latest publications include: (2014). Evaluative discourse and politeness in university students' communication through social networking sites. In G. Thompson & L. Alba-Juez (Eds.) *Evaluation in Context*, pp. 387–411. Amsterdam: John Benjamins; (2017). Emotional and Educational Consequences of (Im)politeness in Teacher–Student Interaction at Higher Education. *Corpus Pragmatics* (*1*)3, 233–255; (in press). A semiotic and multimodal analysis of interactive relations in picture books that challenge female gender stereotypes. In J. Moya-Guijarro & E. Ventola (eds.) *A Multimodal Approach to Challenging Gender Stereotypes in Children's Picture Books*. London: Routledge.

Carmen Santamaría-García

(Im)politeness in Computer Mediated Discourse at Work

Theoretical Framework and Practical Implications

The study of (im)politeness and rapport management have developed from early studies in face management, mostly triggered by Brown and Levinson's (1978, 1987) seminal work on politeness and their portrayal of face as individuals' wants that can be threatened in interaction. They made a distinction between the want for positive face (i.e., their desire to be liked and/or admired) and negative face (the need to have one's freedom unimpeded). Politeness was described as a set of linguistic strategies oriented to face preservation and gave a lot of importance to addressees' needs. More recent studies, however, note that speakers' face deserves more attention that it has received: "(...) much work in face and politeness theory has focused on the face concerns of the hearer and has paid less attention to those of the speaker" (Spencer-Oatey, 2009, p. 137). For this reason, she argues "that a speaker's own face concerns may emerge as crucially important in authentic interaction, and that a speaker's self-presentational concerns thus need to be incorporated into the study of face and given equal weighting to those of the hearer".

Within maxim-oriented approaches, (Leech, 1983), politeness was conceived as a set of politeness maxims, such as the Tact Maxim (minimize cost to other, maximize benefit to other) and the Approbation Maxim (minimize dispraise of other, maximize praise of other). This approach implies, as Spencer-Oatey (2005) notes "that the more a maxim is upheld, the more polite the person will be" (p. 97). This perspective has been widely challenged, (e. g., Watts, 2003; Locher, 2004) mainly on the grounds that politeness is a contextual judgment, as "no linguistic structures can be identified as inherently polite or impolite" (Watts, 2003, p. 160) and that the "universal valences" of Leech's politeness maxims do not apply in all cultures or speech contexts (Spencer-Oatey, 2005, p. 97). Several authors have also pointed out that the illocutionary acts identified by Brown and Levinson (1987) as face threatening are not always so, (e. g., Gu, 1990; Spencer-Oatey, 2000).

The above mentioned changes in orientation have extended the framework for the study of (im)politeness and given way to an approach to face as relational and interactional, rather than an individual phenomenon (Arundale, 2006; Bargiela Chiappini, 2003 and 2009; Haugh, 2009). This means "that the social self is interactionally achieved in relationships with others" (Arundale, 2006, p. 193) and that "it presupposes evaluation by others of the behaviour of individuals as well as groups (Arundale, 1993, 1999; Haugh & Hinze, 2003; Ho, 1976, 1994)" (Haugh, 2009, p. 6).

This wider conception of face has made room for the exploration of its connection with rapport, which is understood as "the relative harmony and smoothness of relations between people" (Spencer-Oatey, 2002, p. 96). Rapport management, defined as "the management (or mismanagement) of relations between people" (Spencer-Oatey, 2009, p. 96), pays special consideration to the factors that may influence the judgments people make of (im)politeness and rapport, namely, *behavioural expectations*, *face sensitivities* and *interactional wants* (Spencer Oatey, 2005, p. 98).

Individuals can hold differing types of rapport orientations towards each other: "a rapport-enhancement orientation, (a desire to strengthen or enhance harmonious relations between the interlocutors), a rapport maintenance orientation (a desire to maintain or protect harmonious relations), a rapport-neglect orientation (a lack of concern or interest in the quality of relations, perhaps because of a focus on self), or a rapport-challenge orientation (a desire to challenge or impair harmonious relations)" (Spencer-Oatey, 2005, p. 96). Judgments "as to whether rapport has been enhanced, maintained or damaged", which may be "conscious or otherwise", are based on the assessment of "behavioural expectations, face sensitivities and interactional wants" (Spencer-Oatey, 2005, p. 96) and individuals may change their judgments during the course of interaction.

Within this context, (im)politeness is "the subjective judgments that people make about the social appropriateness of verbal and non-verbal behaviour" (Spencer-Oatey, 2005, p. 97). Such judgments are based primarily on individuals' expectations on what is socially appropriate, which in turn are derived from their beliefs about behaviour: "what is prescribed, what is permitted and what is proscribed" (Spencer-Oatey, 2005, p. 97) or, in other words, sociality rights and obligations (Spencer-Oatey, 2008, p. 13).

Judgements can also be derived from individuals' face sensitivities, which are described by drawing on work in social psychology on self-aspects (Simon, 2004). Self-aspects are cognitive categories that serve to process or organise information about oneself, such as "traits (e.g., introverted), physical features (e.g., red hair), roles (e.g., father), abilities (e.g., bilingual), tastes (e.g., preference for red wines), attitudes (e.g., against the death penalty), behaviours (e.g., "I work a lot") and explicit group or category membership (e.g., member of the Communist party)" (Spencer-Oatey, 2005, p. 104).

In the third place, judgments on what is (im)polite can be made on the basis of interactional wants or goals, which refer to equity and association principles. According to the first: "people have a fundamental belief that they are entitled to an association with others that is in keeping with the type of relationship that they have with them" (Spencer-Oatey, 2005, p. 100). With respect to the association principle, people "have a fundamental belief that they are entitled to an association with others that is in keeping with the type of relationship that they have with them" (Spencer-Oatey, 2005, p. 100). The association principle has three components: "involvement (people should have appropriate amounts and types of "activity" involvement with others), empathy (people should share appropriate concerns, feelings and interests with others), and respect (people should show appropriate amounts of respectfulness for others)" (Spencer-Oatey, 2005, p. 100).

Knowledge of the factors that influence the judgments that people make of (im)politeness and rapport, i.e. behavioural expectations, face sensitivities and interactional wants, will have practical implications in the study of (im)politeness in computer mediated discourse (CMD) at work and will hopefully lead to better communication in work environments.

Relevant Case Studies in the Literature

The current spread of virtual teams show proof that advances in information technology have made it possible for people to communicate and work together while being at different places. Success of virtual teams seems to be of crucial importance for competitiveness in the course of globalization. In this vein, several authors are exploring (im)politeness in the management of different communicative situations by virtual teams. A selection of up-to-date, relevant studies is presented below.

The importance of communication in virtual teams is explained by reference to the following reasons in Darics (2010) , p. 130:

> Firstly, the work processes are accomplished through conversation and communication practices, and because the participants do not share the same physical environment, all understanding must be achieved through linguistic exchanges. Secondly, workplace talk is the essential means of constructing and negotiating social identities (Holmes 2009, p. 167) and the language choices of the team members play an important role in how they are perceived (Adkins and Brashers 1995: 315). Thirdly, communication is the means of team formation and the means of the establishment of shared knowledge

> and shared practices, especially if the members do not meet in person. The team's and the organization's culture and knowledge are transmitted only through these interactions: online communities and conventions are brought into existence through merely textual, linguistic exchanges (Cherny 1999, p. 21; Herring 2001, p. 624).

Therefore, as she notes, the analysis of naturally occurring data from virtual teams is necessary to shed light both on the linguistic practices of computer-mediated discourse and the non-linguistic phenomena, such as the transmission of individual and team identity, team formation, norm negotiation, cooperation, power relations, etc. With this purpose, Darics (2010) explores the strategies used in virtual teams for compensating for the lack of audio-visual information in CMD, strategies to compensate for the technological constraints of the medium and strategies to aid interaction management from an interactional politeness viewpoint. She compares findings to previous CMD analysis and suggests that the endeavour to communicate along the lines of politeness norms in a work-based virtual environment contradicts some of the previous findings of CMD research (unconventional orthography, capitalization, economizing), and that other areas (such as emoticons, backchannel signals and turn-taking strategies) need to be revisited and re-examined from an interactional perspective to fully understand how language functions in this environment.

The acquisition of skills for computer-mediated communication is mentioned as a "fundamental tool for performing work activities" (Darics, 2010, p. 130), a phenomenon widely explored by Tavčar et al. (2005), who present a systematic discussion of the specifics of communication and work within a virtual development team, noting that virtual teams require intense communication and that special knowledge and skills of virtual team members are a greater obstacle than technical equipment in the process. Their work provides a set of recommendations on how to develop the necessary skills for effective communication and work in virtual development teams, grounded on experiences from an international course on European Global Product Realisation that provided students with initial experiences in working within a global team. Their recommendations can be applied to both university and industrial environments.

(Im)polite behaviours are explored in a range of professional settings in a recent volume edited by Archer et alia (2020). In the thirteen chapters assembled in this collection, authors demonstrate the importance of understanding how interactions are negotiated and managed in such settings. I will be focusing on the two chapters that deal with business discourse contributed by Debray and Freytag. The contribution by the latter, quoted as Freytag (2020a) will be discussed together with a her monograph on the same topic, quoted as Freytag (2020b).

Debray (2020) draws on Spencer-Oatey's (2000, 2008) rapport management framework and defines conflict as the result of the violation of one or more of the bases for rapport, that is, behavior that has been perceived as face-threatening, violating sociality rights and/or obligations or incompatibility of interactional goals. Relational conflicts are part of everyday life and interlocutors are likely to spend a lot of resources on managing potentially conflicting positions harmoniously in talk, hence the importance of research in the topic. Debray (2020) gives support to this idea by referring to Omdahl and Harden Fritz (2006), who mention that all the participants in their study (over 1000), reported having to deal with problematic relationships at work. Her chapter explores conflict management in a very diverse team of MBA students who had to work together on a number of projects over a span of eight months. The nature of the work to be done and the age and prior experience of team members (team managers and leaders from different companies in different countries) put them more in the context of a workplace than a student team.

Soon after the team was organised, two areas of conflict emerged that harmed rapport and lowered affect between its members. How exactly they managed these conflicts and tried to maintain rapport throughout is the focus of this chapter. Debray identifies four different strategies for conflict management, following Holmes and Marra (2004): Conflict avoidance; diversion; resolution through negotiation; and resolution by authority (Holmes & Marra, 2004). Conflict avoidance seems to be recurrent in homogeneous groups, with members frequently inclined "to avoid creating any discordant arguments or schisms" (Janis, 1991, p. 237).

Results of her research show that, despite the diversity of the group under research, avoidance of open conflict was the most common strategy in the team. Team members claimed to avoid open conflict to maintain functionality in the team and sacrifice their performance for the appearance of a positive relationship. This went against the expectation to find open discussion of differing views, which is characteristic of diverse groups and often results in a more "realistic appraisal of alternatives" (Debray, 2020, p. 130) when compared to homogeneous groups. This is the reason why the challenges faced by diverse teams, such as different working styles and unfamiliar approaches, can turn into benefits, when their members are freer to avoid conflict. In this view, conflicts around tasks become not only necessary but desirable for successful task achievement and become institutionally ratified, as discussed in Spencer-Oatey and Dauber (2017).

It is important to note that "being able to honestly disagree" was identified by team members as a positive relational feature that often seems to be "an enactment of intimacy" (Debray, 2020, p. 146). However, the data showed the need for positive relationships for disagreements to happen, as "team members were much more willing to disagree, argue and provide negative feedback to interlocutors with whom they had positive relationships than with those with whom relationships were strained" (Debray, 2020, p. 146).

Freytag's chapter (Freytag, 2020a) is explored here, together with her wider study in Freytag (2020b), which has been reviewed in Santamaría, (in press). Both studies investigate politeness phenomena in directives in British English (BE) and Peninsular Spanish (PS) business emails, analysing authentic language data and attempting at exploration of the perception of linguistic strategies through a questionnaire. They are worth mentioning as pioneering studies in business discourse and CMD, due to their combination of quantitative and qualitative methods of data collection and analysis with a pilot study on metapragmatic insights, which provides an innovative approach to the study of politeness in the field of cross cultural pragmatics (CCP). Regarding the data, a strong point is made for the collection of real instead of elicited discourse (Freytag, 2020b, p. 48).

BE and PS email directives are analysed along four research dimensions, i.e. pragmalinguistic, cross-cultural, sociopragmatic and the perception dimension, focusing on the following aspects: (Freytag, 2020b, p. 200).

> From a pragmalinguistic dimension, it investigates how directives are realized in British English (BE) and Peninsular Spanish (PS) business emails and what strategies can be identified. The cross-cultural dimension systematically compares the two data sets and statistically measures the differences between the BE and PS directive realizations. From a sociopragmatic perspective, the effects that the social and discourse context, namely the sex, social distance (SD) and power (P) between sender and addressee, relative imposition (RI) and purpose, have on the linguistic choices are measured. Finally, from a perception dimension, I address the question of how the English and Spanish email writers perceive the directive strategies identified in terms of directness and politeness

The corpus contains 300 email messages exchanged between 69 first language users of BE and 300 between 72 L1 users of PS based in Spain. Users include managers, business partners and employees of either a Spanish hotel resort or one of the British and Spanish travel agencies with which they cooperated. Messages include reservation and room availability, price negotiations, task allocations and other issues arising in the mentioned workplaces. The head acts in directives have been analysed in terms of sentence type, perspective and head act strategy, modification and sequencing strategies.

Several cross-cultural differences between BE and PS are presented in the results, such as PS higher frequency of pre-decided statements at head act level or a stronger preference for the use of the second-person addressee by BE email writers "58.3 % in the BE compared to 47.1 % in the PS data" (Freytag, 2020b, p. 88). This difference is interpreted as a higher level of directness and stronger orientation to positive politeness in BE versus a higher concern for negative face wants in PS (Freytag, 2020b, p. 90). Blum-Kulka and Levenston (1987, p. 58) are quoted to support this interpretation: "Because requests usually threaten the hearer's face, to avoid naming the hearer as the performer of the requested act is to minimize the imposition" (p. 88).

However, I would argue that differences in perspective alone do not suffice to account for politeness orientation, as it is the case with different levels of (in)directness, and that the rank of imposition (RI) of a particular act is of crucial consideration. For instance, a request with a low RI such as "(46) Please could you confirm a room" seems to be less coercive than "(47) Necesito todos los contactos de las diferentes personas (S357) 'I need all the contacts of the different people' " (p. 87) despite (46) is second-person oriented and (47) shows first-person orientation. Therefore, even when the author argues that the level of comparability between the corpora is sufficient on the grounds that "the emails of both data sets covered the same set of purposes" (Freytag, 2020b, p. 49), the fact that these discourse purposes do not occur in the same proportion in both data sets of BE and PS seems to be responsible for some "limitations for comparability", as the author herself admits (Freytag, 2020b, p. 49).

The distinction of social variables sex, social distance (SD), power (P) and ranking of imposition (RI) in the corpus is very much appreciated, although a more refined, in-depth classification would have been useful in order to maintain the claim for control of their effect on the choice of directive realization strategies in BE and PS business emails.

In order to explore the perception of linguistic strategies in terms of politeness and (in)directness, metapragmatic insights were collected by means of online questionnaires in order to investigate "the email writers' perception of directives in terms of politeness and directness (…)" (Freytag, 2020b, p. 44). The questionnaire contained 10 tasks: "two rating scales for politeness, six questions on general email use and behaviour and two rating scales for directness" (Freytag, 2020b, p. 44). Although hers is a praiseworthy attempt to consider participants' perception of linguistic strategies, the fact that participants were requested to rate pre-fabricated examples in terms of politeness and (in)directness instead of a sample of authentic data can be hinted as a caveat. I would argue for the importance of the collection of perception tests on authentic data in real context in future research in the field.

Concluding Remarks

This chapter has discussed some theoretical concepts of importance for the study of (im)politeness and rapport management in CMD at work, indicating possible practical implications and new directions of research. Early studies in the field were mostly concerned with face as individuals' wants that can be threatened in interaction and mainly focused on addressees' needs. More recent trends, however, are proceeding to explore both speakers and addressees' face concerns as emerging in authentic interaction and resulting from speakers' contextual judgements.

A selection of up-to-date relevant case studies in the literature has shown the potential of studies in (im)politeness and rapport management and their applicability to the improvement of relational work at CMD. It has been argued that research in these areas should not only focus on language production, but also take into account the perception of linguistic strategies. A claim is made that future research in the field would benefit from perception tests on authentic data in real context, instead of using questionnaires on pre-fabricated examples.

References

Archer, D., Grainger, K., & Jagodziński, P. (Eds.). (2020). *Politeness in Professional Contexts*. Amsterdam: John Benjamins Publishing Company.

Arundale, R. B. (1993). *Culture Specific Assumptions and the Concept of Face: A Proposal toward a Cultural Universal for Studying Face Management in Using Language*. Paper presented at International Pragmatics Association Conference, Kobe, Japan.

Arundale, R. B. (1999). An Alternative Model and Ideology of Communication for an Alternative to Politeness Theory. *Pragmatics*, *9*(1), 119–154.

Arundale, R. B. (2006). Face as Relational and Interactional: A Communication Framework for Research on Face, Facework and Politeness. *Journal of Politeness Research. Language, Behaviour, Culture*, *2*(2), 193–216. https://doi.org/10.1515/PR.2006.011.

Bargiela Chiappini, F. (2003). Face and Politeness: New (Insights) for Old (Concepts). *Journal of Pragmatics*, *35*(10), 1453–1469.

Bargiela Chiappini, F. (2009). Facing the Future: Some Reflections. In M. Haugh & F. Bargiela-Chiappini, (Eds.), *Face, Communication and Social Interaction* (pp. 307–326). London: Equinox.

Bargiela-Chiappini, F., & Haugh, M. (Eds.). (2009). *Face, Communication and Social Interaction*. London: Equinox.

Blum-Kulka, S., & Levenston, E. A. (1987). Lexical-grammatical Pragmatic Indicators. *Studies in Second Language Acquisition*, *9*(2), 155–170.

Brown, P., & Levinson, S. C. (1987). *Politeness. Some Universals in Language Usage*. Cambridge: Cambridge University Press. Originally published as Universals in language usage: Politeness phenomenon. E. Goody (Ed.), (1978). *In Questions and Politeness: Strategies in Social Interaction*. Cambridge: Cambridge University Press.

Darics, E. (2010). Politeness in Computer-Mediated Discourse of a Virtual Team. *Journal of Politeness Research. Language, Behaviour, Culture*, *6*(1), 129–150. https://doi.org/10.1515/jplr.2010.007.

Debray, C. (2020). Managing Rapport in Team Conflicts. Dealing with "the elephant in the room". In D. Archer, K. Grainger & P. Jagodziński (Eds.), *Politeness in Professional Contexts* (pp. 129–150). Amsterdam: John Benjamins Publishing Company.

Freytag, V. (2020a). *Exploring Politeness in Business Emails: A Mixed-Methods Analysis*. Bristol: Multilingual Matters.

Freytag, V. (2020b). "I always use the word please" The Production and Perception of English and Spanish Workplace Emails. In D. Archer, K. Grainger, & P. Jagodziński (Eds.), (2020). *Politeness in Professional Contexts* (pp. 199–224). Amsterdam: John Benjamins Publishing Company.

Gu, Y. (1990). Politeness Phenomena in Modern Chinese. *Journal of Pragmatics*, *14*(2), 237–257.

Haugh, M. (2009). Face and Interaction. In M. Haugh & F. Bargiela-Chiappini (Eds.), *Face, Communication and Social Interaction* (pp. 1–30). London: Equinox.

Haugh, M., & Hinze, C. (2003). A Metalinguistic Approach to Deconstructing the Concepts of 'face' and 'politeness' in Chinese, English and Japanese. *Journal of Pragmatics*, *35*, 1581–1611.

Ho, D. (1976). On the Concept of Face. *American Journal of Sociology*, *81*, 867–884.

Ho, D. (1994). Face Dynamics: From Conceptualization to Measurement. In S. Ting-Toomey (Ed.), *The Challenge of Facework* (pp. 269–285). Albany, New York: State University of New York Press.

Holmes, J. (2009). Discourse in the Workplace Literature Review. *Language in the Workplace Occasional Papers, 12*(1).

Holmes, J., & Marra, M. (2004). Leadership and Managing Conflict in Meetings. *Pragmatics 14*(4), 439–62. https://doi.org/10.1075/prag.14.4.02hol.

Janis, I. (1991). Groupthink. In E. Griffin (Ed.), *A First Look at Communication Theory* (pp. 235–246). New York: McGrawHill.

Leech, G. N. (1983). *Principles of Pragmatics*. London: Longman.

Locher, M. A. (2004). *Power and Politeness in Action. Disagreements in Oral Communication*. Berlin/New York: Mouton de Gruyter.

Omdahl, B. L., & Harden Fritz, J. M. (2006). Introduction. In J. M. Harden Fritz & B. L. Omdahl (Eds.), *Problematic Relationships in the Workplace* (pp. xiii–xix). New York: Peter Lang.

Santamaría-García, C. (in press) Freytag, Vera. (2020). Exploring Politeness in Business Emails. A Mixed-Methods Analysis. *Journal of Politeness Research.*

Simon, B. (2004). *Identity in Modern Society. A Social Psychological Perspective.* Oxford: Blackwell.

Spencer-Oatey, H. (2000). *Culturally Speaking : Managing Rapport Through Talk across Cultures*. London: Continuum.

Spencer-Oatey, H. (2002). Managing Rapport in Talk: Using Rapport Sensitive Incidents to Explore the Motivational Concerns Underlying the Management of Relations. *Journal of Pragmatics, 34*, 529–545.

Spencer-Oatey, H. (2005). (Im)Politeness, Face and Perceptions of Rapport: Unpackaging Their Bases and Interrelationships. *Journal of Politeness Research, 1*(1), 95–119. https://doi.org/10.1515/jplr.2005.1.1.9

Spencer-Oatey, H. (2008). Face, (Im)Politeness and Rapport. In H. Spencer-Oatey (Ed.), *Culturally Speaking: Managing Rapport through Talk across Cultures*, (2nd ed., pp. 11–47). London: Continuum.

Spencer-Oatey, H. (2009). Face, Identity and Interactional Goals. In F. Bargiela-Chiappini & M. Haugh (Eds.), *Face, Communication and Social Interaction* (pp. 137–154). London: Equinox.

Spencer-Oatey, H., & Dauber, D. (2017). The Gains and Pains of Mixed National Group Work at University. *Journal of Multilingual and Multicultural Development, 38*(3), 219–36. https://doi.org/10.1080/01434632.2015.1134549.

Tavčar, J., Zavbi, R., Verlinden, J., & Duhovnik, J. (2005). Skills for Effective Communication and Work in Global Product Development Teams. *Journal of Engineering Design, 16*, 557–576.

Watts, R. J. (2003). *Politeness*. Cambridge: Cambridge University Press.

Introduction to The Multifaceted Feature of Politeness: An Interdisciplinary Review

By Hairong Feng

The next chapter examines politeness research across the three disciplines of pragmatics, interpersonal communication and intercultural/cross-cultural communication. Pragmatics is interested in analyzing the contexts of messages and how these contexts influence the meaning of messages. Interpersonal communication studies the verbal and nonverbal exchange between individuals under consideration of the internal, personal, and contextual facets of such exchanges. And intercultural/cross-cultural communication looks at the impact of culture on verbal and nonverbal communication. Politeness, in turn, is a multi-dimensional social phenomenon largely manifested through the use of language; but it also involves the use of face and face threats and serves the function of maintaining and strengthening relationships. It is pointed out that effective communication involves choosing the right amount of politeness for a specific social and relational context. However, culture has also an impact on politeness because the verbal and nonverbal communication associated with politeness various from one culture to another. When considering culture, one needs to be also aware that microcultural differences can play a considerable role in what is considered polite or not; for example, teenagers versus parents. The differences in the language used during relationship building communication in various social classes are an indication of different meanings associated with politeness. That is why the chapter investigates the research of politeness in these three disciplines. Such an interdisciplinary approach is able to provide a richer analysis of politeness. And these considerations need to be kept in mind when attempting to be polite in an intercultural context; especially in the world of business where positive relationships are essential in establishing and maintaining beneficial business relationships. After all, impoliteness often leads to conflicts.

Michael B. Hinner

Hairong Feng (PhD, 2007) is a Professor of Communication at the University of Minnesota Duluth (UMD). Her research interests include supportive communication across cultures, politeness across cultures, as well as intercultural competence. Her publication has appeared in major communication journals, books, and encyclopedias of Communication. She has received top-paper awards from her professional fields and grants from domestic and international collaborations. She has taught Intercultural Communication across nations using both in person and virtual teaching modalities. She served as President for the

Association for Chinese Communication Studies from 2014 to 2015 and currently she is the faculty advisor for the Chinese Students and Scholars Association at UMD.

Hairong Feng

The Multifaceted Feature of Politeness: An Interdisciplinary Review

Politeness is a multi-dimensional social phenomenon largely manifested through the use of language. The study of language use and its meaning to speakers and hearers is pragmatics which aims to explain phenomena of language use in context, especially contextually determined interpersonal meanings. Pragmatics is interested in communicative behavior, and politeness in a pragmatic sense is a matter of conveying meanings in accord with politeness strategies. This is the point where human communication connects with pragmatics of politeness. Communication is viewed as a rational, social, and cooperative activity in linguistic politeness theory (Brown & Levinson, 1987) and politeness model (Leech, 2014) albeit communication involves complicated internal, personal, and contextual facets. Politeness is both universal and cultural specific. There are a number of studies on politeness examining cultural variations in politeness (e.g., Blum-Kulka et al., 1989; Feng et al., 2011; Gu, 1990; Trosborg, 1995). In this chapter, I will review politeness research across the three disciplines of pragmatics, interpersonal communication and intercultural/cross-cultural communication. The goal is to generate implications for future theoretical building of politeness and to have implications for practical use of politeness in mundane communication.

The Pragmatics of Politeness

Five Linguistic Characteristics of Politeness

Leech (2014) delineates five characteristics of politeness calling for theoretical explanations. They are *indirectness, reciprocal asymmetry, gradations of politeness, opposite interpretations of elliptical expressions, and preference and dispreference. Indirectness* refers to the gap between explicit sense and implicit force, and the relation between them – we need to explain why it is that people, in communicating with one another, so often "beat about the bush" – say something different from what they mean. In addition, it is necessary to explain degrees of indirectness and how these correlate with degrees of politeness. *Reciprocal asymmetry* means the asymmetry of self-reference vs. other-reference in politeness needs to be explained. Why is an acceptable thing for S (speaker) to say about H (hearer) not acceptable thing for S to say about S? Similarly, why is an acceptable thing for S to say about S not an acceptable thing for H to say about S? *Gradations of politeness* means politeness has different degrees. It is important to explain gradations of politeness – such that it can be generally agreed that, in a given situation, X would have been a less/more polite thing to say than Y, and Y would have been a less/more polite thing to say than Z. Speakers of a language routinely have to weigh degrees of politeness in communication, and hearers likewise. *Opposite interpretations of elliptical expressions.* Good luck means that S wishes H to have good luck. Bad luck means that S is sorry, and commiserates with H about H's bad luck. Why is it that Bad luck means "I'm sorry about your bad luck" and cannot mean I wish you bad luck? and that Good luck means "I'm glad about your good luck" and cannot mean I am sorry about your good luck? A theory of politeness is needed to explain this anomaly. Finally, *preference and dispreference*. Conversational analysts have noted that in adjacency pairs, where a particular kind of turn spoken by speaker A is typically followed by a response turn spoken by A 's interlocutor B, there is often a preference for one kind of response rather than its opposite. For example, in response to a request, the preferred second turn is to indicate compliance, while the dispreferred one is to indicate refusal.

Current Theories or Models of Politeness

Most extant theories or model of politeness are from linguistics/pragmatics research. Among them, Brown and Levinson's (B&L) politeness theory (1978/1987) is the most influential one, which has been applied to many empirical research across disciplines. Other politeness theories or models (e.g., Gu, 1990; Leech, 1983/2014; Spencer-Oatey, 2008; Watts, 2003) are more or less built in reference (with compliments and criticisms) to B&L's politeness theory. I will review B&L's politeness theory following by other major theories/models (e.g., Leech, 1983/2014; Watts, 2003).

B&L's Politeness Theory

Face is the central concept in B&L's politeness theory. B&L (1987) make a distinction between negative face and positive face. Negative face means 'the basic claim to territories, personal preserves, rights to nondistraction – i.e., to freedom of action and freedom from imposition. Positive face refers to 'the positive consistent self-image or "personality" (crucially including the desire that this self-image be appreciated and approved of) claimed by interactants' (p. 61). Politeness theory posits that many speech acts *intrinsically* are face threatening.

Such acts are labeled intrinsic face threatening acts (FTAs). For instance, challenging or expressing disapproval can threaten a person's positive face wants for approval, whereas ordering a person to do something, or reminding a person of an obligation, can threaten that person's negative face wants for freedom from imposition. The weightiness of any FTA depends on three social factors: the speaker's power relative to the hearer (P), the relational distance between the speaker and the hearer (D), and the ranking of imposition in a culture (R), which means the absolute level of obligation the speaker intends to communicate to the hearer, often culturally defined. The combination of P, D, and R affects the "weight" of action in a specific context. When the weight is greater, one should choose a more polite strategy; when it is less, a less polite strategy is more appropriate. There is no exact calculus for determining when a speaker might choose which politeness strategies, but P, D, and R help model some of the social considerations involved in selecting a politeness strategy.

According to politeness theory, when considering performing an FTA, a speaker might choose any of five super strategies that are presumed to be ordered from least to most polite: (1) do the FTA baldly, without redress; (2) do the FTA on record, with positive politeness; (3) do the FTA on record with negative politeness; (4) do the FTA off record; and (5) do not do the FTA. Do the FTA on record, with positive politeness, means doing the FTA with the attempt to counteract the potential positive face damage. Positive politeness offers assurances that the speaker shares similar wants with the hearer. For example, when presenting a gift to a close friend, one says, "I choose this gift for you and I think you will like it." Do the FTA on record with negative politeness means performing the FTA with the attempt to counteract the potential negative face damage. Negative politeness offers assurances that the speaker respects the hearer's autonomy. For instance, when presenting a gift to a powerful figure, one may say, "I don't know whether you like it or not." Do the FTA off record refers to doing it in a way that the speaker's intent is ambiguous. An example could be: When one wants a person who is next to the door to shut the door, he says, "I feel cold." Do the FTA badly and Do not do the FTA are self-explained.

A speaker chooses a superstrategy based on the perceived weightiness of the FTA. B&L predict that as the weightiness of an FTA increases speakers would choose an increasingly polite, higher numbered strategy. Moreover, a speaker should choose a less polite superstrategy when concerns about efficiency outweigh face concerns. A speaker also is likely to choose a less polite superstrategy when the degree of face threat is low. Politeness theory assumes that individuals are "rational" in the sense of being able to reason from ends to linguistic means for accomplishing their interaction goals. Effective communication involves choosing the right amount of politeness for a specific social and relational context.

Politeness theory also recognizes cultural variations in the concept of face, such as what kinds of speech acts threaten face, what kinds of people have special rights to face-protection, and what sorts of personal interaction style are appreciated. On the other hand, they contend that notions of face contain the most fundamental ideas about the nature of the social persona, morality and virtue, embarrassment and redemption. Thus despite the rich cultural elaborations of face, the mutual knowledge of members' face, and the social necessity to orient oneself to it during interaction, the notions of face are universal. B&L believe their politeness framework provides a primary descriptive format to accommodate such cultural variations.

Leech's Politeness Principle

Leech (1983, 2014) proposes six maxims of the Politeness Principle: the Maxims of Tact, Generosity, Approbation, Modesty, Agreement, and Sympathy. Generosity maxim gives a high value to O's wants such s offers, invitations, and promises are "generous". For example, "*You must come and stay with us next time. I won't take "no" for an answer*!" Tact maxim gives a low value to S's wants such as requests. Requests are often indirect, tentative, giving an opportunity to refuse. For example, "*Could I help myself to a tiny sig of sherry*?" Approbation maxim gives a high value to O's qualities. We like to pay compliments if it seems appropriate to do so: "*Your garden looks so lovely.*" Modesty maxim gives a low value to S's qualities. Self-deprecation (if sincere) is often felt to be polite. For example, "*I'm so dumb, I don't even know it. Hhh! heh*" Agreement maxim gives a high value to O's opinions. In responding to others' opinions or judgments, agreement is the preferred response and disagreement is dispreferred: "*A: It's a beautiful view, isn't it? B: Yeah, absolutely gorgeous.*" Sympathy maxim gives a high value on O's feelings. Sympathy maxim explains why we give a high value to other people's feelings in such speech acts as congratulations and condolences. For example, "*I was so sorry to hear about your father…*"

A maxim is a constraint influencing speakers' communicative behavior and can conflict or compete with one another in context. The General Strategy of Politeness (GSP) comprehends all these maxims: In order to be polite, S expresses or implies meanings that associate a favorable value with what pertains to O or associates an unfavorable value with what pertains to S. Leech argues that S supposes to follow those maxims when interacts with H, albeit in reality individuals may have different internal motives. For example, a speaker could have selfish motives under the disguise of being polite in his/her verbal or nonverbal messages.

Leech agrees with B&L with regard to the fundamental concept of face, the distinction between positive politeness and negative politeness, and the three social cultural factors which influence the degree of linguistic politeness strategies, power (P) social distance (D), and R (rank of imposition). However, Leech has different interpretations on each of them. Leech's revisits of these fundamental concepts offer useful lenses toward understanding of politeness.

Social and Psychological Explanations of Politeness

Face is the central concept in B&L's politeness theory which is founded primarily on the psychological notion of face (Leech, 2014). For B&L, face is assumed to be a positively evaluated property possessed by individual human beings. Leech argues that although face is projected as an element of the psychology of the individual, it is very much a reflection of the individual's relation to other individuals and to society, that is, the social face. Leech backs up his point from the Chinese origin and conception of face. The Chinese societal view of face is illustrated by this quotation from Ho (1976): "Face is lost when the individual either through his action or that of people closely related to him, fails to meet essential requirements placed on him by virtue of the social position he occupies." Hence, in Chinese culture, face is the positive self-image or self-esteem that a person enjoys as a reflection of that person's estimation by others.

Maintaining face gives individuals the motivation to be polite, and therefore it contributes to the cohesion and stability of human societies. According to Leech (2014), politeness contributes to face on two levels. On the first level, politeness serves the face of O (observer). On the second level, it also serves the face of S (speaker). The reason is that politeness is judged as a socially desirable quality, a social norm in the evaluative sense, raising the esteem in which S is held by O and by observers generally. The social explanation and the psychological explanation of politeness work together to give a fuller understanding of how politeness functions, both for the individual and for society. The social theory of politeness helps to show why politeness has a function in human society, and why politeness is a more "normal" phenomenon than impoliteness. However, if politeness is to predominate over impoliteness, the psychological disposition toward politeness and cooperation has to be implanted in the individual. This disposition (i.e., face) is acquired by children in the socialization process. Social and psychological tendencies toward politeness are mutually supporting: the preservation of face and the preservation of comity are intimately interconnected.

Positive Politeness and Negative Politeness

Leech perceives positive politeness playing a bigger role than is allowed for by B&L. For B&L, positive politeness is just one means of redress for an FTA. Positive politeness acts in the service of a negative avoidance principle. For Leech, however, positive politeness aims at an enhancement of face: by attributing value to H, for example in offering, complimenting, or extending sympathy, S is primarily performing a face-enhancing act or FEA (Kerbrat-Orecchioni 1997, Suzuki 2007), not a face-threatening act. Leech labels the terms as neg-politeness and pos-politeness. In the case of neg-politeness, to increase the degree of politeness, we diminish or soften the expression of negative value in the transaction. However in the case of pos-politeness we magnify or strengthen the expression of positive value.

Social Cultural Factors Influencing the Degree of Politeness Strategies

The use of politeness in communication is dependent on two major domains: the language and the social or cultural milieu. Hence there are linguistically oriented and socioculturally oriented aspects of politeness. Leech (2014) terms these as pragmalinguistics and sociopragmatics. Pragmalinguistics and sociopragmatics are not to be studied in isolation from one another. They are both facets of pragmatics: one facing toward language and the other toward society. An important part of the study of politeness is to investigate how they interconnect: how the pragmalinguistic resources of a language enable cultural values to be expressed. Particularly, the study of politeness involves the various scales of value that make a particular degree of linguistic politeness seem appropriate or normal in a given social setting.

Leech contends that three scales of value play this role: the scales of horizontal and vertical distance between speaker and addressee, and the weightiness of the transaction. They are corresponding to B&L's P, D and R factors reviewed earlier. The evaluation of a situation in terms of these scales will affect the degree of politeness. Variation in age, gender, social class, and locality will all have a potential impact; and judgments about weightiness will also depend on a range of cultural factors. The main point to observe is that sociopragmatics is concerned not so much with the resources of language used to express politeness, as with the scales of value that cause a culture to assign more social importance to certain transactions than to others. Comparative sociopragmatics is often called "cross-cultural pragmatics," as it compares not languages but cultures: that is, it compares the levels of value that cultures and subcultures apply to determine the appropriate degree of politeness.

Politeness in Interpersonal Communication

How Communication Is Conceptualized in Politeness Theory

B&L (1987) view communication as a rational, social, cooperative activity. By "rational", it means that politeness theory describes principles for reasoned judgement about communication. By social, it means that these principles are socially shared. The theory explains why languages have polite features and how people can arrive at shared understandings of the features. Politeness theory is not useful for probing personal and internal motivations of communicative messages. B&L (1987) also presume we are motivated to cooperatively honor face in most of our mundane interactions. The kind of cooperation they assume involves co-participating in interaction (i.e., we assume that others desire to communicate information, that they are attempting to be relevant and not deceptive, and so on). Politeness theory directs our attention to judgements of what people should say and do, if they wish to be seen as appropriate and effective. It focuses on dilemmas of interaction and on the creative and constructive ways people use language to enact identities and relationships as they pursue tasks such as requesting, advising, criticizing, or expressing emotion.

Research and Practical Applications of Politeness Theory

Lakoff (1990) defines politeness as "a system of interpersonal relations designed to facilitate interaction by minimizing the potential for conflict and confrontation inherent in all human interchange (p. 34)." This definition illustrates a key function of politeness – the relationship maintenance function of "politeness" in human communication. In fact, some linguistic-oriented politeness scholars have recognized this important function of politeness in their research (e.g., Janney & Arndt, 1992; Leech, 2014; Spencer-Oatey, 2008). For example, Janney and Arndt (1992) equates the notion of politeness with "interpersonal supportiveness," which may be manifest not only in language but in paralinguistic and kinesics features: vocal quality, intonation, gesture, eye contact, and the like. Spencer-Oatey (2008) in her introductory chapter to the book *Culturally Speaking: Managing Rapport through Talk Across Cultures* puts forward a framework for analysis of sociopragmatics that enlarges the sphere of politeness to embrace a more general concept of rapport management (i.e., management of interpersonal relations).

In communication and related disciplines, politeness theory has been interpreted in three distinct ways. Most communication scholars have used the theory to predict behavior. For example, Baxter (1984) asked students to imagine they were working on a group project and had to ask a group member to redo part of the project. Different versions of the scenario varied how well the students knew one another (D), whether the speaker was a group leader or just a member (P), and whether the rewrite involved much or little effort (R). Studies in this tradition have found partial support for the effects of P, D, and R on strategy choice. Other scholars have used politeness theory to predict how behavior will be evaluated. For example, MacGeorge et al. (2004) found that advice perceived by recipients as attending to their face needs (i.e., polite) was generally seen as more sensitive, appropriate, and effective than advice that was delivered with less attention to recipients' face needs. Some scholars find prediction problematic because our actions and evaluations are so dependent on who is interacting, their relationship, and the situation. These scholars use the theory heuristically to identify politeness phenomena and understand the processes that lead to our diverse, creative, situated, and often unpredictable use of politeness in specific situations. For example, Aronsson and Rundstrom (1989) showed how pediatricians were bold on record with children (e.g., "WHAT?" "You SHOULD NOT do that") but polite to parents (e.g., "But then it's best to avoid cats, or what would you say?"). The doctor was appropriately polite to this mother of an allergic child, yet directing a bald on record statement to the child with the mother present ensured that neither missed the point. In recent years, politeness theory mostly has been applied in giving advice research in supportive communication. In the following section, I will review some of the important research in this area.

Politeness Theory and Giving Advice as a Form of Supportive Communication

Giving advice as a form of supportive communication has been studied extensively in the past twenty years. Research has found that giving advice happens frequently between close relational partners such as friends, romantic relationship partners, or family members, but advice is not always appreciated. For instance, in a number of studies examining behaviors perceived as helpful or unhelpful by individuals coping with health problems and life crises, advice was occasionally identified as a helpful form of social support but was more often mentioned as an example of an unhelpful attempt at support (Goldsmith, 2000).

One important reason is that advice is intrinsically a "face-threatening" speech act (Brown & Levinson, 1978, 1987). Advice has been conceptualized as an intrinsically face-threatening act because of the negative implications it carries. Advice giving suggests that the targets lack knowledge or competence in managing the problematic situation on their own, thus threatening the targets' positive face (Goldsmith & Fitch, 1997). Advice also threaten targets' negative face by imposing on their independence and autonomy in decision making, especially if the targets feel obligated or pressured to follow the advice (Goldsmith, 2000; Kunkel et al., 2003). A number of studies have demonstrated that advice perceived by recipients as attending to their face needs (i.e., polite) is generally seen as more sensitive, appropriate, and effective than advice that is delivered with less attention to recipients' face needs (Feng & Feng, 2013; MacGeorge et al., 2004). Research also indicates that face concern becomes particularly salient when advice is not explicitly solicited (Feng & MacGeorge, 2006; Godlsmith, 2000; Goldsmith & Fitch, 1997).

Research on politeness in giving advice has two components: advice message and advice interaction. The advice message research program examines the linkage between language features of advice and politeness. This line of research has primarily focused on politeness strategies (i.e., facework) that are instantiated as a component of advice message per se (e.g., Feng & Burleson, 2008; Goldsmith & MacGeorge, 2000). For example, negative face-work in advice is often manipulated in the form of indirectness or hedges (e.g., "Maybe you could try talking to your professor") and positive facework is reflected in words or phrases indicating inclusion or acceptance (e.g., "When things like this happen, we need to step up for the challenge").

The advice interaction program has focused on how emotional support functions as politeness in giving advice interactions (Feng, 2009; Feng et al., 2017). Feng (2009) tested an integrated model of giving advice. The EPA (emotional support, problem analysis and inquiry, and advice) model demonstrated the best effect in advice interactions. By offering support in a manner that is attentive to the recipient's face needs, a support provider can facilitate the target's coping with their negative emotions and problem solving. From the perspective of politeness theory, emotional support, which is typically instantiated by expressions of understanding, sympathy, and concern, can also function as positive politeness strategies that address the target's face needs (Brown & Levinson, 1987; Goldsmith & MacGeorge, 2000; MacGeorge et al., 2015). The provision of sensitive emotional support prior to advice giving encourages recipients' own sense-making of the problematic situation (MacGeorge et al., 2015) and provides the recipient with more space for working through their thoughts and emotions.

Therefore, the move of emotional support prior to advice giving may also serve as a negative politeness strategy that conveys respect for the recipient's autonomy and mitigates the threat to the recipient's negative face.

In a follow up study, Feng et al. (2017) explored reasons why the EPA model worked better. They found that perceived regard for face partially mediated the relationship between the sequential placement of emotional support and recipients' responses toward advice. Specifically, advice that was offered following the provision of emotional support was perceived as being more attentive to the recipient's face concern, which in turn positively influenced the recipient's evaluation of the advice quality, facilitation of coping, and intention to follow the advice. However, when advice was offered before the provision of emotional support, the benefits of emotional support appeared less salient because "damage" to the recipient's face was already done. Meanwhile the results indicated that it was positive regard for face that explained the influence of the sequential placement of emotional support on the advice outcomes. Interestingly, perceived regard for negative face did not appear to have any mediating effect. This finding suggested that, as two sub-constructs of politeness, regard for positive face and regard for negative face function differently in the processes through which they influence advice reception. While the provision of emotional support prior to advice giving was effective in conveying liking and acceptance of the recipient and helped preserve the recipient's desirable self-image, it did not alleviate threat to the recipient's negative face. However, the results revealed that the engagement of problem inquiry and analysis prior to giving advice helped to convey regard for both the recipient's positive face and negative face.

Politeness Theory and Compliance Gaining Research in Interpersonal Influence

Compliance gaining refers to "any interaction in which a message source attempts to induce a target individual to perform some desired behavior that the target otherwise might not perform" (Wilson, 2002, p. 4). Compliance gaining examines influence within interpersonal contexts and explores how individuals seek and resist compliance during conversations with their personal relational partners such as friends, family members, and coworkers. As such, asking for a request, giving a recommendation, or issuing a command are all speech acts people use to seek compliance. These speech acts are labeled as directives, which "are at the heart of any attempt to gain compliance, given that people seek compliance only when they presume that their targets otherwise would not have performed the desired actions" (Wilson, 2002, p. 202). B&L classify these directives as intrinsic

FTAs which threaten the hearer's negative face want of autonomy. Directives predicate some future acts of the hearer, and so put pressure on the hearer to do or refrain from doing the act. In *orders* and *requests*, the speaker indicates that he or she wants the hearer to do, or refrain from doing; and in *suggestions* and *advice*, the speaker indicates that he or she thinks the hearer ought to do some acts. Orders, requests, suggestions and recommendations are typical compliance gaining acts.

Politeness theory therefore has important implications for compliance gaining study. Wilson (2002) indicates that given the centrality of directives to compliance seeking, it follows that any attempt to gain compliance places certain degree of constraint on the target's negative face. Hence, the speaker might worry to some extent about constraining the target's autonomy and independence within any compliance-gaining situation. For example, when I ask my husband to take care of our two young children when I need to do some work on a Sunday, I put all the burdens of childcare on him, so I worry that he may feel the impositions I place on him. Further, Wilson and his colleagues point out that seeking and resisting compliance can threaten both negative and positive face depending on specific situations. For example, if I say to one of my students: "you need to put more effort into this class in order to get a passing grade", I simultaneously attempt to constrain the student's future behavior and communicate disapproval of the student's current work.

When seeking compliance, the more a potential request threatens the hearer's autonomy, the more the speaker will want to choose a more polite super strategy as reviewed earlier. However, when concerns about efficiency are more important than face concerns, the speaker should choose a less polite super strategy. A speaker also tends to choose a less polite super strategy when face threat from seeking compliance is low such as when the request is small or the speaker has greater relative power. In short, politeness theory does not assume that speakers always will be polite when seeking compliance. Rather, the theory predicts that speakers will vary their levels of politeness based on the degree to which their attempts to gain compliance threaten the hearer's face (Wilson, 2002).

Face concerns would shape the form of compliance seeking messages, and politeness theory has been therefore employed to predict and explain why individuals choose one approach over others when seeking compliance. Scholars have used and modified politeness theory to compose questions about people's choice of compliance-seeking and -resisting messages across cultures, genders, and relationship types. In addition, some other scholars have tested whether persuaders who use specific super strategies, such as going off-record, are perceived as polite, appropriate, competent, and/or effective.

Criticism of B&L's Politeness Theory from Interpersonal Communication Perspective

Interpersonal communication scholars pay closer attention to interactional contexts such as relational, situational, institutional, and cultural contexts. Wilson (2002) points out two problems with B&L's politeness model regarding missing contextual considerations. One is that politeness theory's analysis of how face threats arise is grounded heavily in the form of speech acts, without enough analysis of the context in which speech acts are enacted. For example, individuals from a variety of cultural backgrounds report concerns about appearing to be "butting into" the affairs of others when they give advice, but they rarely have this concern when asking favors. In contrast, individuals at times worry that they might "owe" their interactional partner debts when they ask favors, but they rarely have this concern when giving advice. Hence, the goal underlying a specific speech act like a request or recommendation can define the interaction and make particular threats to face relevant. Moreover, threats to face also vary depending on the unfolding sequence of talk. For instance, the degree to which giving advice threatening face varies depending on whether the target has solicited advice, has disclosed a problem, or has said nothing yet about the topic of advice (Goldsmith, 2004). The second problem is about the rank order of the five super strategies. Wilson argues B&L's claim that regardless of context, the five super strategies can be rank ordered from least to most polite is problematic. A few researchers have reported exceptions to this rank ordering. For example, on-record strategies were perceived as more polite than off-record strategies and positive politeness were evaluated as more polite than negative politeness in certain circumstances. These findings suggest that the perceived politeness of any super strategy depends on specific contexts.

These perspectives from interpersonal communication scholars resonate with the discursive model of studying politeness (e.g., Mills, 2003; Watts, 2003; Werkhofer, 2005). For example, Mills (2003) suggests an interactive concept of politeness depending on the reactions and understanding between conversational partners. She argues that this interactiveness, particularly in relation to the community of practice and the context, should play a determining role in the production and assessment of politeness. Recent research about East Asian politeness has adopted this discursive model which analyzes politeness occurring in longer fragments of authentic interactions (e.g., Mills & Kádár, 2011).

Despite these criticisms, B&L's politeness theory remains an influential theory in guiding empirical interpersonal communication research because the theory has implications for important topics such as message production, identity management, and relationship maintenance.

Practical Implications of Politeness Theory in Interpersonal Communication

In everyday interpersonal communication, politeness theory may help us understand our relationships with others, achieve our goals effectively, and appreciate finely tuned language in our life (Goldsmith & Normand, 2015). An important function of politeness is to maintain our personal relationships in interpersonal communication. First, it might explain recurring difficulties in some relationships. For example, it might help you figure out what it is about an ill-mannered friend that you find so off-putting. Second, politeness theory might suggest alternative ways of pursuing our goals. Are we bald on record when it would be more effective to be more polite? Do we too often rely on off record strategies that do not get our point across? Does overreliance on negative redress strategies make us sound less powerful, or do positive redress strategies come across as too familiar? Finally, even in the absence of communication problems, politeness theory can help us appreciate the finely tuned variations in our language that convey images of self and other, construct our relationships, and may potentially benefit our physical and mental well-being.

A Cross-Cultural/Intercultural Approach to Politeness

Cross-cultural politeness research has focused on explicating how politeness arises within particular langua cultures, such as British English, Mandarin Chinese, or Turkish, and then making comparisons of these politeness formats and practices across those cultures. There are a large number of published studies focusing on politeness from a cross-cultural perspective. In this body of research, the focus on speech acts remains prevalent, with the most popular speech acts being requests, apologies, and compliments/compliment responses (e.g., CCSARP, Blum-Kulka et al., 1989) Politeness is analyzed at the level of the individual or pairs of individuals – how the dyads choose to use speech acts and what factors affect the choices of different forms of speech acts. There is an underlying assumption of universality in this stream of politeness research – linguistic politeness can be systematically described across languages and cultures using the same underlying theoretical framework (e.g., Brown & Levinson, 1978, 1987; Leech, 1983, 2014). Although the ways in which politeness manifests itself differ across languages and cultures, underpinning it are the same operational assumptions: a universal notion of "face" and the assumed universal applicability of "rationality." To explain linguistic regularities across cultures, politeness theory posits that speakers in all cultures want to maintain face.

B&L's politeness theory examines how politeness is employed to redress the performance of face-threatening acts across cultures. B&L recognize cultural variations in the concept of face, which depend on what kinds of speech acts threaten face, what kinds of people have special rights to face protection, and what sorts and styles of personal interaction are appreciated. On the other hand, they contend that notions of face contain the most fundamental ideas about the nature of the social persona, morality and virtue, embarrassment and redemption. Hence, despite the rich cultural elaborations of face, the mutual knowledge of members' face and the social necessity to orient oneself to it during interaction are universal. B&L believe that their politeness framework provides a primary descriptive format to accommodate such cultural variations.

Cross-Cultural Variations in Face and Politeness

Politeness theory, and particularly the concept of face, have been examined and extended in a variety of cultural contexts. Scholars studying Asian politeness challenge the conceptualization and universality of face in B&L's politeness theory. They argue that the equivalence between face and personal wants is based on the Western cultural value of individualism. In Asian societies, face is more of a relational, interdependent phenomenon, reflecting the dominant cultural value of collectivism. Matsumoto (1988), for example, contends that B&L's positive face and negative face is not quite applicable in Japan. The Western notion of face consists of the individual's desire for the approval of wants and desire to protect one's autonomy and independence. However, in Japanese culture, the significance of one's position vis-à-vis relational others is emphasized more than the individual autonomy. A Japanese person wants to understand where s/he stands in relation to others of his or her group and society and must acknowledge his/her dependence on the others. Hence the Japanese notion of face involves an "acknowledgement and maintenance of the relative position of others" (Matsumoto, 1988, p. 405).

This illustration of Japanese face shares similarities with the meaning of Chinese face. The Chinese term for face is *mianzi*, which is central to the Chinese construal of social life. On the one hand, the Chinese face is achieved through reputation and success, qualities claimed by the individual through social recognition, which is similar to the Western concept of face; on the other hand, the Chinese face is a quality to be constantly engaged in in the process of carrying interpersonal relations (Chang & Holt, 1994). The Chinese notion of face involves recognition and understanding of complex personal relationships. Face has been a means through which individuals express their emotional concern toward each other according to the depth of their relationships. Chinese need constantly to take care of each other's face in interactions in order to maintain effective interpersonal relationships. Moreover, Chinese culture tends to be more hierarchical and particularistic, therefore different levels of relations must be observed in order for people to appropriately maintain each other's face. By observing different degrees of relationships and by showing respect for the relational partner's face, the Chinese express emotional concern toward each other. Hence, Chinese face is also relational and interdependent rather than independent. On the whole, East Asian concepts of face are qualitatively different from B&L's face definition. This difference transcends the variability of cultural elaboration recognized in politeness theory.

The fundamental difference between B&L's face concept and the East Asian face concept is also the main factor that creates or explains the variations in the degree to which an FTA is face threatening. A speech act that is supposed to be imposing in one culture may not be imposing in another. For example, in Japanese culture, a request for help from a subordinate to a superior is not considered much face threatening; but it strengthens the face of the superior by recognizing the hierarchical power difference between the subordinate and the superior (Matsumoto, 1988). In Chinese culture, speech acts such as offers and requests are not as face threatening or as imposing as they are in Western culture. Under normal circumstances, offering, inviting, and promising will not be regarded as impeding the hearer's freedom, and hence will not threaten the hearer's negative face (Gu, 1990).

Further, the different meanings entailed in the concept of face also cause variations in the motivation for using positive and negative politeness. In an individualistic culture, negative politeness is more motivated by the respect for the other's independence and autonomy, whereas in a collectivistic culture it is more often required by the social norm of respecting hierarchical order (Pan, 2000). For example, deference in Japanese culture focuses primarily on the ranking difference between conversational participants, whereas deference in Western culture is a strategy that is likely to be used among peers. As Leech (2014) points out, from a cross-cultural perspective, it is generally held that English-speaking cultures place more weight on the autonomy of the individual than do most other cultures, so that avoidance of direct imposition on the hearer in directives (i.e., negative politeness or Tact Maxim) shows especially elaborate development in English. In many other cultures, however, more weight is placed on the value of generosity, for example, showing oneself to be generous in offers and invitations (i.e., positive politeness or Generosity Maxim).

Alternative Models of Studying Politeness and Culture

Among the general and specific criticisms, a consistent theme is that the first wave politeness accounts primarily miss the social, cultural, historical, and contextual conditions that shape the formation and use of language and politeness (Mills & Kádár, 2011). This politeness model is relatively goal oriented, instrumental, and strategic: An individual chooses politeness strategies in order to mitigate face threats. But, in interaction, politeness does not just function to reduce face threat and it is also *normative*. People in a culture choose forms of politeness according to their cultural expectations and requirements. Each national culture has its own unique politeness norms. For example, in Chinese culture, politeness functions to grant "*mianzi*" and thus maintain personal relationships. Failure to observe politeness will incur social sanctions. In Japanese culture, honorifics are used to show respect and recognition of an individual's position within the social order. Honorifics are components of the grammatical structure of Japanese language and they are an essential part of linguistic conduct. Omission of honorifics may cause misunderstanding.

Further, politeness also must be examined with consideration of subcultural, social, and contextual factors within a community of practice. This alternative perspective argues that cultures are not homogeneous and that within each culture there are different views on what constitute polite or impolite behaviors. It is important to be cautious about referring to politeness norms within or across cultures. Recent research has examined regional, class, and gender variations in politeness. Within each culture there is variation in terms of what a regional group sees as polite. A regional identity is associated with the use of certain politeness speech style. Each region has its unique politeness expressions and strategies which are different from the wider cultural norms. It is also evident politeness is associated with a class-based refinement and education. For example, within the UK, the middle classes are often referred to as "polite society" and working-class people may reject certain speech norms which they consider to be associated with middle-class speech. Further, along with regional differences, gendered politeness has also been researched. For instance, Mills (2003) has argued that politeness is associated with the speech norms at a stereotypical level of middle-class white women.

Moreover, the alternative perspective contends that politeness is often discursively constructed: the conversation partners constantly reflect on the interaction as it unfolds. When examining discourses of politeness at a societal level and relating these to practices across different social networks with which individuals can identify, it is apparent that even common sense understandings of norms acknowledge the existence of more than one set of norms regarding politeness within that culture. It is thus necessary to recognize the relativity and variability of politeness norms. The variations in politeness norms within cultures raise questions about intercultural politeness research.

It has been popular to compare politeness forms and practices across cultural groups. All the major theories of politeness have focused primarily on explicating how politeness arises within particular cultures, and then making comparisons of these politeness formats and practices across cultures. However, it has been much less common to examine understandings of politeness in interactions among participants who have different socio-cultural backgrounds. Intercultural politeness research focuses on interactions or other forms of data obtained when people from two different cultural groups interact with each other. Many of these studies have focused on the ways in which divergent practices and expectations may cause discomfort or even offence in intercultural interactions. However, there has been a much more limited amount of research focusing on how participants may in fact attempt to accommodate to these diverging forms and practices or expectations. Yet intercultural politeness interactions involve a complex interweaving and emergence of localized, situated normative practices, instead of simply a transfer and possible "clashes" of different sets of norms or expectancies. Such complexity poses a challenge for contemporary theories of politeness. To date there has been few specific theorizing of intercultural politeness. The overwhelming focus on theorizing politeness cross-culturally is questionable and at the same time raising questions about theorizing politeness in intercultural interactions.

Final Thoughts

This chapter reviews politeness from an interdisciplinary perspective. It is in the field of sociolinguistics and pragmatics, politeness has been extensively researched and studied. Interpersonal communication scholars have applied and revisited B&L's politeness theory in their research, especially in supportive communication. How politeness is perceived as supportive and how this affects relational, physical and mental well-being are worthy of future exploration in empirical studies. In everyday interpersonal communication, politeness theory may help us understand our relationships with others, achieve our goals effectively, and appreciate finely tuned language in our life (Goldsmith & Normand, 2015).

Intercultural communication examination on politeness warrants more efforts in future research.

References

Aronsson, K., & Rundstrom, B. (1989). Cats, Dogs, and Sweets in the Clinical Negotiation of Reality: On Politeness and Coherence in Pediatric Discourse. *Language and Society, 18*, 483–504.

Baxter, L. A. (1984). An Investigation of Compliance Gaining as Politeness. *Human Communication Research, 10*, 427–456.

Blum-Kulka, S., House, J., & Kasper, G. (Eds.). (1989). *Cross-Cultural Pragmatics: Requests and Apologies*. Norwood, NJ: Ablex.

Brown, P., & Levinson, S. (1978). Universals in Language Usage: Politeness Phenomena. In E. N. Goody (Ed.), *Questions and Politeness: Strategies in Social Interaction* (pp. 56–289). Cambridge: Cambridge University Press.

Brown, P., & Levinson, S. (1987). *Politeness: Some Universal in Language Use*. Cambridge, UK: Cambridge University Press.

Chang, H.-C., & Holt, G. R. (1994). A Chinese Perspective on Face as Inter-Relational Concern. In S. Ting-Toomey (Ed.), *The Challenge of Facework* (pp. 95–131). Albany: State University of New York.

Feng, B. (2009). Testing an Integrated Model of Advice Giving in Supportive Interactions. *Human Communication Research, 35*, 115–129. https://doi.org/10.1111/j.1468-2958.2008.01340.x.

Feng, B., & Burleson, B. R. (2008). The Effects of Argument Explicitness on Responses to Advice in Supportive Interactions. *Communication Research, 35*, 849–874. https://doi.org/10.1177/0093650208324274.

Feng, H., Chang, H.-C., & Holt, R. (2011). Examining Chinese Gift-Giving Behavior From the Politeness Theory Perspective. *Asian Journal of Communication, 21*, 301–317.

Feng, B., & Feng, H. (2013). Examining Cultural Similarities and Differences in Responses to Advice: A Comparison of American and Chinese College Students. *Communication Research, 40*, 623–644. https://doi.org/10.1177/0093650211433826.

Feng, B., & MacGeorge, E. L. (2006). Predicting Receptiveness to Advice: Characteristics of the Problem, the Advice-Giver, and the Recipient. *Southern Communication Journal, 71*, 67–85. https://doi.org/10.1080/10417940500503548.

Feng, B., Young Jang, J., Kim, I., & Wang, B. (2017). Explaining the Effectiveness of the Integrated Model of Advice-Giving in Supportive Interactions: The

Mediating Roles of Politeness and Normativeness. *Communication Quarterly, 65*, 402–418.

Goldsmith, D. J. (2000). Soliciting Advice: The Role of Sequential Placement in Mitigating Face Threat. *Communication Monographs, 67*, 1–19. https://doi.org/10.1080/03637750009376492.

Goldsmith, D. J. (2004). *Communicating Social Support*. Cambridge, UK: Cambridge University Press.

Goldsmith, D. J., & Fitch, K. (1997). The Normative Context of Advice as Social Support. Human *Communication Research, 23*, 454–476. https://doi.org/10.1111/j.1468-2958.1997.tb00406.x.

Goldsmith, D. J., & MacGeorge, E. L. (2000). The Impact of Politeness and Relationship on Perceived Quality of Advice about a Problem. *Human Communication Research, 26*, 234–263. https://doi.org/10.1111/j.1468-2958.2000.tb00757.x.

Goldsmith, D. J., & Normand, E. L. (2015). In Dawn O. Braithwaite & Paul Schrodt (Eds.), *Engaging Theories in Interpersonal Communication* (2nd ed., pp. 267–278). Los Angeles, CA: Sage.

Gu, Y. G. (1990). Politeness Phenomena in Modern Chinese. *Journal of Pragmatics, 14*, 237–257.

Ho, D. Y.-F. (1976). On the Concept of Face. *American Journal of Sociology, 81*, 867–884.

Janney, R., & Arndt, H. (1992). Intracultural Tact Versus Intercultural Tact. In R. I. Watts, S. Ide, & K. Ehlich (Eds.), *Politeness in Language: Studies in Its History, Theory, and Practice* (pp. 21–42). Berlin and New York: Mouton de Gruyter.

Kerbrat-Orecchioni, C. (1997). A Multilevel Approach in the Study of Talk-in-Interaction. *Pragmatics, 7*(1), 1–20.

Kunkel, A. D., Wilson, S. R., Olufowote, J., & Robson, S. (2003). Identity Implications of Influence Goals: Initiating, Intensifying, and Ending Romantic Relationships. *Western Journal of Communication, 67*, 382–412. https://doi.org/10.1080/10570310309374780.

Lakoff, R. T. (1990). *Talking Power: The Politics of Language in Our Lives*. Glasgow: HarperCollins.

Leech, G. (1983). *Principles of Pragmatics*. London, UK: Longman.

Leech, G. (2014). *The Pragmatics of Politeness*. New York, NY: Oxford University Press.

MacGeorge, E. L., Feng, B., Butler, G. L., & Budarz, S. K. (2004). Understanding Advice in Supportive Interactions: Beyond the Facework and Message

Evaluation Paradigm. *Human Communication Research, 30*, 42–70. https://doi.org/10.1111/j.1468-2958.2004.tb00724.x.

MacGeorge, E. L., Guntzviller, L. M., Branch, S., & Yakova, L. (2015). Advice in Interaction: Quantity and Placement of Problem-Solving Behaviors. *Communication Research*. Advance online publication. https://doi.org/10.1177/0093650215607612.

Matsumoto, Y. (1988). Reexamination of the Universality of Face: Politeness Phenomena in Japanese. *Journal of Pragmatics, 12*, 403–426. https://doi.org/10.1016/0378-2166(88)90003-3.

Mills, S. (2003). *Gender and Politeness*. Cambridge: Cambridge University Press.

Mills, S., & Kádár, D. Z. (2011). Politeness and Culture. In D. Z. Kádár & S. Mills (Eds.), *Politeness in East Asia* (pp. 21–44). Cambridge, UK: Cambridge University Press.

Pan, Y. (2000). *Politeness in Chinese Face-to-Face Interaction*. Stamford, CT: Ablex Publishing Corporation.

Spencer-Oatey, H. (2008). *Culturally Speaking: Culture, Communication and Politeness Theory*. London & New York: Continuum.

Suzuki, T. (2007). *A Pragmatic Approach to the Generation and Gender Gap in Japanese Politeness Strategies*. Tokyo: Hituzi Syobo.

Trosborg, A. (1995). *Interlanguage Pragmatics: Requests, Complaints and Apologies*. Berlin and New York: Mouton de Gruyter.

Watts, J. R. (2003). *Politeness*. Cambridge: Cambridge University Press.

Werkhofer, K. T. (2005). Traditional and Modern Views: The Social Constitution and the Power of Politeness. In R. Watts, S. Ide, & E. Konrad (Eds.), *Politeness in Language* (2nd ed., pp. 155–199). Berlin and New York: Mouton de Gruyter.

Wilson, S. R. (2002). *Seeking and Resisting Compliance: Why People Say What They Do When Trying to Influence Others*. Thousand Oaks, CA: Sage.

Introduction to Emotional Communication in Negotiation and Dispute Resolution across Cultures

By Meina Liu, Mengyuan Chen, and Yi Ren

The chapter examines the role of emotions in negotiations. While early negotiation research often described objective, rational negotiations, recent research has also examined the role of emotions in negotiations. Both from an intrapersonal as well as an interpersonal perspective. It seems that emotions do play an important role and, thus, cannot be ignored. The chapter points out that while emotions are often universally recognizable, the actual display of emotions in specific contexts varies from one culture to another. Because of these differences, the authors point out that cultural intelligence can be helpful in successfully applying, recognizing, and responding to emotional displays in one's counterpart. The authors point out that violations of cultural expectations do not automatically result in negative evaluations of one's counterpart's behavior. It seems that the cultural values of both negotiators and their roles can result in different perceptions of the actual negotiation which can lead more uncertainties and anxieties. However, the authors point out that this does not have to lead to negative outcomes. In order to avoid potential negative outcomes, the negotiators should focus on empathy and perspective-taking. By using more integrative tactics, it is possible to reach productive outcomes. That is why it is important for intercultural negotiators to be prepared as to the other culture and that culture's use of emotions. It is above all imperative to use and create positive emotions amongst the negotiators while at the same time trying to curb one's own negative emotions. Here as well, knowledge of the other culture can be helpful because it will allow one to be more precise in properly "reading" one's counterpart's emotions and intentions. This chapter is, thus, a first step in preparing oneself for negotiations across different cultures.

Michael B. Hinner

Meina Liu is a Professor of Communication and Chair of the Department of Organizational Sciences and Communication at the George Washington University. Her research interests include intercultural communication, organizational communication, and negotiation and conflict management. She received her Ph.D. in Communication from Purdue University. Correspondence concerning this article should be directed to Meina Liu, Department of Organizational Sciences and Communication, George Washington University, 600 21st Street NW, Washington DC, 20052; phone: 202-994-1870; fax:202-994-1881; email: meinaliu@gwu.edu

Mengyuan Chen received her Master's of Arts degree in Communication Management from the Department of Organizational Sciences and Communication of the George Washington University. She is currently applying for admission to doctoral programs in Intercultural Communication and Strategic Communication.

Isabelle Yi Ren is an Assistant Professor of Management in the Feliciano School of Business of Montclair State University. Her research interests center around how actors make sense and make use of the various cultural, status, and professional boundaries in organizations and the broader society. She received her Ph.D. in Organization Studies from Boston College.

Meina Liu, Mengyuan Chen and Yi Ren

Emotional Communication in Negotiation and Dispute Resolution across Cultures

As globalization continues to bring individuals from different cultures into increased contact with each other, negotiating and resolving disputes across cultures are inevitable, whether between two companies' executives for international joint ventures, licensing agreements, mergers, and acquisitions, or between a buyer and a seller at a flea market, or between a couple about what to have for dinner. Negotiation happens when two or more parties have differing interests and must communicate with one another to strike a deal or reach a mutually acceptable solution (Lewicki et al., 2003). Dispute resolution refers to the process of resolving conflicts where one party makes a claim, and the other party rejects it. Given its pervasiveness, negotiation is frequently considered as one of the most important skills for global managers to have (George et al., 1998).

While early negotiation researchers tend to conceptualize negotiators as mostly strategic, rational, and dispassionate actors (Allred, 1999), an increasing body of research in the past three decades has documented the significant effects of emotion in negotiations, ranging from positive emotions (e.g., happiness, compassion, sympathy) to negative emotions (e.g., anger, disappointment, guilt), either intra-personally (i.e., the effects of experienced emotions on negotiators' own behaviors and outcomes) or interpersonally (i.e., the effects of expressed emotions on the counterpart's behaviors and outcomes), or both. In addition, although intercultural negotiation research remains in its infancy (Luomala et al., 2015), recent research has begun to expand our understanding of the role of emotion in negotiations across cultural boundaries. In particular, cultures can vary substantially in regard to people's emotional reactions to an event, the norms of expressing emotions, and the interpretation of observed emotions. In this chapter, by drawing from the research literature on emotional communication in negotiation and dispute resolution across cultures, we hope to provide readers with an overview of major streams of research in this field and highlight practical and research-informed strategies that readers can utilize in their formal or informal negotiations and dispute resolutions.

Earlier Perspectives on Emotion in Negotiation

Emotion as a "black box" in behavioral research was not really opened until the 1980s. As research on emotion in conflict and negotiations increased substantially, negotiation scholars began to offer a wide range of recommendations regarding the strategic use of emotion in negotiations. Three perspectives concerning the relationship between emotion and negotiation outcomes emerged, which are respectively labeled as the rational negotiator, the positive negotiator, and the irrational negotiator (see Thompson et al., 2008). These perspectives offer advice that ranges from maintaining a "poker face" to displaying a "smiley face," and from suppressing negative emotions such as anger to overtly "ranting and raving."

Specifically, the rational negotiator perspective derives from the traditional emphasis on rational thinking in the U.S. culture, where emotion is considered as a signal that one has departed from rational analysis and thus makes one vulnerable to losing one's power or share of the bargaining zone (Thompson et al., 2008). Negotiators are advised to keep a "poker face" as well as a cool head at the bargaining table. However, this perspective has received little empirical evidence. Not only did scholars find keeping a "poker face" may have adverse effects because of the high level of monitoring and control it requires, but accumulating evidence has indicated that emotions, especially positive emotions, can significantly improve negotiation effectiveness (Carnevale & Isen, 1986; Allred et al., 1997).

The positive negotiator perspective argues that negative emotions (i.e., anger, impatience, frustration, indignation, etc.) should be avoided or suppressed because they likely lead to conflict spirals during negotiation and are thus detrimental to negotiation outcomes, whereas positive emotions can improve negotiation effectiveness because they facilitate a cooperative bargaining process and therefore the discovery of integrative solutions. Paradoxically, however, an opposite perspective (i.e., the irrational negotiator perspective) argues that expression of extreme negative emotions – to the point of appearing irrational – can be highly effective. Accordingly, negotiators are advised to "rant and rave." While each perspective received some empirical evidence and appeared to be partially true, these prescriptive maxims are "hardly consistent, and in some cases, downright contradictory" (Thompson et al., 2008, p. 151).

These conflicting prescriptive maxims suggest that emotions play a variety of roles in everyday interactions and function in both positive and negative ways. However, these perspectives assume that emotions have a universal effect on negotiators regardless of their cultural backgrounds, as it was not until the

21st century did researchers on emotion in negotiations begin to empirically investigate cross-cultural variations in how emotion influences negotiations. A more sophisticated understanding of emotional communication in conflict and negotiation across cultures, therefore, requires a differentiated analysis of cultural variations in how emotion is experienced or expressed, how it shapes negotiation, and what we can do to communicate in ways that transform the negotiation towards a productive direction.

The Conceptualization of Cultural Differences in Emotions

Emotion has been notoriously difficult to define. There are perhaps as many definitions of emotion as there are researchers interested in the topic (Van Kleef et al., 2004). While scholars widely disagree on what constitutes emotion, some researchers manage the subtleties by using the word emotion interchangeably with affect, feeling, and mood. In general, affect is considered a "generic term for a whole range of preferences, evaluations, moods, and emotions" (Fiske & Taylor, 1991, p. 410). Emotions differ from moods in that they are differentiated or discrete, of relatively short duration, and intense, ephemeral, and have a discernable antecedent cause (Frijda, 1993), whereas mood is not associated with a particular stimulus, more enduring, and less intense (Barry & Oliver, 1996). Both emotion and mood have an evaluative component that is felt as good or bad, positive or negative (Parrot, 2004). While earlier research on emotion in negotiation focused more on dispositional affect (e.g., Carnevale & Isen, 1986; George et al., 1998), most studies in the past two decades focused on specific types of discrete emotions in negotiations.

Cross-cultural research has suggested the universality of many facial and bodily expressions, physiological changes, cognitive appraisals, and action tendencies associated with certain emotions, especially in terms of the potential of emotions (Mesquita & Markus, 2001). However, considerable cross-cultural differences have been documented at the level of emotional practices. From a cognitive perspective, emotions arise from the judgments people make about events in their environment, and once emotions occur, people often think in a somewhat altered manner and act accordingly (Parrot, 2004). As people from different cultures live in different social realities that tend to activate different cognitive appraisals, they may *experience* different emotions. For example, Luomala and colleagues (2015) found that Finns experience negative emotions of all types (dejection and agitation) in an unsuccessful intercultural business negotiation to a greater degree than Indians, whereas Indians report positive or neutral emotions such as happy, calm, satisfied, and regretful, even in the case of an unsuccessful negotiation. Liu (2012) found that in response to the same negative behavior exhibited by the negotiation counterpart, American participants judged the counterpart as more personally responsible for perceived negative behavior, felt more anger and less compassion toward the counterpart, and placed greater importance on competitive goals than Chinese participants. Both studies demonstrate that members of collectivistic cultures, such as Chinese and Indian negotiators, are better at perspective taking and less likely to experience negative emotions than individualists.

From a social constructivist perspective, emotion is defined as a "syndrome," a "social role," or "a socially prescribed set of responses to be followed by a person in a given situation" (Averill, 1980, p. 308). Culture influences the *expression* of emotion through cultural display rules or norms that prescribe which kinds of feelings can and should be displayed in which kinds of contexts. For example, Indian negotiators were found to engage in greater emotional regulation when intercultural negotiations were unsuccessful than Finnish negotiators (Luomala et al., 2015). In a similar vein, Adair & Semnani-Azad (2011) found that Chinese negotiators had a more restrained and rigid posture and fewer displays of negative emotion than Canadian negotiators. As emotions communicate important information to observing individuals about one's attitudes, social intentions, and behavioral orientations (Keltner & Haidt, 1999), individuals from different cultures may also interpret the expressed emotions differently based on the different cultural display rules or norms, and therefore, have different behavioral responses to the counterpart's expressed emotions. For example, Liu (2009) found that Chinese negotiators used more distributive tactics as their counterparts' anger increased, whereas American negotiators did not, because overt expression of anger may activate perceptions of outgroup membership for collectivists, which tend to activate competitive behavioral tendencies.

Emotions in Intercultural Negotiations

As both theoretical and empirical works suggest cultural variations in the experience and expressions of emotions, negotiation scholars have long noted the importance of understanding the role of emotion in intercultural negotiations (e.g., George et al., 1998). However, despite an increasing body of research on emotion in negotiations, few empirical studies have examined emotional communication in negotiations from a *cross-cultural* perspective (i.e., cross-cultural comparisons of intracultural negotiations), let alone how emotions may shape the *intercultural* negotiation dynamics (i.e., involving negotiators from different cultural backgrounds).

It is widely agreed that the dynamics of emotional communication are more complex in intercultural negotiations than in intracultural negotiations. According to Barry and Oliver (1996), affect is presumed to be a function of prior perceptions and experiences negotiators bring to a particular encounter. One of the problems associated with intercultural negotiations is the potential clash in expectations between negotiators from different cultures. Perceived dissimilarity in values and beliefs may give rise to perceptions of uncertainty and anxiety, and consequently, more anticipatory negative emotional states (Kumar, 2004). The greater cultural distance between negotiators, the less sense of control they may perceive, as they may enter the negotiation expecting the situation to be ambiguous and difficult.

Although cross-cultural negotiation research has generally found intercultural negotiations to yield poorer outcomes than intracultural negotiations due to cultural clashes in values, scripts, or schemas about negotiation (e.g., Brett & Okumura, 1998), recent research noted that violations of cultural expectations do not always lead to negative evaluations of the counterpart's negotiation behavior; other factors, such as the combination of negotiators' cultural values and bargaining roles, may prompt different emotional reactions and therefore shape the negotiation dynamics in different ways (Liu et al., 2019). For example, Liu et al. compared emotional responses, interaction goals, bargaining tactics, and negotiation outcomes of two types of intercultural negotiation dyads – high-status, high-power distance negotiators (Chinese managers) paired with low-status, low-power distance negotiators (American employees) versus high-status, low-power distance negotiators (American managers) paired with low-status, high-power distance negotiators (Chinese employees). They found that the former experienced more anger, placed less emphasis on cooperative goals, used less priority information exchange, and consequently, gained less joint profit, than the latter. According to Liu et al., although cultural distance may cause negative anticipatory emotional states, expectancy violations can be positive when an American manager meets a Chinese employee, because low-PD values cause American managers to be generally more accepting of employees' competitive tactics and to communicate greater concern for employees' needs, whereas High-PD values cause Chinese employee to be generally more accepting of employers' power tactics and tend to show respect and deference by making more concessions.

On a practical level, this example suggests that intercultural negotiations can be more effective when the culture-role combinations are more conducive to empathy and perspective taking, a significant predictor of integrative negotiation outcomes (Galinsky et al., 2008). When a culture-role combination poses barriers for a more productive bargaining process, negotiators can combat the difficulties through a better understanding of the counterpart's cultural background, to avoid exhibiting behaviors that negatively violate the counterpart's expectations. For example, high-status negotiators (e.g., managers) from high-PD cultures (e.g., China) should be mindful of the egalitarian nature of low-PD cultures and de-emphasize power and hierarchy in their interactions with low-status negotiators from low- PD cultures. Likewise, low-status negotiators (e.g., employees) from low-PD cultures (e.g., U.S.) should be mindful of the cultural assumptions of a high-PD culture and show more respect to their high-status counterpart with more humility and less overt display of negative emotions.

The example also suggests that to counter the effect of cultural distance on negotiators' negative emotional states in intercultural negotiations, it is important to develop a greater understanding of how culture may influence negotiators' experience and expression of emotions, as well as their subsequent effects on negotiation behaviors and outcomes. Imai and Gelfand (2010) found that cultural intelligence (i.e., individuals' capability to adapt effectively to situations of cultural diversity) is positively associated with the extent to which negotiators engaged in integrative information exchange in intercultural negotiations, which in turn predicted joint profit. To provide the reader with a better understanding of culture's effect on emotion in negotiations, below we provide a review of research on cultural variations in the effects of experienced versus expressed emotions in negotiations respectively.

Cultural Influences on Experienced Emotions in Negotiations

Research that documented the intrapersonal effects of emotions in negotiations (i.e., how *felt* emotions influenced negotiators' own cognition and behaviors) has been largely informed by the cognitive theories of emotion (e.g., Allred et al., 1997). Cognitive theorists believe that all emotions are initiated by individuals' appraisals of their circumstances in relation to their well-being and what they care about. For example, according to Weiner (1995), attribution of responsibility (i.e., perceptions of the causes of success or failure, such as ability, effort, and luck) is a cognitive appraisal that generates differential emotional responses, such as anger and sympathy, depending on the characteristics of the appraised causes, such as personal versus impersonal, controllable versus uncontrollable. Such emotional responses in turn direct social behavior toward others, such as helping and punishing.

Substantial negotiation research has supported this proposition: The experience of anger has been found to increase contentious behavior (Olekalns

& Smith, 2003), use more positional statements and make fewer integrative offers (Liu, 2009), increase more face-attacking tactics, use more power-based and rights-based tactics, while reducing interests-based tactics in dispute resolution (Liu & Zhu, 2019), and place more importance on competitive and recriminatory goals (Allred, 1999; Liu, 2012). Although much fewer studies have examined the effects of positive emotions on negotiation behaviors, research showed that compassion was associated with greater trust towards the counterpart and greater emphasis placed on cooperative goals (Liu & Wang, 2010), as well as greater joint gains and great desire for future work relationships (e.g., Allred et al., 1997).

Research on cultural differences in the effects of felt or experienced emotions on negotiations, therefore, seeks to understand how culture influences the cognitive-emotional-behavioral processes whereby emotions influence negotiation. Such research tends to draw on two theoretical frameworks to explain observed cultural differences: Nisbett's research on culture and thinking styles and Hofstede's dimensions of cultural values. According to Nisbett (2003), due to different ecologies, economies, social structures, metaphysics, and epistemologies dated back in ancient China and ancient Greece, Easterners and Westerners have developed distinctive ways of thinking. East Asians are considered holistic and dialectical thinkers, whereas Westerners, such as Europeans and US Americans, are analytical and logical thinkers. Holistic thinkers tend to perceive events holistically or within a large context. They assume that individual parts cannot be fully understood unless they are considered as a coherent whole and placed within the interdependent relationships. In contrast, analytical thinkers attend more to focal objects and specific details than what is going on in the environment. They also tend to place focal elements into a cause–effect, linear, or sequential frame.

Researchers found that such cultural differences in thinking styles help us understand why individualists tend to report more anger and less compassion in conflict and negotiation situations (Liu, 2012). U.S. Americans, for example, were found to make more "fundamental attribution error" or "correspondence bias" (i.e., the tendency to over-assign causality to personality traits and under-assign it to situational constraints) than East Asians (Masuda & Nisbett, 2001). As a result, when making causal attributions, U.S. Americans are more likely to locate responsibility for behavior within the individual, whereas East Asians are more likely to take situational constraints into consideration (Choi et al., 1999). Liu (2012) found that given the same set of persuasive messages by a negotiation counterpart, American participants judged the counterpart as more personally responsible for perceived negative behavior, felt more anger and less compassion toward the counterpart, and placed greater importance on competitive goals than Chinese participants.

Cross-cultural researchers have also attributed such cultural differences to cultural values, especially individualism–collectivism. Individualistic societies emphasize individual rights, such as freedom, privacy, and autonomy, whereas collectivistic societies emphasize group goals and needs, expecting individuals to adjust their personal goals and preferences to achieve group harmony. Anger has been considered an ego-focused emotion that derives from and promotes an independent view of the self, whereas compassion (or sympathy) has been considered an other-focused emotion that results from being sensitive to another person's, rather than one's own, feelings and concerns and in turn promotes interdependence (Markus & Kitayama, 1991). Based on this reasoning, U.S. Americans are more likely to experience anger, whereas East Asians, compassion.

Shirako and colleagues (2015) conducted five studies and provided consistent evidence that negotiators benefited from eliciting sympathy (or compassion) in their counterparts. By making sympathy appeals, negotiators were more successful in both claiming value in distributive negotiations and creating value in integrative negotiations. This suggests that sympathy appeals can serve as a potential tactic to claim desired resources as well as facilitate mutually beneficial agreements. Friedman et al. (2004) tested competing theories about whether anger is productive or counterproductive for dispute resolution; they found that expression of anger tends to lower the resolution rate in mediation, partly because this often generates an angry response in the partner; however, they also found that when the respondents are particularly vulnerable, the filer's expression of anger would not hinder dispute settlement.

Given that American negotiators are more likely to subscribe to the correspondence bias, which tends to increase anger and reduce compassion, a practical take-away from cross-cultural research on emotion in negotiation is to mindfully manage one's angry feelings by engaging in motivated information search about the external, uncontrollable factors that may potentially account for the counterpart's apparent negative behavior. This is particularly true for intercultural negotiation involving members of different cultures. As negotiators from contrastive cultural communities rely on different assumptions about social interaction and have different preferred communication styles, unless negotiators are cognizant of culture's influence on the counterpart's behavioral differences, misjudgment of the counterpart's intentions and motives is very likely, which will inevitably generate negative emotions and reduce negotiators' desire to identify mutually satisfactory solutions.

Cross-cultural research has also documented cultural variations in the effects of anger on dispute resolution processes. For example, in a recent study, Liu and Zhu (2019) found that in emotion-laden disputes, angry feelings may activate different dispute resolution behaviors for individuals from different cultures due to different cultural values. When Hong Kong Chinese get angry in a dispute situation, they place more emphasis on gaining power and tend to use a *power-based* approach that forces conciliation through higher authority, threats and pressure tactics. Due to stronger hierarchical values in the Chinese culture, angry feelings can provoke a power-oriented mindset that views rules and regulations as less applicable, but views power and coercion as more effective in achieving their goals. On the other hand, although anger also activates power goals for Americans, such goals tend to activate a *right-based* approach that relies on mutually acknowledged and objective standards, such as contracts or legal terms, likely due to stronger egalitarian values and greater emphasis on perceived fairness and equity in the American culture. Although anger moves negotiators away from an *interests-based* approach to dispute resolution in both cultures, it is helpful to understand the cross-cultural differences in how anger prompts a different set of distributive behaviors in different cultures. When disputes take place between negotiators from different cultural backgrounds, understanding these differences can help negotiators cope with their emotions, adjust their goals, practice perspective-taking and prevent an already difficult dispute from escalating into an impasse.

Cultural Influences on Expressed Emotions in Negotiations

In the past two decades, most research on emotion in negotiations focused on the interpersonal effects of emotion on negotiation and dispute resolution (i.e., how the counterpart's *expressed* emotions influence one's negotiation behaviors and outcomes). This line of research recognizes that emotion has critical social functions and consequences (Van Kleef et al., 2004). The social functions perspective holds that emotions carry essential information, such as the negotiator's goals, attitudes, and behavioral orientations. Negotiators, thus, would interpret the other's emotions and make moves accordingly. For example, Van Kleef et al. (2008) found that when the counterparts expressed disappointment during negotiation, negotiators may interpret it as a message of asking for more; therefore, they would make more concessions and satisfy the other's needs.

Given the importance of emotional expressions, skilled negotiators may want to leverage and strategically display emotions by purposely expressing authentic emotions or feigned (i.e., generated, amplified, or suppressed) emotions based on their assessment of the situation to achieve desired goals (DePaulo et al., 2003; Levenson, 1994). Prior literature suggests that the expressions of positive and negative emotions can both influence the negotiated outcomes, though it can be difficult in some situations than others (e.g., Potworowski & Kopelman, 2008). Positive emotions are conducive to building trust with the counterpart and increasing the use of interest-based tactics, which in turn facilitate value creation and increase the likelihood of higher joint gains (Kopelman et al., 2006). On the other hand, the display of negative emotions can also function as a source of influence (Forgas & Williams, 2001). For example, according to Sinaceur and Tiedens (2006), in situations where asymmetrical power exists, the high-power negotiator's display of anger allows them to claim greater value than the low-power negotiator's display of anger.

However, the influence of strategic emotions is not universal. Cultural values and norms would sway people's responses to strategically displayed emotions, thus impacting their effectiveness in negotiation (Brett, 2001; Gelfand & Dyer, 2000). Kopelman and Rosette (2008) found that although the expression and recognition of displayed emotions may be somewhat universal, negotiators from different cultures may interpret and respond to them differently. The study suggests that East Asian negotiators (e.g., Hong Kong Chinese) who value face and associate respect with humility and deference are more likely to accept an offer proposed by a U.S. negotiator who strategically displays positive emotions, compared to an offer proposed by a U.S. negotiator who strategically displays negative emotions. Israeli negotiators, however, may be just as likely to accept an offer from a positive U.S. negotiator as a negative U.S. negotiator. In a similar vein, Liu (2009) found that Chinese negotiators increased distributive tactics in response to the counterpart's anger, whereas American negotiators did not. This is because the display of positive emotion is more congruent with the East Asian cultural values, whereas the Israeli culture places less emphasis on humility and deference and does not associate the display of emotions with respect.

According to Adam and Shirako (2013), culturally different display norms may trigger cultural stereotypes, which in turn generate different cognitive and behavioral responses for negotiators from different cultures when they negotiate interculturally. For example, negotiators from collectivist cultures tend to regard expressing anger as face-threatening and inappropriate in negotiation, whereas individualist cultures do not make such associations, tend to be more expressive, and view overt displays of negative emotions as relatively appropriate (e.g., Van Kleef, 2009). Based on empirical evidence from four experimental studies that involved both computer-mediated and face-to-face negotiations, Adam and Shirako (2013) found that the stereotype that members of collectivist cultures (e.g., East Asians) tend to be emotionally inexpressive than European American negotiators contributed to the perception that East Asian negotiators are tougher and more threatening than European American negotiators. Therefore, expressed anger by East Asian negotiators elicited greater cooperation from negotiation counterparts than when anger was expressed by European negotiators. The studies not only supported the emotions as social information (EASI) model, but showed that such effects applied to both East Asian and European American negotiation counterparts.

Nevertheless, as Adam and Shirako's (2013) experiments involved only one-shot negotiations, the researchers suggest that the influence of the cultural background of the expresser may be stronger when the negotiators do not know each other well, and the effect may vary in negotiations with multiple phases. A study conducted by Van Beest and colleagues (2008) using a computer-mediated three-player landowner game examined the influence of communicated anger at different phases of the multiparty negotiation process when parties formed coalitions to secure payoffs. They discovered that participants formed negative impressions towards those who expressed anger, thus excluding them from coalitions as well as allocating payoffs when anger was communicated at the initial stage. However, when anger was communicated after the formation of coalitions and participants had to work with their angry counterparts, they yielded and gave more euros to their angry partners. Therefore, the suggests that the timing of expressing emotions plays a critical role in shaping negotiators' behaviors. Although the study used a western sample and did not examine cultural variations in this process, it shed light on how contextual factors may interact with cultural and emotional factors in regulating negotiation processes. Developing greater cultural intelligence and a better understanding of how culture shapes emotional experiences and expressions can help counter the effects of cultural stereotypes on negotiators' interpretations of the counterpart's emotions, as well as their behavioral responses.

Conclusion

Negotiating across cultural boundaries has become increasingly common in a global economy. As the ability to manage emotions is a critically important skill in intercultural negotiations, this chapter offers a comprehensive review of how the effects of emotion in negotiation vary across cultures and what negotiators can do to achieve greater effectiveness in intercultural negotiations. It is hoped that the readers can utilize research-informed, practical strategies to navigate cultural differences in emotion-laden negotiations and dispute resolutions.

The challenge of intercultural negotiations can be exacerbated when negotiators are emotionally charged. One reason that adds more complexity to emotional communication across cultures is the potential clash in expectations and its intrapersonal effects on negotiators' emotion and behaviors. Greater culture distance can lead to more significant disparities in values and beliefs, thus resulting in more uncertainties and anxieties (Barry & Oliver, 1996). But violations of cultural expectations do not always lead to adverse outcomes. When an intercultural negotiation situation is more conducive to empathy and perspective-taking (e.g., when negotiators' power distance values are incongruent with their power status), negotiators may experience positively valanced emotions and use more integrative tactics, heading towards productive outcomes. To cope with the possible negative effects of emotional states caused by cultural distance, intercultural negotiators can either better prepare themselves by understanding their and their counterparts' cultural backgrounds and the subsequent effects on emotional experiences and communication, or learn to strategically induce positive emotions (e.g., sympathy) in the counterpart, while managing one's own negative emotions.

Research that focused on the interpersonal effects of emotions in negotiation suggests that through expressions of emotions, people communicate essential information and attitudinal signals; negotiators, therefore, interpret these signals and behave accordingly (Van Kleef et al., 2004). Experienced negotiators learn to strategically use their emotions during negotiation, such as amplifying emotion, feigning fake emotion, or hiding their emotions to achieve their goals more effectively. However, the strategic use of emotions is not immune from cultural influences (e.g. Brett 2001; Gelfand & Dyer 2000; Kopelman & Rosette, 2008), as negotiators from different cultures tend to interpret the display of emotion differently. Culturally different display norms may also trigger cultural stereotypes, which were found to cause divergent cognitive-behavioral responses among negotiators from different cultural backgrounds. Although culture's effect on emotional communication in negotiation and dispute resolution remains significantly under-explored, through an in-depth look into a few research examples, the chapter concludes that it is critically important to understand how cultural and contextual factors interact to influence negotiators' emotional communication in negotiation and dispute resolution to counter the effect of stereotypes and effectively navigate complex intercultural negotiations.

References

Adair, W. L., & Semnani-Azad, Z. (2011). The Display of "Dominant" Nonverbal Cues in Negotiation: The Role of Culture and Gender. *International Negotiation, 16*(3), 451–479. https://doi.org/10.1163/157180611X592950.

Adam, H., & Shirako, A. (2013). Not All Anger Is Created Equal: The Impact of the Expresser's Culture on the Social Effects of Anger in Negotiations. *Journal of Applied Psychology, 98*(5), 785–798. https://doi.org/10.1037/a0032387.

Allred, K. G. (1999). Anger and Retaliation: Toward an Understanding of Impassioned Conflict in Organizations. In R. J. Bies, R. J. Lewicki, & B. H. Sheppard (Eds.), *Research on Negotiation in Organizations* (Vol. 7, pp. 27–58). Greenwich, CT: JAI.

Allred, K. G., Mallozzi, J. S., Matsui, F., & Raia, C. P. (1997). The Influence of Anger and Compassion on Negotiation Performance. *Organizational Behavior and Human Decision Processes, 70*(3), 175–187. https://doi.org/10.1006/obhd.1997.2705.

Averill, J. R. (1980). A Constructivist View of Emotion. In R. Plutchik & H. Kellerman (Eds.), *Emotion: Theory, Research and Experience* (Vol. 1, pp. 305–309). New York: Academic Press.

Barry, B., & Oliver, R. L. (1996). Affect in Dyadic Negotiation: A Model and Propositions. *Organizational Behavior and Human Decision Processes, 67*, 127–143. https://doi.org/10.1006/obhd.1996.0069.

Beest, I. V., Van Kleef, G. A., & Dijk, E. V. (2008). Get Angry, Get Out: The Interpersonal Effects of Anger Communication in Multiparty Negotiation. *Journal of Experimental Social Psychology, 44*(4), 993–1002. https://doi.org/10.1016/j.jesp.2008.02.008.

Brett, J. M. (2001). *Negotiating Globally: How to Negotiate Deals, Resolve Disputes, and Make Decisions across Cultural Boundaries*. San Francisco: Jossey-Bass.

Brett, J. M., & Okumura, T. (1998). Inter- and Intracultural Negotiation: U.S. and Japanese Negotiators. *Academy of Management Journal, 41*(5), 495–510. https://doi.org/10.2307/256938.

Carnevale, P. J., & Isen, A. M. (1986). The Influence of Positive Affect and Visual access on the Discovery of Integrative Solutions in Bilateral Negotiation. *Organizational Behavior and Human Decision Processes, 37*(1), 1–13. https://doi.org/10.1016/0749-5978(86)90041-5.

Choi, I., Nisbett, R. E., & Norenzayan, A. (1999). Causal Attribution across Cultures: Variation and Universality. *Psychological Bulletin, 125*, 47–63. https://doi.org/10.1037/0033-2909.125.1.47.

DePaulo, B. M., Lindsay, J. J., Malone, B. E., Muhlenbruck, L., Charlton, K., & Cooper, H. (2003). Cues to Deception. *Psychological Bulletin, 129*(1), 74–118. https://doi.org/10.1037/0033-2909.129.1.74.

Fiske, S. T., & Taylor, S. E. (1991). *Social Cognition* (2nd ed.). New York, NY: McGraw-Hill.

Forgas, J. P., & Williams, K. D. (2001). *Social Influence: Direct and Indirect Processes*. New York, NY: Psychology Press.

Friedman R, Anderson C, Brett J, Olekalns M, Goates N, Lisco CC. (2004). The Positive and Negative Effects of Anger on Dispute Resolution: Evidence from Electronically Mediated Disputes. *Journal of Applied Psychology 89(2),* 369–376. doi: 10.1037/0021-9010.89.2.369. PMID: 15065982.

Frijda, N. H. (1993). Moods, Emotion Episodes, and Emotions. In M. Lewis & J. M. Haviland (Eds.), *Handbook of Emotions* (pp. 381–403). New York: Guilford Press.

Galinsky, A. D., Maddux, W. W., Gilin, D., & White, J. B. (2008). Why It Pays to Get Inside the Head of Your Opponent: The Differential Effects of Perspective Taking and Empathy in Negotiations. *Psychological Science, 19*(4), 378–384. https://doi.org/10.1111/j.1467-9280.2008.02096.x.

Gelfand, M. J., & Dyer, N. (2000). A Cultural Perspective on Negotiation: Progress, Pitfalls, and Prospects. *Applied Psychology: An International Review, 49*(1), 62–99. https://doi.org/10.1111/1464-0597.00006.

George, J., Jones, G. & Gonzalez, J. (1998). The Role of Affect in Cross-Cultural Negotiations. *Journal of International Business Studies 29,* 749–772. https://doi.org/10.1057/palgrave.jibs.8490051

Imai, L., & Gelfand, M. J. (2010). The Culturally Intelligent Negotiator: The Impact of Cultural Intelligence (CQ) on Negotiation Sequences and Outcomes. *Organizational Behavior and Human Decision Processes, 112*(2), 83–98. https://doi.org/10.1016/j.obhdp.2010.02.001.

Keltner, D., & Haidt, J. (1999). Social Functions of Emotions at Four Levels of Analysis. *Cognition & Emotion, 13*(5), 505–521. https://doi.org/10.1080/026999399379168.

Kopelman, S., & Rosette, A. S. (2008). Cultural Variation in Response to Strategic Emotions in Negotiations. *Group Decision and Negotiation, 17*(1), 65–77. https://doi.org/10.1007/s10726-007-9087-5.

Kopelman, S., Rosette, A. S., & Thompson, L. (2006). The Three Faces of Eve: Strategic Displays of Positive, Negative, and Neutral Emotions in Negotiations. *Organizational Behavior and Human Decision Processes, 99*(1), 81–101. https://doi.org/10.1016/j.obhdp.2005.08.003.

Kumar, R. (2004). Culture and Emotions in Intercultural Negotiations. In M. J. Gelfand & J. M. Brett (Eds.), *The Handbook of Negotiation and Culture* (pp. 95–113). Stanford, CA: Stanford University Press.

Levenson, R. W. (1994). *Emotional Control: Variations and Consequences.* New York, NY: Oxford University Press.

Lewicki, R. J., Barry, B., Saunders, D. M., Minton, J. W. (2003). *Essentials of Negotiation* (3rd ed.). New York, NY: McGraw-Hill.

Liu, M. (2009). The Intrapersonal and Interpersonal Effects of Anger on Negotiation Strategies: A Cross-Cultural Investigation. *Human Communication Research, 35*(1), 148–169. https://doi.org/10.1111/j.1468-2958.2008.01342.x.

Liu, M. (2012). Same Path, Different Experience: Culture's Influence on Attribution, Emotion, and Interaction Goals in Negotiation. *Journal of Asian Pacific Communication, 22*(1), 97–119. https://doi.org/10.1075/japc.22.1.06liu.

Liu, M., & Wang, C. (2010). Explaining the Influence of Anger and Compassion on Negotiators' Interaction Goals: An Assessment of Trust and Distrust as Two Distinct Mediators. *Communication Research 37(4),* 443–472.

Liu, M., & Zhu, L. (2019). The Role of Relational Goals in Explicating Dyadic Emotional Communication Processes in Dispute Resolution: A Cross-cultural Investigation. *Communication Research,* 1–25. https://doi.org/10.1177/0093650219831595.

Liu, M., Zhu, L., & Cionea, I. A. (2019). What Makes Some Intercultural Negotiations More Difficult Than Others? Power Distance and Culture-Role Combinations. *Communication Research, 46*(4), 555–574. https://doi.org/10.1177/0093650216631096.

Luomala, H. T., Kumar, R., Singh, J. D., & Jaakkola, M. (2015). When an Intercultural Business Negotiation Fails: Comparing the Emotions and Behavioural Tendencies of Individualistic and Collectivistic Negotiators. *Group Decision and Negotiation, 24*(3), 537–561. https://doi.org/10.1007/s10726-014-9420-8.

Markus, H. R., & Kitayama, S. (1991). Culture and the Self: Implications for Cognition, Emotion, and Motivation. *Psychological Review, 98,* 224–253. https://doi.org/10.1037/0033-295X.98.2.224.

Masuda, T., & Nisbett, R. E. (2001). Attending Holistically Versus Analytically: Comparing the Context Sensitivity of Japanese and Americans. *Journal of Personality and Social Psychology, 81*(5), 922–934. https://doi.org/10.1037/0022-3514.81.5.922.

Mesquita, B., & Markus, H. R. (2001). Culture and Emotion: Models of Agency as Sources of Cultural Variation in Emotion. In A. S. R. Manstead., N. Frijda,

& A. Fischer (Eds.), *Feelings and Emotions: The Amsterdam Symposium.* New York: Cambridge University Press.

Nisbett, R. E., (2003). *The Geography of Thought: How Asians and Westerners Think Differently – and Why.* Boston, MA: Nicholas Brealey Publishing.

Olekalns, M., & Smith, P. L. (2003). Testing the Relationships among Negotiators' Motivational Orientations, Strategy Choices, and Outcomes. *Journal of Experimental Social Psychology, 39*(2), 101–117. https://doi.org/10.1016/S0022-1031(02)00520-6.

Parrot, W. R. (2004). The Nature of Emotion. In M. B. Brewer & M. Hewstone (Eds.), *Emotion and Motivation* (pp. 5–20). Malden, MA: Blackwell.

Potworowski, G., & Kopelman, S. (2008). Strategic Display and Response to Emotions: Developing Evidence-based Negotiation Expertise in Emotion Management (NEEM). *Negotiation and Conflict Management Research, 1*(4), 333–352. https://doi.org/10.1111/j.1750-4716.2008.00020.x.

Shirako, A., Kilduff, G. J., & Kray, L. J. (2015). Is There a Place for Sympathy in Negotiation? Finding Strength in Weakness. *Organizational Behavior and Human Decision Processes, 131*, 95–109. https://doi.org/10.1016/j.obhdp.2015.09.004.

Sinaceur, M., & Tiedens, L. Z. (2006). Get Mad and Get More Than Even: When and Why Anger Expression Is Effective in Negotiations. *Journal of Experimental Social Psychology, 42*, 314–322. https://doi.org/10.1016/j.jesp.2005.05.002.

Thompson, L., Medvec, V. H., Seiden, V., & Kopelman, S. (2008). Poker Face, Smiley Face, and Rant 'n' Rave: Myths and Realities about Emotion in Negotiation. In M. A. Hogg & R. S. Tindale (Eds.), *Blackwell Handbook of Social Psychology: Group Processes* (pp. 139–163). Blackwell Publishers Ltd. https://doi.org/10.1002/9780470998458.ch6.

Van Kleef, G. A. (2009). How Emotions Regulate Social Life: The Emotions as Social Information (EASI) Model. *Current Directions in Psychological Science, 18*(3), 184–188. https://doi.org/10.1111/j.1467-8721.2009.01633.x.

Van Kleef, G. A., De Dreu, C. K. W., & Manstead, A. S. R. (2004). The Interpersonal Effects of Emotions in Negotiations: A Motivated Information Processing Approach. *Journal of Personality and Social Psychology, 87*(4), 510–528. https://doi.org/10.1037/0022-3514.87.4.510.

Van Kleef, G. A., Oveis, C., van der Löwe, I., LuoKogan, A., Goetz, J., & Keltner, D. (2008). Power, Distress, and Compassion: Turning a Blind Eye to the Suffering of Others. *Psychological Science, 19*(12), 1315–1322. https://doi.org/10.1111/j.1467-9280.2008.02241.x.

Weiner, B. (1995). *Judgments of Responsibility: A Foundation for a Theory of Social Conduct.* New York: Guilford.

Part VI Intercultural Communication Competence and Cultural Adaptation

Introduction to Intercultural Competence

By Darla Deardorff

The chapter examines intercultural competence, a useful and important skill in today's globalized world. Deardorff provides a brief outline of the topic tracing its origins back to the 1930s and summarizing the most important characteristics of intercultural competence. Like so many topics in social science, many different labels exist to describe the effective and appropriate communication across different cultures, both at the macro as well as the micro level, and within different contexts. Deardorff also points out that in addition to focusing on individual skills, it is necessary to consider one's counterpart. In other words, while one may consider oneself to be a competent communicator across cultures, one's counterpart may not necessarily perceive one to be competent.

Intercultural competence consists of several characteristics. Namely, having the right attitudes like respect, openness, curiosity and discovery. Furthermore, one needs to have the right knowledge, including cultural self-awareness, culture specific knowledge, an understanding of other world views, and socio-linguistic awareness. But knowledge in and by itself often does not suffice, it is also necessary to have the right skills to understand and apply that knowledge in intercultural encounters. It is necessary for individuals to see one's behavior and communication from the perspective of others. This depends on the attitudes, knowledge and skills one has acquired with regard to other cultures. And finally, it depends on the ability to apply these factors in an appropriate and effective manner so that one's counterpart perceives it as such as well. This ability will allow one to build relationships that are based on trust which tends to result in mutually beneficial business relationships. That is why intercultural competence is considered to be key element in today's business world.

Michael B. Hinner

Darla K. Deardorff is Founding President of the World Council on Intercultural and Global Competence as well as a research scholar at Duke University's Social Science Research Institute and holds faculty positions at universities in several countries, including at universities in South Africa, Japan, Canada and China as well as adjunct faculty at North Carolina State University. She was on the faculty of Harvard University's Global Education Think Tank for several years as well as Harvard's Future of Learning Institute and Summer Institute of Intercultural Communication in Portland, Oregon, US. With over 20 years of experience in international education, she is also executive director of the Association of International Education Administrators (AIEA). Author/editor of 11 books and over 60 book chapters and articles, her publications include *The Sage Handbook of Intercultural Competence* (Sage, 2009), *Sage Handbook of International Higher Education*, (Sage, 2012 and 2nd edition, 2021), *Building Cultural Competence* (Stylus, 2012), *Demystifying Outcome*

Assessment for International Educators (Stylus, 2015), and *Intercultural Competence in Higher Education: International Approaches, Assessment and Application* (Routledge, 2017). One of her most recent publication is an open access book entitled *Manual for Developing Intercultural Competencies: Story Circles* (Routledge/UNESCO, 2020) available in 5+ languages. She regularly gives invited talks, trainings and workshops around the world on intercultural competence, international education assessment, and global leadership and serves as a consultant and trainer on these topics, including with UNESCO and OECD. She received her master's and doctorate degrees from North Carolina State University.

Darla Deardorff

Intercultural Competence

To begin, consider these words from one who could be considered interculturally competent:

> *"I grew up in three cultures: I was born in Paris, my parents were from China and I was brought up mostly in America. When I was young, this was very confusing: everyone said that their culture was best, but I knew they couldn't all be right. I felt that there was an expectation that I would choose to be Chinese or French or American ... the process of trying on each culture taught me something. As I struggled to belong, I came to understand what made each one unique. At that point, I realized that I didn't need to choose one culture to the exclusion of another, but instead I could choose from all three.*
> *The values I selected would become part of who I was, but no one culture needed to win. I could honor the cultural depth and longevity of my Chinese heritage, while feeling just as passionate about the deep artistic traditions of the French and the American commitment to opportunity and the future.*
> *So, rather than settling on any one of the cultures in which I grew up, I now choose to explore many more cultures and find elements to love in each. Every day I make an effort to go toward what I don't understand. This wandering leads to the accidental learning that continually shapes my life....As we struggle to find our individual voices, I believe we must look beyond the voice we've been assigned, and find our place among the tones and timbre of human expression."* (Ma, 2008)

These are the words of well-known musician Yo-Yo Ma from which the following insights can be gleaned: Intercultural competence is a p*rocess* of trying on other cultures, with values being shaped by multiple cultures. Intercultural competence is a *choice* that is made to intentionally explore the unknown and it is a process of continual learning, of being curious about the unknown. Finally, the acquisition of intercultural competence involves going beyond our own voice and situating our identity within a broader context. Intercultural competence has become an imperative given the turbulent times of the 21st century, which finds humans more interconnected than ever before and yet increasingly divided, with such divides exacerbated all the more by the pandemic.

What is intercultural competence? This chapter explores intercultural competence, including a research-based framework, and highlights five emerging themes. First, it is important to acknowledge that there is not consensus on which terminology to use to describe this concept. In fact, multiple terms (over 30+) can be used to describe this construct, with each discipline having preferred terms. For example, in business and management, a term that is often used is "cultural intelligence" (see Ang & van Dyne, 2008) or "cross-cultural effectiveness" (Moran et al., 2009; Fisher & Härtel, 2003; Torbiörn, 1985) while in healthcare and social work, the term "cultural competence" (Anand & Lahiri, 2009; Sue, 2001; Fong, 2009) is most often used, although "cultural humility" (Tervalon & Murray-Garcia, 1998; Juarez et al., 2006; Murray-Garcia & Tervalon, 2017) is also used, especially in healthcare. Education uses a wider variety of terms including global learning and global citizenship. There are many other fields that have addressed the concept of intercultural competence including engineering (Grandin & Hedderich, 2009) linguistics and foreign languages, cultural anthropology, psychology, sociology, business (Chaisrakeo & Speece, 2004), tourism and hospitality, military, conflict resolution (Ting-Toomey, 2009), international development, public administration, law enforcement, and even in religious organizations (Yancey, 2009). (See Deardorff, 2009 for more on this). Regardless of the terms used, it is important to understand how the terms are defined as well as the basis of those definitions.

There is a long history of literature on intercultural competence that can be traced back nearly 100 years, particularly in the United States from the 1930s (Dubois, 1938), and this has been shaped by decades of research on this construct in multiple disciplines including in business, sociology, anthropology, psychology, education and communication, to name a few. (For a more detailed overview on intercultural competence, see Arasaratnam-Smith, 2017; Spitzberg & Changnon, 2009; Spencer-Oatey & Franklin, 2009). Much scholarly effort has been invested, particularly among scholars in the Global North (Moosmueller & Schoenhuth, 2009), in defining intercultural competence over the past several decades. Earlier, various anthropological frameworks such as Hall's three dimensions of cultural difference (1976) have sought to explain some of the difficulties involved in cross-cultural interaction. Hofstede's work has long been used, especially within business and management to understand cross-cultural differences (1997). A more recent bibliometric study (Peng et al., 2020) found that the most highly cited work on intercultural competence in the first twenty years of the 21st century is that of Bryam, Deardorff, Kramsch, Hammer and Bennett.

Competence itself is often defined as knowledge, skills, and attitudes. Specifically regarding intercultural competence, scholars prioritize various components as being central to intercultural competence, such as adaptability (Kim, 2001; Spitzberg, 1989; Spitzberg & Cupach, 1984). Hofstede (1997) focuses on the need to understand cultural difference through underlying cultural values while Bennett (1993) presents an intercultural sensitivity model in which one's response to cultural difference, which is developmental in nature, underscores one's degree of intercultural competence. Magala (2005), on the other hand, stresses identity as central to intercultural competence. Meanwhile, Byram (1997, 2021), viewing attitudes as fundamental to intercultural competence, posits five "saviors" for intercultural communicative competence and looks at the influence of social and political factors on defining and assessing intercultural communicative competence. Imahori and Lanigan (1989) developed a model of intercultural communication competence where the focus is on both persons in the intercultural action, not just the individual, which is unique to many other definitions and models. Arasaratnam's (2006) Integrated Model of Intercultural Communication Competence (IMICC) is based on the findings from a study in which thirty-seven participants from fifteen countries were asked to describe a competent intercultural communicator. Arasaratnam and Doerfel (2005) then used semantic network analysis to identify five key variables that were common among all responses, namely empathy, experience, motivation, listening and positive attitude towards other cultures. As Spitzberg and Changnon (2009) point out, while there is obviously no shortage of feasible approaches or models guiding conceptualizations of intercultural competence, there are some common categories within these conceptualizations including motivation, knowledge, higher order skills, macro-level skills, interpersonal skills (categorized under sub-categories of attentiveness, composure, coordination, expressiveness), contextual competencies (including identity), and outcomes.

Research-Based Model of Intercultural Competence

Using an iterative research methodology known as a Delphi in which twenty-three intercultural experts participated, Deardorff (2006) proposed a Process Model of Intercultural Competence (Figure 1) which emphasizes the lifelong process of developing intercultural competence, comprised of key knowledge, skill, and attitude dimensions that result in desired internal and external outcomes, namely effective and appropriate communication and behavior within intercultural interactions, which is the summary consensus definition of intercultural competence. This Delphi study resulted in one of the first research-based frameworks of intercultural competence, which has found resonance in different cultural contexts. This study serves as a more foundational framework on intercultural competence and as such, the specific elements of the framework will be briefly discussed here, as one example of a grounded research-based definition and framework of intercultural competence.

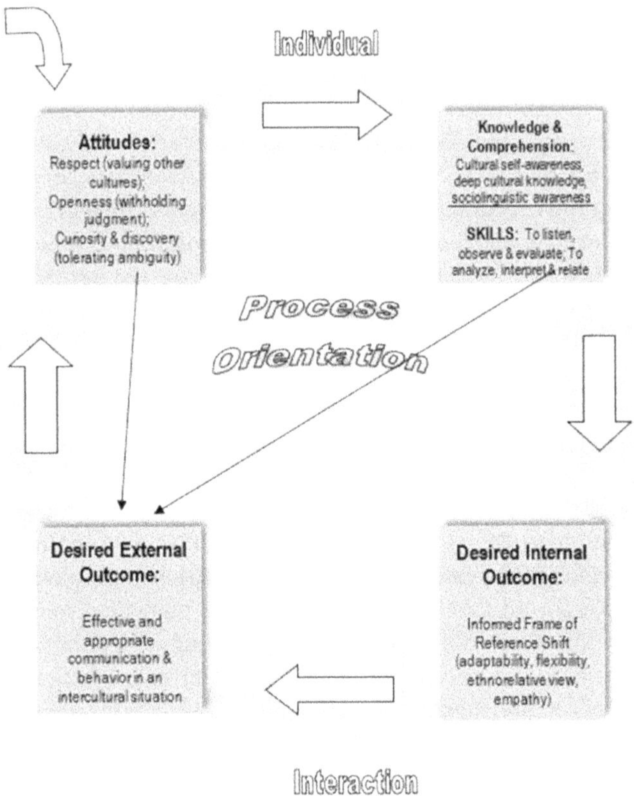

Figure 1: Research-Based Definition and Framework of Intercultural Competence

Attitudes: Based on the Deardorff study, key attitudes emerged, those of respect, openness, curiosity and discovery. Openness and curiosity imply a willingness to risk and to move beyond one's comfort zone. Further, curiosity sets a foundation for more creative ways to turn differences into opportunities while openness allows the possibility of seeing from more than one perspective, which is invaluable when negotiating and mediating cultural difference (LeBaron & Pillay, 2006). In communicating respect to others, it is important to demonstrate that others are valued as fellow humans. This begins by showing interest in others and in listening attentively and deeply, while recognizing that respect itself manifests differently in various cultural contexts. These attitudes are foundational to the further development of knowledge and skills needed for intercultural competence development, with one way to move individuals toward these requisite attitudes being to challenge assumptions. As LeBaron and Pillay (2006) note, "dialogue with genuine curiosity is a precondition for ….addressing cultural conflicts" (p. 94).

Knowledge: In regard to knowledge necessary for intercultural competence, intercultural scholars agreed on the following: cultural self-awareness (meaning the ways in which one's culture has influenced one's identity and worldview), culture-specific knowledge[1], deep cultural knowledge including understanding other world views, and sociolinguistic awareness. The one element agreed upon by all the intercultural scholars in the study was the importance of understanding the world from others' perspectives and thus perspective-taking becomes crucial to intercultural competence.

Skills: The skills that emerged from this Delphi study were ones that addressed the acquisition and processing of knowledge: observation, listening, evaluating, analysing, interpreting, and relating. This concurs with an observation by the former president of Harvard University of the importance of "thinking interculturally" (Bok, 2006, 2021). Knowledge is not static and given the exponential change occurring in the 21st century, it becomes critical that individuals develop the skills necessary to not only acquire knowledge but more importantly, skills on how to make meaning of the knowledge and then apply that knowledge in concrete ways.

Internal Outcomes: The attitudes, knowledge, and skills outlined in this framework ideally lead to an internal outcome that consists of flexibility[2], adaptability, an ethnorelative perspective and empathy. These are aspects that occur *within* the individual as a result of the acquired attitudes, knowledge and skills necessary for intercultural competence. This means individuals are ideally able to see from others' perspectives and to respond to others according to the way in which the other person desires to be treated, thus demonstrating empathy (Calloway-Thomas, 2010; Calloway-Thomas et al., 2017). Individuals may reach these internal outcomes in varying degrees of success, depending on the attitudes, skills and knowledge acquired within this framework.

---

1 There are many definitions that have been used for the word "culture." For purposes of this discussion, "culture" is defined as values, beliefs and norms shared by a group of people.

2 In regard to intercultural conflict resolution, such flexibility becomes vital– in this case, the flexibility of being able to ask questions that interrupt traditional patterns of thinking (LeBaron & Pillay, 2006).

External Outcomes: The summation of the attitudes, knowledge and skills, as well as the internal outcomes, are demonstrated through the behavior and communication of the individual. How effective and appropriate is this person in intercultural interactions? This behavior and communication become the visible external outcomes of intercultural competence. This then becomes the agreed-upon definition of the intercultural scholars in this study, that intercultural competence is the effective and appropriate behavior and communication in intercultural situations. However, it is important to understand that this definition is predicated on particular requisite elements of intercultural competence. It is also important to understand the implications of "effective" and "appropriate" behavior and communication. *Effectiveness* can be determined by the interlocutor whereas the *appropriateness* can only be determined by the other person – with appropriateness being directly related to cultural sensitivity and the adherence to cultural norms and expectations of that person.

This framework highlights essential aspects of intercultural competence noting that there may be additional intercultural elements especially depending on the context. The elements within this framework are placed within the context of intercultural interactions with an emphasis on the process involved in the development of an individual's intercultural competence. One final note on using this framework is that it is not meant to be used solely alone but in juxtaposition with other frames, including ones that address more specifically the developmental, psychological, ethical, interpersonal and engagement dimensions of human interactions.

There are obvious limitations inherent in any framework or model so it becomes important to look at common themes emerging from other cultural perspectives on intercultural competence. Upon closer examination of those different cultural perspectives, several themes emerge including the following: The first theme is the importance of understanding these historical, political and social contexts, particular regarding the role and impact of colonialization on intercultural contact within societies, especially those in African, Asian, and Latin American contexts. In fact, numerous scholars emphasize the importance of context in intercultural competence, and while many definitions and models of this concept tend to view this construct in a vacuum devoid of context, work from Latin American, Arab, and Asian perspectives of intercultural competence note to some degree how crucial it is to consider these contexts. This focus on context points to the importance of awareness in intercultural competence, another theme that emerges from these different perspectives. Another key theme that emerges from different perspectives is that of the importance of relationship within intercultural dialogue and competence. Such a priority on relationship-building has significant implications for trust-building and interpersonal communication skills as well as for conflict resolution. The discussions on relationship also lead to a focus on interconnectedness, which in turn underscores another theme running through the different cultural perspectives, that of identity, in which, for example, the African concept of *ubuntu* epitomizes both relationship and identity (Tutu, 1999; Steyn & Reygan, 2017). UNESCO (2013) published the results of regional perspectives on intercultural competence in which the following dimensions were found in common within a variety of perspectives globally: respect, self-awareness, identity, listening, adaptation, perspective-taking, relationship building and cultural humility. In this age of globalization that often leads to politicized cultural identities, the transcendence of one's identity seeks to defy simplistic categorizations of cultural groups and strives to instead understand the fullness of who one is, moving beyond the traditional dichotomous in/out group mentality to one that embraces and respects others' differences and in so doing, keeps the focus on the relational goals of engagement.

Emerging Themes

In the current discourse on intercultural competence five themes emerge:

1. *Intercultural competence across difference*. More recent work on intercultural competence broadly emphasizes interactions across difference, whatever those differences may be – age, gender, religion, socio-economic status, political affiliation, ethnicity, geography and so on (OECD, 2018; Deardorff, 2020). This broader view of intercultural competence differs from the more traditional views of this competence in which the discourse was confined solely to that of "international" or "cross-border" contexts[3], which is viewed as essentialist and inadequate given complexities of society and human identity (Holliday et. al., 2010).
2. *Intercultural competence as lifelong*. It is important to remember that intercultural competence is an ongoing, life-long process unique to individuals' contexts and experiences, which means there is no "one-size fits all" approach to developing or assessing intercultural competence, pointing to the importance of customizing both interventions and assessment. Further, this increased emphasis on lifelong learning (UNESCO, 2021) means that there is need for intentional support and intervention in developing

3 For example, in the 1980s, Hofstede's well-known work within a global IBM context looked at cultural differences through a national lens.

individuals' intercultural competence beyond the traditional schooling that occurs.

3. *Intercultural competence as holistic.* Increasingly, the complexity of intercultural competence is understood to be within the scope of human development, meaning that this competence is holistically intertwined within emotional, moral, ethical, psychological and cognitive dimensions. For example, the cognitive dimension includes mindfulness, critical thinking, systems thinking, value reasoning, reflective thinking, comparative thinking and meta-thinking, all of which are connected to intercultural competence (Mestenhauser, 2000, Mesternhauser, 2011, Deardorff, in press). Cognitive flexibility may be required, then, in exploring different ways of knowing, being, and behaving in intercultural contexts.
4. *Intercultural competence within context.* Intercultural competence, while having some similar dimensions regardless of context (UNESCO, 2013) manifests differently depending on a multitude of factors include the societal sector (as noted in the beginning of this chapter), geographic and cultural contexts, and those involved in the interactions. One example of bridging these different contexts is the work of a non-profit organization known as the World Council on Intercultural and Global Competence which exists for the purpose of connecting practitioners, researchers, students, and policymakers across disciplines, sectors, languages and countries to learn from and with each other in order to advance the praxis of intercultural and global competence within different contexts.
5. *Intercultural competence within JEDI intersections.* As societies wrestle with justice, equity, diversity and inclusion (JEDI) issues, including decolonization (Steyn & Reygan, 2017), intercultural competence plays an ever increasingly important role in combating racism, addressing prejudices and in strengthening social cohesion. For example, UNESCO has implemented a practical intercultural methodology known as UNESCO Story Circles (Deardorff, 2020) which has proven successful in bridging divides and in engaging participants in racial healing through the power of listening for understanding, a key intercultural competency.

These emerging themes within intercultural competence work provide a broader lens through which to view this construct and have implications within practice and for further research in moving the praxis of intercultural competence forward.

Conclusion

As we continually search for ways to get along together as human beings sharing this one planet, there remains a great need to transcend boundaries, to bridge and transform our differences, to be in relationship with one another and to join in the oneness of our humanity while accepting our differences. These needs will continue to drive us as we seek to overcome differences that may divide us, differences that lead to misunderstandings and conflicts, and even in some cases, to the point of war. This search for intercultural competence underscores the need for genuine respect and humility as we relate to one another, meaning that we arrive at the point of truly valuing each other – and even in loving each other (Curry, 2020). In the end, intercultural competence is about our relationships with each other and ultimately, our very survival as the human race, as we work together to address the global challenges that confront us in this century.

Note: This chapter is adapted from Intercultural Competence in the 21st Century: Perspectives, Issues, Application by D.K. Deardorff. In B. Breninger & T. Kaltenbacher (Eds). Creating cultural synergies: Multidisciplinary perspectives on interculturality and interreligiosity. Newcastle upon Tyne: Cambridge Scholars

References

Anand, R., & Lahiri, I. (2009). Developing Skills for Interculturally Competent Care. In D. K. Deardorff (Ed.), *The SAGE Handbook of Intercultural Competence*. Thousand Oaks, CA: Sage.

Ang, S., & Van Dyne, L. (2008). Conceptualization of Cultural Intelligences: Definition, Distinctiveness, and Nomological Network. In S. Ang & L. Van Dyne (Eds.), *Handbook of Cultural Intelligence: Theory, Measurement and Applications*. Armonk, NY: M.E. Sharpe.

Arasaratnam, L. A. (2006). Further Testing of a New Model of Intercultural Communication Competence. *Communication Research Reports*, 23(2), 93–9.

Arasaratnam, L. A., & Doerfel, M. L. (2005). Intercultural Communication Competence: Identifying Key Components from Multicultural Perspectives. *International Journal of Intercultural Relations*, *29*, 137–163.

Arasaratnam-Smith, L. A. (2017). Intercultural Competence: An Overview. In D. K. Deardorff & L.A. Arasaratnam-Smith (Eds.), *Intercultural Competence in Higher Education: International Approaches, Assessment and Application*. London: Routledge.

Bennett, M. J. (1993). Towards Ethnorelativism: A Developmental Model of Intercultural Sensitivity. In R. M. Paige (Ed.), *Education for the Intercultural Experience* (2nd ed.). Yarmouth, ME: Intercultural Press.

Bok, D. (2006). *Our Underachieving Colleges: A Candid Look at How Much Students Learn and Why They Should Be Learning More.* Princeton: Princeton University Press.

Bok, D. (2021). *Higher Expectations: Can Colleges Teach Students What They Need to know in the 21st Century?* Princeton: Princeton University Press.

Byram, M. (1997). *Teaching and Assessing Intercultural Communicative Competence.* Clevedon: Multilingual Matters.

Byram, M. (2021). *Teaching and Assessing Intercultural Communicative Competence Revisited.* Clevedon: Multilingual Matters.

Calloway-Thomas, C. (2010). *Empathy in the Global World: An Intercultural Perspective.* Thousand Oaks: Sage.

Calloway-Thomas, C., Arasaratnam-Smith, L. A, & Deardorff, D. K. The Role of Empathy in Fostering Intercultural Competence. In D. K. Deardorff & L. A. Arasaratnam-Smith (Eds.), *Intercultural Competence in Higher Education: International Approaches, Assessment and Application.* London: Routledge.

Chaisrakeo, S., & Speece, M. (2004). Culture, Intercultural Communication Competence and Sales Negotiation: A Qualitative Research Approach. *Journal of Business & Industrial Marketing, 19*, 267–282.

Curry, M. (2020). *Love Is the Way: Holding on to Hope in Troubling Times.* New York: Avery.

Deardorff, D. K. (2006). The Identification and Assessment of Intercultural Competence as a Student Outcome of Internationalization at Institutions of Higher Education in the United States. *Journal of Studies in International Education, 10*(3), 241–266.

Deardorff, D. K. (Ed.). (2009). *The SAGE Handbook of Intercultural Competence.* Thousand Oaks, CA: Sage.

Deardorff, D. K. (2020). *Manual on Developing Intercultural Competencies: Story Circles.* London: Routledge/UNESCO.

Deardorff, D. K. (in press). Mestenhauser on Intercultural Competence: Implications for Practice and Research. In A. M. D'Angelo, M. K. O'Brien, & G. Marty (Eds.), *Mestenhauser and the Possibility of International Education.* London: Routledge.

Dubois, R. D. (1938). *Adventures in Intercultural Education: A Manual for Secondary School Teachers.*

Fisher, G. B., & Härtel, C. E. (2003). Cross-cultural Effectiveness of Western Expatriate-Thai Client Interactions: Lessons Learned for IHRM Research and Theory. *Cross Cultural Management, 10*(4), 4–28.

Grandin, J. M., & Hedderich, N. (2009). Global Competence for Engineers. In D. K. Deardorff (Ed.), *The SAGE Handbook of Intercultural Competence.* Thousand Oaks, CA: Sage.

Hall, E. T. (1976). *Beyond Culture.* New York, NY: Anchor Books.

Hofstede, G. (1997). *Cultures and Organizations: Software of the Mind.* New York: McGraw-Hill.

Holliday, A., Hyde, M., & Kullman, J. (2010). *Intercultural Communication: An Advanced Resource Book for Students.* London: Routledge.

Imahori, T. T., & Lanigan, M. (1989). Relational Model of Intercultural Communication Competence. *International Journal of Intercultural Relations, 13,* 269–286.

Juarez, J. A., et al. (2006). Bridging the Gap: A Curriculum to Teach Residents Cultural Humility. *Family Medicine, 38,* 97–102.

Kim, Y. Y. (2001). *Becoming Intercultural: An Integrative Theory of Communication and Cross-Cultural Adaptation.* Thousand Oaks, CA: Sage.

LeBaron, M., & Pillay, V. (2006). *Conflict across Cultures: A Unique Experience of Bridging Differences.* Yarmouth, ME: Intercultural Press.

Ma, Y. (2008). *A Musician of Many Cultures.* In This I Believe, Retrieved from: http://www.npr.org/templates/story/story.php?storyId=87960790.

Magala, S. (2005). *Cross-Cultural Competence.* London: Routledge.

Mestenhauser, J. A. (2000). Missing in Action: Leadership in International Education for the Twenty-First Century. In L. C. Barrows (Ed.), *Internationalization of Higher Education: An Institutional Perspective.* UNESCO/CEPES. Papers on Higher Education. Bucharest: UNESCO.

Mestenhauser, J. A. (2011). *Reflections on the Past, Present, and Future of Internationalizing Higher Education: Discovering Opportunities to Meet the Challenges.* Minneapolis: University of Minnesota.

Moosmueller, A., & Schoenhuth, M. (2009). Intercultural Competence in German Discourse. In D.K. Deardorff (Ed.), *The SAGE Handbook of Intercultural Competence.* Thousand Oaks, CA: Sage.

Moran, R., Youngdahl, W. E., & Moran, S. V. (2009). Leading Global Projects: Bridging the Cultural and Functional Divide. In D. K. Deardorff (Ed.), *The SAGE Handbook of Intercultural Competence.* Thousand Oaks, CA: Sage.

Murray-Garcia, J., & Tervalon, M. (2017). Rethinking Cultural Competence: Cultural Humility in Internationalising Higher Education. In D. K. Deardorff & L. A. Arasaratnam-Smith (Eds.), *Intercultural Competence in Higher Education: International Approaches, Assessment, and Application*. London: Routledge.

OECD. (2018). *Preparing Our Youth for an Inclusive and Sustainable World: The OECD PISA Global Competence Framework*. Paris: Organization for Economic Development and Cooperation.

Peng, R., Zhu, C., & Wu, W. (2020). Visualizing the Knowledge Domain of Intercultural Competence Research: A Bibliometric Analysis. *International Journal of Intercultural Relations, 74*, 58–68. https://doi.org/10.1016/j.ijintrel.2019.10.008.

Spencer-Oatey, H., & Franklin, P. (2009). *Intercultural Interaction. A Multidisciplinary Approach to Intercultural Communication*. London: Palgrave-MacMillan.

Spitzberg, B. H. (1989). Issues in the Development of a Theory of Interpersonal Competence in the Intercultural Context. *International Journal of Intercultural Relations, 13*(3), 241–268.

Spitzberg, B., & Changnon, G. (2009). Conceptualizing Intercultural Competence. In D. K. Deardorff (Ed.), *The SAGE Handbook of Intercultural Competence*. Thousand Oaks, CA: Sage.

Spitzberg, B. H., & Cupach, W. R. (1984). *Interpersonal Communication Competence*. Beverly Hills, CA: Sage.

Steyn, M., & Reygan, F. (2017). New Competencies for Intercultural Communication: Power, Privilete, and the Decolonization of Higher Education in South Africa. In D. K. Deardorff & L. A Arasaratnam-Smith (Eds.), *Intercultural Competence in Higher Education: International Approaches, Assessment, and Application*. London: Routledge.

Sue, D. W. (2001). Multidimensional Facets of Cultural Competence. *Counseling Psychologist, 29*, 790–821.

Tervalon, M., & Murray-García, J. (1998). Cultural Humility Versus Cultural Competence: A Critical Distinction in Defining Physician Training Outcomes in Multicultural Education. *Journal of Health Care for the Poor and Underserved*, May 9(2), 117–25.

Ting-Toomey, S. (2009). Intercultural Conflict Competence as a Facet of Intercultural Competence Development: Multiple Conceptual Approaches. In D. K. Deardorff (Ed.), *The SAGE Handbook of Intercultural Competence*. Thousand Oaks, CA: Sage.

Torbiörn, I. (1985). The Structure of Managerial Roles in Cross-Cultural Settings. *International Studies of Management and Organization*, *25*, 52–74.

Tutu, D. (1999). *No Future Without Forgiveness*. New York: Doubleday.

UNESCO. (2013). *Intercultural Competencies: Conceptual and Operational Framework*. Paris: UNESCO.

UNESCO. (2021). *UNESCO Futures of Education: Learning to Become*. Paris: UNESCO.

Yancey, G. (2009). Neither Jew nor gentile: Lessons about Intercultural Competence in Religious Organizations. In D. K. Deardorff (Ed.), *The SAGE Handbook of Intercultural Competence*. Thousand Oaks, CA: Sage.

Introduction to An Applied Framework for Improving Intercultural Competence in the Workplace Using Assessments

By Kris Acheson, Sundae Schneider-Bean, and Jennifer Wiley

The next chapter takes a closer look at assessments that are used to determine the level of intercultural competence. This is important because an accurate assessment would allow a person or an organization to determine how fit individuals are intercultural encounters. It is also pointed out that intercultural competence is not something that one has or not. Instead, intercultural competence is a process that develops gradually. That is why assessments can tell one where one is, and where one can go in order to achieve intercultural competence. A number of proven assessment tools are introduced (for example, the Intercultural Readiness Check and the CultureConnector). The chapter describes how such tools may be applied. These assessment tools permit one to identify specific values which then allows one to realize why others who hold different values behave and communicate differently. Through these assessments, it is possible to make people become aware of the invisible aspects of culture that influence our perception, behavior, and communication. This knowledge then also lets one undertake steps to overcome specific behavior and to adopt new behavior and communication. From these case studies it becomes apparent that intercultural competence occurs at the personal level which then allows one to interact more effectively and appropriately at the team and organizational levels through self- and other-awareness. Very helpful are also awareness of different communication styles and cultural values as well as emotional intelligence and tolerance for ambiguity. All of these items can be measured with various assessment tools that the authors introduce in the chapter; tools that come in paper and in digital formats. So in addition to presenting the theoretical foundation for intercultural competence, the authors also offer practical advice as to which tools can be used to assess the various aspects of intercultural competence. This chapter is, thus, quite useful to companies selecting, training, and assigning employees to situations that encompass intercultural encounters.

Michael B. Hinner

Kris Acheson earned a PhD in Intercultural Communication from Arizona State University in 2008. Before coming to Purdue University in 2016, she served as a faculty member in Applied Linguistics at Georgia State University for 7 years and was awarded a yearlong Fulbright Scholar grant from the U.S. State Department to research and teach in Honduras in 2015. At Purdue, Dr. Acheson now directs the Center for Intercultural Learning, Mentorship, Assessment and Research (CILMAR) and holds a courtesy faculty position in the Brian Lamb School of Communication. CILMAR's mission is to support intercultural development for everyone in the Purdue community. Led by Dr. Acheson,

CILMAR's staff works with faculty and staff at Purdue to embed intercultural learning across the curriculum and to produce cutting-edge intercultural research. CILMAR's flagship program is the science gateway of resources for interculturalists, the Intercultural Learning Hub (www.hubicl.org). Dr. Acheson is a well-published scholar. While her early studies examined silence across cultures, her more recent research projects strive to identify the best strategies to develop and assess intercultural competence, including innovative externally funded projects to develop virtual reality simulations that foster the attitudes, knowledge, and skills necessary to interact successfully across cultural differences.

Sundae Schneider-Bean is an intercultural strategist and multi-certified coach. Her professional passions are many. She is committed to extending the way we talk about intercultural communication (and its maintenance) within the intercultural field as well as with clients. She is also passionate about intentionally nurturing intergenerational, intercultural relationships through her leadership of the Wisdom Fusion Project. Her expertise has been sought out by clients ranging from European multi-national organizations to international NGOs, from West and East African country directors to seasoned expat spouses. Sundae helps individuals expedite success, create meaningful connections (abroad and at home), and cherish their experience. She is likely most known for supporting others in ambitious transformations. For over a decade, Sundae has served individuals and organizations from over 60 countries across six continents. She is the host of podcast Expat Happy Hour and founder of Expat Coach Coalition. You can find her at www.sundaebean.com.

Jennifer L. Wiley continues to make her career about understanding how learning can be transformative and what that means for the learner. She earned an EdD in Educational Policy Analysis from the University of Missouri-Columbia and a Master's in International Affairs and Administration from Missouri State University. Her work in the field of intercultural learning began in 2004 as she conducted a national survey of high school exchange organizations to better understand how they assessed intercultural learning in the students they supported. She extended her intercultural research and practice as a Peace Corps volunteer in Ukraine by establishing international agribusiness exchanges between the University of Illinois and Poltava State Agrarian University. In 2013, while working at the University of Virginia, Dr. Wiley joined with three colleagues to found CoreCollaborative International (corecollaborative.com), a women-owned consulting firm that conducts program evaluations, intercultural training, and learning assessment. She is currently serving as the Research Fellow for James Madison University's Center for Global Engagement where she has led multi-institution research projects studying the impact and effectiveness of global learning programs such as virtual exchange and education abroad. Her current research involves refining a tool she developed to operationalize programmatic variables of learning experiences (duration, depth of engagement, difference, etc.). She also works collaboratively with intercultural film non-profit Crossing Borders Education to investigate the use of authentic peer videos to model and bring humanness to virtual exchange experiences.

Kris Acheson, Sundae Schneider-Bean and Jennifer Wiley

An Applied Framework for Improving Intercultural Competence in the Workplace Using Assessments

Perhaps we should start with some definitions. Formative assessment is basically a feedback cycle at an early stage of a learning experience, put in place to help support the learning process (Acheson et al., 2020; Lapp et al., 2013). In this case, we are interested in feedback on intercultural competence, or the capacity to interact successfully across cultural differences (Deardorff, 2006; Ting-Toomey, 1999). And, we want to use validated measures – instruments that are researched-based and have been proven accurate and helpful (Anthoine et al., 2014; Heritage et al., 2014). In short, this chapter is about how to make the most of assessments to maximize growth in training, coaching, and other professional development opportunities.

We are talking to you, managers and organizational leaders, coaches and trainers, educators and students, and anyone interested in their own or others' professional development in global organizational contexts. We are writing from our own experiences in all of these roles, with the hope that what we have learned about assessment will become more mainstream than it currently seems to be.

To pique your interest, here are just a few of the many ways that assessment can add value to professional development processes:

- Fast-tracking awareness-raising – There is nothing like looking in a mirror to startle you into a new awareness of how others experience or perceive you. Formative assessment can provide that objective perspective and help people see themselves more realistically.
- Identifying competencies and areas for growth – Intercultural competence is a developmental process, not an innate talent or a switch that gets flipped in your brain one fine day. Assessment is vital for pinpointing where we need to improve and what strengths may help us achieve that improvement.
- Generating motivation for developmental work – This work takes effort, which will not happen unless we are driven by intrinsic motivation. We have to want to grow; it does not happen by accident. The peek in the mirror can spark a deep desire to make our real selves better match our ideal selves.

- Providing a basis for goal-setting and developmental planning – You have to know where you are now in order to both see where you want to go and understand how to get from here to there. Assessment done well gives you a road map for developmental work.
- Analyzing past, current, and future challenges – A good assessment will offer a framework and language to better understand our experiences. We can build on their theoretical foundation to analyze concrete moments in our lives and relationships: times that went well or not so well. We can then also transfer that knowledge to current stressors and future potential challenges.
- Engaging in leadership team building – Assessment is not something you have to do alone. In fact, the same benefits for individuals (self-awareness, goal-setting, etcetera) apply to small groups as well.
- Aligning individual development with organizational values or vision – Leaders who get everyone pulling together, all in the same direction, end up with more horsepower. Assessments that keep individual professional development efforts focused on shared goals benefit the organization as a whole.

Exciting possibilities! Now that we have your attention, we will dive deep into a couple of case studies to illustrate this potential. In Section I of this chapter, you will follow a coach's involvement with Peter and Anna as they process and apply their assessment results. Next, we will extract some lessons learned, from these cases as well as from our general experience. In Section II we synthesize for you some characteristics of effective formative assessments, and in Section III we describe some best practices for implementation of assessment. Feel free to skip around and hone in on what seems most useful to you.

Section I: Intercultural Assessments in Organizational Contexts

Organizations invest to meet upcoming challenges, avoid costly mistakes, and fast-track results. Considering shifts in global economic power, demographic and social change, along with expansion of virtual teams across geographies, investing in measuring and developing intercultural competence across an organization is a wise investment.

Once developing intercultural competence is supported strategically within an organization, the question remains "how?" At the organizational level, due to the benefits and value of assessments mentioned above, internal or external coaches and trainers are often engaged to assess and further intercultural competence among its leaders and key players.

In this section, co-author Sundae Schneider-Bean shares her experience to illustrate how intercultural assessments can further personal and professional development in organizational contexts.

As an interculturalist and coach since 2008, I have partnered with organizations to answer the "how?" While there are many ways this question can be answered, I will make transparent the rationale behind my choices to combine intercultural assessments and coaching to support the professional development of leaders. Drawing on real-life outcomes from my clients, I will offer snapshots of what can happen for a client during this partnership.

Coaching is a common go-to in organizational settings for professional development. The International Coaching Federation defines coaching as "partnering with clients in a thought-provoking and creative process that inspires them to maximize their personal and professional potential" (https://coachingfederation.org/). From this perspective, coaching is an equal partnership. While the coach is responsible for the process, the client is responsible for their own choices. Through this partnership, the coach is there to help facilitate fresh insight. This process empowers the client to move forward with a new awareness, make choices or take action as a result of the sessions.

In the case of organizational contexts where the growth objective is intercultural competence development, the question emerges, "How can a coach optimally evoke awareness when so much of culture is OUTSIDE of awareness?" This is where culture-general and culture-specific know-how, as well as proven intercultural competencies, can serve as catalysts to the coach's original goal of "partnering with clients in a thought-provoking and creative process that inspires them to maximize their personal and professional potential."

Intercultural specialists (as well as coaches with the culture-specific know-how for the relevant context) can add immense value in this awareness-raising and potential competency-building process. Yet, more know-how implies more power, thereby destabilizing the aim of equal partnership. An intercultural assessment can be a means to reestablish a more equal partnership, where the assessment serves as the surrogate container to "hold" the expertise. This allows the coach more freedom to support clients as they make sense of new cultural insight and craft next steps. Verified intercultural assessments give clients ample space to grapple with the results and apply to their own contexts placing them in the driver's seat, as it were, of interpretation, analysis, and goal-setting.

In my years of working with clients in intercultural coaching, I have witnessed the depth that emerges when clients are invited to make meaning of the intercultural assessment results in relation to their current challenges and personal experiences. I will offer glimpses of this by introducing an organizational context and sharing the journey of two participants. The organizational context and cases to follow are based on actual client experiences yet have been adapted and de-identified here to protect anonymity.

The Organizational Context of the Cases

A multi-million dollar company with a very strong brand presence in its home country was simultaneously active in dozens of countries abroad. Not only did the organization have considerable demographic, language and cultural diversity, the corporation itself crossed industries, ranging from cross-border logistics to finance. With global trends and their own business challenges top of mind, the leadership set a strategic initiative to further intercultural competence across the organization. As a first step in this strategic direction, the leadership board committed to raising their own intercultural competence.

The corporation's predominantly male, age 50+ leadership board, while including speakers of several languages, did not reflect the diversity of its employees or clients. As may be common of homogeneous boards who represent diverse interests, there were rumors of personality clashes, blockading and protectionism. I was brought in to support each leader's intercultural competence development process. The board agreed to apply the learnings from the sessions on personal, team and organizational levels, focusing on the following:

The personal level

- Raise the individual's awareness of cultural dimensions and recognize their own cultural preferences and tendencies.
- Assess how actively they tend to apply competencies of intercultural sensitivity, intercultural communication, building commitment and managing uncertainty.

The team level

- Identify how individual preferences could present challenges and assets in collaboration.
- Pinpoint where key differences and common ground exist in a team.
- Experiment with strategies to adjust one's own communication style to better meet the needs of one's culturally diverse team members, explore new ways to actively develop relationships across cultures or build culturally diverse networks.

The organizational level

- Recognize the extent to which one effectively or actively uses cultural diversity as a source of learning and innovation across the department or organization.
- Explore how one's new intercultural perspective could be applied to positively impact a team, a project or the organization.

Considering the dynamics of the board and the learning objectives set out by the board, I proposed 1:1 coaching (over group training) to ensure confidentiality and create space for openness, exploration and deep self-reflection. Because developing and maintaining intercultural competence is a life-long endeavor, the goal to develop intercultural competence over three to six months was ambitious. For this reason, I was eager to integrate assessments into the coaching process so that it would fast-track the participants' level of awareness and deepen personal exploration.

The Intercultural Readiness Check (IRC) is an assessment tool that captures four intercultural competencies: intercultural sensitivity, intercultural communication, building commitment and managing uncertainty (https://interculturalreadiness.com/certification/#validity). The tool was chosen for its area of focus, usability and level of quality. It has been tested for reliability and validity as well as used over the past 10 years with more than 70,000 respondents from all over the world.

CultureConnector (CCO) is a tool that provides personalized feedback on twelve cultural dimensions in four areas: time and space, hierarchy, relationships and dialogue (https://www.argonautonline.com/cultureconnector/). Grounded in over a decade of research and online assessment with an accessible user interface and clear and pragmatic language, this tool was chosen to establish a foundation of cultural-general know-how, which would serve as the base to assess meaningful areas of differences and common ground.

I will guide you through two people's journeys, detailing how they made sense of their own process on the personal, team and organizational level in coaching supported by formative assessment. Having a window into their unique experiences, and thereby witnessing how they are similar and where they differ will shed light on how assessment tools can function to meet concrete learning objectives and enhance an individual's unique learning journey.

Peter

Personal. Peter was responsible for a department within the organization that had a significant financial impact on the business. He had nearly 20 years of experience at the company and was very comfortable with "how it works around here." He spoke the majority language of the country, and, while he also spoke English comfortably, he was less than enthusiastic about speaking other languages. He explained that he is generally interested in other cultures, naming that as one of the motivating factors in taking vacations abroad.

We started our sessions exploring "What is culture?" Peter sheepishly admitted that he had only thought of "culture" as nationality, but after our discussion he realized it was more layered than that. He felt encouraged to hear that he was not alone, and that others often see "culture" and "nation" as synonymous. His curiosity was piqued and he was eager to discover what else he was missing. He completed the CultureConnector assessment, and the following session we walked through each dimension, pausing at the ones he felt less certain on, or where he was struggling to apply concepts to his own life and work context. He reported that the CultureConnector results gave him the "more sophisticated," neutral language he was eager to learn.

By focusing on these twelve preferences and tendencies, Peter came to the conclusion that one of his strengths is attention to detail, but when he reflected on the assessment outcomes he worried that this strength might sometimes be at the expense of building relationships. He set "balance task and relationship" as a goal to monitor in the coming weeks.

Not known for risk-taking, Peter used his results from the IRC assessment to reflect on where he stood with "managing uncertainty." At work, he often hired candidates that came through his trusted network. On his time off, he appreciated adventure…but not too much. He was willing to travel abroad to experience unfamiliar places, but within the safety of a pre-booked resort.

Team. As our work progressed, Peter's motivation and curiosity seemed to grow. In our sessions he would integrate this "more sophisticated" language while describing his experiences and what he was noticing about his team. While describing a challenge from the week, he'd pause and ask (himself) aloud, "I wonder if this is his direct communication style?" or state reflectively "This must be my hierarchy orientation coming out."

As a follow up to the goal he set to "balance tasks and relationships," Peter reported back that during a meeting with a direct report he intentionally built in a few minutes at the start for more personal connection. This was also a way for him to be mindful about trying out new strategies to build relationships. He said he intentionally gave more space for "small talk," breaking from his business-only approach by offering his employee a brief window into his weekend and inquiring about theirs. On this particular day, it served as a useful temperature check of how his team member was really doing.

The identity markers he had previously referenced (gender, nationality) in our initial sessions seemed to go to the background. In their place was a genuine curiosity about discovering his team's preferences and tendencies along the twelve cultural dimensions in the four areas CCO focuses on: time and space, hierarchy, relationships and dialogue.

This curiosity translated into an eagerness to share with his team what he was learning, and a new mission to make these seemingly invisible preferences visible to the team. In a team meeting they explored which dimensions they resonated with, how these tendencies could add value, and when they might spark conflict. Peter's enthusiasm created a ripple effect of curiosity and openness in the team. He used what he was learning in the sessions to focus on building trust and new rules around communication across the team -- what he called "fresh chemistry."

Organizational. Encouraged by this initial success in his team, Peter honed in on an area of development identified in the IRC assessment: actively building commitment. He reported that this felt connected to his tendency to stick with what he feels most certain about, and, when it comes to his interpersonal relationships, a resistance to trying new ways of communicating. As it related to his leadership approach, he was concerned that this may be holding him back from giving his best to the organization. To my surprise, he returned to our last session with big news. He reported that he had stepped out of his comfort zone and tried something he had never done before. Using all that he had been building in our sessions, he proactively approached the "traditionally most difficult member of the board" to get support for something that this board member had typically blocked. With a fresh lens to see himself as well as his colleague, he courageously initiated an effort to build trust and commitment. It worked. This new approach helped them find common ground and paved the way for smoother discussions on strategic initiatives that they both held dear. We celebrated his efforts both for how it impacted the organization in a positive way and by acknowledging all the work he had been doing to lead to that moment.

With only limited time remaining, we turned our attention to how else an intercultural perspective could positively benefit the company on the individual, team and organizational level. Peter shared that he wished there were enough resources for everyone to do the work he did because then they would get it on a "deep" level. The conversation was filled with "What ifs:"

- What if more people learned what I did in the company?
- What if more leaders understood cultural differences in this nuanced way?
- What if we are missing out on business because we're not thinking enough about how we are different?

- What if we built our intercultural competencies more proactively? How would that impact our products? Our business partnerships? Our employee recruitment?

Our time had come to an end, a bit too soon it seemed. Based on what I was observing of his process, it was only at this point that Peter seemed well-poised to start exploring more deeply. Our months of work together prepared him to investigate how intercultural differences could be leveraged for the benefit of the organization, to tap into genuine curiosity, and to utilize grounded strategies to build common ground across cultural differences.

Anna

Personal. Anna was responsible for a small but important division at the company. Her tenure with the organization was relatively short compared to her peers, with only five years at the company. In contrast to the other board members, it was obvious within the first few moments of our session that Anna had culture top of mind. When we kicked off our conversation by exploring how she saw culture, she replied that it was impossible not to see it. It was not that her division was unique in some way or had a more diverse cultural make up, it was that Anna was the only woman on the leadership team. Significantly younger than her peers and speaking Italian as her mother tongue, her connection to cultural differences felt very personal.

She confided that as a "minority" group member she was constantly either "frustrated, bored, fighting or silent." She explained how exhausting it was to spend her days feeling misunderstood or unheard. Her motivations and investment in finding new ways to engage with the leadership board were high. She explained she was simply fed up. In meetings, she often stayed silent because, when she did speak up, it often led to open conflict or her being silenced.

In advance of our second session, Anna had completed the CultureConnector assessment. After we made an initial review of the twelve dimensions, she honed in on the dimensions that covered relationships and dialogue. Two important differences emerged for her and she reported being grateful to finally have language for them. First, she realized that her colleagues had a stronger task orientation while she was more relationship-oriented. This helped her make sense of how many of the conflicts with the board felt so personal to her, but her colleagues seemed more emotionally removed. She also recognized that while she may share a preference for direct communication with her peers, her communication was infused with more emotion. She began to consider how this might be interpreted from her more emotionally reserved board members. She supposed her default responses could lead to some of the defensiveness she was feeling in board meetings.

The results from Anna's IRC assessment supported what she was learning about herself. Her assessment revealed that she had very high intercultural awareness but rated low on adapting her communication approach when faced with cultural differences. She realized this combination was the equivalent of being fully aware of what problem you are hitting up against, but not trying different approaches to solve it. She set herself a goal to explore new ways to express herself in ways that are direct (like her colleagues) but communicate urgency without the charge of emotions. She set the intention to flip her focus from saying what was on her mind to being understood. We tied this goal back to one measure of intercultural competence, an outcome that is appropriate, effective and satisfactory. She was motivated to adapt so that her messages could come across more effectively as a cultural "outsider" in this context.

Team. In a follow up session, Anna explored ways she could express herself with a sense of urgency without tapping into her emotions of defensiveness or even aggression. With surprising ease, she created a list of alternatives she would use to experiment. Instead of relying on showing emotions exclusively through her voice and perhaps animated gestures, she practiced an approach that matched the more neutral tone of her colleagues but expressed urgency. She added phrases to her message such as "that is why this is so critical" and "here is why this is of utmost importance." She also committed to keeping her contributions brief.

Keeping with the aim of being heard, Anna wanted to do more to alleviate a defensive response in her peers. She actively committed to perspective taking and integrating empathy into her contributions while remaining direct. She prepared ways to express this generally, so that she could have something to draw on in a real-life conversation such as, "From your perspective you might be thinking ABC and I understand that. Here is what is important to me." This was her effort to build trust and maintain credibility among her peers.

Anna reported back in a follow up session that she had her new phrases "in her back pocket" during a leadership retreat and kept her communication and relationship objectives in mind. She celebrated that these new strategies were perceived by her peers as "more professional," saved her frustration and energy, and helped her communicate her position more clearly while also steering her relationships more positively.

Organizational. As was characteristic with other board members, there was limited time remaining to turn our attention concretely to how a deeper intercultural perspective across the organization could positively benefit the company. Anna was motivated to take her fresh insights into her work across departments and within her department to intentionally build deeper and more diverse relationships. She hoped that this would support a move away from "taking positions" and toward working on shared (strategic) goals. She knew to do this she would have to build in more time and reflect on when to consciously adapt her approach based on the dimensions of culture highlighted for her in the assessments. Anna knew part of the challenges she faced stemmed from structural issues within the organization, such as the lack of diversity among the board. While she had limited power to address those issues at the highest levels, she was enthusiastic about being more proactive with her own team and department. She wanted to create a culture within her own department that gave language and space for a variety of approaches, rather than allowing others in her sphere to experience what she had on the board: the minority member always adapting to the majority's expectations.

Reflection on the Cases from a Coach's Perspective

One of the most delightful aspects of intercultural coaching of this kind is that you discover alongside clients the breadth and depth of the impact of culture in their lives. The two cases presented here illuminate the deep learning that emerges when using formalized assessments in partnership with a coach. The shifts shared above are progressive, and it is evident that the creative process impacted the clients' mindset, emotions, and behaviors, which ultimately produced new outcomes over time. Thanks to these individuals' shifts both inside and outside sessions, the board as a whole benefited from fresh awareness and deeper competencies collectively. What emerged from the two cases Sundae narrated above mirrors what we have seen in countless other academic and organizational contexts.

The introduction of an assessment that explores cultural-general dimensions (here the CCO), makes the following possible:

- What was formerly "invisible" (or unconscious) is now made visible;
- A dual focus on similarities and differences emerges;
- People move away from a focus on "nationality" (stereotyping based on one cultural group membership) or "personality" (ignoring the impact of culture) toward greater attention to the nuances of observed behaviors and preferences of others;
- Higher awareness of one's own behaviors and preferences is developed and applied to relational work.

The exploration of an assessment that focuses on specific intercultural competencies (here the IRC), makes the following possible:

- People gain language and abstract concepts for relatively quick entrance into developmental work;
- Deep reflection is fostered on one's current level of competencies, including how strengths and gaps present opportunities and risks;
- Shared and neutral language for collaborators offers a new approach to find common ground or resolve latent conflict;
- Individual development work highlights how each person can use their competencies more for the benefit of their team, department, and organization.

In our years of mentoring others' intercultural development, what we have witnessed time and again is that intercultural competence development among leaders emerges most strongly when the application is personal and learning is given the space to become deeply embodied. This takes time, courageous application of new concepts in one's own context and honest self-reflection as well as active experimentation. The more individuals embody the learning, the better teams and the organization as a whole can benefit.

Section II: Characteristics of Effective Formative Assessments

There is no one right answer or universal best assessment choice. Sorry, if you were looking for a simple fix! If it were simple, this would be a really short chapter. However, assessment is not like choosing fruit spread (also known as jam, marmalade, jelly depending on where you live) from the dizzying array of choices between fruit flavors, chunky, strained, no sugar added, where you simply select what appeals to your tastes and preferences.

There are best practice frameworks for choosing an assessment tool that aligns with your objectives and context for assessment (Brown & Glasner, 1999; Lambert et al., 1992). For example, despite its usefulness for other purposes, an IQ or intelligence quotient test (Pfeiffer & Blei, 2008) is not the ideal tool to assess readiness for an executive MBA program, because level of intelligence has little to do with how prepared applicants are to engage in the experience (Sternberg, 1997). Better measures in this case might include those that capture certain relevant skill sets and personal characteristics such as systems thinking, resilience, emotional intelligence, and persistence. Perhaps you can think of other capacities that might predict successful completion of an MBA?

In the following section, we provide a list of criteria that will help you choose the appropriate instruments for your particular contexts. But first, take a moment to reflect.

When you are looking for formative assessment instruments, consider what you and your clients care about most. What do your clients want to know about themselves? What are their goals for coaching? What will they do with the results? Perhaps there are other stakeholders to consider, for example a supervisor who wants everyone in their unit to complete an assessment so they can see the overall group's strengths and points for growth.

Measures What You Want to Know

Assessment nerds typically use the word "construct" to describe what the instrument is measuring. You may identify more than one construct that you need to assess. For example, for team building, it is not uncommon to assess a constellation of constructs because there is more than one skill or attitude that leads to group cohesion and effectiveness, for example open-mindedness, intercultural competence, and tolerance for ambiguity. To make it complicated, each of these constructs could be multi-faceted. Intercultural competence is defined many ways in different contexts, but most agree that it includes a number of skills, attitudes, and knowledge – in other words aspects that are behavioral, emotional, and cognitive in nature (Deardorff, 2006; Spitzberg & Changnon, 2009). To get really concrete, in order to communicate effectively across cultural differences, you need enough knowledge to be able to adapt to a new teammate with an unfamiliar communication style, the willingness to change how you would normally say something, and the skill to put your knowledge into practice by monitoring your own and their implicit expectations and reactions (Ting-Toomey, 1999).

Sometimes assessment tools are focused on only one construct while other instruments may have several interconnected constructs. For instance, the Intercultural Development Inventory or IDI (www.idiinventory.com) is a simpler instrument of 50 items (statements with which you agree or disagree) that identify your orientation towards cultural difference. In contrast, the Beliefs, Events, and Values Inventory or BEVI (https://thebevi.com) has 185 items that capture a constellation of 17 constructs in a whole-self approach that includes your beliefs about gender, the environment, religion, emotionality, and many more aspects of worldview.

Let's take a look at some other commonly assessed constructs for intercultural learning and the tools trainers use to capture those constructs. This is not a comprehensive list, but it will give you a place to start. We are going to talk about these constructs as though they are neat tidy little packages, but actually they are messy and overlapping. Think about the last time you were in a meeting with a business leader who was "tone-deaf" and not paying attention to the needs and emotional states of other stakeholders. You've got a deadline in a high pressure situation, and all the boss can see is that looming deadline not the message from your childcare provider that your kid is sick or the watercooler conversations among the team about how many resumes they have sent out this week. Leaders who are *emotionally intelligent* would acknowledge the pressure the deadline puts on themselves (*self-awareness*) while also holding awareness of how to care for the well being of the team (*mindfulness*).

Self and Other Awareness/Mindfulness. Self-awareness is in essence being conscious of your internal responses to inputs from the environment (to include people and pets) around you (Lu & Wan, 2018; Shealy, 2016; Kegan, 1982). It is a metacognitive process through which you are able to identify how your sociocultural environment and your interactions with it over time have shaped the way you experience the world, your values and beliefs, and your behaviors. Awareness of others is being attuned to how this same process works in other people. Through developing this awareness of self and other you come to understand how and why people are unique in their worldviews and behaviors. These awarenesses are crucial for all sectors of society, and business particularly. When we recognize our biases or come to a new understanding of who we are as cultural beings we are building valuable self-knowledge that can be applied in relationships. Peter's realization that he had been equating culture and nationality was a moment of self-awareness development that could also help generate other-awareness by prompting him to notice and question more about the cultural identities of his colleagues and clients.

Instruments that are commonly used for assessing self and other awareness include the Beliefs, Events, and Values Inventory (https://thebevi.com), the Intercultural Development Inventory, the Intercultural Effectiveness Scale (https://www.kosaigroup.com), and the Character Strengths Survey (viacharacter.org). These tools often identify finer-grained aspects of self or other awareness. For example, the Character Strengths Survey has a construct called *Social Intelligence* that captures how aware people are of their own and others' thoughts and feelings while the Intercultural Effectiveness Scale has a composite construct called *Continuous Learning* that includes both self-awareness and exploration.

Communication Styles and Cultural Values. Another popular construct in intercultural asessments is cultural differences in the ways people communicate and/or the values they hold. Much of this work began with early intercultural scholars such as Edward T. Hall (1959), who coined the terms polychronic and monochronic to describe different categories of time management and developed the concepts of high and low context cultures. Unlike instruments that measure the knowledge, skills, and/or attitudes of intercultural competence, like those discussed in the previous section, these assessments that return feedback about one's communication style or cultural values are not meant to provide information about one's capacity to interact successfully across cultures. They simply reflect back to the respondent who they are and how they naturally operate, usually represented as a score or point on a spectrum between two extremes, for instance between direct and indirect communication styles (Ting-Toomey, 1999) or between values for individualism and collectivism (Triandis, 1995). This information can be helpful to clients in a variety of ways.

Remember Anna's process of gaining awareness that she and the board members of her company had different ways of valuing expressions of emotions and different communication styles? Learning this about herself and her board led her to be more effective in reaching her goals and being heard. Anna's ability to identify differences in the way she and the board members communicated and valued those modes of communication represents both self and other awareness. Having these awarenesses is a step toward adapting styles and behaviors to cross boundaries; however, adapting your communication style takes knowledge, intention and practice. Only the first of these is provided by instruments that identify your natural communication patterns and tendencies.

An instrument that works well in teams to identify diversity in communication styles and cultural values is icEdge (www.icedge.com). When groups take the assessment, the interactive website plots each team member's scores on a spectrum so that individuals can see the team landscape and their place in it (see Figure 1). This tool also offers insightful text about the strengths and challenges of each end of the spectrum. One benefit of icEdge and other tools like it is that it depicts cultural differences as just that – different from each other, not better or worse. This approach validates multiple worldviews and ways of interacting, which promotes acceptance and may even motivate adaptation.

Figure 1: Team Comparison for Recognizing Others' Emotions on the icEdge Website

The WorldPrism assessment on the Country Navigator site (https://www.countrynavigator.com/worldprism-profiling-tool/) is another robust tool that offers comparisons on nine dimensions, both within your organization and across the world. Because you can see graphic representations of your results plotted against group means for many countries around the world (see Figure 2), this tool is ideal for preparing employees for expat assignments to an unfamiliar culture. Just take care not to create or reinforce stereotypes based on the country profiles. The Country Navigator site does a good job of warning not to overgeneralize group means to every group member, but it can still be helpful to emphasize complexity when discussing results with clients. For example, a coach might tease out the nuanced ways in which the client differs from stereotypes of their own cultural groups to highlight that within every culture there is great variation at the individual level (and that it does not feel good for people to assume you are just like everyone else in your community).

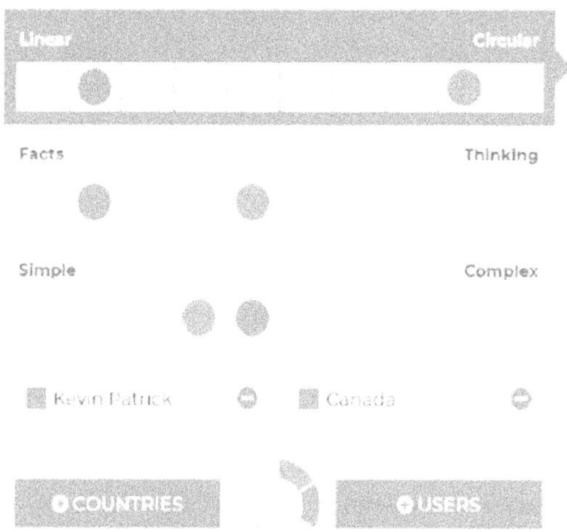

Figure 2: Gap Analysis from the Country Navigator Site

Emotional Intelligence and Tolerance for Ambiguity. Emotional intelligence is the ability to perceive, hold, describe, interpret, use, and make meaning of the feelings within ourselves and others (Salovey, & Mayer, 1989; Goleman, 1996). While there is some disagreement between scholars about whether it is truly a facet of intelligence or a skill (Locke, 2005), the important piece for you to remember is that if you can't demonstrate some level of emotional intelligence, you may struggle to keep healthy relationships. Yes, it is that important.

Another capacity that intersects with emotional intelligence in supporting intercultural competence is called tolerance for ambiguity. This capacity for being comfortable with the unknown, unfamiliar, and unclear is important for creativity (Baer, 2016), risk-taking (McLain, 2009), and openness to new people and contexts (Frenkel-Brunswick, 1951).

Instruments that measure and report on these constructs include the BEVI, IES, and Cultural Intelligence Scale, or CQS (https://culturalq.com/). The BEVI captures both emotional intelligence and tolerance for ambiguity with sub-scales (groups of items/questions that capture a construct). For example, one BEVI sub-scale is Emotional Attunement, which measures value for and comfort with one's own as well as others' emotional processes and expression. The CQS provides insight on tolerance for ambiguity by assessing, along with 9 other constructs, one's level of uncertainty avoidance.

There are many other relevant constructs you might want to measure in different contexts: perspective-taking, quest for meaning or purpose, sense of responsibility to others, global-mindedness or systems thinking, cultural knowledge, critical thinking, and the list goes on. These are all related to the overarching umbrella of intercultural competence.

These constructs related to the ability to successfully navigate differences in interpersonal relationships across cultural differences tend to fall into cognitive, affective, and behavioral categories (Spitzberg & Changnon, 2009). It is important to consider which aspects of the very complex phenomenon we call intercultural competence are most important for the purpose of your assessment. For example, Peter from our case studies identified skills for relationship building as a target goal over knowledge of different cultures. Using an assessment tool that measures affect and behavior were more in line with Peter's goals than one that would have assessed how much he knew about cultural practices around the world or frameworks for understanding culture. Knowledge competencies are important, of course, but Peter had simply identified other priorities that he believed would help him best in his work environment at the time.

Meets Your/Your Clients' Needs

It turns out that being an intercultural assessment measure is a tough gig. Not only do their constructs need to align with client goals in a valid and predictable way, they also need to be interesting, clear, nice to look at, and versatile for different user types. Aren't you glad you aren't the guest of honor at that dinner party?

From a pragmatic standpoint, there are a number of other things to take into account when you are choosing a tool. We wish the conversation could rest with just, "Does it measure the construct your client cares about? And, does it do so with reliability?" As we begin naming them, these other important aspects will begin to come into focus and look familiar. If you reflect for a moment on one of your own survey or assessment experiences you will be able to visualize as you walk through these different aspects of using an assessment instrument: public credibility, user experience, and logistics. All of these aspects of the instrument are important pieces to consider before choosing the right one for your client.

But wait! Even if the tool is a perfect fit for a client's needs, it might still not be a good match for you. It can unfortunately happen that a coach, given their age, gender, language ability, or other aspect of their identity, simply doesn't have the credibility to debrief some clients on some assessment constructs, no matter how skilled or knowledgeable about the instrument they may actually be. So, mentors cannot ignore their own needs, including the need to be comfortable and confident with the assessments they choose.

Credibility. Clients' belief in their results is vital, so choose an instrument with well-demonstrated scientific validity and reliability. Well-constructed instruments take years to create and a large investment of time and capital to maintain. They are likely to brag about the research that shows how wonderful they are. For robust instruments, therefore, you will likely find information about correlation coefficients and other evidence of validity and reliability on their website. You do not need to be a statistician to evaluate these numbers – they always come with arguments about the instrument's accuracy and insight.

All of the instruments we have featured as examples in this chapter have been validated in research studies that you can read about through a quick search of their website or the internet. From those studies you can see the range of application contexts as well as how results have been used. Another resource for finding more information about intercultural assessment instruments is the Intercultural Learning Hub (https://hubicl.org), a free resource site from Purdue University's Center for Intercultural Learning, Mentorship, Assessment, and Research. You will find all of the instruments we have referenced here and dozens more curated and indexed in the HubICL (fondly pronounced hub-ick-el) toolbox.

Be aware that many instruments are subject to confounds that make results untrustworthy, such as social desirability bias. In everyday language, social desirability means that items on the assessment are worded such that it is easy to know what the assessment is measuring and, therefore, easy to know what the socially acceptable answer is. People do not always intentionally answer items untruthfully, although that does happen; it is simply that no one wants to see themselves in an unflattering light, which causes over-estimation of capacity. Complex, well-designed instruments should address the problem of social desirability bias and other potential confounds that could impact the accuracy of assessment results.

In addition to reliability, validity and internal design, use an instrument with a legitimate, easily understandable theoretical framework for explaining development. This criterium is important to your own credibility as a professional. You do not want to have to defend the model every time you present results.

Finally, the more well known and commonly used your instrument, the more reference points you will have from publications and potentially peer organizations to interpret results. Common usage raises credibility, but it may also provide valuable benchmarks for comparison. Some tools even place the respondent on a graph to indicate how their score on a particular construct compares to a global or group average, which can be both intriguing and insightful for clients.

User experience. Take a moment and think about the last assessment, survey, quiz or poll you took. What impression did it leave with you? Were the colors appealing? Was the layout intuitive to navigate? Could you share or compare your results with others?

All of these features and more come together to shape the user experience of the assessment instrument, and they can add to or detract from the user's perception of value for and trust in the constructs the tool is assessing. Imagine you are making an important decision about how to organize a team that will be responsible for a $10 million dollar project. If there are typos in the instructions of the assessment your team will take, how much confidence will you have in the attention the assessment creators put into the inner workings of the instrument?

Specific points to consider when it comes to user experience:

- ***Look and feel***: The graphics in the interface and reports should be clear and easy to understand, not overly wordy, and engaging. In Figure 3, Culture Connector's use of color coding to breakdown complex constructs into understandable bites allows the person reviewing the information to make sense of what they are seeing quickly but with complexity.

Figure 3: Example of Culture Connector Report Graphics

- ***Chunking***: It is advantageous for a user to have a unique login that allows them to save their responses and return later to complete the survey or access their results. Additionally, there should not be a long list of items that participants have to scroll through. Ideally, users would be able to respond to small chunks of the survey and see their progress from screen to screen.
- ***Speed***: In tension with stellar graphics and appealing layouts is how quickly information loads on whatever device your client uses. Time yourself and see how long you can wait before you get bored and move on to Candy Crush. Your selected instrument should load graphics, items, or narrative results quickly and consistently, and reports should be available to users quickly as well.
- ***Sensitivity***: Speaking of patiently waiting, if a skill will help you solve a problem or be more successful in your interactions, how long can you wait to see evidence of your skill-building? As we have mentioned, intercultural competence takes time and intention. It is helpful in maintaining motivation over the long term to be able to track progress along the way. Therefore, the

instrument you choose should be granular enough that it is able to show changes over time. Users will get frustrated if it is too hard to move the needle and their results never seem to change. If marking progress is important, select an instrument that will be sensitive enough to capture these developmental shifts. Likewise, consider if clients can take the instrument multiple times without fatigue.

- ***Comparable results***: If the client is working in a team and has goals related to that larger group, it is ideal to be able to share the results with the team in a supported environment with the coach. Additionally, it is often useful to see the team results as an aggregated mean for the group in order to prompt reflection and dialogue. This is work for a skilled trainer to facilitate, and it holds tremendous power to transform an organization. Even if a team is not involved, many assessment users find it useful to see their results in comparison to others who have taken the assessment, for instance plotted in a graph against respondents from other cultures.
- ***Accompanying resources***: The instrument needs to offer more than just numbers and eye-catching graphs. For maximum impact, there should be related narratives, videos, and/or other interactive materials that support developmental work. Look for tools (like the IES) that support goal setting and planning, have reflection prompts, and provide strategies or activities for doing MORE or LESS of something based upon the assessment outcomes. Take for example the two assessments that Sundae featured in the cases: Intercultural Readiness Check (https://interculturalreadiness.com/) recommends activities for practicing different communication styles, and CultureConnector (https://www.argonautonline.com/cultureconnector/) offers strategies for adapting – that is, if your strength is direct communication, it suggests how you can try more indirect approaches.

*Logistics***.** In addition to user experience, it is important for you to consider what it will be like for you to gain access to the instrument, get the client's results, share results, etc. There are also practical aspects like how much it costs to administer and whether you need training to be qualified to coach with the tool. Some logistics to consider include:

- ***Format***: Is the survey paper-based or digital? Paper based surveys may be acceptable for certain contexts and demographic groups; however, you may find digitally based instruments more versatile. They allow for quick and easy report generation and accessibility from everywhere. Another aspect of format is length. How much time should a client allot to taking the assessment and receiving feedback? For complex instruments, it may take an hour or more to complete the assessment. You will want to prepare your client for that.

- ***Cost***: What are the costs associated with using the instrument? Not only will there likely be a fee per administration of the instrument, the tool may require a license for practitioner use. For most rigorous instruments there is some degree of training you will need before you can make sense of the numbers you see and explain those results to clients. Figure in your time as a cost as well. You should know all the costs involved before you ever have a conversation with the client, and determine how they will be paid. By you, figured into your compensation? Directly by the client to the instrument creator?
- ***Administration***: You will need to understand the administration process well in order to give clear instructions to users. What information do you need to distribute the survey? What is the process? Are you the one controlling disbursement of the survey or do you simply put in an order for a link and instructions to be sent to your client? Some people may prefer to have as much control over the process as possible while others are content to have the process be more automated. Some systems like the IDI and BEVI allow an administrator (someone licensed and trained to use the instrument) to view whether or not the client has taken the assessment, or even send reminders if they have not yet done so.
- ***Results Reporting***: Some instruments will automatically share outcomes with the client as soon as they complete the assessment. In some cases that might be an advantage because the client can use the instant feedback to reflect before you meet. On the other hand, there may be numbers and constructs included that are difficult to understand? How comfortable will your client be looking over a report before you are there to help interpret it? Other reporting issues to consider include: Can you access their report or does your client need to share the information with you? If you are working with a group, are aggregates created for you automatically or do you need to crunch numbers before a group debriefing? And finally, how supportive is the report – do you need to put in a lot of emotional labor as a mentor to create a constructive feedback climate or are the assessment results presently gently and without judgment?

If you are looking for the tl:dr short version of the criteria, here they are in concise bullet points:

- The constructs or concepts that the tool measures should align with the client's goals and the coaching context.
- Your chosen assessment needs to be based solidly on theory and proven effective.

- The client experience of taking the assessment should be accessible, without distracting images or formatting. The assessment should have simple instructions and engaging report materials.
- The instrument should offer resources for how to change based upon the assessment results.
- Clients' logistical needs (time constraints, format preferences, available funding, etc.) should be met.

Section III: Suggested Best Practices for Implementation

We know we have thrown quite a lot at you in this chapter. Perhaps it will be useful to conclude with some very practical tips for how to implement an assessment in intercultural professional development, no matter which instrument is the assessment of choice in your context, and regardless of your role (whether you are a coach, trainer, etc. or on the receiving end of their expertise).

- We cannot stress enough the importance of ***mentorship*** in this work. Learning with any tool can be deepened with facilitation or debriefing from a qualified professional (Jones et al., 2019). A skilled coach or trainer provides cognitive and emotional support in processing assessment results, offers guidance in planning for development, and holds professionals accountable for their development. In higher education, especially in education abroad, contemporary research literature demonstrates overwhelmingly that intercultural development does not occur for most people without such mentorship. In meta-analysis, the quality and extent of mentorship seems to be more important than any other factor – demographics of learners, program/course features such as length and location of study, etcetera. While the scholarship on mentoring for intercultural learning in the professional realm is less well-developed than in post-secondary education, many are beginning to recognize the value of individual attention and support. Many potential reasons probably contribute to the effectiveness of mentorship. For instance, busy people may not have good habits of reflection, relying on experiences alone to prompt change. Sundae often hears from CEOs, for example, "This is the only hour I have all week to actually THINK." Working with a mentor, on the other hand, can draw out transferable knowledge and skills from experiences that can be applied to other current and future contexts. Mentors can also help us avoid cognitive pitfalls like misinterpreting or overgeneralizing across cultures and reinforcing our biases, and support us when the stress and discomfort of developmental work becomes overwhelming. For best effect, mentors should be formally trained and practiced in a variety of assessment instruments so that they can individualize the use of assessments to meet the needs of those engaged in professional development.

- As with most things in life, you get what you pay for. We believe in the value of ***paid assessments***. That is not to say that free options are worthless; they may even be the best choice at times, given available resources. However, we tend to favor validated, proprietary instruments because they often come with great developmental support – individual and/or group written reports, debriefing frameworks, developmental planning guides, and more. From the coach/trainer perspective it can be more efficient, and from the client perspective more credible, to leverage well-packaged turn-key solutions than to create assessment follow-up materials from scratch. Using free tools without this support, we also run the risk that the assessment will be experienced but not deeply reflected on or applied (see the point above about how important these processes are for development). Assessments vary greatly in terms of cost. Some have training as well as usage fees. Others use sliding fee scales that offer discounts for large groups, certain institution types, or research projects. In a nutshell, don't allow sticker shock to discourage the use of high quality assessments. The advantages of proprietary instruments make them worth the investment in many cases. As you decide how much to invest in assessment, keep in mind that cost is one of the many search parameters you can employ in the curated Intercultural Learning Hub toolbox at https://hubicl.org.
- We would also like to caution folks against expecting too much from a single engagement with assessment. Intercultural development work is a lengthy process that requires ***long-term commitment*** and attention (Acheson & Schneider-Bean, 2019). In fact, it is a life-long learning project. Assessment has a place at many points on this path: at the start to give us direction, as we pass milestones to check on our progress, when we need points of comparison with others, and more. Many assessments in the intercultural realm are known for being highly reliable, meaning that the same person taking the instrument again will get similar results. In a statistical sense, that is an advantage because reliability increases predictive power. Theoretically, reliability is also desirable in that it provides evidence of measurement validity. However, high reliability may also mean that it is hard to "move the needle" and see significant change on an assessment, especially over a short period of time. As an example, it would be discouraging for everyone involved if an assessment were given before and after a one-off workshop only to reveal that no meaningful score changes resulted. Instead, it is more productive to frame formative assessment

as the first step in a journey of months, years, or decades, using assessment results to motivate and guide the efforts of sojourners.

- Finally, we want to emphasize that assessment, like development itself, has various ***levels of engagement*** and application that should be attended to. As Sundae modeled in the cases, beyond the individual level, assessment can and should also be utilized with teams, organizations, communities, etcetera. These levels are interrelated, even mutually dependent, although they are not always treated that way. That is, individual growth is tied to team development, and vice versa. Organizations place pressure on members to change, and the reverse is true as well. One mistake we see commonly made is focusing on individual development exclusively, to the detriment of other levels. Perhaps it is easier to get buy-in at the personal level. Maybe it feels less intimidating. It could be that cost or time is a barrier to larger-scale investment in assessment. If individual work is the easiest entry point, wonderful – go through that open door. Just don't stop as soon as you step through. Instead, consider how to scale up assessment processes along with development work in general. How can you best aggregate results to present the birds-eye view to stake-holders? What are the benefits of comparing individual and group-level assessment results? How can you measure impacts on teams, units, whole organizations in the long-term? Finding answers to these questions will step up performance at every level.

We leave you with a final bit of advice: As you let the information from this chapter roll around in your mind and begin to form meaning and connections, try not to be overly concerned about keeping all the definitions and best practices at the ready. These nuggets of wisdom in the abstract are only as good as their application in your context!

So, instead of trying to remember all the concepts and recommendations here, wander in your mind back through the stories that you read about. Think about why they chose to assess intercultural competence. What were the goals they cared about? How do those goals and motivations resonate with you and those you work with?

What concrete outcomes did working towards those goals produce? Focus on the relationships between humans that were enriched or made possible by leveraging assessments in intercultural development work. Note the internal processes that were improved for Peter and Anna.

Once you have committed to this kind of work in either a mentor or mentee role, you can read the chapter, again, for the finer points. It will be here as a resource for you when you need specific guidance for which assessments to choose and how to best implement them in different contexts.

References

Acheson, K., & Schneider-Bean, S. (2019). Representing the Intercultural Development Continuum as a Pendulum: Addressing the Lived Experiences of Intercultural Competence Development and Maintenance. *European Journal of Cross-Cultural Competence and Management*, *5*(1), 42–61.

Acheson, K., Yngve, K. N., Stahl, A., & Jin, L. (2020). Introduction: Recent Research in Assessment in Education Abroad. *Frontiers: The Interdisciplinary Journal of Study Abroad, 32*(Virtual), 1–6. https://doi.org/10.36366/frontiers.v32iVirtual.464.

Anthoine, E., Moret, L., Regnault, A., Sébille, V., & Hardouin, J.-B. (2014). Sample Size Used to Validate a Scale: A Review of Publications on Newly-Developed Patient Reported Outcomes Measures. *Health and Quality of Life Outcomes*, *12*(2), Article #2. https://doi.org/10.1186/s12955-014-0176-2.

Baer, J. (2016). *Domain Specificity of Creativity.* New York, NY: Elsevier.

Brown, S., & Glasner, A. (Eds.). (1999). *Assessment Matters in Higher Education: Choosing and Using Diverse Approaches.* Buckingham, UK: The Society for Research into Higher Education & Open University Press.

Deardorff, D. K. (2006). Identification and Assessment of Intercultural Competence as a Student Outcome of Internationalization. *Journal of Studies in International Education*, *10*(3), 241–266.

Frenkel-Brunswick, E. (1951). Personality Theory and Perception. In R. Blake, & E. Ramsey (Eds.), *Perception: An Approach to Personality*. New York: Ronald. https://doi.org/10.1037/11505-013.

Goleman, D. (1996). *Emotional Intelligence: Why It Can Matter More Than IQ.* New York, NY: Bantam Books. ISBN 978-0-553-38371-3.

Hall, E. T. (1959). *The Silent Language.* New York, NY: Doubleday.

Heritage, B., Pollock, C., & Roberts, L. (2014). Validation of the Organizational Culture Assessment Instrument. *PLoS ONE*, *9*(3), e92879. https://doi.org/10.1371/journal.pone.0092879.

Jones, D. C., Campbell, M. M., & Acheson, K. (2019). Intercultural Learning in Semester-long Study Abroad: A Comparative Analysis of the Effectiveness of One-on-One versus Group-mentored Interventions. *Journal on Excellence in College Teaching*, *30*(4), 7–35.

Kegan, R. (1982). *The Evolving Self: Problem and Process in Human Development.* Cambridge, MA: Harvard University Press.

Lambert, M. J., Ogles, B. M., & Masters, K. S. (1992). Choosing Outcome Assessment Devices: An Organizational and Conceptual Scheme. *Journal of Counseling & Development*, *70*(4), 527–532.

Lapp, D., Fisher, D., & Frey, N. (2013). Feed-Forward: Linking Instruction with Assessment. *Voices from the Middle, 21*(2), 7.

Locke, E. A. (2005). Why Emotional Intelligence Is an Invalid Concept. *Journal of Organizational Behavior, 26*(4), 425–431. https://doi.org/10.1002/job.318.

Lu, C., & Wan, C. (2018). Cultural Self-awareness as Awareness of Culture's Influence on the Self: Implications for Cultural Identification and Well-Being. *Personality and Social Psychology Bulletin*. https://doi.org/10.1177/014616721 7752117.

McLain, D. L. (2009). Evidence of the Properties of an Ambiguity Tolerance Measure: The Multiple Stimulus Types Ambiguity Tolerance Scale-II. *Psychological Reports, 105*, 975–988.

Pfeiffer, S. I., & Blei, S. (2008). Gifted Identification Beyond the IQ Test: Rating Scales and Other Assessment Procedures. In S. I. Pfeiffer (Ed.), *Handbook of Giftedness in Children*. Springer Science + Business Media. https://doi.org/ 10.1007/978-0-387-74401-8_10.

Salovey, P., & Mayer, J. D. (1989). Emotional Intelligence. *Imagination, Cognition, and Personality, 9*(3), 185–211. https://doi.org/10.2190/dugg-p24e-52wk-6cdg. S2CID 219900460.

Shealy, C. (2016). *Making Sense of Beliefs and Values: Theory, Research, and Practice*. New York: Springer.

Spitzberg, B. H., & Changnon, G. (2009). Conceptualizing Intercultural Competence. In D. Deardorf (Ed.), *The Sage Handbook of Intercultural Competence* (pp. 1–52). Thousand Oaks, CA: Sage.

Sternberg, R. J. (1997). Managerial Intelligence: Why IQ Isn't Enough. *Journal of Management, 23*(3), 475–493. https://doi.org/10.1016/ S0149-2063(97)90038-6.

Ting-Toomey, S. (1999). *Communicating across Cultures*. New York: Guilford Press.

Triandis, H. C. (1995). *Individualism and Collectivism*. New York: Taylor and Francis.

Introduction to Adapting to an Unfamiliar Culture

By Young Yun Kim

The following chapter examines cross-cultural adaptation, a process essentially everyone undergoes when living even for a short period of time in another cultural environment. Central to such adaptations is communication. But also stress, adjustment, and the potential for personal growth are associated with cultural adaptation. Most individuals encounter stress in situations of uncertainty, i.e. being unfamiliar with the new culture, including the behavior and communication. Through interaction with natives of the host environment, people learn to adjust to the new cultural environment. This adjustment is a dialectic process that is not linear, but consists of ups and downs. With time, as one adjusts to the new cultural environment, one experiences personal growth from this learning experience. This experience consists of a higher level of cognitive complexity, emotional resilience, and behavioral resourcefulness, according to Kim. Kim, though, points out that people do not experience this growth at the same rate because a number of personal factors come into play; in particular, communication skills and abilities, i.e. communication competence. This competence includes cognitive, affective, and operational competence. Knowledge of the host culture's language and culture play an important role as does a positive motivational capacity and the ability to effectively and appropriately implement the proper behavior and communication for specific situations. In addition to personal factors, the actual social factors of the respective host environment play an important role in the acculturation process as well. It is pointed out that cultural distance can be decisive because it is probably easier for most people to adapt to a new culture that is closer to one own native culture than one that is more distant. Kim describes what can be done to foster cultural adaptation. These include some practical tips on how that may be accomplished. This makes the text quite useful for companies sending employees overseas in that it outlines what needs to be considered when selecting and preparing such employees for an overseas assignment.

Michael B. Hinner

Young Yun Kim is a professor of communication at the University of Oklahoma. Born and raised in Seoul, Korea, she received her M.A. degree in speech communication at the University of Hawaii under the sponsorship of the East-West Center and her Ph.D. degree in communication from Northwestern University in Illinois. Kim has published 12 books and over 120 book chapters and refereed journal articles. She was named in 2002 a fellow of the International Communication Association, and has served recently as president of the International Academy for Intercultural Relations. Kim's first line of research addresses the phenomenon of cross-cultural adaptation. She has conducted original studies among a wide range of immigrants, refugees, and ethnic minorities in the United States, including Korean immigrants, Southeast Asian refugees, and American Indians. Her studies, along with an extensive body of social scientific studies by others, provided the empirical grounding for her Integrative Communication Theory of Cross-Cultural Adaptation. Kim's second line of inquiry is focused on associative and dissociative communication behaviors of individuals when interacting with people of dissimilar ethnic backgrounds. Based on a series of studies examining various psychological, situational, and environmental factors influencing communication behaviors, Kim proposed the Contextual Theory of Interethnic Communication in a book chapter in *Theorizing about Intercultural Communication* (2005). She is currently working to present a fully articulated version of this theory in an upcoming book, *Interethnic Communication in Everyday Life: The Context and the Behavior* (working title).

Young Yun Kim

Adapting to an Unfamiliar Culture

On any given day, numerous people around the world cross cultural boundaries. Immigrants and refugees change homes seeking a new life, along with a wide range of temporary sojourners such as business employees who are dispatched abroad on an assigned job and students studying at a foreign academic institution. While unique in individual circumstances and varied in scope, intensity, and duration, all strangers living in an unfamiliar culture embark on the common project called *cross-cultural adaptation*. Even short-term sojourners are challenged to undertake the process of new cultural learning, so as to be able to navigate their life activities in the unfamiliar environment. Through continuous interactions with the host environment, most cultural strangers become increasingly proficient in their daily functioning.

Cross-cultural adaptation has been extensively investigated across social science disciplines since the beginning of the 20th century (e.g., Simmel, 1908/1950). Although most of the studies in this field have been conducted in the United States, there has been a surge of research efforts in recent decades in various Western European countries experiencing a rapid influx of immigrants and refugees. By and large, researchers have approached cross-cultural adaptation from specific perspectives, typically focusing on isolated segments of the phenomenon specific to disciplinary interests. Psychologists, for example, have focused on psychological responses of individuals to a new and unfamiliar culture (e.g., Berry, 1980), whereas sociologists examined mostly macro-level issues pertaining to ethnic or immigrant groups, such as changes in socioeconomic status of immigrant groups (e.g., Glazer & Moynihan, 1963)

In this essay, we will examine the phenomenon of adapting to an unfamiliar culture based on a broadly-based account provided in Kim's Integrative Communication Theory of Cross-Cultural Adaptation (Kim, 1988, 2001, 2005, 2018). This theory presents a comprehensive, interdisciplinary way of understanding the phenomenon by bringing together a wide range of salient research concepts and theories across social science disciplines into a single communication-centered frame. As such, this theory uniquely provides a "big picture" insight into how and why, newcomers in an unfamiliar cultural environment are able to achieve a relatively stable relationship with the new sociocultural system, both functionally and psychologically.

Cross-Cultural Adaptation

Adapting to environmental challenges, large and small, is a fundamental human condition. Adaptation manifests a natural instinct inherent in all "open systems" that exist in, and co-evolve with, the environment through continuous interactions (Bertalanffy, 1968; Ruben, 1972). Cross-cultural adaptation, then, is simply a special case of the life-sustaining activity people naturally undertake in an unfamiliar environment. Thanks to the built-in human plasticity and "self-organizing" capacity (Jantsch, 1980), each person is capable of acquiring new cultural knowledge and habits and, in so doing, achieve a degree of fitness that is needed to function in a given environment effectively.

Placed at the intersection of the person and the environment, cross-cultural adaptation occurs in, and through, communication. From passive observations and direct one-on-one encounters with members of the host community, to utilization of local and national mass media including various forms of Internet-based "social" media, communication is the very process in and through which individuals adapt to the host environment. Such vital function of communication is highlighted in Kim's (2001) definition of cross-cultural adaptation as: "*the entirety of the dynamic process by which individuals who, through direct and indirect contact and communication with a new, changing, or changed environment, strive to establish (or reestablish) and maintain a relatively stable, reciprocal, and functional relationship with the environment*" (p. 31).

In formulating the integrative communication theory, Kim employs the concept, "stranger." Initially coined by Simmel (1908,1950) and subsequently applied to the study of intercultural communication (Gudykunst & Kim, 2003), this term serves as a heuristic concept for analyzing the social processes involving all people who find themselves, or are regarded by others, as "outsiders" in an unfamiliar social milieu.

Based on these foundational ideas, the theory presents two models explaining the phenomenon of cross-cultural adaptation. The first model describes the *process* in which cross-cultural adaptation unfolds over time. The second model represents the *structure* of cross-cultural adaptation in which key factors facilitating (or impeding) the adaptation process are identified.

The Process of Cross-Cultural Adaptation

The first model accounts for the nature of the process in which strangers adapt to an unfamiliar cultural environment. It is predicated in the fact that life in a new and unfamiliar cultural environment accompanies disorienting and unsettling experiences. Whether relocating in a foreign country temporarily or for long-term resettlement, encounters with an alien culture often present surprises and uncertainties, depending on the severity of cultural dislocation.

Given the inherently challenging nature of crossing cultural boundaries, most investigators of both short-term and long-term adaptation have focused mainly on the problematic nature of cross-cultural experience. The researchers investigating the "culture shock" phenomenon (e.g., Oberg, 1960) have sought to find ways to help ease such predicaments confronting newly arrived temporary sojourners. In studies of long-term immigrants, the problematic nature of cross-cultural adaptation has been examined in terms of "acculturative stress" (e.g., Berry & Annis, 1974).

In contrast, a number of researchers have emphasized the learning and growth-facilitating nature of the same process. Adler (1975), for example, explained that the culture shock experience should be viewed, not as a "disease for which adaptation is the cure," but as a transitional learning experience activating a "movement from a state of low self- and cultural awareness to a state of high self- and cultural awareness" (p. 15). Similarly, Ruben (1983) questioned the problem-oriented perspectives and conjectured that culture shock experiences might, in fact, be responsible for (rather than impeding) their adaptation.

In the process model of the integrative communication theory, Kim (2001) brings together both the problem-oriented and the learning/growth-oriented approaches into a single framework. This model captures the inherently double-edged process of adapting to an unfamiliar culture, one that is both challenging and growth-producing. For strangers in an unfamiliar cultural environment, the acculturative pressure from the new environment and their inability or unwillingness to meet such challenges inevitably brings *stress*, a state of internal disequilibrium.

Yet, as an open system, no human being can stabilize himself or herself forever. The heightened self-awareness in the state of stress serves as the very force that propels strangers to overcome the predicament and partake in the acts of *adaptation,* the forward-looking mobilization of inner resources in order to overcome the unsettling experience of internal disequibrium. In the most stressful moments arises new awareness and that, the darker the frustration, the deeper and more acute the awakening of our mind and its sensibilities for new learning and reformulation of self.

What emerges from cumulative experiences of the stress-adaptation dialectic is a subtle and largely imperceptible psychological *growth*, a form of internal transformation at a higher level of cognitive complexity, emotional resilience, and behavioral resourcefulness. Owing to the creative forces of self-reflexivity of the human mind, each stress experience and the subsequent adaptive moves present strangers with an opportunity to recreate themselves. The dialectic juxtaposition of stress and adaptation lays the very "ground for birth and development of a higher psychic structure – the basis for developmental thrusts upward, the creation of new evolutionary dynamic, and the movement of the personality to a higher level" (Dabrowski, 1964, p. 5). The diminishing severity of fluctuation allows strangers to carry out their daily activities in the new environment with greater ease and proficiency.

The interplay of *stress, adaptation,* and *growth* experiences are represented in a three-pronged process model of *the stress-adaptation-growth dynamic* depicted in Figure 1. Working as the very force behind an individual's adaptive change, this psychological movement does not play out in a smooth, steady, and linear progression, but in a cyclical and continual "draw-back-to-leap" pattern, with an overall forward-and-upward movement in the direction of increasing chances of success in meeting the demands of the host environment. Each stressful experience is responded to with a draw-back, which, in turn, activates adaptive energy to help individuals reorganize themselves and leap-forward.

The stress-adaptation-growth dynamic continues as new challenges present themselves in the host environment, with the generally forward and upward movement in the direction of less stress and of greater adaptation and growth. In this process, large and sudden changes, that are indicative of the severity of difficulties an individual experiences in the host environment, are likely to occur during the initial phase of exposure to a new culture. Over time, the fluctuations of stress and adaptation becomes less intense or severe, rendering an overall calming trend.

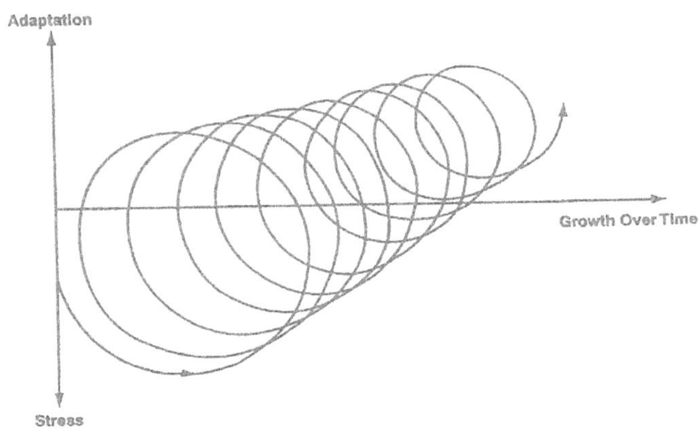

Figure 1: The Process Model: The Stress-Adaptation-Growth Dynamic

Note: From *Becoming Intercultural: An Integrative Theory of Communication and Cross-Cultural Adaptation* by Young Yun Kim, 2001, p. 59. Copyright 2001 by Young Yun Kim.

The Structure of Cross-Cultural Adaptation

Building on the above-described account of the adaptation process, Kim's integrative communication theory presents a structural model addressing the second basic question: "Given the same length of time, why do some strangers attain a higher (or lower) level of cross-cultural adaptation than others?" As shown in Figure 2, this model identifies key factors of communication, environment, predisposition, and intercultural transformation as working interactively to facilitate or impede the process of cross-cultural adaptation.

Communication at the Core

Placed at the center of the structural model, communication factors are highlighted in this model as the primary force facilitating the cross-cultural adaptation process. Communication activities are grouped in two interdependent categories: (1) *(intra)personal communication*, or the mental activities that occur within individual strangers, disposing and preparing them to act and react in certain ways in actual social situations; and (2) *social communication* that takes place whenever they participate in interpersonal or various mass-mediated forms of communication in the host society.

The (intra)personal communication factor refers to the stranger's *host communication competence*, that is, the capacity to appropriately and effectively receive and process information and to design and execute mental plans in initiating or responding to messages from the host environment. The theory identifies key elements of host communication competence in three categories: cognitive, affective, and operational. *Cognitive Competence* includes such capabilities as the knowledge of the host language and culture including the history, laws, institutions, worldviews, beliefs, mores, norms, and rules of interpersonal conduct and relationships, among others. *Affective competence* facilitates cross-cultural adaptation by providing a motivational capacity to deal with various challenges of living in the host environment, including willingness to make necessary changes in one's original cultural habits and openness to new learning and the readiness to partake in the natives' aesthetic and emotional sensibilities. *Operational competence* allows strangers to put their cognitive and affective capabilities in action outwardly, making it possible for them to choose the combinations of verbal and nonverbal behaviors that are appropriate and effective in specific social situations.

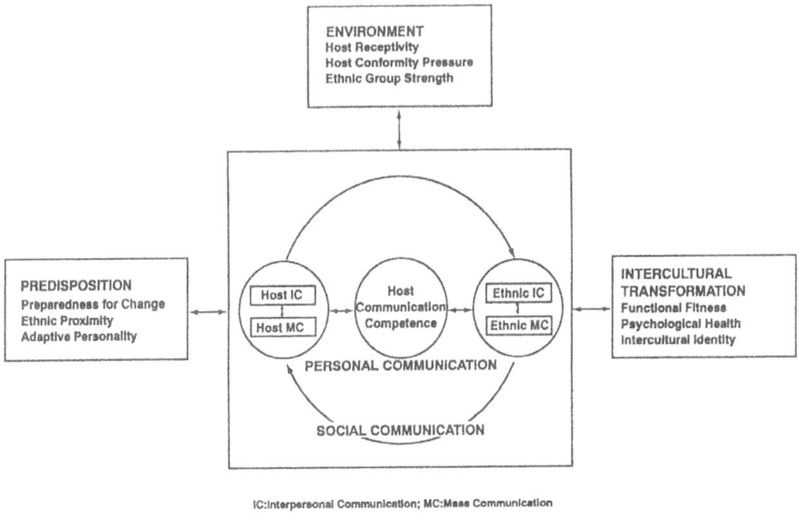

Figure 2: The Structural Model: Factors Influencing the Process of Cross-Cultural Adaptation

Note: From *Becoming Intercultural: An Integrative Theory of Communication and Cross-Cultural Adaptation* by Young Yun Kim, 2001, p. 87. Copyright 2001 by Young Yun Kim.

Directly and reciprocally, the internal development of host communication competence influences, and is facilitated by, an increased participation in external social communication activities of the host environment. The quality of a stranger's experience of the host environment is enhanced by a high level of host communication competence, just as every host social communication event is an opportunity for the stranger to gain an insight into the host culture. *Host interpersonal communication*, in particular, helps strangers to obtain a vital insight into the mindsets and behaviors of the local people, thereby serving as the points of reference for a check and validation of their own behaviors. *Host mass communication* facilitates the adaptation of strangers by exposing strangers to the larger environment. Serving this function are various forms of mediated communication such as radio and television programs, magazine and newspaper articles, movies, museum exhibits, and theater performances, as well as various forms of web-based "social" media communication activities.

In many communities in contemporary societies, strangers' interpersonal and mass communication activities involve co-ethnics or co-nationals and home cultural experiences. *Ethnic interpersonal communication* activities provide strangers with access to their original cultural experiences, often rendering assistance to those who need material, informational, emotional, and other forms of social support. With the advent of the Internet websites, direct satellite- and cable broadcasts, strangers enjoy an increased access to various sources of *ethnic mass communication* that are produced locally or in their home country. Particularly during the initial phases of relocation when strangers lack host communication competence, ethnic social communication activities may serve adaptation-facilitating functions. Due to the relatively stress-free communication experience in dealing with their own ethnic individuals and media, ethnic communication experiences can provide strangers with a psychological relief and a support system. The theory explains, however, that heavy and prolonged reliance on ethnic social communication activities tend to help maintain their original cultural habits and limit their opportunities to participate in the host environment.

Environmental Conditions

To the extent that strangers participate in host social communication activities, the host environment exerts adaptive or maladaptive influences on them. The nature of such influence, in turn, is shaped by the various characteristics of the host environment itself. The theory identifies three key environmental conditions affecting the stranger's adaptation process: (1) *host receptivity*; (2) *host conformity pressure*; and (3) *ethnic group strength*.

Host receptivity refers to the degree to which the environment is structurally and psychologically open to welcoming and accepting strangers into its social processes. A given host environment can be more receptive toward certain groups of non-natives while unwelcoming or even hostile toward certain other groups. Such differences are attributable to the favorable or unfavorable attitudes held among the local population against certain groups of non-natives for various reasons, including the cultural, religious, and political differences and conflicts between

The stranger's host communication competence and participation in host social processes are also influenced by *host conformity pressure*, the extent to which the environment challenges strangers to act in accordance with its language and cultural norms. Ethnically diverse communities in large metropolitan areas in the United States tend to hold greater accommodation of different languages and cultures, thereby exerting less pressure on non-natives to adopt the normative language and communication practices of the host culture.

The third environmental factor, *ethnic group strength*, is associated with the overall size and status associated with the stranger's ethnic group and the material and social support it provides for newly arrived members. Large, well-organized, and active ethnic communities provide its members an informational, emotional, and material support system. Although such an ethnic support system can aid newcomers' initial cross-cultural adaptation, it also tends to exert a level of social pressure to maintain the ethnic practices and discourage an active participation in the host social communication activities.

Individual Predispositions

Along with the conditions of the host environment, a stranger's own background characteristics serve as the baseline for his or her adaptation process. The theory identifies three key predispositional factors: (1) *preparedness*, (2) *ethnic proximity/distance*, and (3) *adaptive personality*.

Strangers come to their new environment with differing levels of *preparedness*, that is, the mental, emotional, and motivational readiness to undertake the challenges of adapting to a new culture. Among the various ways of being prepared are the knowledge of the host language and culture, the psychological readiness to meet the challenges they are likely to face, and the desire to succeed in the new environment. Affecting such preparedness are formal and informal schooling and training in, and the media exposure to, the host language and culture, contacts and experiences with members of the host society, as well as prior experiences in unfamiliar cultures in general.

Also playing a role in the cross-cultural adaptation process is the *ethnic proximity/distance*, the degree to which a given stranger's ethnic (language, culture, religion, and race) background is similar to, or different from, the mainstream ethnicity of the host society. It does so by affecting the level of ease or difficulty each stranger experience in developing host communication competence and participating in host social communication activities. A German expatriate, for example, is likely to face a higher level of adaptive challenges in Saudi Arabia than in another European country such as the Netherlands.

In addition, each stranger faces adaptive challenges in the context of his or her *adaptive personality*, the overall internal resource that would help them endure and persist in his or her adaptive efforts. *Openness* is such a personality resource. As a psychological posture, openness enables strangers to minimize their resistance and maximize their willingness to attend to the new and changed circumstances. The *strength* of one's personality refers to the inner quality that absorbs shocks from the environment and bounces back without being seriously damaged by them. It represents a range of interrelated personality attributes such as resilience, risk-taking, hardiness, persistence, patience, elasticity, and resourcefulness. The *positivity*, an affirmative and optimistic outlook of mind, further helps strangers to endure many stressful encounters with a belief that things will turn out as they should in the end.

Intercultural Transformation

Through extensive and prolonged experiences of communication in the host society, strangers experience a gradual and largely imperceptible internal transformation. Three key facets of such change are: (1) greater *functional fitness* in carrying out daily transactions; (2) improved *psychological health* in dealing with the environment; and (3) an increasingly *intercultural identity* orientation.

Functional fitness of strangers increases as they conduct continuous experiments in the host environment as they strive to "know their way around." Through repeated activities resulting in new learning and mental re-organizing, they achieve some level of appropriate and effective ways to communicate and relate to the host environment. Accompanying increased *functional fitness* is greater *psychological health* with respect to the life in the host environment. Strangers tend to experience a great deal of frustration and anxiety in the early stages of cross-cultural adaptation, most likely due to their lack of host communication competence necessary to carry out their daily life activities with proficiency. As they build their host communication competence through interactions with local people, they are better able to meet their personal needs with greater ease and efficacy.

Long-term adaptive change further includes the emergence of an *intercultural identity*, an individuated and universalized self-other orientation that transcends the boundaries of a single culture. While rooted in the original cultural identity, individuals with an expanded identity are better able to see themselves and others based on unique personal qualities (individuation) and shared humanity (universalization).

Practical Insights

Altogether, Kim's integrative communication theory presents a dynamic and holistic account of how and why individuals adapt to an unfamiliar culture. The stress-adaptation-growth dynamic captures the trajectory of the process through which strangers go through a subtle and largely unconscious transformation and form a workable psychological and functional relationship with the host environment. The structural model identifies a given stranger's communicative ability and participation as the main force driving the adaptation process. The structural model further explains that these communication factors influence, and are influenced by, the conditions of the host environment as well as of the individual stranger.

With these two models addressing the process and the structure of cross-cultural adaptation, Kim's theory illuminates the reality of cross-cultural adaptation, in which each individual is the primary "mover" of his or her own adaptation. Even though host institutions and communities may assist in this process by welcoming and supporting a given stranger, it is the stranger himself or herself who largely bears the "burden" of adapting. The real choice left for the stranger, then, is the *degree* of change that he or she is willing to embrace.

For the readers seeking ways to help themselves for their own adaptive ends, here are some of the basic practical insights emanating from the theory.

Regarding Host Environment as Partner

Cross-cultural adaptation takes place at the interface of the stranger and the host environment. From neighbors and coworkers to public and private institutions, the host environment is an integral part of the new life and our adaptation hinges on the extent to which we are able to work with it, not against it. Embracing this reality enables us to view the adaptation process as a joint, collaborative partnership – one in which our personal well-being is also in the interest of the host sociocultural system. Such an understanding engenders within us a spirit of openness and respect toward the host culture and motivates us to learn and participate in it as actively as possible.

Embracing Internal Change

As we regard the host environment as our partner, we also need to anticipate the likelihood that a part of who we are and what we are may be changed by the new experiences, at least temporarily. This willingness to be changed is vital if we are to attain a degree of host communication competence and, thereby, functional fitness in the new sociocultural system. In accepting change, we may recognize the fact that our basic cultural programming endures even as it is changed by new experiences. Most of us understand and accept that adaptive change is natural and inevitable as part and parcel of living in an alien milieu. This understanding allows us to open ourselves to new cultural learning even in the midst of severe culture shock experiences.

Embracing Adaptive Stress

No matter how welcoming the host environment may be toward us, we are bound to encounter many moments of frustration. During the early phases of the adaptation process, the sheer amount of unfamiliarity with the new environment can invoke an acute and overwhelming sense of uncertainty and anxiety. For most of us, the natural instinct is to avoid stress by separating ourselves from what we see as its source, the host environment itself, thereby passing up opportunities for new cultural learning. Interestingly, however, a basic means we have in managing adaptive stress and countering its potential ill-effects is to accept stress and stop fighting it. It helps to recognize that stress is an integral part of the internal dynamics that helps us mobilize for our adaptation and growth. As Atwater (1983) put it, "growth involves stepping into unfamiliar and potentially dangerous situations that often leave us more vulnerable to hurt and disappointment… .The willingness to take risks is a key to personal growth" (p. 14).

Building Host Communication Competence

Host communication competence is a *sine qua non* of successful adaptation, the very force that "brings the soloists to sing in the choir" (Grotevant, 1993, p. 121). The process of overcoming and managing the uncertainties of an unfamiliar culture hinges on our ability to understand, empathize, and act in ways that are in congruence with local culture. Recognizing the power of host communication competence in adapting to an unfamiliar culture, we can facilitate our own adaptation. Proficiency in the host language, in particular, serves us as an important instrument with which to access to the right of the benefits that native speakers enjoy. We also need to cultivate emotional and aesthetic sensibilities through which we can appreciate and share in local people's experiences of pleasure, joy, and love as well as anger, sadness, and grief.

Cultivating Relationships with Local People

Building host communication competence requires active social interactions with local people. Through actively participate in social activities with local people, we learn the details about how they experience and communicate in various social situations. As Jantsch (1980) noted, "True learning is never rote learning, but always stimulated experience by oneself" (p. 205). Whenever opportunities for communication with the natives present themselves, we need to make an effort to find ways to form meaningful and supportive relationships. Better yet, we may actively look for such opportunities by reaching out to with those coworkers and neighbors around us in our daily life as well as through other opportunities available in the local community.

Celebrating the Gift of Human Resilience

In the end, successful adaptation to an unfamiliar culture rests on the ever-present human resilience. Seldom easy or smooth, life in a foreign land is an eye-opening journey that challenges our habitual cultural assumptions and expectations. We are bound to encounter many stressful moments when familiar relationships and routines are broken. Yet, those unsettling moments are the very force that brings about the unfolding of the stress-adaptation-growth dynamic, in and through which we work through the setbacks and undergo a process of internal transformation in the form of a larger, reconstituted self that reaches beyond cultural boundaries. This insight serves as a guiding vision that helps ease some of our short-term tribulations with optimism and resolve.

References

Adler, P. (1975). The Transition Experience: An Alternative View of Culture Shock. *Journal of Humanistic Psychology, 15*(4), 13–23. https://doi.org/10.1177/002216787501500403.

Atwater, E. (1983). *Psychology of Adjustment: Personal Growth in a Changing World* (2nd ed.). Englewood Cliffs, NJ: Prentice Hall.

Berry, J. (1980). Acculturation as Varieties of Adaptation. In A. Padilla (Ed.), *Acculturation: Theory, Models and Some New Findings* (pp. 9–25). Washington, DC: Westview.

Berry, J., & Annis, R. (1974). Acculturative Stress: The Role of Ecology, Culture, Anddifferentiation. *Journal of Cross-Cultural Psychology, 5*, 382–406. https://doi.org/10.1177/002202217400500402

Bertalanffy, L. (1968). *General System Theory*. New York, NY: Braziller.

Dabrowski, K. (1964). *Positive Disintegration*. Boston, MA: Little, Brown.

Glazer, N., & Moynihan, D. (1963). *Beyond the Melting Pot*. Cambridge, MA: MIT Press.

Grotevant, H. (1993). The Integrative Nature of Identity: Bridging the Soloists to Sing in the Choir. In J. Kroger (Ed.), *Discussions on Ego Identity* (pp. 121–146). Hillsdale, NJ: Lawrence Erlbaum.

Gudykunst, W. B., & Kim, Y. Y. (2003). *Communicating with Strangers: An Approach to Intercultural Communication* (4th ed.). New York, NY: McGra w-Hill.

Jantsch, E. (1980). *The Self-Organizing Universe: Scientific and Human Implications of the Emerging Paradigm of Evolution*. New York: Pergamon.

Kim, Y. Y. (1988). *Communication and Cross-Cultural Adaptation: An Integrative Theory*. Clevedon, United Kingdom: Multilingual Matters.

Kim, Y. Y. (2001). *Becoming Intercultural: An Integrative Theory of Communication and Cross-Cultural Adaptation*. Thousand Oaks, CA: Sage.

Kim, Y. Y. (2005). Adapting to a New Culture: An Integrative Communication Theory. In W. Gudykunst (Ed.), *Theorizing about Intercultural Communication* (pp. 375–400). Thousand Oaks, CA: Sage.

Kim, Y. Y. (2018). Integrative Communication Theory of Cross-cultural Adaptation. In Y. Y. Kim (Ed.), *The International Encyclopedia of Intercultural Communication* (Vol. 2, pp. 929–941). Hoboken, NJ: Wiley & Sons. https://doi.org/10.1002/9781118783665.ieicc0041.

Oberg, K. (1960). Cultural Shock: Adjustment to New Cultural Environments. *Practical Anthropology*, *7*, 170–179.

Ruben, B. (1972). General Systems Theory: An Approach to Human Communication. In R. Budd & B. Ruben (Eds.), *Approaches to Human Communication* (pp. 120–144). Rochelle Park, NJ: Hayden Books.

Ruben, B. (1983). A System-theoretic View. In W. Gudykunst (Ed.), *Intercultural Communication Theory* (pp. 131–145). Beverly Hills, CA: Sage.

Simmel, G. (1908/1950). The Stranger. In K. Wolff (Ed. and trans.), *The Sociology of Georg Simmel*. New York, NY: Free Press.

Introduction to Looking for Ties and Bonds: Intercultural Social Networks in the 21st Century

By L. Ripley Smith

The next chapter examines intercultural social networks from an intercultural perspective within the overall context of cultural adaptation, or as Smith prefers to call it, adjustment. Studying social networks, he argues, can be helpful in explaining how and why or why not individuals adjust to a new cultural environment. The chapter reviews the relevant literature. It is pointed out that social networks refer to the social architecture of multiple dyadic interactions that influence each other. It is noted further that network relations are interpersonal, inter-positional, and inter-organizational which is why they these relations can be used to interpret the behavior of the units on multiple levels in the system. That is why social networks can be described in terms of quantitative, structural indices as well as situated, relational contexts. In an intercultural context, the cross-level capabilities of social network analysis can be used to uncover the complex reality of social relationships and structures existing in intercultural interactions. In fact, social networks can depict the relational processes inherent to cultural adjustments and represent the data of culture acquisition mechanisms. Indeed, personal social networks can provide an indication as to how well a person is integrated into the host society. Research has shown that the inclusion of host nationals in one's personal network is helpful in accessing resources outside of one's co-national network. But it seems that the benefits gained are dynamic and not static, varying by length of time in the host culture and the intention to remain in the host culture. At the same time, though, contact with co-nationals is also helpful, in particular during the early phases of adjustment.

Another aspect to consider is identity within a multicultural context. It is pointed out that every structure seems to reflect choices or opportunities for the inclusion or exclusion of host nationals, co-nationals, or internationals in the support framework because these choices impact the stability and the character of one's identity. Some research indicates that multicultural persons are able to dynamically code-switch between cultural identities depending on the context. That is why analyzing a person's identity from a social network perspective can help understand how that identity was formed and is maintained. However, Smith points out that in today's global world it is necessary to consider an intercultural or a multicultural perspective because in the past many studies were only of a cross-cultural nature. In other words, it is pointed out by Smith that many people have contact with any number of other people who may all be coming from different cultures instead of having only a dyadic relationship between oneself and the host culture. And it seems that contact to individuals from different cultures or lack thereof is decisive as to whether one successfully integrates into a host culture or not. This is important information for human resource departments prior to sending employees on an overseas assignment or in fostering the integration of foreign employees into the existing work environment at home.

Michael B. Hinner

L. Ripley Smith is a scholar/professor at Bethel University in St. Paul, MN, USA. His research and teaching focuses on the topics of intercultural social networks and cultural adjustment, particularly as they pertain to the circumstances of immigrants, expatriates, study abroad students, and refugees. He has also investigated intercultural competence and new media technology. A Fellow in the International Academy of Intercultural Research, his work has been published in The International Journal of Intercultural Relations, the International and Intercultural Communication Annual, The International Journal of the Sociology of Language, the International Journal of Communication, and the Arizona Communication Association Journal. His favorite teaching experience comes from a semester-long study abroad program he leads in Europe every other year. He is currently working on several projects looking at the effects of study abroad and service learning on intercultural competence as well as the social support networks of persons experiencing homelessness.

L. Ripley Smith

Looking for Ties and Bonds: Intercultural Social Networks in the 21st Century

Intercultural relations is one of those areas of research that has significant real-world implications. Phenomena like acculturation, the search for identity resources, and acquiring host communication competence have very personal outcomes for people in those circumstances. And with more than two hundred and eighty-one million migrants around the world as of late 2021, the increasing reality and consequences of cultural pluralism demand our ongoing pursuit of valid, reliable insights (International Organization for Migration, 2021). It is with that motivation in mind that I offer this chapter that hopes to identify ties and bonds in a scattered body of research and chart a course for the future. A great deal of important research has been done in intercultural relations using the concept of a social network, but the attention has been spread among several sub-areas and disciplinary perspectives. Consequently, even though studies of social networks are advancing knowledge in a number of areas in the field we are not benefiting fully from what was once listed as one of the most open and promising theoretical and methodological avenues for future research (Poole & McPhee, 1985).

This chapter aims to provide a background on social network analysis as it has been applied to intercultural relations, detailing its theoretical and methodological origin in the fields of anthropology and sociology, tracing the development of an intercultural social network theory, and then surveying findings related to intercultural adjustment and specific social network properties based upon their salience in the literature. In the process, I hope to bring together the diverse lines of research being conducted in the area of intercultural social networks under a single umbrella in order to illustrate the enormous potential these principles and concepts have for understanding the complexities of intercultural adjustment and communication. In order to do that, an interdisciplinary literature from across the sociological, psychological, second language acquisition, migration studies, and communication disciplines involving social network concepts and methodologies will be consulted. Unfortunately, many of those disciplines do not "talk" to each other, and as a consequence we run the risk of missing out on potential *Medici Effect* insights.[1] For that reason, this chapter will pull the widely scattered insights about *intercultural* social networks together and provide a foundation for the untapped value of an under-utilized perspective in the field.

However, before we dive into the current knowledge base surrounding intercultural social networks, it is important to distinguish that literature from the now ubiquitous mediated channels like Facebook, Instagram, Snapchat, WeChat, and TikTok that saturate our lives. Certainly, there is an overlap, and a few scholars have explored the role of digital social networking sites on intercultural relations (e.g., Croucher, 2011; Smith et al., 2011), but for the most part Kim's (1991a, 1991b) assumption that local interpersonal relationships have a stronger impact on cultural adaptation than mediated channels remains the working hypothesis. And for that reason, we will focus on the former in this chapter.

The Origins of Social Network Research in Intercultural Relations

Some of the earliest work in intercultural social networks can be traced back to the research of Emile Durkheim (1912, 1961) and his book, *The Elementary Forms of Religious Life*. In that book he provided an initial formulation of the socio-structural point of view. The representations of ourselves and those around us, he said, are collective representations. That collective force exists both without and within the self, becoming a source of integration and identity. Other early 20th Century anthropologists and sociologists like Elizabeth Bott, J.A. Barnes, and Jacob Moreno were also charting new territory in socio-structural explanation (Freeman & Wellman, 1995; Wolfe, 1978).

It was Durkheim's notion of integration that attracted and inspired anthropologist, A.R. Radcliffe-Brown. Radcliffe-Brown (1952) emphasized Durkheim's integrative forces in the form of societal structures and how they produced interdependence and equilibrium. Each part in a social structure functions in such a manner as to preserve the continuity of the entire structure. And for Radcliffe-Brown these individual parts were relations between people, as he described, "direct observation does reveal to us that these human beings are connected by a complex network of social relations. I use the term 'social structure' to denote this network of actually existing relations" (1952, p.190).

1 Frans Johansson (2004) describes the breakthrough insights that are made possible at the intersection of disciplines, ideas, and concepts in his book of this title.

For Radcliffe-Brown, each particular social relation between two persons is found within a web of social relations called a network. Thus, the structure is distinct from the relation. It is the framework for a given relation. He suggests that as living organisms are more than the composite characteristics of molecules and atoms, so a social structure and its attendant phenomena are more than the nature of the individual human beings comprising, or filling up the positions in, the structure. The social structure is a social force that unites the human members: "In the study of social structure the concrete reality with which we are concerned is the set of actually existing relations, at a given moment of time, which link together certain human beings" (Radcliffe-Brown, 1952, p. 192).

Here Radcliffe-Brown is referring to a present, existing structure in which a person, or persons, may currently be included, and at the same time a structure which also exists in time, and possesses a certain constancy, or stability, in the form of recurring patterns of relationship. These ideas in turn shaped the thinking of his Manchester University anthropology students, John Barnes and Clyde Mitchell (Scott, 1991).

The influence of Jacob Moreno (1934) should also not be underestimated as an innovative thinker in early social network research. Influenced by Georg Simmel, he introduced the sociogram, making the connection between psychological adjustment and structural "configurations." By allowing visual inspection of system variables, he was able to identify isolated individuals, gatekeepers, influencers, reciprocal relationships, and numerous other network indices. The network thinking of these researchers lead to the understanding that the social object is, to some extent, constituted by the system to which it belongs.

Two of the earliest scholars to apply social networks to the study of intercultural communication were Rogers and Kincaid (1981) who describe several intercultural network studies in their book, *Communication Networks: Toward a new paradigm for research.* They argued that the four conceptual variables of connectedness, integration, diversity, and openness provided a network model that allowed for a holistic, multi-level analysis of communication phenomena. It is that methodological capability that marks the value of the social network perspective to the field of intercultural relations.

The Value of a Social Network Perspective

A social network, or socio-structural perspective, really rests on the idea that interaction behavior can be explained by examining relational data. A social network essentially represents the social architecture of "multiple, inter-influencing dyadic interactions" (Smith, 1999, p. 640). Relationships, or "ties" in network analysis, reflect flows of resources, patterns of exchange, types of support, or qualities of relationship, all of which define the nature of the connection. More specifically, on the dyadic level the properties of the link define the capacity and potential of a relationship in a manner that is far more concrete than abstract notions of acquaintance, friendship, or romantic partner. But not only can a tie represent a connection between two individuals, it functions as a multilevel indicator of a relationship between two persons, two groups, or two systems depending on the embedded features of the nodes, or alters (the individuals being connected). For that reason, network relations are at once interpersonal, inter-positional, and inter-organizational and can be used to interpret the behavior of the units on multiple levels in the system (Warriner, 1981). That unique multilevel quality allows social networks to be described simultaneously in terms of quantitative, structural indices and as situated, relational contexts. The combination of which has provided a means for not only corroborating, illustrating, and nuancing established psychologistic findings in the field, but also for generating novel insights based on the unique methodology of social network analysis. As a heuristic and methodological tool, social networks provide ways to think about relationships that diverge from the typical group affiliation or kinship pattern approaches (Wellman, 1999).

A variety of scholars writing in intercultural communication have expressed the benefits of, and need for, intercultural research employing social network methodology. Beginning with Weimann (1989), who suggested that the cross-level capabilities of social network analysis (SNA) are perfect for uncovering the complex reality of social relationships and structures that exist in intercultural interaction, it became increasingly clear that a network approach was useful given that *inter-cultural* research is keenly interested in what occurs between interlocutors amidst an interaction. A social network approach allows examination of not only the nature of the phenomena, but also an account of how the system's parts fit together and simultaneously facilitate and constrain the interaction. Kim (1977, 1991a and 1991b) also identified personal network analysis as a method that "uniquely has the capacity to capture *emergent* properties of an individual's daily social context by focusing on the structure and contents of relational ties that a person maintains at a given time" (p. 90). Marsella and Snyder (1981) hinted as well at the value of a social network approach, indicating that "The social network model is a systems approach for describing, quantifying, and analyzing the complexities of the social milieu" (p. 157). Smith (1999) agreed with the growing interest in SNA and articulated an argument for specific application of network thinking to the field of intercultural relations, and specifically to acculturation research.

Smith (1999) described an organic intercultural network theory that offers axioms and theorems to investigate the natural phenomena of social networks in cultural transition as people immerse themselves in a host, or non-native culture. Social networks literally provide a graph, or picture, of the relational processes inherent in cultural adjustment and represent the data of culture acquisition mechanisms (See Figure 1: Example Sociogram).

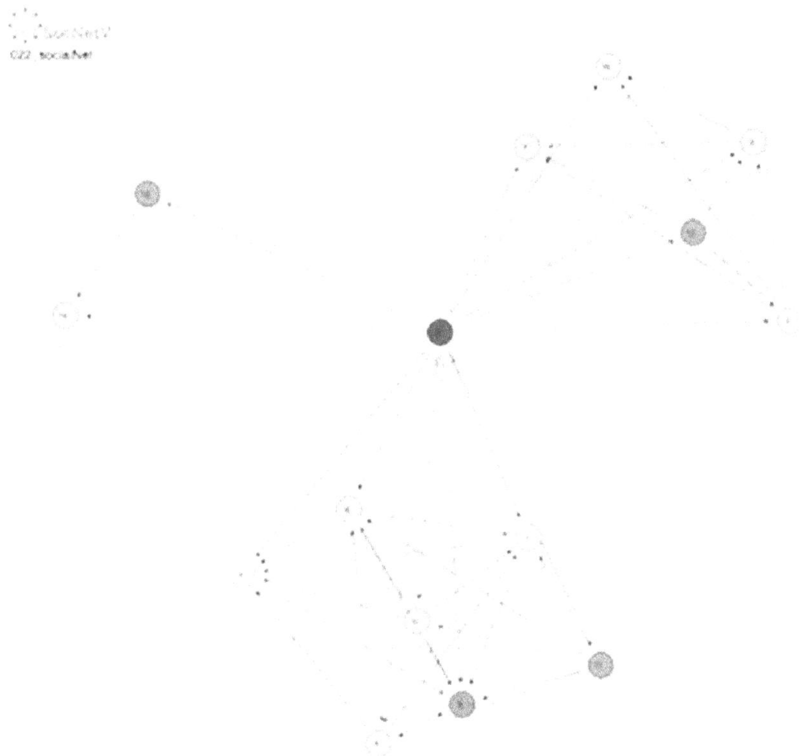

Figure 1: Example Sociogram

Some of the relevant questions to which intercultural networks may offer insight include:

> Do social networks function in the same manner across a variety of cultures? Do these networks consist of similar properties in different cultures? What sorts of relationships facilitate adjustment, and how do these relationships form and how are they maintained?

> What sorts of dependencies develop in an intercultural social network that differ from those characteristic of an intracultural social network? Are there certain properties that facilitate adjustment regardless of culture? Are there significant differences between a person's intracultural- and intercultural links in his or her social network? If so, what is their nature? (Smith, 1999, p. 638)

Despite numerous theoretical and methodological "plugs" in the intercultural literature (see Kim, 1986a, 1986b; Weimann, 1989; Yum, 1984), there have not been enough buyers to adequately tap the social network perspective's storehouse of promise. Part of the reason for its neglect in early years was the impression that it was mathematically opaque, involving computationally complex algorithms better left to statisticians and sociological methodologists. That impression was not entirely false (Scott, 1991). Therefore, the purpose of this chapter is to call attention to the current knowledge base within intercultural social network research; point out some of the contradictory and inconclusive findings in the literature; and offer a challenge for future inquiries that will improve the methodological and theoretical state of that knowledge base. To that end, we will begin with an overview of key intercultural network studies in intercultural relations research. Following that overview, we will identify specific network properties and functions that have become prominent within intercultural adjustment research. Within those examples we will highlight several conceptual and methodological shortcomings and the potential for more sophisticated social network analyses. Finally, the utility of the social network approach for studying intercultural interaction holistically is highlighted in the closing section with multiple avenues for future research identified.

Setting the Stage for Studies of Intercultural Social Networks

The prominence of understanding one's relational environment as an indicator of cultural phenomena has long been a feature of anthropological research, especially in the structuralist stream of thought that took its cue from Durkheim (Barnes, 1971, 2004; Levi-Strauss, 1949, 1969). However, it was another twenty-five years before socio-structural analysis began to appear in intercultural research, and even then, very few studies were examining the structure of social networks across cultural systems (Gudykunst & Ting-Toomey, 1988, p. 78). It required embracing an interdisciplinary literature, and in particular the construct of social support, before social network analysis gained any traction in the study of intercultural relations.

Research and theorizing on social support obtained through one's social network has been extensive from psychological, communication, and sociological perspectives (Albrecht & Adelman, 1987; Belle, 1983; Brownell & Shumaker, 1984; d'Abbs, 1982; Gottlieb, 1981; Henderson, 1984; Janjuha-Jivraj, 2003; Lee & Van Vorst, 2010; Lein, 1983; Lin, 1986; Oommen, 2014; Shumaker & Brownell, 1984; Smith, 2013; Surra, 1988; Wellman, 1981). It didn't take long, however, to determine that the communication of support was crucial on all levels in helping an expatriate adjust to his or her new environment (Fontain, 1986; Kim, 1987). Kim's (1986a, 1986b; 1987) social support network model was one of the most comprehensive, early elaborations of social network methodology applied to intercultural relations, tying specific network properties to communication competence and cultural adaptation potential. This section will review key assumptions and theorems from the primary intercultural network theories in the field of intercultural relations.

Kim (1987) arrived at the conclusion that acquired host communicative competence reflects degree of adjustment to the host culture, while at the same time facilitating further adjustment. In a nutshell, communicative adjustment is achieved by means of gaining host communicative competence through shared networks. In fact, most research recognizes involvement in host communication networks as evidence of intercultural communication competence (Cheng, 2018; Chi et al., 1986; Martin, 1993; 2015; Smith, 2005, 2013; Yum, 1988), or superior language ability as indicative of self-confidence and ability to interact with the host environment (Ying & Liese, 1994). The problem exists in that few studies have identified the relationship between specific structural properties and the various facets of intercultural communication competence.

Kim's (1986b) model posited several important theoretical statements that have served to guide research on intercultural social support networks. Based upon her work with immigrants in the Chicago area, she suggested a mutual causation between host communication competence and relational (network) development. The following assumption was the foundation for three theorems predicting the nature of socio-structural influence on outgroup communication competence:

> *Assumption:* the nature of a personal network reflects as well as influences the ego's overall out group communication competence (Kim, 1986b, p. 92).

Three theorems were generated to describe network characteristics that indicate the type of social integration necessary for outgroup communication competence.

Theorem 1: a higher level of heterogeneity of a personal network is associated with a higher level of the ego's overall outgroup communication competence.

Theorem 2: a higher level of centrality of outgroup members in a personal network is associated with a higher level of the ego's outgroup communication competence.

Theorem 3: a higher level of an ego's tie strength with outgroup members is associated with a higher level of his/her ego's [*sic*] outgroup communication competence (Kim, 1986a, 1986b, pp. 93–94).

Adaptation then, is an outcome of these two causal forces (communicative competence and relational development). A third important insight in Kim's model is the potential for negative long-term consequences from relying on ethnic institutions for a majority of support (i.e., institutional completeness). In terms of network properties, Kim (1986b) suggested that cultural adaptation and host communication competence will be both reflected in, and facilitated by, the integration of host culture natives in the network (network heterogeneity), with centrality and strength of those ties reflecting greater degrees of adaptation/competence.

While Kim created a connection between adaptation factors (specifically host communication competence) and socially supportive networks, Adelman (1988) outlined specific kinds of supportive messages needed for cultural adjustment and where they may be obtained. She echoed several of the conclusions Kim (1987) arrived at, for example, "Strong ties with members of the home culture may undermine the development of close ties with host nationals" (Albrecht & Adelman, 1987, p. 197). Of key theoretical interest is her emphasis on weak ties as sources of critical social support during initial stages of adjustment. Both Adelman and Kim challenged future researchers to explore the myriad of relationships that would further an intercultural social support network theory.

A second interculturalist to tackle social networks related to cultural adjustment was Yum (1988). She was the second researcher to suggest a specifically intercultural social network theory (cf. Kim, 1986b, 1987 under social support theory). Yum (1983) concluded from a study of five ethnic groups in Hawaii that patterns of network properties will vary by culture. Yum (1988) further identified the differences between properties of intercultural and intracultural networks using the base assumption of cultural heterogeneity. She advocated an intercultural social network theory in which networks will be characterized by important variations due to the effects of heterogeneity, difficulty in relationship development, lack of host communicative competence, differing value systems, intimacy levels, role types, and information channels. Consequently, intercultural networks will be more radial, less dense, less multiplex, less transitive, and have generally weaker ties than intracultural networks.

Yum's (1988) formulation was an important developmental stage in the description of a detailed intercultural network theory because she extended the network perspective to the system level, advancing propositions that pertain to clique and whole network features of networks. She suggested that intercultural social networks can be distinguished from intracultural social networks because the variance between cultural groups is greater than the variance within each cultural group. This leads her to the assumption that intercultural networks reflect greater heterogeneity than intracultural networks and the conclusion that heterogeneity affects network outcomes. Among the relationships and properties posited to characterize an intercultural network are the following:

1. intercultural networks will be more radial than intracultural networks;
2. intercultural networks will be less dense than intracultural networks;
3. intercultural networks will be less multiplex than intracultural networks;
4. intercultural networks will be less transitive than intracultural networks; and,
5. intercultural networks will have generally weaker ties than intracultural networks.

Yum's (1988) theorems needed to be tested in multiple cultures in order to refine and extend the theory she set forth. As she notes, her theorems refer to intercultural communication situations in general and lack specificity regarding contexts of networks and combinations of cultures. Relations are generally context-specific, as indicated by the current trend in intercultural studies toward identifying the complexities of relationships and distinguishing between distinct culture-groups. Some of Yum's theoretical propositions will be contrasted with findings on intracultural networks later in the chapter.

Smith (1999) picked up the mantle from Kim and Yum and extended their formulations by offering a formulation of an intercultural social network theory as it applies to a specific cultural process – viz., acculturation. Beginning with an argument for its cross-paradigmatic utility, he argued for a purely socio-structural explanation of intercultural relationships, uniting the study of individual-level phenomena with social processes. The theory described a physics of intercultural social structure, meaning that social networks have natural properties whose characteristics and interactions can be described. In an effort to identify prototypic social architectures, he defined key network properties of intercultural networks and their underlying assumptions. Seven assumptions were identified:

1. behavior can be explained through social relationship analysis;
2. networks are multi-level phenomena consisting of hierarchical structures;

3. proximity in social space and contact opportunities increase the probability of social relations;
4. network ties are reciprocal, and may be asymmetrical or symmetrical;
5. limitations of time and space require that the number of ties any single ego can maintain are finite;
6. network structures hold situational logics that reflexively shape the nature and function of the structure, and;
7. social networks comprise systems of reference points in the formation of social identities. (pp. 642–645)

These assumptions were offered as the ground for seven theoretical propositions about intercultural identity, network composition, and acculturative resources. *Social Network Acculturation Theory* suggested that "networks are places of meaningful association" and inform us of identity formation within relational attachments (Smith, 1999, p. 646). Two propositions were put forward about networks and identity:

1. intercultural identity strategies are discernable within social network structures, and;
2. culturally influenced perceptions shape the function and experienced nature of social networks. (pp. 646–7)

Three propositions were also extended with respect to network composition, arguing that interethnic networks promote acculturation:

1. as socio-structural heterogeneity increases, the probability of acculturation increases;
2. rate of change in an intercultural social network is a dynamic function dependent on the stage of integration with the host community, and;
3. structural constraints will impact the size of intercultural networks, in turn affecting the adjustment process. (pp. 647–8)

Finally, Smith (1999) noted that networks provide the necessary social capital for positive cultural adjustment; two propositions were stated that pertain to acculturative resources:

1. as density increases, the provision of diverse resources within the net[work] decreases, thereby affecting socialization/acculturation, and;
2. intercultural networks will be less dense, with more radial ties in cultures reflecting a contextual-based relationship norm than those found in cultures reflecting a personal-based relationship norm. (p. 650)

In summary, the existing theoretical work in intercultural social networks reflects a uniquely social approach to interpersonal phenomena, as opposed to psychologistic explanations. As we shall see, a great deal of research has been conducted based upon these foundational social network properties and theoretical orientations. Subsequent research has tested these authors' propositions and extended their explanatory scope to specific network properties and salient issues and contexts in intercultural relations.

Intercultural Social Networks and Cultural Adjustment[2]

The issues surrounding cultural adjustment have been, and will continue to be, of paramount importance to the field of intercultural communication. However, most of the early attention the subject has received from both communication and psychological perspectives has been based on psychologistic approaches and not socio-structural in its orientation (e.g., Adler, 1985; Albrecht & Adelman, 1987; Ali et al., 2003; Bochner et al, 1977; Brislin, 1981; Gudykunst, 1979; Gudykunst & Hammer, 1988; Hanvey, 1979; Harris, 1973; Ward & Chang, 1997; Ward & Kus, 2012). Most of these analyses of cultural adjustment assume that the sojourner is an isolated, independent unit to be observed and measured. The contributions of the "multicultural" and "mediating" person are characteristic of this approach and although they represented significant advances in our understanding of adjustment and the "third culture" phenomenon, they inevitably left out some of the social phenomena that to a large extent reflects adjustment (viz., social relationships). Repke and Benet-Martinez (2018) make this argument convincingly, noting that:

> Traditional acculturation research has focused on individuals' culture-related attitudes, behaviors, preferences, and demographics. However, acculturation does not take place solely within the individual... acculturation should be understood as an interactive process between immigrant and host groups, and its resulting behaviors and values mirror not only what happens *inside* of people's minds but also what takes place *between* individuals. (p. 926)

2 I have purposefully chosen the term adjustment over adaptation because of its more general and inclusive meaning. In other words, the idea of adaptation subsumes the notion of acculturation because acculturation is only one means of adaptation. Likewise, adjustment encompasses adaptation since adaptation is only one alternative among many when confronting a new culture. This approach is consistent with much of the historical theorizing on intercultural adjustment (see Berry et al., 1987; Gudykunst, 1979; Herskovitz, 1938; Kroeber & Kluckhohn, 1952).

The strong intuitive connection between intercultural social networks and ability to adjust to a foreign cultural environment has been increasingly supported in the literature (Collie et al., 2010; Gudykunst & Hammer, 1987; Kathiravelu, 2012; Kim, 1986a, 1986b, 1987; Martin, 1993; Smith, 2005, 2013; Yum, 1988). Kim's (1977) original study of immigrant personal communication networks in Chicago began to clarify those interconnections. Regarding social networks, Kim's survey of 281 Korean households in the Chicago area looked at the volume and intensity of the immigrants' relationships with host nationals. She found that interpersonal relationships exerted a stronger influence on perceptions of the host society, and consequently adaptation, than did mass media consumption. Kim (1978) gave more detail on the interpersonal communication patterns of Korean immigrants. She noted an increase in the average number of host national acquaintances from 10.6 in the first year of immigration to 123.8 after seven to nine years in the host society. Kim recognized that communication within one's personal network is central to coping:

> Through communication [a person] acquires control over change in order to cope with the new environment… learning and acquiring new ways to face problematic situations occur through communication, both verbal and nonverbal, and through interpersonal contact. (p. 199)

Kim (1979, 1988a) synthesized her earlier studies to present models for acculturation and adaptation that place central importance on social network integration. She concluded that, "It is very likely that the extent to which an immigrant has incorporated into the interpersonal social network of the host society on the intimate relationship level is predicated on the degree of acculturation" (1979, p. 445). Kim later emphasized the dynamic aspects among three dimensions: acculturation potential, personal and social communication, and communication environment in the host community. She found that a great deal of information about an expatriate is available from his or her network connections:

> We can infer and predict an immigrant's acculturation from the nature of his or her interpersonal networks. An immigrant with a predominantly ethnic interpersonal network can be considered less acculturated and less competent in the host communication system than an immigrant whose associates are primarily members of the host society. In addition, the degree of intimacy in the relationships… is an important indicator of… acquired host communication competence. (Kim, 1988a, p. 347)

However, more recent research suggests that a greater understanding of social network properties is needed; that is, not all host nationals are equal to the task of providing adaptive support (e.g., Bhattacharya, 2011; Fietz & Kaschowitz, 2019;

Ramos et al., 2017). For instance, Jou and Fukada (1995a) found that the source of supportive communication did have an effect on adjustment. Studying Chinese students in Japan, they found that those who received more social support from their Japanese professors were better adjusted. The Chinese students reported that they needed the least amount of support from Japanese friends off campus, received the most support from foreign students, but received less support than they thought they needed overall. Those students who reported higher actual support from Japanese professors had higher adjustment scores leading to the conclusion that the effect of social support varied according to source. Cheng, Meng, and Liu (2018) also found that the strength of the relationship, including the provision of emotional support, but not necessarily the quantity of connections, was a key factor in socio-cultural adjustment.

Smith (1996, 2013) uncovered some of the structural properties that characterize intercultural social support networks in multiple case-studies of expatriates and resettled refugees. He identified three distinct social network structures adopted by expatriates that characterize alternative adjustment strategies. The first structure presented a radial network which spread nodes out to the periphery with a single center, and relatively homogeneous pattern. The radial ties consist largely of home culture alters. The second pattern exhibited multiple centers and a somewhat radial, predominantly weak host national tie socio-structure. While the third structure had an integrated set of heterogeneous, strong ties in an elliptical core of the network. The elliptical core exhibited higher density and stronger node centrality of host-nationals, suggesting a pronounced integration acculturation orientation.

It is clear from the research conducted up to this time that our personal social networks offer a barometer, so to speak, of our integration into a host society. And the evidence is contained in the supportive ties within our network. As network and acculturation models have been developed, certain social network properties have received greater attention in the literature due to their expected influence on adjustment and acculturation. The research surrounding the properties of network composition, multiplexity, density, centrality and clustering have proven most significant. The following sections will unpack what we know about each of these important features of social networks as they relate to intercultural relations.

The Importance of Diversifying Your In-Group

Social network data fall roughly into two categories, either *structural* or *composition* (Wasserman & Faust, 1994). The composition of a network describes the attributes of individual nodes in the network, or actor variables. Features like sex, race, occupation, ethnicity, location, etc. Structural data describe the nature of the relationship between nodes, or in other words, the properties of links in the network. Structural variables include things like density, clustering, multiplexity, and the nature of the tie (e.g., friendship, support resources, reciprocity, etc.). Many social network analyses combine the two kinds of data, providing rich, multilevel insights into intercultural interactions.

Social network composition is perhaps the most prevalent area of study within intercultural social networks. It has been well established that social structure places certain constraints on interpersonal interaction (Blum, 1985). Using that established concept, several researchers have attempted to develop theories of intercultural and intergroup communication that take into account the socio-structural context (Gudykunst, 1986; Yum, 1988). One aspect of network composition that has proven significant is heterogeneity, or sometimes referred to as ethnic diversity (Yum, 1983). Surprisingly, Yum found an average of only 1.65 ethnic others in the communication networks of five ethnic groups and an average of only 1.4 ethnic others in their friendship networks. Gudykunst's (1986) theory of intergroup communication included two theorems regarding the effect of cross-cutting memberships on ingroup and outgroup affiliation.

> *Axiom 14:* as the size of the ingroup increases, the likelihood of outgroup contact decreases.
> *Axiom 15:* the more heterogeneous the social structure, the more contact with outgroup members occurs. (Gudykunst, 1986, pp. 159–160)

These axiomatic statements are well supported not only in intercultural network research, but also in sociological studies and general social network research (Blau, 1993; Monge & Contractor, 2003; Repke & Benet-Martínez, 2018). Repke and Benet-Martínez (2018) studied social networks in a multi-ethnic community and demonstrated that the structure of immigrant networks, specifically those with more heterogeneity, predict their psychological adjustment. In fact, they found that increased presence of, and strong ties with, co-ethnic alters in the network was associated with lower levels of psychological and socio-cultural adjustment. Vinokurov et al. (2017) also found that living in a dense community with low levels of host acculturation was associated with underemployment. In another study looking at the effects of heterogeneity on acculturation, Laroche, Kim, Hu, and Joy (1996) looked at factors accounting for ethnic change in French-Canadian culture and found that the best indicator of acculturation (as opposed to ethnic affiliation) was a reversed measure of intra-ethnic social interaction. Other research on social support networks and ethnicity has identified patterned structural differences in the composition of personal networks. Cantor et al. (1994) reported on the social support networks of elderly living in New York. They found that Euro-American elderly have:

> broad-based networks having the largest number of components… tend to be more geographically dispersed… less frequent face-to-face contacts [with children]… were the most likely to report having a friend/confidant… [and] were the most likely to report knowing their neighbors well. (p. 113)

In contrast, Latino elderly possess:

> more narrow, family-centered networks… greater numbers of children, more children living nearby, and more contact with children… Latinos as a group reported larger networks of siblings and other relatives… whom they see or hear from regularly… Latino elderly were significantly less likely to have a friend/confidant or to know neighbors well. (p. 113)

The social support networks of African-American elderly:

> fall in the middle of the continuum between the narrow, family-centered networks of older Latinos and the broad-based networks of White elderly. African-American elderly were the most apt to report… children in the metropolitan area… have more such children living nearby… were more similar to White elderly with respect to friends and neighbors… the most likely to have friend/confidants, and almost as likely as White elderly to know neighbors well. (Cantor et al., 1994, p. 114)

An understanding of the ethnic-specific structure of social networks opens up avenues for socio-structural explanations of adjustment problems as well. Golding and Baezconde-Garbanati (1990) investigated social integration and provision of emotional support in Mexican-American and non-Hispanic, White social networks. The Mexico-born Mexican-American personal nets give an interesting picture of immigration social architecture. These researchers found that Mexican American networks emphasized nuclear family members, consistently had larger households, and had less contact with friends outside the family than non-Hispanic Whites. Other studies have noted the insular qualities of international student social networks and their consequent effects on cultural adjustment and acquisition of cultural competence (Cao et al., 2017; Meng et al., 2021). More specifically, it is not always interaction with the host culture that yields cultural adjustment and increased global competence. In some multinational settings, the social resources needed for cultural adjustment are acquired from connections within the multinational community, not necessarily from the host nationals themselves (Bhattacharya, 2011; Meng et al., 2021).

Not only has network composition been shown to vary by culture, but the perception of the supportive function network members supply appears to vary by culture. Harrison and Myambo (1995) found that adolescents from the United States and Zimbabwe differed in their perceptions of primary support providers. Adolescents from the United States identified parents and best friends as primary support providers whereas adolescents from Zimbabwe identified a wider variety of persons as supplying significant support. That culture differentially prepares people's perceptions of the functions of social network members has significant implications for the intercultural communicator. Harrison and Myambo (1995) attributed some of the difference in network functions to the cultural dimension of individualism-collectivism:

> In Zimbabwe, one's network members were perceived as providing more intimacy, which fosters competency in functioning within an extended kin system. In comparison, U.S. culture fostered the perceptions of network members providing one with affection, which boosts competency in functioning in traditional nuclear families where intense affect is directed only to a small range of persons. Also, affection from significant others is supportive for competent functioning in individualistic cultures that are highly competitive. (para. 40)

Another significant, recurring finding in the literature is that a same culture, or co-ethnic, social network composition is beneficial in the initial phase of adjustment (Cao et al., 2017; Du & Wei, 2015; Kang, 1972; Kim, 1978; Kuo & Tsai, 1986; Lebon, 1983; Neto, 2002; Smith, 1996; Ying & Liese, 1991, 1994). The research in this area suggests that adjustment is positively related to the size of the local ethnic community and relationships with co-nationals because it contributes to the sojourner's sense of inclusion and security. Ethnic enclaves are a common phenomenon discussed in adjustment research (Church, 1982), and are often seen as obstacles to acculturation or positive social integration (Mok et al., 2007). However, from a network perspective, ethnic enclaves may be a result of ethnocentrism, existing social class structure, language difficulties, lack of common social interests, return migration intentions, or other mobility-limiting conditions related to the host culture which create social distance from host nationals (Small, 1995). That structural condition, combined with the effects of pre-existing social ties may effectively limit the need and/or desire for ties with host nationals (Owusu, 1996). As Small (1995) found in her study of Tongan-U.S. migrants:

> One of the consistent themes of Tongan migration stories is that the critical hurdles in relocating overseas – getting the opportunity to migrate, locating a place to live, finding a job – come from other Tongans. In a typical story, the visa application is made by a sister, brother, parent or child, resident overseas, the airfare is paid by kin with overseas jobs; it is these same kin who will provide a place to live for migrants and their families for months (sometimes years) after arrival. One's first job comes

> from another Tongan – who may come from the same region of Tonga – who brings the new arrival into his/her workplace, or replaces a Tongan who is quitting. (Small, 1995, p. 245)

However, most scholars have accepted the arguments in favor of social integration and have concentrated on patterns evident in the acculturation process. Kim (1978) studied the communication resources available to Korean immigrants through their communication patterns. She found that the volume of ethnic "others" in the immigrants' interpersonal networks steadily increases during the first several years in the host society, though the average number of host culture alters in the network continues to be considerably less than co-ethnic alters. Others have also found similar variation in patterns of dependence on host nationals for adjustment (Jou & Fukada, 1996b). An unexpected finding in Kim's work is that those immigrants who had more extensive involvement in the host culture tended to also be more active in their own ethnic community. Kim also concluded that interpersonal ties, and their resultant communication, is a more powerful acculturative force than consumption of mass media (see also Jun, 1984).

In studies that focused on communicative competence from an intercultural network perspective, Yum (1982) surveyed a large sample of Korean immigrants in Hawaii and found a fairly strong correlation (r =.51) between *communication diversity* and English fluency. Communication diversity is defined in her study as immigrants' use of a wide variety of communication channels that cross ethnic boundaries. Clement (1987) also investigated the relationship between second language proficiency and acculturation. Reminiscent of Schumann's (1978) social distance model, he suggested that L2 proficiency is influenced by motivation. Clement found that a non-native speaker's affiliation with an in-group affects self-confidence in the L2, with members of groups who exhibit less ethno-linguistic vitality showing higher levels of self-confidence and acculturation. Clement established a clear connection between communicative competence and social networks, finding that the "level of acculturation was a function of proficiency in the second language and an interactive function of language status and frequency of contact" (Clement, 1987, p. 271). The causal logic suggested by Clement is given a twist by Erickson (1996), who provides an intriguing rationale for integrating host nationals into a personal network. He suggests that those who wish to possess cultural mobility through acquiring a repertoire of cultures should seek to incorporate variety into their social networks as a means to that cultural variety, not vice versa. Erickson argued that social network variety is a primary *source* of cultural variety, leading to the social capital resources necessary for coping.

Finally, two studies employing network analysis methodology found that network heterogeneity, or diversity, has positive effects on intercultural orientation as opposed to a monocultural orientation (Lee, 2014; Oehlkers, 1991). Specifically, Oehlkers (1991) investigated Japanese sojourners in the United States and found evidence of a relationship between adjustment, network heterogeneity and tie strength. He concluded that a sojourner who includes host culture members in his or her network and develops friendship ties with those nodes will feel more comfort in interacting with host nationals and will feel more a part of the host culture. In particular, he stressed the importance of the reinforcement value of those ties in promoting "belongingness." Oehlkers also concluded that English ability is the best predictor of adjustment in general while heterogeneity is a good predictor of level of alienation and interaction uncertainty.

Pragmatism and Network Composition

Social support describes the resources that are available to someone via social ties to people and groups in a community (Albrecht & Adleman, 1987; Lin et al., 1979). These supportive resources provide a sense of efficacy and confidence in one's ability to cope. To the extent that such resources are available in one's network that can be drawn upon or exchanged, we might say the person has a certain amount of social capital, the social assets available via connections to resources through network relationships (Lin, 2001, p. 19). These resources, both tangible and intangible, are often a critical component in relational satisfaction, emotional well-being, and cultural adjustment in a cross-cultural setting. In a study of the paths of migrant integration into a new community, Guest and Stamm (1993) found that rebuilding new social ties (viz., replenishing depleted social networks) with neighbors or community groups received little priority. They concluded that, "According to this study, the first priority of most migrants is to find a job, a house, and a neighborhood in which to live" (Guest & Stamm, 1993, para. 61). Yum (1983) also found that new immigrants privileged instrumental resources in their relationships:

> Many new ties are formed through activities to satisfy immediate needs: making a living, learning a new language, participating in social life, going to church, and so forth. Social networks put individuals in contact…the particular characteristic of the social networks with which an immigrant becomes associated in the host society are likely to affect many aspects of the adjustment process. (p. 577)

A similar pragmatic ethnic identification pattern was found in expatriate social networks, despite the fact that failure to integrate host nationals into the core of one's social network may effectively marginalize the expatriate and leave them stranded in the periphery of the local community (Smith, 1996). For example, Smith found an average of only 39.8% host nationals in the networks of expatriates across three global regions (East Africa, East Asia, South America). That means when living and working abroad, these expats are composing their social networks of more than 60% co-nationals. Other research has found a significant relationship between better adjustment and international students' efforts to develop relationships with host nationals (Hendrickson et al., 2011; Ying & Liese, 1994). Ying and Liese (1994) failed to find a positive correlation between either size of local ethnic community, or friendship with other similar ethnicities, and adjustment, and concluded that relating exclusively with co-nationals may be insulating. Furthermore, the survival value of inflexible, bounded groups that pool resources as opposed to flexible, integrated social networks utilizing a system of exchange has been contrasted, showing the former to be detrimental in nature (Weiss, 1996). On the other hand, research from a psychology-of-self perspective and integration into superdiverse contexts has found that social capital may in fact be leveraged from both host national ties as well as from "migrant social capital" (Wessendorf & Phillimore, 2018, p. 124). And in some cases, both ties to host nationals or co-nationals, and second language ability, failed to predict either perceived acculturation stress or the quality of social support received (Cross, 1995; Johnson et al., 2003).

In summary, the ethnic composition of social networks does have consequences for different stages of cultural adjustment. It appears that including host nationals in one's personal network is beneficial for accessing resources outside of one's co-national network (e.g., acquiring the second language). However, the benefit gained does not appear to be static, but rather dynamic, varying by length of time in the host culture and perhaps intention to remain in the host culture. At the same time, ties to co-nationals are also instrumental, especially during early phases of adjustment. The complication for the sojourner in all of this is that network composition varies by ethnicity (as well as other factors), increasing the difficulty in knowing where and with whom to develop relationships in a given culture. Acquiring a more nuanced understanding of what kind of relationships are needed, and when, for successful cultural adaptation to occur should be a primary objective for future research.

The Multiplexity Effect

The previous discussion about network composition pointed out that the usefulness of a particular network configuration for cultural adjustment is often a function of the types of relationships in the network. And the types of relationships, and social capital they make available, is a function of the exchange contents that flow through those links. This property of social network ties is known in the social network literature as *multiplexity* and can refer to the idea of a link representing different contexts or roles (e.g., a work colleague and a friend) or alternatively the kinds of content flowing through the link such as advice or finances, etc. (Kadushin, 2012, p. 28).[3] Supportive resources are commonly grouped under labels like emotional support, advice and information, tangible or practical assistance, financial support, and socializing. Adelman (1988) outlined five specific kinds of supportive resources available through social support networks that aid adjustment: (1) perspective shifts that help one modify negative attributions that lead to negative attitudes or depression; (2) skill enhancement that increase the recipients ability to deal positively and productively with their situation; (3) tangible assistance that carries explicit or implicit interpersonal messages of caring, affirmation and encouragement; (4) acceptance messages that reassure the recipient of their self-worth, inclusion and personal identity; and, (5) ventilation opportunity messages which are non-verbal listening behaviors acting as a reflecting surface for the venting partner. All of these messages serve to enhance the sojourner or expatriate's ability to positively adjust to a new environment (Cheng et al., 2018; du Plooy et al,. 2020; Jou & Fukada, 1996a, 1996b; Lee & Van Vorst, 2010). For example, du Plooy, Lyons and Kashima (2020) found that two kinds of social capital, generalized trust and network resources, had a direct relationship to flourishing and positive psychological adjustment in several migrant groups.

As was found with the property of composition, the type of tie or alter that offers these support resources appears to vary by culture. Harrison and Myambo (1995) found that in the United States parents and best friends were the biggest providers of support to their adolescent subjects, with affection being the primary emotional resource. Their comparison sample from Zimbabwe received support from a wider variety of ties in their networks with the dominant resource being intimacy. In addition, the relationships in one's life that provide support during periods of transition and adjustment are not static (Taha & Cox, 2016). These and similar findings have cultural significance in that they advance the notion of culturally specific types of behaviors and competencies promoted within social support networks like differences in residential patterns and relative importance of kin in personal support networks (Cantor et al., 1994; Fietz & Kaschowitz, 2019; Giorgas, 2000; Harrison & Myambo, 1995). For example, Antonucci,

3 Smith (1999) refers to content multiplexity as link multidimensionality.

Fuhrer, and Jackson (1990) found a cross-national difference in reciprocity within supportive relationships; "...the substantially greater number of French elderly compared to American elderly reporting that their relationships are reciprocal and the significantly fewer French elderly compared to American elderly reporting that they receive less support than they provide, suggests that there is a pattern of cultural differences" (p. 529). However, they do conclude that reciprocity in supportive behaviors is positively valued across ethnic and national lines.

Differences in the effects of perceived, actual, and needed support on adjustment has also received attention in the literature (Jou & Fukada, 1995a, 1995b; Oommen, 2014; Zhang & Kline, 2009). Jou and Fukada (1996b) conducted a longitudinal investigation on the support needs of international students. The influence of personality factors versus support factors varied over four periods. The influence of actual support was the strongest in periods one and two, virtually determining adjustment to the exclusion of personality factors. However, in period three the influence of actual support lessened while the effect of personality became stronger. In the fourth period the personality factor of extraversion became much more influential together with a marked drop in the influence of actual support. These findings, along with the findings of variability of support by source, clearly suggest that the need for support during a sojourn, and who one turns to for that support, are dynamic processes.

Understanding multiplexity and the provision of social support more fully would allow us to determine the kinds of supportive resources that are typically available through intercultural relationships. It has been suggested that intercultural ties will be relatively modest in comparison to intracultural links, usually consisting of relationships that span no more than two or three contexts (e.g., family, friend, co-worker); and furthermore, that intercultural relationships will not provide as many types of support (multidimensionality) as same culture ties (Smith, 1996). Research on multiplexity is important because it tells us what qualities are most common in intercultural relationships that in turn promote satisfaction and positive adjustment.

The Social Structure of Intercultural Relations

At the heart of the network, or socio-structural approach, is the assumption that relational structures influence interpersonal relationships (Blum, 1985). Three of the most significant structural properties used in the study of intercultural relations include centrality, clustering, and density. We will discuss each of those indices in this section.

Centrality is a measure of a node's position within the network and indicates whether a person is at the intersection of information flow in the network (Borgatti, 1995). There are several measures of centrality (degree, betweenness, eigenvector, etc.), but in general, it reflects the integration of individuals in the network and the system as a whole. For example, the degree centrality of any given node is the number of ties connecting that node to others divided by the maximum possible ties expressed as a percentage (where each step, or link, representing part of a path to another node, is a degree). The network centralization measure is then the sum of all the node centrality scores divided by the maximum possible value for the network and expresses the cohesion of the network around a few specific nodes/actors.

Numerous studies have demonstrated that certain network configurations either constrain or facilitate communication and the flow of information in cross-cultural adjustment (Kim, 1978, 1986a, 1987; Repke & Benet-Martínez, 2018; Smith, 1996, 2013; Yum, 1982, 1983). Smith (2013) observed a pattern of high density, radial networks among resettled refugees that are also marked by low centrality of host national alters. Yum (1983) reported, "significant ethnic variability in social network patterns" in the communication and friendship circles among five different ethnic groups in Hawaii (p. 588). She found that most ethnic groups were significantly different from the others in terms of communication network size, ethnic diversity, and frequency of interaction. Both Yum and Kim (1977) found the tendency for ethnic groups to maintain strong ethnic boundaries in friendship affiliations, even after living in the host culture for several years. Since an integrated network is assumed to be a key mark of acculturation to the host culture, that type of network structure would seem to work against favorable intergroup contact. Both Kim (1978) and Yum and Wang (1983) suggested that one's perception of a host culture becomes more sophisticated as interaction with members of the host society increases. Yum and Wang (1983) noted that "having a network tie with an ethnic group seemed to have the most influence on the favorableness of the attitude" (p. 298).

The idea behind centrality relates to the broader concept of core-periphery structures within networks (see Figure 2). Many networks are marked by a cohesive, highly interconnected set of nodes at the center with a more loosely connected set of nodes constituting a second tier so to speak around the periphery of the network. Some of those peripheral nodes may only be connected to the network by a single tie with one other node in the entire network. These sets of singular ties and nodes represent important positions in many networks known alternatively as bridges, cut-points, or liaisons, and serve as links between distinct networks. More specifically, these "weak" ties have shown remarkable usefulness in accessing information and resources outside of one's immediate network, and as we shall see, have an important role to play in intercultural relations (Cf., Granovetter, 1973).

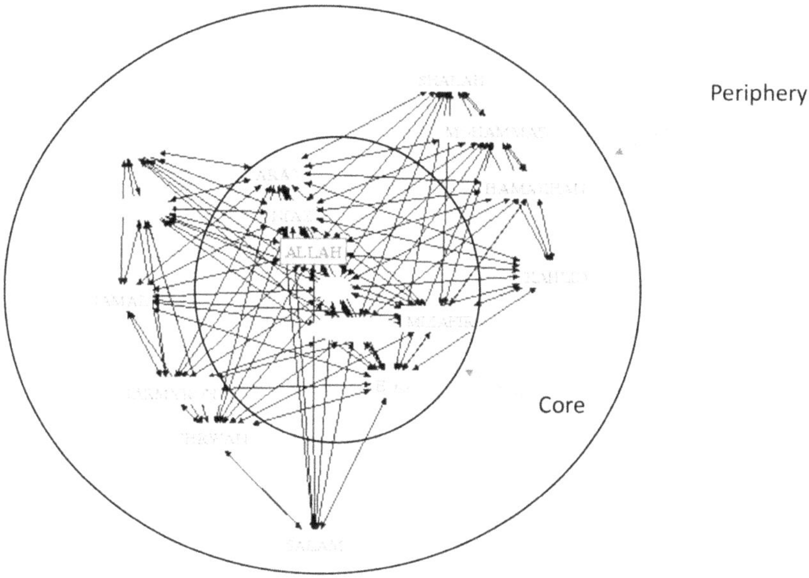

Figure 2: Core-Periphery Network Structure

The notion of a cultural liaison is not new to the field of intercultural relations (Adler, 1975, 1985; Bochner, 1981). The utility of leaning on someone in the host culture who has more experience, more language proficiency, and more social capital is a well-worn strategy for sojourners. Social network research has been able to demonstrate, nuance, and refine our understanding of how those relationships function and describe the resources they actually provide (Faist, 2014; Smith, 2005; Vacca et al., 2018).

Density is another frequently used structural property in the study of social networks because it provides a relatively simple assessment of network connectedness. It is the proportion of the total number of nodes in a network that are connected. Density is a whole network cohesion term that measures the extent to which nodes in a network interact with one another (Smith, 1999). Yum (1983) found an average density of inter-ethnic communication networks of 0.54. Smith (1996) found an average density of expatriate social support networks of 0.47. The literature suggests that low-density networks are preferable for transition and coping situations because they offer enhanced personal control and make available alternative information paths (Albrecht & Adelman, 1984; Repke & Benet-Martínez, 2018). Garrison (1978) found that lower densities in social networks aided cross-cultural adaptation because they provided more freedom to experiment with identity and lowered barriers enforced by tight in-groups. Albrecht and Adelman (1987) view highly dense networks as "stifling" and restrictive in periods of life change. However, most of the work on density has been conducted in an intracultural context, or on immigrants who live in ethnic enclaves (Albrecht & Adelman, 1987; Garrison, 1978). Several studies have found that dense expatriate networks tend to provide positive socialization models leading to cultural sensitivity while loosely connected nets will yield greater chances for growth in communicative competence (Smith, 1996, 2013). For the expatriate, Smith (1996) suggested that a highly dense social structure provides the relational models and positive socialization they need during their search for a fit in the new environment. Expatriates involved in effective cultural adjustment practices are dealing primarily with anomie, or the search for identity, and the reduction of uncertainty.[4] High-density networks provide the necessary reinforcement for positive socialization and tangible assistance to meet both of those needs (Hamburg & Killilea, 1979). Smith also found that higher density nets have larger percentages of "extremely close" ties which tend to be multiplex and offer a wider range of social support.

Of course there are alternative measures of network cohesion such as node connectivity, and some have argued that properties like density need to be assessed alongside other network properties in order to make meaningful observations due to the variation in those properties as a result of the size of a network (Borgatti et al., 2013). Measuring node connectivity is another index of structural cohesion, but it does so by estimating the number of nodes that need to be eliminated in order to disconnect the network (Vacca et al., 2018).

One of the exciting developments in intercultural network studies is the increasing number of studies that are using sophisticated measurements of structural properties. As we refine our ability to measure these social relations

4 Durkheim's *anomie* has been extrapolated to imply a *search* for identity because when the expatriate is confronted with the loss of familiar social codes and supportive ties he or she will undoubtedly attempt to reduce uncertainty. Structurally, I would suggest that a new identity will emerge given the expatriate's location in a new universe of discourse and meaningful relationships.

and apply our findings to issues of acculturation and cultural competence, we are better able to nuance interaction behaviors and orientations like the trade-off between the sense of identity and belonging provided from a dense co-ethnic network and the pioneering potential and access to resources of a more loosely connected, heterogeneous network.

Strength of Ties

Ever since Granovetter's (1973) insightful study on *The Strength of Weak Ties*, a prominent focus in understanding the utility of social networks has been the strength of ties. Research on the strength of ties has revealed subtle effects of both strong and weak relationships. Of course, strong ties constitute rich channels of social capital that can be drawn upon during stressful cultural transitions. But Granovetter's point was that we often overlook the indirect, less influential, more distant connections in our lives, despite the fact that they offer unique kinds of resources. There is a comfort for the sojourner that is found through routine interactions with acquaintances like a familiar clerk at a store that remembers your name, or a parent you see every day as you drop your children off at school. In Adelman's (1988) examination of social support she notes the important connection between weak ties and cultural adjustment, suggesting that these ties provide essential resources during the *initial* period of adjustment when the expatriate first arrives; not only that, they may continue to provide a unique type of cultural information throughout the host culture stay. Weak ties may offer a gradual pathway toward integration that allows for the maintenance of strong heritage culture or co-ethnic ties, the combination of which may reduce acculturative stress. For example, Horn (1980), writing about Vietnamese immigrants to the United States, concluded that Americanization took a toll on the physical and psychological well-being of the expatriates. Those Vietnamese who spoke English well and had better paying jobs were worse for the wear compared to those who were not in the mainstream and preserved their traditional ways. In fact, Lebon (1983) suggested that maintaining ties with your country of origin early in the acculturation process "safeguards" the migrant's identity and personality, contributing to the person's stability which can be crucial to the eventual integration in the host culture. In contrast to multiplexity or intimacy in a tie, Smith (1996) actually found that frequency of communication within the network is *the* crucial supportive resource necessary for developing cultural sensitivity. Furthermore, he found that intercultural ties are rarely intimate, instead most intercultural supportive ties will be "fairly close friends" with balanced reciprocity as the norm.

That is not to say that strong, multiplex ties are unimportant when in it comes to cultural adjustment, the earlier discussion in this chapter has made that clear. Numerous studies on acculturation and migration have noted that the construction of intimate ties is crucial to adjustment, however it matters not with whom (Boekestijn, 1988; Lebon, 1983; van Bakel et al., 2015). But even research that affirms the value of high-quality intercultural relationships often recognizes there is a cost to developing those relationships that manifests in the form of anxiety and jeopardized co-ethnic identification (van Bakel et al., 2015). Furthermore, from whom an immigrant or expatriate accesses necessary supportive resources may well change over time (Taha & Cox, 2016). Very few immigrants, expatriates, or sojourners inhabit a static relational environment. The nature of cultural transition may well be an evolving set of relationship clusters that the sojourner leans into differentially as identity and social support needs demand. Smith (1996) did find, however, that the life sector from which most of an expatriate's intercultural "close friend" and "intimate friend" relationships will evolve from the workplace, though it will vary by cultural region. It is important to remember that developing strong relationships that reflect what Putnam (2001) called "bonding capital" takes a great deal of time and effort. But in the end, acculturation research has made it clear that over time, inter-ethnic tie strength in general is a good predictor of cultural alienation and interaction uncertainty (Kim, 1987, 1989; Oehlkers, 1991). The adaptive evidence of intimate, cross-cutting socio-cultural relationships is perhaps best captured by Kim (1987) as:

> The degree to which natives are incorporated into the [expatriate's] personal network, the degree to which native ties are strong, and the degree to which they are central in network position, are considered to reflect, as well as facilitate, the [expatriate's] host communication competence and adaptation. (1987, p. 205)

Kim is highlighting the hypothesis that our social networks are both the product and process of our intercultural competence, and hence our cultural adjustment.

Our journey of looking for intercultural ties and bonds now returns us full circle back to Radcliffe-Brown and his notion of structure with dynamic continuity – social networks are the mechanism which establishes boundaries and distinctions thereby defining meaningfulness; and communication within one's network is the process of integration and identity-formation (forming one's personhood) within a community. The final subject area we will consider then, while not technically a network property, is identity formation. The very nature of personal social networks implies a systemic dimension that reflects the idea of communication as both functional and expressive in the creation of personal identities within a community (Collier & Thomas, 1988). Cultural identity is a complex idea that can't be reduced to an easy equation. One way to think about it is to approach it analogically, similar to the way anthropologist Clifford Geertz (1973) described culture as "webs of significance." Culture, like music, says Geertz, is not the behavior of performance, nor the instrument played, nor even the memorized score; but it is rather the signifying meaning created when all three come together in concert. He suggests people are "suspended in" these "webs of significance." In a similar fashion to establishing that signifying universe, identity is gained, or rather understood, in the context of one's social network of connections. Thus, like Geertz's culture, identity emerges not as a causal product or agent, but within a context, a networked *universe of discourse* ascribing significance to things that exist within its confines.

Identity Reconstruction and Maintenance

Several facets of identity have been studied in socio-cultural network research. It is commonly held in the literature that cultural identity is formed on the basis of interdependence, or sense of belonging to a culture-group (Nguyen & Benet-Martínez, 2007). Where that is avoided, the relational mechanism for creating a signifying universe in which the expatriate can be defined in a meaningful way by the host culture is absent. Cupach and Imahori (1993) defined identity as "one's theory of oneself" that provides a sense of ontological status and interpretive frame for experience. *A social network approach posits that our ontological status comes from our defining ties to others.* Some have used the term social identity, others cultural identity, to refer to the notion of role identification with underlying cultural assumptions (Durkheim, 1961). Cupach and Imahori (1993) described cultural identity as encompassing social identity, where social identity refers to the set of roles and group classifications which make up one's self image. In the end, however, even cultural assumptions are realized socially and form what Radcliffe-Browne (1952) called the *person* as opposed to the *individual.* It is that person-hood of the expatriate that can be seen in his or her social network ties. More specifically, recent arguments have been made that social networks consist of both form and symbolic, socio-cultural content, and constitute the "frames for the construction of social identities" (Fuhse, 2012, p. 646; Repke & Benet-Martínez, 2019).

Every immigrant, expatriate, or sojourner must negotiate structural features in finding identity in a multicultural context. Each structure seems to reflect choices, or opportunities, for the inclusion or exclusion of host nationals, co-ethnics, or other internationals in the support framework. These choices impact the stability and the character of the ego's identity. As might be expected, some research suggests that multicultural persons have the capacity to dynamically code-switch between cultural identities depending on the context (Lubbers et al., 2007; Repke & Benet-Martínez, 2017). One of the interesting avenues of intercultural social network research has been the description of different relational architectures and the way in which they shape identity. Smith (1996) presented a portrait of that struggle for identity in the descriptions of U.S. American intercultural networks in Southeast Asia, South America, and East Africa. For example, expatriate networks in Southeast Asia were based more on primary role contexts than typical U.S. American social nets. Gudykunst and Ting-Toomey (1988) described the difference as that of relating and communicating contextually versus personally. A contextual style emphasizes social roles and formality, basing identity on status differences. A personal style is informal, less status oriented, and bases identity on individual personhood. Triandis (1978) made a similar distinction in his universal relation dimension of "intimacy – formality." Thus, Smith (1996) found that in a Southeast Asian culture, the Euro-American's personal identity is constructed much differently than in the native, intracultural setting; personal identity is really a combination of roles, built and defined structurally, and interaction is a meeting of those role constructs. Smith used structural and ethnographic data to illustrate the difficulty in defining one's person versus one's individuality. In another study investigating bicultural identity integration (BII), Repke and Benet-Martinez (2017) also found that social network properties like frequency of interaction and interconnections were better predictors of cultural identification than network composition characteristics like nationality or heritage culture.

In studies on migration, particular properties of social structure have proven to be instrumental in the reconstruction of socio-cultural identity and have shown specific stages of development (Boekestijn, 1988; Hamilton, 1985) (Mok et al., 2007; Wissink & Mazzucato, 2018). Wissink and Mazzucato (2018) found that migrant networks evolved toward slightly higher heterogeneity in response to critical events external to the network, such as local political or economic circumstances. Other research looked at specific coping strategies related to the social integration of expatriates, immigrants, and refugees into the host community. Kamya (1997) found a correlation between African immigrants' spiritual well-being and overall coping resources. The study is important in that it identifies the culture-specific function of establishing new social network ties and associated supportive resources they provide. Spiritual well-being may be nurtured through a variety of stress-relieving behaviors like receiving tangible assistance, affirmation, and acceptance from host nationals as well as finding opportunities to vent emotions (Winkelman, 1994).

In research that explored the formation of collective cultural identities, Pfaff (1996) found that informal social groups, or small social networks, were the central spheres within which collective identity was developed and acted as the foundation for collective action. He explored the manner in which people form loosely structured, dynamic networks of collective narratives that provide the beliefs, values, and ideologies which define communities. The strength and security provided by trusted friends yields the identity framework of solidarity from which action is possible.

The construction of social identity structures has also been studied from a linguistic vantage point. Armstrong and Bauman (1993) asserted that a person's identity is formed as they find themselves in common social situations involving the use of significant language features that indicate relational attachments. Since different sets of linguistic features are used to refer to different relational constructs across cultures, expatriates must learn to properly signify, or mark, their relationships through speech; in so doing they form and maintain their social identities through appropriate marked and unmarked speech. For instance, Armstrong and Bauman found that the "use of informal/casual linguistic or discourse features in a previously impersonal relational context can signal an attempt to assert a more personal relationship with less social distance…" (p. 84). People can easily create proper relational meaning within the speech of their native cultures, but when placed in a novel cultural environment it requires knowledge of new linguistic features and their relevance to common social situations. Armstrong and Bauman offered a connectionist model of sociolinguistic influence for accomplishing this task in intercultural training. They employed a cognitive network model that revealed social identity through a process of matching linguistic features to proper common social situations that then indicated appropriate relational rights and obligations; "the effective use of sociolinguistic features in identity negotiations relies on common knowledge of the associations of such features with relationally well-defined situations in a culture…" (Armstrong & Bauman, 1993, p. 96).

Identity as an integrative function in the study of intercultural relations is essentially the outcome, or product, of intercultural competence or acculturation. In that sense, it warrants increased sophistication in our efforts to model and measure it (Fuhse, 2012; Kim, 2015; Lubbers et al., 2007; Repke & Benet-Martínez, 2019). And approaching the sojourner or immigrant's identity path from a social network perspective enriches the clarity, and arguably the validity, with which we understand the subject matter, as well as lending a concrete image to a previously abstract phenomenon.

Tying Things Up: Where to From Here?

We began the chapter by suggesting that a social network, or socio-structural perspective, offers the lens through which we can explain intercultural relations by examining truly relational data. Throughout the chapter, research that addresses intercultural social networks has been discussed and categorized. We have seen that heterogeneity in social network composition reflects an integration acculturation orientation. And that lower density networks that have host national alters in centralized positions suggests stronger host culture identification and communication competence. But although our understanding of intercultural adjustment, identity, and intercultural communicative competence has increased since the early theorizing around intercultural networks, a great deal has yet to be done to investigate these subjects from a social network perspective.

There are bright spots on the horizon, as a few studies are beginning to reflect either longitudinal or causal designs (e.g., Lubbers et al., 2007; Wissink & Mazzucato, 2018). These kinds of studies are required to move us beyond our current understandings and build on previously offered conclusions. And while there are many cross-cultural studies of social support networks, there are fewer studies conducted on *intercultural* social networks. Given the increasing cultural pluralism in many of our local communities, generating solid empirical descriptions, models and theories of *intercultural* social networks is critical to our continued peaceful coexistence. Similarly, much of the extant research has focused on the integrated or non-integrated social network as an end-state, rather than on the process and mechanisms of relational development and maintenance (Fuhse, 2012; Guest & Stamm, 1993).

Clearly there are gaps in our current understanding that open the door to some intriguing opportunities. First, we have the challenge to represent more accurately the complexity of our social arenas. When and under what relational circumstances is cultural competence acquired during a sojourn or migration journey? And what relational architectures mark particular psychological acculturation orientations? Research foci formerly considered distinct areas need synthesis. Second, we have the on-going challenge of focusing specifically on the "social" nature and explanation of social phenomena without resorting to the aggregation of individuated data. Collecting social network data, especially at the whole system level, is time-intensive. Developing instruments and methods to facilitate that process is needed. Third, we have the challenge of detailing network structure and properties across systems, elaborating on the interconnections between structural properties and communicative properties. Finally, little has been done to investigate how expatriates and sojourners construct new social identities – we have the opportunity to identify how social structure impacts self-understanding and its effect on specific strategies of interrelating. I think it is safe to say with Poole and McPhee (1985), that even after thirty-five plus years, the theoretical and methodological ground of social networks still offers one of the most open and promising avenues for increasing our understanding of intercultural competence, adjustment, and identity in the coming years.

References

Adelman, M. B. (1988). Cross-Cultural Adjustment: A Theoretical Perspective on Social Support. *International Journal of Intercultural Relations, 12*, 183–203.

Adler, P. (1975). The Transitional Experience: An Alternative View of Culture Shock. *Journal of Humanistic Psychology, 15*(4), 13–23.

Adler, P. (1985). Beyond Cultural Identity: Reflections Upon Cultural and Multicultural Man. In L. Samovar & R. E. Porter (Eds.), *Intercultural Communication: A Reader* (4th ed.) (pp. 410–456). Belmont, CA: Wadsworth. (originally published in 1975).

Albrecht, T. L., & Adelman, M. B. (1984). Social Support and Life Stress: New Directions for Communication Research. *Human Communication Research, 11*, 3–32.

Albrecht, T. L., & Adelman, M. B. (1987). *Communicating Social Support.* Newbury Park: Sage.

Ali, A., Van der Zee, K., & Sanders, G. (2003). Determinants of Intercultural Adjustment among Expatriate Spouses. *International Journal of Intercultural Relations, 27*(5), 563–580. https://doi.org/10.1016/S0147-1767(03)00054-3.

Antonucci, T., Fuhrer, R., & Jackson, J. (1990). Social Support and Reciprocity: A Cross-Ethnic and Cross-National Perspective. *Journal of Social and Personal Relationships, 7*, 519–530.

Armstrong, B., & Bauman, I. (1993). A Mathematical Model for Intercultural Interactions: Making Connections and Increasing Harmony. *Journal of Communication, 43*, (1), 81–100.

Barnes, J. A. (1971/2004). *Three Styles in the Study of Kinship*. Routledge. https://doi.org/10.4324/9781315017457.

Belle, D. (1983). The Impact of Poverty on Social Networks and Supports. In L. Lein & M. Sussman (Eds.), *The Ties that Bind: Men's and Women's Social Networks* (pp. 89–103). New York: The Haworth Press.

Berry, J., Kim, U., & Boski, P. (1987). Psychological Acculturation of Immigrants. In Y. Y. Kim & W. B. Gudykunst (Eds.), *Cross-Cultural Adaptation* (pp. 62–89). International and Intercultural Communication Annual Vol. XI. Beverly Hills: Sage.

Bhattacharya, G. (2011). Global Contexts, Social Capital, and Acculturative Stress: Experiences of Indian Immigrant Men in New York City. *Journal of Immigrant and Minority Health, 13*(4), 756–765. https://doi.org/10.1007/s10903-011-9444-y.

Blau, P.M. (1993). Multilevel Structural Analysis. *Social Networks, 15*, 201–215.

Blum, T. C. (1985). Structural Constraints on Interpersonal Relations: A Test of Blau's Macrosociological Theory. *American Journal of Sociology, 91*(3), 511–521.

Bochner, S. (Ed.). (1981). *The Mediating Person*. Schenkman.

Bochner, A. P., Kaminiski, E. P., & Fitzpatrick, M. A. (1977). The Conceptual Domain of Interpersonal Communication Behavior: A Factor-Analytic Study. *Human Communicaiton Research 3(4)*, 291–302.

Boekestijn, C. (1988). Intercultural Migration and the Development of Personal Identity. *International Journal of Intercultural Relations, 12*, 83–105.

Borgatti, S. P. (1995). Centrality and AIDS. *Connections 18 (1)*, 112–114.

Borgatti, S., Everett, M. G., & Johnson, J. C. (2013). *Analyzing Social Networks*. Sage Publications.

Brislin, R. (1981). *Cross-cultural Encounters: Face to Face Interaction*. New York: Pergamon.

Brownell, A., & Shumaker, S.A. (1984). Social Support: An Introduction to a Complex Phenomenon. *Journal of Social Issues, 40*(4), 1–9.

Cantor, M., Brennan, M., & Sainz, A. (1994). The Importance of Ethnicity in the Social Support Systems of Older New Yorkers: A Longitudinal Perspective (1970–1990). *Journal of Gerontological Social Work, 22*(3), 95–128.

Cao, C., Zhu, C., & Meng, Q. (2017). Predicting Chinese International Students' Acculturation Strategies from Socio-Demographic Variables and Social Ties. *Asian Journal of Social Psychology, 20*(2), 85–96. https://doi.org/10.1111/ajsp.12171.

Cheng, Y. (2018), How Social Media Is Changing Crisis Communication Strategies: Evidence from the Updated Literature. *Journal of contingencies and Crisis Management 26*, 58–68. https://doi.org/10.1111/1468-5973.12130

Cheng, Y., Meng, J., & Liu, S. (2018). Personal Network Structure and Perceived Social Support in the Context of Intercultural Adjustment [Article]. *Communication Quarterly, 66*(5), 576–594. https://doi.org/10.1080/01463373.2018.1515782.

Church, A. (1982). Sojourner Adjustment. *Psychological Bulletin, 91*, 540–575.

Clement, R. (1987). Second Language Proficiency and Acculturation: An Investigation of the Effects of Language Status and Individual Characteristics. *Journal of Language and Social Psychology, 5*(4), 271–290.

Collie, P., Kindon, S., Liu, J., & Podsiadlowski, A. (2010). Mindful Identity Negotiations: The Acculturation of Young Assyrian Women in New Zealand. *International Journal of Intercultural Relations, 34*(3), 208–220. https://doi.org/10.1016/j.ijintrel.2009.08.002

Collier, M. J., & Thomas, M. (1988). Cultural Identity: An Interpretive Perspective. In Y. Y. Kim & W. B. Gudykunst (Eds.), *Theories in Intercultural Communication* (pp. 99–122). Newbury Park, CA: Sage.

Cross, S. (1995). Self-Construals, Coping, and Stress in Cross-Cultural Adaptation. *Journal of Cross-Cultural Psychology, 26*, (6), 673–698. *EBSCOhost: Academic Search FullTEXT*. [Online]. Available: EBSCO Publishing. 9601095812 [14 Aug. 1997].

Croucher, S. M. (2011). Social Networking and Cultural Adaptation: A Theoretical Model. *Journal of International & Intercultural Communication, 4*(4), 259–264. https://doi.org/10.1080/17513057.2011.598046.

Cupach, W., & Imahori, T. (1993). Identity Management Theory: Communication Competence in Intercultural Episodes and Relationships. In R. Wiseman & J. Koester (Eds.), *Intercultural Communication Competence* (pp. 112–131). Newbury Park, CA: Sage.

d'Abbs, P. (1982). *Social Support Networks*. Melbourne: Globe Press.

Du, Y., & Wei, M. (2015). Acculturation, Enculturation, Social Connectedness, and Subjective Well-Being Among Chinese International Students. *The Counseling Psychologist, 43*(2), 299–325. https://doi.org/10.1177/0011000014565712

du Plooy, D. R., Lyons, A., & Kashima, E. S. (2020). Social Capital and the Well-Being of Migrants to Australia: Exploring the Role of Generalised Trust and Social nEtwork Resources. *International Journal of Intercultural Relations, 79*, 1–12. https://doi.org/10.1016/j.ijintrel.2020.07.001

Durkheim, E. (1961). *The Elementary Forms of the Religious Life*. New York, NY: Collier Books.

Erickson, B. (1996). Culture, Class, and Connections. *American Journal of Sociology, 102*(1), 217–251.

Faist, T. (2014). Brokerage in Cross-Border Mobility: Social Mechanisms and the (Re)production of Social Inequalities. *Social Inclusion, 2*(4), 38–52. https://doi.org/10.17645/si.v2i4.29.

Fietz, J., & Kaschowitz, J. (2019). Counting on Kin: The Satisfaction of Migrants with Their Social Networks in Germany. *International Journal of Intercultural Relations, 71*, 14–23. https://doi.org/10.1016/j.ijintrel.2019.05.001.

Freeman, L. C., & Wellman, B. (1995). A Note on the Ancestral Toronto Home of Social Network Analysis. *Connections, 18*(2), 15–19.

Fuhse, J. (2012). Embedding the Stranger: Ethnic Categories and Cultural Differences in Social Networks. *Journal of Intercultural Studies, 33*(6), 639–655. https://doi.org/10.1080/07256868.2012.735109.

Garrison, V. (1978). Support Systems of Schizophrenic Puerto Rican Migrant Women in New York City. *Schizophrenia Bulletin, 4*(4), 561–596.

Geertz, C. (1973). *The Interpretation of Cultures*. New York: Basic Books.

Giorgas, D. (2000, December 6–8, 2000). *Social Capital Within Ethnic Communities*. [Paper presentation] TASA 2000 Conference, Adelaide: Flinders University.

Golding, J., & Baezconde-Garbanati, L. (1990). Ethnicity, Culture, and Social Resources. *American Journal of Community Psychology, 18*(3), 465–486.

Gottlieb, B. (Ed.) (1981). *Social Networks and Social Support*. Beverly Hills: Sage.

Granovetter, M. (1973). The Strength of Weak Ties. *American Journal of Sociology, 78*(6), 1360–1380.

Gudykunst, W. B. (1979). Intercultural Contact and Attitude Change: A Review of Literature and Suggestions for Future Research. *International and Intercultural Communication Annual, 4*, 1–16.

Gudykunst, W. B. (1986). Towards a Theory of Intergroup Communication. In W. B. Gudykunst (Ed.), *Intergroup Communication* (pp. 152–167). London: Edward Arnold.

Gudykunst, W. B., & Hammer, M. R. (1988). Strangers and Hosts: An Uncertainty Reduction Based Theory of Intercultural Adaptation. In Y.Y. Kim, & W.B. Gudykunst (Eds.), *Cross-cultural Adaptation: Current Approaches* (pp. 106–139). International and Intercultural Communication Annual, Vol. XI. Newbury Park: Sage.

Gudykunst, W. B., & Ting-Toomey, S. (1988). *Culture and Interpersonal Communication*. Newbury Park: Sage.

Guest, A., & Stamm, K. (1993). Paths of Community Integration. [Online]. *Sociological Quarterly, 34*(4), 581–596.

Hamburg, B.A., & Killilea, M. (1979). Relation of Social Support, Stress, Illness and Use of Health Services. In *Healthy People: The Surgeon General's Report on Health Promotion and Disease Prevention*. Washington, DC: U.S. Department of Health, Education, and Welfare, Public health Service.

Hamilton, G. (1985). Temporary Migration and the Institutionalization of Strategy. *International Journal of Intercultural Relations, 9*, 405–425.

Hammer, M. R. (1987). Behavioral Dimensions of Intercultural Effectiveness: A Replication. *International Journal of Intercultural Relations, 2*(1), 65–88.

Hanvey, R. (1979). Cross-cultural Awareness. *An Attainable Global Perspective* (pp. 8–12). New York: Global Perspectives in Education.

Harris, J. (1973). A Science of the South Pacific: Analysis of the Character Structure of the Peace Corps Volunteer. *American Psychologist,28*, 232–247.

Harrison, A., & Myambo, K. (1995). Perceptions of Social Networks among Adolescents from Zimbabwe and the United States. *Journal of Black Psychology*, (no pp.) November. *EBSCOhost: Academic Search FullTEXT*. [Online]. Available: EBSCO Publishing. [14 Aug. 1997].

Henderson, A. S. (1984). Interpreting the Evidence on Social Support. *Social Psychiatry, 19*, 49–52.

Hendrickson, B., Rosen, D., & Aune, R. K. (2011). An Analysis of Friendship Networks, Social Connectedness, Homesickness, and Satisfaction Levels of International Students. *International Journal of Intercultural Relations, 35*(3), 281–295.

Herskovits, M. (1938). *Acculturation*. Glouchester, MA: Peter Smith.

Horn, J. D. (1980). Vietnamese Immigrants: Doing Poorly by Doing Well. *Psychology Today*, (June), 103–104.

International Organization for Migration. (2021, December). *World Migration Report*. Retrieved from https://worldmigrationreport.iom.int/wmr-2020-interactive/.

Janjuha-Jivraj, S. (2003). The Sustainability of Social Capital within Ethnic Networks. *Journal of Business Ethics, 47*(1), 31–43. http://www.jstor.org.ezproxy.bethel.edu/stable/25075123.

Johansson, F. (2004). *The Medici Effect*. Cambridge: Harvard Business Press.

Johnson, E., Kristof-brown, A., Van Vianen, A., De pater, I., & Klein, M. (2003). Expatriate Social Ties: Personality Antecedents and Consequences for Adjustment. *International Journal of Selection and Assessment, 11*(4), 277–288. https://doi.org/10.1111/j.0965-075X.2003.00251.x

Jou, Y., & Fukada, H. (1995a). Effect of Social Support from Various Sources on the Adjustment of Chinese Students in Japan. *Journal of Social Pyschology, 135*(3), 305–312. *EBSCOhost: Academic Search FullTEXT*. [Online]. Available: EBSCO Publishing. 9509274654 [14 Aug. 1997].

Jou, Y., & Fukada, H. (1995b). Effects of Social Support on Adjustment of Chinese Students in Japan. *Journal of Social Pyschology, 135*(1), 39–48.

EBSCOhost: Academic Search FullTEXT. [Online]. Available: EBSCO Publishing. 9504252009 [14 Aug. 1997].

Jou, Y., & Fukada, H. (1996a). Comparison of Differences in the Association of Social Support and Adjustment between Chinese and Japanese Students in Japan: A Research Note. *Psychological Reports, 79*, 107–112.

Jou, Y., & Fukada, H. (1996b). Influences of Social Supports and Personality on Adjustment of Chinese Students in Japan. *Journal of Applied Social Psychology, 26*(20), 1795–1802.

Jun, Suk-Ho (1984). Communication Patterns among Young Korean Immigrants. *International Journal of Intercultural Relations, 8*, 373–389.

Kadushin, C. (2012). *Understanding Social Networks: Theories, Concepts, and Findings*. Oxford: Oxford University Press.

Kamya, H. (1997). African Immigrants in the United States: The Challenge for Research and Practice. *Social Work, 42*(2), 154–166. *EBSCOhost: Academic Search FullTEXT*. [Online]. Available: EBSCO Publishing. 9704091634 [14 Aug. 1997].

Kang, T. S. (1972). A Foreign Student Group as an Ethnic Community. *International Review of Modern Sociology, 2*, (1), 72–82.

Kathiravelu, L. (2012). Social Networks in Dubai: Informal Solidarities in an Uncaring State. *Journal of Intercultural Studies, 33*(1), 103–119.

Kim, Y. Y. (1977). Communication Patterns of Foreign Immigrants in the Process of Acculturation. *Human Communication Research, 4*, 66–77.

Kim, Y. Y. (1978). A Communication Approach to the Acculturation Process: A Study of Korean Immigrants in Chicago. *International Journal of Intercultural Relations, 2* (2), 197–224.

Kim, Y. Y. (1979). Toward an Interactive Theory of Communication-Acculturation. In D. Nimmo (Ed.), *Communication Yearbook, Vol. 3* (pp. 435–453). New Brunswick, NJ: Transaction Books.

Kim, Y. Y. (1986a). Communication, Information, and Adaptation. In B. D. Ruben (Ed.), *Information and Behavior, 1*. New Brunswick, NJ: Transaction Books.

Kim, Y. Y. (1986b). Understanding the Social Context of Intergroup Communication: A Personal Network Approach. In W. B. Gudykunst (Ed.), *Intergroup Communication* (pp. 86–95). Edward Arnold.

Kim, Y. Y. (1987). Facilitating Immigrant Adaptation: The Role of Communication. In T. Albrecht & M. Adelman (Eds.), *Communicating Social Support* (pp. 192–211). Newbury Park, CA: Sage.

Kim, Y. Y. (1988a). Communication and Acculturation. In L. Samovar & R. Porter (Eds.), *Intercultural Communication: A Reader* (5th ed., pp. 344–352). Belmont, CA: Wadsworth.

Kim, Y. Y. (1989). Intercultural Adaptation. In W. B. Gudykunst & M. K. Asante (Eds.), *Handbook of International and Intercultural Communication* (pp. 275–294). Newbury park: Sage.

Kim, Y. Y. (1991a). Communication and Cross-Cultural Adaptation. In L. Samovar & R. Porter (Eds.), *Intercultural Communication: A Reader* (6th ed., pp. 383–390). Wadsworth.

Kim, Y. Y. (1991b). Intercultural Communication Competence: A Systems-Theoretic View. In S. Ting-Toomey & F. Korzenny (Eds.), *Cross-Cultural Interpersonal Communication* (pp. 259–275). Newbury Park, CA: Sage.

Kim, Y. Y. (2015). Finding a "home" beyond Culture: The Emergence of Intercultural Personhood in the Globalizing World. *International Journal of Intercultural Relations, 46*, 3–12. https://doi.org/10.1016/j.ijintrel.2015.03.018.

Kroeber, A. L., & Kluckhohn, C. (1952). *Culture: A Critical Review of Concepts and Definitions*. Cambridge: Harvard University Press.

Kuo, W., & Tsai, Y. (1986). Social Networking, Hardiness and Immigrant's Mental Health. *Journal of Health and Social Behavior, 27*, 133–149.

Laroche, M., Kim, C., Hu, M., & Joy, A. (1996). An Empirical Study of Multidimensional Ethnic Change. *Journal of Cross-Cultural Psychology, 27*(1), 114–132. *EBSCOhost: Academic Search FullTEXT*. [Online]. Available: EBSCO Publishing. 9601293419 [14 Aug. 1997].

Lebon, A. (1983). Maintien des liens culturels et insertion des migrants: quelles relations? *Revue Francaise des Affaires Sociales, 37*(2), 89–114.

Lee, L.-Y., & Van Vorst, D. (2010, December). The Influences of Social Capital and Social Support on Expatriates' Cultural Adjustment: An Empirical Validation in Taiwan. *International Journal of Management, 27*(3), 628–649.

Lee, S. K. (2014). The Impact of Social Capital in Ethnic Religious Communication Networks on Korean Immigrant's Intercultural Development. *International Journal of Intercultural Relations, 43*, 289–303. https://doi.org/10.1016/j.ijintrel.2014.10.001.

Lein, L. (1983). The Ties That Bind: An Introduction. In L. Lein & M. Sussman (Eds.), *The Ties That Bind: Men's and Women's Social Networks* (pp. 3–7). New York: The Haworth Press.

Levi-Strauss, C. (1949/1969). *The Elementary Structures of Kinship (Les structures elémentaires de la parente)* (J. R. Von Sturmer, Bell, J. H., & Needham, R., Trans. and Rev. ed.). Boston, MA: Beacon Press.

Lin, N. (1986). Conceptualizing Social Support. In N. Lin, A. Dean, & W. Ensel (Eds.), *Social Support, Life Events, and Depression* (pp. 17–30). Orlando: Academic Press, Inc.

Lin, N. (2001). *Social Capital: A Theory of Social Structure and Action* (Vol. 19). Cambridge: Cambridge University Press.

Lin, N., Simone, R., Ensel, W., & Kuo W. (1979). Social Support, Stressful Life Events, and Illness: A Model and an Empirical Test. *Journal of Health and Social Behavior*, *20*(2), 108–119.

Lubbers, M. J., Molina, J. L., & McCarty, C. (2007, 12/01). Personal Networks and Ethnic Identifications: The Case of Migrants in Spain. *International Sociology, 22*(6), 721–741. https://doi.org/10.1177/0268580907082255.

Marsella, A., & Snyder, K. (1981). Stress, Social Supports, and Schizophrenic Disorders: Toward an Interactional Model. *Schizophrenia Bulletin, 7*(1), 152–163.

Martin, J. (1993). Intercultural Communication Competence: A Review. In R. Wiseman & J. Koester (Eds.), *Intercultural Communication Competence* (pp. 16–29). Beverly Hills, CA: Sage.

Martin, J. (2015). Revisiting Intercultural Communicaiton Competence: Where to Go from Here. *International Journal of Intercultural Relations 48,* 6–8.

Meng, Q., Li, J., & Zhu, C. (2021). Towards an Ecological Understanding of Chinese International Students' Intercultural Interactions in Multicultural Contexts: Friendships, Inhibiting Factors and Effects on Global Competence. *Current Psychology, 40,* 1517–1530. https://doi.org/10.1007/s12144-019-00280-3.

Mok, A., Morris, M. W., Benet-Martínez, V., & Karakitapoğlu-Aygün, Z. (2007). Embracing American Culture: Structures of Social Identity and Social Networks among First-Generation Biculturals. *Journal of Cross-Cultural Psychology, 38*(5), 629–635. https://doi.org/10.1177/0022022107305243.

Monge, P. R., & Contractor, N. (2003). *Theories of Communication Networks.* Oxford University Press.

Moreno, J. (1934). *Who Shall Survive?* Boston, MA: Beacon Press.

Neto, F. (2002). Acculturation Strategies among Adolescents from Immigrant Families in Portugal. *International Journal of Intercultural Relations, 26*(1), 17–38. https://doi.org/10.1016/S0147-1767(01)00036-0.

Nguyen, A.-M. D., & Benet-Martínez, V. (2007). Biculturalism Unpacked: Components, Measurement, Individual Differences, and Outcomes. *Social and Personality Psychology, 1*(1), 101–114. https://doi.org/10.1111/j.1751-9004.2007.00029.x

Oehlkers, P. (1991, November). *Networks of Social Support and the Adjustment of Japanese Sojourners in the United States.* Paper presentation The International and Intercultural Communication Division of the Speech Communication Association, Chicago, Il.

Oommen, D. (2014). The Relationships among Perceptions of Social Support, Intercultural Communication Apprehension (ICA), and Conflict Management Preferences in the Context of Cultural Adaptation [Article]. *Journal of Intercultural Communication Research, 43*(3), 215–237. https://doi.org/10.1080/17475759.2014.935797.

Oritt, E., Paul, S., & Behrman, J. (1985). The Perceived Support Network Inventory. *American Journal of Community Psychology, 13*(5), 565–582.

Owusu, T. Y. (1997). *The Adaptation of Black African Immigrants in Canada: A Case Study of Residential Behavior and Ethnic Community Formation among Ghanians in Toronto.* [CD-ROM]. Abstract from: Proquest File: Dissertation Abstracts Item NN11825.

Pfaff, S. (1996). Collective Identity and Informal Groups in Revolutionary Mobilization: East Germany in 1989. *Social Forces,* September. *EBSCOhost: Academic Search FullTEXT.* [Online]. Available: EBSCO Publishing. [14 Aug. 1997].

Poole, M. S., & McPhee, R. (1985). Methodology in Interpersonal Communication Research. In M. Knapp & G. K. Miller (Eds.), *Handbook of Interpersonal Communication* (pp. 100–170). Beverly Hills, CA: Sage.

Putnam, R. D. (2001). Social Capital: Measurement and Consequences. *Canadian Journal of Policy Research, 2*, 41–51.

Radcliffe-Brown, A. (1952). *Structure and Function in Primitive Society, Essays and Addresses.* Glencoe, IL: The Free Press.

Ramos, H. M. L., Mustafa, M., & Haddad, A. R. (2017). Social Support and Expatriate Spouses' Wellbeing: The Mediating Role of Cross-Cultural Adjustment [Article]. *International Journal of Employment Studies, 25*(2), 6–24.

Repke, L., & Benet-Martinez, V. (2017). Conceptualizing the Dynamics between Bicultural Identification and Personal Social Networks [Online]. *Frontiers in Psychology, 8*(469). https://doi.org/10.3389/fpsyg.2017.00469.

Repke, L., & Benet-Martínez, V. (2018). The (Diverse) Company You Keep: Content and Structure of Immigrants' Social Networks as a Window Into Intercultural Relations in Catalonia. *Journal of Cross-Cultural Psychology, 49*(6), 924–944. https://doi.org/10.1177/0022022117733475.

Repke, L., & Benet-Martínez, V. (2019). The Interplay between the One and the Others: Multiple Cultural Identifications and Social Networks. *Journal of Social Issues, 75*(2), 436–459. https://doi.org/10.1111/josi.12323.

Rogers, E. M., & Kincaid, D. L. (1981). *Communication Networks: Toward a New Paradigm for Research.* New York: Free Press.

Schumann, J. H. (1978). *The Pidginization Process: A Model for Second Language Acquisition.* Rowley, MA: Newbury House Pub, Inc.

Scott, J. (1991). *Social Network Analysis: A Handbook*. Beverly Hills, CA: Sage.

Shumaker, S., & Brownell, A. (1984). Toward a Theory of Social Support: Closing Conceptual Gaps. *Journal of Social Issues, 40*(4), 11–36.

Small, C. (1995). The Birth and Growth of a Polynesian Women's Exchange Network. *Oceania, 65*(3), 234–256.

Smith, L. R. (1996). *Intercultural Social Support Networks: A Socio-structural Description of Expatriate Adjustment and Communicative Competence*. Unpublished doctoral dissertation, University of Minnesota, Minneapolis.

Smith, L. R. (1999). Intercultural Network Theory: A Cross-paradigmatic Approach to Acculturation. *International Journal of Intercultural Relations, 23*(4), 629–658.

Smith, L. R. (2005). The Structural Context of Intercultural Personhood: Identity Re-formation. *International Journal of Communication, 15*(1 & 2), 89–112.

Smith, L. R. (2013). Female Refugee Networks: Rebuilding Post-conflict Identity. *International Journal of Intercultural Relations, 37*(1), 11–27. https://doi.org/10.1016/j.ijintrel.2012.04.011.

Smith Pfister, D., & Soliz, J. (2011). (Re)conceptualizing Intercultural Communication in a Networked Society [Article]. *Journal of International & Intercultural Communication, 4*(4), 246–251. https://doi.org/10.1080/17513057.2011.598043.

Spitzberg, B. (1991b). An Examination of Trait Measures of Interpersonal Competence. *Communication Reports, 4*, 1, 22–29.

Spitzberg, B. (1991c). Intercultural Communication Competence. In L. Samovar & R. Porter (Eds.), *Intercultural Communication: A Reader*, (6th ed., pp. 353–365). Belmont, CA: Wadsworth.

Surra, C.A. (1988). The Influence of the Interactive Network on Developing Relationships. In R. Milardo (Ed.), *Families and Social Networks* (pp. 48–82). New York: Sage.

Taha, N., & Cox, A. (2016). International Students' Networks: A Case Study in a UK University [Article]. *Studies in Higher Education, 41*(1), 182–198. https://doi.org/10.1080/03075079.2014.927851.

Triandis, H. C. (1978). Some Universals of Social Behavior. *Personality and Social Psychology Bulletin, 4*, 1–16.

Vacca, R., Solano, G., Lubbers, M. J., Molina, J. L., & McCarty, C. (2018). A Personal Network Approach to the Study of Immigrant Structural Assimilation and Transnationalism. *Social Networks, 53*, 72–89. https://doi.org/10.1016/j.socnet.2016.08.007.

van Bakel, M., van Oudenhoven, J. P., & Gerritsen, M. (2015, 2021-09-10). Developing a High Quality Intercultural Relationship: Expatriates and Their Local Host. *Journal of Global Mobility, 3*(1), 25–45. https://doi.org/10.1108/JGM-04-2014-0009.

Vinokurov, A., Trickett, E. J., & Birman, D. (2017). Community Context Matters: Acculturation and Underemployment of Russian-speaking Refugees. *International Journal of Intercultural Relations, 57*, 42–56. https://doi.org/10.1016/j.ijintrel.2017.02.002.

Ward, C., & Chang, W. C. (1997). "Cultural fit": A New Perspective on Personality and Sojourner Adjustment. *International Journal of Intercultural Relations, 21*(4), 525–533. https://doi.org/10.1016/S0147-1767(97)00023-0.

Ward, C., & Kus, L. (2012). Back to and beyond Berry's Basics: The Conceptualization, Operationalization and Classification of Acculturation. *International Journal of Intercultural Relations, 36*(4), 472–485. https://doi.org/10.1016/j.ijintrel.2012.02.002.

Warriner, C. K. (1981). Levels in the Study of Social Structure. In P. Blau, & R. Merton (Eds.), *Continuities in structural inquiry*. Beverly Hills: Sage.

Wasserman, S., & Faust, K. (1994). *Social Network Analysis: Methods and Applications*. Cambridge: Cambridge University Press.Weimann, G. (1989). Social Networks and Communication. In W. B. Gudykunst & M. K. Asante (Eds.), *Handbook of International and Intercultural Communication* (pp. 186–203). Newbury Park, CA: Sage.

Weiss, M. D. (1996). *Japanese Immigrants in Brazil: A Quantitative Study of Exchange and Cooperation in Two Post-war Agricultural Colonies*. [CD-ROM]. Abstract from: Proquest File: Dissertation Abstracts Item 9631803.

Wellman, B. (1981). Applying Network Analysis to the Study Of Support. In B. Gottlieb (Ed.), *Social Networks and Social Support* (pp. 171–200). Beverly Hills: Sage.

Wellman, B. (1999). *Networks in the Global Village: Life in Contemporary Communities*. New York, NY: Routledge.

Wessendorf, S., & Phillimore, J. (2018). New Migrants' Social Integration, Embedding and Emplacement in Superdiverse Contexts. *Sociology, 53*(1), 123–138. https://doi.org/10.1177/0038038518771843.

Winkelman, M. (1994). Cultural Shock and Adaptation. *Journal of Counseling & Development, 73*(2), 121–127. [Online]. Available: EBSCO Publishing. 9505025747 [14 Aug. 1997].

Wissink, M., & Mazzucato, V. (2018). In Transit: Changing Social Networks of Sub-Saharan African Migrants in Turkey and Greece. *Social Networks, 53*, 30–41. https://doi.org/10.1016/j.socnet.2017.03.005.

Wolfe, A. W. (1978). The Rise of Network Thinking in Anthropology. *Social Networks, 1*, 53–64.

Ying, Y., & Liese, L. (1991). Emotional Well-being of Taiwan Foreign Students in the U.S.: An Examination of Pre- to Post-Arrival Differential. *International Journal of Intercultural Relations, 15*, 345–366.

Ying, Y., & Liese, L. (1994). Initial Adjustment of Taiwanese Students to the United States. *Journal of Cross-Cultural Psychology, 25*(4), 466–478. [Online]. Available: EBSCO Publishing. 9610280089 [14 Aug. 1997].

Yum, J. O. (1982). Communication Patterns and Information Acquisition among Korean Immigrants in Hawaii. *Human Communicaion Research, 8* (2), 154–169.

Yum, J. O. (1983). Social Network Patterns of Five Ethnic Groups in Hawaii. In R. Bostrom (Ed.), *Communication Yearbook,* (Vol. 7, pp. 574–591). Newbury Park, CA: Sage.

Yum, J. O. (1984). Network Analysis. In W.B. Gudykunst & Y.Y. Kim (Eds.), *Methods for Intercultural Communication Research* (pp. 95–116). Beverly Hills, CA: Sage.

Yum, J. O., & Wang, G. (1983). Interethnic Perception and the Communication Behavior among Five Ethnic Groups in Hawaii. *International Journal of Intercultural Relations, 7*(3), 285–308.

Zhang, S., & Kline, S. L. (2009). Can I Make My Own Decision? A Cross-cultural Study of Perceived Social Network Influence in Mate Selection. *Journal of Cross-Cultural Psychology, 40*(1), 3–23. https://doi.org/10.1177/002202210 8326192.

Introduction to Case Study of a Multicultural NPO in Kobe: Viewed from the Perspective of Intercultural Communication

By Noriko Hasegawa and Teruyuki Kume

The last chapter presents an intercultural communication case study of a multicultural nonprofit organization in Kobe, Japan. In particular, it examines how and why such a multicultural community manages to have an environment that is essentially free of prejudices which can often hamper cooperation within a diverse (business) organization. Indeed, stereotypes and prejudices often hinder organizational management. The case study attempts to discover why prejudices were overcome so that other organizations can accomplish a similar tolerant environment. With his Contact Hypothesis, Allport had proposed that prejudices can be reduced through mutual interdependence, common goals, equal status, and social norms that promote and support equality amongst all participants. The case study reveals that preparing and sharing common meals at lunch promoted mutual interdependence because if no one prepared the meals, then no one ended up getting something to eat. And people needed food in order to be able to work. So work progress depended on the availability of meals. By working together on specific projects, members from different ethnic groups had to cooperate in order to accomplish their goals. This also fostered tolerance because people had to cooperate which in turn only functioned well if a community was established. It is pointed out that such cooperation should be carried out in work groups composed of a very heterogeneous members consisting of different academic backgrounds, skills, and experiences – in other words, everyone from the community should be involved and not left out. Everyone should be treated equally without preferences or privileges for specific individuals or groups. The case study was able to demonstrate that such community building helped reduce intolerance. It also revealed that support from the authorities, laws, or customs help reduce prejudices. All in all, it is important to create a work environment that is friendly, open to all, and empathetic. This can be accomplished through heterogeneous work groups and communicating actively in those groups so as to achieve a friendly, open, and empathetic work environment. That is why this case study provides important guidelines on how companies can overcome potential intolerance amongst its workforce. If a company manages to create a tolerant environment, then it will profit from the benefits associated with diversity.

Michael B. Hinner

Noriko Hasegawa is a Professor of Intercultural Communication in the School of Humanities at Hokusei Gakuen University, Sapporo, Japan. Her research interests are intercultural communication between Koreans and Japanese, effects of viewing foreign TV dramas on prejudice reduction, and teaching methods of intercultural communication. Her Japanese publications include the co-authored books *Introduction to Intercultural Communication, Intercultural Communication Through Case Studies, Research Methods of Intercultural Communication* (all from Yuhikaku, Japan), *Challenges Facing a Multicultural Japan: From the Perspective of Multicultural Relations Studies* (Akashi Shoten, Japan), and *Encyclopedia of Intercultural Communication* (Shunpusha, Japan). She authored A Quantitative Analysis of Japanese Images of Korea: Perceptual Changes Brought About by TV Drama Viewing in *Intercultural Communication Studies*, and co-authored A Cross-Cultural Comparison of Chinese and Japanese Communication Styles: Focusing on Small Group Discussion in Micheal B. Hinner (Ed.), *Chinese Culture in a Cross-Cultural Comparison*, Peter Lang, GmbH. She received her M.A. in Communication Studies from the University of Kansas in 1990, and her Ph.D. in Media, Society, and Culture from The Graduate University for Advanced Studies, Sokendai, Japan in 2008. Her master's thesis investigated Heroes and Heroines in Japanese Comic Magazines: An Analysis of Sex Role Stereotypes. Her doctoral dissertation explored Effects of Empathic Viewing of Korean TV Drama on Prejudice Reduction. She teaches courses and seminars on intercultural communication, both in the undergraduate and graduate schools of Hokusei Gakuen University. She also serves as a referee / reviewer for the academic journals *Intercultural Communication* and *Multicultural Relations.*

Teruyuki Kume received Ph.D. from University of Minnesota in 1979, and has taught in four universities in Japan, retiring as Professor of Intercultural Communication at Rikkyo University in 2014. Research interests include communication styles, leadership, and decision-making in multicultural organizational settings. He was co-editor and author of *Encyclopedia of Intercultural Communication* (Shunpusha), *Introduction to Intercultural Communication, Intercultural Communication Keywords, Intercultural Communication Through Case Studies, Theories of Intercultural Communication and Research Methods of Intercultural Communication* (Yuhikaku), and *Challenges Facing a Multicultural Japan: From the Perspective of Multicultural Relations Studies* (Akashi Shoten, 2011). He authored *Exploratory Study of Japanese Approaches to Decision-Making in the United States* (Ph.D. dissertation, Ann Arbor, MI: UMI, 1979); Managerial Attitudes Toward Decision-Making: North America and Japan in W. B. Gudykunst et al. (Eds.), *Communication, Culture, and Organizational Process,* Sage, 1985; Contrastive Prototypes of Communication Styles in Decision-Making: Mawashi Style vs. Tooshi Style in Michael B. Hinner (Ed.) *The Influence of Culture in the World of Business,* Peter Lang, 2006); and co-authored A Cross-Cultural Comparison of Chinese and Japanese Communication Styles: Focusing on Small Group Discussion in Michael B. Hinner (Ed.), *Chinese Culture in a Cross-Cultural Comparison,* Peter Lang, 2014. He was Associate Director of Intercultural Communication Institute at Kanda University of International Studies (1990~2000), Fulbright Visiting Professor at Mankato State University (1984), Fulbright Visiting Scholar at East-West Center (1998), and President of Japan Society for Multicultural Relations (2009~2013). He is currently coleader of Proposal Team for Asia Pacific Multicultural Collaboration Center to be established in Okinawa, Japan.

Noriko Hasegawa and Teruyuki Kume

Case Study of a Multicultural NPO in Kobe: Viewed from the Perspective of Intercultural Communication

Introduction

The purpose of this paper is to examine the nature and style of leadership of an NPO named Takatori Community Center (TCC) from the perspective of intercultural communication. Major factors are identified that have contributed to develop and sustain its uncommon organizational culture, which facilitates frank, smooth, and meaningful communication among the multicultural members of the TCC (https://tcc117.jp/).

As of 2000, TCC became a nonprofit organization supporting the local community in Nagata ward of Kobe City, whose residents were predominantly working class, and about 10 % were foreigners when the Great Hanshin Awaji Earthquake occurred in 1995. While its major focus had been various relief activities for about 5 years post-Earthquake, more recently TCC has been engaged in various community-oriented activities, striving to build a better multicultural community, where all of the people with different cultural backgrounds can support each other and work together.

Current Activities of TCC

TCC strives for multicultural community building, where all people can enjoy full participation regardless of their nationality, age, gender, and/or disability. It now holds 10 groups that target different people in the community (see Table 1). These 10 groups share the space allotted by Catholic Takatori Church, and are both independently working and sometimes collaborating with each other. We consider TCC one of the most successful multicultural NPOs, as it has maintained its initial purpose and vibrant activities, while also transforming its organizational structure, as it grew to include a wide range of activities for building multicultural community.

Table 1: Groups of TCC and Their Activities

Group of TCC	Activities of Group
FM YY, Multilingual Community Broadcasting Station	Airs programs in 10 languages
Multilanguage Center FACIL	Offers translation and interpreting service in 28 languages
World Kids Community	Offers children of mixed roots opportunities to express themselves through film production, anime, and so forth
Hyogo Latin Community	Helps Spanish speaking families throughout Japan
NGO Vietnam in Kobe	Provides support for the Vietnamese community
Asia Women's Self-Reliance Support Project	Empowers Asian women through fair trade and so forth
Leaf Green	Supports aged and disabled people
Noda-Kita Furusato Net	Helps the community network in Nagata
Hyogon Tech	Provides IT support for local residents
AMARC Japan Council	International NGO of community radio

Notes. TCC (Takatori Community Center) became an NPO in 2000.

Out of the 10 Groups of TCC, FM YY, Multilanguage Center FACIL, Asia Women's Self-Reliance Support Project, and Leaf Green are also incorporated as NPO.

Research Methods

Our research involved two primary modes of data collection: interviews with key persons, and review of archival material and published materials such as books, articles, and dissertations on TCC. Face-to-face life-story interviews were conducted during the period from July, 2011 through 2012. Also, a total of 200 minutes of follow-up on-line interviews were conducted on August, 2021. A total of seven staff members were interviewed to examine how this uncommon multicultural organizational culture was built and sustained for more than a quarter of a century (see Table 2).

Table 2: Participants Interviewed

Name	Title/Position	Interview Date	Duration
H. Kanda	Representative Director	2011-10-21	120 minutes
J. Hibino	Senior Managing Director	2011-7-24	90 minutes
S. Yoshitomi	Senior Executive Director	2011-7-24 & 2021-8-3	210 minutes
H. Kanaji	Former Staff Member	2011-10-21	120 minutes
K. Murakami	Secretary General	2011-7-6 & 2021-8-13	180 minutes
R. Oshiro	Representative, Hyogo Latin Community	2011-7-6	40 minutes
K. Yoshimoto	Representative, Leaf Green	2011-7-6	60 minutes

Review of Literature on TCC and Its Subgroups

Kanaji (2008) conducted an ethnographic study of TCC based on 6-year-participant-observation from 2002 through 2007. The findings of his research indicated that TCC has succeeded in identifying and claim-making of social problems that foreign residents faced, which both national and local governments were unaware of. Also, he vividly reported how foreign evacuees and Japanese evacuees and volunteers gradually built their rapport, through eating supper together every night and sharing the life stories of the minority members. His report clearly showed that the foundation of TCC's uncommon organizational culture was created and solidified during its first 2 years when relief activities were vigorously undertaken post-Earthquake.

Yoshitomi (2006) described the formative process of a particular self-help organization for newly arrived Brazilians called "Brazilian Community of Kansai," and emphasized the necessity of self-reliance of these self-help organizations. Yoshitomi (2008a, 2008b) explained in detail how she came to the idea of a new type of community business model, which encouraged minority members to be leaders, thus leading to the empowerment of minority foreign residents. Also, Yoshitomi (2013a, 2013b) advocated for the necessity of formulating an inclusive disaster management plan, tailored for the majority as well as minority members. She pointed out the importance of making full use of the multilanguage network and multilanguage community radio to help immigrants, whose human rights are the least protected in times of emergency.

Hibino (2007) explained how they established a mini-FM multilingual radio station called FM YY in order to deliver necessary information to the impacted residents in the community of Kobe right after the onset of the earthquake. He reported that speaking in and listening to their mother tongue in times of emergency warmed the victims' hearts immensely. The listeners as well as announcers felt strongly bonded through the messages exchanged and music aired in their mother tongue. He also described how the minority volunteer announcers regained confidence as their roles changed from being helped to being the helper.

Kume and Matsuda (2013) examined the nature and style of leadership, particularly by the top three directors of TCC, that most likely contributed a great deal to the smooth development and management of TCC. The authors concluded that the uncommon nature and style of collective leadership, as illustrated by the complimentary triangle of relations of the three leaders (see Figure 1), and the three visions they shared were essential factors for the sustenance of TCC.

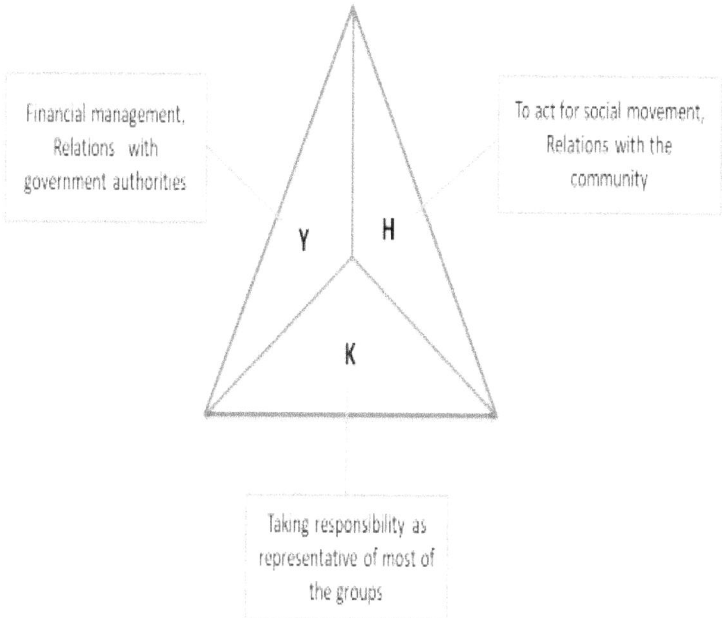

Figure 1: Complimentary-Triangle Relations of the Three Leaders and Their Specialties

The first vision is expressed in the slogan that "unless the minority is saved, the whole society cannot be happy." The leaders of TCC agreed that their mission was to build a multicultural community where every one of the minority members can live their lives fully. The second vision is empowerment of the socially vulnerable. Under this vision, some of the foreign members came to assume leadership in TCC's subgroups. The third vision is making full use of the varied multicultural resources in the community. The authors concluded that their principle of including everybody who needs support as a beneficiary of their efforts, successfully attracted diverse supporters and volunteers, and TCC functions as a Meeting Plaza for those who share the same vision.

Early Stage of TCC from Stories of Top Three Leaders

Kanda's Story

Takatori Church Relief Base (the original name of TCC) was born "accidentally" on the day after the Earthquake within the premises of the burnt down Catholic

Takatori Church. This church was situated in the western end of Nagata Ward, where most of the city was completely burned out. Many volunteers gathered there because someone in the vicinity of the church had kept building a fire every night, making use of wood piled up in and outside of the destroyed church compound. Rescue work developed in various directions depending on the changing needs of the victims, such as preparing warm food, removing furniture from the crashed houses, and providing accurate information to those who had problems in understanding information in Japanese for receiving necessary support. Within 2 weeks after the quake, Kanda, then the Father of the church, organized a group called Relief Committee for the Vietnamese, because there was a sizable number of Vietnamese concentrated in this area, who came to Japan in the 80s and 90s as refugees.

As for why he started the Relief Committee for foreigners, he responded,

> I have great regret for not being able to do rescue work right after the quake. At that time, I did not know who was living in the vicinity of the church. So, I couldn't tell how many people were trapped in the rubble, and I was of no help … 120 to 130 people died, buried, and burned around the church, and still I was useless. So, I started volunteer work for the community with my conviction that I will never feel such bitterness again.

For him, the community naturally included everybody who was living in nearby towns regardless of religion or nationality. He said that after the church building was burned down, he realized that the church was not the building itself. With no wall around the church compound, more people in need of help came naturally, and he knew that the church could be a meeting place where something new and good happens.

Hibino's Story

At the time of the quake, Hibino, an ex-reporter of the *Mainichi* newspaper, was planning to visit Bosnia as a free-lance cameraman. However, after the onset of the quake, he changed his mind and decided to go to Nagata, as it was a famous site of devastation. In Nagata, he visited one of the parks called Minami Komae Park where hundreds of Vietnamese and Japanese had evacuated to. However, the Vietnamese and the Japanese were divided into two groups, quarreling and sometimes lashing out at each other over the relief supplies such as food, blankets, and other necessities. As he came to know Father Kanda was respected by the Vietnamese, he decided to go to the Relief Base to see him. At that time, he started his full-time volunteer work there, going back and forth between the Takatori Relief Base and the various parks, with the Base being his place to sleep.

In March, 1995, Kanda and Hibino met a few Korean volunteers from a community FM radio station from Osaka, and came up with an idea of starting a community multilingual FM radio station. Their radio station broadcast such vital information as the names of surviving friends and relatives, the location of bathing houses, and the ways and means to get some donations, money, and other materials to suffering foreign residents, including Vietnamese, Koreans, and Chinese.

At about the same time, Kanda and Hibino organized a group called the Asia Town Promotion Consultative Body to make the town more multicultural. Their activities included producing multilingual signposts and placing them around the town as well as multilingual advertisements in the market, and promoting an Asian food and goods market. Under Kanda's leadership, Hibino managed the whole group of volunteers including Koreans and Vietnamese. Later, he became the manager of the "Tool de Communication" that provided IT support for the elderly, the disabled, and foreign residents.

Yoshitomi's Story

Right after graduating from college in the early 1980s, Yoshitomi worked for the Spanish Consulate and later for the Bolivia Honorary Consulate in Kobe. Because of her fluency in Spanish, she helped many Latin American immigrants who came to Japan in the early 1990s. After the quake, hearing that Nagata Ward was heavily devasted, she visited Kanda 2 days after the quake at the Takatori Relief Base, and started her volunteer work as his secretary, engaging herself in various kinds of rescue work. Yoshitomi started a community radio station called FM YY with Hibino, and she herself became a voluntary announcer in charge of Spanish and Japanese. She emphasized that in such an unprecedented disaster, it was urgently needed to broadcast the necessary information in various languages, and alleviate the anxiety minority victims felt. This conviction led her to establish Multilanguage Center FACIL in 1999, which is now regarded the most successful of the 10 TCC groups.

Characteristics of TCC that Facilitate Multicultural Community Building

So far, we have provided an overview of the reports, papers, and dissertations on TCC and presented brief summaries of the interviews of the three leaders. In this section, we analyze the interview transcripts from the perspective of intercultural communication. We also identify major factors that have contributed in developing and sustaining this uncommon organizational culture, which facilitates frank, smooth, and meaningful communication among multicultural members of the TCC.

Atmosphere Facilitating Prejudice Reduction

In any multicultural organization, problems concerning stereotypes and prejudice among members are major issues that hinder smooth organizational management. However, at TCC a very low level of threat or prejudice was felt between the members, and every member seemed to feel at home regardless of their religion or nationality. TCC became a safe haven for the minority members, especially during the turmoil in the aftermath of the quake, and it continues to be so even 25 years later.

In this section, we analyze how this uncommon organizational culture was built, using Contact Hypothesis (Allport, 1954) as the key concept. Contact Hypothesis, first introduced by Gordon Allport in 1954, holds that contact between two groups can promote tolerance and acceptance only under certain conditions. Studies and experiments have shown that the following conditions facilitate prejudice reduction: (a) mutual interdependence, (b) common goals, (c) equal status, and (d) social norms that promote and support equality among groups (Pettigrew & Tropp, 2006).

Mutual Interdependence

The first condition for prejudice reduction is intergroup cooperation. Empirical research as well as meta-analysis of the research has confirmed the positive impact of cooperation for building positive peer relationships and helpfulness, both of which lead to prejudice reduction (Johnson & Johnson, 1989; Roseth et al., 2008). At TCC, all of the group leaders met on a regular basis to share the problems each group faced, and to solve them together by giving and receiving advice. These liaison meetings served for sharing and affirming the values of TCC, as well as for building comradery among TCC members. Although only the leaders of each group attended these liaison meetings, lunch meetings were held twice a week, and anybody who worked at various TCC groups enjoyed the international cuisine made by volunteers from Vietnam, Korea, Philippines, and Peru. Kanda said,

> Basically, on Mondays, Korean cuisine, on Wednesdays, Vietnam cuisine, and once a month, Chinese and Peruvian food is served at the TCC cafeteria. Cooks are mostly minority women who are victims of the quake. They volunteered to be the cooks because they wanted to show their gratitude for the volunteers at TCC who worked so hard in helping them.

In this way, the cafeteria served to induce an atmosphere of cooperation and mutual interdependence between the victims and the volunteers.

According to Kanaji (2008), this kind of lunch meeting once ended for a short period of time as older cooks "felt it too much work" (p. 117). However, after they stopped serving lunch and volunteers started having their own lunch at various places independently, the chances of exchanging banter or small-talk among volunteers reduced dramatically, and conflict among members increased. A stiff and unfriendly atmosphere prevailed at TCC then, and Kanda strongly felt the importance of eating the same food together on a regular basis.

Kanda addressed the importance of eating together:

> We as the members of TCC regard cooking, serving, and eating food together as the center of our volunteer work. Everybody enjoyed small-talk between the members and memories at the cafeteria enriched our life itself, and I came to feel as if this kind of experience was "food for the soul" for everybody. I myself sometimes felt as if I had reached an impasse, felt frustrated and irritated for not achieving the goal. But, on those days, once I came to the cafeteria and ate warm food prepared by "Okaasan-tachi [Mothers in Japanese]" with other volunteer workers, I could regain my energy and myself.

It can be seen that the casual and easy atmosphere at lunch time greatly helped in creating TCC's uncommon organizational culture. According to Yoshitomi and Murakami, they had maintained the custom of eating lunch together and holding liaison meetings regularly, until the Covid-19 calamity started. It is clear that TCC's culture of cooperation continues.

Common Goals

Research confirmed that sharing common goals among group members led to prejudice reduction (Gaertner & Dovidio, 2005). At TCC, leaders as well as members from each group shared the slogan that each group must work together for their common goals; that is building a multicultural community where every one of the minority members can live their life fully. Under this superordinate goal, groups worked on problem-solving of their own choice such as helping Asian women, minority children, or foreign immigrants. In this way, the independent activities of each group contributed to attaining the superordinate goal of the TCC. Father Kanda explained how he started the relief activity:

> We realized foreigners living in the community suffered most from the quake, facing language differences, unfriendly social systems, and emotional barriers. Those unsolved social problems did exist even before the quake. But with the shock of the quake, they suddenly came to the surface and started torturing them even more... . Before the

> quake, Kobe had been proudly promoting its image of being an international city and most of us believed it was. However, it wasn't. Kobe was not an international city at all. The local government ostracized foreigners when they really needed help. Realizing their predicament, we started our activities to help them live their lives fully.

The volunteer work that started solely for helping the victims of the quake led to other relief activities, and finally to community building. In Father Kanda's words,

> Struggles with rubble turned to covering roofs with blue tarps, and then we started making furniture and building temporary houses. When we were almost done with the building activity, we changed our focus to making everyone's life back to normal. We started creating our future. Two years passed since the quake, and we finally started walking toward the future. Now, I realized what we need to do is building community.

About how their volunteer work led to multicultural community building, Hibino explained it this way:

> While working for the opening of FM YY, I came to have one conviction. That is, "diversity" does not mean only about living with foreigners. Young and old, and foreigners with different values live together, and are helping each other… . We need to build such a community. Only when we succeeded in building a community where all the residents live happily together based on mutual understanding, regardless of differences, can we call our community a "town of multicultural symbiosis," which we can truly be proud of.

About how to build and sustain such community, he emphasized the importance of involving people who were indifferent to minority residents. Hibino continued,

> While I was engaged in broadcasting at FM YY, I realized the importance of producing programs that appeal to everybody. If our program only broadcast a message about human rights, people would lose interest and stop listening. We may become like an "exclusive club of Minority Geeks" for scholars of minority studies, or people who are into the problem solving of minority people. The same is true for our activities. In order to make our activity of community building truly sustainable, we need to involve everyone in the community.

Yoshitomi also emphasized the importance of involving people who were indifferent to the predicament of foreign residents, and stimulating their concern. She continued,

> Establishing policies and changing laws are of course important. But even if we achieve such institutional changes, we can't change people's true feelings. If the law forces people to accept minorities, people just pretend to accept them. I believe what is important is the process (of causing attitudinal change). I mean, those who have little interest in human rights sometimes changed their attitudes, and gradually came to be concerned about them.

With strong convictions about building a multicultural community, the leaders at TCC started planning various fun activities, such as an Asian Market, Summer Festivals, Folk Art Festivals, and tried to open its door to everyone in the community, so that the chances of interaction between minority residents and Japanese residents would increase. Yoshitomi believed that continuation of such small endeavors would send the message that "difference is fun" to people in the community, which would invite them to open their hearts.

In this way, TCC tried a soft approach to facilitate change in people's attitude toward minority residents. By trying to be a friendly and open organization, where members as well as non-members were always welcome, and volunteers and staff as well as visitors could enjoy an easy and fun atmosphere, they believed that they were getting close to building true multicultural community, where people of different nationality mingle with each other, and minority members would be whole-heartedly accepted by majority members.

Equal Status

Researchers who tested Contact Hypothesis (Allport, 1954) found equal status between members was an important condition for prejudice reduction. Basically, differences in academic backgrounds, wealth, skill, or experiences should be minimized because they hinder achieving equality among members (Paluck & Green, 2008). However, in the first phase of the TCC, volunteers came from all over Japan and their age, social class, educational background, skills, and experiences differed greatly. Still, they seemed to enjoy equal status and help each other regardless of their differences.

The equality rule was first introduced in the aftermath of the quake by one of the volunteers who started calling other volunteers by nicknames he improvised (Kanaji, 2008). In Japan, where being polite, modest, and formal is regarded as a matter of the utmost importance in every aspect of social life, it is very rare for NPO staff or volunteers to be on a first-name basis. But at TCC, especially in the first 2 years when so many people at Nagata were in dire conditions and in desperate need, this unusual casual atmosphere of everybody being on a nickname basis helped greatly in generating a sense of comradeship among volunteers.

As for minority members, they are regarded as beneficiaries as well as benefactors, and three leaders at TCC endeavored to make minority members be equal partners. For example, Yoshitomi talked about an immigrant woman from Peru, who came to Japan in 1991 with her Peruvian husband. When the quake hit Kobe, she was panicked, not knowing what to do with her limited Japanese.

But, later with help and encouragement of Yoshitomi and other TCC members, she became the leader of Hyogo Latin Community. She explained how she came to take the leader's role:

> I visited TCC for receiving counseling service in 2000. My son was attending Japanese school, but, not only he but also I did not understand Japanese. I asked Yoshitomi-san what to do about my son, school, and hospital, and so forth. She helped me a lot, giving me various concrete advice. Since I was helped, I realized that I should help others, too. She suggested I could start a Latin Community. So, I did.

This is a typical example of TCC leaders' endeavors of empowering minority members as equal partners. We can find a similar idea in the manner that Leaf Green, which supports aged and disabled people, is being operated. According to Yoshimoto, who then was a leader of Leaf Green, the basic principle there was that helpers should stand on an equal footing with those helped. To embody this kind of basic principle, Leaf Green adopts a policy of asking the same membership fee for those who help and those who are helped.

Similarly, in managing Multilanguage Center FACIL, Yoshitomi emphasized the importance of creating employment opportunities for foreign residents. She believes that only with financial security, can foreign residents empower themselves, leaving the position of charity recipient, and being in control of their life. Also, she believes in the power of sharing, helping each other, and learning together, and thinks TCC's endeavors will help rectify some of the problems of Japanese society. She said,

> Those of us who were born in Japan have many advantages, thus [we] have the responsibility to make a minority-friendly society, where everyone has an equal chance, and those with talent and good education should be rewarded with suitable jobs. I repeatedly told the minority members, "We are learning from you. You are helping us realize the problems of Japanese society, which Japanese people are ignorant or unaware of."

Yoshitomi also spoke of the role of the minority members:

> Communicating with the minority members made me realize what's missing or wrong in Japanese society. The Japanese people can't see what foreign residents notice easily. We need to rectify what's wrong with our society with the help of their perspective. They present us the chance to change our society.

With her conviction and endeavors, Yoshitomi appeared successful in instilling a spirit of cooperation, which was conducive to the acknowledgment of equality among members with various cultural backgrounds.

Social Norms that Promote and Support Equality Among Groups

The result of research shows that the support of authorities, laws, or customs work for reducing prejudice toward minority groups (Crandall & Stangor, 2005). As for Hyogo Prefecture, where TCC is located, under the slogan of multicultural symbiosis or building multicultural community, "Guidelines for Promotion of Internationalization of Hyogo Prefecture" were first published in 1994, updated in 2016, and they continue trying to make the city more friendly for its foreign residents. Thus, authorities of Hyogo Prefecture and Kobe City were both supposed to be supportive of minority groups. Most of the NPO groups at TCC received monetary support from the local government, especially during their launching period.

The Catholic Takatori Church, which belongs to the Osaka Congregation, gave TCC permission to share its space. In Japan, it is very unusual for the Catholic Church to give an NPO with no religious connection, permission to use the church compound. This fact alone shows how the church gives special attention to TCC and its activities. Also, a Representative of the Osaka Congregation, as well as the Pope himself, sent warm messages and blessings for the opening ceremony of the FM YY in 1996, for facilitating bonding among members with different cultural backgrounds and beyond national, ethnic, and religious differences.

Thus, it could be seen that both the government and the Catholic Church supported TCC's activities. Their position of regarding friendships between minority members and Japanese residents or among minority members positively, may in fact have helped in inducing its multicultural organizational culture.

TCC's Laid-Back and Friendly Atmosphere that Welcomes Diversity

The literature on decreasing prejudice and stereotypes has shown that a friendly and informal atmosphere may contribute a great deal (Brewer & Miller, 1984; Wilder, 1986). At TCC, as was explained above, by eating together regularly, calling others by nicknames, and empowering minority members, equality among members was beginning to be established, all of which helped in creating a laid-back and happy atmosphere. Murakami, now the manager of TCC and FACIL, explained TCC's culture this way:

> At the TCC, those of us with different backgrounds and values just get together naturally. Even when we have different opinions, we can enjoy working together, laughing with each other, and sharing the space. That's what's nice about the TCC. We try not to eliminate those with different opinions. Our slogan is Yuru Yuru Tabunka Ito-okashi, that is, loosely [connected] multicultural [community is] enjoyable. Multicultural community we aspire to is one where people with different backgrounds live together, loosely connected, and enjoying each other's company. We will keep appealing to the

> necessity of making a climate where everybody can just be themselves. That will always be our motto.

Hibino also talked about the culture of TCC that embraces differences in the following manner:

> Many volunteers joined and left TCC. The main reason why TCC attracted them is the space of TCC, cuisine, and time. Sharing of these things is quite important for our communication and discussion. What's more, we had Koreans and Vietnamese and others. Various kinds of people joined us and did so many things together to get our ideas materialized… . There have always been people of diverse cultural backgrounds, meeting and working with us here. Together, we learned about flexible ways of living together.

In a similar context, Yoshitomi said, "Working with diverse cultural groups gives me sharper viewpoints." These statements imply that the leaders' positive attitudes toward foreign residents greatly contributed in begetting TCC's most unusual culture that welcomes cultural difference.

Empathy Building

Decades of research on prejudice reduction have indicated that empathy for the outgroup members can reduce prejudice, and significantly improve intergroup relations (Batson et al., 2009; Eisenberg et al., 2010; Mealy & Stephan, 2010; Stephan & Finlay, 1999). Also, it has been demonstrated that empathy induced for a single member of the outgroup tends to generalize to the entire group that the individual belongs to (Batson et al., 2002; Finlay & Stephan, 2000). In this section, we explain how empathy toward outgroup members at TCC helped in reducing prejudice among members, and thus helped to solidify the group itself as well as building multicultural community.

Kanda and Hibino both repeatedly talked about the empathy inducing narrative of one Vietnamese man. According to Hibino, the memorable event of reconciliation between Vietnamese and Japanese who had been bickering with each other occurred at the Minami Komae Park, where evacuees who had lost their houses were temporarily living.

> The leader of the Vietnamese group started talking about their history. Like, Vietnam became a French colony, and then was divided into North and South and the War with U.S. started… . They were squeezed into a small boat and left the country, and were rescued by a ship. He talked of various things at that time. After his talk, Japanese men who had been severely prejudiced sincerely apologized to the Vietnamese… . Those who had openly professed their dislike of the Vietnamese changed their attitude drastically in just 30 minutes. The Vietnamese man sincerely talked with his faltering Japanese, and

> his narrative moved Japanese men. In the end, they finally shook hands and affirmed their comradeships. When I saw what had happened … institutional barrier, emotional barrier, language barrier … there are many barriers between majority and minority members … I realized that we can cope with them. After the quake, we had many such similar experiences. Old volunteer members like us treasure these experiences dearly.

Hibino named this day their important "starting point," and cherished this memory as their "day of reconciliation." He continued:

> I saw and experienced the process of reconciliation. In 3 months, volunteers started recognizing each other and then calling each other by name. Before, the conflict between them was so severe and sometimes even the police had to intervene. But, through such everyday common experiences and chatting, teaching, and learning together at the cafeteria or meetings, we set about making the foundation of our organization.

It can be seen that the life story of one Vietnamese man made the Japanese men realize that the person in front of them was not just a foreigner with whom they felt no connection, but rather a human being who had experienced extreme hardship, as they had. The commonality those Japanese evacuees found with the Vietnamese men was even more important, as everybody at the Komae Park felt completely closed, shuttered, with their houses burned down and so little left with them. Through listening to the heart-felt narratives and taking the perspective of the Vietnamese men, the Japanese evacuees were able to empathize with them, and thus greatly changed their attitudes.

Taking the perspective of the minority groups has continued on to the leaders of the TCC even after 25 years. In his interview conducted this year, Murakami, who has been working as a manager at several TCC groups since 2001 explained:

> We need to be a bonding agent, or person who works as a liaison, and connect minorities and the majority members of the community. For example, local people often say they don't like foreigners, as they disregard rules for garbage disposal and have bad manners. However, from our viewpoint, foreigners are not to blame. They just don't know how, as nobody explained the rules to them. Even we Japanese sometimes have trouble sorting garbage out based on the complex rules City of Kobe made. Foreign residents try to follow what Japanese residents seem to do just by looking at them, but get scolded for not keeping the rule. They just get so confused, not knowing what to do. We must change perspective from ours to theirs. It's not "their manners are bad," but "it's our society that vexed them." We at TCC feel responsible for making a system for conveying important and necessary information to foreign residents, so that they can lead their lives without trouble. Also, I believe we need to work as a liaison and help majority members to be able to see such an incident from the perspective of foreign residents.

Twenty-five years after the quake, TCC's spirit of empathy toward minority members of the community appears alive and well. The good use of such leaders' empathic attitudes communicates the message that they are welcome and accepted as equal members of the community.

Implications

In this paper, we examined a most unusual NPO that has been successfully carrying out its activities for more than 25 years since its inception, utilizing the perspective of intercultural communication. Analysis showed that TCC's leaders, staff, and volunteers basically follow the conditions given by Contact Hypothesis (Allport, 1954) for reducing prejudice, without their conscious effort. They reported following their hearts and/or doing what they believed they had to do. They cooperated with each other, strove to maintain positive peer relationships, and helped each other. In each phase, holding to common goals worked as the key agent that united members. A new goal was set depending on the demands of the situation, thus their focus changed from rescuing victims of the earthquake to helping all people and contributing to building a viable multicultural community. In its early phases, members spontaneously developed collegial relationships, and later, minority members were empowered and became equal partners with the support and help of Japanese leaders. The City of Kobe and the Catholic Church also supported TCC's activities.

The authors consider the fact that TCC satisfied the four conditions for reducing prejudice as specified by Contact Hypothesis (Allport, 1954), is part of the reason that TCC has been unusually successful in establishing and managing its multicultural organization. Among the factors that contributed to reducing prejudice, we believe that the most important factor is empathy, as that worked as the bonding agent between members with different backgrounds.

As can be seen from the example of the Vietnamese man's narrative, which led to prejudice reduction of the Japanese, empathy sometimes worked miracles. For example, Hasegawa (2005a, 2005b, 2007a) found a strong effect of empathy in reducing prejudice toward Koreans, through a questionnaire and interview study of viewers of Korean drama. As Japan and Korea have a long and sad history ever since Japan colonized Korea, Koreans and Korean Japanese have long been the target of prejudice in Japan. Scholars as well as educators regarded reducing the long-standing prejudice against Koreans as one of their most challenging tasks.

However, the result of a series of research studies defied conventional beliefs. Japanese participants who empathically viewed 20-hour Korean Drama, Huyu no Sonata (Winter Love Song) changed their attitude drastically, and came to have positive feelings toward Koreans. A questionnaire study found positive correlation between the level of empathy toward the main character(s) and the attitudinal change towards Koreans (Hasegawa, 2007a). In an interview study of 57 viewers, most of the participants who watched the drama empathically, talked happily about their drastic attitudinal change toward Koreans (Hasegawa, 2005b). Many said that before watching the drama, Korea was a place with no appeal, and they admitted to having been prejudiced against Koreans. After watching the drama though, the image of Korea turned into a precious place with beautiful scenery, where open and kind people live.

A longitudinal interview study showed that the attitudinal change that occurred by watching the drama had been maintained at least for 2 years (Hasegawa, 2007b). Twenty-eight interviewees who were randomly selected from the 57 original members basically maintained positive feelings toward Korean people, or in some cases, became more positive by making Korean friends, eating Korean food regularly, going to Korea, and watching Korean dramas.

Now in 2021, media reports a 4th Korean boom is underway in Japan. It seems that Korean food, singers, actors, and almost everything about Korea attracts young Japanese people. It is highly likely that mothers who fell in love with Korean dramas introduced Korean culture to their children, thus a love of Korea was being passed down to the next generations. We can say that Winter Love Song, which moved the hearts of Japanese women, paved the way for such drastic attitudinal change in Japanese people.

In conclusion, we offer suggestions for leaders of multicultural organizations which are plagued by frequent conflict between members of different cultural backgrounds, based on what we found through our case study of the TCC. Today, all over the world, people are moving beyond borders, migrating, or going abroad to study, and even a small organization in a small town may face the problem of conflict between members with different cultural or religious backgrounds. Even a Japanese organization that once had boasted its mono-culturality was an advantage, now faces the necessity of reducing conflict among its workers with mixed identity or different cultural backgrounds. Most of us now know that simple proximity between groups does not reduce but rather exacerbates tension and hatred, as the Contact Hypothesis (Allport, 1954) acknowledges.

As can be seen from our analysis, if the leaders of the organization really are willing to work hard to build a multicultural organization with low levels of threat or prejudice between its members, achieving the four conditions specified by the Contact Hypothesis (Allport, 1954) seems to be the most reliable way, challenging though it may be. When there is no time or energy to address interpersonal relations already problematic in a multicultural organization, empathy or perspective taking may be a useful remedy for reducing tension between the members.

However, empathy has relevant preconditions. First, it is advisable to bring about an atmosphere that is conducive to empathy. Research has shown that a friendly and informal atmosphere may contribute in reducing prejudice (Brewer & Miller,1984; Wilder, 1986) as can be seen from the TCC case. Thus, if you are the leader, we suggest that you first create an easy and happy atmosphere, as TCC leaders did.

Second, welcome dialogue between members. Let the members talk about themselves, how and why they think as they do, what they like and dislike, what bothers them, and what makes them happy. In order to create opportunities for sharing thoughts, propose regular agenda-free lunch meetings or longer coffee breaks for just that purpose. Once an open and easy atmosphere is achieved, then encourage an understanding of the importance of trying to take the perspective of others, especially if conflict is underway. Although empathy cannot be an all-purpose remedy for prejudice, it may plant the seeds of a positive attitude, as the Korean drama did for Japanese women, or it may drastically reduce prejudice as the narrative of the Vietnamese man did, after the quake.

At every organization, each member is responsible for building its climate and culture. Leaders can make rules, and they cannot force members to behave in just the way they want. TCC's endeavors taught us the importance of communication in creating a happy organizational climate; sharing stories, building an easy and comfortable relationship, and above all, being empathic toward others, all of which contributed to the sustainability of the organization. When TCC's members felt that other members or leaders were consistently open and trying to see the problem from their perspective, they were engaged and could feel that they were accepted as an equal partner in building the organization and community. If you adopt this approach and try to understand people around you, you may be an agent of change in shifting the atmosphere of your organization from stiff and rigid to one that is easy, flexible, and resilient.

References

Allport, G. (1954). *The Nature of Prejudice.* Oxford, England: Addison-Wesley.

Batson, C. D., Ahmad, N., & Lishner, D. A. (2009) Empathy and Altruism. In S. Lopez, & C. Snyder (Eds.), *The Oxford Handbook of Positive Psychology* (pp. 417–426). New York, NY: Oxford University Press.

Batson, C. D., Chang, J., Orr, R., & Rowland, J. (2002). Empathy, Attitudes, and Action: Can Feeling for a Member of a Stigmatized Group Motivate One to Help the Group? *Personality and Social Psychology Bulletin, 28,* 1656–1666.

Brewer, M. B., & Miller, N. (1984). Beyond the Contact Hypothesis: Theoretical Perspectives on Desegregation. In N. Miller, & M. B. Brewer (Eds.), *Groups in Contact: The Psychology of Desegregation* (pp. 281–302). Orlando, FL: Academic Press.

Crandall, C. S., & Stangor, C. (2005). Conformity and Prejudice. In J. F. Dovidio, P. Glick, & L. A. Rudman (Eds.), *On the Nature of Prejudice: Fifty Years after Allport* (pp. 295–309). Malden, MA: Blackwell Science.

Eisenberg, N., Eggum, N. D., & Di Giunta, L. (2010). Empathy-Related Responding: Associations with Prosocial Behavior, Aggression, and Intergroup Relations. *Social Issues and Policy Review, 4*(1), 143–180.

Finlay, K. A., & Stephan, W. G. (2000). Improving Intergroup Relations: The Effects of Empathy on Racial Attitudes. *Journal of Applied Social Psychology, 30,* 1720–1737.

Gaertner, S. L., & Dovidio, J. F. (2005). Understanding and Addressing Contemporary Racism: From Aversive Racism to the Common Ingroup Identity Model. *Journal of Social Issues, 61*, 615–639.

Hasegawa, N. (2005a). TV drama Huyuno-Sonata no Jyuyo Kenkyu---Nikkan communication no Shiten kara [Gauging the Impact of a Korean TV Drama upon Japanese Viewers: From the Perspective of Japan-Korea Intercultural Communication]. *Tabunka Kankeigaku.* [*Multicultural Relations*], *2*, 1–30.

Hasegawa, N. (2005b). Taikan image no Shitsuteki Kenkyu---Drama Shicho ga umu sinriteki henkano kenkyu [Changing Attitudes toward Korea: A Qualitative Analysis of the Influence of Drama-Viewing upon Japanese]. *Ibunka Communication* [*Journal of Intercultural Communication*], *8*, 67–86.

Hasegawa, N. (2007a). Kankokusei TV drama shicho ni yoru taido henyou no kenkyu---Ibunkakan Kyouiku no sitenkara [A Study of Attitudinal Changes Caused by Korean TV Drama Viewing: From the Perspective of Intercultural Education]. *Ibunkakan Kyouiku* [*Intercultural/Transcultural Education*], *25,* 58–73.

Hasegawa, N. (2007b). Taikan image no shitsuteki kenkyu II---Drama shicho ga umu sinritekihenka no kaijiteki chosa [Changing Attitudes toward Korea II: A Longitudinal Study of the Influence of Drama-viewing Upon Japanese]. *Ibunka Communication* [*Journal of Intercultural Communication*], *10,* 63–82.

Hibino, J. (2007). Community radio ga hatasu yakuwari [The Role Played by Community Radio]. In N. Tamura & S. Shiramizu (Eds.), *Gendai Chiiki Media Ron: Media of the Community, by the Community, for the Community* (pp. 50–67). Nihon Hyoronsha.

Hyogo Prefecture. (2016). HyogoTabunka Kyousei Shakai Suishinsisin [Guidelines for the Creation of a Multicultural Society in Hyogo]. English version, Retrieved from: https://web.pref.hyogo.lg.jp/sr13/documents/tabun kasisin_english.pdf]

Johnson, D. W., & Johnson, R.T. (1989). *Cooperation and Competition: Theory and Research*. Edina, MN: Interaction Books.

Kanaji, F. (2008). NPO jizoku no jyoken [Conditions for Sustainability of NPO]. (Doctoral dissertation). Graduate School of Business, Kobe University.

Kume, T., & Matsuda, Y. (2013). Leadership in Recovery Support for Foreign Residents Since the Great Hanshin-Awaji Earthquake: A Case Study of Takatori Community Center in Kobe. *Communication, Language, Culture, Journal of the College of Intercultural Communication, 5*, Rikkyo University, 153–167.

Mealy, M., & Stephan, W. G. (2010). Intergroup Empathy. In J. M. Levine & M. A. Hogg (Eds.), *Encyclopedia of Group Processes and Intergroup Relations* (pp. 475–478). Los Angeles: Sage.

Paluck, E. L., & Green, D. P. (2008). Prejudice Reduction: What Works? A Review and Assessment of Research and Practice. *Annual Review of Psychology, 60*(1), 339–67.

Pettigrew, T. F., & Tropp, L. R. (2006). A Meta-analytic Test of Intergroup Contact Theory. *Journal of Personality and Social Psychology*, *90*(5), 751–783.

Roseth, C., Johnson, D., & Johnson, R. (2008). Promoting Early Adolescents' Achievement and Peer Relationships: The Effects of Cooperative, Competitive, and Individualistic Goal Structures. *Psychological Bulletin, 1342,* 223–246.

Stephan, W. G., & Finlay, K. (1999). The Role of Empathy in Improving Intergroup Relations. *Journal of Social Issues, 55*(4), 729–743.

Takatori Community Center. (n.d.). *Data*. Retrieved September 8, 2021, from https://tcc117.jp [English version retrieved 2021-9-21] https://tcc117.jp/tcc/pdf/0905tccPamphlet_en.pdf

Wilder, D. A. (1986). Social Categorization: Implications for Creation and Reduction of Intergroup Bias. In L. Berkowitz (Ed.), *Advances in Experimental Social Psychology* (Vol. 19, pp. 239–355). New York: Academic.

Yoshitomi, S. (2006). The Formation Process of the Newcomer's Self-help Organization: In the Case of Hyogo Prefecture. *Multicultural Relations,* 3,17–32.

Yoshitomi, S. (2008a). *Tabunka Kyosei Shakai ni okeru shintonichigaikokujin jijososhiki keisei process: Hyogo ken no jirei kara kosatsu suru gutaiteki shisaku* [Formation Process of Newly Arrived Foreigners to Japan in Multicultural Symbiotic Society; Concrete Policies Viewed from a Case Study in Hyogo Prefecture]. (Doctoral dissertation). Graduate School of Kyoto University.

Yoshitomi, S. (2008b). *Multicultural Society and the Power of Foreigners in the Community; Do Self-help Groups that Would Avoid Ghettoization Really Exist?* Gendai Jinbunsha.

Yoshitomi, S. (2013a). *Global Shakai no community bosai: tabunka kyousei no sakini* [Community Disaster Prevention in Global Society: A Step toward Multicultural Symbiosis]. Osaka: Osaka University Press.

Yoshitomi, S. (2013b). Community Business to shite no Iryo Tsuyaku [Medical Interpreter as Community Business]. In Y. Nakamura, & K. Minamitani (Eds.), *Iryo Tsuyakushi to iu Shigoto: Kotoba to Bunka no Kabe o koete* [Profession Called Medical Interpreter; Beyond the Walls of Language and Culture] (pp. 165–175). Osaka: Osaka University Press.

www.ingramcontent.com/pod-product-compliance
Ingram Content Group UK Ltd.
Pitfield, Milton Keynes, MK11 3LW, UK
UKHW021830100926
8556IPUK00004B/249

9 783631 897669